... of
...ney Income Flows
for
the United States

CORPORATE PROFITS TAXES

SOCIAL INSURANCE CONTRIBUTIONS

PERSONAL TAXES

INCOME

PERSONAL INCOME

DISPOSABLE PERSONAL INCOME

CORPORATE SAVINGS

PERSONAL SAVINGS

EXPENDITURES

2-23-60

THE
INCOME
OF
NATIONS
AND
PERSONS

Alvin E. Coons

Professor of Economics
The Ohio State University

RAND McNALLY & COMPANY · Chicago

THE
INCOME
OF
NATIONS
AND
PERSONS

AN INTRODUCTION TO ECONOMICS

RAND M^cNALLY ECONOMICS SERIES

WALTER W. HELLER, *Consulting Editor*

This book is set in Intertype Baskerville,
with display headings in Foundry Gothic
and tabular matter in Intertype Futura.

Design by Mario Pagliai
Charts and diagrams by Ralph Chevis

THE
INCOME
OF
NATIONS
AND
PERSONS

Preface

THIS BOOK has been written for the college student or the general reader who is beginning the systematic study of economics—one of the traditional fields of social inquiry. It is designed to acquaint the reader with the work which economists do in their attempts to illuminate an aspect of human experience.

Reasonable men differ on what should be contained in an introductory textbook on economics, perhaps even more so on how it should be presented. Substantive economics is admittedly mercurial and elusive. A part of the problem of the transmission of meaning stems, of course, from the fact that the term economics carries with it a whole menagerie of associations. It serves as the workhorse of ordinary discourse as well as the litany of a society of specialists—although even here the ultimate referent for the term is not as single-valued as is sometimes assumed (the not infrequent characterization of a colleague's work as "interesting and important, but hardly economics" bears testimony to this fact).

What is meant by economic understanding? Is there a special form of economic reasoning? Are there unique economic events? Do they add up to some kind of total economic experience? Is there an economic reality? Are there desirable economic goals? These, of course, are broad questions, on which there is likely to be even greater controversy. Should they even be raised at the introductory level? Probably not. These are questions which cannot be answered adequately within the frame of reference of economics. Most economists, who as social scientists aspire to be scientific, recognize that they are issues which relate also to the "state of the arts" in the theory of knowledge and its relation to experience. Nevertheless, the manner in which they *are* answered is likely to be reflected in what is regarded as important.

The task of an author is further complicated by the heterogeneity of the needs and interests of those who take the course in introductory economics. A great majority will have little or no intention of continuing in the field. For those who become majors or minors in economics, lacunae and ambiguities in the first exposure are not likely to be troublesome, since repeated exposure eventually establishes its familiar bench marks in language and reference models, collated with selected events of experience. It is the great majority—those who take only the initial course—about whom there has been mounting concern lest the little economics they get should turn out to be not what they *really* ought to have. Academic economists seldom meet together, even for merriment and diversion, but the conversation ends in a conspiracy to raise the level of economic understanding. Except for an agreement on the desired end, however, unanimity is usually absent.

In the pages that follow, the influence of modern positivism will be apparent. The structure, the language, and general frame of reference also reflect certain beliefs about the order of learning as well as the substantive content of economics. Learning, except perhaps for initial learning, progresses with the "recognition of error," through perceiving events from a different point of view. The groundwork for the recognition of error begins, at the more abstract levels at least, with the examination of language—the medium through which common experience is communicated and shared. Accordingly, the approach here is to acquaint the student with the point of view, the concepts, and relationships used by economists, as found in what they have written and said. Attention is directed to the background and evolution of these concepts, as well as the more important figures who assisted in their development.

The relation between language and events is a complex one in any field of inquiry. Concepts and relationships form part of the world of ideas, linked with the real world of experience in a manner that is not always self-evident, but one that is always selective. Methodology, in the modern logico-empirical tradition, offers at least a working hypothesis of this relationship. As a preparation for the logic of what follows, somewhat more attention is given to method at the outset than is customary.

The age-old controversy between theory and experience (or practice, as they see it) not infrequently comes to the fore with students in the first course in economics. This is because the minds with which we work are not *tabulae rasae* with respect to the materials covered. Images of many of the phenomena discussed are already there because, as a part of everyday language, they are associated with familiar events as well as with received beliefs and feelings. By showing the tentative, exploratory nature of all theory as a tool for inquiry, this problem, even if not resolved, can be shown to be a general one and not peculiar to economics.

Long tradition has given the term economics a *material* association, albeit a tenuous one, usually filtered through the intervening variable, money. There is thus created a kind of double detour along the path which leads from the concepts and relationships of abstract ideas to the so-called *real world*. If, as social scientists, we take as the object of economic inquiry that part of human behavior associated with the acquisition, ownership, and disposition of material goods and immaterial services, a central concept of income linking man's drives for satisfaction and the limited want-satisfying materials of his environment becomes a convenient symbol with which to refer to it. Thus income has been given primary emphasis in the title of this book, and a major portion of Part 1 is devoted to its development as a concept.

Two considerations influenced this decision. A more or less operationally defined national-income concept has become a major tool in the kit of most present-day economists, and defines a large part of what they do. For purposes of continuity it seemed useful to extend the income reference to the microlevel of inquiry. Measures of national income have become practically household terms, even where vaguely understood. Moreover, when members of most beginning classes in economics are asked at the outset what they expect to study in the course, most of them make some reference to money. The step from a common-sense concept of money to that of money flows or money income is not too difficult to make. The link with real-income flows, their origin in production, and their distribution and use in consumption can then follow with a logic which parallels experience.

Most topics that have interested economists, past and present, are discussed. The book consists of six parts, each of which is divided into three parallel sections. Subject-matter identification of the major parts is quite conventional. Following the development of a concept of national income in Part 2, microanalysis is discussed under the headings of Production, Distribution, Consumption, and International Trade. Although defined initially with respect to their links with the circular flow of income, their subsequent development covers most of the topics usually treated under these four constructs.

Within each part, the first section, consisting of one chapter, is primarily descriptive and suggestive, making use of concepts familiar at the common-sense level. In the second and largest section, the principal concepts are refined for more precise analysis and linked with relevant empirical data or examples. The third section treats related policy problems as they are perceived in the framework of different value assumptions. Discussion questions follow each chapter of the text, and at the end of each part there is a selected list of books in which will be found a more complete, and somewhat more difficult, presentation of most of the ideas contained in that part.

This organization is designed specifically to assist the student in distinguishing between different levels of discourse in economic literature or popular discussion. These are: (1) theoretical or analytical statements relating to systems of classification, definition of concepts and relationships, and general consistency in the use of language; (2) factual or empirical statements which can be supported or rejected by data; and (3) normative statements which can be related to value assumptions likely to involve noneconomic criteria.

Somewhat more economic history and history of economic ideas has been included than is usual in "principles" texts. This history has been woven into the main fabric of the book as a means of highlighting the relation between institutional change and changes in emphasis of economic theory. For those curricula which offer economics as part of an integrated core of the social sciences, this should provide something of a bridge to the other disciplines.

One departure from convention is the absence of separate treatment for the government or public economy. Taxation is included under distribution, public expenditures under consumption or income use. This appears to be consistent with the institutional realities of our time. Nor is there separate treatment for comparative economic systems. This discussion has been incorporated in the normative or policy sections of the different parts. Internally consistent ideal models of capitalist, socialist, communist, and fascist economies have become increasingly difficult to square with observations in experience. The permutations and combinations of centralized and decentralized control systems refuse to be contained in manageable form.

During the preparation of this book the author has benefited in many ways from the reactions and criticisms from colleagues at The Ohio State University and from professional associates elsewhere. Professor David M. Harrison used an earlier version of Part 1 in an introductory class, and on the basis of student reactions offered helpful suggestions. Some of the same materials were presented before Professor Virgil Hinshaw's seminar in Philosophy of Science and were constructively criticized. The book's title came from a suggestion by Professor Meno Lovenstein, who maintains a continuing interest in economic education. All parts of the original manuscript were read by Professor Henry T. Buechel of the University of Washington and Professor Robert A. Lampman of the University of Wisconsin. Their suggestions and detection of errors were most helpful. Dean Addison Hickman of North Carolina State College, Professor Harlan M. Smith of the University of Minnesota, and Professor Andreas G. Papandreou of the University of California have seen parts of the manuscript in an earlier form, and their criticisms have produced some revisions. Richard von Glatz of the Rand McNally editorial staff has been most helpful in the final preparation of the manuscript. For whatever errors and shortcomings remain, the author alone is responsible.

ALVIN E. COONS

Columbus, Ohio
January, 1959

CONTENTS

PREFACE   vii

PART 1 · ECONOMICS
An Approach to a Science of Income

section ONE: INTRODUCTION   2

chapter
1   The Economic World and the Economist's World   3

section TWO: ECONOMICS IN THEORY AND EXPERIENCE   18

chapter
2   The Nature and Limits of Economic Science   19

3   The Background and Meaning of
Some Basic Economic Concepts   48

section THREE: ECONOMIC POLICY   60

chapter
4   Normative Systems in Economics   61

PART 2 · THE SOCIAL ECONOMY
National Income and Product

section ONE: INTRODUCTION   78

chapter
5   Aggregate or National Income   79

section TWO: NATIONAL INCOME IN THEORY AND EXPERIENCE   90

chapter
6   Concepts and Models in National Income Accounting   91

7   The National Income Accounts   111

8   An Approach to the Analysis of National Income Variations   132

9   Spending, Saving, Investment, and Income Levels   149

10 Money and Banking Institutions in the United States   175

section THREE: NATIONAL INCOME AND PUBLIC POLICY   208
    chapter
        11 Alternative Routes to Full Employment   209

PART 3 · PRODUCTION
The Creation of Output and the Origin of Income

section ONE: INTRODUCTION   228
    chapter
    12 Production in an Industrial Society   229

section TWO: THE INDIVIDUAL FIRM IN THEORY
            AND EXPERIENCE   244
    chapter
    13 A Simple Theory of Production   245

    14 Production for a Market   263

    15 The Competitive Market   274

    16 Monopoly   294

    17 Different Degrees of Monopoly   303

    18 A More Inclusive Model of Production   315

    19 Economic Analysis and Economic Institutions   325

    20 Production Organization: Formal Aspects   335

    21 Production Organization: Financial Aspects   350

section THREE: PRODUCTION AND PUBLIC POLICY   366
    chapter
    22 Who Should Make Production Decisions?   367

Contents

PART 4 · DISTRIBUTION
Factor Allocation and Income Shares

section ONE: INTRODUCTION   386
> chapter
> 23 Who Gets What and How?   387

section TWO: DISTRIBUTION IN THEORY AND EXPERIENCE   394
> chapter
> 24 Simple Distribution and Allocation Theory   395
> 25 Wages   404
> 26 Rents   420
> 27 Interest and Profits   429
> 28 Personal or Household Income Distribution   441
> 29 Government Income   456
> 30 The Role of Interest Groups in Distribution   471

section THREE: DISTRIBUTION AND PUBLIC POLICY   488
> chapter
> 31 How Should Income be Distributed?   489

PART 5 · CONSUMPTION
The Final Use of Income

section ONE: INTRODUCTION   506
> chapter
> 32 Consumption in an Industrial Society   507

section TWO: CONSUMPTION IN THEORY AND EXPERIENCE   515
> chapter
> 33 A Simple Theory of Consumption   516
> 34 Consumer Budgets and Consumer Spending   528
> 35 Scales and Standards of Living   547
> 36 Consumption and the Public Economy   556

section THREE: CONSUMPTION AND PUBLIC POLICY   570

chapter

37   Attending the Interest of the Consumer   571

PART 6 · INTERNATIONAL TRADE AND INCOME

section ONE: INTRODUCTION   590

chapter

38   The Trade of Nations   591

section TWO: INTERNATIONAL TRADE IN THEORY
         AND EXPERIENCE   607

chapter

39   Balance of Payments, Foreign Investment, and Levels of Income   609

40   Patterns of World Production and the Terms of Trade   629

section THREE: INTERNATIONAL RELATIONS
         AND COMMERCIAL POLICY   639

chapter

41   Alternative Routes to Optimum Trade   641

EPILOGUE: *A Simple Restatement*   662

INDEX   665

That's the best account I can give off hand of my predilection for the concrete. Of course, it seems to me rather a predilection for problems one can treat with some approach to scientific method. The abstract is to be made use of at every turn, as a handmaiden to help hew the wood and draw the water. I loved romances—particularly William Morris's tales of lands that never were—and utopias and economic systems, of which your father's, when I came to know it, seemed the most beautiful; but these were objects of art, and I was a workman who wanted to become a scientific worker, who might enjoy the visions which we see in mountain mists but who trusted only what we see in the light of common day.

WESLEY C. MITCHELL
letter to J. M. Clark,
August 9, 1928

PART 1

ECONOMICS

An Approach

to a Science of Income

SECTION ONE

Introduction

THIS SECTION is only incidentally about economics. A few economic terms, most of which will be familiar, are introduced. The emphasis, however, is on the relation between thinking about economics and thinking about any other field of inquiry. Such thinking, or reasoning, is not essentially different. That is the principal point made here.

Straight thinking involves careful use of language (logic) and observation with a purpose. In our time straight thinking is most closely identified with science.

CHAPTER 1

The Economic World and the Economist's World

THERE IS an *economic world* of jobs, and money, and things with price tags on them. We know that such a world exists because we live in it and have learned to refer to it by that name. We experience it in our modern industrial society through the work we do to make a living, through the money we get and, finally, in those things we are able to buy and use when the money is spent.

To say that *economics* is about the economic world would not be wrong. But such a definition would be too trivial to be of much use. It would be like saying that physics is about the physical world.

The physical world is what we "know" directly from what our senses tell us. The physicist's world of laws and measures and complicated mathematical descriptions is something else. The two, however, are linked together—the language of the latter with the events of the former—in ways that only careful study and training can show.

There is also a biological world, a social world, a psychological world, a world of sports, and innumerable others. We also speak of *dream worlds,* sometimes contrasting them with the *real world*. But we also believe that there is one world which contains them all, even though we would probably have difficulty if asked to define or describe it.

Each of these "other" worlds is simply a different way of looking at (or perceiving) events in the "one world," a point of view or frame of reference, together with the special language men have invented for describing aspects of experience. By putting on a kind of mental blinder (like the devices used on race horses to limit their view to the track in front of them), we can ignore all aspects of experience except those that we want to observe or analyze at any given time.

The word for this process is abstracting; the result an *abstraction.* Without the help of abstractions, what we call thinking would be impos-

3

sible: we could not even imagine the one world that we believe exists, since we can never see more than a small part of it at any one time. We would be reduced to an existence which encompassed little more than immediately perceived colors, sounds, tactual sensations, tastes, and smells. Memory, one form of abstracting, enables us to superimpose what we have experienced in the past upon our experiences of the present. This is how we build up an increasingly comprehensive view of the way in which the "real world" fits together. In the words of John Dewey:

> . . . man lives in a world where each occurrence is charged with echoes and reminiscences of what has gone before, where each event is a reminder of other things. Hence he lives, not, like the beasts of the field, in a world of merely physical things, but in a world of signs and symbols.[1]

Among the more important of these signs and symbols are *language,* which helps us to distinguish and remember different *sorts* of things, and *mathematics* (also a form of language), which helps us to describe the *size, order,* and *number* of things.

Economic Thought and Language

The word *economics* is one of these symbols. It has come down to us as a term of our everyday language which we have learned to associate with particular kinds of experience. Together with other related terms or concepts, it helps to form the word pictures or ideas in our minds with which we communicate with one another. When we read the term in print or hear it spoken, or when we use it ourselves, we usually have in mind the things we do in the "everyday business of making a living." The economic world that each person knows best is his own very private one—his job, his income, his expenditures, his property, or perhaps his expectations about what the future holds for each of these categories.

The *economist's* world is linked to the private economic worlds of each of us. But the economist, like the physicist, is a specialist, who has concentrated his attention more specifically on the broader economic environment. He has developed conceptual tools for thinking about the way in which the economic experiences of individuals are connected to form the broader and more abstract public world or economy. To study economics as a specialized field of inquiry is to study what the economist does. It is the study of his language and his thought and of how these are related

---

[1] *Reconstruction in Philosophy* (Boston: Beacon Press, 1948), p. 1.

4

to experience, to events which recur with some regularity and which we would like to predict and control. To speak of *the economist,* of course, is to speak in general terms. The *discipline of economics* comprises the scientific tradition of many generations of economists.

Economics and Everyday Affairs

At this point a word of caution may be in order. Nearly everyone fancies himself as something of an economist. Probably in no other field of inquiry does the specialist meet more amateur competition.[2] The physicist, the chemist, and the physician can retreat behind their cyclotrons, their complicated formulas, or their Latin phrases without being challenged by anyone who has not spent years in study and research. When they speak on matters pertaining to their "world" (or field), their judgment is usually accepted. But the economist seldom encounters anyone who is not willing with the slightest encouragement to air his views on economics, especially on how economic affairs ought to be conducted.

There is a reason for this. Although the world of the physicist or chemist attracts our interest directly only now and then, and the physician is consulted chiefly when we are ill or planning to buy insurance, the events which the economist studies are of continuing concern for all who have outgrown the dependency of childhood.

From the time when we begin to participate in the adventure of ideas, we are conditioned by the printed page, by radio or television, and by the spoken word of ordinary conversation to label certain activities "economic affairs." These same activities can also be viewed in other ways. Consequently, economics, as we use it in everyday speech, is likely to be a term with many different associations. For ordinary conversation, when we express opinions and listen to those of others, we do not always need to clarify our meanings. Each has his own private world, a mixture of reality and dreams in which he sees events not only as they are, but also as they ought to be. These are perceived not only as true or false, but as good or bad, desirable or undesirable. We do not always make clear the sense in which we are speaking.

The drawing-room or the "cracker-barrel" economist is likely to change worlds in the middle of his conversation, ringing in for good measure his dream world, which is designed to fit his own feelings. For social gatherings and political speeches, this does not matter much. Here the

---

[2] Psychologists might disagree with this statement, and perhaps rightly so. A good subject for a Ph.D. dissertation would be the proportion of time spent in drawing-room conversation on the ills of the economy and on the psychological dissection of absent acquaintances.

5

purpose is not necessarily to inform, but more often to impress people or express feelings. An assertion about the "law of supply and demand," "economic waste," "economic necessity," or "sound economics" seems impressive and fits the need.

If the purpose, on the other hand, is insight or understanding, clarification, accuracy, or the posing of meaningful questions (to which meaningful answers may be found), there is more involved. We want to acquire new and sharper tools for thinking, and to gain command over an increasing range of those elusive things called *facts*—statements about reality that can be checked and verified by others.

In approaching economics as a specialized study, therefore, it will be well to keep in mind that we shall be engaged in an inquiry which differs from much of our everyday discussion, just as the systematic study of chemistry differs from the amusing pastime of producing minor explosions and unpleasant smells with a Christmas chemistry set. The difference is in the procedure, in the systematic linkage between thinking and observation or experience. It involves learning to use the methods that have produced the growing body of knowledge we call science, as well as the history, the concepts, and the observations of economists.

Can Economics Be Scientific?

When we talk of being scientific in our thinking about economics we need to add a note of warning. As we progress from the economics of everyday conversation to the more specialized version of the trained economist, we do not necessarily achieve greater certainty. There will be times when convictions that have been firmly held will be replaced by doubts. We sometimes "know" things from our own everyday experience that are not true. Nor will conclusions arrived at be easily translated into immediate recipes for action. They will not tell us what we *ought* to do. The atomic scientist can provide us with a new source of energy, but he cannot determine how we shall use it, whether for manufacturing bombs or for generating power. The great body of economic thought does not contain any fixed conclusions which are immediately applicable to personal, business, or governmental use. Training in economics can help the individual to order his thinking about problems just as other disciplines can. It does not necessarily tell him how to make money as an individual— if that is his chief objective—or how to vote exactly on specific public issues as a citizen.

Economics is scientific insofar as it can be characterized as a way of thinking, a frame of mind. But this is no exclusive possession of the economist. Most of this approach to "reality" is borrowed from the great fund

6

of social or human knowledge. Thus, we reject at the outset any claim to a unique form of "economic thinking." As a discipline, economics is distinguished rather by the problems it undertakes to solve and the questions it asks.

Scope and Method
in Economics

In their efforts to make sense out of a complex and changing world, most trained economists try to be scientific in outlook and method. If any single term can describe the scientific tradition—which is so closely associated with the more important intellectual achievements in the modern world—it is *objectivity*. Whether complete objectivity can be attained in economics, or in any other social science, is a much debated question, and we cannot hope in this book to deal with the problem in detail. The position one takes with respect to this question will depend partly on one's definition of science. It will be useful, therefore, before proceeding with the special problems of economic science, to outline briefly the working definition of science which underlies much of what is to follow.

We have indicated in a general way the broad field within which the economist operates as a scientist or investigator. He begins with events, experience, or observations in what we have described loosely as the "economic world." By means of systematic ordering of observations, by reflection, and by the refinement of language so that it can be used for more precise (and hence more meaningful) statements, the economist attempts to increase our understanding of, and ultimately our predictions about and control over, events in the "real world." His procedures are similar to those of scientists in other fields.

In later chapters we will become acquainted with the specific observations, the concepts, the analysis, and the conclusions reached (sometimes to be rejected later) in the evolution of economic thought and language. In this introductory section, however, we can save ourselves confusion later on if we concentrate for the moment, not on what is unique in economics, but on what it shares with other disciplines.

The Method and Spirit of Science

Science *begins* with the things we already "know" from the trial and error of everyday life. As an authority for this observation, we can cite Albert Einstein:

> Scientific concepts often begin with those used in ordinary language for the affairs of everyday life, but they develop quite differently.

7

They are transformed and lose the ambiguity associated with them in ordinary language, gaining in rigorousness so that they may be applied to scientific thought.[3]

The concepts used in ordinary language are the words we use when we refer to events in the shared environment, the meanings we give to common experiences. They are linked with the mental images or ideas we use when we think about the "real" world and how it fits together. Usually these common-sense concepts are colored by the emotions—the feelings of approval or disapproval we have about the world. That is why they are usually described as *nonobjective,* since they do not always mean the same thing to everyone.

These concepts, at the hands of specialists, are refined and given more limited meanings, which can be used with greater precision for scientific purposes. This precision enables us to handle the more involved mental images or models that scientists have built up to help interpret experience, and which often seem so different from the things we know directly. The atom of the physicist and the molecule of the chemist are such models. So, too, is the *economic system* used by the economist. Such models are not perceived directly; they are inferred or constructed as devices for tieing events together.

Like so much in our complex and constantly changing world, we cannot say precisely what science is. As individuals we cannot possibly know all it has to teach us. We know only that it exists in the books, the pictures, the papers of learned societies, and the blueprints and machines that have been built with such knowledge. No one person owns it, for science is *social knowledge.*

Private knowledge exists in the beliefs and feelings of the individual. This exclusive possession, which each of us has, is a valued thing, but not always one to be trusted. Our beliefs are the things we *think* are true; and our feelings are the reactions that comfort us or disturb us in an environment that often seems harsh, sometimes cruel, but which is usually merely indifferent to our needs.

Beliefs may be wrong, and so mislead us; feelings sometimes blind us. As individuals, we are not always certain where beliefs end and feelings begin. But through interactions among ourselves, we are forced to reexamine our thinking. We can sometimes agree on some things that are true, or on the conditions under which they can be made to come true.

---

[3] Albert Einstein and Leopold Infeld, *The Evolution of Physics* (New York: Simon & Schuster, Inc., 1938), p. 14.

8

If we look at the same thing and call it by the same name, we enjoy a sense of having shared the same experience. And when many know the name of a certain type of event, and share it as a sense experience, they can believe with confidence that "this thing did happen." Sometimes, however, "knowing" consists only of discovering what is not true.

The Detection and Measurement of Error

Inquiry begins with the recognition of error—the sensing of a problem. This problem arises when experience fails to confirm our preconceptions or when drives originating in felt needs are not satisfied. In other words, when new experience differs from past experience we want to know why. Sometimes we are forced to reorganize our previous view of the real world. Somewhat simplified, this is what the process of thinking and learning involves. The impetus for rethinking our personal "world view" may come from being stimulated by others, whose beliefs and valuations are different because their experience has been different. All such differences are related to the past and to how well the trial and error of experience has taught us to interpret our clues. *That part of human knowledge which has undergone elaborate refinement in order to reduce error and personal feeling to a minimum is usually what we designate as scientific knowledge.*

As living organisms we are in a continuous process of adjusting to our environment, which is itself changing continuously. In this process we learn to interpret clues and to respond to them. The use of past experience to interpret the relatedness of events—the nature of cause and effect—is the essence of intelligent behavior and the foundation of "common-sense," on the one hand, and of that more sophisticated form of common sense we call science, on the other. In our time much of this scientific knowledge has been recorded for us, and we can draw upon it as an aid in understanding the world about us. With the growth of scientific knowledge has come a better understanding of the nature of science. A whole new discipline, the philosophy of science, is now devoted to exploring the meaning of science itself.

If we examine what scientists do when they work on a problem and succeed in bringing order out of what was previously ambiguity or indefiniteness, we usually find that the process can be described by the following steps: observation, definition, theory or model construction, testing, and the reserving of judgment. We will treat each of these in turn.

1. *Observation.* Observation is treated first in our discussion of the methods and spirit of science in order to emphasize the primacy of sense experience as the source of our knowledge about the *real world.* This is what is implied when modern science is described as empirical in its orien-

9

tation. The empirical tradition is very old, and the term itself is derived from an ancient Greek school of medicine which used experience as its guide in medical practice (rather than deductive logic, based upon what was assumed to be *innate* needs of the body). Its modern development, however, begins with scientists of the seventeenth century who trusted their senses more than their intuition. In the form of *logico-empiricism,* the method of modern science, logical inference and creative imagination are given parallel importance, but the final test of knowledge is in experience (observation) and, wherever possible, in the controlled experiment. At any given time it is the agreement among observers, the checking of one another's facts and analyses, which gives to scientific knowledge its social or public characteristic.

2. *Definition and Classification.* Identifiable events (things) are distinguished and classified according to similarities and differences, either in the "mind's eye" or as a systematic operation. Various phyla, species, types, and varieties, or classes and sets, are established, and the separate events are assigned to them and distinguished by symbols. With familiarity, these symbols become the *concepts* which represent events in the real world, helpful for the recall of past experience when similar events are encountered again. Definition is basically a problem of language, enabling us to think in terms of our symbols or signs even when we are not observing events directly. Similar or related events are grouped together, and our language takes on the richness of ordered experience. Things which are not relevant to our particular field or world, which do not fit the criteria determined by our problem, are neglected or ignored. Thus the chemist identifies the elements by atomic weights and valences. As we shall see, the economist identifies forms of property, markets, factors of production, and so forth. The most precise definitions are operational, which means describing the events according to the operations performed in identifying them. In the exact sciences these operations are capable of precise mathematical statement.

3. *Theory or Model Construction.* Theories or models are like maps or blueprints of a feature of the real world (for example, the physical world or the economic world), in which concepts are arranged in some order (distance, time, weight, value, etc.) with respect to one another. Like road maps, which help us to understand direction and distance in the territory through which we are traveling, theoretical models are simplified analogues which help us to think our way around that aspect of the real world in which we are interested. As our knowledge of a field becomes more detailed and exact, knowing the values of some of the variables in the model enables us to deduce or predict others. If our road map is ac-

curate, and if we drive at a given speed, we can estimate how long it will take to travel between one town and the next. Knowing the relation between temperature and volume and pressure of gases, the physicist can predict what will happen to pressure if volume remains constant and temperature is changed. With less exactness, the economist can estimate direction of change in one variable, say price, when another variable, say available income, changes, if there are no other offsetting influences. Thinking in terms of a model is usually described as deductive reasoning, and the test for judging such reasoning is logical consistency.

4. *Testing.* Testing may be described as the act of checking experience to discover whether inferences drawn from the theoretical models or maps are verified, whether predictions that are made are realized in the real world. Thus, if in theory two events or variables are believed to be related in some consistent way, so that we can predict that a change in one will be followed by a change in the other, we can put the matter to test. Mendel performed such a test by crossing different colored peas to test his theory of heredity. Testing is observation with a purpose and with a background of ordered experience to draw upon. In the exact sciences, this is done in a laboratory under controlled conditions. Geology, astronomy, biology, and the social sciences generally have only limited ranges of questions that can be answered by laboratory tests. These sciences are empirical, but testing is done under actual conditions that are only approximately constant. Modern statistics provides useful techniques for collecting and ordering observational data both outside and inside the laboratory. In economics, particularly, most observations must come from "facts" gathered under conditions only roughly the same and analyzed statistically to remove observable but nonsignificant differences.

5. *Reserving of Judgment.* The final step in scientific method can be described best as an attitude of mind rather than any specific thing that is done. It means not believing too strongly in any conclusion until the weight of evidence is very strong. This, in a complex world, usually means rejecting many more conclusions than are accepted. The desire for certainty and security, as modern psychology has taught us, is a compelling influence on us all. We often fool ourselves because we *want* to believe something, because we feel that it *ought* to be true. The determination to continue to question conclusions is a safeguard against personal bias.

Of course, where human observers are involved, it is easier to recognize sources of error than to avoid them. In each of the steps outlined above, it is possible for error to occur. Confusion and disagreement may arise over the use of language. These are errors of definition and logic. Events may be erroneously perceived, or observed in different ways. Super-

11

ficial resemblances may cause the observer to ignore significant differences. Biases may creep into observations if the observer feels strongly about what he *ought* to see. This is a type of error to which the social sciences are especially subject.

Social Science and the Problem of Value

As a technique for inquiry, science has steadily improved its methods of guarding against errors in observation. Repeated observations by many scientists, trained in the same tradition and serving as checks on one another, have helped to reduce errors of this kind.

Errors of feeling are more difficult to guard against, except within narrow ranges in the exact sciences, where a specialized language has been created to serve specific purposes, and where the events with which they deal vary with a more consistent pattern. An elephant on a slippery river bank becomes, in the language of physics, "a mass on an inclined plane under conditions of reduced friction," and all of the other associations of humor, sympathy, or horror no longer complicate the mental picture. A mass of elephant and a mass of inert matter behave about the same under similar conditions.

But in the social sciences, which are centered on man himself, the problem is more involved. First of all, the scientist is not able to place himself entirely outside his subject, since what he studies often includes himself. Events which the physical scientist observes are more independent of the observer, and what he feels or what he does has little effect on them. In social relations, however, the fact that a subject is being studied frequently changes his behavior, so that the conditions with which an investigator starts are not repeated exactly.

The social scientist has often relied upon language drawn from everyday affairs. He has been expected to do so because of the nature of his subject, and is regarded as something of an exhibitionist when he attempts to develop more neutral concepts for the events of everyday experience. He tries to make his concepts usable by careful definition, and by stating his interpretations of their meaning; but his statements, even so, may not mean the same to everyone because of the tricks that language can play on us. Language can convey meaning or it can be used as an instrument to influence behavior. The same word, spoken in different contexts, may convey information on one occasion or express a feeling or attitude on another. This is particularly true where problems of value are concerned— problems of *good* and *bad*. In social affairs relationships may be described as they are, or as they ought to be. The thinking model, the concepts and

12

relationships of which it consists, may be realistic, or it may be "ideal" in the sense of being desirable.[4]

This dualism accounts for the peculiar meaning sometimes associated with theory in the social sciences. "Theoretical" is often regarded as the opposite of "practical," hence idealistic or dreamy, concerned with achieving goals that are unattainable because they are not realistic.

The concepts used in describing the two worlds—the dream world and the real world—may be the same, but the relationships that are posited may be quite different. For example, economists use a model of the market which they call "perfect competition." With inferences drawn from this model, some have then advocated policies for practical affairs, as though the conditions described in the ideal or theoretical model prevailed in the world of experience. By thus concretizing feelings or value judgments implicit in the ideal model, such advocates committed the fallacy of *misplaced concreteness*—treating an abstraction invented only as a thinking tool as though it were "reality." This fallacy is not confined to economics alone, nor to the social sciences. The point here is simply that in this area it is easier to fall into this kind of error.

An important part of learning to think scientifically is to distinguish between the value judgments sometimes implicit in language and the verifiable or testable predictions. The scientist, as a scientist, does not use his fund of knowledge and his methods of inquiry directly to answer questions in the field of value. He does not finally settle the issues of good or bad, desirable or undesirable. This does not mean that the scientist, as a citizen or as a human being, does not make such judgments. It means only that in his role as scientist he tries to keep separate the areas of belief and feeling.

The nature of this rather thin dividing line is pointed up when we consider questions of social policy. Policy is invariably linked with problems of value, because it is associated with goals or ends. These are usually some desired condition or set of events, which it is proposed to attain at some future time, as a result of present and succeeding actions. *Policies* are specified rules of action intended to achieve desired results. Social policies can be defined, accordingly, as *rules of behavior, which people in their social and political roles adopt or have imposed upon them, to make actions predictable and goals realizable.*

---

[4] Both types of model are ideal, in the sense that they are thinking models or "ideas." Constructs used for ordering observations, such as *economic system, capitalism, democracy*—all of them used by one or more of the social sciences—have been described as "ideal types" by Max Weber, German social scientist.

Value conflicts arise in our society because goals or ends are seldom universally agreed upon. Individuals and groups, whose experiences have differed, do not share the same objectives. The social scientist can study different value systems as they are reflected in different cultures. He may classify and describe patterns of values, and point out mutual inconsistencies and contradictions. Science can provide knowledge which tells us whether goals are attainable, or how they may be attained most effectively. It does not tell us (except for the obviously unrealistic and unattainable) whether they should be sought. Through scientific method we can learn to identify value positions, and to associate them with the individual and group characteristics of those who hold them. This is usually regarded as the province of sociology, and perhaps of political science. As individuals we can try to know those of our opinions which rest on value judgment and those which are more or less objective.

Economics as a Social Science

Because it is concerned with man and his actions in the face of problems, economics is classified as a social science—that general field of inquiry which focuses on human behavior. At the point where the economist begins to abstract from events of experience, therefore, there is likely to be an overlap of other social sciences, such as sociology, political science, psychology, and anthropology. It differs from them, however, in the nature of the problem with which it starts.

The Economic Problem

There is one *general problem* which economists usually list as basic to their field of inquiry. It stems from a fact of experience that has been a matter of continuing concern to men since they became conscious of problem solving. This is the problem of scarcity in the means for satisfying human needs and desires, relative to the extent and variety of those needs. When means are scarce, when there is not enough to satisfy all the uses man would like to make of a thing (whether it be money or resources or time), he is forced to choose.

Choices are made because they must be made. If they are not made consciously, they become choices by default. For when limited means have been used up, some of the ends (needs) they might have served are unsatisfied. Through experience, therefore, men learn the art of choice making, as individuals and as groups. An important part of human adjustment to environment is learning to make those choices in a manner which experience has shown to be the most satisfactory.

This necessity for choosing extends to all aspects of life, but it is

14

nowhere more important or more evident than in the use of the materials of the environment which are required for satisfactory living. In the sharing of these scarce resources, men have worked out patterns of behavior (social institutions) which reflect such adjustments and which determine in part how future adjustments will be made. However, although many of the means that satisfy human needs are of a physical or material nature (in the ordinary, common-sense meaning of those terms), they are not exclusively so. There has been a tendency to concretize the objects of the economist's concern, but, as we shall learn, this can be overdone. In modern economic life many of the scarce things are services performed by people, and cannot be called material in any "real" sense.

The study of this choice-making process in the use of scarce resources (including man's working time) has been the task which economists have set for themselves. The existence of this necessity for choosing is usually implied by the term economics, as it is used in everyday language.

The statement of the problem we have just given is one with which most economists would agree. To the beginner, however, it may be somewhat disturbing, since this is not the form in which it is most commonly encountered in experience. This is rather an abstract formulation, an inference from many facets of man's experience, and as such it can be better appreciated at the end rather than at the beginning of the introductory economics course. We have introduced it here as a preview of what is to come, and it should be kept in mind as something which ultimately ties together many different kinds of economizing behavior.

Because it is concerned with scarce materials and energies in the physical environment, economics may appear at times to overlap the boundaries of technology. However, economics is not technology, although it is linked to it because of the way this growing knowledge of the control of the external environment has of changing the underlying conditions of scarcity and the way men perceive their needs. The concern of economists is rather with human actions as they are reflected in a set of complex relationships between men and things, and among men themselves, as these affect decisions in the allocation of scarce materials to different uses. In organized society the key to these relationships is to be found in the institution of property. This has been the basis, at times, for describing economics as the science of wealth. We will develop this idea further in Chapter 3.

Let us now relate our specific task to the general discussion above. We begin with the language in which affairs of the economic world are recorded and communicated. This includes the words and associations of everyday affairs (in which a sense of the economic problem is reflected), as well as the literature of economics, which contains the observations and reflections of students of economic affairs. Much of an introductory course in economics (as in any field of inquiry) is devoted to learning this language.

Any discipline can be treated almost exclusively in terms of its abstract symbols, its theory, its logic. Some economists try to do this, and to them the study of economics is synonymous with economic analysis. But *pure theory,* or analysis by itself, is incomplete. The role of theory is to suggest hypotheses to be tested by further observation; that is, to raise questions rather than settle them. Those who sought a *pure theory of choice* of universal validity could do so only by making some rather simplified assumptions about human motivation and behavior. (It should also be noted that many economists recognized the nature of their assumptions and claimed for them no more than logical validity. Others did not.) We will return to this in the next chapter and thereafter.

There have been other students of economic affairs who at times have cast themselves in the role of critics of theoretical economists, stressing the importance of direct observation of "reality." To them, economizing behavior occurs within a framework of institutions and social habits, and hence cannot be viewed as having universal validity. Emphasizing "facts" rather than "theory," they have in turn been criticized for producing only an endless description of the past, a hodgepodge of arbitrarily selected observations. Facts do not speak for themselves. They are meaningful only if they can be related to other facts in some kind of pattern. Economists in this tradition have accumulated large quantities of observational data of use to the analyst.

Some economists have been frankly "normative" or value oriented, in the sense that they have argued for specific public policies. Guided by deductions from such ideal models as laissez faire[5] and central planning of economic activity, they have sought to influence legislation and individual or group actions toward goals which they regard as desirable for their own sake or because they lead to other desirable consequences such as freedom or security. Their "world" is also a part of economic literature. Their utopias provide us with insight into men's dreams of a better world, dreams that have sometimes stirred large numbers to action and played a part in shaping social goals.

We can now turn to the more systematic exploration of economics as a field of inquiry. Bear in mind that the pattern that has been de-

---

[5] This term will be explained more fully later. Briefly, it refers to a theory of organization and policy which minimizes the role of government in economic affairs.

scribed above is woven into the fabric of what follows. The next two chapters treat economics as theory (language) and as experience, while the last chapter of Part 1 deals with some of the normative (value) aspects of economics.

Discussion
Questions

1. What is meant by a statement of fact? By an economic fact?

2. Describe briefly your concept of science. Of scientific method.

3. Make a list of statements of economic events from a newspaper or magazine. Classify these statements according to whether they are analytical, factual, or evaluative.

4. What kinds of data would you expect to find in a book of economic statistics? Would these be of use to other social sciences?

5. Reread the quotation from Wesley C. Mitchell at the beginning of Part 1. What kind of economic model does he favor?

6. What does the term reality mean to you? Economic reality? Social reality?

Economics

in Theory

and Experience

THIS SECTION is concerned with preliminary definition and background of some basic concepts and relations—the symbols and their referents in experience used by economists to express ideas and organize data. Economics, particularly economic theory, has a history: it has a beginning and it has undergone development and change. While a comprehensive history of economic thought cannot be included in an introductory text, some background on how the concepts and relations developed will contribute to a better understanding of their uses and limitations.

Any society, according to Harold Lasswell,[1] has three benefits to confer on its members: *income, security,* and *deference.* Income is that aspect of social relations with which modern economists are chiefly concerned.[2]

In perspective, it is possible to trace a shift of emphasis in economics from *wealth* to *income.* This shift, it can be argued, is linked with changes in the nature of property, that is, with changes in methods of production and the way in which people establish claims against "society's" output of useful things.

---

[1] *Politics: Who Gets What, When, How* (New York: McGraw-Hill Book Co. [Whittlesey House], 1936).

[2] Similarly, security is a concept which is of interest to political scientists, while deference has had primary attention by sociologists, social psychologists, and other behavioral scientists. It should be pointed out, however, that these concepts, because they refer to phenomena that are interdependent, are ambiguous until they are carefully defined and developed for thinking and observational purposes.

18

CHAPTER 2

The Nature and Limits of Economic Science

SINCE INQUIRY usually begins with the recognition or framing of a problem, our first task will be to examine the meaning and usage of the term *economic*. If there is a common denominator in experience for the different contexts in which people use this word, it will provide a clue to the problem situation.

We read in the press that a "conservative" senator has issued one of his periodic statements that the government must *economize* or the country will face financial ruin. During a coal strike or an unusually severe cold spell or a war, business and local government leaders get together to discuss ways to *economize* existing coal stocks. A manufacturing establishment, announcing a layoff of workers, explains that decreasing sales revenues have made it necessary to *economize*. An embarrassed hostess, apologizing for the sour cherry pie she has placed before her guests, reveals that she tried to *economize* on sugar, after she discovered that she forgot to include it on her shopping list.

In each of these examples the term appears as the verb *to economize*. Other forms of the root word will come to mind. As an adjective, it appears in such everyday expressions as an *economy-minded* administration, an *economy-size* package, an *economical* wife. As a noun, it is *economy,* which is a widely-used term, and one to which we shall return. The examples cited here will serve our purpose.

The above usages are so common that we seldom question what they mean. They have associations, both of feelings and belief, which are based upon shared experiences in a common problem. This problem consists of some form of constraint upon the actions and aspirations of people, a constraint (or limitation) which can be traced to two characteristics of the environment.

19

Basis of the Economic Problem

The first of these characteristics relates to the general physical environment. While this environment varies widely over the earth's surface, with few exceptions it is not a particularly "friendly" one. The biological processes on which life depends require that an organism obtain from its surroundings the nourishment to live and grow and the appropriate materials to maintain body temperature within the limits of tolerance. For human beings, this means food, clothing, and shelter. In most areas inhabited by man, these requirements are found in sufficient quantities to make life possible, but rarely easy or automatic. In the fringe areas (the arctic, for example) the environment is harsh, indeed.

The second characteristic of the environment which gives rise to the constraints which create the economic problem is the fact that human existence is a group or social phenomenon. In everyone's environment are many other people who all have the same desires and needs. On the same "niggardly nature" all must depend, frequently in competition with one another. This is especially obvious in the heavily populated, underdeveloped areas of the world, such as India, China, and the Indies.

However, human beings also aid one another.[1] Organized group life is the result of long co-operative effort. Men have learned enough about the predictable processes in nature to turn them to account in satisfying their needs.

Despite a long-run increase in man's capacity to satisfy his needs, however, the constraints mentioned above have not been erased. Nowhere can the great body of mankind attain satisfaction without effort. This is partly due to a characteristic of human beings themselves: the capacity "to want" is not fixed or static. Basic needs are overlaid with social needs, so that the wanting or desiring process is a continuing adjustment, in which the felt need from any particular drive, such as hunger, sex, curiosity, display, or entertainment, may be satisfied, but the total process is insatiable so long as life remains. Moreover, modern civilization has developed a new and different environment in which the job of making people desire more and better things is an occupation of advertising men and salesmen.

In all of its forms, the economic problem emerges as one of underlying scarcity. This need not be scarcity in any absolute sense. It is rela-

---

[1] Recent research in biology indicates that mutual aid is also important for all forms of life. While Darwin's idea of survival of the fittest as a force in the process of evolution is not contradicted by this hypothesis, the capacity to form group interdependencies appears to be necessary for survival. Compare Ashley Montagu, *The Direction of Human Development,* pp. 38–47.

tive scarcity in the face of man's dynamic capacity for wanting things. To the extent that this scarcity is imposed from without by circumstances of the natural environment, making it necessary to choose which wants will be satisfied and in what order, economic action means coming to terms with that environment as the price of individual and group survival. To the extent that scarcity is a condition imposed by the rivalry of human beings, modified by co-operation and joint effort, economic action means finding methods for sharing the scarce means of satisfaction among members of society in a way that makes group life tolerable.

Economic Systems

All known societies, past and present, in adjusting to the physical environment, and in their members adjusting to one another, have had certain arrangements which can be abstracted from others and designated *the economy*. While the economy (or economic system) is not something that can be observed directly, it can be inferred from institutionalized behavior, that is, from customary practices for sharing the work, for the distribution or sharing of goods and services, for decisions of what and how much to produce, and for the accumulation of useful things to be used in future production, such as seed, tools, buildings, and inventories. This, by and large, is the system of relationships to which the concept of *the economy* refers.

When we use the term economy in everyday affairs, it calls to mind many different things, such as the geography of industry and agriculture, and patterns of trading habits and routes over which goods move. But mostly it suggests the things that we and others own, the system of property claims. In any society this is the part of social organization which assures access to limited goods and services.

We know from history that the forms or structures of economic systems have varied widely. They have ranged (and still do, to some extent) from self-sufficient household economies, through nomadic tribal organizations and the medieval manorial systems, to the modern exchange system, with its complex property and credit structures.

Precision in thinking about economic affairs becomes possible only when the system of calculation is fairly advanced.[2] For, while the problem of economizing is one that has concerned men as far back as historians

---

[2] The coming of the Arabic numbers to Europe after the twelfth century greatly facilitated the development of bookkeeping or accounting, and taught men to think about what was behind those accounts. Luca Pocioli (1445–1509?) has provided us with the earliest systematic treatment of double-entry bookkeeping, the forerunner of modern accounting systems.

can discover, it is only in fairly recent times that a systematic ordering of ideas about the process and the accumulation of reasonably accurate data have begun. In one sense, then, the existence of an economic system originates in the systematic thinking about it.

The study of the language of economics can begin with the evolution of the term itself. *Economy* derives from the Greek *oikonomia,* which initially referred to the household.[3] Tracts on *oikonomikos* outlined the "best procedures" for getting the maximum usefulness from the services of slaves and women, both the property of the master of the household. Thus we see that economics began as a "normative" prescription. There was a transfer of meaning, however, and the term came to be applied to the affairs and management of the city-state. As men moved out of the narrow confines of tribal and largely self-sufficient households, they took their language with them and made it do for larger affairs.

While a term for economics, or its equivalent, is to be found in the surviving works of writers and savants through the ages (as they recorded their reflections on trade and wealth), it was not until comparatively recent times that economics was treated as a separate discipline. Plato and Aristotle treated it as an aspect of political affairs. The Scholastics of the Middle Ages, of whom Thomas Aquinas is perhaps the best known, regarded their prescriptions on money and wealth as logical inferences from the more general revelations of divine law. Because such things were regarded as "worldly," they were given but minor attention, chiefly to minimize their importance, but also since they were marks of status. Each station in life was accorded a "just price" or income, which would enable a person in that station to maintain himself in it.

Classical Economic Thought

Adam Smith (1723–1790) is ordinarily credited with establishing economics as a separate discipline, although the name he gave it (which persisted for a century) was political economy.[4] His most influential work (though he did not regard it his most important) was titled *An Inquiry Into the Nature and Causes of the Wealth of Nations,* published in 1776. We know it simply as *The Wealth of Nations.*

In this book Smith was not completely original. He borrowed liberally from predecessors and contemporaries, including the Physiocrats in France and the Mercantilist writers in England. His contribution consisted of fitting together into a more unified structure the preceding

---

[3] This usage survives today in our term "home economics."
[4] French historians are inclined to credit the Physiocrats of their own country with establishing economics as a separate field.

piecemeal observations and interpretations of financial, production, and exchange data. Professor of Moral Philosophy at the University of Edinburgh, student and friend of David Hume (regarded by many as the founder of modern empiricism), and extensive observer of the European scene, Smith established a pattern in economic literature which lasted a long time and had widespread influence.

Adam Smith's analysis focused on his concept of wealth, which he interpreted to mean the *material* basis of well being. The problem that interested him was "What actions by government and citizens will contribute most to an increase of the 'wealth of the nations'?" Production and exchange were viewed as basic processes in the creation of wealth. The system of classification he used for the main body of his analysis was a fairly obvious one based on observation of events around him. He identified three broad classes of variables (factors of production) as important to the production process:

1. *Land,* which includes everything existing in nature, such as soil, minerals, climate, rainfall, flora, and fauna;

2. *Labor,* which is the energy or effort expended by human beings to bring new and more useful material things into existence; and

3. *Capital,* or "stock," which consists of the produced means of production, such as tools, machines, buildings, and all other useful things which have been created from "land" as a result of past human effort. These, Smith maintained, are the "real" foundations of wealth, in contrast with the mercantilist thesis that gold, obtained through trade with other countries, represented a measure of the "real" increase in national well being.

The major sections of *The Wealth of Nations* described these factors and how they are combined in the production, exchange, and final distribution of wealth among people. While his interest was in the material aspects of well being, Smith perceived that the process of creating these materials was a reflection of adjustments among men, more specifically among different classes of men. The specialization and division of labor then developing fascinated him.

The exchange value or price of different goods, Smith believed, was proportional to the amount of labor that had been incorporated in them. For example, if a beaver skin cost three times as much as a deer skin, this was because it took a man, on the average, three times as long to trap a beaver as to kill a deer. Hence he is described as having had a labor theory of value.

Speculating on the developments then in process, Smith attempted to construct an ideal type (model) of social and political organization best suited to economic growth and development. Beginning with the human individual, whom he viewed as basically self-centered, constantly calculating his own advantage, the problem of social organization was how best to turn this human nature to account and harness it to the interest of the nation. His conclusion was that everyone would benefit if each individual were left free by government to advance his own self-interest. Each could be expected to serve others only if it were made to appear advantageous. The following passage from *The Wealth of Nations* will illustrate the burden of his belief and the form of his language:

> It is not from the benevolence of the butcher, the brewer, or the baker that we get our dinner, but from their regard to their own interest. We address ourselves not to their humanity, but to their self-love, and never talk to them of our own necessities, but of their advantages.

The individual was a reasoning person, weighing advantages against disadvantages in his relations with others. This was coupled with a "propensity to truck, barter and exchange," which Smith regarded as a natural and dominant characteristic of all men. Despite the essentially selfish and self-centered nature of man, society could still turn this human nature to account in the market. For there each individual would tend to be regulated by every other individual, and no one could advance his interest indefinitely without coming to terms with the others, subject, of course, to the state's enforcement of order, respect for property, and observance of contract.

Thus Adam Smith (and the school he founded) was inspired by this view of human nature to favor *laissez faire* or nonintervention by government. By leaving men free to seek their greatest advantage, the factors of production would find their most rewarding use in creating the goods and services other people wanted. In this way would the wealth of the whole nation be increased.

Those who followed in the Smith tradition developed his theory with increasing refinement. T. R. Malthus (1766–1834), who is remembered chiefly for his theory of population, underlined the basic problem of scarcity by focusing attention on the tendency of a people to outrun its food supply. Jeremy Bentham (1748–1832), English philosopher, economist, and reformer, and an exponent of a utilitarian philosophy of the "greatest good for the greatest number," was instrumental in promoting not only a belief in the free market, but also in persuading politicians to put it into practice. David Ricardo (1772–1823), a financier and Member of Parliament, not only wrote an influential book on political economy, but also fought the battle for laissez faire in Parliament, particularly against the landed aristocracy. His theory of rent was a political weapon, as well as an instrument for analysis. John Stuart Mill (1806–1873) was the British economist who in 1848 gave a final, systematic presentation of classical economic thought in his *Principles of Political Economy*. In this book he adopted an arrangement which became characteristic of most textbooks on economics, namely, a division into production, distribution, exchange, social progress, and the influence of government.

Finally, Alfred Marshall (1842–1924), another British economist of the classical tradition, rounded out formal economic theory in his *Principles of Economics,* published in 1890, in which he formulated with mathematical precision many of the basic concepts. This book was widely used as a text for more than forty years. Along with the *material* or *real* basis of economic life, which had been developed by the classical school, Marshall incorporated the idea of a subjective value, which made the value of things dependent not only upon the fact of material scarcity but also upon the relative value men gave them by desiring them. He made *supply* and *demand* equal partners in the valuing or pricing process. His concepts of equilibrium or "normal price" in the market and of the optimum or normal firm in the industry were refined statements of how the balancing of interests in a free and competitive market—the balancing of supply and demand—results in the most satisfactory settlement of the scarcity problem.

There were many who contributed to the main stream of nineteenth-century economic thought, but those listed here were perhaps most influential. From their works come many of the concepts still used in economic literature.

Classical and neoclassical economic thought, from Smith through Marshall, was deductive and abstract. On the basis of a few rather simple assumptions, the classical or "orthodox" theorists proceeded to construct a model that was logical, neat, and certain.

With the human individual (atom) as datum point, they asked the question, "How does the rational human being organize his effort and the scarce materials of the environment to maximize his satisfaction or well being?" Some economists in this general tradition delighted in using Daniel Defoe's lonely Robinson Crusoe as their prototype of *economic man.* Decisions about how much work-time to spend fishing, how much to devote to goatskin suits and an umbrella, how much to devote to shelter and the laying in of supplies for a rainy day (or to enable him to build a boat) could be neatly portrayed in such a simple setting. With the

25

coming of Friday, the idea of division of labor and specialization was introduced. Finally, by lifting these narrow limitations, an entire economy could be organized, ideally, without doing serious damage to first principles. Even the introduction of money was not supposed to make any difference, since under ideal conditions money simply "stood for" things.

When Robinson Crusoe produced something, he had a purpose in mind. The product was the result of his individual effort. Once he had a helper, it was more difficult to determine who had "produced" the good. This problem was solved, in a system of private property, by attributing the product to the one who thought of the idea and persuaded the other to help him. Although the latter had an interest in the product, this could be liquidated by the payment of a wage. The initiator was the *entrepreneur,* and output was regarded as his property. Exchange consisted of a transaction between individuals in bartering one good for another. The agreement on the rates of exchange thus determined the relative value of the products. When many were active in the process, the value that emerged was a social value or consensus. Through the use of money, or a medium of exchange, this process was made easier. The price (value in money terms) under specified conditions became the "true" or social value of the good. (The development of the money process will be explored more fully in the next chapter.)

Thus the theory of value or price became central in classical and neoclassical thought. The social process, by means of which price emerged as the "true" measure of social evaluation of men and things, was comprehended by the term *competition.* Where competition prevailed, price became the criterion of worth of all scarce things. The process operated in the market. Each individual brought his mite to the market for valuation. The price set for it largely determined (when multiplied by the quantity offered) what the individual could claim of other things. Thus each unit of goods or productive factor supplied became a source of demand for other goods.

"Supply creates its own demand" was a truism elevated to the dignity of an economic law by Jean Baptiste Say (1767–1832), French economist and interpreter of Adam Smith. Say maintained that a free market, where prices are allowed to find their "natural" level, where all individuals are governed in their economic behavior by competition, will tend toward a stable situation or *equilibrium* in which the demand for goods will equal the supply. (In other words, all goods brought into the market would be taken back by someone else, with each supplier in turn acquiring things he most desired.)

Inferentially at least, it was accepted that a price established in this

26

way was a *just* price, since it would be just sufficient to clear the market of all goods offered for sale. On the other hand, it measured usefulness of the good to the purchaser, since it would represent the amount of claims against other things he would be willing to give up in order to obtain a particular good.

The individual enterpriser or entrepreneur (in the beginning the individual capitalist who risked his wealth in business ventures, but later to become the organizer who risked other people's wealth) was viewed as the moving influence in the free economy. By employing the factors of production (land, labor, and capital) he sought to earn a *profit*, thereby increasing his own claims against others. Free enterprise became known as the *profit system*. In following their own interests in maximizing their profits, by producing the things most desired by people as consumers, these entrepreneurs were regarded as the benefactors of society.

Social and
Ideological Setting

The men and the ideas described above represented the main stream of systematic economic thought (in academic circles, at least) until quite recently. Their influence has left its imprint on our culture, our language, and our values. Even to talk about many of the problems that interest us we must use the concepts they framed. In Parts 3 and 4 of this book, when we examine the problems of production and distribution, the analysis will borrow extensively from the classical tradition.

Before proceeding, however, it will be helpful to reconstruct some of the setting from which their outlook evolved. Two important influences on classical thought can be distinguished, one ideological, the other an emerging new world of experience, although practically the two are intermingled.

Background of Liberalism

The economics which began with Adam Smith and attained its fullest refinement with Alfred Marshall was a product of a world view which emphasized the individual. Specialists in the history of ideas generally refer to that climate of opinion which emerged during the eighteenth and nineteenth centuries as the "liberal tradition." Its distinguishing characteristic was a revolt against authoritarianism in its various forms. Political, religious, and economic thought all came under its influence.

In politics the absolute power of monarchs and the influence of the aristocracy gradually gave way to democracy, which conferred on a widening circle of citizens a voice in governmental affairs. In religion the splintering of established church groups and the proliferation of new sects and denominations can be interpreted as a consequence of the free exercise of individual conscience.[5] And in the writings (as well as the Parliamentary debates) of the classical economists was to be found a justification for the freedom of the individual to pursue his own economic interests, independent of all but minimum interference by government.

This eruption of the individual was a product of the Industrial Revolution, a major force in the transformation of society and the breakup of feudal institutions. The spread of scientific knowledge had been in progress since the beginning of the Renaissance, and in 1776—the year of the Declaration of Independence and the publication of *The Wealth of Nations*—a steam engine was constructed according to Watt's design, to be used for industrial power. This was the first of the great releases of inanimate energy (to be followed in the next century and a half by others) which were to accelerate man's conquest of space and time. The effect was to free men in great numbers from a narrow dependence on the land and those who owned the land. It created powerful tools for changing the environment and shaping it to new needs and desires. It also altered the relations among individuals and groups, so that old ways of life and old ways of thinking no longer seemed meaningful.

Economic liberalism was at once an explanation and a prescription for individualism in the area of man's wealth-getting and wealth-using activities. To the rising merchant and industrial classes, particularly, individualism provided clear "ideological" justification for what they saw as their own advantage, and a weapon to be used against the established order.

The gradual refinement of formal economic thought and method parallels the growth of the new industrial society itself. Adam Smith perceived the emerging relationships of the new society indistinctly, and his statements were correspondingly vague. The following excerpt from Arnold Toynbee, nineteenth-century economic historian, gives one interpretation of events of the period:

> . . . Adam Smith lived on the eve of an industrial revolution.
> Ricardo lived in the midst of it. Assumptions which could never have

---

[5] Two economic historians have advanced the thesis that the liberal development in religion was not simply a parallel to liberalism in economics but that it was an active ingredient in the growth of the enterprise society. Compare R. H. Tawney, *Religion and the Rise of Capitalism,* and Max Weber, *The Protestant Ethic.*

occurred to Adam Smith, because foreign to the quiet world he lived in, a world of restrictions and scarcely perceptible industrial movement, occurred to Ricardo almost as a matter of course. That unceasing, all-penetrating competition—that going to and fro on the earth in search of gold—that rapid migration of men and things, the premises of all his arguments were but the exaggeration, however wild, of the actual state of the industrial world of Ricardo's time. The steam engine, the spinning jenny, the power loom, had torn up the population by the roots; corporation laws, laws of settlements, acts of apprenticeship, had been swept away by the mere stress of physical circumstances; and with all that visible movement of vast masses of people before his eyes, with that ceaseless tossing and eddying of the liberated industrial stream ever before him, is it to be wondered at that, with the strong native bias of his mind already in this direction, he should make without hesitation that postulate of pure competition on which all the arguments of his treatise depend?[6]

To recapture the experience on which this body of thought was based, one needs to imagine the activity which attended the beginning of the Industrial Revolution. A hint of this is given in the above passage from Toynbee. Immediately preceding and during the period of economic liberalism's greatest development, the nations of the Old World, and particularly England, were busy filling up the unoccupied areas of the earth, slowly but surely linking them together through trade. This process continued even when the various colonies separated from the mother country. Into the older countries, from which the explorers, traders, and settlers set out, there poured a flood of new products, raw materials, and gold. *Real goods* were multiplied many fold, making possible the rapid increase of population. By the middle of the nineteenth century, the wheat fields of England had moved to the New World, and her population was increasing and "eating" more than Malthus had believed possible.

Men had once thought of land as the limiting factor of production. Those who controlled its use could not but be accorded status and deference. Now attention shifted to *capital* as the dynamic or creative factor, and the accumulation of capital became the key to growth of the production economy. The position of influence shifted to the merchant and the industrialist in the minds and hearts of men no less than in the tracts of the economists. As capital, in the form of new machinery, ships, buildings, and technological processes expanded, the size of individual business units

---

[6] *Lectures on the Industrial Revolution* (New York: Humboldt, 1884), pp. 5–6.

also grew. Private companies increasingly adopted the organizational form of the corporation, welding together the property and the efforts of many. The individualism of classical doctrine was very flexible. In economics, as in law, the public corporation was accorded the status of a person. As changes took place, however, the complex system of property, production, consumption, and investment relationships of the real world attained an ever increasing variety not dealt with by the classical model.

There were increasing weaknesses in the classical model as a tool for organizing experience. It ceased to have contact with "real" problems and became more and more a system of formal logic deduced from a very simple set of assumptions. There is little doubt that during its early development it had helped men to order their thinking about events of the then developing system of social and economic relations. Especially was this true for the field of international trade. But as the century wore on, classical theory sacrificed realism for formal elegance. Here is how Alfred North Whitehead summed it up in 1925:

> It is very arguable that the science of political economy, as studied in the first period after the death of Adam Smith (1790) did more harm than good. It destroyed many economic fallacies, and taught how to think about the economic revolution then in progress. But it riveted on men a certain set of abstractions which were disastrous in their influence on modern mentality.[7]

Whitehead is here referring to the fact that the ideal model which the economists constructed, and in terms of which they speculated about what men could do if freed from the restrictions of the feudal property system, resembled closely what was actually taking place at the time. These new freedoms paid off in expanded production and trading activities once rigid government restraints were lifted. Later on, when other restraints began to develop, the growth of powerful private economic controls (outside government but often relying on its protection) rendered the model out of date and policy recommendations which relied upon it at least questionable.

Critics of Classical Economics

To leave the impression that economic ideas of this period were influenced only by classicism would be wrong. There were other schools of thought. Karl Marx and the socialists cannot be ignored. The Historical school

---

[7] *Science and The Modern World* (New York: The Macmillan Co., 1925), p. 280.

in Germany and later the Institutionalists in the United States were both critical of the accepted doctrine of classicism.

Common to all these critics was a point of view which focused on another aspect of economic life. They believed that the wealth-getting and wealth-using activities should be viewed in a social or political setting. They placed less emphasis on the relation between man and wealth—the material aspects of the environment—and more on the relation between man and man. They were less interested in the purely "rational" aspects of behavior, more interested in the evolution of institutions and in the way they influence actual behavior in coping with the economic problem.

Karl Marx (1818–1883) stressed the division of men into classes based on property systems. In contrast to the classical school (a name, incidentally, which he first used), Marx organized his thinking in terms of broad aggregates, of the interrelatedness of individuals and groups as the fabric of society. It was he who first used the term *capitalism* to refer to the economic system which followed feudalism. He focused attention on evolution and change, and the effect of capital in binding individuals more closely together in groups and classes. To some, this represents his positive contribution to social science.

Marx, however, was more interested in political action. He believed that his "scientific" studies had provided him with a clue to history and to socio-political change. His theoretical system is sometimes called the economic or materialist interpretation (determination) of history. Within that system the class struggle was treated as the factor which induces change to new economic forms, somewhat in the manner that Darwin viewed the "survival of the fittest" as the dynamic factor in biological evolution.

Under capitalism Marx predicted that the proletariat or the working class, subjected to increasing exploitation by the capitalists, would become the "engine of revolution," transforming society into its next phase, which he envisioned as some form of socialism.

Not content with the role of scientist, Marx also worked in the Socialist International to promote the system whose coming he viewed as inevitable. He sought by his writings and other activities to stimulate a class consciousness among working people and to hasten the overthrow of capitalism.

Together with Friedrich Engels (1820–1895), his collaborator and sometimes "meal ticket," Marx gathered considerable empirical data and published numerous "tracts for the times." Some of his principal concepts (his labor theory of value, for example, on which he based his theory of exploitation) he borrowed from the classicists, particularly Ricardo, and his model of social dynamics derived chiefly from the German philosopher Hegel.

The German Historical school, which emphasized the institutional and political aspects of "economic" relations, was influenced by the value system of romantic nationalism, and had a tendency to wander off into a dogma of narrow statism. The members of this school did, however, contribute to a tradition of empiricism in economic science and several of them made contributions in statistics. Some of the better known names associated with "historismus" are Wilhelm Roscher (1817–1894), Bruno Hildebrand (1812–1878), Karl Knies (1821–1898), and Gustav Schmoller (1838–1917).

In the United States the Institutionalists, of whom Thorstein Veblen (1857–1929) and John R. Commons (1862–1945) were perhaps most influential, likewise questioned the limited view of human nature which made of man a "lightning calculater of pleasures and pain," motivated only by pecuniary advantage. Veblen, especially, was influenced by developments in the other social sciences—in psychology and anthropology, specifically. He was fascinated by the complexity and variety of institutional arrangements by means of which men have organized the economic processes. He viewed the institutional arrangement of Western civilization not as something "natural" but merely as one of many possible arrangements. Moreover, he believed the enterprise society to be changing from one of many relatively independent small business firms, regulated by competition, to one with a growing core of giant corporations and powerful economic pressure groups, which created a division between those who "make money" and those who "make things."

The Institutionalists gave direction not so much to what economists "think" as to what they do. Both the Historical and Institutional economists stressed observation and description of business organizations and government practice, the collection of statistics on production, resources, population, industries, and family consumption units, with the ultimate purpose of deriving from the "facts" an empirical model of the economy as it "really" is.

The division in economic thought between those who emphasized the deductive, idealistic aspects of knowledge, and those who stressed details, facts, and experience is not, of course, unique. It appears at some point in the history of virtually all fields of inquiry, and has been especially evident in philosophy. In economics, as elsewhere, the divergent points of view managed to coexist. The terms *theoretical* and *applied* economics persisted as a common, if not always useful, description of the work turned out by exponents of the two approaches.

More recently the tendency has been for disputes over methodology to moderate. A shift of emphasis in theory, the improvement of empirical methods, and the increasing availability of more reliable statistical data about the economy, have contributed to a greater unification of what economists do, and of the concepts with which they work.

Some More Recent Developments

During the 1930's formal economic theory (at least, the analytical model of the academic discipline) came under the influence of a new generation of thinkers and writers, with the result that it was considerably broadened in its scope. Two treatises on the problem of monopoly[8] appeared almost simultaneously in the United States and England. The former, by Edward Chamberlin, was called the *Theory of Monopolistic Competition,* and the latter, by Joan Robinson, *The Theory of Imperfect Competition.* These books dealt with problems of pricing and the allocation of factors under conditions other than those of competition. Both were more or less in the classical framework, but with somewhat different assumptions. They took into account circumstances which had become increasingly apparent from experience—the fact that a decreasing number of firms dominated more and more markets. This tendency had begun in fields now characterized as public utilities (transportation, communications, power, the supplying of money and credit), but after the turn of the century had extended to more and more areas of the production economy. The influence of these writers will also appear in Parts 3 and 4.

This integration of the problem of monopoly in economic affairs into the main body of theory, however, was only the beginning of change. By the end of the 1930's an increasing number of references to the "new economics" began to appear in the literature.

At the center of this ferment of ideas among economists, one name in particular figures prominently, that of John Maynard Keynes (1883–1946). The son of a respected Cambridge economist and a student of Marshall, Keynes had been trained in the English neoclassical tradition and had earned a creditable reputation working within that frame of reference. Struggling with the problems of economic affairs in the twen-

---

[8] The problem of monopoly had been recognized and treated theoretically much earlier by a French economist, A. Cournot (1801–1877). It had been given passing reference by Marshall, but he regarded it as of little significance and hence not particularly interesting.

tieth century, however, he reached a point in the development of his ideas where he no longer found the concepts used by the classicists the most useful.

Although it is possible to trace the evolution of his ideas in a succession of books and articles over nearly two decades, his most widely known and his last major work was *The General Theory of Employment, Interest and Money.* Some of the ideas contained in this volume were not new, some were borrowed from others (and acknowledged),[9] and the book itself was hastily and not always well written. While his rejection of traditional economics may prove to be less complete than at first appeared (and as Keynes, in fact, claimed), the effect of his work has been to change markedly the language and order of problems with which economists deal. Before exploring the nature and significance of those changes in more detail, however, it will be useful to review the background of experience which, in a sense, was forcing the hands of economists and of which they now began to take account.

The Changing Content of Economic Experience

In modern industrial society men had been subjected periodically to a disturbing new experience in the form of recurring periods of declining economic activity, of unemployment and widespread deprivation, even though there existed large unused production facilities. Men spoke of "poverty in the midst of plenty" (never quite accurate, but containing enough truth to be convincing and disturbing), while communists and other radicals demanded the abolition or drastic reform of existing institutions.

Instability was, in fact, the notable weakness of industrial society. Evidence supports the fact that these alternating periods of prosperity and depression date from the early nineteenth century when, after the end of the Napoleonic wars, the institutions which Marx called "capitalism" began their more rapid growth and development.

For the persons affected, the industrial workers especially, depression usually meant the loss of jobs and the consequent loss of income. Farmers and small businessmen experienced falling prices, decline in the value of property holdings, and substantial, if not complete, loss of income. Many lacked the means to acquire the things they and their families required—things that could still be observed in store windows and in warehouses. The family might continue to consume for a time by drawing on past savings (if there were any), by selling things that they owned,

---

[9] Some of Keynes's ideas had, in fact, been anticipated by a group of Swedish economists, of whom Knut Wicksell (1851–1936) is usually regarded as the leader.

or by purchasing on credit as long as it could be had. To all such make-shift solutions there was always a foreseeable limit, and the personal problem of insecurity could only be reduced, finally, if a job were found. Psychologically, insecurity was not limited to the actual loss of a job, since many who remained employed experienced great uncertainty by anticipating further layoffs.

In the nineteenth century there was a succession of such crises. Recovery always came, sometimes sooner, sometimes later, and the extent of the crisis varied widely. The century between 1815 and 1914 was relatively peaceful. The minor wars in various parts of the world, and the American Civil War in particular, were associated with wide variations in economic activity, so that wars were frequently credited with being the disturbers of economic activity.

The belief persisted, however, that other important causes were connected with the so-called "commercial crises," since wars themselves, despite their waste and destruction, were usually periods of prosperity and high-level economic activity. Depressions usually came after the war had ended. This was an experience that was quite new in the history of mankind. 1117458

One of the earliest studies of commercial crises was by a French physician, Clement Juglar (1819–1913), whose thoughts and observations on the subject were published in 1860. He believed that prosperity and depression were aspects of a single phenomenon, and that depressions were not simply cases of economic illness. Both prosperity and depression could be understood, he asserted, as functional characteristics of the existing economic institutions.

Others searched for causes outside the economic institutions. William Stanley Jevons believed he had found a clue to the cause of cycles in the sun spots (which had just been observed to follow a cyclical pattern). Marx and the socialists, of course, viewed industrial depression as further proof of the inherent weakness of existing economic institutions and additional evidence of the inevitable breakdown of capitalism.

Economists of the orthodox tradition, for the most part, had no theory of the business cycle as such. Their competitive model of economic life was designed to explain how a laissez faire enterprise economy worked to bring about a balanced use of the factors of production. It was not adapted to inquiry into the failures. They were aware, of course, of business fluctuations, of booms and depressions, of unemployment, falling prices, and declining output. These phenomena they saw as departures from the long-run natural tendency for the economy to achieve equilibrium with a full use of scarce resources.

In their analysis these economists stressed factors which could "cause" prices of different commodities to get out of balance with one another, thus creating an imbalance between demand and supply. There were two such factors emphasized: (1) flexibility of the money and credit supply, and (2) rigidity of certain prices in the short run, particularly wages. Increasing the amount of money (either through the use of bank credit or the discovery of new gold deposits) would tend to increase effective demand, particularly for the factors of production. This would result in a rise in prices, since people had more money to spend. As prices rose, labor unions would demand, and get, higher wages. These events occurred during the boom period. As production rose, the less efficient workers would find jobs at union rates, producers costs would rise, causing profits to decline. Sooner or later employers would be willing to continue high level production only if the price of labor (wages) could be reduced.

To the extent that they made recommendations concerning policy, the classical economists emphasized stability of the money and credit supply on the one hand, and greater flexibility of wages (the largest element in costs) on the other. By cutting costs, and thus prices, while the money supply remained stable, the money demand could again be brought into equilibrium with the supply of goods when labor was fully employed. When unemployment appeared, they maintained that this was because the price of labor was too high. Unions, by resisting wage cuts, were in effect choosing unemployment.

Thus, an apparent "logical" conclusion of their analysis was that the ups and downs of the economy were a natural and inevitable consequence of imperfections in human institutions, if not in man himself. They did not favor concerted action through the agency of government to get out of depressions, since this might delay the "natural" processes of correction and adjustment. A few of the extreme laissez faire advocates did believe that government intervention against unions would have beneficial effects, since such combinations were themselves an interference with a free market. When economic theory began to take account of monopoly in general, the neoclassical economists favored public policies to break up monopolies in business as well, because of their tendency to raise prices in the monopolized areas and to create an imbalance in the economy.

By the third decade of the twentieth century an extensive literature on the business cycle had accumulated. Empirical economists and statisticians (in the service of government, private organizations, and the universities) had gathered and organized numerical data portraying the long-run growth and the short-run setbacks for many facets of economic life. Thus, when the great depression of the early 1930's affected the economic activities of a large part of the industrial world, those who undertook to analyze the order and magnitude of the changes had more to work with than at any previous time. Theories or hypotheses of the nature and causes of depression could be subjected to more rigorous testing with the facts of experience. "Practical" proposals were legion, from autarky ("buy American," "buy British," etc.) and subsistence farming ("back to the land") to international monetary reform and co-operation. For most of such piecemeal proposals there was lacking a general body of theory, a frame of reference, to relate specific actions to one another in a meaningful system.

When Keynes published his *General Theory* in 1936, the attention it received and the influence it exercised stemmed from the fact that what he believed and taught appeared to have relevance for the problems of depression.[10] The concepts and relations he developed were adapted to the whole economy, not as an arithmetic sum of "representative" individuals (all conforming to a rather simplified pattern of economic behavior), but as a complex structure of individuals and groups interacting through a common cultural medium of money income.

The "new economics" is distinguished by the emphasis it gives to national income analysis. Its difference lies not so much in concern with the central variable of national product, as in the frame of reference from which it is viewed. Smith, Marshall, A. C. Pigou, and others were interested in the growth of "real income" from specialization, capital accumulation, the expansion of enterprise, and other factors which are more or less "long run" in their influence. Keynes and his followers were concerned with economic events which resulted in "short-run" changes in the level of employment and output caused by money-income flows.

Price analysis moves to a position of secondary importance in economic literature after 1940. Perhaps it is more accurate to say that problems involving price no longer get the attention in economic analysis they did once, because they are not the problems regarded as of crucial importance. This can be illustrated by an example used earlier. In suggesting policies to cope with unemployment, we noted that economists had previously stressed flexible wages. They argued that if wages were reduced, thereby lowering costs, it would again become profitable for producers to expand output and employment.

Keynes questioned this reasoning. He noted that while a reduction of wages, generally, might reduce costs, the income of the workers would

---

[10] Some critics of Keynes maintain that the *General Theory* was only a theory of depression, that policies which derive from it are not applicable once full employment is reached.

be reduced at the same time, thereby causing purchasing power or *aggregate demand* to decline. The position of producers as a group would not thereby be improved. This was a case in which analysis applicable to an individual business or industry could not be generalized. He discounted the conclusions of such price analysis on theoretical grounds, and he did not believe that wage reductions were "practical" because of the strength of modern labor unions.

The new frame of reference was based on an assumption that unemployment and a declining national income are problems of *aggregate demand*—a sufficient purchasing power in the hands of spending units willing to purchase available goods and services at prevailing prices. Such purchasing power depends on two variables, the total amount of liquid funds (money and credit), and the willingness of those who control them to exchange their holdings for goods or factors of production. The extension of economic knowledge requires an analysis of spending and saving behavior, and understanding of the income units whose actions determine the total amount of spending and saving.

The details of Keynes's theoretical model, the concepts and system of classification, the relationships, and the policies he proposed for understanding economic reality and using that understanding to control the modern economy will not be developed further here. These have now been assimilated into the main currents of contemporary economic thought, and developed and altered by his followers and critics as they have been put to test. They will be our concern through much of the remainder of this book. Part 2 in particular, which is devoted to national income measurement and analysis, bears the greatest imprint of his influence.

The space devoted above to the contributions of one man may seem excessive to some. It is true that a reading of economic literature, the proceedings of learned societies, the important books (in the field of theory, particularly) written during the past fifteen years will testify to his impact. But no man, even the most brilliant, creates an ideological system out of whole cloth. Each builds on the insights, observations, and interpretations of others. From the history of science we learn that new directions in thought are generally accepted only when the world is ready for them. As experience accumulates, old ways of "ordering the real world" cease to be productive of new insights, of new directions for inquiry. Then by happy accident, or by brilliant insight or dogged perseverance, the so-called catalyzers of human thought signal a new direction. Historians of ideas, reconstructing events at a later date, can usually point to the fact that the groundwork for such ideological revolutions has usually been laid in advance.

38

When the appearance of the *General Theory* officially signaled the shift in emphasis of economic theory to what has since been called the "national-income approach," much spadework had already been accomplished at the empirical level. Estimates of the national income of the United States had been published for the first time in 1929. These were chiefly the work not of theorists but of applied economists and statisticians. A prime mover in the development of these estimates had been Wesley C. Mitchell (1874–1948). A student of Veblen, with a pronounced institutional bent, Mitchell had already made a significant contribution to knowledge about the business cycle while Keynes was still working on refinements of the classical tradition in which he had been trained.

Other aggregate studies of the whole economy had provided indices for measuring total economic activity. These were all necessary operational tools which had to be at hand before a concept of national income could be given empirical content. And behind these measures, there had to be a development of "economic" institutions linking people ever more closely together in a complex and interdependent relationship.

To a nation of largely self-sufficient households, even though politically united, the idea of *national income* would be unlikely to occur.[11] For what meaning would it have to add together the value (even if it were possible to put a value on things that were never compared) of what the families created for themselves in food, clothing, living space, and fuel? Until nearly the middle of the nineteenth century the United States had been predominantly a nation of farmers, and farmers (until comparatively recently) produced much that they used.

Modern technology, expanding markets, the growing size of business units, increasing organization and specialization, the exchange of a constantly increasing range of goods and services against money all combined to bring about a change. The proportion of the population working directly for wages and salaries expanded steadily, until by the second decade of the twentieth century it was the majority. Men no longer worked to create things, but to create a money income. Far from being a veil behind which "economic reality" was to be discovered, money became the warp and woof of the economic fabric. When people think of income, they think at first (if not exclusively) in money terms.

---

[11] This point should not be stretched too far. The *idea* of national income is, in fact, quite old. According to Joseph Schumpeter, the concept of the flow of income was grasped by some as early as the fourteenth century. As we shall see in the next chapter, and particularly in Part 2, the need for a concept of national income was understood quite early in the history of economics. What these early economists lacked were the operational tools and the raw data for actually deriving a usable measure of income.

With this brief summary of the history of economic ideas and experience, we can now attempt a restatement and definition of the frame of reference of modern economic thought.

Restatement
and Definition

For the modern economist, as a social scientist, the objective of inquiry is to reconstruct the "economic reality" to which the concept *income* refers. In furtherance of this inquiry, the economist attempts to identify and describe (as precisely as his tools will permit) the factors affecting its size, its origin, its distribution, its use, and its rate of growth or decline. Data include the patterns of production organization, the structure of property claims against the scarce and useful output of society, and rates of destruction in the use of the goods and services with which people sustain life and give it meaning. He is aided in this search by countless records kept in the common denominator of money value, which are the clues from which consistencies in past economic behavior must be inferred, and on the basis of which predictions of future actions are attempted.

What Income Is

When we think of income the image which comes first to mind is that of money, the paper bills and small change we get from the paymaster or salary clerk each week or month. It may be the figures on a check which has to be "cashed" before it is spent, or the sum of all such receipts which we total up when we figure our annual income tax.

This is a starting point, but no more than that. A concept of income which refers to a process of counting the number of times a dollar comes into our possession is operational, but it does not go very deep. For money does not usually stay put, and its subsequent history is part of the concept of income also.

What we *really* have to show for our effort at the end of any period of time (a month, a year, a lifetime) is a small accumulation of things we now own—clothes, car, equity in a house or business, a figure in a bank book which tells us how much the bank owes us—plus the remembrance of the goods and services we ate up, wore out, or otherwise "enjoyed" during that time. Most of these we obtained by translating money income into things through purchase, and these things we can call *real income*.

If this concept is projected onto the national level, national income

40

consists of all the money incomes of individuals, businesses, and governments added together on the one hand, and the mountains of goods and hours of services created—by means of which everyone is fed, clothed, sheltered, entertained, protected, and sometimes corrupted—on the other. To this should be added the accumulation of new things such as buildings, roads, bridges, and unused goods—the new "stock" as it was called in Adam Smith's time.

Economists have repeatedly cautioned against the pitfalls of thinking in terms of money. Money income can be an "illusion." But this, too, can be overstressed. The ultimate reality is human behavior, and in the world of symbols and signs money can be very "real." We need only to recognize that our common-sense meaning of income is a starting point. There is nothing wrong with starting with an "illusion." After all, the astronomer also starts with an illusion (a foggy spot on a photographic plate), from which he has to work his way back to the "reality" which may be a star a million light years away.

The economist's concept of income, although more precisely stated, is not so different from that of the common-sense concept of income. He totals the figures which stand for dollars that have passed through peoples' hands. Ultimately his interest is in the size of the parallel flow of goods and services which the labor, the machines, and the natural resources together helped to create. But to count, measure, or weigh all the millions of things produced would be a hopeless task, since none of these units of measure can be reduced to a common denominator for purposes of measuring the different sorts of things. Tractors and permanent waves, diamonds and blue-plate lunches, cement and tulip bulbs possess one characteristic in common for income purposes, and that is their value. Value, for the economist's purposes, is measured in money. Thus, *income* is literally "that which comes in"—first in money, and then in what the money buys.

Income flows would not command our attention as such, were it not that they pose certain problems. The most central, of course, is the fact that income (money) is difficult to come by. From the time we first are aware of the thousand-and-one good things (goods) which may be had from shops and soda fountains, it has been impressed upon us that such things cost money, and "money doesn't grow on trees." This is the *form* in which we experience the problem of scarcity relative to our wants. For most of us, those of us, at least, who are heads of households, the major part of our waking hours in adult life will be spent in the pursuit of activities aimed at securing a money income. The problem confronting the modern economist, then, is the observed fact that income is scarce in

41

relation to the desire for it. Here are some questions which he explores: What sets the limits to income at any given time? Why is it more difficult for some to get than for others? What use do people make of it after they get it? To find these answers involves the economist in still other questions How do incomes originate? How do we measure them? Where do they go when they are spent?

These are questions with which we will be dealing from now on. They will carry us back through appearances to "reality." But it will be well to remember throughout, to remind ourselves again and again, that all of reality is in fact a process—a process of change. If at times the subject matter seems to be a bit abstract, it can be recalled that thinking is itself a process of abstracting. Most of the errors in everyday economic discussion stem from the fact that there is too little awareness of just how abstract are the words we use.

Definition of Economics

For present purposes, then, the following concise definition of economic science can be kept in mind. *Economics is an application of the scientific method to the study of income, with a view to understanding how it is produced, measured, distributed, and spent.*

Definitions, however, are only a convenience. They serve as a starting point for inquiry, as tools for ordering our thinking and our observations as they relate to a problem. The study of income would scarcely engage our attention were it not for the fact that it is a term agreed upon to designate an aspect of our society, our common experience as members of society, associated with questions which we think important.

The problem of income scarcity is not unique. It can be traced back to the physical or natural limitations on *real income,* to social and institutional limitations, and to human motivation and effort.

In the succeeding chapters we will be concerned with the income problem as it appears in a modern industrial society, such as that of the United States, where the principal institutional characteristics are: (1) considerable freedom of enterprise, which includes the right to own and use natural resources, factories, goods of all kinds, and the right to free association for income purposes; (2) substantial freedom of choice to consumers to spend income without great restriction by government (except in wartime) on goods that are preferred; and (3) a system of markets where, within limits, individuals are free to buy and sell goods and services under varying degrees of competition and in which prices (money values) of goods are not set by a single central authority, except in times of emergency. A fourth characteristic might be added. That

42

would be the absence of rigid central planning in which individuals are controlled in their income-getting and spending activities by government. This is more or less implied in the other three. To say that the American system is one in which government plays no part in economic affairs would be incorrect. Government, as we shall see, plays a considerable role. But in the United States the traditions of nineteenth-century liberalism are still partially adhered to, particularly in opinions of "what ought to be." It is not so strong as it once was, however, and economic literature has increasingly characterized ours as a "mixed economy," by which is meant an economy in which the role of government is positive.

Differences in economic systems can be reduced, very largely, to variations in the way the fundamental problem of scarcity is met. Authoritarian societies, whether of fascist or communist variety, control the efforts of their citizens in meeting the problem of scarcity by means of coercion as well as rewards. These rewards determine income distribution. Nations do not change the basic facts of scarcity (discussed at the beginning of this chapter) by changing the form of their economic or income system. The scarcity problem is one that must be met by all systems.

From what we know about the past from historical records, no previous society has produced as much from its resources as our own, or for so large a proportion of its population. In terms of life expectancy and the elimination of suffering from cold, hunger, and disease, modern industrial society has made the greatest progress in the struggle to lessen the basic problem imposed by the "niggardliness of nature." We call this "economic progress," and we measure it by the growth of per capita *real income.*

Specialization
in Economics

In economics, as in other fields of inquiry, the complexity of the subject fosters specialization. The separate tasks which economists perform are related to their interests and their abilities; they range from constructing the most abstract models to the collection of detailed statistics on some minute aspect of the economic or income process. Some of these areas of specialization, framed in terms of the income concept, are described below.

Economic History

The economic historian investigates the structure and development of past economic or income arrangements. He is interested in how people have adapted their behavior and their institutions to the constraints imposed by the "economic problem" at different periods in history. He attempts to provide insights into how people made their living, how the different individuals and groups shared the real income created by their combined efforts. He is interested in their technology, its impact on the production economy, and in the ownership patterns determining the distribution of goods and services.

A primitive economy can be described as one in which people live largely by direct appropriation from nature. Hunting and fishing rights would be the most important property forms. Division of labor in such societies was based largely upon some form of status, related to sex, age, or social class. Division of the product, within the tribe, was frequently equalitarian during times of scarcity, by capacity to consume in times of plenty.

Early organized societies, with their military legions and subject peoples, were usually characterized by the exercise of naked power as an important element in determining work load and distributive shares. The feudal system, which followed the breakup in the Western world of Imperial Rome, evolved into a society of rigid classes based upon the ownership or control of the land. The peasants who tilled the soil, gave up predetermined amounts of their product as *rents* to those who controlled the land. The freer society which followed the breakup of feudalism saw the development of new means of acquiring goods and services through trade or exchange.

While certain fairly distinct periods in the evolution of the present economic institutions can be identified, there has always been wide geographic and cultural variations. It is the job of the economic historian to reconstruct and organize, from evidence he can discover, the variety of past economic experience as well as the present stages of economic development.

Economic Theory

Theorists are those specialists who concern themselves with the more abstract generalizations. They build models and other symbolic representations which enable us to conceptualize broad central tendencies and relationships from the variety of detail. To the extent that these symbolic analogs can be verified in experience, they provide the means of understanding "reality."

Such models are of two kinds. In economics they may be a symbolic representation of actual income flows in relation to other variables, or they may be hypothetical models of a "desirable" economic system, in which the income flows conform to some predetermined pattern of behavior.

A special branch of economic theory, *econometrics,* has carried the technique of abstraction to a high level. Combining economic theory, mathematics, and statistics, specialists in this branch of the discipline translate the important concepts and relationships into mathematical language, thereby abstracting completely from meanings and associations of everyday language. When they have constructed a model which appears to resemble the relationships that hold for an existing economic or income system, they derive inferences from their model to test in experience. By giving their concepts and relationships empirical content, such as numerical values for national income, consumption, savings, investment, and others, they attempt to test the reliability of their model by predicting future values for these variables.

The econometricians also develop *ideal* models, by constructing "desirable" relationships for certain functions, then attempting to determine what other relationships would have to be in order to attain this goal. Some of the criteria for judging such models are equality, stability, or growth of real income.

Historians of economic theory or economic thought are specialists in the evolution of economic language.

Economic Statistics

Workers in the field of economic statistics are of two general types. The first group gathers historical data or time series on various aspects of the income or economic process. The second group attempts to extract from these data the maximum information about the variations in the different series and their representativeness. They also construct indices, by means of which large bodies of numerical data can be represented. Both groups must work closely together, of course. The first can be regarded as specializing in observation, the second in the application of statistical theory.

Most statistics about the economy are not gathered directly by economists, but by governmental and private agencies, often for other purposes. The departments of Labor, Commerce, Agriculture, Treasury, and various other bureaus and commissions are the sources of many of the basic data economists use in empirical research. Economists frequently serve as advisers to these agencies in an attempt to improve the usefulness and accuracy of statistics. A general textbook, such as this one, draws its material from an economic literature which includes the work of all such specialists.

Limits
of Economics

As we develop our income concept in succeeding chapters, it will be apparent that some aspects of the "everyday business of making a living" will escape the measuring rod of our discipline. No attempt will be made to get at the intangible satisfactions (or dissatisfactions) we get from living where we do and performing the job of our choice, sometimes called *psychic income*. Even the productive services of the housewife will elude us. To try to get a measure of everything would involve us in an attempt to measure the meaning of life itself.

Although our attention is focused on a phase of social relations which appears to be closely related to the materials of the external environment, it still cannot be separated from man himself. His decisions, his actions, and how he views his world will enter into and affect the income flow. Yet, these cannot all be taken into account. The other behavioral sciences, viewing the same social world from a slightly different frame of reference, have their contributions to make also. Some economists once believed seriously that theirs was the only true science in the social field. This view is no longer widely held.

Income and *power* are often closely intertwined. Each can unlock the door to the other. Some of the problems we encounter will overlap with those that interest the political scientist. Status, as sociologists and social psychologists point out, is closely correlated with income in our culture. The study of economic behavior can never be complete if it is isolated from other disciplines.

There is evidence that as the social sciences grow in maturity, cooperation among the separate disciplines becomes increasingly desirable. In an expanded science of man in the future, economics may well become a minor technology. The things economists know, though only a small part of the total picture, would still be important.

Discussion
Questions

1. Using the different parts of speech, prepare a list of terms which can be derived from the verb "to economize." Is there a common association in experience which corresponds with these terms?

2. What was your income last year, in dollars? Make a list of things for which this income was spent.

46

3. List the ten wealthiest persons you know. What criterion did you use in deciding who should be included?

4. The aristocracy of the Old World, and the pre-Civil War South in the United States, frequently regarded business or commerce with disdain. Why?

5. What is the money illusion? Why is money regarded as desirable?

6. David Riesman has commented that people once judged a person by the extent of his wealth, whereas we now judge him by his expense account. Discuss.

CHAPTER 3

The Background and Meaning

of Some Basic Economic Concepts

IN THE PRECEDING CHAPTER we have used a number of terms without developing them as concepts. The full meaning of some of these will not be clear until they are more fully explored in succeeding chapters. There are a few terms, however, that are so much a part of economic language, so commonly identified with it, that an examination of their etymological and semantic background will be helpful at this point.

Wealth

Of all the terms used in economic literature, none suggests, on first impression, greater objectivity and "material fact" than *wealth*. The meaning of the term most frequently given is "all goods which are material, transferable, scarce, useful, and owned."

However, few terms have lent themselves more to poetic license and ambiguity. "There is no wealth but life," opined John Ruskin, nineteenth-century romantic who was appalled by the materialism of the emerging industrial society. Like Carlyle, who characterized classical economics as the "dismal science," Ruskin rejected the spirit and teaching, the concern with wealth and materialism, of political economy.

Etymologically the term wealth is involved and circular. Those well placed with respect to the material requirements for living were said to "fare well" and hence, by inversion, "welfare." Whatever contributed to welfare was wealth. To conclude therefore that wealth is what contributes to welfare brings us full circle.

Like most words, this one carries its history with it. The concern with wealth, in material form, was closely related to the experience of people at the time of economics' early beginnings. All were closely dependent on the land, on agriculture, forestry, and fishing for the simple requirements of living. Those who owned, or controlled, the land and the relatively simple capital equipment obviously fared best.

The early emphasis on materialism by economists led to a rather barren system of classification. Writers on economics attempted to distinguish between *productive* and *nonproductive* occupations. A nonproductive occupation was one which resulted in no new "material wealth." This excluded personal services from the production process. Lawyers, doctors, teachers, white-collar workers, and many others were classified as nonproductive, in the sense that they added nothing new to the flow of material goods or wealth. A shadow of these earlier assumptions lingers on in popular discussion. When people try to decide which occupations are most important to the social welfare, the farmers, miners, lumbermen, and fishermen appear to have the most to contribute, because the results of their handiwork are concrete, and obviously necessary. Yet nations with a high proportion of their population in these *primary* industries are the poorest in *real income,* as will be brought out later.

The shift of emphasis in economic science from wealth to income is in part a recognition of this important fact of experience. A nation at war will place more emphasis on material things, for wars are wasteful of materials as well as of men. But a high-income society in times of peace will have a larger proportion of personal (nonmaterial) services in the composition of its *real income.*

Property

For some purposes it is useful to keep a second concept in mind, the concept of property. What, for example, does a man mean when he says, "This house is my property"? The association seems to be *material.* A house is a physical object. That physical object is his property.

This association can be misleading. The owner is referring to a relationship between himself and a physical object. The property aspect of that object is a right, the right to use or otherwise dispose of it. Thus, there is implied some further link with a social, legal, or power system by means of which the owner's right can be defended. His right to the use of the object presumes the authority or power to deny its use to others. It was this aspect of property which led the French social philosopher Proudhon to declare, "property is theft." He believed that he had discovered in the property system of his time, in the legal rights of the owners of property to deny its use to others, the cause of the poverty and suffering about him.

In contrast to this view, the right of the individual to ownership and control over that which he has obtained through his efforts has usually been regarded in organized societies as an important motivation for the creation of a stable society. Where protection of property rights does not exist, where physical goods and property claims cannot be accumulated with a sense of security in their use, few have exerted themselves to produce beyond the minimum needed for survival. In such a society accumulation of material things takes place slowly. A country in the throes of revolution, as China has been for many years, rarely has a large output or national real income. The individuals, and hence the society, accumulate little, not because the population consumes much, but because of small production.

Some form of property, some system of ownership of both the instruments of production and the goods and services produced, has characterized most societies known to history.[1] Common ownership by the family, the clan, the tribe, has sometimes been the rule. At other times, while *ultimate* ownership has been vested in the group, the right to use and control has been assigned to the family or the individual.

Under feudalism title to the land—the principal form of property in a predominantly agricultural society—was vested in the king or overlord, and assigned to the lesser lords as long as they remained loyal. Lords of the manor, in turn, assigned land to peasants, who worked to produce their own subsistence and paid rent *in kind* for the privilege of using the land. For centuries those who worked the soil were permanently attached to it as serfs, a part of the overlord's property like fences, ditches, and hedgerows. With the rise of the towns, serfs who were freed (or escaped) from the land found work there, and sometimes managed to "own" their artisan's tools and their domiciles, and to have a clear property right to the goods they produced. But with the coming of the factory system the tools again passed to someone else. Their only property rights were in the contractual obligations of the employer to pay wages.

Property in human beings was common throughout much of recorded history. During the last hundred years, however, this type of ownership has been frowned upon in most societies, although baseball players may still be bought and sold, and film stars are sometimes rented out. Of course, in these cases the contract, not the person, is property.

The debate over property, particularly in whom it should be vested, is a very old one. It is recorded in the earliest documents left by man,

---

[1] Security of property does not necessarily imply that it must be security of private property. In our own society the courts enforce security provisions on public as well as private property.

and is specifically dealt with by Plato and Aristotle. The former inclined toward ownership in common, the latter toward private property.

The importance of property rights, of course, is related to the fact that they are one consideration in settling the question of how to divide claims against the national income—the question of "who gets what?" Since the *real income* is a joint product of human effort and materials of the environment, and since these materials are limited, the assignment of property rights in materials as well as in effort helps to establish claims against the joint product. Thus, when idealists express their feelings toward judicial decisions or legislation by saying that "property rights have been put ahead of human rights," they are indulging in a fallacy of misplaced concreteness. Only people have rights under the law. Legal decisions which uphold a property claim against some other type of claim, less clearly or less easily defined, do not hold in favor of things in opposition to people. They sustain the claims of property holders against other persons.

This concept of property needs to be remembered if another feature of man's relation to a social environment is to be understood. This is the limited nature of property. No property right is absolute. It is more like a bundle from which separate rights can be withdrawn, as a twig can be withdrawn from a bundle of twigs. Society, which we have defined as the complex of social groupings and institutionalized patterns of behavior, imposes limits on property rights in things, and hence in the manner of use of those things. Ultimately this means a limitation on the kinds of income claims that will be honored. A person who owns a piece of land in a residential section of a city will be prevented from building a glue factory there by zoning laws. This means that he cannot earn an income by processing dead horses. Much of the legal structure of any society is devoted to defining property rights and to procedures for settling disputes over such rights.

A second characteristic of property rights in most things is that they can be transferred from one owner to another, either wholly or in part. The sharing of property rights is an important feature of the development of co-operation among people. One person may own, but for a consideration may transfer the right to use what he owns to another. Thus, in our society, property has become an involved pattern of rights and claims in the useful and scarce materials and personal services around us, and to the income they help to create. Shares of stock, mortgage bonds, liens, and so forth are abstract titles or property rights in things held by persons other than those actually using them. A share in a company by a stockholder who does not participate in management is a general property right, entitling the holder only to a certain claim against the income of the company.[2]

Capital

One reason for discussing property at some length is to provide background for the third of our concepts, *capital,* which as a factor of production has come to occupy a central position in the production process. Capital has a common association with wealth, as well as with property, both collective and private. The division between ownership and use in the field of capital is an important aspect of the division of labor and joint effort. Broadly speaking, capital consists of all useful things which, at any given time, have been inherited by society from the past. So defined, capital includes land, buildings, machines, technology, and every other aid which, when combined with human effort, creates the flow of goods and services we have identified as *real income.*

A customary practice is to attribute to goods a *material* characteristic, and to classify as services those things which men do for one another. The distinction is more apparent than "real." A suit of clothes is a physical object. Its usefulness as a piece of property and a consumption good is not, however, anything material. In the process of being worn out, it performs the service of protecting its owner from the elements, from the public's disapproving stare, and from being arrested. It may, if it is the work of a skilled tailor, get him recognized as a man of distinction. Likewise, a machine used in the manufacturing process performs a service through being worn out over time in changing the forms of materials to make them more useful. Real capital, then, consists of the multitudinous aids to production which, when combined with human labor, add to the flow of service-rendering things. Such "tools" at any given time reflect the knowledge of society about the material universe, the accumulated body of experience which enables workmen to shape such material to human requirements. Thus, even the material universe is, in a sense, social. In the words of Wesley C. Mitchell:

> We shall come to think even of natural resources as cultural products. Are they not, to all intents? The aboriginal inhabitants of this continent north of Mexico had little farm land, virtually no coal, no metal beyond bits of virgin copper, no petroleum, no plastics.

---

[2] In case of liquidation, shareholders have a residual claim in company assets. Certain voting rights also go with ownership of common stock. See page 341.

European settlers brought some of these resources with them in the form of knowledge; their descendants have invented the rest; . . . Science is beyond all comparison the greatest of resources.[3]

These resources and accumulations of machines, tools, buildings, roads, drainage systems, reserves of immediately useful goods, and knowledge constitute the reservoir of *real capital,* which when combined with human effort provides the flow of *real income.* From this real income we are all fed, clothed, sheltered, amused, and one day buried. From this real income the stock of capital goods is replaced and increased, in order to make possible the still further increase in production. This process will be explored in detail in Part 3.

The services of capital, combined with the services of men, generate the service-yielding goods and the usefulness they embody. Capital without human effort would not produce a flow of usable things, save at a very primitive level, as when a bountiful nature drops fruit into waiting hands. Labor without capital likewise could produce little or nothing. The difference in productivity between an American worker and a Chinese worker results mostly from the fund of capital which the former has to work with, and the training which has taught him how to use modern tools.

There is another aspect or meaning of the term capital—that is, capital as property. An individual who contributes to production directly through his personal efforts establishes a claim against income called a wage or salary. An individual who has established a property right in any of the various forms of real capital, and who can therefore decide to use it (or allow it to be used) in the production process, likewise creates a claim against the income flows.

It is this aspect of capital that occasionally leads to confusion. When we speak of capital, we sometimes mean *real capital,* at other times capital as property, or a claim against income. We may also mean something still more abstract—the money value of real capital. This aspect of the property concept will be elaborated when we discuss money as our next topic.

When an economic system is described as capitalistic, more is implied than the fact that real capital is used in the production process. The reference is to the private ownership of the capital goods, and the role of individual decisions in combining these with hired labor to create an output of goods and services. This was the term which Marx coined to refer to the institutions which succeeded feudalism, and was contrasted

---

[3] "Economic Research and the Development of Economic Science and Public Policy" (twelve papers presented at the twenty-fifth anniversary meeting of the National Bureau of Economic Research, New York, June 6–7, 1946), p. 16.

with his "ideal" system of communism, in which all capital used in the production process would be collectively owned. Marx, adopting Ricardo's labor theory of value, maintained that all capital was the result of past labor, and thus was not entitled to any claim against income beyond that necessary to maintain itself. The classical economists held that capital, both real and as property, was made possible through postponed consumption or waiting. Since saving made possible an increased future income, owners of property which resulted from saving were entitled to claims against that income.

Money

When money was first invented or came into general use is not known for certain. Examples of money as a physical object can be traced back to antiquity. The earliest known coins of gold and silver came from Lydia. References to money as a form of wealth occur in the oldest written documents.

The English term "money" derives from Juno Moneta, or Juno the Adviser, in whose temple at Rome coins were made. We see, therefore, that the name itself reflects the fact that the money function has commonly been performed throughout history by the metals, particularly gold and silver. These metals have always been highly regarded as ornament and treasure. In isolated societies where the metals were unknown, the function was usually performed by some other treasured item, like the wampum of the American Indian. The Roman word for money was *pecunia,* derived from *pecus,* meaning cattle. This important animal, used very early for power, for food, and as a source of primitive instruments or tools from hide, hair, horn, and bone, became a standard of value for other things. In Colonial Virginia a hogshead of tobacco was for a time the unit into which the value of all other items were converted; and in the prison camps during World War II, the cigarette, an almost universally desired commodity, became a medium of exchange, the standard of value, and a source of power and control.

The function of money is to make comparisons among items that are traded. The "money function" becomes a necessity whenever men begin to trade. A barter agreement may be arrived at through a process of bargaining, putting up three hens against a rabbit, two cows against a horse, or pieces of silver against all of these. An item which is highly valued and often traded is compared with many things. It begins to function as a standard, or a unit of account. Other items acquire a "value," expressed in terms of this standard. If the item is durable, divisible, and easily recognized so that it passes freely from hand to hand, it may become a *medium of exchange*. In other words, it becomes an item traded against all others, with the expectation that it can be exchanged at a later date for something else. This is why some economists have called it a *store of value*. It is a claim against other things which need not be exercised right away. This facilitates exchange. A man who has two cows to exchange for a horse need not hunt until he finds someone who has both a horse and a desire for two cows. In similar manner it becomes a standard for deferred payment or debt. A man who needs a horse, but has neither cows nor money, may still get the horse by agreeing to pay at a later date. He could agree to pay in cows at the time of the exchange, but again the other party might not want cows. A sum of money agreed upon between the two is usually to be preferred.

Here a fascinating complexity begins to develop. In organized society the one who has received the "promise to pay in money," or the debt, may transfer his claim to someone else as part of some further exchange. When this happens money as a physical entity begins to drop out of the picture. All that changes hands is a set of figures stated in terms of money as a unit of account. Like the Cheshire cat that disappeared and left only a grin, the "thing" on which trade subsists is an abstract statement of a promise to pay. All that is implied is a belief that sometime, somewhere, someone will pay to someone else a sum of money.

What money *really* is has bothered men for ages, and no brief definition has been formulated that does not leave out something that money is and does. As a claim against other things, against goods and services in general, it usually is accepted only if it possesses qualities that inspire confidence. For that reason kings and monarchs often had their seal or escutcheons embossed on pieces of metal as a guarantee of weight and purity, or on paper as a testament to the fact that their wealth and power stood behind it. A group of German students of pecuniary affairs, observing its history in these symbols, formulated a "state" theory of money. Its acceptance as a medium of exchange and store of value, they maintained, was based upon the power and authority of the state. This theory, however, is too simple as a description of experience. Rulers have been notable backsliders from their pledges. They have "sweated" their coins and debased them with cheaper metals to increase their number. They have printed paper money beyond their power to collect taxes and make good on their promises. It is perhaps more realistic to say that confidence in a country's currency as a standard and store of value rests ultimately upon the stability of the social organization and the capacity of the nation to produce and deliver the goods and services against which money claims have been issued. *For money is basically a form of property.*

It is a property right in its most abstract form, a claim against things in general, which members of a stable society will honor.

Everything that is owned is potentially a claim against other property. An owner can surrender his property claim in a car in exchange for money or for some other property right. A *debt* is a negative property right—or negative wealth, if that is preferred. Money is a property right with which a debt may be settled with the greatest convenience. When money is in the form of cash or paper bills, it is acceptable for tax obligations, for debt payment, or acquisition of other property rights. Because of this quality of easy transferability, which is analogous to a "flow," money is characterized as "liquid." A person (or a business) who has converted property or capital into money is said to be in a highly liquid position.

Property rights in real capital are bought and sold. Their value is expressed in money terms. Hence, when a businessman states that his business is capitalized at $20,000, it may mean that he has paid $20,000 for real capital represented by asset entries in his balance sheet. Capitalization may mean something else. Property rights, we have seen, are a source of claims against income. The present value of these rights is based upon the future income which the owner may expect to get from them. We will come back to this point in Parts 3 and 4.

The Market

We have noted that money emerged as a by-product of exchange. A term closely allied to exchange is the market.

The market, as an idea and as experience, is at least as old as recorded history. References to the "market place" abound in Biblical literature and other ancient records. Markets rose and declined as civilizations flourished, developed arteries of trade and communication, and then decayed or fell to invaders. During the medieval period *fairs* emerged as interregional institutions for selling merchandise. Much of the trading was by barter, since money was itself a commodity, that is, gold and silver. Credit was not unknown, but was less extensive than it later became.

With the development of modern means of transportation and communication, the connotations of the market have changed to cover new situations. The ancient and medieval market was both a place and an activity. Usually it was an area set aside in the towns where peasants brought their products from the country, and where craftsmen displayed their wares. There the people of the town came to higgle and bargain over exchange ratios among goods. During periods of strong guild organ-

56

ization prices were administered collectively by these associations. When travel became more general foreigners from a distance set up shop and sometimes undersold the home producers, and the market was steadily expanded.

The modern market is not so clearly marked off. It may be world-wide, or it may be strictly local. For different purposes a market may be defined by geographic area, by nature and type of product, or by conditions of entry or exit, that is, by the degree of control exercised over traders and conditions of trade. Market classification is thus highly varied.

Some producers sell in a market that is well organized or capable of absorbing practically any amount of output, as in the case of the commodity exchanges. Some producers and sellers have established routine contacts with purchasers who take periodic consignments, like the customers on a milk route or retailers visited by bakery trucks. Producers of other commodities (new, unusual, or luxury goods) find it necessary to carry on a continuous selling campaign through salesmen and special representatives. Generally, the conditions for the existence of a market are present when buyers and sellers are able to make contact for purposes of exchange, whether by mail, by telephone or telegraph, through agents or representatives, or by face-to-face contact. For purposes of analysis, however, we can abstract from all of these and refer to the marketing process. The meaning then is not unlike that of everyday usage.

The Firm

Business and industrial organizations are of many different types. We will have occasion to look at them more closely later on. However, we need a general concept which abstracts an element common to them all. This is the idea of control. A term which has now been widely adopted by economists is that of the *firm*. The word is derived from the Latin *firmare,* meaning to confirm by signature. In the form *firma* it appears in many Romance languages as the word for a signature. In English, *to firm* was *to sign* until the eighteenth century. For early partnership agreements the term referred to the person or persons who could sign for the others. In the British Partnership Act of 1890 it was first used to designate the collectivity of persons making up a business.

Thus, by accepted usage it has come to mean, particularly in economic analysis, the business as an entity apart from the owners. It implies control in the form of a central bookkeeping office of the establishment where property rights are administered and an accounting of them rendered. It is the basic unit for carrying on the production process.

Wants

The term *want* will be used from time to time as a shorthand expression or concept for the wanting (or desiring) process of the individual. It comes close in its meaning to the concept of *need* as used by the psychologist. The term has found its way into language by concretizing a process: the individual wants something; he therefore has a want. Such a process begins with the physiological needs of an organism for nourishment and protection. Through inhibition, customs, and habit these basic drives have been overlaid with social meaning and form. The individual wants not just food, but food of a socially accepted sort. A lady wants a hat, but not just something for her head; it must be different from that of her neighbor —but not too different.

Alfred Marshall distinguished between wants and activities. The first he defined in terms of basic biological needs. The second he linked with needs which are social in origin. We speak sometimes of necessities and luxuries, not always a useful distinction. This idea will be developed further in Part 5. The term *wants,* as used here, will abstract from all of these details and will refer only to felt needs of individuals and groups as expressed in behavior through spending.

Goods

In contrast with wants—a concept obtained by concretizing behavior— the concept of a good is the result of concretizing a quality. The term derives from God: a goodly man is a godly man; he is a good man. A thing characterized by desirable qualities is good; it becomes *a good.*

A good is therefore defined as anything which has the quality of being good for something. Evolution and accepted practice have made of good a concept which means to fill a purpose. A consumer's good fills an immediate want of an individual or household. A producer's good is anything that fills the requirement of a firm in carrying on its activities. Soft goods and durable goods, durable consumer goods, and capital goods are classifications found in treatises on economics as well as in newspapers and everyday discussion. In its most general form the concept of a good may also include the services rendered directly by human beings. This concept will be developed in Part 3.

Household

Finally, the term used to designate the basic consumption or spending unit is the *household.* It is the ultimate recipient of income, the smallest organization exercising choice in the use of income. A family may be a

58

household, but not all households are families. A single individual, receiving a money income and deciding how to spend it, is also a household.

Discussion
Questions

1. Prepare a list of persons you would classify as wealthy. What was your criterion for selection?

2. Look up the different property forms defined by law. Distinguish between personal property, real property, and intangible property.

3. What are the advantages of holding part of your property in the form of money? Disadvantages?

4. Radicals have often used the slogan, "Down with property!" Do they want to destroy the machines? Does capital exist in the Soviet Union? Property?

5. All useful things are really no more than a bundle of services. Discuss.

Economic Policy

ECONOMIC POLICY, as distinguished from analysis and empirical description of economic events, usually involves some form of explicit or implicit value judgment. Statements about policy are linked with goals or ends that are preferred.

Goals may be axiomatic—that is, accepted as good in and of themselves. Or they may be judged desirable because they have consequences that are favorable. For example, the old saying, "honesty is the best policy," can be treated as axiomatic. The Ten Commandments exhort us not to lie. They can also be supported on purely practical grounds, because if we lie we may be exposed and suffer unfavorable consequences.

An extended treatment of the general problem of ethics and values is beyond the scope of this book. We merely note that problems of policy sooner or later get involved in these broader philosophical considerations, and for purposes of clear thinking we need to recognize them as such. As acting and feeling human beings, we do make value judgments. As scientists, we are warned against them, since ultimate values do not lend themselves easily to scientific treatment.

If economists recommend a policy as preferable, what are the criteria by which it can be judged? Will such a policy result in greater total income, in more suitable distribution, greater security, or will it contribute to other values of a "noneconomic" nature? These are some of the questions to be introduced in this section.

CHAPTER 4

Normative Systems in Economics

POLICY HAS BEEN DEFINED as a "set of rules or canons of behavior which individuals and groups adopt (or have imposed upon them) to make future actions predictable" (see page 13). We shall now try to give this definition more depth as it is related to economic affairs.

To argue for a particular policy is to argue for a pattern of behavior or program of action which, if accepted or imposed, is calculated to make the attainment of some desired goal more likely. An economic policy would be one which, if followed, might be expected to increase the real income of individuals (or the whole economy) as a means of reducing constraints imposed by scarcity.

Most economists believe that the findings of economic inquiry serve a useful purpose as guides for action in practical affairs. Like all scientific knowledge, economics may provide a recipe for doing things, a body of rules which if followed will have foreseeable consequences. Given certain goals or ends, economists can sometimes provide information and suggestions on means for achieving such ends. One tax may raise required government revenue with less disturbance to other phases of economic activity than another. If the nation is experiencing inflation, a given monetary and credit policy may be more likely to restore stability than some other one.

Goals or ends themselves may be in conflict, however. Social and political objectives, in the larger affairs of the nation, will also require attention. Choice among competing goals involves still more fundamental questions of value. For analytical purposes the economist, as economist, can avoid this problem by assuming that the goal or end is given. The basis of policy recommendations then becomes axiomatic.

As long as the economist remembers that conclusions about policies arrived at in this way are not likely to be final, his recommendations may be suggestive and helpful. They cannot be authoritative. The problem and its frame of reference with which the economist starts is a partial or limited view. Income-getting and income-spending activities, while they may (for most of us) occupy more of our time and attention than any other single aspect of life, are not the whole of life. In our own culture, particularly, the money symbol pervades much of what we do and think. As we have already noted, wealth has a way of conferring power and status, security and respect. Yet economic behavior is not total behavior. Other symbols and associations which give life meaning and purpose are carried into the "market" and help to determine what people do there. This is why the economist must at some point in his thinking about social "reality" take into account the insights and knowledge provided by other social sciences.

Philosophies of life, loyalties to value systems, are compounded not only of what we believe to be true and accurate about the real world, but of our dream worlds as well. Economists are no exception. In public policy debates economists are often found opposing one another. Differences among them arise not so much from analytical and empirical questions, or the content of economic science, but from broader normative judgments.

Welfare Economics

Welfare economists have attempted to formulate certain principles to serve as a measure or criterion for policy. Their objective has been to explore and give "real" content to a concept of *general welfare*.

Such a criterion in its most general form has been suggested by A. C. Pigou. A policy, he believes, can be said to promote "economic welfare" if it results in at least some people being made better off from an income standpoint without at the same time making others worse off.

This welfare "principle" would rule out mere redistribution of wealth and income, which takes from the rich and gives to the poor (or vice versa, assuming that those who have wealth are better able to appreciate it), since those who lose are presumably "worse off" than before. It would permit a relative leveling downward of new (additional) income by channeling a greater proportion of the increase to lower-income groups.

Some would argue that growth in per capita real income, regardless of its distribution, is the most important measure of economic welfare. Let us examine some implications of this criterion. Can we say, for example, that any policy which leads ultimately to an increase in production and a higher level of total real income represents an increase in general welfare? A question still more crucial in terms of our present discussion would be: Granted that such a policy, if undertaken, would *in fact* increase the quantity of real goods and services available and the general level of consumption, could it be supported with the authority of economic science?

Even if the answer to the first question were, Yes, the answer to the second question would have to be, No! Other considerations would have to be taken into account. We will illustrate with an example. Assume that our sole objective were to increase the level of income, that this single motivating force determined the behavior of individuals and groups. There can be little doubt that the resources of a nation, human and otherwise, could be organized so that the total output could be greater than any we have attained. There would still remain the knotty problem of which specific goods and services to produce, but that can be neglected for the moment, assuming merely that some fixed proportion is maintained among goods and services now being produced. This comes fairly close to what actually happens in wartime. Then the people of a nation can achieve a singleness of purpose not usually attainable at other times. Individuals, motivated by patriotic duty and kept in line by social pressures, identify themselves with the single goal—defense of the country and defeat of the enemy. The estimated needs of the military and the minimum requirements of civilian workers to maintain efficiency determine the composition of output, while only available resources and human endurance set its limit.

At other times this degree of co-ordination and agreement cannot usually be attained. This is particularly true in our Western culture, with its traditions and habits of individual freedom. In a society already rich in material things, and characterized by considerable "freedom from want,"[1] the value placed on freedom is high. Policy prescriptions, therefore, are likely to conform to multiple-value criteria on which the individual scientist, as scientist, is not equipped to pass judgment. Conflicts arise between knowledge which follows the "real model" of experience and the "ideal model" of how things *ought* to be.

When economists who share the same scientific frame of reference and who have access to similar statistical or observational data differ on matters of policy, this is not necessarily an indication that one is the better economist, or that one may be right and the other wrong. Equally competent men may differ, because they differ with respect to other values as well as in their interpretation of income experience. They may differ on their assumptions about human behavior. They may have greater reser-

---

[1] Perhaps a better phrase would be "freedom to want."

vations about inferences to be drawn from the statistical summaries and indices of income-getting and income-spending actions. But basic differences are likely to be on what is *good* or *desirable*. These opinions are not subject to verification or test because they stem in part from sources that are nonrational.

What, then, is the role of the economist in this area of policy formation? Granted the tentative nature of the hypotheses which the economist derives from empirical models of relationships among important economic or income variables, he can still estimate what will happen to other variables, such as spending or saving, if investment or government deficits vary. Or if a given objective is desired, say a stable price level or a reduction of unemployment to some given level, he can recommend what appears to him to be a policy most likely to achieve that end.

As a citizen he can make known what in his opinion are desirable goals. But he cannot claim the authority of his science as evidence to support what he thinks is the best objective. If his preference has been influenced by what he believes will happen in fact, because of behavior patterns inferred from his knowledge of economic behavior in the past, then his "ideal model" and his empirical model may move very close together. On the other hand, if policy recommendations are shaped to other objectives which the economist believes are good because they promote other values—such as freedom, revered tradition, self-sufficiency, or national interest—then he must look elsewhere for support for his position. The economist, as scientist, has but one responsibility to his discipline, and indirectly to the society of which he is a part, and which in a sense provides him with an income for doing his job. That is to continue the research, the testing, and the questioning of his own scientific beliefs to the end that dependable knowledge is accumulated.

Individuals differ on important value questions, presumably because their experiences have been different. In the light of their beliefs and feelings, there is not always a clear-cut dividing line between the possible and the desirable. There is room for differences. The psychologist can tell us some things about personality differences which are likely to be correlated with different value positions. The sociology of knowledge is another branch of the social sciences which investigates value commitments as group or cultural phenomena.

Economists are sometimes classified as conservative or liberal. These terms, however, are ambiguous. They have been used for a long time and thus have a history behind them. Specific policy proposals, which were classified as liberal during one period, may be regarded as conservative in another. As we have already noted, liberalism was once identified

64

with a climate of opinion in economics associated with minimal government intervention in economic affairs. Today it is more frequently associated with a body of opinion favoring an increasing role for government.

Attitudes toward the role of government or social control of economic affairs serve as a basis for classifying normative or value systems reflected in the policy prescriptions of economists. Using this criterion, we shall distinguish three such positions: (1) laissez faire or market supremacy; (2) planned or central direction; and (3) pragmatic or mixed direction. As categories for purposes of classification, and as "ideal" systems, these terms do not refer to actual or existing systems. They are constructs which emphasize certain features of societies or of the idealized models of such societies when they are used as criteria for evaluating policies. When used in the latter sense, they could perhaps be described as *economic philosophies*.

Laissez
Faire

Few students of social and economic affairs today would advocate extreme laissez faire. Even as an ideal model, complete laissez faire has found expression only in the doctrines of the anarchists. Sometimes conditions approximating this ideal have existed for brief periods, as in the early frontier days of our own West. However, associations for the safeguarding of life and property were always the necessary prelude to ordered economic development.

As a set of values and a prescription for public policy, the *laissez faire philosophy* rests first of all upon the assumption of potential evil *inherent* in all government. All government relies upon a delegation of power to (or usurpation by) some individuals, enabling them to use coercion to regulate the actions of other people. This constitutes a limitation upon the freedom of the individual. While some such limitation may be necessary, if the freedom of each to act is not to interfere with the freedom of others to do likewise, any delegation of authority to impose such limitations ought to be kept at a minimum. Such authority needs to be carefully circumscribed and defined. The ideal should be "a government of laws and not of men."

A value system cannot be interpreted in terms of its logic alone. For ideologies, like societies, have histories. They are inherited from the past. While nineteenth-century liberalism, the most important expression of the laissez faire tradition in economic affairs, recognized a positive role for government, it also stressed the desirability of a minimum of government. Provision for national defense and an internal police force to maintain order and protect property, an elected legislature to enact certain "rules of the game" (such as monetary standards and other objective criteria for describing and measuring things owned or traded), and a system of courts to enforce these rules were regarded as the central core of *proper* government functions. In addition, it was acknowledged that government could best provide for some services so general in their social utility, of such long-range benefit to all, and productive of such small immediate returns that private individuals would be unlikely to undertake them. These included a postal system, public education, and a system of streets and highways.[2] With the rise of great cities and the development of modern industry, the list was extended, although not always easily or automatically. Outside of these areas it was argued, economic activity could be best carried on by private individuals and associations. This system, characterized as free enterprise, was perceived as resting upon a solid foundation of free contract and an entirely voluntary set of social relationships entered into by individuals following their own best interests as they saw them.

The driving force of this system was believed to be universal human needs and wants and the motivation they provided for each individual to act. In the face of unlimited wants and the freedom of consumers to pick and choose, no enterprising worker or property holder need lack the opportunity to turn his productive services to account in earning his own income. Possessing such income, none need search in vain for those to satisfy his wants.

From the millions of individual decisions to spend, to save, and to invest, the organized economic life of free men, it was believed, would emerge. Conforming to no prior design, no single integrated plan, the end result would nevertheless have all of the appearances of such a plan. The rule of law in economic life would be achieved in a free market by the workings of an inexorable law of supply and demand. Such a law need not be enacted by any government. By no action of government could it be repealed.

However, while the law of supply and demand could neither be enacted or repealed, it could be inhibited and distorted. Government interference with the free market to achieve some immediate objective, such as the development of a new industry or the protection of a favored

---

[2] Even these activities were not accepted in the beginning by many laissez faire advocates, but were attained only after prolonged debate and increasing public sentiment for them.

group or class, was viewed as likely to create more problems in the long run than it solved. Free enterprise can only be expected to function in an atmosphere where government is not periodically upsetting its plans by arbitrary action. When it does, all enterprise is discouraged. Even those enterprises which benefit from a specific subsidy or special privilege from government are not likely to act with confidence, since what governments give they can also take away. The free market, on the other hand, distributes its benefits and its penalties impartially. No individual or firm can curry favor save by doing a better job, by producing a better or a cheaper product. Investments undertaken to finance a new and better practice will be sound investments. Those undertaken because of special privilege are not likely to be so. For these reasons a nation can best insure the effective, high-level use of the factors of production by maintaining an environment favorable to private enterprise. Errors in judgment will occur, but these errors will be small compared with the total successes, smaller than when decisions are concentrated in the hands of a central organization.

This was the ideal model adopted by those who preferred the free market and justified a policy of laissez faire. The central value around which it was built was freedom of the individual. But this freedom was to be harnessed to the general welfare by checks provided by every other free individual.

To what extent was this ideal model based upon experience? Economists and economic historians differ in their answers to this question. Some maintain that during the transition from a predominantly feudal society to modern industrialism this admittedly simplified model of the *good* economic system came very close to experience. For this was the time of the emergence of the small trader and the limited market. Enterprises were many, and none was large enough to exercise a disproportionate influence in the market.[3] The higgling and bargaining between small traders was, in fact, a form of social control, since competition in the market place functioned as an assurance to all that no one could dominate a system of trading among equals.

To those who, like Adam Smith, had observed these beginnings and, like Ricardo, who had intimate knowledge of trading on the stock exchange, the link between what they saw around them and the abstract logical model of their speculations about it was close enough to warrant accepting it both as explanation and justification.

However closely the two models may have approached each other

---

[3] This type of market will be developed and discussed in detail in Part 3.

in those earlier times, other economists have stressed the fact that quite soon thereafter the gulf between the two began to widen. The *real* model continued to undergo changes; the *ideal* model, while it was refined and provided with an elegant, logical superstructure, did not.

As discovery and invention provided a new, more complex technology for the production processes and large-scale industry moved in to displace trade at the center of the income process, the private decisions of many small traders ceased to perform their functions. Before the law all production units were treated as individuals. The individual corporate firm had the same rights, the same contractual obligations. But this individual was different. It was an aggregation of property holdings, a growing center of economic and financial power.

In these circumstances those who believed in laissez faire were faced by an ever widening paradox and dilemma. Government had been relegated to a minor role and purposely made weak in order to prevent it from intervening in the free market. As the conviction grew that the market was being rigged through the increasing control by a decreasing number of giants, whose influence on prices and output had become determining factors, the demand arose for government to intervene. For a weak government to intervene would be ineffective. After the first third of the nineteenth century[4] a slow but steady growth of government intervention began. A policy aimed at directing human behavior back into the ways of the free market required an increasing amount of undoing.

Nowhere was there greater disparity between those who believed in the desirability of a free market (as represented by the classical economists) and the actual emerging practice than in the United States. Groups organized for purposes of obtaining special advantage in the market sought and obtained tariff protection from competition outside the country. That such protection from competition promoted concentration of economic power is acknowledged by most students of the problem. Year after year advocates of laissez faire continued their advocacy of free trade; year after year the proponents of tariffs had their way. Railroad enterprises undertaken by private associations sought and were granted public subsidies, land grants from the public domain, and special privileges from states and cities. These became the first of the giant corporations. Parallel growth occurred in oil, tobacco, sugar, textiles, steel, meat packing, and other industries. As the concentration of capital or property claims increased, other groups sought and obtained government intervention designed to curb the railroads, "trusts," "big business," "Wall Street," and the various "interests"—all of these terms

---

[4] This intervention came in England earlier than in the United States.

standing for "private" groups that were seen as dominating the market.

It is arguable that laissez faire as a criterion of policy and a bulwark of human freedom foundered on its neglect of this important body of experience. Even though the formation and enforcement of the rules of the game were an acknowledged part of the ideal, the task proved more difficult than it had appeared in the first blush of emerging liberal thought. The increasing complexity of economic life produced divisions and jars which only the intervention of a more powerful force could keep from erupting into open conflict. In the words of Ernest Barker, one of the more discerning political scientists and students of democracy, "Government intervened to prevent a more damaging intervention than its own."

To focus attention on the widening gap between laissez faire in theory and practice is not to diminish its attraction and its power as an ideal. There can be no doubting its profound influence in the shaping of Western thought and institutions—particularly the language and the philosophy of the law—and nowhere more than in the United States. As a political slogan and expression of an ideal, it possesses a powerful attraction. The law of supply and demand is still regarded by some as being specific and as "natural" as the law of gravity. The oft repeated phrase "less government in business and more business in government" continues as an expression of the understandable ambition of a free people to manage it own affairs.

However, freedom in economic affairs is not absolute. The choice may be not between more or less freedom to earn, to spend, and to invest, but between the freedom of one individual or group versus the freedom of other people. More yachts may mean fewer houses or schools or public parks. Of greater importance, the right to security and advantage for a few may mean shrinking real income and insecurity for many.

No special interest group in society, seeking its own privilege or private advantage, has ever failed to make use of one or more of the value associations of free enterprise, when that has served its purpose. Representatives of industries seeking tariff protection do so on the grounds that this instrument of special benefit is a protection of free American enterprise. Organized labor, when it seeks exclusion of foreign goods, presents as an argument the "safeguarding of an American standard of living," even when it means the raising of prices for domestic consumers. Organized farm groups seeking price supports or subsidized exports will ordinarily use as their argument the safeguarding of the independence of the family farm or the protection of important commodities vital to national welfare. In each case the objective sought is the use of an instrument of public policy to accomplish some income shift for the advantage of some special group.

Few economists would today support the view that mere government withdrawal from all economic affairs could re-establish the impartial arbitration of income affairs by a "free market." Professor Ludwig Von Mises would probably come closest to this position. Because he has experienced in the European countries where he lived formerly the rise of absolutism and complete economic domination by fascist and other totalitarian governments, he has adopted an extreme position. Professor F. A. Hayek occupies a position on policy questions slightly less extreme. However, his *The Road to Serfdom* can serve as an example of this type of normative judgment. He stresses the dangers inherent in government action to achieve full employment and high-level production.

The Policies of Positive Laissez Faire

A less extreme position than that of Von Mises or Hayek is another which is also influenced by the nineteenth-century liberal tradition. Aware of the wide gap which exists between what is and what ought to be if a free market is to function effectively, economists who hold this view place less emphasis on the extent of government intervention and more on the kind of intervention. They are likely to be vigorous in their opposition to monopoly of all kinds. Since a free market cannot function if the institutions of private property result in concentrations of economic power (which bias the market through restrictions of *real output* in order to increase prices and income), their prescriptions for public policy stress the importance of *enforcing* a free market.

This point has been emphasized by the late Henry Simons in his *Positive Program for Laissez-Faire*. According to his view, private enterprise and a free market can function only in an environment where any business firm is free to engage in the type of production that promises a profit income. New firms must be able to compete with old established firms. If they cannot, then competition breaks down and the market ceases to do its job. Wherever competition has been demonstrated to be ineffective (as in the "natural monopolies"), then the industry may be taken over by a public corporation and operated in the general interest, which means that the service would be provided to all at "cost."

Planned or
Central Direction

The value orientation to be discussed now, under the heading of Planned or Central Direction, is in many respects the opposite of laissez faire. A wide range of variation is to be found among its advocates, combining in different degrees political, social, and economic considerations. A common characteristic is a denial of the effectiveness of a private enterprise system in providing: (1) sustained high-level production and full employment, and (2) planned use of modern technology to achieve the widest possible distribution of real income benefits.

Central planning or collectivism places primary emphasis on the group, on society itself, as a means to the end of individual realization and security. Two terms are likely to be familiar from everyday affairs: *socialism* and *communism*. Socialism has been derived from the same etymological root as the term society; communism from the same root as community. Both of these terms have acquired other associations, primarily political in nature, because of their identification with parties dedicated to the changing of existing institutions. Neither of these ideals, or dogmas, has attracted a wide following in the United States. As "ideal" political systems, both have appealed to the working class of countries more highly stratified, with rigid class barriers to economic as well as social improvement. The United States did not inherit the predominantly feudal institutions which continued to influence attitudes and values down to the present time in many European and Asian countries. On the contrary, our frontier society had from the beginning a much more equalitarian culture, and an environment which put a much greater premium on individual self-reliance. However, it is a fact of the world in which we live that the basic philosophy of collectivism or socialism has a larger following, in terms of the number of people who believe in it, than does free enterprise. Joseph Schumpeter, who was an economist with an abiding interest in the history of ideas, concluded in his *Socialism, Capitalism and Democracy* that as a value system socialism appears to be winning in the struggle for men's minds. This conclusion is no expression of Schumpeter's own preference, since he was throughout his lifetime a careful student and ardent defender of free enterprise.

The dominant economic characteristic of the various ideal models of a collectivist society is the proposal that private ownership and control of the factors of production—land and capital goods—be abandoned or greatly modified in the direction of *social ownership*. In such an economy property income would be nonexistent, except for government bonds. All household incomes would originate from some type of personal service (physical or intellectual labor), performed as part of the production process, or from "income transfers" which presumably would be provided for those unable to work.

The idea of a centrally-directed economic system is very old. Many early religious groups believed in a form of community organization, in which plans for the group economic life were made by a council, usually

71

the older members of the society. Most of these had no clearly thought-out body of theory or doctrine to guide them in resource use, no rationale for the general guidance of decisions. The socialist economist gets little help from the experience of these groups to guide him in economic decision making in a planned, democratically-controlled industrial society. Present-day experience cannot provide us with answers to these problems either. No socialist nation, which is at the same time democratically controlled and industrially advanced, has ever existed.

Great Britain under a socialist (Labour) government remained predominantly a private-enterprise economy. At no time did the Labour government advocate the nationalization of more than about twenty per cent of industry. Hence, those industries which were socialized operated in a predominantly market environment. Public enterprise tried to show a profit the same as any other. Its labor and materials were purchased in the "market." Its revenues or receipts were from private enterprise and the households.

In the Scandinavian countries, where socialist coalition governments have been in power for more than a quarter of a century, the extent of nationalization has been no greater than in England. Public enterprises, in their accounting practice, behave much as would private corporations.

The only nation that is avowedly communist in orientation is the Union of Soviet Socialist Republics (USSR), and now perhaps her satellites also. For ceremonial purposes at least, the value system espoused by Soviet leaders is declared to derive from Marx's *dialectical materialism* through Lenin (and, until recently, Stalin). The Soviet state is not a democracy, and free consumer choice is not emphasized. Private property in land and other major capital resources was abolished by stages after the 1917 (Bolshevik) Revolution. Labor unions are essentially agencies of the state, and freedom of choice of occupation is limited. For many in forced-labor camps it does not exist at all. This does not mean that all decisions on resource allocation and income distribution are wholly arbitrary or whimsical. How these are made will be treated in later chapters, when we deal with the separate aspects of the income process.

Pragmatism and
the Mixed Economy

In the economic literature concerned with "comparative economic systems" the term "mixed economy" has been used with increasing frequency in recent years. There is an implication in this concept, when applied to a nation like the United States, that the criterion for policy lies somewhere between that of laissez faire liberalism and central planning. In popular idiom such terms as modified capitalism, regulated free enterprise, the welfare state, and others of similar connotation occur frequently.

Is the mixed system, then, simply a compromise between the older rival ideologies of laissez faire and central planning? On a purely logical basis it might be argued that such is the case. However, there is another approach to the value problem which we have chosen to call the *pragmatic*. Although pragmatism can be described as a philosophical position (for which the American philosopher John Dewey has provided elaborate underpinnings), it is a philosophy with a difference. If it can be said to have an ideology or dogma (and some professional philosophers would argue that it has), it would be that experience, not the ideal model or value system, comes first. The criteria for value judgments are themselves subject to change and are reinterpreted in the light of experience.

Moreover, there is the suggestion that this is how it ought to be, not because it is in the nature of things to do so, or because there is an absolute value in doing so, but because it works. Such an approach lends itself to experimentation. The mixed economy is, in fact, more the result of experimentation than a compromise between laissez faire and central planning.

As a socio-economic environment, the United States has always been more receptive to experiment and change than some of the older, tradition-bound cultures. The student of ideas might even argue, as Bertrand Russell has, that it is no accident that the pragmatist philosophy was an understandable outgrowth of the dynamic American scene. William James and John Dewey in all likelihood developed pragmatism as a philosophical system because it appeared to fit the type of social adjustment they saw around them.

Since the onset of the great depression and the "revolution in economics" which followed in its wake, one could argue that economics as a discipline has become more pragmatic and less concerned with orthodoxy either of the classical or the collectivist persuasion. Economists trained during the past twenty years are likely to view the "free" market as a useful (and desirable) instrument for providing the "feedback" of information on price movements which provide clues on consumer preferences and guides for the allocation of factors of production to the firm and industry. At the same time they are likely to acknowledge that in a period of giant industrial combinations and labor unions, depressions, international crises and wars, the economic policies of governments must be evaluated by criteria other than whether they advance the interests of

73

free enterprise and a competitive market or whether they are consistent with socialist first principles.

As a case in point, we may cite A. P. Lerner, whose *Economics of Control* was published near the end of World War II. Lerner, who had been a student and associate of Keynes, spent much of his early intellectual life attempting a marriage of classical analysis with the Utopian value system of a more equalitarian socialism. When events in the Soviet Union demonstrated that an authoritarian political party, professing the ideals of socialism, can achieve a tyranny over people and resources to advance the goals of a relatively small group, he rejected a socialist dogma as he had previously rejected the laissez faire dogma. In this book Lerner reaches conclusions about policy not much different from that of American (and British) pragmatism, although his analysis follows the classical equilibrium form.

On the question of private ownership versus collective ownership of capital, Lerner is unwilling to give an arbitrary answer. Where private enterprise functions effectively in getting goods produced and distributed (and he develops rather an abstract criterion for testing this effectiveness), there is no a priori reason for assuming that a collective or planned production would be superior. When competition cannot operate, public intervention is indicated. Moreover, if the private sector fails to maintain full employment, or if income distribution interferes with other social values or with the effective operation of a mass production economy itself, then government intervention can be defended.

Lerner's position is more or less typical of the new economics which emerged from the discussions, the research, and the analysis of the Keynesian revolution. This does not mean that all who follow this tradition would subscribe to the whole of his analysis or his conclusions.

One can argue, as Alan Gruchy has,[5] that for an understanding of contemporary attitudes among economists on economic policy the influence of American institutionalists and pragmatists should be taken into account more than they have been. Gruchy has analyzed the work of a group of heterodox (in contrast with orthodox) economists,[6] and adopted the term *economic holism* to designate their point of view. Most of these economists (some of whom we shall have occasion to refer to later on) were empirically minded rather than theoretical. However, this empiricism included an awareness of relationships transcending individual economic

---

[5] *Modern Economic Thought: The American Contribution* (New York: Prentice-Hall, Inc., 1947).
[6] Thorstein Veblen, John R. Commons, Wesley C. Mitchell, John M. Clark, Rexford G. Tugwell, and Gardiner C. Means.

units (firms and households), even when its exponents had no precise model of what they were. In their teaching and writings Gruchy shows the growth of an inclination to take into account the interrelatedness of institutions of a whole socio-economic system—an inclination which he links with the growing complexity and interdependence of the institutions themselves. With respect to public policy, he emphasizes their willingness to experiment with programs for dealing with recognized problems, even though information may be incomplete. Their willingness to experiment is partly because this is the only thing we can do, and partly because this is also how we learn from experience about the workings of a changing economy.

Specific Policy Areas

In succeeding chapters, as we explore the income process and break it down into particular parts or components, we will be able to illustrate more specifically how these value orientations are applied (and justified). We will examine their implications for levels of resource use, for decisions on what and how much to produce, for income distribution, for the ultimate use of income by consumers, and for trade among nations.

Discussion Questions

1. What, in your opinion, are the dominant values of American life? What do they imply when applied to economic and business affairs?

2. Thomas Jefferson once stated that "that government is best which governs least." Do you believe this view is widely held today?

3. What do the terms conservative and liberal suggest to you? Do you find these useful terms for describing people you know?

4. If you were in a position to influence public policy, insofar as it relates to the getting and spending of income, what present arrangements would you change? On what would you base your recommendations for change? Are your recommendations realistic?

5. What do you understand by the term "practical"? What do you use as your criterion of the "practical"?

6. Under what circumstances might it be said that the economic welfare of a country had improved?

Selected References for Part 1

Frank, Phillip. *Modern Science and Its Philosophy*. Cambridge: Harvard University Press, 1949.

Galbraith, John K. *The Affluent Society*. Boston: Houghton Mifflin Co., 1958.

Myrdal, Gunnar. *The Political Element in the Development of Economic Theory*. London: Routledge and Kegan Paul, Ltd., 1953.

Pigou, A. C. *Income: An Introduction to Economics*. London: Macmillan & Co., Ltd., 1948.

Polanyi, Karl. *The Great Transformation*. New York: Rinehart and Co., 1944.

Rapoport, Anatol. *Operational Philosophy*. New York: Harper and Brothers, 1953.

Reichenbach, Hans. *The Rise of Scientific Philosophy*. Berkeley and Los Angeles: University of California Press, 1951.

Robinson, Joan. *Marx, Marshall and Keynes*. Delhi: The Delhi School of Economics, University of Delhi, 1955.

Russell, Bertrand. *Human Knowledge: Its Scope and Limits*. New York: Simon & Schuster, Inc., 1948.

Zweig, Ferdinand. *Economic Ideas: A Study of Historical Perspectives*. New York: Prentice-Hall, Inc., 1950.

The study of real and money national income, and the causes determining their movements, not as theoretical concepts but as observed facts, is now fully recognized as the essential subject-matter of economics.

COLIN CLARK

PART 2

THE SOCIAL ECONOMY

National Income and Product

Introduction

How DOES ONE comprehend the income of an entire nation? Is it simply the sum of all individual incomes?

The idea of the national income is quite old. Reasonably accurate estimates are relatively new. Today most people are familiar with the national-income and product estimates published by the Department of Commerce. What do these estimates actually measure?

We present first the background and development of a national-income concept. We then treat it more rigorously, showing how the same income process can be viewed in different ways to provide not only a knowledge of its size and variation, but also insights into the structure of the economic system, how the component parts fit together, and how changes in one part can be related to succeeding changes in other parts.

Exchange against money is the process which links together the services of people and things, and by means of which these acquire a "price tag." For thinking about this process in the aggregate, economists and national-income accountants have developed a system of classification, a language and a logic of variation and change. Concepts useful for the analysis of *micro-* or individual-income problems often cannot be applied in the same sense to the larger scene. Savings, for example, may have quite different consequences for a whole economy than for an individual household or firm. Some forms of individual assets or properties cancel out one another when they are viewed in the aggregate or *macroeconomic* sense.

78

CHAPTER 5

Aggregate or National Income

WHEN THE SURVIVING American Pilgrims had gathered their first harvest and surveyed the results of a year of effort, they agreed to set aside one day for Thanksgiving and the contemplation of their bounty. The "blessings" they counted for the year, and for which they gave thanks, if added together would have constituted the group (colony) income.

Precise measurement of the total was not required and was not attempted; it was comprehended more or less subjectively. The winter of starvation and suffering through which they had passed the previous year would not be repeated. Capital accumulation had begun, for above and beyond the requirements for living through the next winter there was seed for the spring's planting. The reserve of natural resources, of land, timber, and game constituted a fund of capital which would insure an increasing flow of real income in the future, providing for economic growth. In time the separate colonies would be linked together by new arteries of trade and communication with one another and with the outside. Crude systems of money and credit would emerge, and the development of markets would make it possible to assign a money value to things that were traded. In a predominantly self-sufficient agricultural society, however, where much that was produced was used in the household, very little of the total came under the measuring rod of money.

In such a setting much of the interdependency was "noneconomic" in the modern sense. Members of a family worked together as a close-knit social unit. Neighbors co-operated in house raisings, husking bees, and mutual defense. Help was exchanged on a basis of rough equivalence, and debts to one another were remembered and paid back in kind. Each adult was something of a Jack-of-all-trades, although specialized skills such as midwives, carpenters, cobblers, blacksmiths, millers, and others did exist.

While the fortunes of all members of the society might rise or fall together (as a result of good or bad harvests, devastating storms, or the gains from the discovery of new resources), the fortunes of the individual household were most closely related to family effort and skills.

The Modern Setting

The great contrast between the economic environment just described and present conditions will be apparent. Specialization, division of labor, large-scale industry, transportation and communication, and an all-embracing financial structure have linked more than 170 million people together into a social economy. This social unit or aggregate is perceived chiefly through the unifying influence of the dollar symbol, the common denominator of social evaluation in a pecuniary culture.

In thinking about the economic or income process, each person tends to begin with his own experience. A $2,000 income in 1939 is compared with a $6,400 income in 1957. If we are asked to account for the change, a number of explanations come to mind. With age and experience, our skills on the job have improved and thus command a higher wage or salary. If we own a business, the fact that new capital has been invested to enlarge and improve it may be the basis for the larger income. If debts have been paid, our equity in the business enlarged, part of the income may be due to what property contributes to our "earning power." Each of these explanations can be traced to personal efforts and judgments.

Anyone who has lived through the period between 1939 and 1957, however, is aware that part of the difference cannot be attributed to individual or household effort. Nearly everyone's income has increased. A 1939 dollar means something different from a 1957 dollar. Earlier the experience would have been reversed. From 1929 to 1933 peoples' incomes shrank, although there had been no loss of skills or physical endowments. To describe this difference quite obviously involves us in problems associated with the whole economy. Although it may be less obvious, some of the causes of increased personal income which we credited to the individual are traceable to the social or over-all economic climate. To comprehend this economic world outside ourselves requires a language and logic of its own.

Development of a National Income Concept

Attempts to conceptualize the economic system as a whole—which in terms of our frame of reference means a model for the study of *national*

80

income—can be traced back to the very beginning of economics as a separate field of inquiry. The need for such a concept was recognized, but the analytical techniques of those who tried to work with it were circumscribed by the limitations of their times, and particularly by the lack of reliable statistical data and methods.

The Physiocrats in eighteenth-century France designed a rather crude model of the over-all economy of their time. The *Tableau Économique* of François Quesnay (1694–1774) was a diagrammatic analogy of the circulation of wealth (income), that is, the flow of goods and the opposite flow of money among the different classes of society. But the Physiocrats were prisoners of their own culture. They believed that only agriculture was productive of new wealth or income. Hence, their "produit net," or a measure of the real income of society, was a very limited concept.

Adam Smith can also be said to have had some idea of income. He, however, focused on wealth as the central concept, and his primary emphasis on the individual did not lend itself to the development of a separate frame of reference with which to handle aggregates. He was disposed to locate the broader aspect of the system in some "unseen hand" which co-ordinated economic affairs according to plan. The same was true of Ricardo, but less so of Mill, who possessed a more elaborate and complex view of society. There is some indication that Malthus came nearer to grouping aggregate relationships than his contemporaries.

Karl Marx's concept of the economic system as a whole offers something of a contrast to the basic ideas of Ricardo, from whom he otherwise borrowed heavily. Marx's thought ran to aggregates. He developed an analysis of the income of society which sought to prove that the distribution of that income, in addition to being unjust, made ultimate breakdown inevitable. He was not interested in the size of the aggregate income, because to him this was not an important problem.

Although he had much less empirical data on output and income than we have today, Alfred Marshall understood what would be involved in framing a concept of national income (national dividend as he called it). Here is how he expressed it:

> . . . this national dividend is at once the aggregate net product of, and the sole source of payment for, all the agents of production within the country: it is divided up into earnings of labor; interest of capital; and lastly the producer's surplus, or rent, of land and of

81

other differential advantages for production. It constitutes the whole of them, and the whole is distributed among them; and the larger it is, the larger, other things being equal, will be the share of each of them.[1]

While each of the above economists can be said to have had a rather general concept, credit for the most rigorous formulation of a model of the national economy goes to a group of economists now referred to as the Lausanne school. The best known members of this group were Léon Walras (1834–1910) and Vilfredo Pareto (1848–1923), professors of political economy at the University of Lausanne. Their hypothetical model of *general equilibrium* attempted to take into account complex interrelationships of the various parts of an economic system. They were interested not only in particular markets, but in the links among all markets, the income flows, the aggregate demand functions, and so forth. This was in contrast to the model used by the English classical economists, who were interested in a theory of prices of particular goods—in the forces which bring supply and demand into equilibrium in a single market (*partial equilibrium*). The sophisticated theoretical work of the Lausanne school did not immediately adapt itself to empirical application, although some of the concepts influenced later developments.

The Modern Income Concept

A concept of national income and, what is perhaps more important, usable data to give it realistic content had to await the development of reasonably accurate statistics as well as a more acute awareness of need. It is undoubtedly no accident that organized efforts to develop some empirical measure of national income dates from the period of World War I. Modern total war is a great unifier of the production and distribution processes. Logistics—the equipping and supplying of armies—requires an ability both to estimate needs and to know what it is possible for an economy to produce.

The fact that the United States did not possess adequate knowledge in 1917–19 to do this job effectively, set economists like Wesley C. Mitchell (a government consultant during the war) to thinking about the problem. Shortly thereafter he and his associates initiated the inquiry which subsequently produced the first estimates of our national income. A few years before his death, on the twenty-fifth anniversary of the

---

[1] Alfred Marshall, *Principles of Economics* (8th ed.; London: Macmillan & Co., 1920), p. 536.

82

founding of the National Bureau of Economic Research, Mitchell recounted the experience:

> In 1920, our Board of Directors had the wisdom to select as the National Bureau's initial project one that envisages an aspect of the whole economy. National income embraces the output of all commodities and services that can be thought of without overstraining conventions as passing through the market, with due allowance for the fact that a portion of this output merely offsets the wearing out of certain durable possessions. . . . When the country entered this war[2] estimates of national income covering twenty years and classified in several ways were available.[3]

The National Bureau published its first estimate of the national income for the year 1929. The time was significant, for that was to be the year of our greatest income attainment for more than a decade. The great depression began the following year, and the level of economic activity plunged downward. In 1932 the task of preparing annual income estimates was taken over by the Department of Commerce.

Since then sources of data have been greatly extended, the concept of national income or product has been refined, and the statistical techniques for handling the data improved. These estimates have now become part of the language of everyday economic affairs. They are reported in government publications and widely used as the most familiar index of our economic attainments. Table 1 shows the annual income estimates since 1929, as reported by the Department of Commerce.

National income is made up of the dollar claims against goods and services, generated in the process of producing those goods, which accrue to the factors that have co-operated in production.

What can we learn from a set of data such as this? The most obvious clue it gives us is to the level of economic activity during these years.

We see the dip from 1929 through the early 1930's—the years of the great depression. If we think in terms of money—as we usually do in our society—a mental image is created of the slowing down of money income passing from hand to hand. And behind this image we can recall, if our experience goes back that far, what was happening to people. There were the unemployed, the bread lines, the factories that were closed, houses and apartments that were empty. Moving down the columns, further

---

[2] World War II.
[3] National Bureau of Economic Research, *Twenty-Fifth Annual Report*, 1945, p. 16.

Table 1. National Income in the United States, Annually, 1929–1957
(billions of dollars)

Year	Income	Year	Income
1929	87.8	1944	182.6
1930	75.7	1945	181.2
1931	59.7	1946	179.6
1932	42.5	1947	197.2
1933	40.2	1948	221.6
1934	49.0	1949	216.2
1935	57.1	1950	240.0
1936	64.9	1951	277.0
1937	73.6	1952	290.2
1938	67.6	1953	302.1
1939	72.8	1954	299.0
1940	81.6	1955	324.1
1941	104.7	1956	343.6
1942	137.7	1957	358.2
1943	170.3		

Source: *Economic Report of the President, 1958.*

changes in the figures reflect the slow recovery that took place, followed by the bustling efforts of the war and postwar years, when the outpouring of goods and services reached unprecedented volume, and levels of employment rose.

The full meaning of these figures will not be clear until we get behind them, until we know the operations by which they were derived. Even then we still have to comprehend the kinds of activity which constituted the human experience for which these are but abstract symbols. While these figures tell us much, they do not tell us all. There are dangers in treating them too literally.

Macroeconomics: the National Inventory

As we have to project our thoughts behind the arithmetical symbols in which the above estimates are stated, in order to link them with the real incomes of goods and services, so must these estimates themselves be built up from elements of *real* economic activity.

Basically the economy of the United States is the organized activity by means of which some 170 million people obtain the requirements for living. Human effort and knowledge applied to existing materials in the environment constitute the foundation. Linking effort and materials together is a continuous flow of transactions among people, each involving a change of ownership or access to service-rendering material goods and immaterial human services.

A national inventory or system of classification focuses on those variables which enter into or influence the number and level of transactions. At the highest level of abstraction two categories can be distinguished: *things* and *people*. Under these headings would be listed various subclasses, according to their relation to the producing and income-getting activities. Natural resources and capital equipment would be included under things. Total population classified for income purposes would make up the other category.

Natural Resources

The natural resources of a nation include all materials and energies of the physical environment of actual or potential use to man. Among these would be the land surface capable of sustaining animal and vegetable life (as well as the terra firma on which men move and have their being), the minerals below the surface, the rivers, the lakes and surrounding oceans, and the larger influences we call climate and weather.

Further subdivisions could be made for more detailed treatment. Land can be broken down into soil types, fertility, slope, and accessibility. The minerals and other elements that we identify from our storehouse of scientific knowledge could be listed and inventoried. For the present, however, we need only call attention to the existing physical environment in its broadest sense. (The classical economists lumped all such variables under the heading of *land*.)

Capital Equipment

Under this classification we would include all of the various artifacts, such as buildings, tools, machinery, and stocks of goods in varying stages of readiness for use. Most of these would consist of materials of the first category (things), modified by the physical and mental energies of man —the congealed efforts of hand and brain locked up in new physical forms of iron and steel, mortar and stone, wood and clay, and now the countless other forms of matter created by modern chemistry. These are the produced means of production. This category would also have to include a form of capital invisible to the eye—except as it can be seen in books and blueprints—the mental capital of technology.

Population

For present purposes we will also require a classification of people. Not all will be of equal importance to the national inventory. From the total population we will have to make certain deductions to arrive at the subtotal with which we will be concerned.[4] Those to be eliminated from consideration include:

Children (too young to work);
The retired (too old to work);
Students (training for work);
Housewives (whose work is not counted for income purposes);
The incapacitated (physically or mentally incapable of work);
Voluntary unemployed (too rich to work, too lazy to work, or resting); and
Armed forces (since World War II a significant withdrawal from civilian production).

Those remaining after these deductions constitute the civilian labor force, which in turn might be classified according to many varieties of skill and specialty. Table 2 shows the relation between population and labor force for selected years.

The potential efforts of the working force and the service-rendering things of the environment comprise the *factors of production*. The capacity of an economy to create want-satisfying goods and services depends upon

Table 2. U. S. Population, Civilian Labor Force, Unemployment
in Selected Years
(in thousands)

Year	Population	Civilian Labor Force	Unemployment
1939	130,879	55,230	9,480
1950	151,683	63,099	3,142
1952	157,028	62,966	1,932
1953	159,636	63,815	1,870
1954	162,417	64,468	3,578
1955	165,270	65,848	2,904
1956	168,174	67,530	2,822
1957	171,220	67,946	2,936

Source: Adapted from U.S. Bureau of the Census and Department of Labor Statistics.

[4] These categories cannot be neat and fixed. Exceptions will occur in any practical application where the assignment of a particular individual to one of these classes will be arbitrary. Children do some productive work, though less than formerly. Retired persons may move back into the labor force, as they did during the war, and as also may housewives and students. There are different degrees of incapacity and voluntary unemployment. During periods of high-level production, the working force increases through recruitment from these classes.

these factors: the quantity and quality of resources, the amount and composition of the capital goods, and the size and skills of the working force. If two such national environments are compared, and if the available factors are similar in all respects save one—either the fertility of the soil or the richness of the ore deposits, the extent of accumulated capital equipment, or the number and skills of the workers—the one with the advantage in any of these will be capable of the greatest output. A nation with superiority in them all would be capable of outproducing any other. The high output potential of the United States can be attributed to a subcontinent of rich resources, a vast accumulation of capital improvements, a highly skilled population, and the organizing abilities developed in an environment favorable to business undertaking.

In addition to capacity, however, output will depend upon the extent to which these factors are actually used. This means purposive use, for they not only need to be used, but must also be used in effective combination and for the kinds of things that members of the society want in their roles as consumers. We will return to this point in Part 3 when we develop more fully the meaning of production. Here we need only note that rate of use helps to determine the level of transactions.

A society or nation need not be limited in its capacity to obtain the requirements for living by the factors within its boundaries. By exchange with (or plunder of) other societies, access to materials from the outside can be obtained. This is the basis of international trade, which becomes very important for many nations lacking important subclasses of the factors of production.

By convention the general term adopted by economists for this fund or inventory of useful things is *wealth*.[5] From this working fund is derived the *flow* we call income. An important distinction needs to be kept in mind. When we are discussing wealth in terms of aggregates, we will mean something slightly different from our everyday usage of the term. A wealthy individual drawing up an inventory or balance sheet of his holdings would probably include among the *things* he owns intangible securities, such as stocks and bonds and money. For that individual this would be quite correct. From the point of view of society, however, these are only evidences of property ownership or claims against the things held by other people and by businesses. A totaling of all such property claims in their positive and negative aspects would cancel out, and we would be left with the fund of "wealth," which represents the "real" factors of production.

---

[5] This concept was developed in Chapter 4.

The Economic System as Income Process

Economists speak of the basic decisions an economic system must make in coming to grips with the problem of scarcity. As already indicated in Part 1, these are:

1. How currently produced goods and services are distributed among the members of society.

2. What new goods and services should be produced in anticipation of future consumption.

3. How should they be produced—that is, by what combination of factors of production. Should they be produced largely by hand, or by machines; should the land be farmed extensively or intensively.

4. How much of what is produced should be used for current consumption, and how much should be devoted to replacing capital as it wears out and in enlarging the capital stock.

5. At what level or how near to its capacity will the economy operate.

To say that the economic system makes these decisions is only a manner of speaking. The economic system does not make decisions. It is rather a consolidation of the millions of decisions made every day by people in their roles as housewives, business executives, workers, professionals, government officials, and others. When our frame of reference is this over-all economic system, the thinking model consists of the structure which economists and others have invented for organizing these millions of decisions into a pattern of logically consistent relationships. Production can be defined here as the social process by means of which all useful goods and services come into existence, and claims to income are established. Consumption consists of exercising such claims against the flow of goods and services, and channeling them into the hands of those who will destroy them in use.

If the rates of production and consumption are different, the fund of usable things in a nation will either accumulate or be drawn down. An accumulation we call investment, a drawing down is disinvestment. Professor Kenneth Boulding employs a vivid analogy which he has named the "bathtub theorem." The economic system, he suggests, is like a bathtub, in which the faucet represents production, the drain consumption. The level of water in the tub represents the fund of real capital. In rich societies, with a high "water level," consumption need not be tied directly to production. Either may run ahead of the other by building up or drawing down the fund of capital.

Money-income flows and real-income flows, the two sides of every transaction, move in opposite directions. They need not always move at the same rates, although they are interdependent and affect each other. We experience this interdependence as inflation and deflation, and its consequences for business and household decisions. To study the ebb and flow of income we must first have in hand a usable model of the basic variables, together with scales for measuring changes. In the next section we shall develop such a model and measures more systematically.

Discussion
Questions

1. During the great depression of the 1930's some areas were affected very little. Subsistence farmers of the southern Appalachian region and the Ozarks continued to live much the same as they did during the prosperous 1920's. Why do you think this was true?

2. Since that time a number of areas have been developed as vacation resorts and many of these farmers now depend upon the tourist trade for cash income. How would you describe what has happened?

3. China has a much larger population than the United States. The national product is probably much smaller than that of the United States. A numerical measure of the total product in China would be rather difficult to arrive at, however. Why?

4. How would you estimate how much housewives add to the total production of a country like the United States?

5. During the 1930's the output of manufactured goods decreased; that of agriculture actually increased. Why do you think this happened?

6. Describe in your own words what the term economy or economic system means to you. Is this something you can observe directly, or is it a handy abstraction for relating observable events to one another?

National Income

in Theory

and Experience

TRANSACTIONS among three basic income-creating and income-receiving sectors—households, business firms, and government—comprise the source of national-income flows. Each transaction is a two-sided affair. Expenditures by one of these units becomes income to another.

Balancing each money transaction is a change of ownership of some good or service. These goods have price tags on them. A summation of these price tags, minus certain deductions to avoid double counting, gives an aggregate value of national product. A summation of the money transfers gives a corresponding statement of national income.

It is useful to perceive these transactions as a flow measured over a period of time. Rates of flow vary with the number of transactions and the volume of money and credit in the system. Thinking about and observing these flows requires a simplified model of the basic relationships. The number of different accounts that must be kept for the social economy are suggested by the model. By collecting and estimating relevant data called for by these accounts, we have the materials for measuring national-income flows. Having measures of these flows for successive periods, we can analyze the changes that occur, calculate different relationships among the component parts, and derive hypotheses concerning "causes" of changes. That is what this section deals with.

CHAPTER 6

Concepts and Models

in National Income Accounting

BASIC TO an operational concept of national income is a system of social accounting. This means a system of bookkeeping for the nation.

In a strict semantic sense the nation does not have an income, if by that we mean what we do when we say that an individual's income is $5,000, or when we say that the revenue of the Federal government is $71 billion. National income is more abstract (a construct), which nevertheless has a meaning of its own. We can illustrate this by means of a "scale" model of the larger thinking model used in national-income accounting and analysis.

A Simple Model of Money Flows

For our purpose, a group of 30 students in a classroom can be treated as a closed economic system. The instructor has just distributed to each member of the class a crisp one dollar bill, thereby creating for the group an economic and financial history. Every minute, on a signal from the instructor, each student passes the dollar to his neighbor. All receipts and expenditures are entered in an account book. At the end of twenty minutes each person will have taken in $20. This is his money income for the period, as shown in his account book or income statement. This is the amount of money that passed through his hands. Figuratively speaking, he has had the experience of "pocketing" a dollar bill twenty times, and his income has an operational meaning in that sense.

We can now set up a *national-income account* for our simple "society." Each of the 30 students received $20 during the period. The total for all such income statements is $600. Each individual's expenditure was income to his neighbor. If everyone had spent his money more rapidly, or if each had possessed more money at the start, the aggregate income account would have been larger. If, instead of signaling each minute, the instructor had given the cue to spend the dollar every thirty seconds, each person would have taken in, and spent, $40 during the period. The class income would have been $1,200. If instead of giving each person one dollar at the beginning of the period, the instructor had distributed two dollars, this would also have doubled the income. At the first rate of spending the "economy's" income would then have been $1,200. At the faster rate it would have been $2,400. In each instance the "national income" figure we attain is a construct, a nonbehavioral datum, but we observe in this example that it is the consequence of behavior.

If the student had used a system of double-entry bookkeeeping, he would have had entries for receipts in one column and for expenditures in another. In every case in our example the two items would be equal. Thus it does not matter whether we count the money as it comes in or as it is spent, if it is all spent. We would not want to count them both and add them together because we would be adding two sides of the same *transaction*. We shall see presently that in the greater complexity of the national economy a double-entry system which shows source and allocation gives us two measures of the same process.

Our analogy is not particularly "realistic." It is little more than a money-passing game. But let us assume now that in the interval between "dollar passing" each person manufactured or produced some kind of good or service valued at one dollar,[1] ownership of which he transferred to his neighbor as he received the money income. We now have two parallel flows moving in opposite directions, the one a *money flow,* the other a *real flow.*

The concept of total (national) income acquires added meaning now because it is closely associated with the real income flow. At constant prices for goods and services an expansion or contraction in the total money flow would represent a parallel change in real income.

Saving

What happens if some student (in our example) varies his behavior from the prescribed rules? What if one individual (or more) decides to

---

[1] For purposes of this illustration we take this value as given. The economic process by means of which this value is arrived at will be our concern in the next three parts of the book.

build up a stock of dollar bills? He can convert more of his property or assets into cash by continuing to "sell," and at the same time reducing purchases. He might decide to do this for a variety of reasons. In the language of the economist, we would say his "liquidity preference" had increased.

For a time the dollar bills might continue to come in. The neighbor from whom he was buying, however, would soon find his income source drying up. His stock of "goods" have ceased to move and *real property* begins to accumulate involuntarily. Unless he gets money from another source his own purchases will have to be reduced. Sooner or later, if this action continues, the total money flow and the real flow will be affected. If the instructor were to step into the breach and inject new money, or if those who are saving were to lend the money to others, this might restore the flow. When those who desired to hold dollar bills had been satisfied, the flow would expand again. On the other hand, if the quantity of money or the rate of spending were to increase, without a parallel increase in the goods and services produced, more would be spent for the same goods and the price paid for each would tend to rise.

Like all very simple analogies, this one has limitations as an analytical or thinking tool. We have exhausted the usefulness of our small closed society of homogeneous individuals in a strictly limited environment. It will be helpful, however, as we inquire into the wider compass of the whole economy, to remember the relationships described. Here are illustrated some paradoxes that show up if we try to think of "society's income" in the same frame of reference used for an individual. For example:

1. Expenditure to one person is income to another. Income and expenditure are simply two sides of the same transaction. The individual sees it from only one side.

2. Money flows and real flows move in opposite directions. Money is a claim against goods, and the more rapidly these claims are taken up, the greater the volume of real income at constant prices. The money flow is a measure of the real income flow, but if prices rise or fall the money flow will overstate or understate the real flow.

3. With a fixed quantity of money, it will be impossible for all members of society—or for any substantial number—to build up cash balances. A desire by some for cash balances can only be satisfied if others are reducing their cash, or if new money or credit is forthcoming.

4. Attempts to accumulate net cash balances or saving will result in unsold goods piling up. As we shall see later, unsold goods will usually mean that those producing them will stop doing so, and the size of the

national income will shrink, thereby reducing the amount of saving that can take place.

The Real Income Flows

Instead of keeping our attention on the money flows, we might have watched the goods and services changing hands. Ultimately, of course, this is what interests us, since it is from this flow that the wants of all must be met. In connection with this flow a number of questions arise.

Are the factors of production being used in such a way that the national income is as large as it could be? Would a different combination of these factors provide a higher level of desired goods and services? Is the national real income for this year larger or smaller than last year or five years ago? Is economic progress providing a rising scale of living?[2] Is there more food, clothing, house room, medical service, and leisure time than a year ago, a decade ago, a century ago? If so, and to the extent that these things contribute to well-being, to human satisfaction and adjustment, we can say that the people of a nation are better off.

If we knew exactly how many units of every commodity and the hours of personal service that had been created in any given year, we could compare this information with another year and presumably determine which was larger. There are difficulties, however.

Assume that in Year 2 more of every type of good or service had been produced than in Year 1. We could then say that the nation was better off in terms of scarce goods and services in Year 2. But how much better off? If there were exactly 10 per cent more of everything, the real income would clearly be larger by 10 per cent. If the rate of increase had been uneven, as probably would be the case, comparison would be more difficult.

Assume, too, that no single commodity increased by less than 5 per cent, although some commodities were larger by as much as 25 per cent. What could we then say that would be unambiguous? Only this: national real income in Year 2 was at least 5 per cent larger than in Year 1. But suppose some commodities increased by as much as 50 per cent, while others decreased as much as 50 per cent. Clearly we are in difficulty. Our process of counting breaks down.

To take a very simple example, let us say that two commodities—rockets and refrigerators—are produced from a given set of factors; that in 1951, 1,000,000 refrigerators and 10,000 rockets were turned out. In 1952, as labor and other factors were diverted from appliances to

---

[2] This concept is developed in Part 5.

the production of rockets, the output of refrigerators falls to 500,000 and the rockets increase to 50,000. Has total output increased or decreased?

Clearly, it is impossible to tell by inspection. What we can do, of course, is to resort to a type of averaging—a measure which we will encounter in different problems and which is usually referred to as *index numbers*. These are useful devices, widely employed by government agencies, newspapers, economists, and others for purposes of description and comparison. But they need to be used with care lest they give the unwarranted impression of exactness. Here is how the process of averaging or index construction would operate in the case of our two-commodity problem. Since we want to compare 1952 with 1951, we will construct a ratio of output for each of the two products. Output for 1951 will appear as the denominator, called the *base*, and that for 1952 as the numerator.

$$\text{Refrigerators} \quad \frac{1952}{1951} \quad \frac{500,000}{1,000,000} = .5$$

$$\text{Rockets} \quad \frac{1952}{1951} \quad \frac{50,000}{10,000} = 5$$

If we convert our ratios to percentage terms (by multiplying by 100) we see that the output of refrigerators is 50 per cent of the base year while the output of rockets is 500 per cent. If we add these percentages and divide by 2, we get an average change in the two products.

$$.5 \times 100 = 50$$
$$5 \times 100 = 500$$
$$2 \overline{\smash{)}550} (275$$

If we say that the total output in 1951 equalled 100 (which is what we mean when we call it the base year), then the output in 1952 is 275, or 2¾ times that of 1951.

There is a joker in the deck, however. By using 1951 as the base, we have made it the *norm* against which to measure change. The relationship which existed between refrigerators and rockets in that year becomes absolute for purposes of measurement. In that year, when 1,000,000 refrigerators and 10,000 rockets were produced, the ratio was 100 refrigerators to one rocket. In making this the basis of our index system, we have arbitrarily made 100 refrigerators the equivalent of one rocket for purposes of measuring rates of change. With that ratio fixed, with the relatively smaller decrease in refrigerators and the very large increase in rockets, of course, the output in 1952 will appear larger.

We can pinpoint this problem still more if we reverse our procedure and measure the combination in 1952 against the preceding year. 1952 becomes the base.

$$\text{Refrigerators} \quad \frac{1951}{1952} \quad \frac{1,000,000}{500,000} = 2 \times 100 = 200 \text{ per cent}$$

$$\text{Rockets} \quad \frac{1951}{1952} \quad \frac{10,000}{50,000} = .2 \times 100 = \underline{20} \text{ per cent}$$

$$2\overline{)220}(110$$

Here we are confronted by a paradox. The output of 1951 is here shown to be 10 per cent larger than that of 1952. Obviously, the output for each year cannot be larger. The cause of the paradox is, of course, the shift in the base. The 1952 combination now becomes the standard against which to measure change. One rocket is now treated as the equivalent of 10 refrigerators. Which base is correct? This is an unanswerable question as long as we are dealing with unlike things. The choice of a base and equivalencies will always be arbitrary.

In making index numbers of physical output much depends on the units selected and how they are weighted with respect to each other. There is no common denominator to all of them which can be used as a measure or standard. As was pointed out earlier, when we are considering the combined output of goods and services, each has its unit of measurement and there is no easy way to combine these. We cannot do it on the basis of number (for example, carats of diamonds with tons of hay), on the basis of weight (beef on the hoof with the voice of a Metropolitan soprano[3]), or indeed on the basis of any other physical characteristic. The change of quality is more important than the change in amount, and our measuring system does not get at that. This is sometimes referred to as the index problem.

A group who called themselves Technocrats created a stir in the 1930's by proposing to convert everything from labor to finished goods into *ergs* of energy. This was supposed to give a common basis for measurement. Aside from producing a few articles and pamphlets about how convenient it would be if this were done, they never made much progress toward their objective. Ergs cannot capture the subtle difference between a masterpiece and a pedestrian musical composition, or for that matter between a well prepared omelet and a bad one. In social valuations these things make the difference.

---

[3] Even though for certain purposes there may be merit in such a comparison with the soprano herself.

96

In computing total output of goods and services produced for any period, allowance has to be made for previously existing materials used up in the production process each year, such as natural resources and capital equipment. There must be some way of subtracting this from the gross output, so that the final figure is net income. Otherwise we are using up our capacity to produce. If more of such materials are required to produce rockets than refrigerators, or vice versa, this fact should be taken into account. But these things are likely to have physical characteristics quite different from what is produced, thereby further complicating the measurement problem.

A Money Measure of Output and Income

The task of computing total output is simplified when we introduce *money* as our measuring rod, although the index number problem does not disappear. Actually, the whole procedure is very tricky and has to be used with caution. Nevertheless, we can get over some difficulties, and if certain conditions are fulfilled (which will be explained later) the measure becomes a meaningful and useful one.

Money is a measuring device which has evolved from the social process of exchange.[4] In this process a unit value or price is established for most of the different goods and services which enter the income flows. If we could imagine a perfect process for "social evaluation," an ideal money would provide us with a precise measuring rod. The money measuring rod we have is an imperfect one, but it is the best we have, and by learning some of its shortcomings we can make it serve a useful purpose. By multiplying the number of units of different commodities by their price, and totaling these amounts, we obtain a *money measure* of them. If we can compute or estimate the money value of an important part of the goods and services produced during a year, we can then make comparison with other years. By subtracting the value of equipment and resources used up, we can determine net income. It can then be stated, within limits, whether the national output or income has changed— whether it is larger or smaller and by how much. An illustration will be given following our discussion of the actual measures of national income to show how the process of constructing indices of "real value" from money value is accomplished (see pages 197–98).

In our simple model the "national income" emerged from the exchange of goods and services against money. What one person spent became income to the person with whom he traded. However, we neg-

---

[4] See discussion in Chapter 4.

lected an important consideration. If the members of our hypothetical "class economy" were actual producers, the dollar they received would not be net income, unless they were selling a personal service. If they had purchased raw materials or paid wages, then the price of their product would include these amounts and something more. Otherwise the sellers would have no income of their own. What they had paid out would be cost to them. These cost payments would already have become income to the persons who received them and we would not want to count them again as part of total income.

We can clarify this point if we follow a specific product, say a linen handkerchief, through a number of transactions. Since we cannot possibly include all of the transactions associated with even so simple a product as this, we will assume at the outset that at each stage of production the producer hires no outside labor and incurs no other costs than the amount he pays for the "handkerchief in process."

The handkerchief starts with raw flax produced by a farmer. Assume that the price received for the flax is 3 cents. The manufacturer who buys and transforms the flax into thread pays the 3 cents to the farmer, and after processing has a product (thread) worth 5 cents, which he sells to a weaver. His *income* is 2 cents. The weaver who processes the thread into cloth has a product worth 10 cents, and a net income of 5 cents. If the one who dyes, hems, and embroiders the handkerchief creates a product which wholesales for 60 cents, his income is 50 cents. Finally, the one who stocks the handkerchief and holds it until a customer buys it for $1.00 realizes an income of 40 cents.

The amount of income generated is $1.00. This is the final selling price of the product. However, it is the result of five transactions. If we counted the full amount of money that each agent took in, our total money income would be greater than the real income that has resulted. This is shown in Figure 1. Gross transactions total $1.78.

This example can be used to illustrate in simplified form the two methods for computing (estimating) national income and national product. If it were possible to collect data on the selling price for all finished goods turned out during a period, in this case the handkerchief, we would have a money measure of the national product. Alternatively, by determining the *value added* by firms at the different stages of production, we would arrive at the same figure—$1.00. Since in practice it is easier to get data on sales and cost of sales from various industries, the second method has proved to be the more practical.

Any accounting system must avoid the error of double counting, or the national-product figure will be too high. When the additional

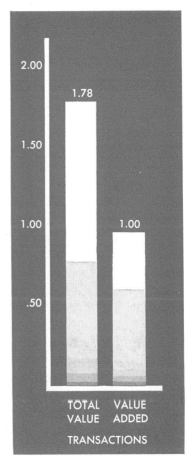

Figure 1.   Difference Between Total Value
of Transactions and Value Added

transactions which would ordinarily be involved are considered, even in such a simple example as that given above, it will be apparent that the task we have set up for ourselves is not a simple one. In all probability the 3-cent income of the farmer is in fact already partially committed for costs of seed, fertilizer, gasoline, depreciation of machinery, and other necessary expenditures. The processor of the flax would undoubtedly be a large manufacturer with labor costs, rents, interest payments, and machine costs, in addition to the raw materials. The same would be true of the other producers. And when this process is projected onto the broader screen of the whole society or nation, with its enormous number of transactions, the task of measuring income flows is complex indeed. To accomplish this task will require a system of classification for the different transactions, and a corresponding set of accounts. As a preliminary to the treatment of these accounts, a set of visual models will be presented to assist in conceptualizing the relationships among them.

Basic Models
of Income Flows

Households require a money income to purchase their consumption requirements. For four out of five in the adult working population this means working for someone and being paid a wage or salary. Some householders receive their claims to income through ownership of property. Any particular individual may receive income from several sources, through working for many employers (who are called clients or patients), or through distributing property rights rather widely by owning *shares* in different business organizations.[5] Still other claims, called income transfers, are the result of institutional provisions and chance. These include the incomes of the members of families who are the dependents of the principal income receivers, those who rely on charity, public relief, swindling, and theft, as well as on certain other distributive shares which cannot be assigned a clear function in the production process. For purposes of measuring national real income, these *transfers* have to be excluded; not to do so means counting dollars for which there is no corresponding flow of new goods and services. They are counted, however, as personal income.

A system of classification used for constructing a model of income flows will distinguish between income receivers on the basis of how the income is used—whether for consumption purposes, which withdraws real income from the system and uses it up, or for production, which has the effect of continuing and expanding future real-income flows. The system of classification also has to differentiate between factor owners and factor users.

The most common consumption or spending unit is the family. This spending unit will ordinarily consist of husband and wife, together with dependents. However, in the United States roughly one-fourth of such spending units (13.5 million of the 52.2 million) consist of single individuals earning and spending their own incomes. The spending unit may include more than one provider, as when the wife or children have jobs which supplement the family earnings. The term *household* is used to refer to all such consumption units.

---

[5] An analysis of these claims—who gets what and how—will be found in Part 4.

Production is carried on in a great diversity of establishments. The term *establishment* is used by the Department of Commerce to mean any business unit which has an independent central accounting office. The characteristics these establishments have in common is control over, but not necessarily ownership of, the factors of production. Whether this control is exercised by an individual or a group of individuals is not important at our present level of analysis. These units will be classified together as the *business firms*. This classification does not divide people into producers and consumers, but according to functional roles in the income process.

To conceptualize the national-income flow of the private consumption and production economy, it can be imagined as a circular process carried on between the aggregates of our two basic units. Both the money flows and the real flows move between them. Figure 2 will serve as a convenient visual aid.

The outer circumference of the circle represents the real flows.[6] The inner circle represents money flows which give access to (or control over) the real flows. Both flows are shown passing through markets where transactions take place. In the lower half of the diagram, the direction of the money flow is from firms to households. Viewed by the firms, these are money costs paid out to the owners of factors of production. From the point of view of the households, this same flow represents the money claims or income from property rights and personal services, including wages and salaries, rents, interest, fees, royalties, dividends, and so forth. Balancing these money flows is the transfer of control to the business firms of the factor services such as labor and professional services, physical equipment and resources, liquid funds or cash, and more abstract things such as patented processes. Across the upper half of the diagram are the balancing flows moving in the opposite direction. Here the money transfers are from the households to the business firms. They are the expenditures of the households which, looked at from the other side, become receipts or gross business income. Balancing these money flows are the goods and services which are the output of the business firms. These move through markets to the consumers, and when the flow is in equilibrium they are priced to cover all of the various costs incurred in producing them.

If we can now refer to our example of the linen handkerchief, the lower money flow would be the total of all the *net* income payments in

---

[6] The particular shape of these diagrams is not to be regarded as having significance. They are not drawn to scale and are intended only to show direction of flow.

Figure 2. A Simple Income-Flow System
of the Private Economy

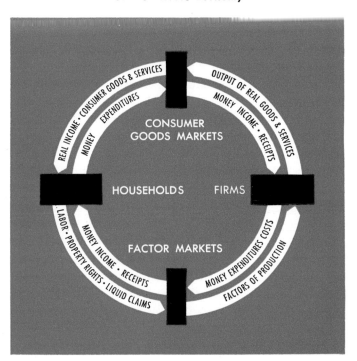

the five transactions, or $1.00. The factor flow would include the various productive services that went into making the linen handkerchief. The $1.00 which had been distributed would just be sufficient to buy back the finished article priced at $1.00. We are, of course, limited in our illustration by the fact that we chose an indivisible item which could not be bought back, since not all of the income is in the hands of a single individual. However, when we use the handkerchief as a *symbol* for many different goods and services of various sorts and sizes, the principle illustrated still holds.

Going behind these symbols, we can imagine the households (factor owners) delivering control over the productive services to the firms and receiving their receipts or money claims in return. On the other hand, we can visualize these claims being presented in the market for purposes of withdrawing real income for use. When the flows in both directions are equal, there are just enough claims to take over the ownership of goods made available during any given period. The amount of all of the price tags on the goods and services is equivalent to the money receipts of the firms. The total of the income flows to the households is equivalent to the amount spent for these goods.[7]

How do we measure the flow of income for a period such as a year? Without stretching the imagination too far, we can think of some kind of income meter that can be attached at a point on the circular flow of our diagram. It might be attached at the output point of the firms to measure money value of all new goods and services as they are offered for sale by the firms. Since our symbol for firms is all-inclusive, abstracting away interfirm payments, the meter should measure the total money value of the firms' output. Entering our readings in the proper account, for some unit of time, we get a figure for national product.

Totaling the net value added to goods and services by all of the individual firms for the time period under consideration, we get the value of all goods and services produced, or the total value of the national output. However, this figure still would not give us the net national output. At the beginning of the measurement, we would start with a set of firms as going concerns, that is, production organizations with machinery and plant, representing a carry-over from some previous period. In other words, the individual firm would possess a stock of real capital, and the aggregate capital controlled by all firms would represent the total accumulated private production capital of the nation. In the process of creating the national output a part of the machinery, the buildings, and the inventories of previously accumulated parts and raw materials would be worn out or used up. Each firm attempts to maintain its capital value intact. Since equipment is only replaced at intervals after it is worn out or obsolete, the individual firm provides for its replacement by creating depreciation reserves. These are in effect costs which are assessed against the output, and which are included in the selling price of the products. Thus, taken altogether, the value of national output of goods and services would include the value of capital used up. This should not be counted as new or net national product (real income). Hence the term applied to this first measure of national output is *gross national product*. This would be the real income as measured by its dollar value before deducting for depreciation.

Instead of setting up the hypothetical income meter to value the goods and services as they flow from the firms, we might have set it up to measure the flow of money income as it is paid over to the households. These are the expenditures (costs) of the firm which become the incomes

---

[7] Again we need to emphasize that this concept of equilibrium is not a description of reality. It is a construct, a thinking tool.

of the households. These incomes are the result of multiplying the total units of factors supplied by their prices, as determined in the factor markets. Ideally, when the twin flows are in balance this money flow should just buy the net national product, leaving that part of the "real" flow representing the depreciation still in the hands of the firms.

To the economist engaged in national income research these two points of measurement serve as checks on each other. Because of the complexity of our income-producing and income-using system, it is never possible to obtain all of the facts. Available information is seldom complete, and much of it must be pieced together from samples and estimates. Thus, if two estimates of the twin flows, arrived at from these two approaches, are in substantial agreement (particularly if the two are carried on independently of each other), confidence in their reliability is increased. If the two diverge significantly, a recheck is warranted.

The simple model described above leaves out of account an important consideration. Not all output is designed for immediate, direct consumption. Some things are *producer goods,* which are sold to other firms for use in turning out consumer goods. These firms can be represented as drawing on the same real flows of productive services or factors of production. They contribute, therefore, to the personal incomes of the households as factor owners. They also receive a money income which can be represented as coming directly from the consumption goods firms and in a roundabout way from the expenditures of households. This relationship is shown in Figure 3.

These two diagrams represent the income flows originating in the *private economy,* which until quite recently accounted for more than 95 per cent of the value of the gross national product.

Role of Government

In the United States the several levels of government—local, state, and Federal—have been from the earliest times a factor influencing both money- and real-income flows. As providers of services, such as roads, river and harbor improvements, a postal system, a school system, a police and defense force, these governmental agencies purchase materials, employ people, and provide real income of various kinds. When the volume of purchases and the extent of services were small relative to the rest of the total economic or income process, the influence of government could be largely ignored. While the influence of government decisions on income flows has always been evident to the local citizens of communities that sought army posts, public buildings, veterans' hospitals, state penitentiaries and universities, as well as many other agencies of public service, the tendency of most of those who thought about the economic process was to treat them separately. Indeed, public finance was once treated as a separate branch of economics. More recently, as the size of government purchases and the number of services provided have increased, particularly those of the Federal government, to treat them separately would mean neglecting an important influence on the total income flows, both real and money.

To complete the map of the income process, we need to include the *public economy*. Most government incomes derive from taxes and fees, which are collected both from firms and households. Services are rendered to citizens both as producers and as consumers. Thus the most convenient location for this function on our diagram is in the center.

To continue our twin flows as before with separate lines representing the money flows and real flows would make a two-dimension diagram very complicated. Accordingly, we will use a simpler chart, letting a single line indicate the two-way flow process. Government can now be represented as one of the income-generating units, receiving and disbursing money, purchasing goods and services, and hiring employees to perform public functions. Some actions of government are linked only to the purely monetary flows. These are income transfers, and do not contribute directly to real income, although as we shall discover later on they may influence those flows. The relationships when the influence of government is introduced are shown in the two models of Figure 4.

Interaction

So far the influence of time has been neglected. A production period was mentioned, and the idea of measurement of income flows during some unit of time has been suggested. Actually, the income-getting and income-spending process is continuous, although the rate is not constant. The channels of trade, the movement of goods and services, the production of raw materials have all come down to us as part of an evolutionary process. Unlike the flow of water through a city's water mains, or the flow of electricity through the lines of a public utility, the process cannot be stopped to install a meter. Any time period we impose has to be eased in gradually.

Most enterprises and household units, as well as government bodies and bureaus, keep accounts or records on the basis of either a calendar or fiscal year. Account books are closed, a balance is struck, and the results of the year summarized and analyzed. This is purely arbitrary, however, since the income effects of actions taken earlier will not yet be fully realized, and actions taken in the present may have effects that continue into the future.

105

Figure 3.   A More Complex Income-Flow System of the Private Economy

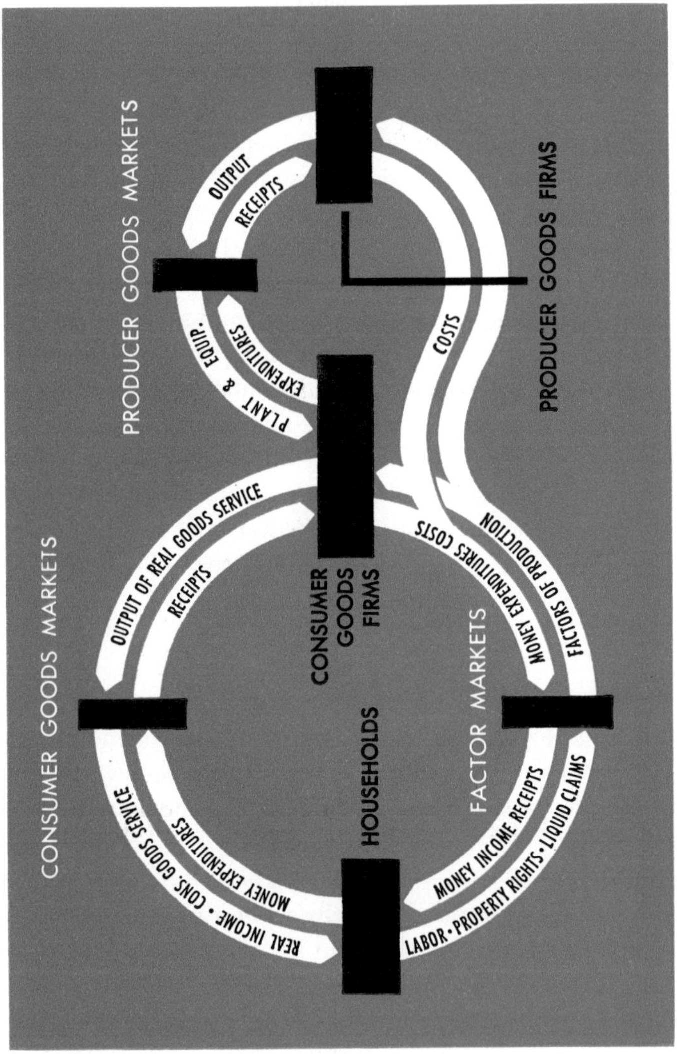

The Social Economy

106

Figure 4. Income-Flow System of the National Economy

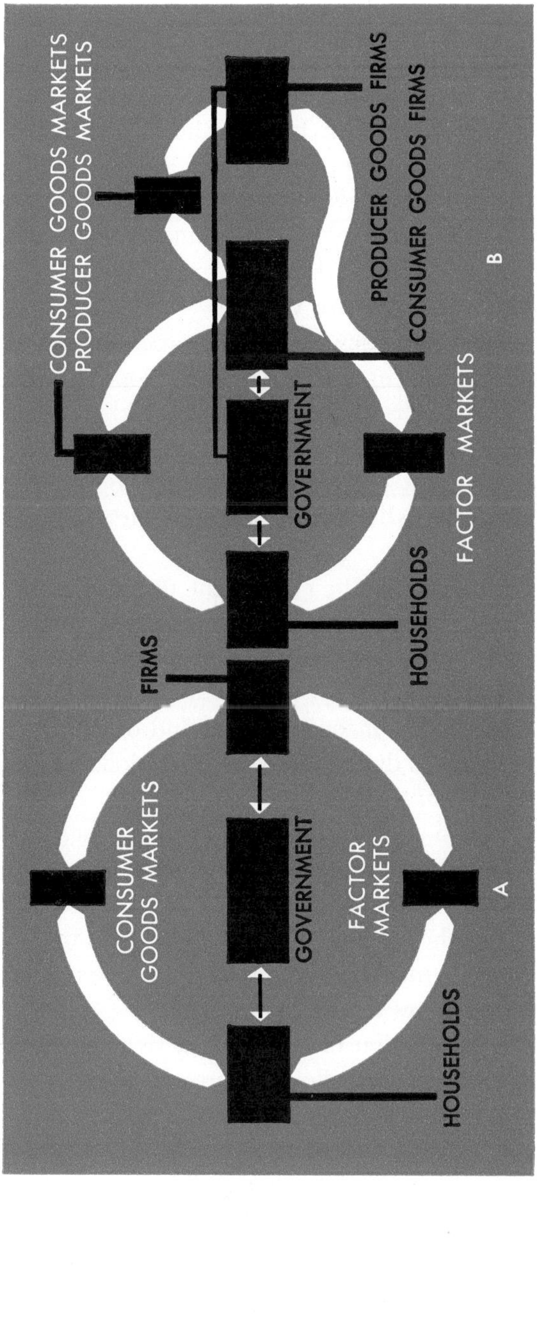

From these annual audits judgments are made on whether or not economic activity, or the income flows, are expanding or contracting. Actually, the twin flows are quite uneven. If it can be imagined that a measure were taken for very short periods, the flow of goods and services to consumers would vary markedly. One need only think of buying habits to see that this is true. Some marketing is done every day for the staple goods, but in most places during a week's time Saturday is the big shopping day. In September, just before school opens, families stock up on children's clothing and supplies. There are the Christmas rushes, the Easter buying, and countless other "peak" periods. Production patterns follow these buying habits, although ordinarily firms have learned to anticipate such periods, so that the goods are turned out in advance in order to be available when they are wanted.

In the earning of money income the process may be regarded as more or less continuous as long as we (or our property) are employed. Payments, however, are discontinuous. Some workers are paid by the day (mostly transient workers and those doing odd jobs); some are paid quarterly or annually; but the majority of employees are paid weekly or monthly, and people who own a small business may take in something every day.

In our analysis it will be convenient to use a more abstract concept of an income period which can be conceptualized as some kind of average of these different actual periods. If we can determine the total income of the household sector for a year, we can divide this number by the average number of dollars in the income stream, and determine (on the average) about how many times during the year those dollars became income. This we will call the *turnover*.

Referring again to our classroom example used at the beginning of the chapter, when the 30 students had a "class income" of $600, and the number of dollars in the system was 30, our turnover during this period was twenty. While the turnover for the whole economy will vary from year to year, the estimate most nearly agreed upon by economists and others is from three to four times a year.

As the time dimension of economic activity is extended, the money-income and the real-income flows approach equivalence. A society cannot consume more than it produces for an indefinite period. In the shorter period, both as individuals and as a society, we can consume more than current production by drawing on past accumulations. This is especially true in rich societies such as our own. Inventory stocks may be drawn down. Capital equipment can operate without full maintenance, and fertility can be withdrawn from the soil. This is what happens during wartime. Over a long-run period, however, the "bathtub" would run dry and the capacity to sustain income flows would diminish without continuous renewal through production.

A Note on the
Limits of Income

As represented in our models, the real (outer) flows are linked together: consumption goods depend upon the services of the factors used to produce them. When consumption-goods firms and producer-goods firms are shown separately, we see that output intended to replace and expand productive capacity must attract part of these factors. When the relationships of our model are given empirical content, it should be apparent that to the extent that there is some fixed amount (or supply) of factors, there is some upper limit to real income. Up to that limit (which cannot be determined precisely) the actual level of real income depends upon the extent to which the factors are used. If they are not all used, the size of that real income will be less than the hypothetical limit.

This limit, while possible to imagine, is best perceived as a shifting horizon, in the sense that historically it has expanded as factors of production have increased and technology has been improved. Population growth, particularly growth of the working force, results in an increase in total real income. As will be demonstrated later, the rate of increase in total output may be less than that of the population, if the other factors of production do not increase also. Then the total output may increase, but real income per person falls. Low-income nations are those whose population presses against a limited supply of the other factors of production. On the other hand, a rate of increase in the other factors (particularly capital) which exceeds the rate of population growth, makes possible not only a greater total real output, but also an increase in output per capita or per employed worker. Between 1929 and 1950 population in the United States increased by one-fourth; employment in the private economy rose by 22 per cent, while output rose by nearly 75 per cent.

For any nation it is a warrantable assumption that an economic or income objective is to approach as close to the maximum limit as possible, due consideration being given to the leisure preference of people. Some such meaning as this is implied when we speak of "America's capacity to produce."

The purely monetary flows, the money and credit side of transactions, represented by the inner flow of the diagram, are also tied together, consumer expenditures with factor payments and income transfers. In addition, these are interwoven with the real flows, as we have already noted. The upper limit of the money income flows and of the money values of the real flows are not equivalent to the real flows. Even if a nation had reached its full capacity to produce goods and services, the money income could conceivably go on increasing, as could the money statement of the national product. We have to conceptualize economic growth in part through the illusion or "veil" of money, working back from the dollar values to the goods and services for which they stand.

Discussion
Questions

1. Think of an ordinary transaction such as the purchase of a new pair of shoes. Describe the action of each of the parties to the transaction. Describe the results of the transaction in terms of the changes in the property ownership of the parties to the transaction.

2. What would happen if everyone in the country suddenly decided to to save one-half of his income?

3. Why, in times of war, do governments usually urge citizens to save more of their income?

4. Distinguish between the value-added measure of production and the value of final product.

5. John Doe is the head of a household, which he supports by managing a branch store of a large retail chain store. What two economic roles is he performing in the economy?

CHAPTER 7

The National Income Accounts

THIS CHAPTER will be concerned with the definition and associations of the principal concepts used by the Department of Commerce in estimating income flows in the United States. These will be illustrated with the actual figures for selected years.

Space does not permit us to treat in detail such matters as data sources and certain other problems of national-income accounting. Some of these problems are quite technical, involving techniques and reliability of sampling and data sources. Not everyone is agreed on the classification of all income data. For example, interest payments on the government debt were formerly classified as income payments, the same as payments for other borrowed funds. Since much of the national debt was incurred in fighting a war, it was decided that there was no current production which corresponded to such payments. Accordingly, these are now treated as income transfers—payments which are income to those who receive them but for which no current production service is performed. There are other disagreements or interpretations of accounting meanings.

In the early part of our discussion we will make frequent reference to the diagrams of the income-flow system presented in Chapter 6. Although the national-income accounting system is considerably more detailed than this very simplified diagrammatic flow system indicates, the latter should be helpful in visualizing the substantive nature of the process behind the accounts.

For the consolidated accounts of the basic consumption units shown in the diagrams we will use (by convention) the term *household sector*. The consolidated accounts of all firms (which include all individuals and organizations producing goods and services) become the *business sector,* the aggregation of the accounts of governmental units the *government sector*. A fourth aggregation not shown on our diagrams is the foreign sector, which shows the net effect of all transactions—household, business, and government—with the rest of the world. Because this sector is relatively small in the total of all income transactions in the United States, it can be largely neglected until we treat foreign trade as such in Part 6.

Ideally the household-sector account would consist of a consolidated statement of the income accounts of all households, in which are entered all receipts from and all expenditures to the other two sectors. These would include under receipts all payments received for factor services (labor and property) from firms and governments, and all income-transfer payments. Under expenditures would be included all payments to business firms and governments. Transactions among households themselves are neglected in the consolidated account, except for the compensation of household employees.

Analogously, the business sector accounts should include all income-generating transactions between the basic production units and the household and government sectors. In the process of consolidating accounts, all interfirm transactions disappear, with the exception of expenditures on new plant and equipment and on inventories. As will become apparent later on, these expenditures are the basis for measuring new investment which represents the growth of the income-generating system itself.

Consolidated government accounts show the receipts of all taxes and fees and all government expenditures: to households as payments to government employees, and to business for goods and services.

In practice, of course, it would be impossible to collect the accounts of the nearly 53 million households for each income period. Many households keep no systematic records. The task of assembling them would be too great if they did. Consequently the National Income Division has had to piece the information together from other sources, including sample budget studies and data from receipts and expenditures of business firms and governments, whose numbers are not so great and whose records are better kept.

The task is complicated by the fact that not all transactions generate income, although in appearance they do not differ too much from those that do. Some transactions represent simply a change in ownership of existing assets or properties. If A has $5,000 cash and B has a lot in a residential area valued at $5,000 (unless B is a real estate agency which has been developing the lot), nothing is changed if they exchange properties. The same would be true of a purchase of an existing share of stock. No income would be generated if a father sent his son a check for $100. One phase of social accounting procedure is to eliminate non-income-generating transactions and double counting, as when a firm buys a partially finished product from another firm, adds something to it, and then sells it to a consumer at a price which includes the first transaction plus the value added by the second firm.

The combined profit and loss statements of all business firms become the income and product statement for the production economy. The adjusted balance sheets of business firms (plus household investments in housing) become statements of savings and investment from income. By combining and arranging these data in different ways, income accountants are able to derive the various aggregates which give us our measures of the national-income flows.

A Family
of Aggregates

There are different vantage points from which to "view" the national-income flows. A measure of the flow at these different points of entry and exit gives a value for the aggregate transactions which create the flow. The social accounting system is designed to record these flows, according to source and disposition. We have then a family of aggregates, all more or less connected but which give us different information about what has been happening in different parts of the system.

Social accounting procedure parallels that used in the basic income units. The parts that make up the total value of transactions, both of receipts and expenditures, can be combined in different ways and for different purposes, that is, to obtain different information. The terms *gross* and *net* will be familiar. For example, gross income to a household will be a measure of income before certain costs of earning it have been deducted. Gross income to a firm is the amount received from sales transactions (and other sources) before deducting costs. For the national economy we can start with an analogous measure.

Gross National Product

During any period of time the combined actions of all firms in the United States (something over 10 million in number, of which 4.9 million are farms), together with government employees, produce some aggregate volume of goods and services.[1] The total value of these goods and services, as determined by the market or exchange system (except for government services), is called the gross national product or GNP.

---

[1] Household production, that is, the homemaking services of the housewife, are not included in the national estimates.

113

Broadly speaking, the GNP is made up of three types of goods: consumer goods, producer goods, and services. Referring to Figures 3 and 4b, we can associate this real flow with the outer circumference of the upper half of the diagram, plus the goods and services purchased by government and the total of government services rendered, valued at cost. It includes the real income which moves from the consumer-goods firms to the households and to government. As physical goods and services, these embody the materials and services firms have incorporated in them. For this period, however, the firms may have sold more or less than was produced. Most firms maintain inventories. If sales have been greater than production, inventories are reduced. If production has been greater than sales, inventories are larger. Total production, measured in dollars, is the total net value of sales,[2] plus or minus the change in inventories. In addition, GNP includes the equipment which producer-goods firms furnish consumer-goods firms, government, and one another. In this part of the business sector, output consists of finished plant and equipment sold, plus or minus inventory changes.

When the outputs of these two classes of firms are added together, we need to note something else. New producer goods serve two functions: (1) to replace depreciated equipment, and (2) to expand productive capacity. The latter is a part of net investment. Total net investment (which includes inventory accumulation) plus depreciation equals gross investment. Total net investment is usually positive, although it need not be. Gross investment will always be positive. Thus the contribution of private firms to the GNP is made up of consumer goods sold plus gross investment. Government's contribution is largely the services of all government employees, valued at their actual cost, since we do not ordinarily think of government services as passing through a market.[3]

Gross national product, the basic aggregate income concept, overstates the total value flow of *new* goods and services by the amount of depreciation incurred in producing them. For shorter periods it is useful as an indicator of total output, to tell us whether output is expanding or contracting. In wartime particularly, when an all-out effort is being made to increase output and capital maintenance can be neglected temporarily to further the war effort, it is an indicator of the amount that can be made

---

[2] Aggregating net value of sales for all firms gives the total of value added.

[3] This is not absolutely true, of course. Governments must compete to a certain extent with private firms for the personnel they hire. Government salaries are usually lower than those in business, but the discrepancy cannot be too wide. Other purchases are ordinarily made on the market at the going rate, although for some services, such as those of land-grant railroads, the government pays lower prices.

available. A nation could not consume its total GNP indefinitely, however, without impairing its capacity to produce.

Net National Product

To get a measure of *net national product,* therefore, it is necessary to deduct depreciation.[4] Net national product or NNP tells us in effect how much can be consumed during a period, while still leaving the economy with as high an output potential at the end as at the beginning of the period.

Both GNP and NNP are most usefully conceptualized as *real income,* even though they are stated in terms of our dollar measuring rod. Net national product is not included in the series of figures published by the Department of Commerce, and hence is chiefly of theoretical interest.

National Income

National income consists of the flow of money claims which accrue to the factors of production. For this reason it is sometimes called "national income at factor costs." In Figures 3 and 4 it would be represented by the inner flows of the lower part of the diagram.

National income and net national product approach each other as equivalent values under equilibrium conditions, if we consider only the private economy. However, indirect taxes collected by government from business are included in the prices of their output. These taxes help to pay for government services, but that part of the net national product does not flow to the households through the market. Thus national income is essentially of the same magnitude as net national product less indirect business taxes, which are paid chiefly by households.

Personal Income

Not all income claims established are actually received by households during a period such as a year. Corporations retain part of their earnings instead of paying them over to the stockholders as dividends. In addition, corporate income is subject to an income tax, and this further reduces income claims households would otherwise have against corporations. On the other hand, government transfers (in the form of veterans' allowances, old age retirement, unemployment compensation, and interest payments on the national debt), increase household receipts over factor payments in a given period.

---

[4] Depreciation reserves from the balance sheets of individual firms constitute the source of this information.

115

Disposable Personal Income

Income actually received by households is not available for spending in its entirety. Personal taxes, of which the personal income tax is the most important, together with payroll deductions for retirement and unemployment compensation, are paid out of income. The remainder is called *disposable personal income*. This can be spent for consumption purposes or saved.

Some Relationships
Among the Aggregates

We can now examine some relationships among the aggregate measures defined above. These will be useful to have in mind in the next chapter when we consider certain hypotheses about changes in the level of income.

Consumption and Economic Activity

Economists from the time of Adam Smith have usually "observed" that all economic activity is for the ultimate purpose of satisfying consumer wants. This statement, as it stands, is difficult to reduce to a precise operational meaning, because "ultimate" can mean many things, and "consumer wants" is correspondingly ambiguous. We can, however, give it meaning in terms of our model.

In an economy with a complex monetary system and a high degree of specialization and division of labor many transactions have an indirect relation to consumption. All factors of production are linked by some type of property relationship with households, however indirect. All income eventually accrues to persons. It may be diverted, however, and at any particular time may be quite inaccessible.

At this point, we can ask one relatively simple question: for any period for which we have data, how much of the money spent by all sectors on GNP passed through the household sector again as income?

During any accounting period, such as a year, household expenditures on consumption goods and services enter the business sector (firms) as sales—the inner flows of the upper half of our simple flow charts. On an income and product statement of the business sector this would be recorded (in a double-entry accounting system) as a source of income from the households. As these receipts come in, however, some disposition is made of them. A substantial part will be allocated to the payment of factor services such as wages, interest, rents, and profits, and will thus flow back through the factor market as household income.

Government expenditures, as we have noted, enter our flows at two

116

points. Payments to government employees enter the household sector directly as income (the same would also be true of government transfer payments to households). Government purchases from firms appear on the latters' accounts as sales income, and the disposition of this income is the same as that from households. A substantial part of it goes for payment of factor services, and this becomes household income.

The remaining expenditures on GNP will consist of interfirm purchases on capital account. Again, transactions among firms may be of two types—those involving goods in process, and purchases on capital account which represent investment expenditures. These expenditures are for maintaining and expanding the production economy itself. Expenditures for maintaining capital do not directly become income to the households. New investment, however, does result in new income being generated through payments to the factors to correspond with the new property or wealth being created. On our flow models this relationship can be perceived by a comparison between Figure 4a and Figure 4b. In the former all firms have been grouped together. All income to the firms is shown coming directly from households (or government). These receipts flow back through the factor market to the households, though not directly. We can perhaps imagine this movement in terms of pools or reservoirs within the sector. In Figure 4b, where a separation is made between consumer-goods and producer-goods firms, we have shown this diversion as a flow between firms, illustrating the fact that income received from the household sector does not flow back directly, but is diverted through the firms producing capital goods. From there it does move back into the main stream of household income in factor payments.

We can clarify the income-flow process further by examining some of the pools and eddies in the system, which in roundabout production are not clearly shown in our simple models. These help us to account for the differences between the receipts of firms and the earnings of households. They also help us to link these with the real income processes. Some of the more important of these are depreciation, business taxes, business savings, and household savings.

Depreciation

Existing plant and equipment wear out through being used in production, from the deteriorating influence of age and fatigue, and from obsolescence. On the basis of estimated productive life for buildings and equipment, firms allocate the cost of this depreciation, over the life of the facility, to the cost of their output, thus providing for eventual replacement. Such costs are included in the price (value) of the GNP.

What happens to that part of gross business receipts allocated to depreciation allowance? It disappears into the general assets of the firms used in production. When equipment is replaced, payments are made to the producer-goods firms. This is part of gross investment, and such transactions result in payments being made to the factors of production by the producer-goods firms. The depreciation funds are not themselves paid out directly, however. They are part of the reservoir of values that is maintained as long as production is an on-going process, or as long as consumption expenditures flow into the business sector. (A useful analogy might be a power dam with a given head of water, which helps to maintain the flow over the dam while remaining constant itself.)

Depreciation allowances subtracted from the gross income of one firm are eventually spent with other firms, and all households taken together earn as much less from one firm as they earn more from another. When we eliminate interfirm payments in consolidated sector accounts, the firms have only the total receipts entering their area from household expenditures, plus the government purchases. As we noted above, gross national product and net national product differ by the amount of depreciation allowances. Money spent for replacement is accounted for by these allowances. When we think of all firms together, we can see that the production of replacement equipment merely maintains the productive capacity, and money spent for this purpose does not add directly to the incomes of households.

Business Taxes

Business firms pay indirect taxes on many of their products. We can imagine these firms as the collecting agent for these taxes, which have been included in the purchase price of the commodities. Their amount is deducted from total consumer expenditures, and hence is not returned to the households in factor payments.

Government also collects corporate-profits taxes, which means that this part of the income of the firm is not returned to the households as dividends. Since taxes are spent by the government they eventually reenter the income flows. The parallel real flow to these taxes can be conceptualized as government services valued at cost.

Business Savings

Business firms, and particularly corporations, may retain a part of their net income (profits). Thus this represents a withholding of part of the claims of households. We can call this business saving.

Accordingly households receive less in personal income than the na-

118

tional income generated by their efforts and the use of their property. However, household (personal) income is increased by transfer payments by government and business. The income received by the household sector is reduced again by personal taxes (income, property, fees) which are paid over to government. What remains is disposable personal income. This aggregate in turn is broken down into the part which is spent on consumption and that which is saved.[5] Savings in turn can be represented as a counterflow in the main current, turning back from the household sector into the channel of factor services as loanable funds.

We are now ready to look at the national-income accounts of the United States for 1956 and other selected years. It will be well to bear in mind that economic activity, of which these figures are a measure, is a continuing process moving at varying rates. When we impose an accounting structure based upon a period of time, such as a year, the events (flow) of that year are figuratively frozen and the irregularities averaged out. Thus these figures can be perceived as the average rate of flow maintained during the period.[6]

National Income
Accounts for 1956

The Department of Commerce estimate of GNP for 1956 was $414.7 billion. This comprised the total value of goods and services sold to consumers, the gross private domestic investment, the purchase of goods and services by government (transformed into government services), and net foreign investment, which represents the difference between our debit and credit transactions with the rest of the world. Each of the principal components, as shown in Table 3,[7] will be analyzed in sequence.

1. Household expenditures on goods and services (consumption) amounted to $267.2 billion. This corresponds to the upper money flow from households to all firms in Figure 4a or to consumer-goods firms in Figure 4b. It can be imagined as the money side of transactions in consumer-goods markets which resulted in household acquisition of goods and services.

---

[5] For any individual household, and for the household sector, total expenditures could exceed income. This relationship will be explored in the next chapter.

[6] Department of Commerce estimates are now quoted on a quarterly basis. These estimates are stated in "annual rates."

[7] In some cases the figures do not add up to correct totals. To simplify the table, some of the smaller adjustments are omitted; the aggregates for the principal measures are given as they are published by the Department of Commerce.

Table 3. GNP, NNP, NI, and Other Related Aggregates in the United States, Selected Years

(billions of current dollars)

	1956	1955	1949	1939	1933	1929
1 Consumption Expenditures	267.2	254.4	180.6	67.6	46.4	79.0
2 Gross Private Investment in Plant & Equipment	61.4	56.4	35.3	9.0	3.0	14.5
3 Depreciation Allowances	34.3	31.6	18.4	7.8	7.2	8.6
4 Net Investment in Plant & Equipment (2 — 3)	27.1	24.8	16.9	1.2	—4.2	5.9
5 Net Investment—Inventories	4.6	4.2	—2.7	4.2	—1.6	1.7
6 Total Gross Investment (2 + 5)	66.0	60.6	32.6	13.2	1.4	16.2
7 Total Net Investment (4 + 5) or (6 — 3)	31.7	31.7	14.2	5.4	—5.8	7.6
8 Government Purchases	80.2	77.1	43.6	13.3	8.0	8.5
9 Net Foreign Investments	1.4	—.4	.5	.9	.2	.8
10 GROSS NATIONAL PRODUCT (1 + 6 + 8 + 9)	414.7	391.7	257.3	91.1	56.0	104.4
11 NET NATIONAL PRODUCT (10 — 3)	380.5	360.1	238.9	83.3	48.8	95.8
12 Indirect Business Taxes	35.0	32.9	21.6	9.4	9.1	7.0
13 NATIONAL INCOME (11 — 12)*	343.6	324.1	216.2	72.8	40.2	87.8
14 Corporate Retained Profits	9.1	8.0	8.3	1.2	—2.4	2.4
15 Corporate Profit Taxes	22.0	21.5	10.4	1.4	.4	1.4
16 Government Transfer Payments	22.9	21.3	16.2	3.7	2.7	1.9
17 PERSONAL INCOME (13 — 14 — 15 + 16)†	326.9	306.1	206.8	72.9	47.2	85.8
18 Personal Taxes	39.7	35.8	18.7	2.4	1.5	2.6
19 DISPOSABLE PERSONAL INCOME (17 — 18)	387.2	270.2	188.2	70.4	45.7	83.1
20 Personal Consumption Expenditures	267.2	254.4	180.6	67.6	46.4	79.0
21 Personal Savings (19 — 20)	20.0	15.8	7.6	2.9	—.6	4.2

* These figures have been adapted for the statistical discrepancy.

† Deductions for social insurance contributions, which have become increasingly important, are not shown. This accounts for discrepancies in the total.

Source: Adapted from reports of the Council of Economic Advisers.

2. Gross private investment in plant and equipment was $61.4 billion. Depreciation allowances were $34.3 billion, making net investment in plant and equipment approximately $27 billion. Inventory changes were positive, amounting to $4.6 billion. Thus total gross investment was $66 billion. We can think of the expenditures on plant and equipment (and housing) as transactions in the capital-goods markets. Inventory increases show that output exceeded sales.

3. Government purchases of goods and services were $80.2 billion in 1956, of which $47.2 billion were purchases by the Federal government and $33.0 billion by state and local governments. This flow is illustrated on our diagrams connecting the government sector with consumer-goods firms, producer-goods firms, and households.[8]

4. Net national product. If we now deduct the figure for depreciation, in this case $34.3 billion, the net national product is approximately $380.5 billion. Thus we have $267.2 billion for consumption, $31.7 billion for net investment, and $80.2 billion for government services.

5. National income. Government units at all levels collected $35.0 billion in indirect business taxes (and related liabilities) in 1956. In Figure 4a this item represents the money flow from business firms to government. If we subtract $35.0 billion from net national product, we get a national income (NI) of $343.6 billion.

The Circular Flow

Consumer expenditures during a year's time are also the most important source of the households' own earnings in that income period. When each individual household spends for goods and services it helps to maintain the flow of production which is the source of income claims. The $267.2 billion total consumption expenditure (the value of consumer goods sold) became receipts to consumer-goods firms. We note that part of this amount ($34.3 billion) was retained by the firms as depreciation allowances. This flow of household expenditure also was the source from which indirect taxes were paid. If we assume that the producer-goods firms turned out only investment goods, and that all consumer goods were turned out by the other firms, we can show the $267 billion flowing directly into the area of consumer-goods firms as in Figure 3. When these firms have deducted depreciation and indirect business taxes approximately $198 billion remains, which represents the amount returned di-

---

[8] In national income statistics government purchases of capital equipment are treated as government consumption in the year in which they are purchased.

rectly to households as earnings during the year. However, financed by the firms' own expenditures were inventory increases of $3.4 billion. This means that factors of production earned income for producing goods not yet sold. Hence the $3.4 billion of inventory investment must be added to consumption expenditure to give the complete story of the current year's production from which the earnings of households came.

Consumer-goods firms paid out $27.1 billion to the producer-goods firms for replacements. When this is added to the $34.3 billion of new investment, we get a total of $61.0 billion gross investment. If no net investment had taken place, and if depreciation allowances had not been spent on replacements, disinvestment would have occurred and national income would have shrunk by this amount, unless the shrinkage was otherwise offset. Actually, of course, 1956 was a year of rather heavy investment as well as of extensive consumer purchases.

The rest of national income was made up of government disbursements and purchases, together with business transfer payments.[9] Gross national product was estimated to be $23.0 billion greater (in current dollars) than in 1955. A part of this increase was attributable to inflation.

Simplified Income Statement

Before leaving the national-income accounts as they relate to 1956 it will be useful to view them in a slightly different frame of reference. By consolidating the various accounts we can present them in the form of a simplified income statement for the economy as a whole. We can look at the gross national product (or income) in two ways: (1) where it comes from, and (2) what was done with it. The following table shows the disposition and source of all accounts in 1956.

GROSS NATIONAL PRODUCT
(billions of dollars)

Disposition		Source	
Consumption Expenditures	$267.2	Consumption	$267.2
Taxes	96.7	Domestic Private Investment	65.9
Savings (Business, Personal, & Government Surplus)	50.8	Government Purchases	80.2
		Net Foreign Investment	1.4
Total	$414.7	Total	$414.7

[9] Business transfer payments are gifts of various kinds, particularly to charity and education, and bad debts. In the latter case someone received the goods or real income, but no payment was made. For accounting purposes they are treated in the same way as gifts.

Presenting the accounts in this way highlights an important relationship. Consumption expenditures appear on both sides, representing both source and disposition of income. Consumer spending determines the largest proportion of income, and hence, indirectly, the level of use of the factors of production, particularly the level of employment. This gives us a partial answer to the question raised earlier—the extent to which production activity serves the consumer.

On the disposition side of our account savings and taxes represent withdrawals from the income flows. Savings represent income not spent on consumption. However, this is balanced by investment expenditures.[10] Taxes, too, represent a siphoning off of disposable income, and unless or until they are passed on through government spending, they are withdrawn from the income pipelines.

The relationship can be seen more clearly if we show it symbolically, letting C stand for consumption expenditures, S for savings, T for taxes, I for investment, G for government expenditures, and D for government deficit:

$$C + S + T = C + I + G.$$

If we cancel out C from both sides of the equation we get

$$S + T = I + G.$$

This can then be put into the form:

$$S = I + G - T.$$

Thus, for any given period, such as a year, the amount that is saved from the national income will be equal to the amount of investment that has taken place, plus the government expenditures minus the taxes.

If government expenditures were exactly equal to taxes, savings would equal investment. In other words, the part of the gross national product not taken off the markets by household purchases would be the amount held by firms as the additions to their plant and equipment and inventories.

For any past period savings and investment must be equal, because real income produced—and not destroyed—by consumption accumulates. However, assume that government has spent more than it has taken in taxes. The government debt has increased. Government spending has contributed to national income, thus serving to maintain effective demand. Because government has not raised taxes to the full amount of its spending, households and business firms are left with the ownership of property

---

[10] In the above balance sheet the figure for savings is not a separately derived item, but is simply the residual figure after deducting taxes and consumption from GNP. It includes Social Security payments, since these were not included under the heading Taxes. It would also include the government surplus.

(claims) they would not otherwise have had. Thus the government deficit represents a form of investment. We can therefore add another equation to our series:

$$S = I + D.$$

The government may, of course, collect more in taxes than it spends. This does not alter the fundamental equality of savings and investment for the nation as a whole, but again merely changes the distribution of the ownership of property or wealth.

The effects on national income and the level of resource use of aggregates represented by savings, investment, and debt will be treated more extensively in the next chapter. Here we merely need to note that the source and disposition of the national income affects the relationship between effective demand and the available output of goods and services. For any period such as a year an excess of either flow over the other will have an effect on prices. If the money flows exceed the real flows, prices will rise and the income measures, stated in dollar terms, will also rise. Then if we compare the measures of the current year with previous years, real-income differences will be magnified. On the other hand, a decrease in effective demand relative to the real-income flows will cause our income measure to understate real income relative to other years.

Consistency Among the
Three Larger Aggregates

Data drawn from different accounts can be arranged to give us our three principal measures of national income. These are related to one another in a fairly consistent way. In terms of the theoretical model we have set up, this means simply that the relationships as drawn are internally consistent, that we can work our way around the circular flow in either direction and come out with results for a year that are equivalent.

If the three measures are so related, they should vary through time with respect to each other in a consistent manner. If we plot our three income measures—GNP, NNP, and NI—for a series of years, we see that they do move together over time (Figure 5 and Table 4). The differences among them are relatively constant, and when they do vary we can explain this fact in terms of what we already know—changes in taxes, in retained corporate earnings, in savings.

For most purposes we can use any of the three measures to describe what was happening to economic activity for any given period. Any of the measures can also give us a picture of how the whole economy was per-

124

Table 4. Relationship Among Three National Income Measures, 1929–1956
(billions of dollars)

Year	GNP	NNP	NI
1929	104.4	95.8	87.8
1930	91.1	82.6	75.7
1931	76.3	68.1	59.7
1932	58.5	50.9	42.5
1933	56.0	48.8	40.2
1934	65.0	57.9	49.0
1935	72.5	65.3	57.1
1936	82.7	75.2	64.9
1937	90.8	83.0	73.6
1938	85.2	77.4	67.6
1939	91.1	83.3	72.8
1940	100.6	92.5	81.6
1941	125.8	116.8	104.7
1942	159.1	149.0	137.7
1943	192.5	181.6	170.3
1944	211.4	199.4	182.6
1945	213.6	201.0	181.2
1946	209.2	197.6	179.6
1947	232.2	218.1	197.2
1948	257.3	240.8	221.6
1949	257.3	238.9	216.2
1950	285.1	264.6	240.0
1951	328.2	304.8	277.0
1952	345.4	321.6	290.2
1953	363.2	336.7	302.1
1954	360.7	331.9	298.3
1955	391.7	360.1	324.1
1956	414.7	380.5	343.6

Source: *Economic Report of the President, 1958.*

forming during different income periods—whether it was expanding or contracting from year to year.

The gross and net national products have been defined as real meas-

Figure 5. United States Gross National Product, Net

National Product, and National Income, Annually,

1929-1956

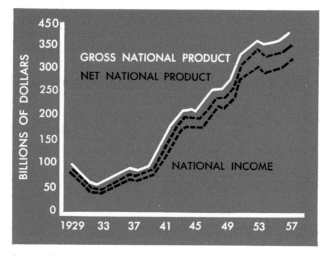

Source: U. S. Department of Commerce.

ures. National income is the money flow which moves in the opposite direction to balance these real flows. But as we have noted, and as was amply demonstrated by the pronounced price rise in 1950 and again in 1956, rising prices distort the money measure. We therefore encounter a further complicating factor of an elastic measuring rod, superimposed upon the index-number problem mentioned earlier. Consequently, as an aid to the linkage of these two flows, we must now return to a consideration of index numbers.

When prices are fairly stable, and if comparisons are not made between periods too far removed from each other, the national-income measures give a reasonably reliable general representation of real output stated in money terms. When prices vary, however, these figures must be deflated by means of an index. Results need to be interpreted with greater care. We can illustrate this index with a greatly simplified example, which will show us the essential nature of the operation used in deriving it.

Let us say that United States pig iron production in a given year was 50 million metric tons, crude petroleum was 1,714 million barrels, and so on. Production of several commodities during two successive years is given as follows:

126

Commodity	1st Year	2nd Year
Pig iron (millions tons)	50	56
Coal (millions tons)	574	591
Crude petroleum (millions bbl.)	1,714	2,016
Electric energy (millions kw-h.)	222,486	282,594
Corn (millions bushels)	2,880	2,400
Wheat (millions bushels)	1,109	1,364
Cotton (millions bales)	9	11

In terms of these important commodities, it appears that production in the second year was greater than the first. Corn production alone was smaller. We know from our earlier discussion that the base for any index of physical production would be an arbitrary one. Therefore, let us convert these figures into total value of output, using assumed prices.

	First Year			Second Year (price the same)		
	Production	Price	Total Value (000)	Production	Price	Total Value (000)
Pig Iron	50	$ 20	$1,000	56	$ 20	$1,120
Coal	574	6	3,444	591	6	3,546
Petroleum	1,714	2	3,428	2,016	2	4,032
Electricity	222,486	.03	6,686	282,594	.03	8,478
Corn	2,880	2	5,760	2,400	2	4,800
Wheat	1,109	2.10	2,327	1,364	2.10	2,864
Cotton	9	150	1,350	11	150	1,650
			$23,995			$27,490

Using constant prices (first year figures), we find that total value of output was roughly $24 billion in the first year and $27.5 billion in the second. The latter is clearly larger. But how much larger? Using the first as a base year, we obtain the following:

$$\frac{27,490}{23,995} = 1.19 \times 100 = 119.$$

Value of output for these commodities in the second year is 119 per cent of the base, or larger by 19 per cent. If we were to reverse the procedure, using the second as the base, we would find the first year's output to be approximately 81 per cent, or 19 per cent smaller. However, we cannot get off so neatly as that. Let us assume that prices had risen considerably in the two year period. We shall need to value the second year's output at current prices.

127

Second Year
(current prices)

Pig Iron	56	$ 24.00	$ 1,334
Coal	591	8.00	4,728
Petroleum	2,010	2.10	4,234
Electricity	282,594	.035	9,890
Corn	2,400	1.90	4,560
Wheat	1,364	2.00	2,728
Cotton	11	145.00	1,595
			$29,069

Value of production is now a little more than $29 billion. When we compare this with values of the base year, we get these results:

$$\frac{29,069}{23,995} = 1.26 \times 100 = 126.$$

We now discover that the production of these commodities was 26 per cent larger, or 7 per cent more than when we used constant prices.

There is a dilemma here, one that statisticians have been unable to solve completely. It is a compounding of error because of the change in the value of money and changes of physical composition. We could use base-year prices for both years (eliminating changes in price), but that brings the problem of relative physical weights in by the back door. We are treating a 10 per cent increase in tons of coal exactly the same (relatively) as a 10 per cent increase in kilowatt-hours—assuming that the relationship between them was a normal one, and that the social valuation of these commodities does not change. We might work backwards, valuing both outputs at second-year prices. Some statisticians favor this. But this would make the most recent combination the norm. Other statisticians have worked out a compromise by cross-multiplying the output of each year by the prices of the other year and then averaging the two. If we had done this the result would have been a splitting of the difference between our two figures 119 and 126. Other formulas are also used, such as averaging the squares of the differences, reducing this again by extracting the square root. These statistical problems need not concern us further. Any actual index, of course, will be a composite of many more commodities than we have used in our example, which was simplified deliberately to make it easier to follow the arithmetic.

We are now in a position to comprehend the process of correcting for changes in the value of the dollar. Throughout our discussion of the different income measures the values were stated in current dollars. Prices generally were low in the 1930's, and since World War II and the Korean war they have risen markedly. In comparisons between 1929 and 1933 a money measure for the second year would understate real income because of falling prices (a rise in value of the dollar). To compare a measure of 1956 income with either 1933 or 1929 in current prices would magnify the real-income differences even more. In Table 5 the values of gross national product and consumption expenditures are given for selected years from 1929 to 1956, first in current dollars and then in dollars that have been converted by an index using 1956 prices as the base.

Table 5. Gross National Product and Personal Consumption Expenditures for Selected Years

Year	GNP		CONSUMPTION	
	Current Prices	1956 Prices	Current Prices	1956 Prices
1929	104.4	187.1	79.0	129.1
1933	56.0	130.1	46.4	104.7
1939	91.1	196.2	67.6	139.4
1949	257.3	301.8	180.6	206.7
1950	285.1	329.9	194.0	219.1
1951	328.2	354.2	208.3	220.6
1952	345.4	366.9	210.3	227.6
1953	363.2	382.0	230.5	237.2
1954	361.2	375.6	236.6	241.4
1955	391.7	402.5	254.4	258.3
1956	414.7	414.7	267.2	267.2

Source: *Economic Report of the President, 1957.*

The ambiguities of the index remain. The things we do as individuals and as a nation, the technical bases of production, and the types of goods we consume are continuously changing. From year to year these changes may be slight and go unnoticed, but go back ten years and try to list the content of real income then and now. Go back twenty years, a half-century, a hundred years; one by one the things we use and take for granted drop out of the picture. Television, a most recent acquisition, is but a few years old. The days when frozen foods, radios, automobiles, nylon, rayon, cellophane, and countless other items were unknown are still within the memories of living people.

Thus we find that our money measures do not take account of many aspects of everyday living. All a money income gives to any generation is freedom to choose from what the environment has to offer, and when those offerings change comparisons rest on rather shaky foundations. When we say that income is 10 per cent greater than last year, the statement is meaningful. To say that it is 50 per cent greater than twenty-five years ago also has meaning, but it requires more qualification, the filling in of detail, and the use of other measures.

Supplementary Measures

A physical production index of goods and selected services can supply added detail regarding past production activity, although here again care must be exercised in the use of these figures. Measures of total production activity are obtained from a breakdown of national product by converting the current value into that of a base period.

For purposes of keeping track of economic activity other physical measures may be helpful. Freight car loadings, steel ingot production, petroleum output, and electric energy generated during specified periods are particularly useful, because these commodities and services are used in many of the particular consumption and production goods which typify a modern industrial society.

National Income and International Trade

A complete concept of the national income requires one additional item— the foreign trade balance. This appeared as a net item in our national-income accounts for 1956, but so far we have not discussed it.

Goods and services are exchanged across national boundaries. Exports give rise to income claims against foreigners. They reduce the real income available for domestic consumption. Goods and services imported expand available real income and increase the claims of foreigners against the United States economy. During any given period these opposite flows need not balance each other. For any year a given country may have a positive or a negative balance. A positive balance for the United States against a given foreign country represents certain property claims against individuals, firms, or government agencies in foreign countries. These may range

130

from short-term commercial loans to long-term equities in foreign properties. In each case they represent a form of investment.

Because of its general acceptability, gold has long been a useful commodity in the settlement of such claims. A country which has a long-run negative balance is likely to experience an outflow of gold. When this happens, the country can attempt to make investments more attractive, or to take steps to reduce purchases abroad. Since World War II the dollar has become almost equally desired as a form of property.

While the total volume of goods and services traded by the United States is small relative to gross national product, foreign sales are quite important to a number of industries. As we shall see in Part 6, the United States has become increasingly dependent upon foreign trade for a number of essential materials. We will also explore in more detail the purely monetary aspects of international trade in Chapter 10.

Discussion
Questions

1. Does the term sector, as used in this chapter, refer to something in the *real world* which is clearly distinguishable, or is it rather a part of a logical system of classification? What determines whether a given transaction falls in one sector or another?

2. If a father hires his son to mow the lawn, would you expect this transaction, ideally, to affect the national product? Practically?

3. The figure for the gross national product can be viewed either as income or product. Why? Do you find it useful to try to perceive this figure in real terms?

4. Suppose a nation consumed its entire gross national product. What would be the likely consequences of such action, if indulged in for a long time? When might such an action occur?

5. What kinds of changes in the national product are very inadequately represented by the measures of national income and product?

CHAPTER 8

An Approach to the Analysis

of National Income Variations

THE MODEL of income flows developed in the preceding chapters is a useful guide in arranging observational and estimated income data by source and disposition, so that for any period the various measures of national-income flows can be related to one another in an internally consistent system.

As a logical model, this system of classification of money income receivers and income users has few contradictions that cannot be explained, or traced to actions by the income-generating units. The actions of households, firms, and government agencies in their income-getting and income-using roles can be fitted into this theoretical system.

The most important use of these measures, however, is for purposes of discovering relationships that help to explain variations in national income and in the levels of factor use. This means developing a theory of income and employment.

Long-Run Growth and
Short-Run Setbacks

Measures of national income have been available on a year-to-year basis only since 1929. Using the experience gained in deriving these measures, and the information they provide on different relationships, government agencies, university researchers, and independent research agencies have worked backward in filling the gaps in existing data until we now have reasonably accurate estimates of national income since 1909. Prior to that we have less reliable estimates pieced together from many sources. The staff of the National Bureau of Economic Research, building on the early work of Wesley C. Mitchell, has performed yeoman service in this field. In 1926 Willard L. Thorpe published the *Business Annuals,* a compilation of all that could be gathered together from disparate sources about economic activity. From old records, newspapers, government documents, the decennial census, and elsewhere, bits and pieces of information were fitted together to supply details on production, income, capital formation, and consumption. Simon Kuznets, another pioneer in the field of income estimation and measurement, has prepared a study titled *National Product Since 1869,* which includes estimates of income and capital formation on a year-to-year basis since that time. These are all useful materials, providing a time perspective of the successes and failures of our economy. As a background for our present inquiry, we will examine briefly the history of economic progress or income growth.

From the period immediately following the Civil War to the onset of the great depression in 1929 it has been estimated that the average annual rate of growth of income was 3.7 per cent. Since part of this was "plowed back" in the form of capital accumulation, the increase in real income available for consumption was somewhat less. Joseph Schumpeter estimated the rate of increase in available output at 2 per cent per year. This is a compound growth, since the increase in successive years is computed on an expanding base. This was the growth which brought the United States to the high level of real income achieved in 1929.

Actually, if all the annual outputs between 1870 and 1929 were represented by points on a graph, the line which they formed would be highly irregular. There were long periods, as in the 1870's, when the national product declined. Men and machines "rusted" in idleness, while people lacked the necessary requirements for living. A news note from Harper's Weekly in 1873 gives a graphic picture of economic events and their human consequences in this period of depression:

> New York City alone saw nine hundred people starve to death; saw the Children's Aid Society providing shelter to more than 11,000 homeless boys, while thousands more got no help; found three thousand infants abandoned on doorsteps; found more than a hundred dead babies in ash barrels, area ways and dumps; watched thirteen hundred of its citizens die violent deaths; and had the disturbing knowledge that one out of every seven people in the city had at some time been convicted of a crime. For several years the nation faced disastrous poverty. Businesses failed by the thousands, hundreds of

thousands of laborers lost their jobs, and disease, vice and crime increased alarmingly.

By 1929, when our measures of national income indicate a gross national product of approximately $104 billion and a national income of $87 billion, economic progress seemed to preclude such experiences as those reported in 1873. Those who lived through the depression which began that year, however, saw the national income fall to $40 billion in 1933, with an estimated unemployment of nearly 13 million men and women—approximately one-fourth of the civilian labor force. By 1930, however, a much wealthier nation in terms of accumulated capital, with reserves of all kinds, had insulated itself against physical deprivation such as that described in 1873. It is doubtful that, with a much greater population, the number who experienced physical suffering in the great depression approached that of the earlier period. The psychological suffering, of course, is something else and can only be filled in by a sensitive imagination to complete the reality which lies behind the income figures.

Estimates of national income provide an objective measure for making comparisons, which, although less colorful, serve as a criterion for evaluating the potential of the national economy, and of how well it is performing at any particular time. The highest level of output achieved up to a given time becomes an experience datum for pinpointing what the economy can do. Any recession from peak levels achieved under peacetime conditions, becomes a problem to be explained.[1]

Variations Relatively Easy to Expialn

Income variations for short periods which recur year after year can be explained by buying habits related to holidays, seasonal influences of climate and weather, as well as customary practices. These form a pattern in the statistical series repeated year after year. Statisticians have developed techniques for eliminating them from the income measures. Most published series carry the notation "adjusted for seasonal variation."

Business firms and governments have learned to anticipate such fluctuations in economic activity, and to "live with them." Factories plan their work so that production is more evenly distributed through time. Seasonal employment creates some difficulties, particularly from the standpoint of providing a steady source of income to those in the seasonal trades, but for the most part these are minor problems compared with the larger issues of prosperity and depression.

---

[1] This, of course, assumes that no catastrophe such as earthquakes, floods, mass bombings, or other identifiable physical events has reduced productive capacity. In such cases no further explanation is needed.

134

Trend

Another measure of change in economic activity—one associated with relatively long periods of time—is called the growth curve or *trend*. If one looks at a graphic presentation of the statistics of national income for the entire period for which they are available, the irregular path it describes appears to have a distinct upward tilt. We can draw a straight line through the scatter of annual income data in such a way that squared deviations from it are equivalent above and below the line. Such a line or regression curve would show the tilt very distinctly.

We know in general why the growth of national income, thus portrayed, has taken place. It is connected with the fact that population has increased, and the number and size of firms and the equipment which they use have expanded. Production is better organized and better managed, and technological processes have been improved.

Business-cycle analysts sometimes remove the trend by subtracting the upward bias from the figures for each year. The resulting statistic is said to have been "corrected for trend." This, however, is a tricky business. Any decision on where to start the trend must be abitrary, although some bases will be more useful for certain purposes than others.

Kondratiev, a Russian statistician who studied nineteenth-century data for industrial countries, believed that he had found evidence of long waves or cycles in economic activity of fifty years duration. The implications of his theory would be that what appears as a long-run trend might simply be the upward phase of one of these long cycles.

The National Bureau of Economic Research in its business-cycle studies does not remove the trend from its data on the grounds that trend and business fluctuations are too intertwined in the data to be separated. When their analyses of successive cycles are connected, however, the trend effect can be observed.

A crude, common-sense measure of the economic growth which has occurred over the last two hundred years is the great increase in population now supported by world resources and industries. In Western industrial countries particularly this has taken place with a steady, if at times spotty, rise in scales of living.

Variations More Difficult to Explain

The variations we have come to associate with the term "business cycles" have not in the past been such that business could adjust to them, nor households adapt easily to the burdens they impose. Economists and others once regarded these wide swings of income and employment as "natural" phenomena, which like drought and plague must be endured. Many theories or explanations have been advanced for them. The most frequent explanations and proposed cures have usually involved some kind of preconceptions about money. Money panaceas have been advanced as cures for booms and depressions, particularly the latter.

Modern students of the variations in money income and real income have ceased searching for a single cause of business cyles, seeking rather to comprehend the sequence of changes that occur and to associate them with the behavior patterns of individuals and groups in the economy, whose actions give rise to income flows in the first place. From these patterns it is the task of the social scientist to formulate hypotheses of economic behavior, perhaps as a special case of behavior in general, and to use these as axioms for further inquiry into the economic process.

An axiom of our national-income model is that the sources of household income during any period are consumption expenditures, net investment, and government expenditures. If this be true, then an increase in any one of these will result in an increase in national income, and also in national product if there are unused resources and if there are no offsetting factors.

What are the circumstances under which such increases take place, and how are they passed on to complete the circular flow of expanded income flows? The discussion below is based upon modern income-expenditure analysis as it appears in much of contemporary literature.

The Concept of Equilibrium in National Income

Our analysis can begin with the assumption of an equilibrium between the twin income flows. Consumer expenditures or effective aggregate demand are just sufficient to take from the market the goods and services being offered for sale at stable prices during the period under consideration. Depreciation reserves are adequate to take from the producer-goods markets the equipment being produced. Taxes and fees collected by government are just sufficient to pay for the goods and services for current operations, and for the transfer payments to which government has been committed. This equilibrium could occur at different levels of factor use. We shall assume that unemployed reserves of manpower and resources exist. Such a situation might be described as one of stagnation or "sidewise movement" of the national-income indicators.

In this situation let us assume further that consumer-goods firms decide to increase production either by stocking up on goods (increasing inventories) or by enlarging their plants so that they could at some future time, when the expansion has been completed, turn out a larger volume of goods and services. The reasons for such a decision can be neglected

136

for the moment. Of the unemployed factors—labor, plant capacity, or land—some will now be employed. If the level of employment were relatively high, increased activity would mean longer hours, utilizing both machines and manpower more intensively. In either case the earnings of households would rise. Potentially, at least, the increased personal-income flows would make it possible for households to increase expenditures. Households would have more income. Inventories would be drawn down at points nearest the consumer until new production made it possible to replace them. In such circumstances supply would be said to create demand.

An expansion could start from the other direction. If for any reason the flow of household expenditures should increase in advance of production (perhaps through relief payments or other transfers, or from savings), sales managers and production executives of business firms would find their old rates of output inadequate. Existing inventories would be reduced. With consumers more eager to buy, bidding against one another for the existing goods, *money demand* would be in excess of the supply of available goods. With a willingness to pay higher prices, the general price level would show an upward tendency, and producers would respond with increased output.

Finally, such an expansion might be initiated by government. Under the assumed circumstances a rearmament program or a public works project which called for an expenditure of new funds would mean increased effective demand, new production, and an increase in personal incomes. In each of these last two instances it would be meaningful to say that demand created its own supply. When an expansion of money flows occurs, the real-income flows can be expected to follow.

Anyone who has lived through the post-World War II years and the Korean war, can understand the order of these events. During the World War employment rose, with a consequent heavy disbursement of wages and other incomes. At the same time the production of many consumer goods was curtailed, so that materials and labor might be used for the war effort. Households, unable to spend their incomes because of rationing and other controls, accumulated money or other liquid assets. They were encouraged to invest in war bonds and to pay off old debts. At the end of the war a backlog of savings to the credit of households had been built up. After the war consumers were eager to buy the things they had been denied. The result was a rising volume of consumer purchases, with a consequent rise in prices and the incomes of business and industrial firms. Eventually, of course, plants were reconverted to the production of civilian goods, new plants were built, and the flow of real income began to rise to balance the money flows. Continued high government expenditures for foreign relief and disbursements to veterans and the armed services prevented a balance from being achieved, with the result that prices continued to rise. This situation was intensified after the outbreak of the Korean war, when government expenditures for defense rose sharply and consumer expenditures were increased in anticipation of possible shortages.

This is an example of what happens when an increased flow of money income occurs at a time when the factors of production are employed at a high level and the economy is pushing close to the hypothetical limit of capacity. Increased money flows can only register their effects in higher prices and money income. The dollar buys less, that is, has less value in terms of real income. Money measures overstate the increase of real income, even though these have been substantial.

Budgets and
the Income Flows

An important question is suggested by the order of events just described. How can a firm, a household, or a government increase its expenditures beyond its income? The answer is, of course, by *going into debt,* by spending previous savings, or by changing the form of its assets. For the purposes of later analysis it will be helpful to explore what is meant by going into debt, and how this is possible in an industrial society.

First, let us consider again some of the qualities of that highly "liquid" form of property called money. Specifically, we need to understand its function as a store of value and a standard of deferred payment. Debt or credit is a money statement of negative property claims (see pages 55–56). Debt is most interesting to us, in the present context, when it functions as a *medium of exchange.*

We shall begin with the concept of a budget, which can be defined as a planned relationship between income and spending. Each of the three basic income-receiving and income-spending units can be perceived in terms of its budget for income purposes. For any period of time, but particularly for a short period, these units may operate either on a *deficit budget* or a *surplus budget*. This means that spending may exceed income, in which case the budget is described as deficit; or income may exceed spending, in which event the budget is described as surplus. A deficit budget is possible because modern financial organization makes it possible to use a promise-to-pay-in-the-future as money. A surplus budget is possible because money as a store of value enables an income unit to accumu-

138

late claims or to transfer them readily in the settlement of debt. What kinds of action ordinarily undertaken will result in deficits or surpluses? We shall consider each of the income units in turn.

Households

Many households do not spend all of their current receipts for immediate consumption. Some of them save in considerable amounts. When they do so they build up property claims in the form of cash holdings, bank deposits, or by purchasing abstract titles, such as bonds or stocks from which they expect to earn a future income. This is an example of a surplus budget. The household withdraws from income flows more than it returns in new income transactions with the consumer-goods firms. Conversely, a household may spend more than its current income by drawing on cash balances previously accumulated, usually by reducing bank balances, converting less liquid assets into cash, or by going into debt. This is the deficit budget.

If, on balance in a given period, more households are accumulating assets from a given level of income than are going into debt, the income that is passed on from the household sector will be smaller than that received. Effective demand will be shrinking. There will not be sufficient spending to take from the market the available consumer goods from the production of which household income has been earned. On the other hand, if on balance more households are operating on deficit than on surplus budgets, the income flows from consumer sources will be expanding and will tend to run ahead of real-income flows.

Firms

In a parallel manner the firm can operate during a given period on a surplus or deficit budget. When a firm is operating on a deficit budget it is usually investing—hiring the factors of production to produce goods it will not sell until later, expanding buildings and equipment which will be used in the future to turn out a larger volume of goods or services, or purchasing new equipment in excess of its depreciation reserves.

If on balance firms are operating on surplus budgets, they will be accumulating cash balances or paying off debts, and will pass on in income claims to the households less than they are taking in from the stream of household expenditures. On the other hand, with a net deficit budget for all firms the amount passed on to households in the form of national-income flows will be expanding.

When these two income-receiving and income-spending units of the private sector of the economy act in concert, whether through surplus or

139

deficit budgets, the effect is to expand or contract national income immediately, and subsequently the gross and net national product, unless the economy is already at or near the limit of capacity. *Balanced budgets, of course, have the effect of maintaining* a constant income flow.

Government

Government budgets can be viewed in the same light as budgets of households and firms. They are two-sided affairs—income and expenditure. They too may be unbalanced. When governments spend more than they are currently withdrawing from the income flows in the form of taxes, the effect is to expand money flows. During the past two and a half decades government deficits have been the result of attempts to get the economy out of a great depression, of the prosecution of wars on many fronts, or of building up defenses against anticipated aggression.

Governments run into debt by borrowing. When they spend money that has been saved by households or firms—who lend to the governments by buying government bonds—the effect is to offset a failure of the private sector to generate new income. On the other hand, the Federal government may borrow from the banking system. This results in generating an entirely new source of income. We should perhaps hasten to add that the spending units of the private sector utilize the services of the banking system too—firms in particular—and for that reason banks will be given special attention shortly. When governments collect more in taxes than they spend, they are practically forcing the other units to "save," and the effect is likely to slow down the income flows.

The Money and
Banking Function

To understand how it is possible for households, firms, and governments to operate with surplus and deficit budgets, we will now expand our earlier discussions of money. Specifically, we need to examine an aspect of the money process which we know from everyday experience as *banking*.[2]

Money is most usefully defined as a form of property. It is a generalized claim against what the nation or the society has to offer in goods and services of all kinds, just as any other form of property represents a claim which may be exchanged for still other property. It differs in that it is the most liquid or the most easily exchanged form of such claims.

---

[2] The United States banking structure is presented in Chapter 10.

We noted in Chapter 4 that promises to pay, which circulate from hand to hand and function as money, are claims against some future delivery of property or value. Usually these are referred to as credit money. Their legal designation is *negotiable instrument,* which is another way of saying that this particular form of debt can circulate from hand to hand, and the holder, provided he is a holder by due process,[3] is the rightful owner of the property claim. An ordinary check or bank draft is perhaps the most familiar form of this instrument.

In every organized nation the provision of a circulating medium (money) has usually been a function of government. The Constitution of the United States reserves this right specifically to Congress, in Section 8 of Article 1. In the language of that document, Congress is granted the power "To coin money, regulate the value thereof, and of foreign coin, and fix the standard of weights and measures." Today, however, the function of coinage is limited mostly to minor coin and the issuance of silver certificates, which are rather like warehouse receipts for silver bullion stored in vaults at West Point.

The great majority of transactions in the United States are made with credit money in the form of Federal Reserve notes and checking accounts. Commercial transactions, roughly 85 per cent (in terms of value) of all purchases and sales, are accomplished by the use of credit. This credit is created by the banking system. Specifically, it is generated by the commercial banks, in conjunction with a central banking setup which in the United States is the Federal Reserve System.[4] Commercial banks are a specialized type of business firm, whose particular function is to "manufacture credit or liquidity." They are also depositories for the surplus cash of people and firms. This reservoir of cash serves as reserves for the credit money otherwise known as demand deposits or checking accounts.

Banking institutions convert assets or property of less liquid form into money, so that they may be used for facilitating the production and consumption process. The largest users are the business firms, although banks perform a function in the field of consumer credit as well.

What is the nature of the *banking function* thus performed? Let us examine the case of a manufacturing firm which is accumulating inventories it prefers not to market at once. If the firm has good market contacts and there is reason to expect that at some future date the goods can be sold at a price which will cover costs and return a net income to the firm, it will be regarded as a sound credit risk. A loan would enable the firm to

---

[3] If he has come by it in a manner prescribed by law; that is, if he has not stolen it, obtained it under false pretense, or otherwise gained possession illegally.

[4] Details of the operation of the Federal Reserve System will be discussed in Chapter 10.

meet its payroll and contract for additional raw materials. This company can secure a loan from a commercial bank, using inventories or expected future income as *collateral* or backing for the loan. What, precisely, does this term collateral mean? The firm in effect transfers a part of its property rights in real assets to the bank, in exchange for a more liquid form of property. When the goods are sold, or income is available from other sources, the loan can be repaid, together with an interest charge (which is the price paid for the credit), and the debt erased. Full and unencumbered ownership of the firm's property reverts to its original owner. The bank has created a medium of exchange which is spent, thereby generating additional income. The act of spending is linked to continuation of production, bringing into existence a new flow of real goods to balance the new money flows thus created.

When the Federal government borrows from the banking system, exchanging its bonds for demand deposits, the effect on the money-income flows is similar. Governments spend in advance of tax collection, and that spending adds to the money-income flows. Government deposits pass into the accounts of private firms or households.

What about the collateral of a government agency, and particularly of the national government? Here we will note a shift in the referent of the term. Although a less specific property right than that of a private borrower, the collateral behind a government loan is the sovereign power of that body to tax, to levy claims against all private property rights or ultimate income claims. It is also linked with the power of the sovereign authority to issue its own money. A government might obtain its requirements for goods and services by simply printing new money to pay for them. With the government then accepting such money in payment for taxes, fees, and other obligations to itself, the general acceptance of such money would be established, as long as the authority of the government remained unchallenged and the capacity of the economy to produce remained intact.

The money and banking process gives flexibility to an industrial economy, making possible the very great divisibility of property and specialization typical of modern production, distribution, and consumption. Some have even assigned money a causal role in economic affairs. It will be worth our time, therefore, to consider certain relationships which come to the fore when income variations are viewed in their purely monetary aspects.

The Quantity Theory of Money

Since the first emergence of money as an abstract claim against things of

142

value its role in human affairs has been debated. As a physical object and a symbol of "wealth," it has been desired for the power it confers upon whoever holds it. Practical men (politicians and businessmen), noting the apparent abundance of money during periods of prosperity with their high prices and vigorous trade, and its scarcity during periods of stagnation when prices are low and business depressed, have focused on money itself as the active agent. Depending upon what preconceptions they held about what "good money"[5] ought to be, they assumed a connection between the quantity of money and the level of business activity.

In the United States during the last quarter of the nineteenth century the money question was a burning political issue. Members of the Greenback movement, with an implicit belief in the State theory of money and an explicit conviction of a close relationship between the quantity of money and prices, advocated the printing of paper money by the Federal government as a cure for depressed incomes and low-level production. At a later date the "silver question" became the issue of the day, and William Jennings Bryan stumped the country in 1896 and again in 1900 as an advocate of the "free coinage" of silver. The coinage of silver, he maintained, would expand the quantity of money (which he believed had been unduly constrained under the gold standard), thereby promoting "prosperity." Those who espoused such expansion of the currency have usually been classified as "naive quantity theorists" or "money cranks."

In a different form, however, the quantity theory of money has at times been credited with a "hard central core" of truth which has made it quite respectable as an analytical tool. In this form it was assigned not necessarily a causal role, but a permissive role which made it useful for expressing a relationship between business and household transactions and the level of prices.

Classical and neoclassical economic analysis minimized money's role in the long-run determination of income; but because money was needed to explain short-run variations, it was ushered in by a side door as the transactions form of the *quantity theory* of money. In substance that theory is this: If the quantity of money in the hands of the public is increased, and the quantity of goods and services remains constant, the prices of those goods and services will rise because there is more money to be spent on them. Money income will be larger, but this larger money income rep-

---

[5] Sir Thomas Gresham (1519–1579), English trader and financial adviser to Queen Elizabeth, on the basis of observations in his time concluded that "bad money" tends to drive "good money" out of circulation. In economic literature this is called "Gresham's Law."

resents the exchange of the same goods and services. With a constant quantity of money, an increase in the exchange of goods and services (transactions) will be associated with a fall in prices, since with the relatively smaller ratio of money to goods the former could only do its job if prices per unit were lower.

This relationship can be stated in the form of an equation:

$$MV = PT.$$

In this equation M represents the quantity of money, V the number of times it changes hands, P the average level of prices, and T separate transactions involving the transfer of ownership of goods and services. In this form the equation is a tautology. It involves viewing both sides of the total exchange process at once. In simple terms it states that the amount of money multiplied by the number of times it changes hands will be equal as a statement of value to the quantity of goods and services traded, multiplied by their price. Since the relationship is an aggregate, representing all of the transactions in a total system, the P represents an average or general price level.

If we express the equation in a slightly different form, it can be made to state explicitly the relationship between money and prices. Dividing both sides of the above equation by T we get the following form:

$$\frac{M\,V}{T} = P.$$

This tells us that the general level of prices will be a ratio obtained by dividing the product of money times velocity by the goods and services traded, or the work that money has to do in facilitating transactions. If the quantity of money in the system increases, while the transactions remain constant, the numerator will increase while the denominator stays the same. Under these circumstances the general level of prices will rise. For example, suppose we substitute a set of figures for the symbols:

$$M = 200$$
$$V = 5$$
$$T = 10$$
$$\frac{200 \cdot 5}{10} = 100.$$

Now, if we double the quantity of money, assuming that the velocity does not change, and that goods traded remain the same, the price level will be double:

$$\frac{400 \cdot 5}{10} = 200.$$

The dollar, or whatever monetary unit is used, would on the average buy just half as much in terms of real goods and services as before. If this can be imagined as actually happening, it will be apparent that the money value of national income would be double what it was before, although the real income would be the same. This would be unlikely to happen unless the level of output were at or near its maximum, that is, during full employment.

In the small "classroom economy" which was used for purposes of analogy in Chapter 6 we noted that a doubling of the quantity of money resulted in doubling the "national income." But this was a forced draft situation. Money was spent on signal. In everyday affairs money is not spent in this way. It influences the income flow only as people *decide* to spend it. To gain an insight into how the quantity of money becomes effective demand, we have to inquire into circumstances in which money, when it is received, will be spent. This involves us in peoples' attitudes toward money as an asset.

The naive quantity theorists assumed that money received would be spent, and that it would be accepted at face value by those who received it. In classical economics the quantity theory of money was used as a justification for the *gold standard*. A unit of money, defined as a certain quantity of one commodity (gold), would always mean the same thing. Thus money would be the one form of property whose value would always remain the same. If prices of other things changed, the property owner could always convert his holdings into money of constant value. A stable measure of value would also function as a store of constant value. This was supposed to inspire confidence and encourage enterpreneurs to undertake their business ventures without fear of the future, since they would always be able to convert their wealth into money of constant value.

Critics of the gold standard, on the other hand, maintained that the limited supply of gold constituted an undue restriction on the extent to which property (assets) could be translated into liquid form. For money to do its job, prices would have to fall. An expanding economy in the real sense would require falling prices unless the quantity of gold could be increased or used more efficiently. We shall return to this point later.

As an analytical tool the quantity theory of money is a difficult model with which to work except at an abstract level. Measures of the quantity of money are obtainable. The measures of credit money are more difficult to handle, but at the present time are available. The velocity of money or rate of turnover is even more difficult to obtain, although bank clearings provide something of a clue. However, even when we obtain the values to substitute in the equation, it is still largely descriptive, and while it may indicate what happened, it gives few clues to how it happened.

145

Another theoretical model for organizing observations of how households and firms act with respect to the quantity of money has been thought more useful in modern times. This model includes certain hypotheses about the "motives" for holding cash.

The Cash Balances Form of the Quantity Theory

At any given time the quantity of money in existence can be classified in two ways: (1) money which is working by being spent, and (2) money which is idle or in some hoard. D. H. Robertson refers to these as "money on the wing" and "money at roost." Only money on the wing, that engaged in promoting exchanges of goods and services, affects the income level. Money at roost is unemployed.

We can ask the question, "Why doesn't money stay in circulation to stimulate the exchange of goods and services?" To answer this question we can try to discover why people hold cash. On an *ad hoc* basis a number of reasons for wanting to hold money will come to mind.

The Need for Pocket Money

All of us keep a sum of money in our pockets to take care of customary or habitual expenditures. The amount we carry (or maintain as balances in the bank) depends upon how frequently we are paid, and how much we are paid. This can be illustrated by a simple example. Let us say we are paid $50 cash once each week. If we are paid on Saturday and distribute our expenditures uniformly throughout the week, we will be "broke" when next payday comes around. On Wednesday we will have $25. On the three preceding days we will have more, on the three succeeding days less. But the average amount of our cash balance is $25. Suppose we get exactly the same salary, but are paid by the month. On the last day of the month we receive $200. Next payday we are broke. Prior to the middle of the month our cash balance will be more than $100, after the middle of the month it will be less. Our average cash balance for the period, however, will be $100.

The longer the time between paydays, the larger will be the cash balances needed to take care of ordinary expenditures. Also as prices rise individuals will ordinarily begin to carry more money. Everything costs more. The average of all such cash balances for any period gives a partial figure for the quantity of money which will be idle or at roost.

Reserves for Contingencies

While it is not an unusual experience for most of us to be broke on payday, we usually try to hold back something for unforeseeable expenses if we

146

can. We have a nest egg for the rainy day or for the unusual item we may want to buy. Such reserves may be partially held in cash, and all together may constitute a sizable demand for liquid funds.

Speculative Hoards

Some withholding of spending is done for speculative purposes. This applies both to households and to business firms. We may be expecting to buy some consumption item. If there are indications that prices may fall in the future, there is an incentive to wait. Thus in periods of falling prices an increasing number of persons may withold liquid claims from the income stream, with the consequence that less is passed on to others to create new income. When this happens the money on the wing diminishes, and unless it is augmented in other ways effective demand will decrease and incomes will fall. Firms act in the same way. If prices of raw materials or other factors of production are expected to fall, management may hold off buying. Moreover, firms will try to reduce inventories and increase cash holdings. The effect on national income is similar to that outlined above when households decrease purchases and accumulate cash. With a fixed quantity of money the amount left to do money's work is smaller, and prices may decline still further. On the other hand, rising prices are likely to affect people in the opposite way. They will not want to hold so much cash, but will ordinarily attempt to convert money into real property or goods.

Income variations may be explained in terms of what people do with respect to money. The tendency of these reactions to be cumulative can go far to explain the wide range of variations in the national income during different periods.

However, while it is possible to see why the ups and downs go on once they are started, it is not so easy to relate the reasons for the reversals to purely monetary explanations. The income-expenditure approach makes use of the money concept, not by bringing it in by a side door, but by relating it more specifically to the actions of income-getting and income-spending units. This will be our topic in the following chapter.

Discussion
Questions

1. National-income flows vary from time to time because people vary their rates of spending. List all the different seasonal factors you can think of which might influence spending rates.

2. If a household is currently spending more than its income, does this mean that it is spending unwisely? What are the conditions under which a household could spend more than it received, say during a year?

3. If the entire household sector showed a deficit, what would you expect to be happening to consumer credit?

4. Under what circumstances, ordinarily, will a firm be operating on a deficit budget? A surplus budget? What would be the effect if the entire business sector were operating on a surplus budget?

5. For what purposes do you find money useful? Under what circumstances would you prefer to hold other kinds of property or assets?

6. When you "really" need money, the bank is not likely to be much help. Discuss.

CHAPTER 9

Spending, Saving, Investment

and Income Levels

WE ARE NOW PREPARED to consider some important relationships associated with the variation in levels of national income. They apply to transactions among the three principal income sectors, and how these affect the aggregate. Our concern now will be not only with the direction of their influence on national income, whether toward expanding or contracting it, but also with their timing. In other words, we shall put "dates" on income receipts and expenditures.

Our analysis so far has been of the hen and egg variety. We have noted that expenditures create income and income in turn creates expenditures. The problem now is to pay attention to the sequence of events, to discover when and under what conditions one becomes the other and how changes in one can be associated with changes elsewhere.

This will involve examination of other aggregates from the national-income accounts. *Disposable personal income* can be further subdivided into aggregate spending and aggregate saving. Investment will be viewed with closer attention to the reasons for its being undertaken; we will distinguish between what is called autonomous and induced investments, what their implications are for income levels, and their effect on stability and growth of real income.

The concept of a budget will have to be extended, because when budgets are "dated" it is necessary to distinguish between *planned* consumption and saving, and *realized* consumption and saving. We know from personal experience that these need not be the same. Plans are usually concerned with what we intend to do with the incomes we expect to get. These plans are subject to change. If our income changes, or if

149

prices of the things we plan to buy go up, expectations have to be altered. Sometimes we plan to save a certain amount. If prices go up, or if our income drops, planned saving can only be carried out by reducing consumption or our plane of living. Usually it is saving that gives way, although not necessarily in every individual case.

We will also make use of the *income period,* a more abstract concept than time we mark off on the calendar or note on a clock. An income period, as we defined it above, is the average time it takes money flows to complete the circle from household expenditures to firm receipts and back to household receipts from firm expenditures.

Timing in Household Budgets

Most household incomes are not spent during the period in which they are earned. This may be difficult to conceptualize, since the income process is continuous. There is no obvious starting point. For purposes of analysis, however, it is useful to construct one. Households will ordinarily have for expenditure in the "present period" income claims already earned in a previous period.[1] Most households have plans tentatively committing this income to consumption expenditure or to savings. These plans may not be realized. If incomes or prices change, actual or *realized saving* may be different. Realized savings can be determined only at the end of a period.

Consumption expenditures tend to follow national income, rising when national income rises, falling when national income falls (Figure 6). Since consumption expenditures of households are the largest single item entering the national-income flows, the question arises whether or not national income is not determined by consumption. On the basis of the best evidence available, the answer to this question is, No! The "causal" relationship appears to be the other way around, at least within significant ranges of variation. National income determines consumer expenditures. Of course, national income itself is comprised of the three aggregate expenditures—consumption, investment in the private sector, and purchases and transfer payments in the public sector. But our interest here is not only in the fact that each affects national income, but also by how much and by what kind of timing.

A hypothesis basic to much of modern economic analysis postulates that consumption expenditures tend to be rather stable in the short run (from one period to the next), but that they follow national income with

[1] Any household possessing property claims of whatever sort can usually convert these into liquid form, whether with the pawnbroker or with other banking and credit institutions. The more nearly liquid an existing claim—for example, a government bond—the less likely will be the loss of value if it is converted into cash.

Figure 6. National Income and
Personal Consumption Expenditures

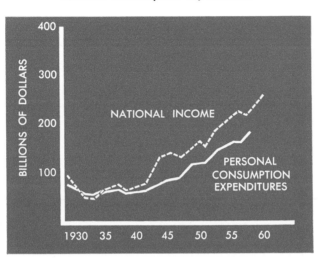

Source: U. S. Department of Commerce.

a slight lag. In other words, planned household expenditures follow the most recent income experience. This means that if national income is rising, consumption expenditures will rise, but at a slower rate. On the other hand, if national income is falling, households will ordinarily act to protect their past levels of consumption, reducing expenditures more slowly than income.

If this is true, it means that in the cyclical ups and downs of national income other sources of national income will have a determining role. Investment expenditures appear to vary directly with national income and to fluctuate more widely. For example, in the great depression of 1929–33, when national income dropped by more than 54 per cent in current dollars, consumption expenditures decreased by slightly more than 45 per cent. Gross private saving decreased by 82 per cent between 1929 and 1933, while gross private investment, which reached its low in 1932, dropped by more than 94 per cent. Realized saving in many cases became negative, that is, disinvestment took place, and consumption declined as the national income continued to fall.

The Propensity to Consume

A relationship developed by Keynes and others serves as a useful analytical tool for dealing with the interaction between the purely monetary flows

151

and the real flows at the aggregate level. It has provided new insight because it focuses attention on the fact that saving and investing in a monetary economy are separate functions performed by different people and for different reasons.

This would not be the case in a self-sufficient economy. For if saving in the real sense be defined as producing without consuming the entire output, then whatever is accumulated automatically becomes investment or *capital accumulation*. A primitive community which makes its living by catching fish may devote its whole effort to that task by hand or with very crude tools. By reducing its total consumption for a certain period (or by keeping its per capita consumption constant, if it happens to get a lucky catch or surplus), some of its members may devote their time to making new or improved equipment, by means of which future output (or income) can be increased. Thus the saving is linked in a direct way with capital formation, which is, of course, the same as investment. Savings and investment are equivalent.

In a modern enterprise economy, with large accumulations of real capital and a highly developed monetary and credit system, this equivalence is no longer automatic. What is saved is not simultaneously invested. Investment does not depend on specific acts of saving by households. However, for the nation as a whole, for any period once it is past, the amount that is saved will necessarily represent investment. We can therefore think of what happens in a monetary economy over a period of time as a process whereby variations in the different income aggregates are a "balancing of forces," by means of which savings and investment are brought into equivalence. Keeping this in mind, we can now develop through a series of steps the concepts of the *propensity to consume* and its half-brother the *propensity to save*. We will begin with an *ex post* identity[2] which we can state symbolically:

$$Y = C + S,$$

where Y represents income, C consumption, and S saving. To fix the referents of these symbols in our mind, let us illustrate first with an example where our data is for a single household. Assume that such a unit receives an income of $3,000, spends $2,400 on consumption, and saves $600. Our identity becomes

$$\$3,000 = \$2,400 + \$600.$$

We can now state this relationship another way, as a ratio of the income spent and saved. Our notation becomes:

---

[2] *Ex post*, meaning "after," in this context refers to a period that is past, so that the identity has been realized.

$$\frac{C}{Y} = \text{Average Propensity to Consume}$$

$$\frac{S}{Y} = \text{Average Propensity to Save;}$$

or in terms of our example:

$$\frac{2400}{3000} = .8$$

$$\frac{600}{3000} = .2.$$

It will be apparent that $\frac{C}{Y} + \frac{S}{Y} = 1$. Thus for the period under consideration 80 cents from each dollar became income to someone else, while 20 cents was saved and not passed on directly.

In aggregate analysis, where we seek to understand income changes over time, we need to think not in terms of a single static relationship between income and consumption as we did above, but of a schedule or series of such ratios. If for each year for which we have available statistics on national income we plot the consumption expenditures against disposable income, we obtain a scatter of points such as that shown in Figure 7. By fitting a straight-line regression curve to this scatter (a line which averages out the spread among them), we obtain the relationship shown by *cc*. If we now construct a 45° curve *OL*, which describes a one-to-one correspondence between income and consumption, we will have a bench mark against which to measure what actually happens.

With very low incomes, such as we had in 1932–33, the expenditures on consumption lie above the base line and saving is negative. However, as soon as income increases from this low point the consumption line lies below the base line and diverges from it more and more at higher incomes. This gap represents saving[3] for the nation or the economy.

Consumption of Individual Households

Another source of data on the relationship between income and consumption is available from budget studies from individual households. Sometimes called income-expenditure studies, they enable us to trace on a slightly different dimension the relation between consumption and income. If these budgets are classified and arranged in an ascending order according to size of income (along the horizontal axis), and if expenditures on

---

[3] As indicated in Chapter 7, if we were to plot consumption against national income, saving would include business saving, government surplus, and net foreign investment.

Figure 7. Disposable Income and Consumption Expenditures

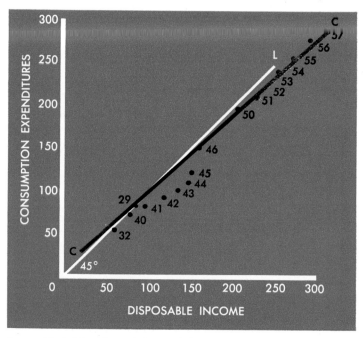

Source: Adapted from Economic Report of the President, 1929 to 1957.

consumption are plotted against them, we obtain a relationship between income and consumption resembling that shown in Figure 7. When household incomes are very low, consumption (on the average) exceeds income. As we move to the higher income classes, however, the income-consumption relationship diverges from the 45° line, showing a tendency for savings to increase relative to consumption. Some have interpreted this to mean that, on the average, as a household's income increases, as it moves to a higher income bracket, the expenditure pattern (particularly saving) conforms to that of the new class, but only after a lapse of time. These data, too, appear to support the thesis of the essential stability of consumption.

Having examined the consumption function as embodied in empirical data, we will now restate the relationship in its theoretical form and consider certain of its implications.

The Marginal Propensity to Consume

Another relationship derivable from the consumption function gives additional insight into the economic processes. This is called the *marginal*

154

Figure 8. Theoretical Consumption Functions When Savings Increase at a Constant Rate and at an Increasing Rate

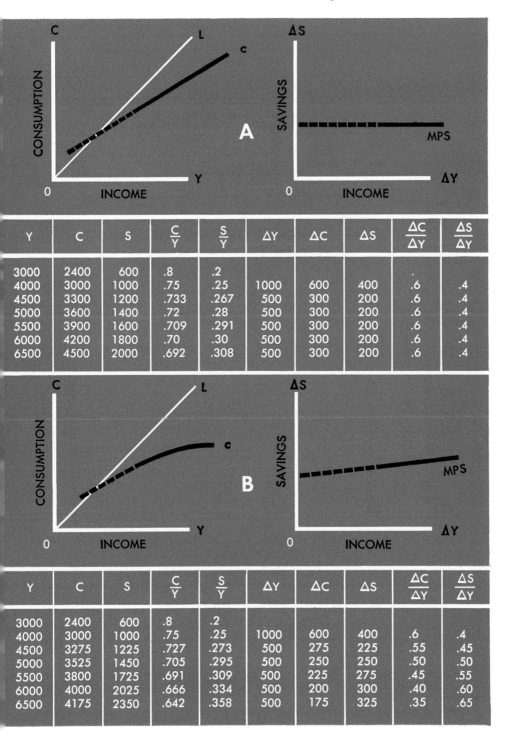

Y	C	S	$\frac{C}{Y}$	$\frac{S}{Y}$	ΔY	ΔC	ΔS	$\frac{\Delta C}{\Delta Y}$	$\frac{\Delta S}{\Delta Y}$
3000	2400	600	.8	.2					
4000	3000	1000	.75	.25	1000	600	400	.6	.4
4500	3300	1200	.733	.267	500	300	200	.6	.4
5000	3600	1400	.72	.28	500	300	200	.6	.4
5500	3900	1600	.709	.291	500	300	200	.6	.4
6000	4200	1800	.70	.30	500	300	200	.6	.4
6500	4500	2000	.692	.308	500	300	200	.6	.4

Y	C	S	$\frac{C}{Y}$	$\frac{S}{Y}$	ΔY	ΔC	ΔS	$\frac{\Delta C}{\Delta Y}$	$\frac{\Delta S}{\Delta Y}$
3000	2400	600	.8	.2					
4000	3000	1000	.75	.25	1000	600	400	.6	.4
4500	3275	1225	.727	.273	500	275	225	.55	.45
5000	3525	1450	.705	.295	500	250	250	.50	.50
5500	3800	1725	.691	.309	500	225	275	.45	.55
6000	4000	2025	.666	.334	500	200	300	.40	.60
6500	4175	2350	.642	.358	500	175	325	.35	.65

propensity to consume, and it focuses on the additional or marginal income when total income increases. Whereas before we asked the question, "What happens on the average to each dollar of a given income?" now we ask, "What happens to the additional or marginal dollar of income?"

We will use for the sake of simplicity the example of the $3,000 income considered above. Let us say that this income increases to $4,000, and when it does consumption increases by $600. The increase in income we will designate as $\triangle Y$, the increase in consumption as $\triangle C$, and the additional saving as $\triangle S$. Using the same ratios as before we get

$$\frac{\triangle C}{\triangle Y} = \text{Marginal propensity to consume}$$

$$\frac{\triangle S}{\triangle Y} = \text{Marginal propensity to save.}$$

Substituting the actual figures we get

$$\frac{600}{1000} = .6$$

$$\frac{400}{1000} = .4 .$$

Thus of each additional dollar of income above the previous base 60 cents is spent on consumption and 40 cents is saved.

The question of what happens to the additional income as total income rises is an important one in a rich industrial society with large accumulated reserves of capital. Conceivably, even with zero income some consumption could still take place in the short run (curve *cc* would intersect the vertical axis at some point above the origin). At some level of income a rising consumption curve intersects the reference line. Beyond this point saving becomes possible, and in the real world is positive. Moreover, as income increases still farther the distance between the two lines (representing saving) increases.

A question of some importance to our later analysis is whether or not the *rate* of increase in saving is constant or whether it too increases. Since the rate of increase is measured by the marginal propensity to save, this is another way of asking if the consumption function is linear or curvilinear.

The two situations are illustrated by the accompanying tables and diagrams of Figure 8. Table A and the two charts with it illustrate a situation in which the marginal propensity to save is constant, that is, the same proportion of the additional income is saved no matter how much total income increases: $\frac{\triangle S}{\triangle Y}$ is constant at .4. In this situation both

156

consumption and saving rise with each increase of income. The average propensity to consume $\left(\dfrac{C}{Y}\right)$ falls, while the average propensity to save $\left(\dfrac{S}{Y}\right)$ rises. Thus, as shown in the chart, the gap between consumption and income widens as income increases.

Table B and the accompanying charts illustrate the situation in which the propensity to save increases at an increasing rate. The marginal propensity to save can be shown as a rising curve, and the gap between consumption and income is greater than in the first example.

Which of these two situations is the more realistic? The evidence is not conclusive. Some empirical studies appear to indicate that the marginal propensity to save is rather constant. As we shall see shortly, the question of which relationship appears to hold true is an important one, since it gives some indication of the magnitude of the task of maintaining the level of income in an enterprise economy, in the short run particularly (in the long run this problem seems to disappear as people adjust to higher levels of living).

When income is not spent on available output, effective demand will tend to lag behind supply. Unless saving is offset by investment, money-income flows will diminish, and a fall in production and employment follows. If the propensity to save increases at an increasing rate, the implications for an enterprise economy are great. In order to maintain national-income flows, investment would have to increase at an increasing rate. The problem would exist, of course, if the marginal propensity to save were constant at all income levels. This latter relationship is the more conservative, and is all that is needed to predict a basic instability in the private sector of the economy.

The Linkage of Saving and Investment

The essentials of the above relationship can be illustrated with a simple numerical example and three income situations. We can assume that government budgets are in balance so that their effect is neutral. At the end of an income period (called Period 0) $100 is available and of this $100 it is planned to spend $80 on consumption and save $20. If during the following period (called Period 1) this plan is carried out, $80 is the amount of new income generated by household expenditure. In our first situation, assume that the consumption-goods firms decide to invest $20, and this amount is returned to the households as factor payments. This is the case of stable income, national income at the end of Period 1 being the same as at the end of Period 0. When planned investment is exactly equal to planned saving, the flow of money income will be constant at the rate of $100 per period and realized saving will be equal to planned saving.

Now let us consider a second situation. At the end of Period 0 the income stands at $100 as before. The household's plan is to spend $80 and save $20. What happens if planned investment for the period is only $10? Income for Period 1 now becomes $90. Realized savings can be only $10, because the income flow has dropped to the point where savings and investment are equal. Once the process of income decline has set in, it will work itself out over a series of income periods. Since with falling incomes consumption is not likely to remain constant, even though it declines less, relatively, than does income, firms will have unsold stocks. In the face of this situation, investment can be expected to decline further. With unsold stocks business firms will ordinarily begin to reduce prices to accumulate cash. Falling prices tend to discourage buying rather than encourage it, particularly of durable goods. The liquidity preference of both firms and households rises, since with the prospect of still lower prices money will buy more later on. An equilibrium between savings and investment may not be re-established until a much lower level of consumption and income has been reached, with a consequent rise in unemployment. In fact, if producers resist lower prices, unemployment may rise even more. This is likely to occur if a degree of monopoly exists, a problem which will be treated in Part 3.

Finally, there is a third situation. Again for Period 0 assume an income equal to $100 and a planned consumption of $80. However, through dishoarding or from newly created credit, we will assume that firms have decided to invest $30. In consequence, national income for Period 1 rises to $110. Realized saving is increased above the planned saving of the previous period. It is likely that an expansion of consumption—in this situation a rise in effective demand—would be a stimulus to still further investment, resulting in a cumulative effect quite the opposite from the second situation above. Indeed, once the process is initiated, with a gradual rise in effective demand and an upward pressure on the price level (particularly if there is no unemployment), it is the very thing which characterizes the upswing of the business cycle. The stimulus to national income of any *given* investment will be dissipated through saving in the course of several income periods, unless otherwise renewed by other investment decisions. These decisions are made by the management of firms attempting to establish claims to income, and they are guided by clues which this management gets from the environment in which it operates.

158

The complete picture of this environment must await our treatment of production and distribution in Parts 3 and 4. With what we have learned up to now, however, we can fill in the broad outlines of the roundabout production process as it generates the national-income flows.

Investment

If we neglect the influence on national income of the public sector of the economy on the assumption that it is neutral,[4] a balance between the twin income flows of the private sector will be one in which national income is equivalent to the value of net national product. Given the propensity to consume, household earnings for the production period are sufficient to purchase the aggregate output of consumer goods and services. Planned investment is sufficient to take over the ownership of new capital goods, including inventories.

In the preceding chapter we offered the hypothesis that consumption is a function of income; that is, consumer expenditures within limits depend upon income. The relationship was stated more precisely in terms of our two concepts, the average and marginal propensities to consume.

Unlike expenditures on consumption, investment is a highly variable aggregate. We have observed from our national-income accounts that net investment may vary from a negative quantity (disinvestment) in some years to substantial amounts in others. From the evidence it would not appear that any kind of stable relationship exists between national income and investment. In other words, it would seem that investment is an independent variable upon which income depends.

However, while this hypothesis appears to be a reasonable one, it is subject to some qualifications. Decisions to invest are made on the basis of clues which the firms' managers get from changes in consumption. This is particularly true of the investment category listed in our accounts as inventories. When consumption expenditures (experienced as sales by the firms) are increasing, inventories will ordinarily be built up in anticipation of rising prices. The reverse is true when sales are falling. Inventories are reduced to avoid losses. Plant expansion will also be undertaken when effective demand presses against capacity. Thus, while total net investment cannot be realistically perceived as dependent on national income, decisions to invest are linked to the variations in income through the changes in consumption.

As in the case of savings, it will be desirable to think of investment

---

[4] That is, the government is operating on a balanced budget.

as taking place over several income periods and to distinguish between planned and realized investment. In an uncertain and changing world plans may not work out. When an income period is past, net investment (capital accumulation) must equal realized net savings (output not destroyed in consumption and money claims not spent on consumption). If we think in terms of our simple model of income flows, it will be apparent that all firms together may turn out more than is sold to households in any given period. This may be because the firms planned it that way. When expectations about the future are favorable, the firms will want to add to their inventories and to increase plant and equipment by more than current depreciation allowances. On the other hand, inventory investments may occur because goods remain unsold if firms have overestimated consumer demand. At the end of the period realized investment will have occurred in either event, but only in the first case will realized and planned investment be equivalent.

If current consumption exceeds current production, firms will find that realized investment is smaller than they planned, that disinvestment occurred when they had planned to accumulate inventories or had only intended to reduce them slightly. For example, following World War II business encountered difficulty in building inventories (filling the pipelines, as the financial pages of the newspapers expressed it), because goods moved into consumers' hands as fast as they were turned out and many purchasers had to wait.

If we imagine that at the beginning of any income period all firms have plans for their output during the period,[5] the net national product and the national income from the private sector will be tentatively determined in the combined plans of the firms. Based upon experience and their estimates of consumption for the period, the firms decide on an output which will satisfy the effective demand and give them the investment or disinvestment their plans call for.

When consumption is about what was expected, investment plans (or disinvestment) will be realized. Otherwise there will be an error in prediction, a surprise which may be pleasant or unpleasant. Ordinarily, an accumulation which was not planned is undesirable from the firm's point of view. It is associated with unsold stocks or unused capacity which tie up a firm's assets in real goods, reduce liquid funds at its disposal, and subject it to the risk of loss if prices should decline. In such circumstances firms are likely to desire greater liquidity and to slow down production until sales have caught up. On the other hand, sales larger than

---

[5] These may be conscious plans or the result of habit from following rules of thumb.

expected are likely to increase liquid or cash claims and to encourage greater production in the following period in the hopes of expanding profit income. Thus a difference in planned and realized investment provides the clue on which management acts, and can be regarded as the "proximate cause" of production changes and changes in national income from one period to the next.

Planned net investment during a period ordinarily requires that a firm operate on a deficit budget. This, of course, is in addition to depreciation reserves, since depreciation allowances are a cost of production recovered from sales receipts. When they are spent for replacement equipment they do not, like net investment, add anything to national income.[6]

There are two ways in which a firm may spend more than current income. For any given period these funds may come out of savings of past periods or from the banks. We will consider each one briefly:

1. Savings from income may be spent at a later time. Thus planned investment can be financed from retained corporate profits or from the sale of securities to households to absorb their savings. While saving withdraws money flows from the income stream, investment adds to it. If planned saving could always be used at once to finance new investment, and if no other source of investment existed, national income would remain relatively constant from period to period. Net national product or real income could be expected to expand as technology improved, or as capital and population increased. This would be the condition under which supply would create its own demand. But where saving and investing are done by different persons or persons acting in different capacities, there is reason for questioning the faith expressed in Say's Law that effective demand will automatically equal supply (particularly in the short run).

2. Credit institutions may be both a help and a hindrance in this situation. They may facilitate communications between savers and investors so that savings are translated into investment. The commercial banks, by creating new credit money in the form of checking accounts (demand deposits), can cushion the effect of a lag in the time it takes savings to get "back to work." When firms secure their investment funds from savings institutions (savings banks, insurance companies, and others), investment comes out of realized savings from previous periods.

---

[6] This should perhaps be qualified. Depreciation allowances are largely set by statute and administered by the Internal Revenue Bureau. A depreciation allowance which overstates the actual depreciation may be a source of net investment to the firm. Calculation of depreciation costs is a complex accounting problem.

When investment is restricted to the amounts of previous savings, there is a financial limit to which new investment can take place. Commercial banks can expand the supply of money, making it possible for businesses to undertake the ownership of new real property, particularly in inventories. This increases the income of households in advance of currently available supply and results in an upward pressure on prices. Whether or not the general level of prices will rise depends on the extent of unemployment.

Autonomous and Induced Investment

Plans for investment are made by the directors and management (or owners) of firms as part of their function in promoting company and individual objectives. These include the payment of dividends to stockholders, maintaining and increasing the net worth of the production unit, and enlarging the company's share of the market. Most of these economic objectives depend upon firm profits for their attainment.

Common sense and the intuitive judgments of those in control of the firm's affairs are the "stuff" from which such plans are made. The profit and loss statement, the balance sheet, departmental budgets and sales ledgers (past and present), plus information from the "market" (the actions of other firms and industries), all form part of the environment taken into account when investment plans are made.

For analyzing their impact on the level of national income and employment, economists have adopted a dual classification for investment decisions. *Autonomous decisions* are so named because they are motivated by factors relatively independent of the level of national income. Investments in this category help to determine national income rather than being determined by it. *Induced investment,* as the name suggests, is inspired by rising income levels (disinvestment by falling income), particularly as these create expectations of still further increases in prices and incomes. While the dividing line between the two would be difficult to establish in any actual situation where plans are being made, it is useful analytically to distinguish between them.

While no investment decision is totally independent of general economic conditions, because all investments are likely to be made with an eye to what they will add to net income or profits, there are some types of investment which are based upon circumstances which can be called *real*. The management of most firms will have plans for improving plant layout, equipment, or product, to increase its efficiency, or make the product more desirable. Investments to achieve such objectives are likely to appear desirable quite aside from changing price levels, because they

162

are related to such factors as technological improvement,[7] plant design, product appearance, and changing consumer needs. They are not likely to be undertaken on any very large scale while national income is falling. By the same token management is unlikely to undertake them when national income is high or rising, since profits are usually favorable in any event and costs are likely to be regarded as excessive.

Induced investment is that part of planned investment undertaken in response to *changes* in consumer demand or consumer spending. Here inventories play an important role, although the expansion of plant and equipment also enters the picture during periods of rising effective demand and levels of factor use. This type of investment may be particularly marked during heavy defense and war expenditures, when government purchases are high. It is always of marked importance in a rich industrial economy, with its great variety of accumulated real capital, much of it highly specialized. Economists have recognized for some time the importance of a relationship which appeared to exist between the demand for consumer goods and the demand for the output of producers goods and services used to produce them. This relationship is known as the accelerator or the *principle of acceleration.*

The Acceleration of Derived Demand

Experience has shown that changes in the rate of consumer spending tend to be reflected backward in the stages of production at an accelerated rate. This can be illustrated by what happens in firms whose outputs can be located on different time scales according to their remoteness from final consumption.

1. We shall consider first an example of a semidurable consumption good which is stocked by retailers. In the case of a shoe merchant we can assume that a retailer's sales are 1,000 pairs per period (the income or turnover period would vary for different types of merchandise; for some it might be a week, for others a month, for items like jewelry much longer). To serve his customers the retailer ordinarily maintains an average inventory, say one period's sales, and once he has built up his stock, he would order replacements at the rate of 1,000 units each period.

What happens if the retailer's sales increase by 10 per cent, that is, to 1,100 per period?[8] The retailer will now need to order 1,100 shoes to restore the depleted inventory. Moreover, if he expects the increased

---

[7] This type of investment will be discussed more fully in Part 3 under the heading Technology (page 328).

[8] This increase need not be an actual increase. It may be an estimate by the retailer based upon what appears to be a trend in his sales.

demand to continue, he will need to keep a larger stock. Hence he will order an additional 100 shoes, making 1,200 in all, if he follows customary practice. Thus a 10 per cent increase in retail purchases results in an immediate increase of 20 per cent in purchases from the supplier. However, unless the demand of the retailer continues to increase by 10 per cent over the base period after the initial increase, the retailer's purchases will drop back to 1,100, and a stable consumer demand will then mean a reduced order for the manufacturer compared to the initial adjustment. Of course, the principle works in reverse as well. A 10 per cent drop in demand will induce the retailer to draw down his inventory, thereby reducing his regular purchases from the supplier by a greater percentage than the decrease in sales.

2. In our second case we will consider the effect of the acceleration principle upon an industry still further removed from the ultimate consumer—the manufacturing of shoe-making equipment. We will begin the analysis with a stable situation, where employment and income have found a level at which there is no tendency either to expand or contract. In this situation let us say that the amount of the output of shoes per period is valued at 1,000.[9] To produce this value of output, equipment valued at 5,000 is required. If this investment has been built up over a time, as will usually be the case, it will be represented by machines in varying stages of depreciation. We can assume that the average life of a machine is ten years, and that at present, in order to maintain physical capital intact, one-tenth is replaced each year. This would involve a replacement demand for machinery of 10 per cent of 5,000, or 500. If consumer demand has been relatively stable, the industry producing these capital goods will have adjusted its operations so that little excess capacity exists.

What happens when the demand for shoes increases by 10 per cent? To produce the additional goods will require an expansion of capital (investment) in the consumer-goods industry of 10 per cent. In short, the value of *new* equipment needed will be 500. This is equivalent to the present output of the capital-goods industry for its regular replacement demand. Thus a 10 per cent increase in demand for the consumer good is reflected back as a 100 per cent increase in the demand for investment goods. Where no excess capacity existed, this would mean a substantial increase of investment in the capital-goods producing industry. Moreover, because of the durability of the capital goods, replacement require-

---

[9] These numbers can be perceived as indices. They are intended only to portray relationships.

ments for the new investment will not recur for ten years. Thus, unless demand for the consumption good increases by another 10 per cent in the following period, the capital-goods producing firms will have excess capacity.

What if consumer demand increased by only 5 per cent in the second period? To satisfy this smaller increase will require machinery only of the value of 250. With a replacement demand of 500, total demand for the output of shoe machinery will fall to 750. Thus it appears that if demand for a consumer good continues to increase, but at a slower rate, the result after the first upsurge will be a decrease in demand for the output of investment-goods firms.

3. Finally, we need to consider the effect on the more roundabout industries (those more remote in the production process from the consumer) of the nature of an increasing number of consumer goods. We refer, of course, to the durable or hard good which renders its service to consumers over an extended period. Automobiles for family use, refrigerators, radios, television sets, and many other labor-saving and amusement items fall in this class. All of these require considerable capital equipment to produce. All are exhausted of their service-rendering capacity only over time, so some time must elapse before replacement is necessary. During this interval, if output is to be sustained, total demand for such durable goods must expand.

Replacement demand occurs partly as a consequence of wearing out, partly as a result of obsolescence, since these are products that are highly stylized and subject to almost continuous "improvement." Consequently, the period during which they may perform satisfactorily is variable. During periods of high-level income, replacement and new demand increase together, with new purchasers frequently acquiring the castoff models of those with high incomes and style consciousness who want replacement before the old model is worn out. During periods of falling income, new demand coming from the lower-income groups virtually ceases, and those who formerly purchased replacements while the old item was still usable postpone their purchases. This is passed back to the industry and to the machine-tool makers for the industry in a magnified form.

The acceleration principle for the capital-goods industry has become an analytical concept or convenient hypothesis for predicting wide fluctuations of investment on the one hand, and the very great instability of employment in the capital-goods industry on the other, once the level of national income changes, no matter what the cause.

165

The Principle of the Multiplier

In the final relationship to be discussed in this chapter we will examine the link between investment and the propensity to save. The multiplier can be described as a hypothetical relationship showing the effect on national income of a given injection or increment of new investment.

A simple case can be used to illustrate the concept. Let us say that a firm decides to undertake an autonomous investment in a new plant of the most modern engineering design. This involves the expenditure of $1,000,000. The venture is to be financed partly by retained earnings, partly by the sale of new securities.[10] The actual construction is undertaken by a contractor who hires the workers, purchases the materials, supervises the project, and turns it over to the firm when completed. The expended funds will pass into the hands of laborers, foremen, engineers, architects, materials suppliers, and so forth, and a certain part of this income will be spent on consumption goods during the period following that in which it is earned. It thereby becomes income to consumer-goods firms, who in turn pay it out to the workers and property owners who supply the factors of production. Each time the initial investment-expenditure turns over it adds to the national income in the manner already discussed.

How long will the effect of this initial investment continue? If there were no leakages it might go on indefinitely. But the effect of any given investment eventually wears out. Why? The answer is "because of the propensity to save." Each time the income completes the circuit it becomes household income. The amount passed on will be reduced by the amount saved.

This can be illustrated with the example we just used. We will assume that the marginal propensity to save is .2. The accompanying table shows the income passed on each turnover period.

We have carried the series through only 10 periods, but it is apparent what is happening. In each turnover period the income effect of a single initial injection gets smaller. If we add the above series we get $4,494,750.24 as the total addition to national income from our initial injection. Had we continued it, we know from a simple rule of mathematics that the sum of such a decreasing series will approach some whole number as a limit. In this case the limiting value is 5 million dollars. In other words, the addition to income is five times the initial investment. This is called the *multiplier effect,* and in this case the multiplier is 5.

---

[10] For an investment of this type the company might enlist the services of an investment-banking firm, which would raise the funds from the public but which would advance the money immediately. This type of institution is described in the next chapter.

Income Period	Net Income Resulting from $1,000,000 New Investment	Savings from Income
1	$1,000,000.00	$200,000.00
2	800,000.00	160,000.00
3	640,000.00	128,000.00
4	520,000.00	104,000.00
5	416,000.00	83,200.00
6	332,800.00	66,560.00
7	266,240.00	53,248.00
8	212,996.00	42,599.22
9	170,396.80	34,079.60
10	136,317.44	37,263.49
Total	$4,494,750.24	$898,950.31

If the propensity to save could be determined, and if this theoretical model corresponded to experience, the multiplier could be defined as follows:

$$\frac{1}{MPS} = \text{Multiplier.}$$

Substituting the values of our example: $\frac{1}{.2} = 5$. Now assume that 50 per cent of all additional income were saved: $\frac{1}{.5} = 2$.

The greater the marginal propensity to save, the smaller the income effect of a given investment, and the larger the investment required to maintain the national income at some previous high level.

Now let us consider the savings column. At the end of ten income periods this total is nearing $900,000, and is approaching $1,000,000 as its limit. In other words, when the savings from the income process generated by a new investment has reached the amount of the initial injection, the total effect on national income has run its course.

The Leverage Effect

The principle of acceleration as a strategic factor in business cycles was first developed as an analytical tool by J. M. Clark, and further elaborated by Roy M. Harrod, an Oxford professor and student of Keynes. The multiplier principle was first given prominence by Keynes, although credit for first formulating it is usually given to R. F. Kahn. More recently a number of economists have used the term *leverage effect* to refer to the process of interaction between the phenomena covered by these two concepts. According to this principle an initial injection of new investment has the effect of increasing household income above some previous level. Out of this additional income some increment of consumption will result. This increase will bring the acceleration effect into operation, which in turn exerts an additional multiplier effect, and so on until the physical or psychological limitations on output prevent further expansion of real output.

As should now be apparent, the leverage effect provides a more systematic concept for analyzing the process described rather loosely in Chapter 8, in which we noted that an increase in national-income flows could be generated either by an expansion of consumer expenditures or by a new flow of investment expenditures. We can specify with greater precision—analytically, at least—the circumstances in which each of these increases attains its maximum effect and then diminishes in its capacity to further affect national-income expansion, or even to maintain it, unless continuously renewed.

Both the accelerator and the multiplier play a role, in an enterprise economy, in the observed tendency of income and employment to fluctuate rather widely around the long-run growth curve or trend. Each implies a certain economic inertia present in a dynamic economy such as that of the United States. An expansion once started tends to keep going for a time, but frictions and leakages keep it from going on indefinitely. A contraction likewise continues until capital depletion goes so far that replacement is necessary.

So far in our discussion of the leverage effect we have neglected the role played by government in this process. We have kept it out of the discussion by assigning it a neutral role—assuming a balanced budget at a fixed level for the public sector of the economy. We can now drop this restriction and inquire briefly into how government expenditures fit into the picture. Government budgets, like those of the household and the firm, can show a surplus or a deficit. Taxes and expenditures need not be equal, and the effect of each on income flows will be quite different. How taxes are raised and how they are spent can also be important influences on income flows, but this aspect of the public economy will be reserved for fuller treatment later. Here we are concerned only with the direction of their influence.

Government investments in such capital improvements as roads, public buildings, armaments, flood control, irrigation, power development, and similar items will bring the multiplier effect into operation just as do investments in the private sector. Transfer payments, particularly when the shift is from individuals and groups with a high propensity to save to others with a high propensity to consume, may increase effective demand and bring the accelerator into play.

With regard to the timing between taxes and expenditures, the effect on income flows is likely to be especially marked if the government is operating on a deficit budget, borrowing through the sale of bonds. If this borrowing is from the banking system, resulting in the creation of new credit money, the multiplier effect may be more pronounced than if the expenditures are from taxes which would reduce spendable funds, some of which might be used in the private sector. This inference is consistent with the point made in our discussion of the national-income accounts, that the government debt is analogous to investment. In other words, during a period of depressed economic conditions, when both firms and households have a high liquidity preference, a government deficit sustains investment by satisfying demands for cash, thereby slowing down the forced liquidation of other assets. This leaves in the hands of individuals and firms assets comparable in value to the public debt—since had the government exercised its full powers to tax the equivalent property values would have had to be surrendered in order to pay the tax.

Stability and Use of the Leverage Relationships

What can be said about the stability of the leverage relationships? Are the propensities to consume and to save, as measures, sufficiently stable to be assigned values that can be determined empirically? Having determined such values statistically, could we use them for prediction? Assume that income after reaching a given peak has fallen by 45 per cent—as it did between 1929 and 1933. Would the injection of a given investment restore it to the previous level? How high would national income have to go to ensure full employment without running off into inflation? What about a situation at the beginning of a depression, when a million unemployed have appeared in the capital-goods industries? By how much would expenditures on consumption have to be increased to bring the accelerator into operation and create jobs for these workers?

Any economist who is honest with himself and his profession would have to assent that precise answers cannot be given to these questions. Throughout our discussion we have constantly reminded ourselves that the measures, even of past income periods such as a year, are still rather crude. Although national-income accounting has improved remarkably, and although it is possible to derive values for these relationships historically, it must be kept in mind that these are aggregates or averages. Many of the values are indices. We can do the mathematics involved but the values arrived at are not very stable.

Estimates of the long-run average propensity to save appear to be near .3. There is no doubt that it varies with the business cycle which it is presumed to aggravate. This would give the multiplier a value of approximately $3\frac{1}{3}$. With an income period of three to four months, as has been estimated, the upward stimulus of an investment can be expected to run its course in a little more than 40 months—a time estimate not far different from that sometimes assigned to the duration of the most characteristic business cycle.

In the case of the accelerator, the assignment of a precise value is even more difficult. The possible variation in the life of any durable good or durable equipment in the production process gives rise to other variables. The existence of excess capacity, even obsolete equipment which is still usable, will condition the impact. As we shall note in Part 3, the presence of monopoly is likely to result in a permanent excess capacity in some industries.

Granted the difficulty of precise prediction, are these relationships useful tools for estimating the direction of change? There is some evidence that they are. Since the depression, when most of these relationships were conceived and developed, events have occurred which tend to support at least their partial validity. The large investment, both public and private, which attended the war effort solved the unemployment problem which had existed throughout the 1930's. Income, both money and real, expanded substantially, as did consumption and saving. The backlog of demand, built up during the restrictions of the war years, proved to be a considerable factor in the induced investment which followed the war. It may be significant that this force proved stronger than most economists, even the most ardent "Keynesians," had imagined. Most of them had predicted large unemployment shortly after hostilities ceased.

What guides then can these relationships provide for prediction and control? This question will be explored further when we deal with questions of policy, and consider what the above analysis may suggest as "desirable." Meanwhile, the following may be considered.

We need to keep in mind that this general theory of income variations is a greatly simplified picture of a very complex reality. It is a construct, an *ideal type,* which has attempted to focus attention on key factors which appear to be of primary importance, in the aggregate, for the determination of the national-income flows. When those have been singled out—in this case the relation between income and consumption (consumption function), the relation between investment and saving, and the questioning of an earlier hypothesis that supply always creates its own

170

demand—the rest of the theoretical conclusions are largely deductive.[11]

Since 1945 the Federal Reserve Board has sponsored an annual survey of consumer finances. In these studies techniques developed by statisticians and psychologists have been brought to bear on the general area of "economic behavior." Using concepts and relationships developed by economists, these investigators have attempted to find out how changes in some of the larger aggregates—income levels, cash holdings, income changes, price changes, and so on—have affected behavior of carefully selected samples of households and firms. As a source of testable hypotheses, the developing models of economic theory helped to suggest areas of research which can add to our fund of knowledge of how our economy operates under varying conditions.

Meanwhile, however, economists are called upon to contribute their research findings and their speculations about them to the market place of ideas where issues of immediate policy are threshed out.

Income Variations and Cycle Theory

The preceding analysis does not come out with a neat theory or single cause for business fluctuations to serve as a basis for prediction or forecasting. On the contrary, it tends to reinforce a skepticism of any theory based upon a single cause. Time and again in the past such theories or explanations have been advanced and gained a following, only to be discounted or replaced. Each served a function, perhaps, in that it emphasized an aspect of the real world, and served as a basis for further inquiry.

William Stanley Jevons late in the nineteenth century became convinced that he had a purely "natural" or physical explanation for the business cycle. Observations of the sunspots had established the fact of a solar cycle repeated about every eleven years. This seemed then to coincide with the time period of business ups and downs. Jevons' reasoning was essentially as follows. The sunspots affect crop production, and variations in crop production are diffused throughout the whole economy as these raw materials move through the stages of production. Too many other relevant facts, however, could not be fitted into the theory. Variations in crop yields are highly uneven over the earth's surface. Agriculture has decreased steadily in relative importance to total economic activity. Vast accumulated reserves have made us less and less dependent on any year's output.

---

[11] See Arthur F. Burns, *Economic Research and the Keynesian Thinking of Our Times* (New York: Twenty-Sixth Annual Report of the National Bureau of Economic Research, 1946).

171

When the sunspot theory proved inadequate as a purely physical influence, attempts were made to relate this phenomenon to human psychology, on the assumption that the sun's radiation may have the effect of producing alternating periods of optimism and pessimism about the future.

Monetary causes of the business cycle, as we have already noted, have had a considerable following. Naive quantity theorists saw this relationship as simple and direct. Others attempted to relate money and credit factors to behavior, acknowledging that a flexible money and credit system was a necessary but not sufficient cause of business ups and downs.

Overinvestment theories of the business cycle stressed both a physical and a monetary aspect. Those who stressed the "real" causes believed that the breakdown came because too many of the factors of production had been allocated to the building of factories, machines, and other capital goods, resulting in a marked imbalance between producers' goods and consumers' goods. Such imbalance must inevitably be followed by a period of reorganization to restore some kind of "normal" balance. Monetary overinvestment theories stressed the role of flexible money supply in bringing about this disproportion between consumers' goods and producers' goods.

Others approached the problem quite differently. To them the principal causal factor was *underconsumption*. In its crudest formulation this theory stated simply that households did not get back from the market enough money (income) to buy what they had produced. Moreover, the underconsumption theory stressed the inequality of income distribution as a factor affecting spending and saving, with disproportionate saving being done by the very high income groups.

A so-called psychological school of business-cycle theorists from the later sunspot theorists on attempted to relate "economic behavior" to such psychological factors as optimism and pessimism, alternating between expectations of unlimited economic progress and impending economic catastrophe. Certainly evidence exists that mass expectation in many areas contributes to excesses of various kinds. Prosperity or a belief in prosperity can become contagious and affect rather markedly what people do.

Joseph Schumpeter stressed the unequal distribution of such psychological qualities as willingness to take risks, to attempt new ideas. Like other characteristics (intelligence, height, weight, etc.), these qualities follow the so-called normal distribution. An enterprise economy provides the widest scope for the relatively small number of persons with extraordinary initiative to try out new ideas, some of which succeed. These *innovators,* believing in their capacities for initiating new enterprises, make the investments and start the upswing which marks the prosperity phase of the cycle. As their successes become known, the *imitators* move in and attempt to secure some of the profits now being realized by the more enterprising. Eventually the economy approaches the physical limit of its output. More and more of the imitators begin to encounter disappointments. Withdrawal begins, and then the imitators "rush out" as they had "rushed in." The result is a downswing of economic activity and income, although the real results of the innovations remain as contributions to progress.

Following our earlier discussion, it should now be apparent that these theories are not mutually exclusive. Each represents a different frame of reference for the same events. Overinvestment and underconsumption are opposite sides of the same coin, two ways of viewing the income flows. Psychological factors are likewise part of that same process since the income flows, as we have seen, are not independent entities, but the consequences of human behavior. If we start with the income-expenditure flows as the "immediately perceived events" and their variations as problems to be explained, our model offers possibilities for weighting many of these factors according to their contribution without assigning to any the character of an absolute cause.

Discussion
Questions

1. In 1933, in the midst of the great depression, the editor of an Iowa newspaper, addressing himself to the question, "What happened to the money?" concluded that "We spent it!" He won the Pulitzer Prize. Would you have given it to him on the basis of "economic wisdom"?

2. Accounts are usually kept and analyzed on an annual basis. Assume you are a retailer whose sales amount to $1,200,000. Assume further that your average inventory is $100,000, which also constitutes your working capital. How many times, on an average, did you turn over your stock of goods? Approximately, what is your income period?

3. Assume that you are on your first job, supporting a family on $5,000 a year. You get a raise of $1,000. Which items in your budget would you increase? Do you think your imagined behavior would be typical of households in this income class?

4. A manager of a manufacturing plant has realized for some time that the equipment being used is out of date and the building poorly arranged for the most efficient flow of production. Plans have been drawn up for remodeling and rearrangement. Is this an example of autonomous or induced investment?

5. A school teacher with a modest savings states that she has decided to invest in A.T.&T. She buys a few shares of stock through a broker who forms a trust fund. Is this transaction an investment in the sense in which we have been using this term?

6. Distinguish analytically between the accelerator and the multiplier.

CHAPTER 10

Money and Banking Institutions

in the United States

UP TO NOW we have been adding piecemeal to our knowledge about money and our understanding of the role of money in the income processes. We will now bring what we have learned together and relate it to our financial organizations and their roles in the economy. We will need to review some of the history of our money and banking institutions, because what we have now has largely developed out of experience with financial affairs in the past. First let us review some of the things we have learned.

1. Money is a form of property, the most abstract form—a kind of disembodied claim which may be used to acquire property rights in other things of value (wealth) or to settle debts (negative wealth).

2. Because money functions as a measure of value, all things of value acquire in the process of being exchanged a money aspect or "price tag" which facilitates exchange and the keeping of accounts.

3. Money began its career as a type of commodity which, by being exchanged against many things, got itself adopted as a standard. Like any other unit of measure, it was abstracted from the physical object with which it was initially associated. (We can think of a linear measure of one foot without remembering that it was once linked with the pedal extremities of man.)

4. With the development of a money system and monetary institutions, together with the division of labor and specialization which characterize an exchange economy, economic activity is comprehended by a vast number of transactions.

5. These transactions, which are two-sided affairs, give rise to the twin income flows. When money is facilitating such transactions it is

175

said to be working. It can do more work if there is more of it, or if it passes from hand to hand more rapidly.

6. The demand for money originates with the basic production, consumption, and governmental units.

7. The supply of money originates with the branch of government charged by Congress with that responsibility and with banks. Banks have been defined as firms whose function is to produce or generate liquidity, that is, money.

We now turn to these monetary institutions and to the general financial structure of the United States.

The Standard Monetary Unit

Unlike many of our other social and political institutions, the monetary unit of the United States was not British in origin. Before the Revolutionary War many different types of money circulated in the colonies, much of it metal coins. The most common was the Spanish silver dollar or "pieces of eight,"[1] which had entered the country as a consequence of the smuggling trade with the West Indies. Alexander Hamilton, first Secretary of the Treasury after 1789, advised that this monetary unit be adopted on the grounds that less of a conversion problem would be involved and less confusion created than if the pound sterling or any of the hodgepodge of other currencies were selected as the basic unit.[2]

At the outset the *standard dollar* was defined as either gold or silver, the relative weights of the two metals being about fifteen to one. There followed, however, a period of struggle between groups who advocated a single gold standard for the dollar and those who preferred the bimetallic standard, both metals being made into coins at some fixed ratio. By *standard money* was meant "that form of money in which all other forms of money are redeemable."

Throughout most of the nineteenth and well into the twentieth century, the belief was widely held that having money defined in terms of some specific commodity such as gold or silver was the answer to the need for a measuring rod for value which would be stable. Their argument was that a dollar backed by gold would provide a benchmark or guide for orderly processes of production and exchange. Confidence in the means of payment was regarded as of first importance.

How was a gold standard supposed to operate? We can illustrate by means of the standard established in the Currency Act of 1873

---

[1] This is the source of our designation of the quarter as "two bits."
[2] The United States thereby obtained a more "logical" monetary unit (based as it is upon a decimal system) than the more cumbersome British pound. This is in contrast to the system of weights and measures which were patterned after the mother country.

(described by William Jennings Bryan as the "Crime of '73"). The dollar was defined as 23.22 grains of gold. Since there are 480 grains of gold in an ounce, this established the mint price of gold at $20.67 an ounce:

$$\frac{480}{23.22} = 20.67.$$

Under the gold standard the Treasury stood ready at all times to buy or sell gold at the established rate or to coin it, at a small cost, into gold coins. Individuals were free to melt coins down into bullion for sale on the open market, but not to recast it into money form. Under these rules the "logic" of the gold standard was as follows:

If the price level were to fall, with a decline in the price of commodities generally including gold bullion, people would prefer to hold their property in money (we would say now that the liquidity preference would increase). They could in these circumstances take gold to the mint and have it coined into money. As the quantity of money in peoples' possession increased and their desire to hold money was satisfied, spending would be resumed, the income flows would increase, the fall in prices would be arrested, and the previous level of income would be restored.

Where would this gold come from? Stocks of gold exist at all times in the commercial inventories of goldsmiths, in the ornaments and jewelry of people, as well as hoards in private possession. Mining operations are constantly bringing in new supplies. A general fall in prices, leading to a decrease in the cost of labor, mining equipment, and so forth, while the price of gold remained constant, could be counted on to stimulate gold production. Gold in hoards and in unused trinkets would have more value at the mint than in the hands of their owners. From these sources the flow of gold to the mint was supposed to come.

On the other hand, if a boom were to start both real and money income flows would expand. The market prices of commodities including gold would rise. Gold would then command a premium as bullion in the market. People would no longer want to hold property in the form of cash, since the value of money is fixed. Rising costs would make gold mining less profitable (with the Treasury price still $20.67 an ounce). People would thus be encouraged to melt gold coins down into bullion, and this would be exported for the purchase of goods in other countries with lower prices, thus reducing the money flows at home and increasing the real flows.[3] Eventually the general price level would be brought back into line with the price of Treasury gold.

---

[3] One of the most important points in support of the gold standard has always been that it is international, and during certain periods it was. But in order to function as it was supposed to nations had to be internationally minded, and observe the rules of the game both at home and abroad. This, as we shall see, was often not the case.

The "logic" of the gold standard was impeccable. It was balanced and, like the dreams of perpetual motion, practically automatic. Its only flaw was the same flaw in the perpetual motion idea: it wouldn't work, and for the same reason—friction. As a model of human behavior it was too simple, since it was based upon the particular circumstances which obtained when it had in fact worked and when the exceptions could be ignored.

One of the arguments for gold as the single monetary standard was its essential durability and scarcity. It was stated that its rate of destruction is infinitesimal, so that the existing stock accumulates from year to year, and this accumulation should parallel the economic growth of society. But is this the way gold production really reacts? The answer is, No! Aside from the panning operations of a few prospectors, gold production is a large-scale, costly operation. Entry into and exit from the business are neither simple nor easy. Moreover, the history of the industry shows that gold mining is not a steady year-after-year proposition. The great gold strikes in California, the Black Hills, Alaska, Australia, and South Africa all precipitated gold rushes, which for a time channeled quantities of the metal into circulation. Nor did the response of people with gold accumulations conform to the prescribed pattern. For years large amounts of gold disappeared into the hoards of East Indian princes. During periods of depressed and falling incomes gold coins and gold certificates were withdrawn from circulation and from the banking system, and secreted in strong boxes, mattresses, and fruit jars. From 1930 to 1932 nearly two billion dollars disappeared into hoards, undermining the whole money and banking structure. Despite official pleadings and assurances, these funds could not be coaxed out of hiding.

When nations in the midst of a boom saw their gold stocks threatened by increasing purchases abroad, few of them hesitated to suspend payment of specie or alternatively to restrict foreign imports (it is an interesting fact of history that the American political party which so long stood for the "virtues" of the gold standard was also the party of high protective tariffs). Nearly every major war or crisis saw governments suspend the payment of gold. Defining standard money in terms of a single commodity stabilized the dollar only in terms of that one commodity—and in the case of gold not a very useful one at that. Other prices, including incomes, could vary widely, and with them employment. We review this history here, because it persisted long enough to create a habit of thinking that still creeps into our longings for an easy solution to a knotty problem. Now we can examine another facet of our monetary history because of its contribution to the monetary system we now have.

Forms of Money Other Than Standard

When a nation has developed beyond a rudimentary industrial stage, so that the number and size of transactions become large, metal coins get to be a nuisance. In the case of gold, coins of low denominations are so small that they are easily lost or misidentified. Larger values are difficult to carry around, and there is a risk of being robbed.

An early expedient was to issue a form of *representative money*. This was paper money, a kind of warehouse receipt stating that there was on deposit in the national treasury a specified amount of gold. A second form of money has always been that of very small denominations (less than a dollar), the minor coins used for change making and small purchases. These are issued by the mint, and because their metal content is worth far less than the value stated on the face of the coin, they are sometimes called *token money*, but are now usually listed in treasury reports simply as *subsidiary* and *minor coin*.

A third form, once called *fiat money*, was simply paper currency engraved with some face value stated in money terms, issued by government without reference to any specific "backing." The *greenbacks* or United States notes issued by the Federal government during the Civil War were of this type. These notes usually specified that they would be redeemed in other forms of money. Fiat money is money because the government says so. It usually circulates, and is accepted if it can be used for paying taxes or customs. As long as we were on a gold standard these forms could be regarded as credit money or promissory notes of the government. They were thus a form of credit money, based in the last analysis on the stability of the government and its power to levy taxes against the property claims of its citizens.

Although these and other forms of credit money circulated freely before 1933, there was a subtle distinction sometimes made between them and representative or full-bodied money. They were designated as *lawful money*, and their acceptance was fairly general because they could be redeemed in standard money on demand. They might be used for the payment of debt, as long as the creditor did not object. If he did, and especially if the contract had been so drawn, he might demand payment in *legal tender*, which was the standard money.

Silver Money

Although in 1873 the United States formally adopted gold as its monetary standard, some concessions were made to the silver interests and the advocates of bimetalism. Silver lost its job as a monetary standard, but under the provision of successive acts passed by Congress the Secretary of the

179

Treasury has been required to purchase specified amounts of newly mined silver (at times involving the entire output) for use in coinage and as "backing" for silver certificates issued in denominations chiefly of $1 and $5. To the imaginative mind these silver certificates might be construed as *representative money*. Since, however, the silver in a silver dollar has been consistently valued in the market at less than a dollar, these are, like the minor coins, essentially token money.

The Dollar after 1933

The economic collapse of the 1930's was an experience which had its impact on many aspects of economic thought and action. The gold standard, as it had existed for a little more than a half-century (except for a brief interruption during World War I), was abandoned. Contrary to predictions, "grass did not immediately grow in the streets," and out of this new experience there came the increasing awareness that there had been nothing particularly "natural" or automatic about a freely convertible gold standard. It is now viewed as one form of money management, which under certain conditions can facilitate transactions. Under other conditions, when the desire for liquidity takes the form of large-scale hoarding from the income flows, it may produce the opposite effect, as it did in the early 1930's.

In 1933 the dollar was revalued in terms of gold. This meant a decrease in the gold content of the dollar or alternatively an increase in the dollar value of gold. Under enabling legislation passed by Congress, the President announced a sequence of increases in the price of gold, from the long-time Treasury rate of $20.67 an ounce to $35.00 an ounce. Now if 35 is divided into 480 (grains of gold in an ounce), it will be apparent that the symbolic gold content of the dollar has decreased from 23.22 grains to 13.71 grains. What did this mean in terms of the gold stocks in the Treasury? A large paper profit appeared. The devaluation of the dollar was approximately 41 per cent. The gold stocks held by the government now represented that much of a potential increase in the number of dollars.

However, matters did not rest there. The entire gold stock of the country, including the gold certificates, were *nationalized*. It was made illegal for private individuals to own or to hold coins, gold bullion, or representative gold certificates, except for industrial, artistic, or souvenir purposes. Holders of this form of property were required to exchange it at the Treasury or banks for other money: United States notes, silver certificates, or various forms of credit money to be described shortly. All profits accruing from the revaluing of gold, including that held by individuals, be-

180

came the property of the Treasury—about $2.8 billion. The circulating media were simplified and redefined. The distinction between *legal tender* and *lawful money* disappeared.[4] All lawful money became legal tender.

Since 1934 the U.S. Treasury has been the sole purchaser of newly mined gold, except for industrial users who are licensed to acquire needed supplies. Gold imports are likewise purchased by the Treasury and become part of the gold stock at Fort Knox, Kentucky, in the form of metal bars. Table 6 tells the story of what happened to United States gold stocks as the world output expanded with the stimulus of the new high price and as other countries exchanged their gold for dollars.[5]

Table 6.   U. S. Monetary Gold Stocks, 1932–1940
(millions of dollars)

1932	$ 4,226
1933	4,036
1934	8,238
1935	10,125
1936	11,258
1937	12,760
1938	14,512
1939	17,644
1940	21,995

During the period of transition between the old and the new monetary standard of the United States, an important problem arose because of the presence in many debtor-creditor contracts (including some government bonds) of a so-called gold clause. This clause usually provided that, on the option of the creditor, payment must be made in gold coin of the United States of "present standard weight and fineness," meaning the value prevailing when the contract was made. Had such provisions been interpreted literally, every dollar of debt contracted under the old standard would have become $1.69 under the new. To prevent the hardships which such an interpretation would have imposed upon debtors, Congress by resolution (approved by the President on June 5, 1933) abrogated all such provisions and made their inclusion in future contracts illegal.

The constitutionality of the Act of Congress authorizing change in the gold content of the dollar was immediately challenged in a series of

---

[4] A creditor may still refuse to accept minor coin in settlement of debts above a certain amount. This is based solely upon considerations of convenience. In other words, a debtor could not pay a large debt with a truck load of pennies.

[5] Not all of this increase can be attributed to the increase in the Treasury price of gold. Part of the inflow was due to financial insecurity in other parts of the world.

cases brought before the Supreme Court. In deciding these cases the Court (1) upheld the powers of Congress to regulate the content of the dollar, as provided by the Constitution, and (2) refused to uphold existing gold clauses, for the reason that this would have constituted an unjust enrichment of creditors and imposed unjust burdens upon debtors.

Thus was the standard monetary unit of the United States changed. The price of gold has remained unchanged from 1934 to the present. What have the actions taken in 1933 meant in terms of our monetary standard? Are we still on a gold standard? Is our money *backed* by gold? An answer sometimes given is that we are on a *nominal* gold standard. A common-sense translation of this would be "gold standard in name only." What we have had in fact since 1934 is a system of currency managed by monetary and fiscal authorities in a manner which still preserves a part of the symbolism of an earlier standard.

The final test of the value of money, its acceptability, and its usefulness in promoting income activity, is the extent to which it gives its owner command over other property and the goods and services which are exchanged. The existing management of the monetary system, while using gold, reserves that form of property to government, the agent of the social economy. However, the part of our actual money supply or *currency* which originates with the Treasury is small—approximately 15 per cent. The rest consists of Federal Reserve notes, which are issued by our central banking system. Both, however, are of minor importance when compared with "check book" money which is generated by our commercial banking system.

A breakdown of the stock of currency in circulation (millions of dollars) in the United States as of April 30, 1957, is as follows:

A. *Notes and Currency*

  1. TREASURY CURRENCY

	(millions of dollars)
Standard silver dollars	$ 250
Silver certificates and Treasury notes of 1890	2,100
Subsidiary silver coin	1,301
Minor coin	469
U.S. notes	315
Federal Reserve bank notes	135
National bank notes	62
Total Treasury Currency	$ 4,631

2. FEDERAL RESERVE NOTES	$25,855
Total Notes and Currency	$30,519
B. *Demand Deposits*	$107,000

Banking

Banking as a function (see pp. 140–47, The Money and Banking Function) and an occupation is no doubt as old as money itself, if indeed the two can be separated. Any society which has progressed beyond the stage of narrow self-sufficiency to the point of accumulating reserves of wealth or capital develops the means to carry out transfers of ownership or control over such a reserve. This is essentially what the banking function does.

Biblical literature abounds with references to moneylenders and money-changers, not always in a favorable light. The medieval commercial civilizations of Venice and Genoa were famous for their highly developed banks, which exchanged the currencies of many nations and granted credits to merchants as well as governments. In 1682 Gerard Maylnes, one of the earliest English publicists to begin the systematic observation and analysis of financial and economic activities, wrote:

> A Bank is properly a Collection of all the ready money of some Kingdom, Commonwealth, or province as also of a particular City or Town, into the hands of some persons licensed and established thereunto by public authority of some King, Prince, or Commonwealth.

Many English banks began with the goldsmiths, whose strong boxes were used for safekeeping by the general public (at least one private English bank in fact traces its history in an unbroken line to the leading goldsmith of the late medieval period). The *receipts* which these craftsmen issued to depositors became the basis later of bank-note issue, passing from hand to hand as money. The notes of instruction to the goldsmith from depositors to pay over to some third party a specified sum from the depositors' funds evolved into the *draft* or *check,* as we know it, and the demand deposit on which it operates. The lending at interest of several times the actual amount of deposits became the forerunner of the later practice of basing demand deposits on fractional reserves. This began when goldsmiths discovered that not everyone was likely to demand his gold at once, hence he could earn an extra income by lending "other people's" money.

The unhappy experience of many persons and even whole commu-

183

nities with the consequences of overambitious banking practices (involving large expansion of credit, misappropriation of funds, and lack of responsibility) led quite early to increasing regulation by governments and to the formation of central banks[6]—institutions closely allied with governments, public in outlook if not in organizational form, which served as bankers' banks and attempted to co-ordinate banking activities.

Types of Banks and Credit Institutions

Specialization in banking, as elsewhere, has developed to fit the needs of those served. From the pawnbroker to the large investment banking house the capacity to serve the liquidity needs of the community is the basis for incomes earned by those performing the banking function. It is possible to make a relatively simple classification which describes these banking functions. We have included certain other institutions which, while not banks in a strict sense, perform similar functions.

1. *Savings Banks.* As the name suggests, savings banks are the banking institutions which accept deposits of money usually saved out of income. In exchange for such funds the bank gives an acknowledgment of its debt in the form of a deposit slip or entry in an account book. The deposit, plus the interest it agrees to pay, then becomes a liability of the banking firm. This debt may be payable after some specified time or after required notice has been given.

Funds thus received are available for loan to others. Those who have need for funds, and who can demonstrate responsibility for them, borrow by note from the bank, paying a rate of interest higher than that paid the depositor. The difference between the two interest rates becomes income to the bank. Such loans need not be made directly. They can be made indirectly through the purchase by the banks of notes, bonds, mortgages, and other forms of debt.

Other institutions which perform this same function, but which are highly specialized as to type of loan, include: building and loan associations, credit unions, farm credit associations, land banks, and household credit corporations. Their size also varies widely.

2. *Investment Banks.* Investment banking firms are to be distinguished from savings institutions chiefly on two counts: size, and type of client. Most investment houses are very large, dealing in credit operations involving millions of dollars. Until comparatively recently the large investment banks, such as Morgan-Stanley and Kuhn, Loeb & Company, were

---

[6] The Bank of England was organized in 1694, and existed as a private institution until nationalized by the Labour government in 1948. The Bank of Sweden, oldest of the central banks, was established in 1626.

individual proprietorships or partnerships.[7] Their owners were men of large private fortunes. More recently they have been incorporated, although their stock is rather closely held.

The clients of these banks are the relatively large business and manufacturing corporations, and both foreign and domestic governmental agencies. Most of their loans are for long-term capital improvements to be financed by stocks or bonds. They are staffed with investment specialists having broad acquaintance with industry and commerce. The investment bank serves as a bridge between savers and investors, but the process is usually an involved one. It begins with an investigation by the bank of the firm's plans for investment or expansion, of its management, and of its market prospects. If the request is evaluated favorably, the bank will underwrite the investment by making the needed funds available at once. If a stock or bond issue has been planned, the bank will take over the certificates of equity or indebtedness, discounting them at a certain rate. It then begins the *distribution* of these securities, selling them to investors, large and small, all over the country (or the world). When they have been disposed of, the bank will have recovered its original advance to the company, plus whatever it has been able to make by way of a premium over the discounted purchase price.[8]

3. *Other Savings Institutions.* Insurance has become an increasingly important form of household saving, with insurance companies becoming some of our largest enterprises. In 1957 the largest companies reported assets of nearly 15 billion dollars, while sixteen companies reported assets of more than 1 billion. As agents for their policy holders, these institutions are leading sources for investment funds.

The incorporated business is able to supply its own funds for investment purposes, a type of "savings" of increasing importance. The retained earnings and depreciation reserves have become so important in the business sector that commercial banks particularly have come to rely increasingly on governments as borrowers. Like the insurance companies, modern large-scale business has to be taken into account as a reservoir of liquid funds withheld from household income flows and which is available for investment, and thus part of the money and credit supply.

Government agencies have likewise acquired significance among savings institutions. Old Age and Survivors Insurance, a Federally administered program, receives the compulsory contributions of employees and employers to the retirement of millions of workers covered by this legisla-

---

[7] These organizational forms will be taken up in Part 3.

[8] The bank may retain a part of the issue for its own portfolio. If the issue is a very large one, it may share its distribution with other banks.

tion, and most of these funds are invested in government bonds. The Railroad Retirement Board performs a similar function for railway employees. Examples of such funds could be multiplied many times at local, state, and national levels. We shall return to further implications of these types of savings in Part 5, which deals with Consumption.

Capital for a wide range of credit agencies serving production units has also been provided by government. The Farm Credit Adminstration, for example, supplies both long-term and intermediate credit to farmers and farm organizations (such as co-operatives), while the Commodity Credit Corporation makes loans on farm products. During the depression the Reconstruction Finance Corporation was created to make loans to banks and other strategic business organizations in distress. When World War II broke out the RFC became an important source of liquid funds for war production, a service which continued throughout postwar reconversion and the Korean defense period, until it was liquidated after 1952.

4. *Central Banks.* Central banks are ordinarily public or quasi-public corporations, and are sometimes called bankers' banks. Their usual function is to maintain a stable money and credit system rather than to earn an income for shareholders. In the United States the Federal Reserve System performs this role, supervising and controlling the operation of the commercial banks.

5. *Commercial Banks.* The stock in trade of the commercial banks is commercial paper. This represents the short-term credit on which merchants, brokers, and manufacturers operate, and which helps sustain such money-income flows as wage payments and purchases of raw materials.

Commercial banks influence these flows by making short-term credit either easier or more difficult to get. They receive deposits and they create them by lending, that is, by granting businesses the right to draw checks against newly created accounts. These accounts are debts or liabilities of the bank. Balancing them, as assets to the bank, are the notes (commercial paper) which businesses owe the bank and which they will pay at a later date. As a group and in concert with the central bank, they can expand the total volume of liquid funds by making loans available to business, to government, and to households through holding in reserves a fraction of their total liabilities in cash.

How a Bank is Organized

The basis of any bank operation has to be a pool of property, more or less liquid in form. This constitutes its capital, and some plan for raising it is a prerequisite to being granted a charter. This is usually done through the sale of shares. The impetus for the formation of a new bank usually originates with a group of commercial and industrial leaders who feel the need of such a service in the area, as well as from persons experienced in bank- ing who see it as an opportunity for earning an income. The time for forming new banks in the United States has pretty well passed. The trend appears to be in the opposite direction, with the number of separate banks actually on the decline through mergers and consolidations. The total of all banks in the United States in 1955 was 14,309, which was 156 fewer than in 1954, and in considerable contrast to the 29,715 in 1920.

However, for the purposes of illustrating how it would be done, we can imagine a situation in which a productive community with a need for banking service and unable to obtain it from existing institutions, decides to start a commercial bank. The evolution of such a banking enterprise can be told by a series of dated balance sheets.

Let us say that an organizing committee for the Gibraltar National Bank has sold ten thousand shares of stock at $100 each and has been granted a charter. Its balance sheet would appear as follows:

BALANCE SHEET
GIBRALTAR NATIONAL BANK
January 1, 1956

Assets		*Liabilities*	
Cash	$1,000,000	Capital Stock	$1,000,000
Total	$1,000,000	Total	$1,000,000

In January the bank acquires a building and equipment, and opens its doors to the public. At the end of the first month its balance sheet would appear somewhat as follows:

BALANCE SHEET
GIBRALTAR NATIONAL BANK
February 1, 1956

Assets		*Liabilities*	
Cash	$ 900,000	Deposits	$3,000,000
Building and Equipment	100,000	*Net Worth*	
Loans & Discounts	2,000,000	Capital Stock	1,000,000
Investments	1,000,000		
Total	$4,000,000	Total	$4,000,000

During this interval the bank has altered the form of its property holdings
and has acquired debts to the extent of $3 million, which in this case are
in the form of deposits. Of these, $1 million were acquired through accept-
ing funds from the public and $2 million through loans to borrowers.
These loans are offset in the assets column by entries labeled loans and
discounts (commercial paper). Part of the original capital has been converted into buildings and equipment. The bank holds cash in the amount
of $900,000. Investments (high-grade bonds to the extent of $1,000,000)
have been purchased. The bank has thus acquired income-earning assets
(loans and investments) of different degrees of liquidity and profitability.

Here we have illustrated two important considerations in bank operation. The more liquid the assets, that is, the closer they are to money or
cash, the safer the position of the bank with respect to meeting any demands that may be made upon it by its depositors. In periods of crisis the
more liquid a bank can be, the less likely it is to have to cease operations
because of inability to meet its obligations. On the other hand, the larger
the proportion of loans and investment, the greater the prospective earnings of the bank. An important problem of bank management, therefore,
is to steer a course between the conflicting goals of liquidity or security on
the one hand and profitability and risk on the other.

A bank could be maneuvered into a position, through careless planning of invesments, where the maturity dates of its loans are bunched too
far in the future. When this happens the bank finds itself unable to meet
current liabilities without outside help, even though its investments in the
economic processes are perfectly "sound." An insolvent bank, on the other
hand, is one with too many loans that have "gone bad" through the failure
of its debtors.

In terms of its role in the income process, a highly liquid bank is not
helping to generate income. Its money is "at roost," so to speak, not doing
its job. On the other hand, an overzealous bank management can do its
enterprise harm as well as great damage to the community by making
loans and encouraging indebtedness which generate inflation and eventual
collapse.

Today our bank would be subject to certain legislation and enforced
banking practice intended to give assurance that it would meet its responsibilities on both counts. Thus our presentation of the balance sheets of the
Gibraltar National Bank, while useful for illustrating certain principles of
bank operation, would be quite unrealistic in terms of present-day legal
requirements. In a national bank the first-line reserve in the form of cash
would not be this large. The bank would be required to deposit in its
Federal Reserve Bank an amount equal to some percentage of its deposits.

For present purposes let us assume that this is 18 per cent. Accordingly, cash would be smaller and we would have in its place an asset item: Federal Reserve Deposits. Also, as a member of the Federal Reserve System, this bank would be required to have stock in the Federal Reserve Bank to the extent of 3 per cent of its own capital account. Thus a more realistic balance sheet would be as follows:

BALANCE SHEET
GIBRALTAR NATIONAL BANK
February 1, 1956

Assets		*Liabilities*	
Cash	$ 330,000	Deposits	$3,000,000
Federal Reserve Deposits	540,000		
Building and Equipment	100,000		
U.S. Government & Other Bonds &		*Net Worth*	
Investments	1,000,000	Capital Stock	1,000,000
Loans & Discounts	2,000,000		
Stock in Federal Reserve	30,000		
Total	$4,000,000	Total	$4,000,000

A brief review of our past banking experience will help to explain why these items would now be there and the function they perform—particularly the reserves.

Some Highlights of United States Banking Experience

We can abbreviate this excursion into history if we point up at the outset what appears from the present vantage point of hindsight to have been violations of "sound banking practice."

1. The United States was the last of the important industrial nations to organize any kind of central bank.

2. In our commitment to a laissez faire philosophy and our distrust

of any centralization of financial power, we opened the way during our so-called "free banking" period for many bankers of doubtful ability, if not questionable integrity, to engage in practices that were not in the public interest.

3. Lacking a central bank to act as its fiscal agent after 1836, the Federal government set up a system of subtreasuries to receive taxes and other public revenues and to disburse them for government expenditures. When receipts exceeded expenditures money was withdrawn from the economy and periods of "tight" money developed as a restraint on transactions.

Development of State Banks (1781–1863)

To finance the Revolutionary War, the Bank of North America was founded in Philadelphia in 1782, and chartered by the Pennsylvania legislature. The Bank of New York and the Bank of Massachusetts followed in 1784. These were the only incorporated banks existing in 1790.[9]

These banks, and others like them which followed, were able to create "money" by issuing their own *bank notes*. Such notes were obligations of the bank of issue (in form and appearance much like the representative money issued by the Treasury), and usually stated that an equivalent value in gold or silver would be paid to the bearer upon presentation at the bank. Backing for the notes was some paid-in capital—various securities and deposits—a portion of which was held in hard money or government obligations. As long as a bank could meet (or was believed to be able to meet) its agreements, its notes circulated and might not even come back for redemption. The lending of these notes at interest was a source of income to the bank. If the notes were not presented for redemption, this was an added source of gain. With poor travel and communication, the bank at any event could often count on a considerable time lag in the process. This was an encouragement to liberal issue. Days of reckoning were common, however, and distrust widespread; few who used the banks in those days were strangers to the hardship and loss involved in bank failure. Often during this period redemption in gold and silver virtually ceased.

There was an interlude during this period when we did have a central bank. The first Bank of the United States was founded by Alexander Hamilton and chartered in 1791 by the Federal government for twenty

---

[9] Few banks and no orderly banking system existed in Colonial times. There was little need for them in a predominantly self-sufficient economy. Any loans that were made were largely on a personal basis.

years. It served as the depository for Federal funds, and made some attempt to collect the notes of state banks and present them for redemption.

A stronger bank—the Second Bank of the United States—was chartered in 1816. It was capitalized at $35 million, and these funds were raised from individuals, corporations, and states, as well as 20 per cent from the Federal government. Private subscriptions had to be paid at least 25 per cent in gold or silver, the remainder in other currency or securities. The Federal government appointed a minority on the board of directors. A number of rather severe restrictions were placed on the bank, as far as acquiring property or contracting debts were concerned. It did function, however, both in the capacity of a central bank and as a commercial bank, issuing its own bank notes, making loans to business and government, accepting deposits, and transferring funds from area to area. As agent for the government it collected and disbursed funds, and as a central bank it exercised control over state banks by collecting their notes and presenting them for redemption.

Both the First and Second United States banks were unpopular with frontier peoples, who were frequent debtors and favored "easy money." The bank became involved in Federalist politics, and when its charter expired in 1836 Andrew Jackson refused to renew it.

Thereafter banks which were chartered by the various states under widely different standards, together with private (unincorporated) banks, took over the field. At first each bank had to receive its charter by a special act of the legislature. Beginning in 1837, with Michigan in the lead, the states gradually set up "free banking" laws under which any banking firm meeting specified standards might be granted a charter.

There followed a period of confused and highly variable banking practice. The number of state banks rose from 506 in 1834 to 1,601 in 1861. State bank notes outstanding increased from $95 million to $202 million in the same period. The value of the notes varied widely. As they circulated more and more, their value declined in proportion to the distance from the bank of issue. Holders of the notes saw their property claims dissipated. It was a period of "wildcat banks," which were set up in remote and inaccessible places.[10] Notes sometimes continued to circulate after the issuing bank had failed. Some states, notably New York, Massachusetts, and Louisiana, attempted to remedy the situation by more severe requirements and bank supervision. But the problem was only corrected when banking entered a new phase.

---

[10] And inhabited chiefly by "wildcats."

National Banking System (1863–1914)

In 1863 a national banking system was initiated, which provided for chartering individual (free) banks by the Federal government. The legislation under which such banks were permitted to operate was known as the National Banking Act (passed in 1863). The purpose of the Federally chartered banks was (1) to create a group of responsible institutions which could issue a uniform currency (notes) in which the public would have confidence; and (2) to create a new source for loans to the Federal government to finance the Civil War.

The first of these objectives was achieved by giving the national banks a monopoly of *note issue*. A bank which had met the capital requirements received a Federal charter and was granted the privilege of issuing its own national bank notes. Each such bank was required to accept the notes of the others at face value. A tax of 10 per cent on all state or other bank notes was imposed to (a) force them out of circulation, and (b) to put pressure on state banks to apply for Federal charters. The tax achieved its objective on the first of these counts, but failed on the second, for reasons that will soon be made clear.

Under the National Banking Act government bonds could be used as backing for the national bank notes, thereby serving the second purpose—that of financing the war—but also creating an arrangement which was to persist for fifty years. This is how it operated. A national bank might purchase interest-bearing government bonds. By depositing these bonds with the Comptroller of the Currency, the bank could then issue new notes up to 90 per cent of the value of the bonds (par value[11] or market value, whichever was smaller). The result was an expansion of the money supply. The bank earned interest both from the bonds and its notes. While this system served a useful purpose during a period of rapid expansion and development, it did not function to the satisfaction of the economic community and was ultimately replaced.

This period also saw an increasing use of demand deposits and personal checks as the circulating medium. Such instruments became practical as transportation and communication improved and as cities grew and industries expanded. Many state banks neither joined the national banking system nor went out of business when their right to issue bank notes was cut off, because the demand deposit replaced the bank note. The regulation of banks by the states was less strict. Smaller amounts of capital were required, and more diverse types of loans could be made—for example, on

---

[11] Par value was the face value printed on the bond and the amount the government would repay when the bond matured.

real estate (such loans were not permitted the national banks on the grounds that this was the function of savings banks).

While an expanding use of "check book" money permitted the co-existence of state and national banks, and became increasingly important in the operation of the latter, a need persisted for a supplementary form of currency. To meet the requirements of a rising national income, which was at the same time varied widely, a currency with some flexibility was needed. This the national banking system did not provide because its reserves were inadequate or poorly located. For example, seasonal variations in production required that the amount of currency be expanded during peak activity. This was especially true in rural areas at harvest. Payrolls were commonly met in cash, and farm people persisted in their preference for holding currency. Money withdrawn did not return until it was actually spent. Periodic money "panics" developed. During these periods the voices of the money "cranks" resounded throughout the country.

Several reasons can be advanced for the lack of flexibility in the national banking system as then constituted.

1. National bank notes were based upon government bonds. The limit of their issue was thus determined by the extent of government borrowing. Since during this period a policy of balancing the Federal budget annually was usually regarded as desirable, the bonds outstanding did not change substantially from year to year, and particularly from seasonal peaks to lows. Moreover, the volume of notes was not constant with respect to these bonds. When market value was above par, as it usually was during depressed periods, a bank which paid $120 for a bond could issue notes on the basis of 90 per cent of its $100 par value. This reduced reserves and credit.

2. The reserve requirements set up under the National Banking Act had a tendency to concentrate currency in the large cities and to "starve" the more remote sections. Three classifications of national banks had been made, based upon the type of area they served, and different reserve requirements were set for each:

a) *Country Banks,* in small cities or towns (not over 6,000 population), were required to maintain reserves of 15 per cent against both notes and deposits. Of this amount two-fifths had to be in the banks' vaults in cash; the remaining three-fifths could be either cash in the vaults or deposits with city banks of either of the other two classifications.

b) *Reserve City Banks* (cities from 6,000 to 50,000 population) were required to maintain 25 per cent reserves against notes and demand deposits. Of this amount one-half had to be cash in the vaults, while the remaining one-half might be in banks of the next higher classification.

193

Figure 9. Federal Reserve Districts and Bank Locations

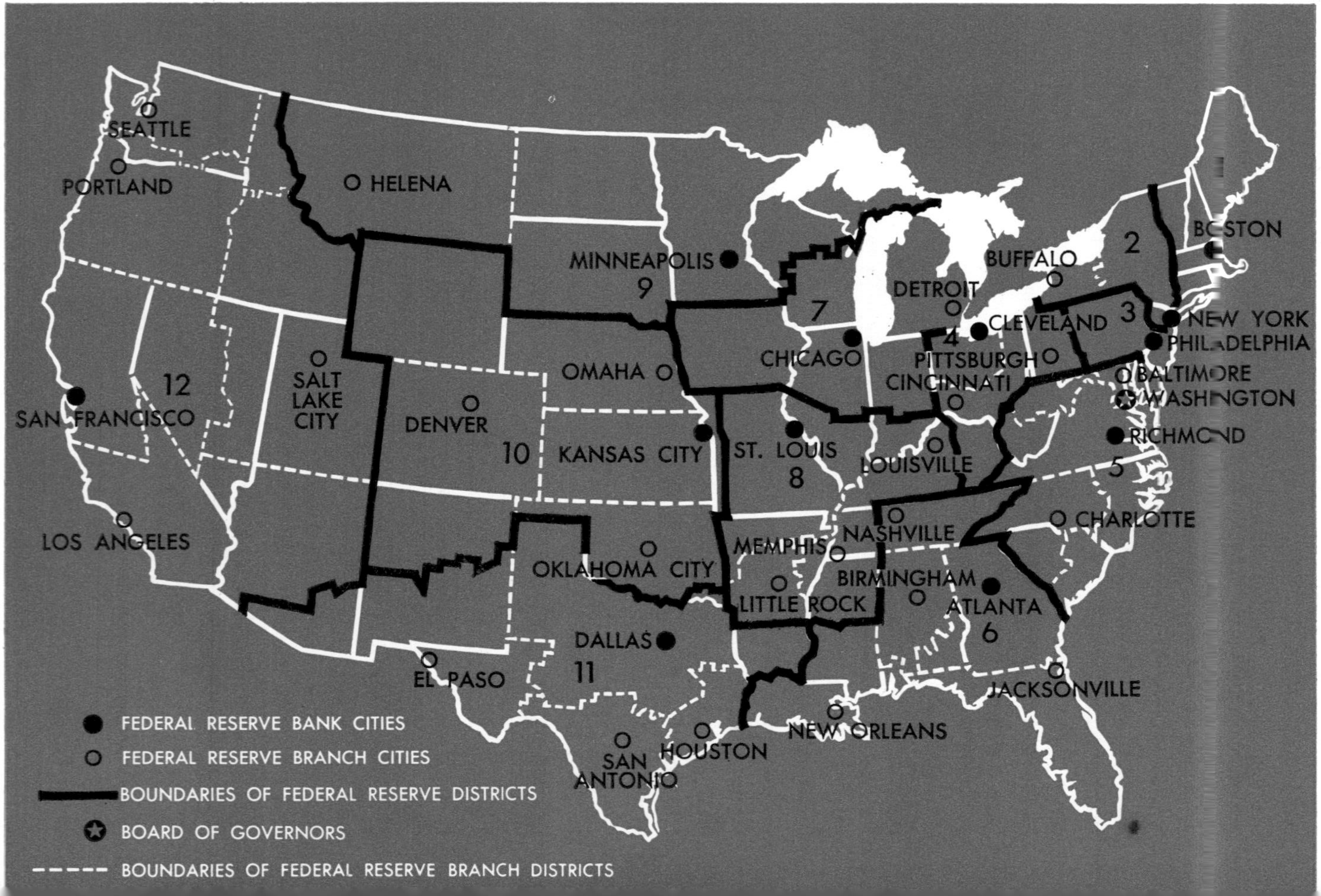

BOSTON

NEW YORK
PHILADELPHIA
BALTIMORE
WASHINGTON
RICHMOND

2
3
BUFFALO
CLEVELAND
PITTSBURGH
CINCINNATI
4
DETROIT
CHARLOTTE
5

ATLANTA
BIRMINGHAM
NASHVILLE
LOUISVILLE
MEMPHIS
LITTLE ROCK
6
JACKSONVILLE

CHICAGO
7
ST. LOUIS
8

NEW ORLEANS

MINNEAPOLIS
9
OMAHA
KANSAS CITY
OKLAHOMA CITY
10
DALLAS
11
HOUSTON
SAN ANTONIO

DENVER
EL PASO

HELENA
SALT LAKE CITY

SEATTLE
PORTLAND
12
SAN FRANCISCO
LOS ANGELES

● FEDERAL RESERVE BANK CITIES
○ FEDERAL RESERVE BRANCH CITIES
━━ BOUNDARIES OF FEDERAL RESERVE DISTRICTS
✪ BOARD OF GOVERNORS
- - - BOUNDARIES OF FEDERAL RESERVE BRANCH DISTRICTS

c) *Central Reserve City Banks* (cities above 50,000 population) were also required to maintain 25 per cent reserves in cash against notes and deposits, all in their own vaults.

The country's cash reserves tended to be pyramided in the larger cities. In off seasons, when the need for cash was slack in rural areas, any amount above the required reserves gravitated toward the larger cities where it could be deposited at interest. This would encourage the expansion of loans there. During peak seasons the smaller banks would withdraw their deposits. With a 25 per cent reserve requirement, the loss of each dollar of cash would necessarily reduce notes and loans by four dollars. This meant enforced liquidation of loans and an increased demand for cash.

3. Finally, Treasury policy contributed further to the problem. The subtreasury system, as has been noted, tended to slow down money flows by tieing up cash reserves.

From 1914 to the Present

In 1914, after extended study and discussion of banking reform, Congress established the Federal Reserve System, the counterpart of the central banks of other countries. Strictly speaking, there was established not *a* central bank but twelve such institutions, each functioning as *the* central bank of a region (Figure 9). Initially the separate banks were linked in a rather loose confederation, with a Federal Reserve Board sitting in Washington to act as a co-ordinating body. Later amendments and revisions of the original act have integrated the banks into a more centralized organization, supervised by a Board of Governors of seven members. Each governor is appointed for fourteen years by the President (confirmed by the Senate), with terms initially staggered so that now one new member is appointed every two years, and may not be reappointed after completing a full term. Members are selected for their knowledge and experience in banking and finance. The Board sits in the System's own building in Washington where its needs are served by a staff of trained specialists and research workers. The Board of Governors and the System are charged with the responsibility for maintaining, within the limits of authority and ability, a money and credit supply to fit the "needs" of the whole country.

The Reserve Banks

Each of the twelve Reserve banks[12] serves the affiliated banks of its district.

---

[12] There are also 24 branches, not, however, equally distributed among the 12 districts.

As a system, they also serve the Federal government as *fiscal agent*—collecting taxes, marketing its bonds, holding government deposits, and disbursing funds. They also serve the needs of individual firms in commerce, industry, and agriculture, as well as households, by continuing efforts to eliminate bottlenecks in orderly money flows and the channelling of credit resources to productive enterprises.

Each Reserve bank, named for the city in which it is located, has as member banks *all* national banks in its geographic area, and as many state banks as want to belong and as have met the necessary requirements. Each Reserve bank has its own board of nine directors, three representing the interests of industry, commerce, and agriculture, three representing the member banks, and three the public. The public or Class C directors are appointed by the Board of Governors; the other six are elected by the member banks. One of the Class C directors, "a person of tested banking experience," is chairman of the Board and Federal Reserve Agent; another is vice-chairman. Each bank also maintains a staff of trained administrative and research personnel.

Ownership and Operation of Reserve Banks

Why did Congress decide to set up regional banks rather than a single central bank? The answer is that the final form of the Act was a compromise. Conflicting opinions and fears, typical of most issues that come before Congress, were expressed to committees charged with reforming the banking system. Some were suspicious of control by the Federal government, some were afraid of domination by "Wall Street," and others feared sectional domination and interference with access to credit by established "big business." The United States is a large country, made up of forty-eight "sovereign" states and a diversity of regions, whose interests have often been in conflict. Congress attempted to define the twelve regions so that they would not be too different in relative economic importance and credit requirements. The task was not an easy one, and as many had feared, New York has become increasingly the dominant bank in terms of assets and reserve bank capital. Chicago is second, San Francisco third. The remaining nine are more nearly the same size (Table 7).

Another issue was raised over who should own the Reserve banks—who should subscribe the initial capital. Some wanted government ownership, others favored public subscription. In the end the capital stock was sold to member banks, who are required to hold an amount equal to 3 per cent of their paid-up capital and surplus, on which they receive 6 per cent dividends. Any earnings above the requirements for maintaining a predetermined surplus are paid to the Federal Treasury.

196

Table 7.   Federal Reserve Banks Ranked According to Total Assets,

June 30, 1957

(thousands of dollars)

Bank	Total Assets	Bank	Total Assets
1 New York	$13,190,157	7 Boston	$2,756,085
2 Chicago	8,915,203	8 Atlanta	2,562,309
3 San Francisco	5,783,373	9 Kansas City	2,181,601
4 Cleveland	4,591,461	10 St. Louis	2,077,357
5 Richmond	3,332,629	11 Dallas	2,028,368
6 Philadelphia	2,892,051	12 Minneapolis	1,051,027

Source: *Federal Reserve Bulletin*, July, 1957, p. 780.

Function

Unlike other banks, the primary objective of the Reserve banks is not to make a profit, although they do. These are "bankers' banks," and their responsibility is to provide services for the member banks, regulate and control the operations of the system according to some criteria of the general interest, and to serve as the fiscal agent of the Federal government.

All member bank reserves—a predetermined percentage of their total deposits[13]—must be deposited with the Reserve bank of their district. The pooling of these reserves at the central bank speeds up the velocity of circulation, thereby increasing the effective "working" time of money. It brings into play the "clearing" principle which we can now describe as it operates at different levels.

1. *In a particular bank.* People with deposits in the same bank transact business without handling their money. Assume that A has a deposit with a bank. He makes a purchase from B valued at $100, giving him a check on the bank. B, who also has an account with the bank (or who now decides to open one), sends the check to the bank for deposit. The bank accountant merely adds (credits) $100 to B's account and deducts (debits) the same amount from A's. The money has been working, even though it did not leave the bank. Such transactions are repeated many times daily, and while some cash may be withdrawn for small purchases, it usually is returned by businesses in short order. This illustrates how a bank can do a very large business with a relatively small amount of till money.

[13] These reserve requirements can be varied and are determined by the Reserve banks for member banks in their district, though operations among districts are closely coordinated. The maximum reserve requirement that can be set is 26 per cent for Central Reserve City banks. The minimum requirement in the case of Country Banks is 7 per cent. Reserve requirements for time deposits are 3 per cent.

197

2. *Between banks in the same city*. What happens if *B* does business with another bank in the same city, and sends the check there for deposit? The same process operates between banks. Ordinarily, over any extended period any particular bank will have as many checks drawn on other banks as they will have drawn against its deposits. In any one day this may not be true—hence the *clearing house*.[14] Messengers from each bank bring all checks drawn on other banks to a central point, usually one of the banks. There offsetting claims between each pair of banks are matched and arrangements made for paying any net difference either way. Banks usually maintain an account with the clearing house, which is either debited or credited. If one bank were losing business to the others, its clearing house account would be reduced and would have to be replenished with cash. Otherwise the account would not change from time to time.

3. *Between cities*. When a check is cashed in a city other than that of the bank on which it is drawn, the Federal Reserve banks come into the picture. If it is cashed or deposited with another bank in the district, it will be forwarded to the Reserve bank (or branch) of that district. Since reserves of all member banks in the district are on deposit there, the amount of the check is added to the reserve of the bank forwarding it and deducted from the reserve account of the bank on which it was drawn. The canceled check is sent back to the bank so that the account of the drawer may be debited. Again, a bank will be receiving out-of-town checks as well as losing reserves to out-of-town banks. Consequently, its reserves do not fluctuate widely under ordinary circumstances. Sometimes, of course, if industry in a particular town is expanding and the banks of that town are making substantial loans, out-of-town purchases of raw materials and supplies by the borrowers may reduce the reserves. When this happens the bank can borrow from its reserve bank by selling or discounting commercial paper. For example, a $5,000 note drawing 6 per cent interest may be discounted at 3 per cent for the length of time remaining until its maturity, the amount being added to its reserves. Or the local banks may sell government bonds from their portfolio of investments to the Reserve bank, the sale price being added to their reserves. As out-of-town purchases give way to sales, when finished products are ready for market, a return flow sets in.

---

[14] Legend has it that the idea of a clearing house was invented by London bank messengers who passed each other daily going to each others' banks. They discovered that if they all met at a "pub" they could save their legs and enjoy themselves while still clearing the checks. The story is probably false, but in view of the reputation of the bankers of that day (shades of Dickens!) it would have served them right if it were true.

4. *Between districts.* When a check goes out of the district in which it is drawn, the process is a little more involved. We will illustrate with an example.

Assume that a student from Detroit is attending college at Columbus, Ohio. He receives a $1,000 check from home, drawn on a Detroit bank, which he deposits in a Columbus bank. His account is credited with that amount. The Columbus bank forwards the check to the Cleveland Reserve bank, where $1,000 is added to its reserve account. The check is sent to the Detroit Branch Reserve bank, and the amount deducted from the reserve account of the bank on which it was drawn. When the member bank receives the check, it debits the account of the student's father. Through this clearing of checks there has been an effective transfer of funds without the need for actually transporting the currency across country. However, the process is not complete. As it stands, the Cleveland bank is "holding the bag." It has added to its obligations to its member bank, but has received no offsetting credit.

To make the example simple, let us say that a Cleveland student is attending school in Detroit. He receives a $1,000 check drawn on a Cleveland bank. Now the clearing is reversed. The Cleveland banks (Reserve and member bank) reduce obligations by $1,000 and the Detroit banks increase theirs. The Cleveland student will be drawing on and spending money already in Detroit, while his Detroit counterpart will be doing the same in Columbus.

Clearings among districts tend to balance out, unless income in some districts is increasing relative to others. To take care of this each of the twelve Reserve banks maintains an account at the headquarters of the Federal Reserve System in Washington. Transfers among the accounts there are used to settle positive and negative balances. If a Reserve bank depletes its account in Washington, funds must be transferred out of the district to renew its Washington balance.[15] A district which builds up a surplus will eventually transfer it out of Washington. Money and credit reserves are thus shifted to areas where there is more work for money to do.

5. *Nonmember banks.* Some 7,845 of the 14,309 banks in the United States are not members of the Federal Reserve System. How do they clear their checks? Most banks maintain deposits with other (correspondent) banks. This is a device by means of which nonmember banks can use the clearing service of the Reserve system. By keeping an account

---

[15] These transfers are accomplished by means of the gold certificates in which Reserve banks keep their reserves.

with a member bank, it can deposit out-of-town checks there and they will then clear through the system.[16]

Other Services

In addition to holding reserves, making loans, and discounting commercial paper, the Reserve banks examine the member banks to see that they are complying with banking regulations, furnish them with cash for till money, and provide other services. Through these large credit pools, a much greater volume of money "on the wing," in the form of checks, is kept busy facilitating exchanges, thereby promoting a high level of real-income flows.

Influencing Transactions Through Monetary Policy

As originally conceived by its founders, the Federal Reserve System was not intended as an agency with any very direct part in determining income levels. The prevailing view then was that the level of income is determined by real forces. In other words, the decisions of industrial, commercial, and agricultural firms were regarded as independent of outside influences. To facilitate these decisions, there was a need for a flexible currency which could be expanded and contracted as these basic economic units desired. The general regulator of the price level was still the gold standard.

The Federal Reserve System was granted the monopoly of note issue formerly held by national banks. Prior to 1945 these Federal Reserve notes were backed by 40 per cent gold and 60 per cent commercial paper (after 1933 this was a nominal gold backing, the Reserve Banks holding gold certificates; in 1945 this was reduced to 25 per cent, and the remaining 75 per cent may now include government bonds as well as commercial paper). Until 1933 Federal Reserve notes circulated as lawful money. Since then they have become *legal tender* and the principal form of currency in circulation for denominations of $5 and above. The ability of the Federal Reserve System (the Reserve and member banks) to expand the money and credit supply operates chiefly through the power to expand demand deposits, plus the issuing of Federal Reserve notes to serve as till and "pocketbook" money.

The expansion of deposits is accomplished through the lending operations of the commercial banks. The role of the Reserve banks in this process was originally envisaged as that of facilitating these loans, in

---

[16] Although nonmember banks are more numerous than member banks, they do only about 15 per cent of the total banking business.

accordance with the desires of business and industry, by increasing member bank reserves. When the Reserve banks discounted commercial paper for their member banks, crediting their reserves with the purchase price, the latter would experience what is known as excess reserves. In other words, their reserves would be larger than required by law and their liquidity position would be an indication that their profits might be increased if more loans were granted.

There was a limit to the extent that credit could be expanded. This limit was determined roughly by the gold supply the Reserve banks had to maintain behind their deposits and their notes. However, if it appeared that through liberal loan policies money-income flows were increasing so rapidly that the price level was rising, the Reserve banks had the power to *increase the reserve requirements.* In this way commercial banks would be forced to reduce their loans to build up their reserves. Thus income payments would cease to rise until effective demand and effective supply (real income) were brought back into balance.

Reserve banks also have another technique for discouraging loans. This is the *discount rate.* By raising or lowering the discount rate, rediscounting of commercial paper by the commercial banks can be made either more attractive or less attractive. There is no additional profit to be made by rediscounting paper already held, because with the higher discount rate a bank can only expect to earn on the new loan about what it was already earning on the old. The effect of this policy, however, does not end here. The higher discount or interest rate, it was formerly believed, would encourage households to save more and to loan it out at the higher interest. The greater saving would mean smaller consumer expenditures for the time being. Of course, a decline in the interest rate was believed to have the opposite effect, that is, to discourage saving, promote spending, and encourage new investment expenditures. This form of control was relied upon to maintain stability during the 1920's, and was the technique used in an attempt to head off further price rises in 1929, particularly in stock market prices. The failure of this effort led to a decline in confidence that the interest rate could be relied upon as an instrument for controlling inflation.

A third method available to the Federal Reserve System for influencing loans by the commercial banks is that of *open-market operations.* An open-market committee—before 1933 dominated by the Reserve banks, but since that time by the Board of Governors' majority— affects reserves directly by buying (or selling) government bonds on the open market. These may be purchased (or sold) by banks or by depositors. If they are purchased by member banks, they are paid for by reducing reserves with the Reserve bank; if purchased by individuals, the checks in clearing through the Reserve banks are deducted from the member banks' reserves. The contraction in these reserves has a still more pronounced effect on the credit supply. If the legal reserves are 20 per cent, this means that for every dollar reduction in reserves, deposits must be reduced $5, providing, of course, no excess reserves exist. To bring deposits in line with reserves, old loans may not be renewed as they fall due, nor new loans made until old ones are paid off. The effect is to restrain the flow of new income payments, thereby serving as a check on money income flows and the pressure on prices.

By way of summary then, the Federal Reserve System has three methods for influencing the amount of money and credit in circulation and—through the effect of this on loans—the rate of national-income payments. These are: (1) increasing or decreasing the reserve requirements; (2) raising or lowering the discount rate; and (3) open-market operations.

Modification since 1933

An almost complete collapse of the banking and financial system of the United States in the winter of 1932–33 inspired changes and shifts of emphasis in Federal Reserve organization and practice. We have already noted some of these changes as they were reflected in modification of monetary standards.

These reforms paralleled an increasing participation by government in the income processes. At the time this was called "pump priming." The analogy should be clear. Like the priming of an old-fashioned water pump, the injection of liquid funds into the circular income flow was regarded as a means for filling the money and credit pipelines. To insure against a future drying up of money and credit flows, however, there was built into the Federal Reserve System a number of permanent features which marked a departure from the primarily laissez faire philosophy which characterized the original act.

From the outset the Federal Reserve banks were intended to be privately owned institutions. Although there were some who advocated their outright nationalization in 1933, this was not the prevailing view and they remained private institutions owned by the member banks. Some of their freedom of action, however, was circumscribed. The governing body, renamed the Board of Governors as noted above, was given greater powers to regulate the types of loans a commercial bank could make. More rigorous inspection was imposed, and compliance was enforced through threats of loss of membership in the system and the withdrawal of borrowing privileges. Membership in the open-market committee was changed to give a majority voting power to the Board of Governors rather than to the representatives of the Reserve banks.

In the Banking Act of 1933 and subsequent amendments, especially during World War II and the postwar years, the Board of Governors was granted powers to regulate specific types of credit, particularly for consumer purchases,[17] and loans to speculators on the security and commodity markets.

Federal Deposit Insurance Corporation

The bank failures in the early 1930's aggravated the great depression and contributed to the decline of national income and product. By immobilizing deposits they cramped the production and purchasing plans of many. The psychological impact was also very great, discouraging buying and encouraging efforts to increase liquidity. Many withdrew deposits in order to hold their savings in cash. Banks were unable to renew or make new loans, and households were forced to liquidate property holdings. Banks became the owners of farms and other business properties which they could neither sell nor operate efficiently.

In March 1933 all banks were closed on executive order of the President. Only those regarded as solvent were permitted to reopen. As confidence in banks returned, action was started to create another institution, which would represent a still higher pooling of credits that could be used only for meeting the obligations of banks which in the future should become insolvent. This was to become, in 1935, the Federal Deposit Insurance Corporation. The sources of funds for this institution were four: (1) capital funds of $289 million, subscribed by the Treasury and the Federal Reserve banks, (2) sale of the corporation's own bonds, (3) insurance premiums paid by insured banks, and (4) earnings from the investment of unused funds.

All member banks of the Federal Reserve System, both national and state, were required to join the FDIC and to pay an annual premium of $\frac{1}{2}$ of 1 per cent of total deposits. At the outset $5,000 of each depositor's total deposits were insured. After World War II, as the fund expanded, coverage was extended to $10,000.

The purpose of the FDIC is to safeguard the banking system against the runs of panicky depositors, such as occurred in the 1930's. The knowledge that funds are insured reduces such fears and saves the banking system from strain. An effect of creating this type of institution was to bring under closer supervision and control of a Federal agency most of

---

[17] The power to regulate consumer credit was a temporary grant during the Korean war. It is not now in force.

the remaining state banks which had remained outside the Federal Reserve System. The right to insure their deposits under the FDIC was extended to the nonmember state banks. Most of them did so, of course, since depositors were unwilling to do business with banks which could not afford them the same security available at member banks. Thereby they came under the regulation and inspection of the FDIC, as strict in most respects as those of the Federal Reserve System.

From our past experience with the money and banking system, and from the trial and error of revision and modification we have derived what we now have. In recent years voices have been raised in favor of a thorough inquiry (preferably by an independent commission) into the many institutional changes that have occurred since the last such investigation preceding the founding of the Federal Reserve System. They point to the rise of a whole new set of influences on liquidity—the giant insurance companies, health and welfare funds and investment trusts, internal financing by large corporations and consumer-credit agencies—all exercising an influence on money flows. Many of these are not subject to controls, or to the same controls, as the older banking institutions. We can perhaps ask of the present arrangement, "What has been its performance during our recent years of expansion?" Table 8 shows something of what has happened with several aggregates.

Table 8. Parallel Changes for Selected Years in National Income
and Money Supply
(billions of dollars)

Year	National Income	Total Deposits and Currency	Demand Deposits	Currency Outside Banks
1929	87.8	54.7	26.4	3.6
1939	72.8	64.7	36.2	6.4
1949	216.2	173.9	111.2	25.4
1954	299.0	214.8	134.4	27.9
1955	324.1	221.0	138.2	28.3
1956	343.6	226.4	139.7	28.3

Source: Economic Report of the President, 1958.

Foreign Exchange

There is a purely monetary aspect of international trade and the balance of payments mentioned earlier which can be treated most conveniently here. It will be discussed under two headings: the exchange rate, and the clearing process in international trade.

The Exchange Rate

National currencies are bought and sold as part of the trading operations among nations. The *exchange rate* is simply a price of one of these national monetary units in terms of another. For example, the British pound during 1948 could be purchased at $4.03. In 1949, as a result of actions taken by the British Treasury, it dropped to $2.80. This exchange rate can be viewed two ways. A pound, which in 1948 could purchase $4.03, in 1949 could buy only $2.80. Dollars had become more expensive in terms of pounds. On the other hand, one who used dollars to buy pounds had to pay $4.03 per pound in 1948, but in late 1949 could buy the same for $2.80. For the American tourists traveling in England, this lower rate for the British pound meant that the dollar would now buy more of whatever goods and services the economy of that country had to offer. For the importing firm, it meant that the same amount of British goods, in terms of pound value, could be purchased for fewer dollars.

Nationals of one country, whether households or firms or government agencies, buy foreign currencies because they cannot use their own money in the country in question. Because the volume of exchanges between countries runs into large amounts, it is useful to think of these exchanges or flows in real and money terms, just as in the case of the national-income flows. For any extended period real flows must be balanced by real flows, hence the monetary aspects of this exchange are simply another case of clearing, such as we observed in operation between Federal Reserve districts.

International Clearings

We can begin with the simplest case, where the goods and services exchanged under a given rate of exchange balance each other exactly. Assume that a New York importer desired to purchase in England 500 cashmere sweaters, which he expects to sell at $20 each. The price in England is £5. At an exchange rate of $2.80 = £1, the cost will be $14 each, or $7,000 total. Since the American importer has only dollars to spend, let us say he pays this amount over to a New York bank to facilitate the exchange. Through an arrangement with a correspondent in London, this bank arranges for the payment of £2,500 to the British manufacturer. We will now assume that at the same time a British textile firm arranges to import 200 bales of cotton at $35 per bale, a total cost of $7,000. The textile merchant pays £2,500 (the cost of the cotton

205

in pounds) to the same London bank, which arranges for the New York correspondent bank to pay $7,000 to the New Orleans cotton broker.

We can now generalize the process illustrated by the example. Imports into the United States give rise to a supply of dollar exchange and a demand for pound exchange. Exports from the United States give rise to a demand for dollar exchange here, and a supply of pounds in England. In the example cited the supply of money available for foreign exchange is exactly equal to the demand for it. The two cancel out, and we can regard the cotton as having been exchanged for cashmere sweaters. (Other costs, such as transportation, insurance, banking services, etc., were neglected for purposes of simplification.)

Actually, of course, the specific exchanges do not balance so neatly. The markets for foreign exchange are highly developed, and the clearings become general rather than specific. Let us say that during a period such as a year American importers make available a $280-million supply of dollar exchange, which means that there is created at the same time a demand for £100 million. On the other hand, British imports equal $420 million, or a supply of £150 million. There would be $140 million worth of American exports not balanced by imports. If this situation occurred under conditions of free market exchange, the exchange rate would change under pressure of an excess of pounds. The pound would fall (or the dollar rise), with a resulting shift in the real flows. Pressure on the pound might be eased by borrowing, and the positive United States balance of trade (negative British balance) could continue so long as credit sources were available.

When the two nations operated on a gold standard trade balances could be brought about by shipping gold back and forth. By means of triangular trade a three-way balance might be achieved, as was the case when England had a negative balance with the United States but a positive balance with southeast Asia where we purchased rubber and tin. If, as was true prior to 1914 and for a period during the 1920's, the pound and the dollar were both defined in terms of gold, the exchange rate would ordinarily remain fairly close to the ratio of the two gold contents. The pound, defined as 113 grains of pure gold, and the dollar as 23.22 grains, had an exchange ratio to each other of £1 = $4.87.

Following the abandonment of the gold standard in the 1930's most countries set up stabilization funds to maintain their exchange rates. From the profit it made on devaluation of the dollar the United States created a $2 billion reservoir which was used to buy up any excess of dollar exchange. Other countries did the same, except for periodic devaluations calculated to stimulate exports by making their markets an attractive place for foreigners to buy.[18]

Since World War II the chronic dollar shortages of England and other Western nations have been an indication of the very large surplus of real goods and services these countries have had to purchase from the United States. We have become the great creditor nation of the world. Only through the granting of large credits (and gifts) have these countries been able to buy as much from us as they have.

Discussion
Questions

1. Can you state what money "really" is in terms of a gold standard? Why was it believed that people would prefer to hold gold as an asset?

2. What is the "state" theory of money? How much validity does it have?

3. When someone says, "I keep my money in the bank," is he speaking literally or figuratively?

4. Why, in your opinion, are banks vested with a higher degree of public interest than other business firms?

5. What philosophy lay behind the belief in a system of free banking? What experience appears to indicate that this philosophy was not well founded?

6. Argue the case, pro and con, for a nationalized central bank.

7. Describe how a commercial banking system, operating on a 100 per cent reserve system, might function.

---

[18] This will be discussed in Part 6.

National Income

and Public Policy

ECONOMISTS SOMETIMES DISAGREE on what policies are best suited to maintain high-level employment and income—though perhaps less than formerly. In modern economic literature as well as popular discussion these disagreements concern the relative effectiveness (and desirability) of *monetary* and *fiscal* policy, piecemeal government intervention versus long-range government planning.

To some, such discussions are now regarded as academic. We have already had the longest period of sustained high-level employment and rising income in history. Have we found the way to make depressions obsolete, to flatten the business cycle? Some would argue that the Keynesians have carried the day. Others worry about inflation and a possible time of reckoning. Still others feel that high-level employment purchased with increasing government intervention may be too high a price to pay. Behind these attitudes toward questions of public policy, of what can be done and what ought to be done, the subtle influence of the value judgments discussed in Chapter 4 can be detected.

This section explores the relation of these value judgments to the evaluation which different economists make of public policy, where the latter is concerned with the level of resource use. Some experience data from nations with different value commitments are also cited.

CHAPTER 11

Alternative Routes to Full Employment

UNDER THE CLASSIFICATION established in Chapter 4 we will describe policy prescriptions as they are influenced by three general ideal models: (1) laissez faire or market supremacy, (2) planned economy or central direction, and (3) pragmatic or mixed control.

Laissez Faire

To those who desire a minimum of government, the level of resource use and employment is not regarded as a separate problem. Specifically, they do not perceive it as a problem which government should attempt to deal with other than in an indirect way. Fearing bureaucracy, distrusting centralization, and convinced of the virtues of private enterprise regulated only by free consumer choice in a competitive market, economists like Von Mises and Hayek, publicists like Henry Hazlitt, and many others would rely on what they regard as the natural laws of supply and demand to achieve the objectives of optimum real income. Among these laws or forces they would include: an almost unlimited capacity in human beings to want goods and services, and hence to seek an income in order to obtain them; an understanding by consumers of what they want that is superior to any that could ever be available to a central planning agency attempting to maintain full employment by directing factors of production into public projects; and finally the essentially self-centered nature of man, which appears to render him incapable of putting forth his best efforts whenever he cannot be made to feel that he is responsible for his own welfare, his own property, and his own actions. In short, those who share this system of values believe that viewing the economy as a whole and attempting to deal with the economic problem at the macro-level will render the other important economic or income problems of what to

209

produce and how to distribute the product more difficult if not impossible of solution.

This does not mean that those who adhere to the traditions of nineteenth-century liberalism (particularly those who follow a point of view described earlier as positive laissez faire) see no role for the central government in economic life, or discount entirely the usefulness of an over-all view of the economy. Many of them have accepted the hypothesis of the essential instability of investment behavior, and of the importance of investments in maintaining income levels. They reject, however, the inference from the "new economics" that such instability is inherent in an advanced industrial society or that a high propensity to save makes it increasingly difficult to offset such saving by new investments. Accordingly, they oppose the idea of increased investment in the public sector of the economy as a means to compensate for a failure of investment to keep pace in the private sector.

They stress, rather, government action to maintain an economic (income) environment favorable to *private* investment. Since the multiplier principle, if it can be regarded as a realistic relationship, will operate whether the investment be public or private, income levels and employment *can* be maintained equally well by the latter, without risking the continued encroachment of government in economic life.

There is an inherent distrust of any substantial use of deficit financing by government. Government budgets *ought* to be balanced, or an attempt made to balance them. The influence of the public sector of the economy can thus be kept neutral. Otherwise a fluctuating price level will bias market allocation of the factors of production, through induced investment, to the extent that production decisions by firms will be distorted and the kinds and quantities of specific goods will lose contact with consumer preferences.

Monetary policy, namely, the control of money and credit, rather than government budget manipulation, is more highly regarded as an instrument for maintaining a favorable environment for investment. Investment, except for obvious public improvements such as parks, roads, flood control, public buildings, and so forth, should be left in private hands to be decided on the basis of profitability.

Recognizing that profitability loses contact with real contributions to output if a fluctuating price level stimulates excessive *induced* investments, market defenders favor a monetary and credit management which permits flexibility, but which holds in check the inflationary pressures that stem from monetary overinvestment. Some who hold this position would take away from the commercial banking system much of its present discretionary control over money and credit. They would, in effect, abolish reserve banking by requiring *100 per cent reserves*. A national monetary authority (central bank) would issue currency equivalent to the value of all bank deposits, to be held in the reserves of every type of bank. No bank could then loan more than the amount of money "stored" with it. This would give a monetary authority, operating under strict rules, the control needed to execute a consistent policy. Falling prices and the appearance of unemployment would be a clue to the authority that liquidity preference was increasing. The issuance of more money through the purchase of bonds and commercial paper would result in an immediate increase of bank money available for lending. On the other hand, rising prices would be a cue to the monetary authority that it should decrease the supply of liquid funds and thus slow down the rate of making new loans.

Not all economists who see themselves as upholding the private enterprise tradition would go this far. They maintain, rather, that a monetary authority or central banking system based upon some modified gold standard or nondiscretionary type of managed currency would be adequate. The stability assured by this type of monetary policy would encourage autonomous investments adequate to assure high-level income and employment. As long as there are segments of the population with many unsatisfied wants, no nation need be limited by lack of investment opportunities, they believe, provided rigid controls over income getting and income spending, either public or private, are prevented from developing. Technological changes can supply, and have in the past supplied, new and better ways of providing for old needs, and have created new goods and services to satisfy new wants. These require continuing investments.

The other area of "legitimate" government intervention in economic life, in the view of this ideological position, would be at a lower level, in the searching out and breaking up of monopoly. We will postpone this aspect of their policy prescriptions until Part 3.

Centralized or
Planned Economy

To the convinced socialist or communist and others who believe in a planned and centrally-directed economic system, thinking in terms of a macromodel is neither unusual nor new. To them, complete freedom of the individual per se is an illusion. So much of what the individual is, and what he can become, is conferred upon him by the society of which he

211

is a part that even to imagine an individual in isolation does serious damage to reality.

Property rights have always been conferred upon the individual by society, and even in Anglo-Saxon common law no right can be defended which does not at the same time imply an obligation. Modern economic life, along with the co-operative effort which it entails, is already a system of discipline which needs only to be recognized and "rationalized" to make way for purposive planning for a frontal assault against the problem of scarcity. All that stands in the way is a system of property rights and special privilege inherited from the past. If the nonhuman factors of production were to be nationalized and their allocation or use *determined by a plan* which seeks to achieve the optimum output of goods and services, the economic problem as we know it could be solved in a manner at once more purposeful and equitable than is possible under the "anarchy of capitalism."

Those who advocate a centrally-directed economic organization would insist that the instabilities arising out of the inequalities between savings and investment, characteristic of an enterprise economy, would not be a problem under planning. The central bank of such an economy would be strategically situated to maintain an equilibrium between the real-income flows and the national income. Household income would either be spent as consumption expenditures or saved. Since savings could only be held as cash, deposited in the banks, or used to purchase government bonds, central banking statistics would provide at all times an accurate estimate of funds available for investment and the level of investment required to maintain the income flows.

A planned program for economic development would at the same time provide a continuing source of new investment opportunities. If at any time aggregate demand were inadequate to absorb the current output, a system of consumer credit through lending by the banks could prevent goods from piling up and prices from falling.

Central Planning in the Soviet Union

That a centrally-directed economy, with sufficient powers for creating or reducing new income claims, could more easily attain an equilibrium between the twin income flows does seem likely from the only evidence we have. For example, at the end of World War II, when most countries were plagued by rising prices induced by excessive liquid funds in the hands of consumers, the Soviet Union was no exception. Governing authorities there met this problem by wiping out vast quantities of money. All outstanding currency was withdrawn from circulation and replaced by new money.

212

During a prescribed period the old currency could be exchanged for new. Those with small holdings were able to convert at an almost equivalent rate. Beyond a specified amount, however, the old money could only be exchanged at a rate of ten (old) to one (new). A balance between liquid holdings and stocks of available goods having been re-established, price control and rationing could be abolished without fear of further inflation. This action by the authorities wiped out large hoards held by so-called speculators, who had accumulated large sums through *black-market* operations during the war.

Since its founding in 1918 the Soviet Union has never known an investment problem. Predominantly agricultural and ambitious to be an industrial power, the country has always had a backlog of investments. Under such circumstances the claims of the Soviet Union that it has never had unemployment are unimpressive, and not especially meaningful as an indicator of how well a wealthy industrial society, democratically controlled, might function under socialism. However, a brief examination of the procedures followed in balancing its national-income flows will be of interest in illustrating their methods for dealing with levels of resouce use.

In 1929, at the beginning of the first of her five-year plans, the Soviet Union initiated an ambitious investment program to transform the predominantly peasant society into an industrial economy. To do this without the aid of outside capital required that labor and other factors of production be shifted from consumption-goods industries (chiefly food) to heavy industries. Policies were aimed at increasing human effort, while holding in check any desire for greater consumption. Initially, large exports of grain and timber were used to pay for machinery imports. To secure labor from the farms, the mechanization of agriculture was speeded up. Tractor stations to provide mechanical power for the new collective farms were established. As income payments to the large new army of workers increased, prices in the regular markets were allowed to rise, limiting consumption to the level of available output. For favored workers special factory stores were established where limited amounts of basic necessities could be purchased at lower prices. To encourage effort prizes were awarded for production records. To secure food and fibres for the favored industrial workers taxes were collected "in kind" from the collective farms. Propaganda campaigns were launched by the Communist party, medals and special orders of Lenin and Stalin were created to give *status in lieu of income*. Registration by a system of passports was instituted to prevent workers from changing jobs without permission, thereby insuring that labor, as well as materials, could be channeled into the planned new industries. Prices became an important instrument of policy, adjusting avail-

213

able supply to the rising effective demand generated by the large new investments in industrial development.

Finally, "savings" were channeled through Gosbank, the Soviet central bank. This so-called *rationalized* banking system was established with specialized banking services to different industries, such as agriculture, the tractor stations, and regional industrial trusts. Credit was distributed among the different branches and divisions of industry allocating the factors of production according to the plans of the Central Planning Board. Since World War II this system of directing and controlling resources has continued, with the creation of large new financial institutions whose function is to channel goods and raw materials from the satellite countries to the Soviet Union.

Employment Level Under Democratic Socialism

Immediately following World War II Great Britain, under a Labour government, embarked upon a program of planned investment, nationalization, and important social-welfare services to all consumers. Both major political parties had been committed to "full employment" policies or the use of the government's full financial strength to insure against the kind of unemployment England had known between the two world wars (the social-welfare program adopted by Labour had been designed by William Beveridge, an economist of the older Liberal tradition). The Labour party argued that, with its program of nationalization for coal and transport (both in need of new capital) and for other basic industries, investment would be accomplished on a more "rational" basis, insuring against the erratic, piecemeal investment of the past.

During Labour's one term in office Great Britain struggled under a very large burden of foreign debt. Successive loans and grants from the United States and Canada cannot be minimized as factors which assisted in new investment and the reconstruction of war-damaged industries. It is true that no serious unemployment problem arose, as had been feared. In this, England was no exception among the industrialized nations. Thus the evidence cannot be said to have been conclusive as far as Labour's claims of its ability to maintain high-level output is concerned. The fiscal policy of the Labour party, which advocated rather mild central planning, cannot be said to differ markedly from that espoused by a more pragmatic approach.

A second example may be cited where a moderate form of central planning, particularly in fiscal policy, has had a longer history. The Social Democratic party (allied with the Agrarian party since 1951) has been in office in Sweden for more than thirty years. Among the party advisers have been a number of Swedish economists whose attention to fiscal policy as a means of stabilizing a whole economy antedates that of Keynes. With a core of nationalized industries (including power) and a tax and spending policy managed with an eye to levels of employment, the Social Democrats have maintained a rather stable economy, which has at the same time achieved a level of living second only to that of the United States.

Pragmatic or
Mixed Control

Some have claimed that the public policies of the New Deal, as well as similar policies of other Western nations after 1930, can be traced to the influence of Keynes and his followers (who included an increasing number of professional economists after 1936). It is arguable, however, that far from being an influence which brought about a change in governmental practice and produced institutional changes, the shift in the economists' point of view was a belated recognition of a major shift in the income processes. The concept and model of the "mixed economy," with its greater interdependence, and an expanded public economy can be interpreted as a closer approximation to economic "reality" than the highly individualistic model of pure capitalism or free enterprise.[1]

What were the policy recommendations which resulted from this shift in point of view? On the assumption that a sustained high level of resource use is an objective generally acceptable, many economists believed that the financial strength of the national government should be used to intervene in the income process. For the immediate objective of getting out of the depression the government ought to unbalance its budget by spending more than its current receipts. This was a departure from accepted doctrine and the prescriptions of most economists up to that time, who had usually regarded it as "sound finance" to balance the government budget annually.

The *deficit budget* could be realized in either of two ways, or by a combination of both: (1) through increased spending for public works and relief (transfer payments), to be financed by borrowing; or (2) through a reduction in taxes, leaving more money in peoples' hands while continuing to maintain or to increase levels of government expenditure.

---

[1] For a book which throws some light on the above observation see *Beckoning Frontiers* (Knopf, 1951) by Marriner S. Eccles. Mr. Eccles, a successful banker and financier who experienced the banking collapse of 1930–33 (and, incidentally, weathered it successfully), reached conclusions very similar to and somewhat in advance of those of Keynes. Later Mr. Eccles was to become chairman of the Board of Governors of the Federal Reserve System.

215

As a consequence of either action it was predicted that liquid funds in the hands of households would increase until the desire to hoard or to hold cash had been satisfied. Then a rising level of consumer expenditures, an increase in total effective demand, would provide an incentive to business firms, who, seeing new opportunities for profit, would increase output, employ more of the factors of production, and thereby generate still further increases in disposable consumer income through the leverage effect.

It will be apparent from our foregoing discussion why this might be expected to happen. Increased consumer expenditures, setting into motion the acceleration effect on the capital-goods industries, would stimulate increased employment there. Government investment, as well as private investment, would exert an upward influence on national income and employment through the multiplier.

Would such a policy result in a price rise that would cause living costs to rise faster than wages, because of time lags and delays inherent in the production process? Keynes answered this question in the affirmative. In an enterprise economy this is not only likely, but desirable. For as prices of consumption goods rise, even slightly, profit opportunities improve, thereby serving as a stimulus to production. However, it is a hypothesis of macroanalysis that this price rise will not be significant as long as unemployment persists. Industries can secure additional productive services without substantially increasing the costs of their output. Keynes believed that the habitual perception of income in dollar terms would obscure the fact of a slight fall in real wages due to the decline in the value of the dollar. In other words, when there is unemployment prices of goods can rise slightly without creating immediate union demands for wage increases.

The classical economists, it will be recalled, had usually advocated a a cut in money wages as the means to reduce costs and encourage the expansion of production by firms. Such cuts, however, usually have been resisted by organized labor, and are unpopular with employees. The decrease of real income through the rise in the price of wage-goods was thus regarded as a simpler way to achieve the same objective.

Critics of the above policy maintain that it represents a depression philosophy, a spending philosophy, shortsighted and conducive to waste. Defenders of the policy hold that this criticism stems from a misunderstanding of what Keynes believed. They submit that this policy can be applied equally to depression and to boom conditions.

When should deficit financing by government be reversed? Certainly if money-income flows continue to increase indefinitely inflation will result. Once high-level employment of the factors of production has been achieved and the economy has reached an output close to its physical capacity, inflationary pressures can be predicted. Then deficit financing needs to be reversed. A higher income level will have increased the yield of taxes, bringing the Federal budget more nearly into balance. If necessary to stop inflationary pressures, taxes could be increased, the surplus being used to retire bonds issued during the deficit period.

Estimating the precise point at which capacity output has been reached is admittedly a difficult task. No measure of full employment of all factors of production is possible. We now estimate unemployment in the labor force. At any given time, even at high-level output, a reservoir of unemployed is likely to exist. Many of these will be persons in transit from one job to another, since ordinarily some industries are expanding, others contracting. Such a reservoir functions to provide flexibility in the industrial system, to permit shifts in production as tastes change and new products appear. At a high-level output, however, individuals who occupy the reservoir will be changing jobs, and no one who is otherwise employable need remain for very long. When the number of unemployed begins to increase and individuals remain out of a job for an extended period, this is an indication of contraction in the economy and becomes a signal for action in reversing the trend.

On the other hand, the general price level serves as a signal for inflationary tendencies. A slowly rising price level, when there is unemployment, may be desirable. At high-level employment rising prices create inflationary pressures and distortions.

Thus these two indices have been offered as clues to when action should be taken, if an economy is to avoid unemployment on the one hand and inflation on the other. This can be described as an *equilibrium* between the money-income flows on one side and real-income flows on the other, at or near the upper limit of productive capacity. Its justification rests on a belief that high-level production is in the general interest. A defense of this pragmatic position must be made in terms of answers to several important questions.

1. *In view of past production records, which show a long-run growth of real income that is unparalleled, why has it been necessary to depart from the time-honored policy of fiscal or budgetary neutrality in the public sector of the economy?* Past records, it can be pointed out, do not show an unbroken record of economic progress. Ups and downs in the income processes have been experienced as gluts and shortages of purchasing powers, with resulting ups and downs in real income. These variations are associated with changes in levels of resource use, which can be traced to shifts in human expectations and decisions rather than to "real" causes. In other words, without loss of skills, without the destruction of important re-

sources, and with a technology which has improved from year to year due to the growth of scientific knowledge, there have been periods when the annual product has fallen behind the high levels previously obtained. Wesley Mitchell, after many years devoted to the study of the business cycle, concluded that far from being due to a malfunctioning of a free-enterprise society these instabilities were inherent in it. The fact that decisions to save and decisions to invest are made by different functional groups in an enterprise society, and that there may not be very close coordination between the two, makes the attainment of equilibrium a matter of chance rather than design under a laissez faire ideology.

Early in the history of economic thought Malthus foresaw such a contradiction in the logic of the "capitalist" process. In an exchange of letters with Ricardo he warned that oversaving might cause a breakdown in the income process. When investments are made with the expectation of larger sales and greater profits at some future time, these sales will be forthcoming only if the income claims generated in their production are used to buy them. Too great emphasis on saving, he believed, might so restrict effective demand that unsold goods would discourage investment and cause the whole process to break down.

Malthus' solution was novel. He felt that there should be a professional consuming class—the churchmen, the landed aristocracy, and the capitalists themselves. With a leisure class devoting itself to the arts, to the advancement of culture, the incentive to continue production would be maintained.

Malthus' concern with an internal contradiction in the free-enterprise model was ignored by the main body of the classical tradition in economic thought until Keynes "rediscovered" it, reproducing it in the *General Theory* along with other notes on the underconsumption theories of the trade cycle.

Alvin H. Hansen, one of Keynes's earliest interpreters on the American scene, has hypothesized on some possible explanations for national-income variations. His analysis has been called the "stagnation thesis," the substance of which is as follows. As long as the frontier existed in the United States (and in other nations of the New World), the spatial expansion of economic activity required a continuing large volume of investment. The building of canals, railroads, and highways required large capital expenditures. While the virgin resources, rich farm lands, timber reserves, and mineral deposits remained unexploited, they held out income opportunities for individuals both at home and from abroad. However, the passing of the frontier, the filling up of intervening space, and an increasing accumulation of capital little by little removed the "urgency" for investment. It

218

became less automatic, while the increased savings from higher income levels reduced the relative effectiveness of aggregate demand, and with it the prospects for investment returns high enough to induce firms to risk their funds in new ventures, except under the most favorable circumstances, such as prevailed after a depression. Hansen has also pointed to the fact that, while early development was largely capital using in its requirements, modern technology and management efficiency have resulted in capital saving. Machines are more efficient in design, since modern lubrication and alloy steel have lengthened their productive life. Large corporations with substantial depreciation reserves can finance their own investments without having to borrow household savings. Hansen sees all of these influences creating the buildup of instability which resulted in the tremendous collapse of the 1930's.

Critics of Hansen and Keynes (and their followers) have sometimes charged them with undermining free-enterprise society by a lack of faith in the capacity of human beings to want, particularly in the light of the many low-income households in even the richest nation. Keynes insisted that he was basically a "capitalist," concerned lest the free-enterprise society, in failing to prevent collapse of the income processes, bring down its whole social structure because of pressures created by idle men and idle machines. Hansen, too, has denied that his recommended use of government fiscal policy or compensatory spending to promote investment means a denial of the capacity of an enterprise society to continue its economic progress. He says only that we can no longer rely on investments being made automatically. Only if they are consciously promoted may we possess any kind of assurance of stable growth.

Such hypotheses are not easily proved or disproved. They are derived from selected historical observations. They leave unexplained why the breakdown of the income processes came in 1930, not earlier or later. As a model of past experience, the system contains paradoxes which are not fully resolved.

2. *Can we point to any body of experience as evidence that a controlled, flexible federal budget can be effective in maintaining high level income?* During the 1930's when "pump priming" was being tried, many critics pointed to the slow recovery from the depression lows compared with other economic breakdowns in the past. By 1939 there were still nearly 9 million unemployed. In 1937 a sharp "recession" occurred, despite efforts of the Federal government to prevent it.

Some economists, on the other hand, point out that the early efforts at deficit financing were half-hearted and inadequate, and that the 1937 recession occurred because of a "premature" attempt to achieve a balanced

219

budget.[2] As support for their position, they stress the fact that once the defense and war spending got under way after 1939 the nation rapidly achieved full employment and unprecedented levels of output. Since the war we have had large government budgets and the level of employment has continued high. The ideal of 60 million jobs, once emblemed as visionary and impractical, was attained and surpassed. Large governmental expenditures, coupled with high-level consumption and investment expenditures, however, have been associated with a steadily rising level of prices (at times rapidly rising), which poses another important question.

3. *In a predominantly private-enterprise economy, operating in an environment of political democracy, can a program of government spending, once embarked upon, be reversed?* This question in turn raises two corollary questions:

a) What is the effect of a constantly expanding public debt?

b) Will the struggle for income advantage among different economic interest groups through political pressure result in undermining the entire private sector of the economy?

Economists who support the pragmatic approach to national-income stability have assumed that government agencies charged with control of the Federal budget, with money and credit policies, and with debt management, can reverse their programs when the twin indicators of employment and price level provide the clues. They do not foresee or desire rigid controls for the entire economy beyond the control over aggregate money-income flows. *Size* of debt, they maintain, is not a matter of primary concern; its *rate of growth* is. The reason the rate of growth is important will be clear if we consider the nature of the public debt. A national debt which is owed by a government to its own citizens is something different from one that is held by foreigners. National debt accumulates when government spending exceeds taxes. This means that citizens are left with property or income claims they would not have had if the taxes had been collected at the time income was created by government spending. The debt thus becomes an accounting figure which represents, operationally, at least, a delay in balancing the national books in order to discover who finally owns what. If the debt were to be paid, this is what would happen. The government would collect taxes from some or all of us, depending on the kind of taxes employed, in order to pay off its bonds. Payments would likewise be made to some or all of us, depending on who held the bonds. If this were done, some might be worse off, others better off.

The same physical assets, the same skills and capacities for producing goods and services, would be as they were before. The pattern of owner-

---

[2] See especially Marriner Eccles, *op. cit.*, pp. 287–323.

ship, however, might be quite different. The situation would be somewhat analogous to that of a corporate enterprise which, as a going concern, is confronted by all of its creditors (including the stockholders) demanding that they be paid off in cash or in kind, so that they can see what they *really* own. Such a "settling up," of course, does not ordinarily occur. As long as creditors are being paid their interest or their dividend income, they are getting all they ever hoped or expected to get. Property represents a claim to income, and is not ordinarily valued for any other purposes.

Interest on the public debt, as we have already noted, represents an income transfer. It is not balanced by an equal and opposite real-income flow. Thus, if the national debt were to grow at an extremely rapid rate at a time when the national income was not also expanding, interest payments could result in significant redistribution of the income flows. This would in all likelihood be upsetting to income expectations, and therefore to consumption and investment decisions. That is why some economists have counseled only that care be exercised to keep the rate of expansion of the government interest payments less than that of national-income growth.

Experience since the 1930's has indicated a debt "tolerance" far greater than once was believed possible. Congress, fearing "national bankruptcy," enacted legislation in the 1930's limiting the Federal debt to $40 billion. However, the requirements of World War II and the reluctance of Congress to raise taxes to finance the war on a pay-as-you-go basis, for fear of discouraging productive effort, resulted in Congress lifting this limit. In 1945, at the end of the war, the Federal debt stood at approximately $279 billion. The debt in 1930 had been $16 billion, when the gross national product was $91.1 billion. In 1957 the debt was $275 billion, gross national product $433 billion.

Much of the expenditure which accounts for this debt accumulation, of course, was not made as a matter of choice. It was imposed by the requirements for achieving victory and by commitments for postwar reconstruction. Pressure for additional expenditure continues as part of the attempt to underwrite security in the face of a new drive for world power by the Soviet Union. The unemployment problem which characterized the 1930's has been replaced by inflationary pressures. The diversion of real income from civilian use to that of the military services and to our allies abroad has meant that national income continues to expand at a rate greater than the goods and services available for purchase.

In order to keep down the costs of servicing the public debt the Treasury during the immediate post-World War II years followed a policy of keeping interest rates low. To insure a market for government bonds the Federal Reserve System stood ready to purchase unsold issues. These purchases were financed by creating demand deposits credited to the Treasury. As new liquid funds were spent by government agencies and moved into the possession of firms and households, they added to the reserves of member banks, thereby enabling them to create additional purchasing power. This resulted in an undermining of the traditional controls which the Federal Reserve System had exercised over the creation of new deposits by the commercial banks.

The presence of excess reserves meant that the raising or lowering of reserve requirements for the member banks, within the limits provided by law, had little influence on lending practices. Raising the discount rate for commercial paper was also less effective because of the high proportion of government bonds in the portfolios of member banks. In order to obtain reserve credits which would enable it to create new demand deposits, the commercial bank needed only to deposit bonds with its reserve bank. Open-market operations were similarly restricted, since the Federal Reserve System was committed to support the price of government bonds, and thus could not make them attractive to private purchasers by lowering their sale price.

During the second term of the Truman administration, and particularly after the outbreak of the Korean war (which set in motion a new round of price increases, with some resumption of government controls), a conflict developed between the administration of the Federal Reserve System and Treasury officials over the "proper" role of monetary policy. While recognizing that monetary policy may not be effective in stimulating new transactions once a recession is under way, Federal Reserve officials insisted that little attempt was being made to use it to control inflation, where it is generally believed it can be effective by controlling new investments.

After 1952 a new national adminstration embarked upon a program aimed at the increased use of monetary controls (one of the planks of the 1952 Republican platform stressed the importance of returning to "sound money"). Successive increases in the discount rate by the Federal Reserve Board had raised the interest rate by 1957 to its highest level since the 1930's. An effort was also made to get a larger proportion of the national debt (bonds) into the hands of the "public" and out of bank portfolios. While an attempt has been made to reduce Federal spending, progress in that direction has been slight. By the close of 1957 there was some relaxation of a restrictive monetary policy.

The Role of Fiscal Policy

Since the years of the great depression and the concern with unemployment which characterized the thinking of that period many economists as

222

well as political leaders in the United States have accepted the philosophy of the mixed economy. In 1946 Congress passed the Employment Act in which the maintenance of high-level employment was set forth as official policy. The act created a Council of Economic Advisers, with the responsibility for conducting continuous observation, research, and analysis into the American economy. The advisers' findings are transmitted to the President, who uses them in his own report to Congress, with recommendations for legislation aimed at coping with the problems that appear to be developing.

At the policy level, however, economics and politics are linked. The limited role of economic science, and of economists as scientists, needs to be re-emphasized. In a political environment where various income groups are able to exert influence and apply pressures the outcomes of specific programs cannot be predicted.

For the economist this often poses an important value problem itself. Changes in the income and price levels do not affect all persons or groups in the economy in the same way. A rising price level benefits debtors and makes creditors worse off in terms of income. Farmers benefit because they have traditionally been debtors. Business firms usually gain. Holders of cash, persons on money incomes fixed by contract (such as bondholders), wage and salary workers (particularly those who are not organized), and other creditors become worse off in terms of real income. Their fixed money incomes buy less. Up to the limits of productive capacity, inflation has ordinarily in the past benefited those most actively engaged in production and production decision-making. For that reason a "little inflation" has usually not been distasteful to governments in power. Beyond this point, however, hyperinflation and loss of confidence in money has usually resulted in social dislocation, speculation, and even a decline in production.

More recently a number of economists, including Sumner Slichter of Harvard University, have expressed a belief that, because of some important shifts in the institutional structure of our economy, a "little inflation" may not only be desirable but necessary. This problem, however, takes us beyond the model and data presented to assist in aggregate analysis. We will now take a closer look at the economic processes, sector by sector and function by function.

Discussion
Questions

1. Under a policy of complete laissez faire, on whom would responsibility for maintaining employment rest? Under what conditions would those

most responsible be likely to act in such a way as to sustain employment?

2. Why is a concept of the national economy more easily comprehended in the ideological system of central **planning** than in that of laissez faire?

3. How would investment decisions be made under central planning?

4. Would you describe the pragmatic approach to national-income policy as a compromise position between laissez faire and central planning?

5. Why would declining marginal productivity for capital tend to discourage investment in the private economy?

6. A deficit budget for the Federal government can result from different actions by government. Describe these, and trace the different income consequences of each.

Selected References for Part 2

Clark, J. M. *Strategic Factors in Business Cycles*. New York: National Bureau of Economic Research, 1934.

Dillard, Dudley. *The Economics of John Maynard Keynes*. New York: Prentice-Hall, Inc., 1948.

Hansen, A. H. *Business Cycles and National Income*. New York: W. W. Norton & Co., 1951.

Hart, A. G. *Money, Debt and Economic Activity*. New York: Prentice-Hall, Inc., 1953.

Keynes, J. M. *The General Theory of Employment, Interest and Money*. New York: Harcourt, Brace & Co., 1936.

Maisel, S. J. *Fluctuations, Growth and Forecasting*. New York: John Wiley & Sons, Inc., 1957.

Marshall, Alfred. *Principles of Economics*. London: Macmillan & Co., Ltd., 1920.

Robertson, D. H. *Money*. New York: Harcourt, Brace & Co., 1922.

As it is the power of exchanging that gives occasion to the division of labour, so the extent of this division must always be limited by the extent of that power, or, in other words, by the extent of the market. When the market is very small, no person can have any encouragement to dedicate himself entirely to one employment, for want of the power to exchange all that surplus part of produce of his own labour, which is over and above his own consumption, for such parts of the produce of other men's labour as he has occasion for.

ADAM SMITH

PART 3

PRODUCTION

The Creation of Output

and the Origin of Income

Introduction

BACK OF THE MEASURES of national product described in Part 2 stand the more than ten million firms of the economy of the United States, where decisions are made on what to produce, how much, by what combination of factors, and when. This is also where claims to income originate. In economic literature this is usually referred to as the problem of allocation. Both statements say essentially the same thing, since the allocation of factors of production to one commodity usually precludes their being used for another.

Our frame of reference is shifted as we focus on details of individual and group action, and on the different sorts of things that move in the real-income flows, along the assembly lines, over the rails and highways, en route to a final destination—ownership and use by persons.

Beginning with the common-sense meanings of production, productivity, and efficiency, we refine and develop them as concepts for more rigorous analysis. These are then made parts of a model which has come to be most commonly associated with economics as a discipline.

This, along with Parts 4 and 5, is the part of economics referred to as *microanalysis*. If we could call what we have covered in Part 2 the anatomy of an economic system, this by a similar analogy would be called its physiology. If one prefers to think in terms of systems analysis, the social economy now becomes the environment.

CHAPTER 12

Production in an Industrial Society

TIME HAS BROUGHT about many changes in the way the people of the United States live, in the kinds of jobs they hold, and in the composition of goods and services they produce and consume.[1]

In one frame of reference the size and composition of this output reflect the technological conditions of production. At any one time it will be made up of the material and service income it is possible to have, given the kinds and amounts of factors of production combined according to the institutional controls which co-ordinate and regulate their use. Shifts in size and composition of output are principally the result of technological changes (new knowledge of resource use), population changes, and the discovery of previously unknown factors of production.

From a different reference point changing patterns of production are a reflection of the shifts in what people want and are willing to use their efforts and ingenuities to attain. The fact that few today would buy even the finest surrey, preferring instead the most battered "horseless carriage," explains why labor and materials are no longer used to produce surreys. While both vehicles provide transportation, the surrey has been outmoded by scientific discoveries and the increased tempo of modern life.

Either frame of reference provides its own insight into the production process. Perceived needs and the production activity devoted to their satisfaction are linked with what it is possible to do with known resources and processes. These are constantly revised and extended as the dreams of one generation become the realities of the next. Here we shall confine our discussion to the first frame of reference, leaving for later chapters the exploration of changing consumption patterns.

---

[1] The interested student who wants a vivid portrayal of what life was like even early in this century will find Frederick Lewis Allen's *The Big Change* rewarding.

The Structure of
the Production Economy

The structure of the American production economy is revealed in what broad subgroups of the population do, the roles they perform in the production processes, the things they make, and the places where they live and work. From the studies of the economic historian, the records of the decennial census, and surveys of other agencies (public and private) we can trace the changing structure of the production economy.

Population Changes

One clue to how the economy of the United States has grown and changed can be found in the population statistics. The first phase of population development consisted of filling up largely unoccupied continent with a continuous drift of settlers and immigrants to the frontier regions. Population growth was linked with a steady increase in the acres of cultivated land and the number of households occupied in transforming the resources they thus brought into being into the requirements for family living.

The simple diagram in Figure 10 shows the continuous rise in total population from 1790 to 1956, and the distribution of that population between urban and rural domiciles. In 1790 slightly more than 5 per cent

Figure 10. Total Population of the United States, and Number Residing in Urban and Rural Communities, by Decades, 1790-1950 (Farm Population Since 1910)

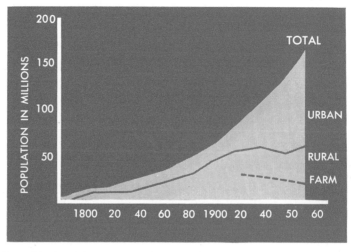

Source: *Statistical Abstract of the United States* and 1954 *Census of Agriculture.*

230

Figure 11.   Working Force of the United States by Industry, 1870-1950

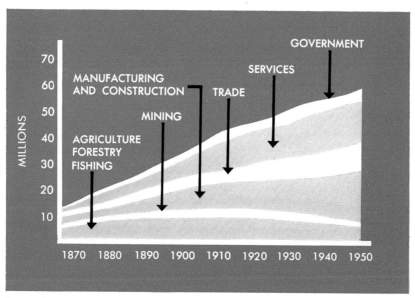

Source: Adapted from Harold Barger, *Distribution's Place in the American Economy Since 1869* (Princeton: Princeton Univ. Press, 1955), p. 4.

of the population lived in cities of 2,500 or more. By 1900 urban population had increased to nearly 40 per cent and at mid-century the figure was approaching 60 per cent. Persons actually living on farms had decreased by then to approximately 18 per cent, while the proportion of the working force in agriculture was about 10 per cent.

As early as 1870 the westward movement of peoples was already paralleled by this other population shift. By 1890, when the historian Frederick Jackson Turner noted the final disappearance of a frontier, the movement of people from country to city was well under way as developing industries sought manpower. While the number of people on farms continued to increase, the proportion of the total population in agriculture declined. After 1910 the number of farms actually began to decrease and this shift in the structure of the economy has continued to the present. Rural areas have always been important sources of population for the cities and manpower for industry because of their higher birth rates. While among individuals there were undoubtedly many motives for making this shift, there can be little doubt that one of the important influences was the better income prospects offered in the new and expanding industries.

Throughout much of the nineteenth century the natural rate of population increase was supplemented by immigration. Until well into the last

231

quarter of the century a majority of immigrants came from northern and central Europe. Peasants and farmers, they came to settle the new lands.[2] Shortly before the turn of the century immigrants began to come increasingly from eastern and southern Europe. Their destination was the new urban centers, where they gathered in ethnic neighborhoods and found jobs in industry and trade. After World War I legislative limitations on immigration curtailed this type of population increase.

Occupational Changes

Figure 11 shows a breakdown of major occupational groups of the gainfully employed from 1870 to 1950. Until 1920 manufacturing and mining showed the greatest increase. Since that time the services, or tertiary industries, including government, have grown most rapidly. Table 9 illustrates another occupational classification and shows the number in each group whose work now represents a specialized type of contribution to production.

American industry began in New England and the Middle Atlantic states, where capital accumulated in the early shipping trade very largely gave industry its start. There the first cities developed. For many years these cities' influence gave an eastward bias to the population center of

Table 9. Selected Occupational Groups, 1956
(in thousands)

Occupation	Males	Females
Professional and semiprofessional workers	3,928	2,125
Farmers and farm managers	3,683	199
Proprietors, managers, and officials except farm	5,363	932
Clerical and kindred workers	2,952	6,104
Salesmen and saleswomen	2,522	1,480
Craftsmen, foremen, and kindred workers	8,237	253
Operatives and kindred workers	9,313	3,548
Domestic service workers	31	2,111
Service workers, except domestic	2,712	2,597
Farm laborers and foremen	1,549	832
Laborers, except farm and mine	3,427	93
Total	43,718	20,272

Source: *Statistical Abstract of the United States*, 1957, p. 208.

[2] An exception was the large influx of immigrants from Ireland during the potato famine; they settled mostly in cities.

232

the United States. Gradually, decade by decade, this population center inched westward on the map, as first the railroads and then the motor carriers made it easier to move men and materials. It lingered longest in Indiana, where the regional influence of the associated manufacturing processes of iron and steel gave work and created markets. More recently the southward extension of industry (textiles, power development in the TVA area, and oil) and the population and industrial development of the Far West have brought population center and geographic center closer together.

Table 10 and Figure 12 show the civilian labor force, the number of farms, and business firms by major regions. They show too, comparative figures for value added in industry and cash sales (with government payments) of the farms.

The year 1900 marks a dividing line in the industrial history of the United States. It was then that the rate of development quickened and then accelerated. By mid-century 231 cities claimed more than 50,000 population. There were twelve states in which population density was more than 100 per square mile. Rhode Island, the most densely populated state, had more than 737 persons per square mile. California, which has emerged in recent decades as an industrial state of significance, had less than 100 persons per square mile, only because it is such a vast area of land, much of it mountainous or desert. Its urban areas are among the most extensive.

We have already examined evidence of the phenomenal growth of

Table 10.   Regional Economic Differences

Region	(1954) Estimated Population (000)	(1950) Civilian Labor Force (000)	(1954) No. of Farm Firms (000)	(1950) Cash Receipts & Gov't. Payments all Farms (000,000)	(1954) No. of Business Firms (000)	(1953) Value Added in Industry (000,000)
New England	9,652	3,846	81.8	$ 751.9	270.0	$ 9,904.7
Middle Atlantic	31,949	12,551	257.2	1,915.7	953.2	31,654.9
East North Central	32,703	12,389	798.7	5,395.4	828.7	39,926.4
West North Central	14,463	5,511	905.2	7,107.4	417.2	7,050.3
South Atlantic	22,137	7,965	859.0	3,423.4	564.2	10,686.2
East South Central	11,338	3,992	789.5	2,010.6	208.2	4,666.9
West South Central	15,026	5,218	668.1	3,352.5	398.2	5,646.8
Mountain	5,564	1,845	180.0	1,944.3	125.3	1,501.6
Pacific	16,245	5,755	242.7	3,500.2	462.4	10,620.9

Source: The Conference Board, *The Economic Almanac, 1956*, p. 428.

Figure 12. Regional Differences in Agricultural and Industrial Output and Income for the United States
(Percentages Based on Statistics in Table 10)

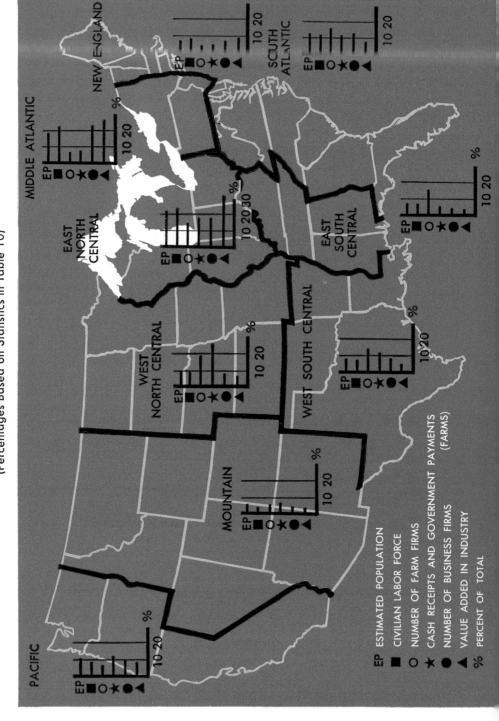

aggregate output (income) which accompanied the movement and growth of population. We can now look more closely at patterns of production and of the factor combination from which it stems. A breakdown of the national-income statistics into industrial origin provides a clue to the contributions to production of the different parts of the production economy. This is a rough indicator of the allocation of factors. Certainly it does not correspond to the distribution of the human factor, because factor combinations (men, machines, and resources) vary widely, depending on the type of industry. However, it does give an insight into our economy and the direction of its development (Table 11).

Table 11.   Percentage of National Income by Industrial Origin

Industry	Percentage of Total 1954	1929
Agriculture, Forestry, and Fisheries	5.5	9.4
Mining	1.7	2.3
Contract Construction	5.2	4.3
Manufacturing	30.0	27.1
Wholesale and Retail Trade	17.4	15.2
Finance, Insurance, and Real Estate	9.3	14.5
Transportation	4.9	7.6
Communication and Public Utilities	13.6	3.7
Services	9.9	11.8
Government and Government Enterprises	11.8	5.8
Rest of the World	.5	.9

Source: The Conference Board, *The Economic Almanac, 1956*, p. 428.

A necessary prelude to the present arrangement was the technological revolution which made possible the increased productivity of agriculture, so that the population surplus of the rural areas might be released from the land to take up jobs in the processing and fabricating industries. A little more than a century ago it required 20 workers on the land to supply surplus food and fibre for three in the city. Today a single worker in primary production is able to provide basic raw materials for 17.9 persons.

In the development of machine power lies much of the secret of increased productivity. In 1850 it has been estimated that approximately 15 per cent of the power generated for production was from human energy. Draft animals provided approximately 79 per cent of all of the energy expended. Machines supplied a mere 6 per cent. By 1900 the energy of man had dropped to 10 per cent, while that of draft animals had fallen to 50 per cent, and 38 per cent was provided by machines, largely steam. By 1930 man power accounted for only 4 per cent of the total energy expenditure, while draft animals created only 12 per cent. By 1960 it is estimated that not more than 3 per cent of industrial power will be supplied by human energy, that a bare 1 per cent will be provided by draft animals, while 96 per cent will be accounted for by machines. What the dawning age of atomic energy portends is still a question mark.

The decline in human effort can be seen in the reduction of the number of hours that men must work. In 1850 the normal work week was 72 hours—six days of twelve hours each. By 1900 a 60-hour week had become the rule, and by 1930 the average had fallen to 48 hours. Now 44 hours is typical, and men speak with confidence of the 35- or even the 30-hour week. For an increasing number of workers the job consists not of the backbreaking toil of former years but of an increased use of skill and knowledge in the tending and direction of machines. While the skilled craftsman and handy worker have declined in importance, statistics of the labor force show that the percentage of engineers, professional workers, white-collar workers, and so forth has increased much more rapidly than the total population.

Distinctive Features of American Production

There are two important characteristics of industrial output in the United States: (1) the very large proportion of durable capital goods, including consumer durables, and (2) the volume of basic raw material production in the form of minerals—the metals from which this vast outpouring of capital goods is fabricated and the energy sources which drive the engines of production.

These features can be pinpointed if we look for a moment at a sample of the manufacturing firms and the nature of their principal output. Table 12 presents the twenty largest industrial corporations in the United States, ranked according to sales (if assets had been the criterion only four would have been displaced[3]). Of this list of twenty, seven are producers of petroleum products, that source of energy which drives so many of the machines on which other forms of production depend. Two are producers of steel, one of chemicals, and three of automobiles. Electrical equipment is represented by three firms. Three of the twenty produce nondurable consumer goods; one firm produces rubber goods. The table also shows the number of employees of each of these firms. All told a little less than three million persons are employed by these industrial giants.

---

[3] They would have been "bumped" by three oil companies and a chemical firm.

236

We can accent this aspect of American production by comparing it with the rest of the world. Of the total world production of coal, nearly one-third is produced in the United States. In crude petroleum the United States is even farther out in front, with nearly 50 per cent of total world

Table 12.   Twenty Largest U. S. Industrial Corporations, January 2, 1957

Rank*	Company	Assets (000)	Employees	Sales (000)
1 General Motors		$7,400,351	599,243	$10,796,443
2 Standard Oil (N.J.)		7,901,530	155,530	7,126,855
3 Ford Motor		3,071,478	178,061	4,646,966
4 U.S. Steel		4,108,950	260,646	4,228,877
5 General Electric		2,221,147	280,497	4,090,016
6 Socony Mobil Oil		2,819,619	76,000	2,750,300
7 Chrysler		1,294,760	143,873	2,676,334
8 Swift		561,640	77,200	2,429,302
9 Western Electric		1,223,724	129,540	2,372,726
10 Gulf Oil		2,872,270	57,700	2,339,715
11 Bethlehem Steel		2,089,998	150,126	2,326,705
12 Texas Company		2,574,130	52,689	2,046,305
13 Armour		468,308	60,000	2,011,446
14 Standard Oil (Ind.)		2,437,196	51,765	1,890,228
15 Du Pont		3,568,585	89,449	1,888,446
16 Shell Oil		1,368,035	39,903	1,635,435
17 Westinghouse Electric		1,264,469	125,050	1,525,376
18 Standard Oil (Cal.)		2,041,373	37,318	1,452,521
19 Goodyear Tire		888,213	101,135	1,358,764
20 National Dairy Products		534,114	46,496	1,352,878

* Ranked by sales.

Source: *Fortune Magazine*, July, 1957 (Supplement). As an indication of the dynamic nature of the American economy, the Fortune Directory of the 500 Largest Industrial Corporations for 1958, which appeared after the above was written, showed two of those listed (Goodyear and National Dairy) no longer among the first 20, having been replaced by Boeing Aircraft and General Dynamics. Copyright by Time, Inc.

production. Of the world's total of pig-iron production in 1950 the United States accounted for more than 44 per cent.

Table 13 is a breakdown of the manufacturing industry according to product groups. Here we see the number of firms in the various categories, classified according to the kinds of goods produced, together with the average number of workers and the value added by manufacturers.

As has been repeatedly emphasized, however, production is more than

Table 13. Major Industry Groups, 1954

Group	Establish-ments (no firms)	Number of Em-ployees	Value Added (000)
Food & Kindred Products	42,374	1,647,204	$13,400,318
Tobacco Manufactures	627	94,863	988,001
Textile Mill Products	8,070	1,037,440	4,750,461
Apparel & Related Products	31,371	1,189,923	5,146,294
Lumber and Wood Products	41,485	645,936	3,188,434
Furniture & Fixtures	10,273	340,694	1,966,410
Pulp, Paper, & Products	5,004	530,210	4,581,944
Printing & Publishing	32,531	804,386	6,264,558
Chemicals & Products	11,075	739,389	9,444,629
Petroleum and Coal Products	1,381	215,843	2,582,623
Rubber Products	1,406	246,526	1,903,702
Leather & Leather Goods	4,845	356,578	1,637,417
Stone, Clay & Glass Products	11,162	491,814	3,820,959
Primary Metal Industries	5,838	1,117,059	9,372,910
Fabricated Metal Products	22,516	1,019,406	7,596,175
Machinery, except Electric	25,601	1,541,725	12,309,016
Electric Machinery	5,758	959,126	7,403,134
Transport Equipment	5,348	1,704,572	13,925,908
Instruments and Related Products	3,142	272,586	2,128,706
Miscellaneous Manufactures	17,010	695,917	4,473,050
Total	286,817	15,651,197	$116,914,639

Source: *Census of Manufactures, 1954.*

the transformation of materials in the manufacturing process.[4] To supply the mass markets of today an increased proportion of productive effort is devoted to the movement of goods and to the direct supply of peoples' needs in the form of services. It is in the use of human skills to minister to these needs that the professional and service workers contribute to production.

Retail establishments of all kinds numbered 1,720,920 in 1954. Included in this figure are firms which range from the corner grocery and drug stores to supermarkets and department stores. Servicing these retail

[4] There are, in fact, indications that the term manufacturing has become one which no longer suggests the nature of the secondary industries. Etymologically the term means "to make by hand." In the continuous processes, controlled by automatic machinery, which characterize an increasing number of the industrial firms (perhaps best illustrated by the great chemical industries) fewer and fewer hands are required. This has led to the suggestion by Robert A. Brady and others that "machinofacturing" is a better term.

establishments were 252,127 wholesale houses, while manufacturers sales branches numbered more than 23,000. Agents and brokers firms made up another 24,000. To operate their associated facilities and more than 220,000 miles of trackage the railroads of the United States required about 1.1 million employees in 1953. More than $12 billion is the estimate of total advertising costs, representing materials and human effort devoted to persuading people to buy the output of our private economy.

While this overview of growth and development in the field of production fills in details which were neglected in our analysis of the social economy in Part 2, we still have not focused on the area of decision making which initiates output and parallel income claims. Back of this over-all design such decisions take place in the offices, the shops, the factories, and on the farms, which are separate to some degree, yet linked together as part of the income system.

Conceptualizing
Production

An enterprising Hollywood director, given the task of creating the illusion of modern production to serve as the background for action involving some captain of industry, might proceed as follows. A fade-in shot of giant smokestacks belching forth smoke would move slowly downward, broadening the angle of view until a plant comes into focus. A twin line of trucks, loaded with crates or sheets of steel and tubular parts, would roll in and out of the main gates. The figures of men moving here and there, manipulating cranes or directing loading and unloading operations, would create the impression of bustle and purposeful action. Then the eye of the camera might travel out through the gate and into a front-office building, passing through a room where batteries of typists and clerks create a pattern of noise and movement. As it moves through a doorway and into a private office we are aware of a "distinguished looking" man behind a desk. He is pouring over some papers. On a large chart which hangs on the wall behind him a heavy line cuts horizontally across a graph, somewhat uncertain as to its direction up or down. For the moment it appears to be following an upward trend. We infer that this accounts for the look of satisfaction on our hero's face. He will shortly repair to the board room, there to give his report, on which the board will act and decisions will be made which eventually may affect the activity we have just been observing.

A totally different type of scene might have also created a convincing illusion of production. In a search for some ultimate referent for the term, any one of hundreds of activities would do. Two artists commissioned to

239

draw their conception of production would be unlikely to approach it in the same way. A combine slicing through the wheat of a Kansas field, a freight train moving across the countryside or into a terminal, a truck backed up to a loading dock, or women workers in the needle trades stitching sleeves to blouses—all these would suggest production.

As a technical process we might study the intricate control system of an assembly line, where materials, human efforts, and inanimate machine power are combined to turn out finished products. But this is the province of the industrial engineer, the production manager. We might even follow the finished products until they are delivered into the hands of the ultimate consumers. This, however, is the concern of the marketing specialists. Both are forms of technology. Our interest is broader, more abstract. It concerns the manner in which production relates to our earlier discussion of income flows.

The Semantics of Production

Production is a term of everyday use. We all know in a common-sense way what it means. To produce something is to *make* something new, to change the *form* or state of matter in such a way as to adapt it to some purpose. Anyone engaged in activity related to this process may be said to be producing. One who does it better, or faster, or who wastes less material than another, can be said to be more productive. An acre of land that grows more corn than another, or than the average (provided the seed and tending are the same), will also be described as more productive.

A definition of production depends upon our point of view. From the standpoint of the ultimate consumer, the one who uses the end product, production may be defined as the creation of something useful—sometimes called utility. When productive activity takes place near to consumption it may indeed be easily recognized as the creation of utility. In simple societies it was. The primitive hunter produced in order that he and his family might eat, or that the tribe might eat. In agricultural societies the cave or storehouse was somewhere between the field and the kitchen, but the movement from production to consumption was never indistinct or blurred. The early craftsmen of our own country produced *on order;* the journeyman cobbler measured the family for shoes and made them on the spot.

Today the distance between production and consumption has lengthened and become more roundabout. The modern equivalent of the journeyman cobbler works not in the home or even in his own shop. He tends a machine which does not make a whole shoe. Division of labor requires that he stitch soles, fit heels, or fashion uppers, not according to a specific foot, but to fit a last which is an abstraction, a kind of average designed to

240

accommodate a million feet. Back of him will be the designer, the market research analyst, and a whole battery of others. Ahead of him in the production process will be salesmen, advertisers, and others whose efforts will "touch" the shoe before the final transaction which puts it on a foot.

It does not matter what role the individual worker plays in the hierarchy of the production organization, whether as workman, foreman, or manager. The end in view, for those who participate all along the line, is not the satisfaction of any specific want or need. The purpose is to establish a money claim, which may itself be exercised against the real flow of goods and services of society. When that claim is finally exercised it forms one side of a transaction which is itself an aspect of the process.

The Role of the Market

Where the ultimate consumer is not known production is shaped by another abstraction—the market. The modern producer exchanges mostly for a price against some form of money payment or claim. The flow of goods passes to buyers willing and able to pay the highest price. These buyers may not even be consumers, but another type of producer who passes them on to a still more remote consumer, conferring on the goods the added usefulness of *place* or *time*.

In this way, producers add to the real-income flows new goods and services. They withdraw from the money-income flows, only to channel the withdrawal back when they exercise their claims over other goods and services which may be for further use in production, or for personal use by themselves and their families as members of households and ultimate consumers.

So far we have used the term producer as though it referred to some single individual or person. Yet all that has been said implies a process, interrelated and complex. Assimilated into even the simplest consumer good of modern society will be the concerted efforts of many hands and brains, as well as the services of tools and machines worn out or resources used up. All have co-operated in helping to create it. The good itself is the consequence of countless acts and decisions, all contained within the field of forces that is modern industrial society. Here and there it is possible to single out an act or a decision that appears to be of special importance. These are the decisions which are made at the centers of control in an economic system, which for our purposes at least possess important characteristics of causation. They are associated with a striving for income, particularly that special claim called *profit*. Such claims, as we shall see, are the *promised* rewards for initiating the chain of events which results in the bringing together of the factors of production for the creation of goods and services for the market.

But the process is complicated by the fact that in so complex a system money incomes or claims may be realized not only by *adding* more to the flow of services but also by *restricting* production.

Production and Exchange

Where exchange is mostly for money or credit, the dividing line between production and exchange becomes indistinct. Both contribute to the flow of real income. Both are sources of claims against income. The large marketing organizations, whose business is exchange (sometimes called distribution in popular speech[5]), are an integral part of production as we know it. Through storage, transportation, and the maintenance of available stocks of finished goods (inventories) they give to products the added usefulness of *time, place,* and *convenience.*

Specialization and Division of Labor

The difference in individual abilities or skills for particular job operations is a phenomenon we know from observation. We know, too, from experience the possibility of improving such skills through practice and training. Earlier economists gave extended treatment in their analysis to the division of labor and specialization. This was the theme with which Adam Smith began in *The Wealth of Nations.* His illustration, which has become classic, described how men in his day, working together at specialized tasks rather than separately, were able to multiply the output of pins per man-day several thousand times. This increased productivity he attributed to (1) improved dexterity, (2) saving of time and elimination of waste motion, and (3) invention of a machine, once a particular task had been reduced to a fairly simple pattern of repeated motion. For his time these observations showed insight and originality and were an aid in thinking about the industrial society then emerging. Unlike Adam Smith, we live in a world where it requires no special insight to see these advantages, since they are all about us. The assembly line has reduced time saving to a science and elevated it to an art.

Although specialization can be credited with the tremendous expansion in the output of goods and services, relative to human effort, it is not without its "costs." A man or a machine, specialized in or designed to perform one task or operation with great efficiency at high-level output, is likely to be less adaptable and perhaps quite inefficient at lower outputs. Specialization makes for rigidities and for high fixed costs, which, as we

---

[5] Not to be confused with distribution as it is used in economic analysis—a concept treated in detail in Part 4.

shall see, make it difficult for some firms to adjust when they encounter the kinds of instabilities described in the preceding chapters.

Exchange follows as a necessity where division of labor and specialization exist. For if an individual is to concentrate all effort on one specialty, he must obtain the means of satisfying the bulk of his needs and wants indirectly through exchange. Once it develops, specialization appears to generate still further specialization and division of labor. Out of this process of interaction, and the striving for efficiency it promotes, has come an important motivating force in the recombination and adaption of factors of production called *economic progress*. One after another of the old production operations which were once performed in the household or in family workshops have been transferred to the economically separate firm. The heads of households derive income by performing some specialized type of labor or service (or by owning), while wants are satisfied through spending a money income.

In describing the production economy in bold strokes we have been gradually bringing into focus the concepts and relationships which are of primary interest to the economist. In succeeding chapters these will be abstracted from their more specific referents, generalized, and cast into analytical models for organizing more systematically our knowledge of the income aspects of production.

Discussion
Questions

1. What are the factors which account, very largely, for the more rapid growth of the service types of industry?

2. Compare the proportion of the working force of the United States employed in agriculture with that of India, Brazil, Mexico, Great Britain, and the Soviet Union. What does this indicate about their industrial development?

3. What are the four principal types of production? Give examples of occupations or professions which can be identified with each.

4. If all housewives in the United States were suddenly to resume baking their own bread, what would be the effect on national product, as measured by social accounting?

5. What accounts for the very high productivity of labor in the United States?

243

The Individual Firm

in Theory

and Experience

OUR POINT OF VIEW in this section is that of the individual firm. The objective of our inquiry is to answer the question: How are decisions made which determine the kinds and amounts of goods and services to be produced?

In order to deal conceptually with such decisions we must change our focus from historical and current aggregates to the partial analysis of a microsystem. The basic production units, which are our concern, function within the larger economic and social environment already described. Actions taken by agents of the firm can be regarded as adjustments to that environment, differentiated for analytical purposes to correspond to the way it is experienced by the firm—as a network of markets, of potential purchasers, and as rival firms and products.

The analysis follows fairly closely that of neoclassical economics. It focuses on the institutions and stimuli of the monetary economy, where property in the factors of production is predominantly in the control of private persons and associations (which for present purposes are treated as legal persons), who seek to maximize the profit income of the firm.

CHAPTER 13

A Simple Theory of Production

A THEORY OF PRODUCTION and productivity can begin most conveniently with a simple situation, where the number of co-operating factors is small and where all but one is fixed. We can use the example of an acre of land planted to corn and tended by a single producer, using given tools, seed, and his own labor time. He will know from experience, or he can find out from the reports of experiment stations, that the amount of seed he plants per acre will affect directly the size of his harvest.

Output When One Factor Varies

The results of an experiment designed to measure the effect of different quantities of seed on yield per acre might appear approximately as follows:

Table 14. Input-Output Relationships
(seed variable)

Units of Input (pounds of seed)	Total Product (bushels)	Average Product (bushels)	Marginal Product (bushels)
1	3	3	—
2	7	3.5	4
3	12	4	5
4	18	4.5	6
5	25	5	7
6	33	5.5	8
7	40	5.7	7
8	45	5.6	5
9	48.5	5.4	3.5
10	51	5.1	2.5
11	52	4.7	1
12	51	4.3	—1

As the amount of input (seed) is increased, the output also increases. But while the output increases it does not always increase by the same amount with each unit of seed. In other words, the *rate of output* per unit of input varies. This relationship can be made more explicit by performing a few simple arithmetic operations on the figures for input and output.

By dividing total output (product) by total input for the different applications of seed, we obtain relationships which show units of output per unit of input, a simple average: if the producer desired to get the largest output per unit of seed, as he might if the seed were unusually scarce, he would plant about 7 pounds per acre. At that input he would expect to obtain an average output of 5.7 bushels per pound.

Figure 13. Basic Input-Output Relationship

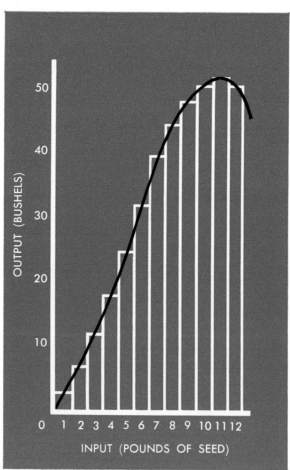

Figure 14. Total, Average, and
Marginal Output Curves

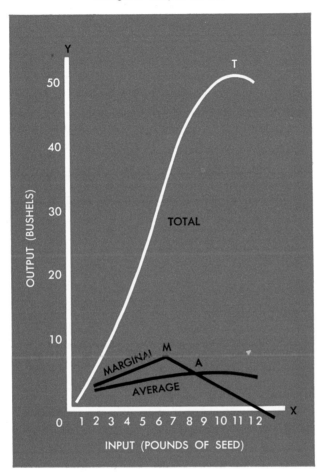

In practice the question most likely to be asked is, "Shall I plant a little more or a little less than I have been planting?" To answer that question the producer would be more interested in the column headed *marginal product*. This gives the rate of increase in the output, or the amount which is added to total output if the input is increased by an additional small unit—in this case one pound. Assume that 6 pounds to the acre had been planted the previous year. The table indicates that the seventh pound of seed on the average will add 7 bushels to total output.

Let us examine this concept of the marginal unit a little more closely. We have already had some experience with it in connection with the

247

propensity to consume. It will have other uses as we proceed. The concept is derived from differential calculus, and is a measure of rates of change. The marginal unit is the additional unit of whatever is being measured. Here it is additional output associated with an additional unit of input (a little later we will use it as a measure of costs and revenue resulting from the production and sale of one more unit of a good).

To assist in conceptualizing the relationships in the table, we shall convert them to a geometric diagram (Figure 13). On a simple bar chart we can show this relationship by measuring total output at each of the different inputs, output being measured on the vertical Y axis of a two dimensional diagram, input on the horizontal or X axis.

The bars of the chart take this form because inputs are measured by discrete units (one pound of seed) which are relatively large. If the additional inputs were made sufficiently small, say one kernel at a time, the bars would become very fine lines, and the upper ends of those lines would become points on a continuous curve such as has been drawn through the mid-points of the bars. This assumes continuous variation, and implies that quantities can be divided into infinitely small units. The figures for the average and marginal outputs can be shown in like manner. Combining all three on a single graph, we get the relationships shown in Figure 14. Each of the curves rises to a maximum and then declines. These are significant turning points, useful in analyzing production and productivity.

Total Productivity Curve

As we have indicated, the output of corn is the result of a combination of several factors of production—land, capital, labor, and seed (itself a form of capital carried forward from a previous production period). In determining total output, each factor contributes something, and is helped by each of the other factors. Here only one is assumed to vary—the seed. As the input is increased, the amount of corn produced will increase until it reaches a maximum. Beyond that point nothing can be added to output by increasing the variable factor, and beyond a point the total will actually decline. The point of maximum output is called the point of diminishing absolute or total returns, indicated by T on the chart. To get more corn, it would be necessary to have help from one or more of the other factors. The producer could increase the land, add more capital in the form of fertilizer (which would imply more labor), or expend more labor time cutting away the weeds which compete with the corn for moisture, fertility, and sunlight.

Average Productivity Curve

Total production divided by the number of units of input gives us average output, or output per unit of input. Moving along this curve, the average rises slowly as long as the amount added to total product by an additional unit of input is more than the previous average. As the additional or marginal product begins to decrease, the average product levels off and reaches its maximum at the point where the marginal product attributable to the variable factor is equal to the average product. Thus under the assumption of continuous variation the marginal productivity curve will always cut the average curve at its highest point. This is the point of *diminishing average returns,* indicated by *A* on the chart.

Marginal Productivity Curve

If the initial application of the variable factor is small, an additional small application will produce a greater than proportional increase in total output. If only a little seed is available, the seed is the limiting factor and an acre of land is too much. Scattered over the whole acre, even the labor would be ineffectively used. It would be better to reduce the other factors. But a small increase in seed, as the land and labor are more effectively used, results in a greater than proportional increase in output. If the seed is increased, as the combination of seed with the other factors reaches its greatest effectiveness (in terms of the variable factor), the point is reached where the next added unit of input will not add as much as the previous one. This is the point of diminishing marginal returns, indicated on the chart by *M*. No producer would operate before the point is reached. He would, as indicated above, vary the other factors—land in this case—until the factors were combined in more *productive proportions*.

The Physical Law of Diminishing Returns

We have been discussing a purely physical relationship. The tendency discussed here was first formulated by Turgot in France in the eighteenth century, and was further developed in England after 1815 at the time of the debates over the Corn Laws. It has come down to us as the law of diminishing returns or nonproportional output. As a technique of analysis and a guide to decisions, it states that "successive additional applications of one factor of production in a given production process, if the other factors do not increase, will reach a point where a less than proportional increase in output will be realized." An implicit assumption which underlies the law is that the basic technology does not change during the period considered.

This process of measuring productivity illustrates the technique of marginal analysis in its simplest form. By holding all factors but one constant, we can measure the effect of one variable on production. Given this knowledge for each of the various factors, we can maximize the return from any one of them.

The knowledge of productivity alone, however, does not provide the basis for making production decisions. If there were unlimited quantities of all resources, it would not matter how they were combined. But as has been pointed out and as we know from experience, the available factors of production are not ordinarily unlimited, at least not unlimited in the face of all the uses to which they might be allocated. To produce a given output of a good or service, we usually have available a variety of combinations of factors. The same results may be obtained by using large amounts of raw materials, with little labor and capital, or with a relatively greater application of skilled labor and capital equipment to lesser amounts of resources or raw materials.

In a primitive economy the individual producer would solve the production problem by making the most effective use of the limiting factor, the one most difficult to come by. He would employ it in different uses as sparingly as possible, seeking to attain the highest productivity or the largest average output per unit of input of the scarce factor. In the case of the more plentiful factors the producer might use them to the point of diminishing absolute returns. The scarce factor would tend to be regarded as fixed by nature or the existing supply conditions, while the more plentiful factors would be the variables. However, other factors might also be available in different proportions. Here again, in different combinations, the individual would attempt to use more sparingly the least plentiful factors. It is perhaps more accurate to say that, to the extent that this was done, the producer would be acting in a way to get the most out of his scarce resources.

The population problem in "underdeveloped" areas is one case where the concept of diminishing returns applies. Each new person added to the population brings "two hands and only one mouth." But the additional two hands, when applied to a static amount of land, become successively less effective. Unless other factors of production in the form of tools or new sources of land are forthcoming, output per person falls. Population pressure against the food supply becomes ever more intense, as it has for so long in India and China. This is why there is now great emphasis in those countries on capital development. While social reforms have received great attention there, these are likely to succeed only if they contribute to the increasing productivity of the human factor.

Efficiency as an Economic Concept

Closely related to productivity in economic or income analysis, but separate from it, is the concept of efficiency. Productivity is a technical concept. Efficiency is a social concept, in the sense that it refers to factors with price tags on them. It is a measure not of physical output but of the cost of output derivable from the cost of the co-operating factors of production. With given costs of the factors, a combination which results in a lowering of the costs of production will be described as a more efficient combination.

Decisions to produce are made in this social setting. As a consequence of the market-valuing process, the producer is confronted not only with different factors and different ways of combining them, but also with factors that have themselves been valued in the economic process. His immediate variables are costs on the one hand and revenues or money receipts from the output on the other. If the number of units of the combined factors of production are multiplied by their prices, and the total of all such operations added together, the result will be called *total costs*. If the units of output are multiplied by their price, the result will be *total revenue*. These are thus expressed in the standard unit of account.

A simple example will help to clarify this relationship. Production in the example above consisted of using resources (land), capital, and labor to grow corn. The acre of land was a fixed quantity; so too were the services of the machinery (capital) and the labor, since the cultivation of an acre of corn would probably not involve more work if the corn stalks were closer together. We will assume that for all practical purposes the requirements would be the same. Only the seed is assumed to vary.

If the marketing and accounting processes have operated so that each of these services has a money value assigned to it, we can convert our production figures into costs. It will be simpler to take a case where the services of the land and the machinery are hired or rented.[1] The cost of the fixed factors can thus be represented as a fixed sum. We will assign them an arbitrary value as follows: rent for the land, $10; rent for machinery, $20; if the tending of the corn requires ten man-days of labor for the season, and that type of labor earns $5 a day, then the total wage bill is $50. The total cost of the fixed factors will be $80.

When this total is combined with the cost of the variable input we obtain the total cost for each of the different outputs or yields. Assuming $14 per bushel (56 pounds) or 25 cents per pound as the cost of seed

---

[1] This is not necessary, since if the producer owned them he would *impute* to them the same price he would have to pay if he had rented them, or that he could receive if he were to rent them out to someone else.

corn, we can then construct a table of relationships between output and costs (Table 15). While the assumed conditions are not wholly unrealistic, they are arbitrary and intended only to illustrate a set of relations. Under these conditions the cost per bushel would be very high if only one pound of seed were used. The reason will be obvious. The full productivity of the land is not being used, but full cost is being charged. As the seed is increased, the cost per bushel falls rapidly. Again the reason should be apparent. The initial fixed cost is quite large. As we increase the variable

Table 15. Cost of Producing Corn Under Conditions of Nonproportional Output

1 Total Fixed Costs	2 Input in Units of Seed (lbs.)	3 Variable Cost— 2 × .25	4 Total Cost— 1 + 3	5* Total Output (bu.)	6 Average Cost Per Bushel— 4 ÷ 5
$80	1	$ .25	$80.25	3	$26.75
80	2	.50	80.50	7	11.50
80	3	.75	80.75	12	6.73
80	4	1.00	81.00	18	4.50
80	5	1.25	81.25	25	3.23
80	6	1.50	81.50	33	2.46
80	7	1.75	81.75	40	2.04
80	8	2.00	82.00	45	1.82
80	9	2.25	82.25	48.5	1.69
80	10	2.50	82.50	51	1.61
80	11	2.75	82.75	52	1.59
80	12	3.00	83.00	51	1.62

*Column 5 is a reproduction of Column 2, Table 14.

factor, costs rise by an insignificant amount. On the other hand, because of rising average and marginal productivity, the total output is increasing at an increasing rate. Slowly rising total cost, when set off against rapidly increasing productivity, means rapidly decreasing costs per unit of output.

In this example costs continue to decline until the application of the 11th pound of seed per acre, at which point the cost is $1.59 per bushel. For this situation, given the structuring of production opportunities as we have assumed them to be, $1.59 is the *least cost combination*. However, if we can remove our assumptions that all factors except seed are fixed, we can imagine the producer thinking in terms of a number of the factors being increased or decreased. He would then have a series of different possible cost combinations, in which case still lower average costs could be attained. This then is a *special* case of factor combination. We will return to the problem of factor allocation in Part 6, when factor combination is discussed as an aspect of distribution or income determination.

The process described above, the act of allocating successive units of a variable factor of production, is not a description of behavior. It is a mental process, a series of calculations, using previously acquired knowledge of productivity and prices. We have all indulged in this kind of "figuring" to discover if it will pay us to undertake some venture. Our answers are not usually so precise as those in the problem, because even with the best of information we frequently have to make a few guesses or assumptions about some of the prices or productivity items.

We can now frame a definition of efficiency in terms of the relationships we have just discussed. *Efficiency* means the combining of factors of production, where productivity and cost are given, in order to minimize the money cost of producing a good or service.[2] A note of warning is in order. Efficiency does not mean profitability, although again there is a relationship between the two ideas. Efficiency, as has been noted, is a relationship on the cost side of production. Profitability, as will be shown in succeeding chapters, involves a *relationship* between costs and receipts or revenues. Before that can be determined we need another variable— the price that can be obtained for the different outputs.

This imaginary producer might decide not to produce corn at all at a price he could reasonably expect to receive. With the resources available to him, even the most efficient combination of seed might not be a very efficient *scale of operation*. In other words, his lowest unit cost could be higher than the price, and the total costs greater than the revenue he could expect. In that case he would decide to use the factors for something else, or he might seek to get command over more land, so that machinery and labor could be used more intensively, more productively, and thus more efficiently. As we will observe later on, because of rapid changes in technology this kind of decision has been faced by farmers for years.

Advantages in Production

Because of variability in the factors of production, their distribution in geographic space, and the ease or difficulty with which they can be brought together, there exist relationships which are called advantages in production. These are associated with productivity and efficiency. As the pro-

---

[2] The concept of efficiency adopted here may appear to be unduly narrow compared with popular usage. In everyday speech it has many shades of meaning, many of them vague and unspecified.

ductivity of different factors in particular production uses is discovered through previous experience (technology or the state of the arts), this is translated into resource use. For some factors of production, physical productivity in a particular use is so marked that they far outstrip any similar resources or factors known to exist elsewhere. These factors can be described as highly *specialized* for that use. When used to produce a given good or service, the need for other factors in combination with them is less than elsewhere. Such factors can be said to have an *absolute advantage* in that particular use. The fertile prairie soils of the Middle West have an absolute advantage in a particular use—namely, the production of corn. A given combination of labor and capital applied there will produce more corn than anywhere else in the world. The reason is that both soil and climate (deep black loam, an adequate and well distributed rainfall, hot summers to promote rapid growth, and enough frost-free nights to permit maturation) are suited to this particular plant. This advantage has resulted in the establishment there of the Corn Belt. Absolute advantage is closely related to physical characteristics and physical productivity, but not solely. If the uses for corn were not such as to warrant its being grown, or if modern transportation were not what it is, the state of Iowa would not grow the quantity of corn it does. There would not be the justification for such a degree of specialization, for it would have no income importance. (Greenland, after all, has absolute advantage in the production of icebergs, a matter of no great income importance to the Eskimos.) Examples can be given for most factors of production, including the human. Those with unique skills or physical characteristics are so-called "naturals" for certain activities. Mickey Mantle is a great baseball player because skill and training have made him outstanding in that sport.

From absolute advantage it is but a short step to the more income-oriented *comparative advantage*. This concept can be most easily illustrated by means of an example. On the basis of output per acre, Kansas should not be growing wheat. Many states which produce very little wheat could do better. The average yield in Kansas is about 14 bushels per acre. Ohio does better than that. Yet the wheat belt is centered in Kansas. However, Ohio has greater advantages, from an income standpoint, in the production of other things. Kansas has few alternatives, and almost none that is better. Comparatively, its advantage is greatest in wheat.

An example of human factor may point up the contrast even more. A doctor might be both an excellent physician and a first-rate bookkeeper. Even if he were able to make entries and strike a balance in less time than any practicing bookkeeper, it still would not pay him to take time from his medical practice to keep his books. Reductions in revenue would outweigh his savings in cost, thereby reducing his income. He would have an absolute advantage in both medicine and bookkeeping, but his comparative income advantage would be in medicine.

We can now frame a definition of these two concepts. *Absolute advantage in production is framed in terms of some physical measurement, and borders on the purely technological. Comparative advantage is an economic concept, related to efficiency and money costs when compared with revenues.*

These concepts are most frequently used by economists as a conceptual tool for the understanding of international trade. Division of labor and specialization on an international scale can be shown to result in the same advantages in production as on a national scale. If a country can command greater quantities of a commodity through exchange than by direct production, then in terms of real income it will realize an advantage by doing so. Both parties to the exchange can benefit. When there is an absolute advantage this is not difficult to perceive. Thus Brazil has an absolute advantage in the growing of coffee. The exchange of automobiles, which are not at present produced efficiently in Brazil, for coffee, which is not grown in the United States, is obviously of benefit to both countries. Where the advantage is comparative rather than absolute, the benefit is more subtle and for various reasons (usually political) such trade has been opposed by different interest groups. Further discussion of this problem is reserved for Part 6.

Exchange and Value

We can now pose a number of additional questions. What is it that determines the *rate* at which various goods and services are exchanged? This is another way of asking what it is that determines *relative value*. However, in a modern exchange economy, where money is used, this amounts to asking what determines relative price. Is there a difference?

During a sale merchants advertise that "you can now get a $5.00 value for only $4.98." When real estate prices rose rapidly after World War II and private dwellings more than doubled in price, it was a common experience to hear the new property owner complain that he had paid more for his house than it was worth. One hesitant buyer phrased it this way, "Can I afford to pay $25,000 for a $10,000 house?" Implicit in all such statements is an assumption that there is some kind of an objective value or *real value* separate from price.

By way of contrast, others may have a stock answer that all value is determined by supply and demand. Grumpy old Thomas Carlyle once remarked that if you taught a parrot to say "supply and demand" you would have an economist. This is an exaggeration. Economists are less likely to be enamored of the magic in these two words than the public, and more likely to view them as the end product of a *process* rather than as the beginning of all wisdom. The implications of this statement will become clear as the next few chapters unfold. Meanwhile it will be helpful if we trace the historical development of the concept of value as it is used in economic analysis.

Broadly speaking, the problem has been complicated by the fact that there is a larger field of value which transcends economics. We have already treated the problem of value in Part 1. In the early development of economic thought primary emphasis was given to the theory of value as such, because this was regarded as central to the whole problem of production and distribution, or the creation, distribution, and use of wealth. As was noted in Part 2, the French Physiocrats believed that agriculture was the only source of new value (and consequently of income), because it appeared to them that only in the production of basic raw materials did nature co-operate directly with man in the production process. Agricultural labor was described as the father of value, but nature was regarded as the mother—an analogy with the process of reproduction as observed in living organisms. Labor applied elsewhere than agriculture was called nonproductive, since it seemed not to produce anything new— no net product.

Smith and Ricardo regarded labor as the source of value.[3] According to the *labor theory of value*, the worth of useful things was proportional to the amount of human labor incorporated in them. If one good required twice as much labor to produce as another, then their relative values would be as one to two. They would exchange for each other in those proportions. This they called *value in exchange*.

The classical economists recognized another aspect of value which they called *value in use*. They were aware, for example, that an object might be produced at great labor cost and still have no particular value if no one could find a use for it. Other commodities—water and air, for example—might possess a high use value, but because of their great abundance be incapable of commanding other commodities in exchange. Marx, who took over the labor theory of value from Ricardo, attempted to rationalize the first of these apparent discrepancies with the concept of "socially necessary" labor—a kind of average or index. He recognized that one man might spend much time and effort in digging for a diamond, while another might pick one up from a river bed which, if equal in size

---

[3] However, Ricardo was never quite satisfied with this.

256

and purity, would have the same value. But, said Marx, this was not the usual thing. Most people have to dig for them; hence it is the socially necessary labor which determines value. This concept of value suited Marx's purposes, since he used it in his exploitation-theory of wages. But the contradictions of an objective theory of value have remained unresolved. The later neoclassical economists developed a subjective theory which has at least proven more "workable."

Subjective Theory of Value

A group of Austrian economists, of whom Karl Menger and Eugen Böhm-Bawerk are the best known, created something of a revolution in economics when they reversed the frame of reference of the value problem. Instead of looking for value in the object or the good, they located it in the behavior or consciousness of men. That which gave a good its value, they maintained, was the fact that someone found it useful and desired to appropriate it. It remained for Alfred Marshall to reconcile the earlier classical view with the Austrian approach.[4]

That synthesis was essentially the modern formulation of the economic problem and man's efforts to cope with it—the interaction between scarce resources and goods on the one hand and the multiplicity of human wants on the other. If the desired good exists in such abundance that all can have as much as they want, no problem is involved. It is a free good. But if, as is the case with most useful things, it is scarce and many desire it, the chances are that in an organized society it will have been appropriated. To obtain it involves some sacrifice and an act of choice in giving up some other useful thing, or the sacrifice of time and effort in the producing of it. Value emerges then as a relative concept, the end product of a process of choosing. It becomes the balancing of the utilities of different commodities, including the desire for leisure, in a way to achieve maximum satisfaction. Economic value or price expresses the relationships among different goods. It is a result of the social process of exchange, and finally of exchange against the measuring rod of money. Factors of production command prices because they are used in the production of consumption goods that command a price.

---

[4] To attribute such a synthesis to one man is, of course, to oversimplify. The newer view was the product of many minds. The English economist, W. S. Jevons, had arrived at a position very similar to that of the Austrians. Other names associated with the refinement and development of the neoclassical thought are Wicksteed, J. N. Keynes (father of J. M. Keynes), and J. B. Clark, the American economist. The synthesis was accompanied by many controversies and debates, as is usual in all ideological changes, but the details of these need not concern us here. Marshall's synthesis in his *Principles* was merely the one to achieve the widest acceptance.

257

An integral part of this process of price determination is the *allocation of factors* to the production of those goods rated most important by the markets. This is how in an enterprise or mixed economy decisions are made about what to produce. All who participate in the production process do so in expectation of a money income.

The Profit Motive and the Profit System

The enterprise system of production, as we know it, is an economic system organized around the *profit motive*. This term can be broadly or narrowly defined. In normative statements it can be used as a term of praise or of deprecation. To those who believe in it strongly, it has been credited with most of the advances men have made against the scarcity problem and the evils of poverty and want. On the other hand, those who see only the unsolved problems of men, the selfishness and greed that are so often associated with "injustice" and inequality, single it out as an evil influence. Their proposals for a "better world" often contain such references as "production for use and not for profit." These judgments have tended to destroy some of the usefulness of the concept for analytical purposes. It will be helpful, therefore, to attempt to clarify the term and the sense in which it will be used in the chapters that follow.

We can begin with a term which we can call the "income motive," a slightly more general term and one which can be applied to the type of expectation or anticipation which motivates all who participate in the production process in an interdependent economic system. For reasons already discussed, such an economic system would not be possible if some form of money, some unit of account, did not exist. In other words, in any society but one of self-sufficient households some method of acknowledging and keeping track of income claims would be necessary.

Given that system, which is an inheritance from the past for virtually the entire modern world, the *income motive* can be viewed as an adaptation modern man has made to his social environment. In the system of rewards (and punishments) meted out by society, money income is one of the more important. Income is desired, not for itself alone but for what it can command in real income and satisfaction. John K. Galbraith, following his experience as a deputy administrator of the Office of Price Administration during World War II, has remarked that the desire for money income, even in time of war when such motives as patriotism and fear of the enemy run very high, is probably the greatest incentive to get people to produce. All who contribute to production, who perform the labor, who rent their resources and capital goods, or who loan their money do so in

258

hope of gain, in the expectation of claims against the output of the joint effort. This is the income motive.

Co-operative effort of all kinds—groups of individuals working together for common goals—requires co-ordination and leadership. Those who perform this function in production have been called entrepreneurs or enterprisers. Those who act to carry out the entrepreneurial function do so with the same expectation of gain or money income as those who follow their lead by contracting with them to furnish labor and property services. While the stimulus is similar, the mode of operation differs. As initiators and co-ordinators of the production process, the entrepreneurs assume certain obligations in advance. In contracting for the service of factors, they agree in most cases to make certain fixed income payments to those who supply them. They incur costs in the name of the firm. These they plan to meet out of expected revenues. Their hope of income is in a residual claim—a remainder—which is the difference between the costs incurred and the receipts for the output of goods and services. By convention and accepted usage this is called *profit*.

It is in the expectation of profit income that production in the firm is undertaken. When in many different individual firms factor services are brought together and combined for the purpose of creating an output, the economic system has been characterized as a *profit system*. This means the same thing as an enterprise system.

The profit system, modified though it may be by changes in institutions, is one way a society can be organized to get its goods and services produced. It is a method of organizing production in which there is no single plan involved. It is the result of millions of plans and millions of decisions to act on the basis of those plans. Actions taken in the expectation of profit, can be observed as a sequence of adaptations and adjustments. Controls, exercised by those who perform the entrepreneurial function, proceed on the basis of clues. In the light of these clues decisions are made as to what kinds of things to produce and in what quantities.

As an aid in observing, understanding, and (within broad limits) predicting these decisions, a series of abstract analytical models developed by economists can provide us with certain insights. They are focused on the set of conditions which, in a sense, determine the flow of goods and services entering the real-income flows discussed in Part 2. Prices are among the more important of the clues acted upon within the firm, since they furnish the basis for calculating costs, revenues, and expected profits.

If we now recall the historical and descriptive information presented in the preceding chapter, we can interpret the shifts in population and the differences in regions as adjustments which have resulted, in part at least, from the restless quest for income. The discovery and development of new resources and the changes in people's values and wants (both genuine and manufactured) are forces continuously affecting productivity and efficiency, necessitating a reallocation of the factors of production.

Discussion
Questions

1. How are indivisibilities related to factor combination? What do you understand by the term fixed factor? Are physical characteristics of the factors the only consideration in accounting for indivisibilities?

2. What is the economic criterion of efficiency? How is it related to productivity?

3. Are there circumstances under which maximum total product might be significant to the individual producer?

4. When might it be important to maximize the average productivity from a given input?

5. In terms of a total product curve, what is it that the marginal productivity curve measures?

6. Why is it convenient, for purposes of analysis, to assume that the prices of the factor of production are known (given), and that they do not change during the time they are being used in analysis? Do you think this is a realistic assumption?

Appendix to Chapter 13

The Location of Industry

A PROBLEM which has interested economists for a long time is that of the location of industry. Again, there are two aspects to this problem. One may ask the question, "Where ought important industries to be located in order to achieve the 'best' allocation of the factors of production?" Or one may ask, "Is there any order or pattern which can be described by a theory or set of principles which will enable one to predict where industries will in fact be located if the owners or entrepreneurs seek to maximize their income?" It will be apparent that this question is related to the concept of advantage in production discussed above.

J. H. Von Thunen (1783–1850), a German agricultural economist, was one of the earliest to address himself to this problem. Von Thunen created a model of what he called "The Isolated State." He assumed that a city in the midst of a central plain, surrounded by mountains and drained by a navigable river, constitutes a closed economy. The city is dependent upon the agricultural hinterlands for its raw materials and food supplies. Given this situation, how would the pattern of production be arranged or structured?

Factories for the production of finished goods, of course, would be located in the city near the largest market. The principal exchange would be between the city and the agricultural hinterlands. Reasoning deductively, Von Thunen concluded that the patterns of land use or types of production enterprise would arrange themselves more or less in concentric zones, fanning out from the urban center. Nearest to the city would be those perishable products which required rapid transportation—such things as dairy products, fresh vegetables, etc. Next would come industries whose products have a high ratio of bulk to value, such as bricks, hay crops, etc. These would of necessity be located near the center of consumption. Still farther out would be the more durable commodities, higher in value, which could be transported overland to the city. Most remote and totally dependent upon the navigable river for transportation would be items of great bulk and weight such as stone, timber, iron ore, etc., which are difficult to ship.

The full details of Von Thunen's model need not detain us here since it represents a highly specialized case. However, it is important, chiefly because it focuses on some of the important influences which affect the decisions about location. Three considerations are taken into account in explaining location as an aspect of efficiency and in shaping decisions about where an industry ought to be located. There is first of all the geographic location of resources. Important mineral deposits, soil characteristics, and climate are determined by natural forces. Iron ore, petroleum, and other minerals must of necessity be mined where they are located. In general, efficiency will be greater at those deposits or on those soils which are most productive. Secondly, there is the problem of where the materials are to be used or consumed. Large centers of population usually constitute the markets. Ease of transportation and the nature of the transportation facilities will be of paramount importance. Because transportation constitutes an additional cost, examples can be cited in which it is cheaper to use the poorer resources near at hand than to work richer but more distant resources. Finally, the stage of technological development will be an important influence. The rich copper deposits of Michigan, deep in the earth, were once an important source of copper. With the development of newer extractive methods and using the knowledge gained from modern chemistry, copper mining later shifted to the more remote and lower-grade deposits of Montana and Arizona, where the fixed costs of getting the deposits to the surface were less. Moreover, pure copper is a metal with a high unit value and hence can absorb the transportation costs of much greater distances.

Whether the actual processing will take place near the source of supply of raw materials or near the point of greatest consumption will thus depend upon the kinds of transportation, the relative value of the raw materials compared with the finished product, the existing labor supply, and, of course, business judgment itself, in evaluating the importance of these different influences. Bad judgments tend to be corrected by a weeding out process as comparative costs assert themselves. However, this process may be delayed or even reversed by political and social influences. National states, for reasons of self-sufficiency and security, frequently alter the patterns of resource use, supporting through income transfer or subsidies less productive factor combinations and less efficient firms in order to attain objectives other than maximum real income.

While industrial location constitutes an important area for investigation, there is today less optimism among economists that a general theory of location is possible. Specialists in the field can and do offer useful advice, but usually in terms of a particular case, a given situation.

CHAPTER 14

Production for a Market

BUILDING ON A FOUNDATION of the simple model of production, our concern now will be with decisions that occur within the individual firm and with the firm's relation to the market and to the other firms producing similar goods, all of them together constituting an industry. We shall examine first the concept of the market *as viewed by the producer.*

Any market is a two-sided affair. It has a buying side and a selling side. On the buying side are ranged the purchasers, armed with the money or credit claims which they are able and potentially willing (under given conditions) to surrender in order to obtain a desired good or service. This is the demand side. Opposite them are the sellers. They have control of the goods and stand ready to surrender ownership of them for the money claims. This is the supply side.

Demand for a Particular Good

The concept of effective demand or the total demand for all goods and services available for purchase was developed in Part 2. Here we shall consider the demand for a particular good.

The *demand* for a good can be defined as *a hypothetical schedule or table of the amounts of a particular good that will be purchased in a given market during a specified time*[1] *at all relevant prices.* Note the specifications. The good is a particular good—"shoes or ships or sealing-wax." The market is given, that is, it is defined or marked off as a locus within which buyers and sellers communicate with each other. It may be large or small, depending on the nature of the product. The time is specified. Since both real and money incomes are flows, they must be meas-

---

[1] Demand may also refer to the amounts of a good an *individual* would take at different prices at a given time.

263

ured according to some time period. Finally, the price is an expression of the amount of money which will be surrendered per unit when different amounts are involved.

What will determine the amounts of a particular good that buyers will purchase? Since demand has been defined as the amounts buyers stand ready to purchase, to surrender other property in order to obtain, it follows that an important determinant of demand for a particular good will be the money income available. Incomes vary from person to person, and for all but a few are limited. It follows that at extremely high prices a good can be bought by only a few. At lower prices it will come within the income and credit possibilities of a larger number of buyers.

Aside from income, however, people have different *tastes*. Some prefer to spend their income for sleek, shiny roadsters, while others prefer a trip abroad, a baby, a summer cottage, or various less expensive items. Any good is likely to meet with varying degrees of attraction or indifference among the buyers who come to the market. Some will want it even if the price is high. Others will buy it only if it is cheap. Differences in taste affect the demand for a good in much the same manner as differences in income. As a rule, less will be bought at high prices than at low prices.

There is one other influence on buyers' willingness to purchase, and this is related to the amounts of this particular good they may have already. Once they acquire a given number of units, the good becomes less important to them. For unlike the sum total of all our wants, the desire for a particular good or service may be satisfied completely. Only the freak—the dope fiend, the alcoholic, the crank—desires to limit himself to the consumption of a single item to the exclusion of all others. Thus the importance to the individual of having one or more additional units of a good at any given time will depend on how much of it he has already. This aspect of wants also merges into that of the existence of close substitutes and their prices.

If we think of the usefulness of a particular good in terms of the total satisfaction we get from it, then we can imagine successive units adding to that total until satiety is reached. If the total for any given time rises to a maximum, each additional unit adds a little less as that maximum is approached.

We can show this effect by means of a diagram similar to the total productivity curve which we encountered earlier. Consider the example of socks. One pair of socks will possess a great deal of utility for us. It warms our feet, prevents blisters, and saves us from embarrassment. The importance of one pair would be very great. An additional pair would be a great convenience. It would mean that we could have a change and thus permit one pair to be laundered. A third pair would further increase our total stock of utility from the socks. It would lessen the tragedy if the laundry failed to return on time. Moreover, three pairs of socks would permit variety. A fourth and fifth pair would in all likelihood increase our total satisfaction.

To illustrate this point we can set up a hypothetical scale of utility.

UTILITY OF SOCKS

Number of Pairs	Total Degree of Utility	Marginal Utility
1	10	—
2	19	9
3	27	8
4	34	7
5	40	6
6	45	5
7	49	4
8	52	3

Such a presentation of marginal utility is dramatic and a logically rigorous way of saying that when we have enough of a thing we don't want any more. It overstates the case, however. Usually we do not acquire any one good to the point of satiety. What we do is to use our limited income to acquire a specific good only to the point where the desire for some other good commands the focus of our attention, at which point we substitute the second for the first in our purchases. Diminishing marginal utility is in fact a diminishing marginal rate of substitution in our budget, since with a limited income all goods must be to a certain extent substitutes for each other. When we already have several units of a good, its importance is diminished, and we can usually be persuaded to part with additional income to obtain another unit only if we can get it at very low cost.

It will be noted that the effects of this tendency on our consumption habits are similar to those of the other two determinants of demand—restricting purchases at high prices and encouraging them at low prices.

In summary, then, the principal determinants of demand are (1) income, (2) tastes, and (3) diminishing marginal utility or rate of substitution. For our theory of demand these will suffice. There are obviously other things which influence demand. For example, we may be influenced at any given time not only by our present income but by what it has been in the past and what we expect it to be in the future. Our reserves of wealth also are a factor. We may buy now rather than later on the strength of what we expect prices to be in the future. But for the moment we shall ignore the role of expectations, important though they are, and confine ourselves to a timeless or static situation. Further discussion of consumer behavior can await our discussion of consumption in Part 4.

The Demand Schedule

Because of the interrelated determinants of demand, more will be purchased at low prices than at high prices in a given market. The adjoining table represents a hypothetical demand for socks in a given small market area during one week.

DEMAND FOR SOCKS

Price per Pair	Pairs of Socks Likely to be Purchased per Week
$.75	100
.70	110
.65	130
.60	160
.55	200
.50	250
.45	300
.40	360

These figures can be plotted on a graph, using the vertical axis to measure price and the horizontal axis to measure quantity. We get a curve which slopes downward from left to right, as illustrated by the solid line in Figure 15. Movement along the curve shows us the relationship between price and amount purchased. Any given price projected to intersect the curve shows the amount that will be taken at that price. When the price changes, the amount taken changes in the opposite direction.

As long as the basic determinants of demand remain unchanged, we assume that there will be no change in demand and changes in price may be said to result in or cause the changes in amounts taken. When changes occur in the determinants, the whole series of relationships between price and quantity can be assumed to change. A change in income, a change in tastes, or a change in use for the particular good can be represented by a shift in the demand curve. If the change is an increase, the curve will shift upward and to the right and will lie above the previous curve so that more will be taken at the same price; or, alternatively, the

Figure 15. Hypothetical Demand Curve,
Showing Increase and Decrease in Demand

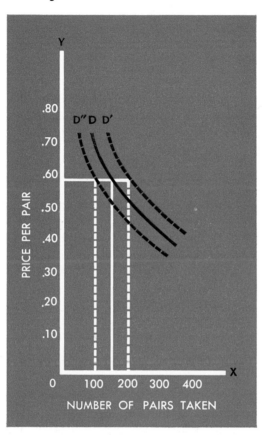

same amount will be taken at a higher price. If the change is a decrease, the curve will shift downward to the left. An increase and decrease in demand are shown by the dotted lines on the graph.

The distinction between a shift in demand and in movement along a given demand curve is important. They suggest that for the analysis of an actual problem we will need to investigate whether the increase or decrease in amounts taken is the result of a change in price (which comes from the supply side) or a change in income, tastes, or rate of substitution (which is an influence from the demand side).

Elasticity of Demand

The *demand curve* will be negatively inclined or downward sloping for any particular good. However, demand curves for different sorts of goods

267

will vary in the steepness of their slope. On some demand curves the increase in amount taken as the price is lowered will be relatively greater than for others. This quality of the demand curve we call *elasticity*.

One approach to demand elasticity is to consider its two extremes. The horizontal demand curve, the one parallel to the X axis, would be completely elastic—an elasticity of infinity. On the other hand, a curve perpendicular to the X axis would have zero elasticity (Figure 16). No such demand curves can be imagined from experience. These are concepts useful as criteria with which to compare any actual demand situation.

On a curve which is elastic the increase in amount taken, if the price is lowered even slightly, will be relatively great. On a curve which is only slightly elastic even a fairly large decrease in the price will lead to only a small relative increase in amount taken.

We can now offer the following tentative definition. *Elasticity is a measure of the change in amount taken in response to a change in price on a given demand curve.* Our first test can be in terms of the total amount buyers would spend on a good at different prices. In Figure 17, the rectangle under the demand curve represents the total expenditure, since its area is determined by the price per unit multiplied by the amount taken. If we lower the price and then compare the total expenditure at the new price with the total expenditure at the previous price, we can learn something of the relative changes in the two variables. If at a lower price more is spent than at a higher price, the demand curve between the two prices can be described as elastic, since the amount taken has increased relatively more than the price has decreased. If, on the other hand, at a lower price the amount spent is less than at a higher price, the demand would be characterized as inelastic, because the amount taken does not increase proportionally as much as the price decreases—hence a smaller total. If the rectangles are the same, the demand will be characterized as unitarily elastic, that is, neither elastic nor inelastic.

If demand is elastic an increase in the price will result in a smaller total expenditure, while if it is inelastic an increase in price will lead to a greater total expenditure. We can state this as a rule. On an elastic demand curve total expenditure will change in the opposite direction from the change in price. On an inelastic demand curve total expenditure will change in the same direction as price. We can formulate our definition more precisely in the form of a ratio. The simple equation for a statement of price elasticity would be:

$$E = \frac{\text{Percentage change in quantity}}{\text{Percentage change in price}}.$$

268

Assume a 5 per cent decrease in price. If the increase in quantity is 10 per cent, the elasticity of demand would be 2. This demand would then be said to be elastic because the amount taken increased by a percentage greater than the percentage decrease in price. If, however, in response to a 10 per cent decrease in price, the amount taken increased by only 5 per cent, elasticity would be .5, in which case the demand would be inelastic. If the percentages were the same, say 10 per cent in each case, the elasticity of demand would be one or unity, midway between elastic and inelastic or the dividing line between the two.

We can now state the definition of elasticity a little more precisely. It is the percentage change in quantity which would result from a one per cent change in price. Thus in our first example, where the elasticity was two, we can say that for each one per cent change in price the amount taken will change in the opposite direction by two per cent. In the second example a one per cent change in price would produce only a one-half per cent change in quantity, and in the third case, the example of unit elasticity, a one per cent change in price results in a one per cent change in amount taken, and there is no change in the total expenditure on the good.

Supply of a Particular Good

In contrast to the buying side of the market, the behavior of sellers is characterized by another pattern. While at a high price buyers would be willing to take only a reduced amount of the good, sellers would ordinarily decide to dispose of a larger quantity. If the price were low they would be unwilling to surrender more than a small quantity of the product for liquid claims. A hypothetical example of the supply schedule for socks on our market might be as follows:

SUPPLY OF SOCKS

Price per Pair	Number Pairs Offered
$.75	300
.70	250
.65	200
.60	160
.55	130
.50	110
.45	100
.40	75

269

Figure 16. Upper and Lower Limits
of Demand Elasticity

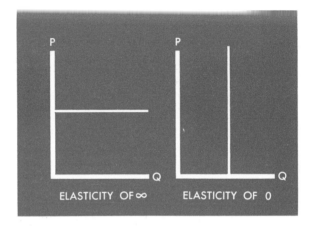

ELASTICITY OF ∞   ELASTICITY OF 0

Figure 17. Straight-Line Demand Curves
of Different Degrees of Elasticity

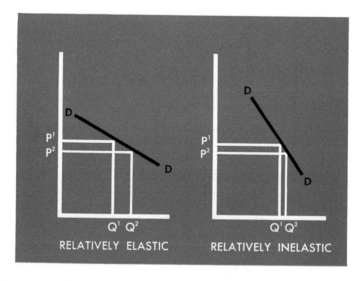

RELATIVELY ELASTIC   RELATIVELY INELASTIC

These figures give us a curve which slopes upward to the right (Figure 18). The relationship between price and quantity is described as a *direct* one. The determinants of supply are related to costs incurred in producing the good. A more complete development, therefore, must await our discussion of costs. However, here we can say that just as the eagerness of buyers to purchase differed among the different buyers, so too

270

Figure 18. Hypothetical Supply Curve, Showing
Increase and Decrease in Supply

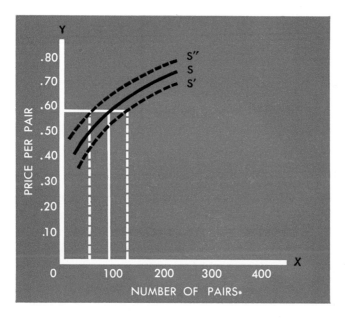

Figure 19. Hypothetical Supply and Demand Curves
with Equilibrium Market Price

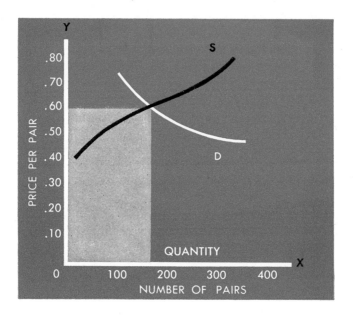

the eagerness of sellers to sell will vary. The need for cash will vary among sellers. Each will be likely to have some *reservation price* below which he would be unwilling to exchange the product for money. If he is hard pressed by conditions he may be willing to sell at a very low price. As the price rises the reservation prices of more and more suppliers will be met and hence more will be offered. At a very high price a much larger quantity will be offered for sale.

The steepness or flatness of the supply curve will depend on the nature of the production process and whether the amount to be put on the market can be expanded rapidly or only after a lapse of time. Thus the elasticity of supply is related to the conditions under which the good is produced.

Market Price

We can now combine the two schedules on the same graph—the downward-sloping demand curve and the upward-sloping supply curve (Figure 19). Under the assumed conditions, it will be apparent that only at one price will the amount offered and the amount demanded be the same. This is the point at which the demand and supply curves intersect, and is called *market price*. It is the price which accommodates both sides of the market. At a higher price more would be offered than taken. Some of the suppliers could not find buyers. At a lower price more would be demanded than offered. Some of the buyers could not find willing sellers. The market price, in other words, would clear the market, and those unwilling sellers would take their unsold goods away with them or wait for another day, while the buyers with insufficient income, or indifferent tastes, or who regarded their present stock as adequate would leave the market empty-handed. Accordingly, we will call the market price the short-run equilibrium price.

Discussion
Questions

1. If, as a result of short supply, the price of beef rises and consumers shift their purchases from beef to pork, does this represent a change in tastes? How would such a shift appear to pork producers?

2. How do you think your family would respond, if the price of salt were to increase by 50 per cent? Would you describe the demand for salt as elastic or inelastic? Why?

3. Prepare a list of goods and services which, in your opinion, would be tied to a purely local market. Compare this list with a list of items for which the market is national or even world-wide. What factors account for differences among these goods?

4. As a result of medical reports on effects of smoking, purchases of filter cigarettes have increased relative to nonfilter cigarettes. In terms of the concepts developed in this chapter, how would you describe this change?

5. As real income in the United States has increased, demand for services has increased (as described in Chapter 12). How would you relate this fact to the discussion of the determinants of demand in this chapter?

CHAPTER 15

The Competitive Market

MARKETS DIFFER in many respects. In this and succeeding chapters we will be concerned with the features which are significant in price formation and which affect the decisions of firms respecting what to produce and how much. This chapter deals with the *competitive market*. The conclusions and relationships follow by inference from a set of carefully defined conditions.

Competition is a term with a variety of meanings. It is most commonly associated with rivalry or struggle. From the playing field or the battle ground to love and romance, from man's everyday affairs to the struggle for existence in nature, the events of experience can be characterized as competitive.

Market competition has some of these associations, but the "spoils" are of a carefully defined sort. Beginning early in the last century and influenced in part by Darwin's theory of evolution, economists viewed competition in the everyday business of making a living as part of the "natural order" of things.[1] Given organized social institutions, and with prescribed limits to action set by property forms and accepted practice, it was viewed as a process and a means of discovering when attempts to achieve further profit-income would cease, in the knowledge that all had been done that could be done. The goal (or the "spoils") of economic activity in an industrial society is income. For the private firm this reward is *profit*. The question the economist asks is: When will profit be maximized? This implies some limit.

In most concepts of competition there is a presumption of *equality*

---

[1] It may be interesting to note that Darwin himself was not without debt to the economists. Darwin has credited to the population theory of Malthus (the tendency for population to outrun food supplies) his own inspiration for the idea of the survival of the fittest, which became the driving principle of his evolutionary process.

among the contenders, and a belief that the results of the struggle cannot be known in advance. The outcome can only be determined by the test of opposing forces, in this instance the market forces of supply and demand. The institutions of private property—free contract and the desire for income—can assure this impartial determination of results. The "ideal type" of the perfectly competitive market is most usefully perceived, therefore, as one in which individual decisions and actions result in an equilibrating or balancing of opposing forces. The requirements for a perfectly competitive market in an analytical sense, as outlined and identified by economists, are six:[2]

1. A large number of buyers.
2. A large number of sellers.
3. A homogeneous product.
4. Free entry into and exit from the market.
5. A knowledge among buyers of their wants and income, as well as full knowledge of other products and relative prices.
6. A knowledge by sellers of their costs, and of what price they must ask to cover these costs.

A large number of buyers and sellers is necessary so that no *one* of them can, by decision to buy or sell, greatly influence the market. Free-

Figure 20. Demand for Output of Individual Competitive Firm

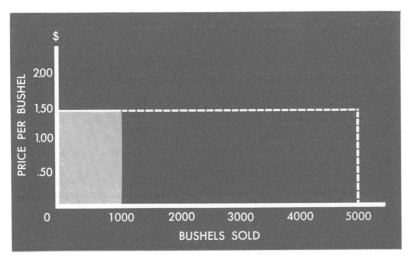

2 A rigorous logical analysis of the assumptions connected with the idea of the competitive market would include more than are listed here. Each of the terms used could be analyzed further. For our present level of presentation, these will do. As it stands, however, the model is the limiting case, rather than a comprehensive one.

dom of entry and exit are necessary if sellers are to take advantage of any rise in price, and if buyers are to be free to fill their needs when prices fall by converting money into goods. The assumption of a homogeneous product is an analytical convenience, a simplifying condition which can be dropped for more complex situations.

Decisions to Produce

In production the significance of the competitive market can be comprehended by the way it appears to the individual producer or firm, and by the relationship among the firms making up an industry. Each firm is one of many; its output is only a small part of the total. The buyers, also many in number, are not known to the firm in any personal sense, nor the firm to them. Since the product offered for sale is assumed at the outset to be homogeneous, there is no reason for preferring the output of any particular firm. Purchasers trade where they can get the good for the lowest price.

The firm has no incentive to undersell the market, which functions as the impersonal arbiter of price. There is no point in trying to undersell the many competing firms, since the output of no single firm is enough to increase or decrease significantly the total supply. At the quoted price for a given time the firm simply decides to sell or not to sell. Having sold, it decides further whether to go on producing either more or less than in the recent past.

This relationship to the market may be clearer if we look at it through the eyes of the individual seller. Demand as seen by the seller is infinitely elastic. This can be illustrated by means of *a demand curve for this firm's output*. We can use as an example the case of a wheat producer who can offer 5,000 bushels for sale. The market price is assumed to be $1.50 per bushel. He can sell one bushel, 100 bushels, 1,000 bushels, or the entire 5,000 bushels at that price. Plotting these amounts against the price we get a series of points which can be connected as a horizontal curve (Figure 20), which we know from our earlier discussion to be infinitely elastic. If the producer decides to sell 1,000 bushels, his total revenue is the area marked off by the solid line—1,000 × $1.50, or $1,500. His average and marginal revenue are each $1.50, since each additional bushel sold added $1.50 to total revenue. This single curve then represents the demand for his *output,* the average revenue curve, the marginal revenue curve, and an extension of the price line to cover the whole lot.

In the example just cited the decision of the producer to sell 1,000 bushels is arbitrary. We have not inquired into how he arrived at that decision. It can be presumed that the market met his reservation price, the price below which he would not sell. What determined that reservation price? More important, what effect will the price he receives have on his decision to go on producing wheat? To answer this question involves us in a concept of costs.

Costs of the Individual Firm

The firm has been defined as the basic unit of production. It is the organization that brings together the different factors of production to produce for the market the goods or services with which it hopes to realize an income. It contributes to the real-income flows of the nation, and receives a money claim.

Decisions to sell or to produce are made by people. Thus there is implied a directing or organizing head of the firm, which we have defined as the *entrepreneur*. This need not be a single person, as we shall see in a later section, and the decision may be made by an agent of the owners of the firm. The *function of entrepreneurship* involves the making of decisions to produce, to sell, or to go out of production. With one eye on the market and the size of the claim, or the price that is being offered, and the other on costs, the entrepreneur seeks to *maximize* profits by bringing together the factors of production for which he must pay, since the owners of these factors, whether labor or capital, are likewise seeking to maximize their incomes.

For the present analysis it will simplify things if the costs or the prices of the factors of production are assumed to be given, and that they do not change during the period under consideration. Later we will extend our analysis to explain how the prices of the factors themselves are determined (Part 4). With costs given, and with a price for the product given, it is possible to determine an output which will maximize profit or minimize loss (where profit is impossible).

Fixed Costs

The act of deciding to go into production involves commitments. If the firm has liquid assets (and usually it must have) it must *invest* them in plant, equipment, and so forth. These are partially nonrecoverable costs, unless ultimately paid out of revenue from production. Even if nothing is finally produced, these costs represent claims of others against the firm or the property it owns. This can be illustrated best by an example. At the outset, the firm will ordinarily require a business site—a building or plant. This it may acquire outright by purchase (the surrender of liquid claims or borrowed funds), through construction (in which case the contractor is paid with available funds), or by lease (in which case a contract arrangement is made for payments). Equipment is secured, permanent personnel hired on a contract basis, and other commitments made before a single unit of output is produced. Accordingly, a certain fixed amount will be assessed against the firm and entered in its accounts. Let us assume that this total is $100 for a given period of time, perhaps a day, a week, or a month. Should the business be liquidated or fail before it gets into production, at least part of this investment would be lost to the owners.

A point to keep in mind is that these costs *do not vary with output* once the scale has been decided. If the output is small, these fixed costs will be apportioned among a small number of units and fixed cost per unit will be very high. As output expands and a larger output bears the cost burden, the fixed cost per unit falls rapidly, and if the output is large enough it will become very small indeed. Table 16 is a compilation of cost figures for an imaginary firm turning out a single commodity. Column 1 shows the output, column 2 the fixed costs, and column 3 the average fixed costs. From our earlier discussion of the simple theory of production, it will be evident that fixed costs are associated with the fixed factor or factors. These costs fall rapidly as the output increases.

Variable Costs

Once the firm is ready to produce for the market, it will incur other costs directly related to the volume of output. Such items as raw materials, nonspecialized labor, power, water, and light will be used in different amounts, depending upon how much is produced. Thus, as the volume of output is increased, the costs of variable factors will increase. Total variable costs divided by the units of output will give another average, the average variable costs per unit.

When output is small the fixed factors will not be used in the most effective combination with the variable. It will be recalled from the discussion of a simple theory of production that the average and marginal product rose initially when certain factors were fixed and others varied. This we saw was because of the increasing productivity in the combination of factors. If the additional physical output per unit of input is rising, it will be evident that when these inputs are converted to money terms the cost per unit output will be falling. The average variable cost curve will fall to the point of diminishing average returns, and will then rise at an increasing rate as the fixed plant or establishment reaches the peak of its most effective operation. The average variable costs are shown in column 5 of Table 16.

278

Table 16. Hypothetical Costs of an Individual Firm

1 Output: No. of Units	2 Total Fixed Costs	3 Average Fixed Costs— 2 ÷ 1	4 Total Variable Costs	5 Average Variable Costs— 4 ÷ 1	6 Total Costs— 2 + 4	7 Average Cost— 6 ÷ 1 or 3 + 5	8 Marginal Costs— $T_2 - T_1$,* etc.
1	$100	$100.00	$ 10.00	$10.00	$110.00	$110.00	—
2	100	50.00	19.00	9.50	119.00	59.50	$ 9
3	100	33.33	26.00	8.66	126.00	42.00	7
4	100	25.00	31.00	7.75	131.00	32.75	5
5	100	20.00	35.00	7.00	135.00	27.00	4
6	100	16.66	40.00	6.66	140.00	23.33	5
7	100	14.28	46.00	6.57	146.00	20.86	6
8	100	12.50	53.00	6.62	153.00	19.13	7
9	100	11.11	61.00	6.77	161.00	17.89	8
10	100	10.00	70.00	7.00	170.00	17.00	9
11	100	9.09	80.00	7.27	180.00	16.36	10
12	100	8.33	91.00	7.53	191.00	15.92	11
13	100	7.69	104.00	8.00	204.00	15.69	13
14	100	7.14	119.00	8.50	219.00	15.64	15
15	100	6.66	136.00	9.06	236.00	15.73	17
16	100	6.25	155.00	9.68	255.00	15.93	19
17	100	5.88	176.00	10.35	276.00	16.23	21
18	100	5.55	199.00	11.05	299.00	16.61	23
19	100	5.26	224.00	11.78	324.00	17.05	25
20	100	5.00	252.00	12.60	352.00	17.60	28
21	100	4.76	283.00	13.47	383.00	18.23	31
22	100	4.54	317.00	14.40	417.00	18.95	34
23	100	4.34	354.00	15.39	454.00	19.73	37
24	100	4.16	394.00	16.41	494.00	20.58	40
25	100	4.00	437.00	17.48	537.00	21.48	43
26	100	3.80	484.00	18.61	584.00	22.46	47
27	100	3.70	535.00	19.81	635.00	23.51	51
28	100	3.57	590.00	21.07	690.00	24.64	55
29	100	3.44	649.00	22.37	749.00	25.82	59
30	100	3.33	713.00	23.76	813.00	27.10	64

* T = Total Costs.

To determine the cost per unit of output, however, the firm needs to know not only the two separate average costs but also the total average cost per unit. Thus, if for every output we add together the fixed and variable costs and divide by the number of units of output, we will obtain the cost per unit, or average cost. Since at very small outputs both

279

the fixed cost per unit and the variable cost per unit will be falling, the average cost per unit will fall very rapidly as output expands. As the fixed costs fall more and more slowly and the variable costs rise at an increasing rate, the average cost per unit will decline to a minimum, after which it too will rise at an increasing rate. Figure 21 shows the relationship among the three curves.

One additional cost curve, which is not a cost in any direct or real sense but expresses a relationship between cost and output, is the *marginal cost curve,* which is analogous to the marginal productivity curve in simple production. It represents the added cost of producing one more unit of output (starting from any previous output), and measures the *rate* at which total cost is increasing. Since as output increases only the variable costs change, the marginal cost curve can be derived either from total variable costs or total costs. The marginal cost curve will intersect the average variable cost curve and the average cost curve at their lowest points, just as the marginal productivity curve cut the average productivity curve at its highest point. Where productivity is rising, given constant costs for the factors, cost will be falling. The four cost curves are now combined in Figure 23 to show the relationships of the firm's costs to one another. These are the cost relationships which a firm will find useful in making its decisions if it desires to maximize profit.

Costs and Revenue

If these costs are known, the answer to the question of how much to produce is a relatively simple one. By plotting graphically the information from column 6 in Table 16, a total cost curve rises from its intersection of the vertical axis at $100 (the amount of fixed costs) at a variable rate until it reaches the capacity shown in the table (Figure 22). If we take $25 as our market price for the product, the corresponding revenue curve would be a straight line rising at a constant rate beginning at an output of one unit. This type of graphic representation can be called a *break-even chart.* Point A on the chart is the *break-even point.* At an output of 6[3] all costs are covered. At a price higher than $25 per unit the break-even point would be reached at a smaller output. At a price below $15.64 there would be no output at which total costs could be covered.

If the firm seeks to produce at the point where the difference between the total revenue and the total cost is greatest, this will be the out-

---

[3] The actual intersection of the curves is between 5 and 6 units.

put directly below the point where the distance beween these two curves is greatest. To locate this point, it would be necessary to compute total revenue and total costs for various outputs, subtracting the one from the other (costs from revenue), and choosing the output where the difference is greatest. In this instance that output is 19. Beyond this point, because of the tendency for costs to rise at an increasing rate, the distance between the two curves will narrow again. At some conceivable output, indicated by *B* on the chart, profit would again disappear and losses would result.

Market Periods

So far our analysis has been static. Time has been left out of account. The adjustments which a firm must make are experienced in a time sequence in which changes in the market price for output occur. Disregarding for the moment changes related to fluctuations in the general price level which affect both factor prices and finished goods (often unequally), we will need to take into account fluctuations in relative prices, particularly of close substitutes, which will affect the demand for a given product and for changes in supply, because of the entry and exit of firms to and from the industry. Three different market situations based upon the length of time involved can be distinguished.

The first has been called the *period of market supply*. In point of time this is the shortest. It is a period during which the amount of a given product has already been produced. All costs, both fixed and variable, incidental to this output have been incurred. Production cannot be undone. Costs can only be recovered through sale of the goods. If the market has turned unfavorable, either because buyers' expectations for income have become unfavorable, because their tastes have changed or because the market is already flooded with this particular good, then the seller (in this case the firm) can only do the best it can to recover costs. Sale may be postponed to await a more favorable market, in which case inventories rise. If the adversity appears likely to be of some duration, then it may not be worthwhile to incur the added costs of storage, and the output will be offered for what buyers will pay. If the good is perishable or subject to changing fashion, the pressure to sell is likely to be greater. Fruit and vegetable markets usually offer special bargains at closing time. Department stores and fashion shops plan their sales sometime after the peak of seasonal buying. In this short period, then, the demand side of the market is all-important and will determine what the market price for goods already produced will be. It will affect the current income of the firm (and industry), but it cannot alter production decisions that have been made.

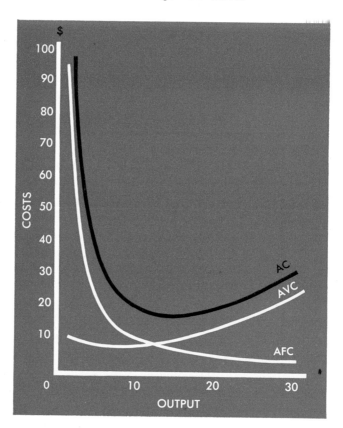

Figure 21. Average Fixed, Average Variable,
and Average Cost Curves

The Short-Run Period

The next period, which is usually called the short-run period, covers a time during which existing firms (with particular reference to the firm under consideration) can expand or contract output with existing plant and equipment through increasing or decreasing the variable input. If the market price has changed, either up or down, then in the short run the firm will expand or contract its output.

What are the limits to this short-run expansion or contraction? A higher price per unit means a larger revenue. It also means a more favorable cost-price relationship, since it extends the range of fixed costs which can be covered in the short run. Analytically, it is here that the cost curves derived earlier find their use. The marginal cost curve provides a short

282

Figure 22. Total Cost and Total Revenue Curves,
Break-Even Points, Under Competition

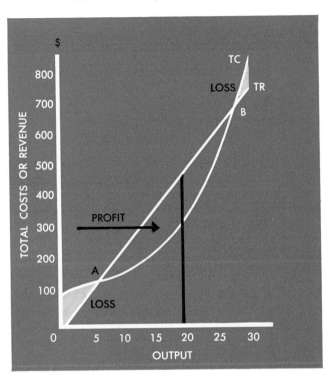

cut for decision, since it is a result of a previous analysis of costs. It shows the cost of an additional unit, starting from any given output.

Generally speaking, if output is determined at the point where the price or marginal revenue curve intersects the marginal cost curve ($MC=MR$), the firm will have made its best short-run adjustment. This is defined as equilibrium, the output from which there will be no short-run incentive to change. For our hypothetical firm this output will be 19 units, if the price is $25 (Figure 23). Here profit will be a maximum. Literally, what the above relationship tells us is that as long as the price that can be obtained for an additional unit is greater than the additional cost, total profit will be increased by producing that additional unit. By the same logic a fall in the market price—a decline in MR—will call for a reduction in output to the point of the new intersection of MC and MR. If the market price falls below the average cost in the short run, this output will minimize the loss.

How low can the market price fall before the individual firm will cease producing entirely? A moment's reflection will make it clear that should the price fall below the variable cost of production, the firm will minimize its losses by closing down. To produce under such conditions would mean that the firm loses not only the fixed costs (which it must pay in any event) but also at least a part of the costs of materials or labor going into the product, and which it could avoid if it stopped producing.

The basis has now been established for determining the entire supply curve for the firm in the short-run period. Since at each market price the firm will produce and sell the output at which the marginal revenue just equals the marginal cost, the marginal cost curve can be said to determine the short-run supply curve of the individual firm. A summation of the marginal cost curves of all firms in an industry will give the *short-run market supply curve*.

How long is the short-run period? For how long would the firm continue to produce if prices were to remain stable at any given level? If this firm were one in a large industry that had overexpanded so that price remained consistently below the average cost of production, it, along with others, would be failing to cover all costs. For a time each would attempt to minimize losses by restricting output. However, no firm could continue to do so indefinitely. While it might be covering its variable costs, it would not be able to meet all fixed costs. This might mean paying no return on the capital invested. It could mean neglect of depreciation reserves to replace physical capital as it wears out or becomes obsolete. If such conditions endured, any firm would of necessity go out of business over the long period. Since this firm is one of many, the final determination of whether or not it would fail would depend upon its ability to withstand losses compared with other firms in the field.

The Long-Run Period

This brings us to the third time period, the long-run period, which defines the conditions for equilibrium in the industry, as well as equilibrium in the firm. Our concern here is not with the individual firm alone, but with all of the firms which together make up the industry. The long-run market or production period can be defined as the length of time required for production to be increased or decreased through the expansion or contraction of the number of firms in the industry, or through the expansion of the size of existing firms.

Assume that the market price rises and remains for some time in excess of the prevailing average cost of production. The representative firm, if it produces at the output at which $MR=MC$, will make a profit. After all costs are paid, including normal returns on investment and the salaries

284

of management, a residual or profit income will remain. This means that purchasers are now willing to pay more than the average cost of production. Evidence that the market could absorb more stems from the fact that those who are producing for the market are making profits. Under the competitive conditions which have been posited, it is unlikely that existing capacity would remain the same. Individual firms might seek still larger profits by enlarging their plants by ploughing profits back into the business. Since a competitive market is relatively unrestricted, however, the entry of new firms into the field would be more likely.

In either event the result would be the same—an increase in the available supply. There would be more sellers and an increased offering on the market. The market supply curve would shift to the right. As this happened, if demand did not increase further, sellers would be seeking buyers. On our diagram the new supply curve would cut the demand curve at a lower point, and market price would decline. If the initial price rise resulted in an overexpansion, as frequently happens in experience, the price would fall below long-run average costs. Firms would now be undergoing a loss. If the costs of all firms were not everywhere the same, those with the highest costs would be incurring the largest losses. Forced withdrawal through bankruptcy or through conversion to other commodities would follow.

Is there a situation in which expansion or contraction over the long run would not take place? The requirements for this condition would constitute *equilibrium* within both the firm and the industry. If the market price equals the marginal cost of the firm at the output which also just covers average cost, then the individual firm would have no incentive either to expand or to contract output in the short run. Furthermore, there would be no incentive either to increase or to withdraw capital from the field. The optimum firm would not be making a profit, but on the other hand it would not incur a loss. It would be covering all costs of production, including full return on capital, necessary reserves for depreciation and obsolescence, plus the wages of management necessary to retain management skills. In terms of our model, this is what is meant by *long-run equilibrium*.

The question will no doubt be raised, "In a profit system and in a situation where firms are motivated by the desire for profits, how can an industry operate over the long run if there are no profits?" The answer is inferred from the special features of competition. In the market situation outlined above, where entry and exit are free and comparatively easy, there is no means whereby the individual firm can protect its profit position. When profits exist, other firms in search of profit will enter the indus-

Figure 23. Marginal and Average Cost Curves,
Basic Decision-Making Tools

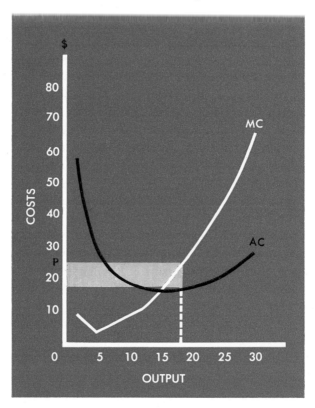

try and profits will be reduced. According to this model, in an economy in which a large proportion of industries were operating under conditions of perfect competition there would be no long-run profits. Buyers in a competitive market would secure the goods they sought at their minimum supply price or their lowest average cost of production. However, the individual firm, making no profit, could not expect to improve its situation by shifting to another industry, since over the longer period it could hope to obtain no more than the going rate of return on its investment and a rate of management return which would itself be determined through competition.

If the owners of factors of production were free to shift them, it would mean that all resources would find their way over a period of time into the fields of production most highly valued by the consumer. They would be allocated to provide for the satisfaction of the most urgent or

286

most important wants. As those wants changed and consumers, tired of old goods, sought new satisfactions, resources would find their most profitable use in providing new goods. Entrepreneurs, as organizers and risk takers, might secure short-run profit incomes as rewards for innovations, but over a long period they would only secure the normal rewards of management and invested capital.

Thus in this abstract model of entrepreneurial behavior it is the *hope of profit income,* not profit as such, which is assumed to motivate production decisions. Short-run profits, which are facts of experience for many firms, are projected in the imagination of the entrepreneur to favorable future income situations, and are acted upon. Accordingly, as an ideal model, competitive free enterprise becomes both a hypothetical description of behavior and a criterion for a "desirable" organization for the allocation of the factors of production.

Economies of Scale

Factors of production can be combined in different ways. This was dealt with in the discussion of our simple production model (see pages 245–53). To produce a given output, more or less fixed capital or equipment may be used. An automobile can be made by hand labor—samples of new models usually are, at great cost. Or it can be made by machines and rela-

Figure 24. Market Price and Short-Run Equilibrium of the Firm

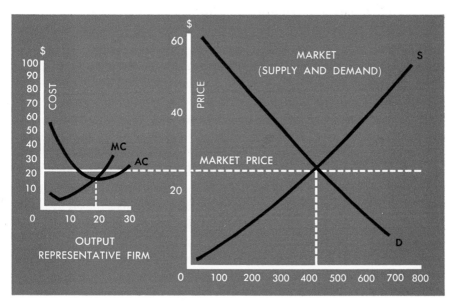

tively small amounts of labor time. Capital and labor are substitutes, within limits, for each other.

Large machines are indivisible, however, and represent large capital investments. This means that a firm which invests heavily in capital equipment will have a greater proportion of fixed costs. As has been noted, fixed costs fall rapidly as output expands, and will continue to fall as long as output can be increased. Hence the greater the proportion of fixed costs to variable costs, the more rapidly will the average cost of production fall as output expands and the lower it will be at the optimum. This is the basis of the economies of large-scale production.

Is there any limit to this process? At any given time is there any combination of factors which, under competition, will give the very lowest cost of production? These are important questions, because on the answers depends the possibility of some kind of equilibrium being established.

The concept used to designate such an adjustment of factors is the *optimum firm*. It is defined as that firm which, with a given state of the arts, has achieved the combination of factors at prevailing prices which gives the lowest average cost, and which can be said to be the most efficient combination. The classical economists believed that under competition all firms would tend toward such a combination. Given sufficient time, the equilibrium or long-run normal price will tend to equal the lowest average cost of production of the optimum firm. Figure 24 is a representation of the market supply and demand curves when the industry is in equilibrium, with the market price extended to show the optimum firm in equilibrium.

Such a situation, of course, could persist only under relatively static conditions, in which all technological change had ceased on the one hand, and in which tastes remained the same on the other. Population also would probably have to remain constant. While some economists have speculated about the possibilities of static conditions, they have mostly recognized that such is not the nature of the world in which we live. The nineteenth century was a period of rapid technological change; the twentieth has been even more so. It may be useful to visualize an economic system as tending toward an equilibrium, but never reaching it because of changing tastes and technology. Firms expand as they adapt their production processes to newer, more efficient technology and to the changing pattern of consumer behavior as expressed in the choice of goods and services.

Competition is an important motivating influence in the adoption of newer, more efficient methods. For if a firm can cut costs by the use of more efficient technology and organization, it can undersell the less efficient organizations. Not only can it realize greater profits, but by underselling the less efficient producers the low-cost firm can command an increasing share of the market. Thus other firms are forced to adopt more efficient methods to stay in the market.

At any given time considerable difference could exist in the costs of actual firms. The most efficient would achieve unit costs below the going market price and would be making a profit. Others would be just covering costs, including normal returns on capital and the wages of management. Still others would be gradually falling back, able to remain in the race only for the short run or as long as prices were sufficient to cover variable costs and pay something on fixed costs. This relationship is shown in Figure 25.

The Marginal Firm

In this setting the firm which is just covering all of its costs, the marginal firm, is of strategic importance. For if the submarginal firms withdraw, the resulting decrease in supply would result in an increase in the market price and other producers, attracted by the profits of the remaining firms, would enter. The marginal firm would then be back at its old position.

Is there a limit to the efficiency of scale? The answer to this question will decide whether or not the special features of competitive industry can persist. For if one firm, or even a small number of firms, can undersell the others because of greater efficiency, the latter will lose in the market. One of the requirements for a competitive market—a large number of sellers—would disappear. On the other hand, if there is some optimum scale of operation it would be perfectly possible for a large number of production units to exist, each of about the same efficiency. This would mean that beyond the optimum output, under competition, long-run average costs would again begin to rise. Some economists have maintained that such is the case. If at some point the supply of an important factor of production ceased to be elastic, costs would increase. In the case of some industries based upon resources that are naturally limited, such as land, the point of increasing costs would be reached relatively soon. Agriculture has long been recognized as an increasing-costs industry. To increase its output, any single firm would be required to pay a higher and higher price for the limited factor, again assuming static technology.

But how about an industry based upon the use of large-scale capital equipment which is not only expanded but also improved? The greater the proportion of fixed costs, the more rapidly average costs will decline. Is there nothing to limit such increasing efficiency?

The limiting factor was once thought to be management, or more

Figure 25. Three Short-Run Equilibrium Situations

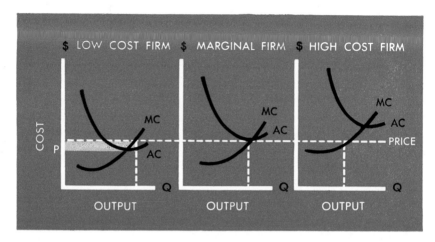

specifically the problem it faces in co-ordination and supervision. A capable enterpriser, beginning on a small scale and by increasing the specialization of his function as manager, can gradually extend his abilities over a much larger and more efficient organization. Eventually, however, as the firm acquires more and more plants, supervision must be delegated to others. Limitations of the human factor become predominant as direct personal contact is diluted. Bureaucracy and red tape increase. Consequently, efficiency declines and costs rise.

Such a tendency can be shown graphically by means of the *long-run cost curve* for an industry, illustrated in Figure 26. This is a sequence of average cost curves for a changing series of optimum scales. As output expands the average cost curve of the optimum firm decreases through successive stages until it reaches a minimum level, and for a time the industry may be able to expand at relatively constant costs by duplicating the optimum firm. Eventually, however, the costs of the industry will rise as it is forced to bid factors away from other industries. The *envelope curve* enclosing the series of smaller average cost curves of the representative or optimum firm shows the long-run costs of the industry. The vertical dotted lines mark off the different stages. Area *A* designates the stage of decreasing costs; *B* shows costs that are fairly constant; *C* is the stage of increasing long-run costs. An industry can expand into area *C* only when the demand for its product is increasing substantially.[4]

---

[4] This same curve can be viewed as a *planning curve* for a firm before it has made commitments regarding size of scale. As it expands it is able to achieve lower costs, until it expands beyond the optimum.

290

Figure 26. Long-Run Planning or Envelope Cost Curve for Industry

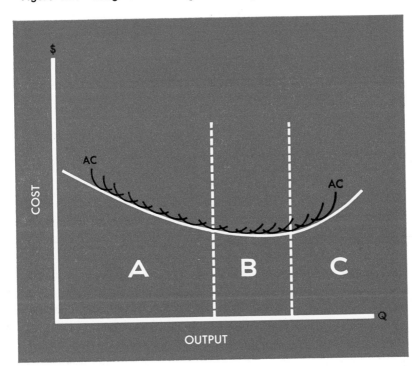

Internal and External Economies

So far we have been concerned with the economies that accrue to the individual firm as a result of actions taken *internally*. Savings in costs brought about through more productive combinations of factors, which are the results of more efficient organization and management, are of this kind.

There are additional income advantages which arise outside the firm and are in effect another aspect of the division of labor and specialization. These are known as *external economies*.[5] An example will help to clarify the concept. Firms of a new industry will find it difficult to secure trained workers for specialized jobs. There may be no subsidiary industries to supply parts of the proper design for assembly into the finished product. Henry

---

[5] The concept of external economies and factor allocation get us involved in questions which concern the factor market. The simplifying assumption adopted at the beginning of our analysis—that factor costs were given—now acts as a brake on extension of the market analysis until that assumption is removed. However, we have elected to discuss factor allocation in conjunction with distribution in answering the question, "Who gets what and how?" We will come back to it in Part 4. It perhaps needs to be emphasized again that we are pursuing an inquiry into the income process, and to do that conceptually we have to "freeze" it in order to examine certain relationships more precisely.

Ford, when he began the manufacture of automobiles, found few suppliers of carburetors, ignition systems, bearings, or even appropriate machine tools. Later on, as his output expanded, he could farm out the manufacture of these separate parts. Subsidiary industries could devote full time to supplying the needs of the automobile industry. Workers from all parts of the country flocked to Detroit as the information circulated that Ford was hiring men at what was then high wages.

When an industry has existed for some time it can benefit from the internal economies or efficiencies of the various supplying industries, including the graduates of trade schools, universities, and business schools which undertake to train people to fit its needs. It becomes difficult to trace the concept beyond two or three fairly obvious steps, because it is soon lost in the complex web of the social process itself. We can only observe that any business operating in a modern, highly organized society realizes benefits therefrom, some of which it pays for directly, some only indirectly, if at all. External economies which contribute much to economic progress can be viewed as an achievement of society itself. By the same token, diseconomies can be transmitted to many remote and seemingly unrelated parts of the economy when the normal channels of trade are blocked because of friction, conflict, or control by interest groups.

Competition and Laissez Faire

One of the advantages long claimed for the competitive market is that it tends to be self-regulating. Where it has operated effectively it has required only a minimum of government interference to ensure the greatest social advantage as far as the *maximizing* of national income (minimizing cost) is concerned.

Free consumers, left to determine their own wants, reward the producer who pleases them by buying his products and punish those who fail to respond to their desires by leaving them with their assets tied up in a surplus of unsold goods. When each individual, in pursuit of his own gain, was checked and balanced by the next individual in search of the same, profits (where they existed) were the rewards for initiative in anticipating the desires of the market and in adopting efficient methods. But they could be no more than short-run profits, since others attracted to the field would copy what had been done and slowly expand the output of goods which had found favor there, until the market price was driven down and until it erased everything above the normal costs of production.

Until the fourth decade of the present century the main body of academic economics, at least, concerned itself with refinements of the theory of perfect competition as an explanation of the workings of the

292

enterprise economy. The focuses of attention were the interaction of the forces of supply and demand in the market, the determination of value or price of the individual commodity, and the forces tending to bring about equilibrium within the firm and in the industry. The fact that not all markets were competitive did not go unnoticed. It may be recalled that the general public had become quite aware of and excited about the growth of large business units which were beginning to dominate some markets. This was especially true in America, where public concern resulted in the passage of the Sherman Anti-Trust Act of 1890. Some states had undertaken to regulate large firms—particularly the railroads—even earlier. The existence of monopolistic tendencies was noted and deplored, but the central body of theory—the general model—was not extended to include the decision making of firms under other than competitive conditions until 1933.

Discussion
Questions

1. The concept of the competitive market has certain value assumptions associated with it. Whom is competition supposed to benefit?

2. What is the basis for time as defined by market periods? Would it be the same for all industries?

3. Why is short-run equilibrium a concept associated with the individual firm?

4. Why is long-run equilibrium unlikely to be fully realized in the world of experience? Would you characterize it as a descriptive or analytical concept?

5. In a competitive market economy, what is the principal criterion for allocation of the factors of production? In a behavioral sense, what does it mean to allocate factors of production?

6. Of what significance, analytically, is the representative firm?

7. Define economies of scale. How do indivisibilities relate to economies of scale?

CHAPTER 16

Monopoly

THE CONCEPT OF MONOPOLY, as it applies to markets, presupposes ideal conditions, which in several respects are completely opposite to those associated with our concept of competition. These include unequal power or control, freedom of action for the monopolist, and the absence of freedom for others.

To the extent that pure monopoly can be imagined, it would consist of a single supplier of a good greatly needed, for which no close substitute could be found. Experience provides us with no such example. To speak of pure monopoly in other than a verbal sense is to commit the fallacy of misplaced concreteness. But a condition of pure monopoly can be approached. In our modern world certain raw materials of strategic importance and limited supply are a case in point. For purposes of our model, however, pure monopoly is perceived only as a limiting case.

Production decisions by a firm operating under conditions of monopoly hinge on how the demand curve appears to the firm. In the previous chapter we saw that the demand curve for the *output* of a competitive firm could be perceived as a horizontal straight line. For a monopolist the market demand for the output of the firm would be the same as the demand for the product. In other words, it would be negatively inclined, sloping downward to the right.

With a downward-sloping demand curve, the monopolist is faced with a choice between high prices with a relatively small output and low prices which would permit a correspondingly larger output. On a given demand curve, when the price is chosen the amount which will be purchased is determined; or if a given output is offered on the market, the asking price cannot be higher than the buyers are willing to pay for that amount, unless changes in demand are induced.

The presumption is warranted that the firm or the entrepreneur will not be interested in price or quantity as such, but in the combination of price and quantity which maximizes profit. To determine the output which will result in maximum profit it will be necessary to know the costs of the firm as well as the total revenues that can be obtained from different outputs. Table 17 is an *assumed demand schedule* for the output of a monopolist. For each of the given prices and corresponding amounts that would be purchased, it is now possible to compute the total revenue. Total revenue, it will be noted, rises to a maximum and then declines. Where the total revenue of the competitive producer increased at a constant rate, the monopolist's total revenue increases at a decreasing rate, and at an output of 26 in our example ceases to increase at all. Beyond this point total revenue declines and marginal revenue becomes negative.

Table 17. Assumed Demand Schedule for Monopolistic Firm

Average Revenue or Price	Amount Purchased	Total Revenue	Marginal Revenue
$50.00	1	$ 50.00	—
49.00	2	98.00	$48
48.00	3	144.00	46
47.00	4	188.00	44
46.00	5	230.00	42
45.00	6	270.00	40
44.00	7	308.00	38
43.00	8	344.00	36
42.00	9	378.00	34
41.00	10	410.00	32
40.00	11	440.00	30
39.00	12	468.00	28
38.00	13	494.00	26
37.00	14	518.00	24
36.00	15	540.00	22
35.00	16	560.00	20
34.00	17	578.00	18
33.00	18	594.00	16
32.00	19	608.00	14
31.00	20	620.00	12
30.00	21	630.00	10
29.00	22	638.00	8
28.00	23	644.00	6
27.00	24	648.00	4
26.00	25	650.00	2
25.00	26	650.00	0
24.00	27	648.00	—2
23.00	28	644.00	—4
22.00	29	638.00	—6
21.00	30	630.00	—8

In Figure 27 total revenue is plotted against total costs[1] to give a *break-even chart*. Point *A* shows the output at which the firm will just cover all costs—approximately 3 units. Point *B* shows the hypothetical output beyond which no profit would be made. The greatest total profit (largest difference between revenue and costs) is realized at an output of 16 units.

Here again, as in the case of the competitive producer, we can simplify the process of locating the point of maximum profit by the use of the marginal revenue and marginal cost curves. Marginal revenue is derived from the total revenue figures, and is the amount added to total revenue at any given output if one more unit is produced or sold. Figure 28 is a graphic representation of the monopolist's demand schedule (or average revenue curve) along with the marginal revenue curve. Note that the marginal revenue curve is below the average revenue curve, and that it falls more steeply. The significance of this relationship lies in the fact that it will therefore intersect the marginal cost curve farther to the left, or at a smaller output.

For a producer seeking to maximize profits (or minimize losses) we now have the necessary information, which we can state in the form of a rule for production decisions under conditions of monopoly. It is the same as the rule for the competitive producer. As shown on the diagram, *if the monopolist produces at the point of intersection of the marginal cost and the marginal revenue curves (16 units), he will maximize profits.* This relationship is shown in Figure 29, which brings together the average and marginal revenue curves with the average and marginal cost curves.

When output is determined at the point where *MR* and *MC* intersect, a perpendicular erected from the base line through this point will intersect the average cost curve and the average revenue curve (price) showing the profit per unit. In this case per unit cost is $15.93 and price is $35, giving an average profit of approximately $19.00. Total profit, as shown by the shaded area, would be $305. Any larger or smaller output would result in a smaller total profit.

Monopoly and Elasticity of Demand

What is the significance to a monopolist of demand elasticity? It has been noted that an elastic demand is one which is sensitive to price changes. A small price change leads to a much greater proportional change in the amount taken. A price increase will result in a contraction in amount taken

---

[1] For purposes of simplification, the same cost figures as those employed in the chapter on competition have been used. If it makes the example more credible, the reader can imagine that the output figures represent hundreds or thousands of units.

and a smaller total expenditure than before the change. A price decrease, on the other hand, will lead to greater total expenditure. If the demand is inelastic, changes in total expenditure are reversed. The change in amount taken is less proportionally than the change in price. When the price is increased more is spent. When the price is decreased a smaller total expenditure results, and less revenue is taken in by the firm. An elastic demand, as has been noted, is one for which substitutes are available. Monopoly, by definition, assumes a lack of substitutability.

How demand elasticity affects the relationship between costs and revenues is of analytical importance. The straight-line demand curve used in our example above (Figure 29) is elastic for the upper two-thirds of its total length. This will be apparent from the fact that as the price decreases total revenue increases until the 25th unit. At that point total revenue reaches its maximum and begins to decline. Where the total revenue attains its maximum the marginal revenue becomes zero.

If a monopolist were selling a good which had no cost of production, he would expand his output to this point.[2] Where costs are involved, however, the profit-conscious monopolist will stop considerably short of that output. What about elasticity and the point of intersection of the MR and MC curves? Suppose the demand curve in our example had been more inelastic. In that case the slope of the average revenue or demand curve would have been greater, more nearly perpendicular. The marginal revenue curve, lying below it and falling more rapidly, would have intersected the marginal cost curve farther to the left at a smaller output.

Conversely, a more elastic demand curve would have been flatter and nearer the type of curve which faces a competitive producer. Average revenue and marginal revenue would have been closer together, while the marginal revenue curve would have cut the marginal cost curve farther to the right—at a larger output. A monopoly of a commodity with a completely elastic demand would be no monopoly at all. We will want to return to this point later when we consider monopolistic competition.

Monopoly and Equilibrium of the Firm

Just as in the case of competition, the firm under conditions of monopoly will be in short-run equilibrium when it is producing at the output where marginal cost equals marginal revenue. In other words, it will pay to go

---

[2] Antoine Cournot, a French mathematician and economist of the nineteenth century, who first formulated a theory of monopoly, chose as his example the sole owner of a mineral spring, the output of which involved no variable costs of production. He concluded that the monopolist would charge a price which maximized total revenue. In short, he would lower price and expand output (or sales) to the point where MR becomes zero.

Figure 27. Total Cost and Total Revenue Curves,
Break-Even Points, Under Monopoly

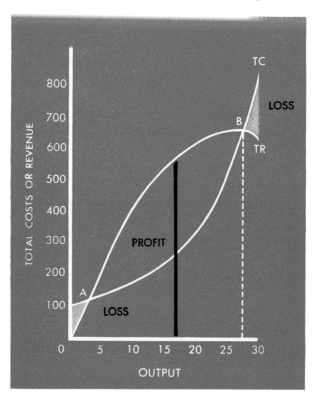

on producing as long as the marginal or additional unit is expected to sell for more than the additional cost of producing it.

What about the long run? If the monopoly were complete, there would be no outside compulsion to change output or price unless the demand determinants were to change or unless costs were to change. Since the field is monopolized, there can be no entry of new firms. Monopoly profits may continue indefinitely. Large profits need not be shared with others.

There may be some technological improvements. If by improved methods the firm can reduce costs, it may add still further to its profits. Moreover, if no change in demand occurs, a lowering of average and marginal costs will usually mean that the marginal revenue curve will intersect the cost curve farther to the right at a larger output. Thus a part of such increases in efficiency will be passed on to the rest of society in the

298

Figure 28. Average and Marginal Revenue Curves
Under Monopoly

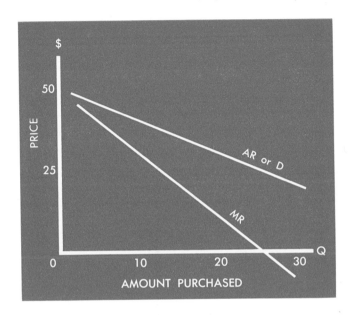

Figure 29. Cost and Revenue Relationships
Under Monopoly

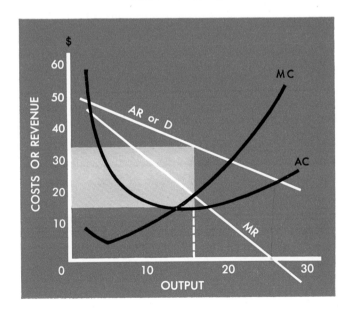

form of greater real-income flows. However, there appears to be some likelihood that the rate for adopting technological improvements under conditions of monopoly will usually be slower. If monopoly profits are substantial and there is no threat of competition, a monopolist would be likely to adopt a more leisurely attitude toward new improvements. It could postpone replacing capital equipment that has become obsolete until costs of the older facilities have been recovered. This is a logical deduction of the model as it has been developed so far, but some empirical evidence appears to support this conclusion as well. We will return to this point later.

Another consideration to bear in mind is that under the stated conditions the monopolist does not usually produce at the optimum or least-cost output. He gains more from maintaining his price per unit than he gains from producing additional units which he could only sell at a lower price; and it should be noted that this would necessarily mean a lower price for all units sold, unless the seller were to discriminate among his buyers. *Price discrimination* means charging different buyers different prices for the same commodity, depending on their willingness to pay higher prices. This in fact is frequently done under monopoly. We will return to this concept in the next chapter.

Social Consequences of Monopoly

What are the implications of monopoly for society? (There is little reason to inquire what the benefits are to the monopolist.) First of all, in terms of real income the existence of widespread monopoly will mean a restriction of scarce goods and services in order to maintain or increase the income of the firm. Any expansion of consumption must be paid for on the monopolist's terms.

Secondly, since the firm does not carry its production to the point that would give society the benefit of least cost, there will be a less than optimum use of scarce productive resources.

Monopoly, of necessity, would have to be based upon some kind of property right which provides effective control over scarce resources and the power to exclude others from their use except on the owners' terms. There is implied, therefore, a link between monopoly control and a governing authority which is prepared to enforce such property rights. It would not be too strong a statement to say that wherever monopoly exists in anything approaching an absolute sense, it must be the handmaiden of government. The greatest monopoly of all, of course, is authoritarian government itself. The salt monopoly was long a favorite monopoly of governments in totalitarian states, or of colonial administrations intent on exploiting undeveloped or backward areas. Salt is required by all living organisms. It has no substitute. Since it is required in relatively small amounts, even a very high price does not impose a great burden on the individual budget. And even when it is cheap not much more will be used. Thus in Spain the salt monopoly was an effective revenue-raising device for the government. The British also used it for a long time in India. But in order to be effective, it had to be coupled with a prohibition against production of salt by private individuals. In both Spain and India even the evaporating of sea water was regarded as an illegal act and an offense against the ruling authority carrying heavy penalties.

Democratically-controlled governments are less likely to make extensive use of such devices, particularly in the case of necessities. Some representative governments have created monopolies in the tobacco and liquor trades, since popular opinion frequently regards widespread consumption of these two items as not particularly desirable, and monopolies here are less destructive of individual liberties and welfare. Near monopolies are to be found in the case of patented items. Here too, the aid of government must be invoked if the patent right is to be enforced. Even so, human ingenuity has usually been up to the task of inventing effective substitutes, which come near enough to the original without infringing the patent law.

With the development of modern technology there has come into existence an important group of monopolies, sometimes called natural monopolies. These monopolies comprise important consumption items in an industrial society electricity, telephone and telegraph systems, and various forms of transportation. All of these services require such large-scale investments in capital equipment that volume becomes a first requirement for low-cost operation. To duplicate these facilities in order to ensure competition would result in an allocation of resources in excess of requirements and often in losses due to excess capacity. If bankruptcy results, services may be interrupted or public subsidies provided. Thus it has become the practice of municipal, state, and national governments to grant a franchise which carries exclusive rights to produce such services. When this is done, however, regulations of the use of the monopoly privilege go along with the grant. Another alternative in this field is the creation of a publicly-owned monopoly to provide such services at "cost." In democratic nations monopolies have been subjected increasingly to regulation. This is to ensure that the monopoly advantage shall not be pushed beyond certain limits.

These are the essential features of an analytical model of monopoly as such, and some illustrations from experience. Realistically, the concept is not too important, save as an idea and tool of analysis. The area between the extremes of pure competition and pure monopoly, where varying degrees of what is called monopoly are present, is likely to be both more interesting and more important. This is particularly true where mass production methods and organization have reduced the number of firms in a given industry. The next chapter will extend our model to include these situations.

Discussion
Questions

1. Compare the associations of the term monopoly in the field of economics with that of monarchy in politics. What are the similarities and differences?

2. An electric power company is granted an exclusive right to supply power for a large city. Ordinarily, why would this not be an absolute monopoly?

3. Using the definition of competition discussed in Chapter 15, what conditions present in competition would be absent in monopoly?

4. The difference between monopoly and competition is not significant, since entrepreneurs merely try to maximize profits in both cases. Comment.

5. A salt monopoly would be more valuable than a diamond monopoly. Comment.

CHAPTER 17

Different Degrees of Monopoly

SHORT OF the pure monopoly defined in the preceding chapter, there may be different degrees of control over output and pricing decisions. In general, these can be noted as exceptions to the conditions specified earlier for the competitive market. The number of buyers and sellers may vary. The entry of new buyers or sellers can be blocked, and exit may be difficult because of large fixed commitments. Knowledge is often incomplete, ignorance and prejudice the rule. Where goods and services vary and the link between quality and performance is not clear, sellers trade upon consumers' lack of understanding. This lack of understanding regarding a commodity, or the absence of a homogeneous product, limits substitution and forms the basis of monopoly.

Bases of Monopoly Power

Even the types of a raw material such as wheat vary considerably. There is hard winter wheat, soft spring wheat, and several grades based upon moisture content and storing qualities. There are the different varieties useful for bread flour and cake flour, and the glutinous wheat used in macaroni. Within each of these classifications the product can be graded so that individual units are more or less uniform.[1]

Among manufactured products, goods that have incorporated in them different amounts of labor and machine services, the range of variation is greater. When *real* differences are combined with the imagined differences in the minds of buyers (created by the persuasive voice of the advertiser) the complexity increases. Are Kellogg's Corn Flakes and Post Toasties the same or different products? Are they likely to be perfect substitutes for

---

[1] The standard quality on which most market prices are based is Number 2 Hard Winter Wheat.

303

each other? What about Camel and Chesterfield cigarettes? Is a blue plate lunch served with a smile and a pleasant remark the same as one thumped down with a silent glare? How about Fords and Chevrolets—not to mention Fords and Cadillacs? One may say that "an automobile is an automobile"; but in the minds of buyers there is a difference, and it may require wide differences in price to persuade the buyer to substitute one for the other in his consumption budget. When this is true, price need not be closely related to costs. Thus *product differentiation* is a source of monopoly control in the supply of specific commodities.

Every producer has a monopoly of sorts. A farmer has a monopoly of the steers he has fattened; but it is not a very important monopoly, because the ordinary consumer (except in rare instances where the chambers of commerce may sponsor an ox roast to consume the prize baby beef from the county fair) does not differentiate between one farmer's cattle and those of another.

The neighborhood grocery, because of its nearness, may possess an advantage in convenience which it can use to maintain a price difference between its products and those of the supermarket downtown. This monopoly advantage is greater than the farmer's, but less than that of General Motors or Ford, or even of Lili Dache, whose monopoly is based upon prestige and what might be called "irrational" consumption by those unable to afford such expensive hats.

Again, a degree of monopoly may exist when a small number of very large firms dominate a particular field of production, as in steel, copper, aluminum, tin cans, and so forth. Where this is true, even when the producers do not act in concert, there is a tendency for active price competition to be nonexistent. There may be in such an industry a price leader—usually the most important producer—whose pricing practices are followed by the others. Varying degrees of monopoly are partially maintained through the absence of easy entry into the field because of the amount of investment required.

In situations such as those described above member firms will frequently insist that their industry is competitive. There may be great rivalry in the struggle for buyers. This rivalry will usually take the form of large expenditures on advertising and high-pressure salesmanship to persuade the buyer that his need is for a particular brand regardless of price differences. This is a different kind of competition from that considered earlier. If it leads to the development of important quality improvements, this feature of real income may elude the measuring rod of money. This is in fact an argument used by large corporations like Du Pont, whose contribution to economic life cannot be denied. Small competing companies would be unlikely to create nylon, orlon, cellophane, and other products based on the findings of expensive research.

Monopoly advantage pushed far enough can defeat itself. Large profits may stimulate research efforts to develop substitutes, similar enough to satisfy the need but different enough to elude patent laws. Large profits may also result in diversification in other industries, as when a manufacturer of automobiles takes on the production of refrigerators. Moreover, a high price for steel has led to its replacement in many uses by aluminum or plastics. Finally, domination by a single firm, or a too narrow practice of price leadership, can lead to government regulation and control.

Within limits, each form of consumption competes with every other for the consumers' dollar. There is a connection, however slight, between markets far removed from one another. Cigarettes and candy can come into conflict, as a leading tobacco company learned a few years ago when weight-conscious ladies were urged to reach for its brand of tobacco instead of a sweet. Summer vacations and the latest automobiles will compete in limited budgets, though they may constitute *joint demand*.

In economic analysis the relation between prices of different goods and services is described as *cross elasticity* of demand. The emergence of a new commodity, which makes inroads on consumer budgets, may result in shifting to the left (Figure 15) what was formerly a relatively inelastic demand for a commodity possessing considerable monopoly control and the injection of a greater degree of price elasticity.

We will now supplement our general survey with a number of more specific types of market classification in this area.

Duopoly

A market in which two firms face each other as rival sellers is called *duopoly*. It is characterized by great instability, an instability likely to be destructive of competition.

Assume that there are two firms of approximately equal size and efficiency, sharing a market for a particular commodity and charging at the outset an identical price. Assume further that each could supply a larger share of the market. If Firm A were to lower its price by a small amount and increase sales, it could expand output, not only by the amount that sales can always be expanded by lowering price, but also at the expense of the rival firm. To the firm lowering its price the second type of expansion would appear as an increased demand for its output (a shift of its demand curve), while to the other firm it would appear as a decrease.

Such unilateral action would not go unnoticed by the rival firm. A reduction of price by Firm A would in all likelihood result in retaliatory action by Firm B.[2] If this course of action were followed to its likely conclusion, both firms would cease price cutting only when both were operating at capacity (least-cost combination) and selling at their minimum average cost. Neither would be making a profit. No one would benefit but the consumer. When one firm possessed greater staying power than the other, the price might even be reduced to less than average cost in the hope of bankrupting and forcing the rival firm out of business. In this case the result would be monopoly. Considerable literature in economic theory has been devoted to an interesting speculation about this type of rivalry. Assuming no direct exchange of information, no collusive agreement between the parties, such an action is like a game of strategy, with feints and probing moves to sound out the opposition's economic strength.

Ordinarily the process need not go so far. When Firm B is producing at capacity, Firm A may actually be able to increase its price, once more realizing a monopoly profit. This is because Firm B cannot, at least in the short run, expand output further due to rising costs. Hence it could not supply the whole market. Eventually, as most price wars do in this situation, the process would be likely to end in a truce, with both parties agreeing to live and let live. Some type of price leadership could be established (assuming outright collusion were illegal and difficult), resulting in a sharing of the maximum monopoly profit for the industry.

One can work out under various assumptions many refinements of the theory of duopoly. But this is hardly worth the effort—at least not in the beginning of our study of economics. It is sufficient merely to note that with only two firms in a market freedom of action and competition are likely to be kept within narrow limits. Each must take into account, in formulating production policies, the possible effect of such action on the other.

Oligopoly

To denote a market situation where the number of rival firms is more than two, but less than enough to assure effective competition, economists have adopted the term *oligopoly*.[3] Relationships in this kind of market are more complex than under duopoly. Individuals are less neatly paired off, one against the other. If one firm cuts its price to attract buyers, the effect of

---

[2] Such action does happen in the everyday world, and will be recognized as what in business language is called "cutthroat" competition.

[3] The root is the same as that for oligarchy, Aristotle's term for government by the few. Thus oligopoly means, literally, a few sellers. The present widespread use of the term derives from E. H. Chamberlin—cf. his *Towards a More General Theory of Value* (New York: Oxford, 1957), pp. 31–42.

the action will be spread among more than one rival producer. For that reason it may not lead to immediate retaliatory action. It would be unlikely to go unnoticed, however. To understand why an individual firm in such a situation might wish to strike out on its own in an effort to attract buyers, it will be useful to consider certain cost and price relationships. Some firms may have advantages of location with respect to given markets, protected from their rivals by the physical fact of distance, which can only be overcome at added cost. At times, however, this may not be a permanent advantage if a distant firm, secure in its own local market, can lower its costs by expanding. This firm may be able to turn out additional units for very little more than the variable cost of production, if its sales in its own local market are covering the fixed costs. By selling in its own market—which up to now has been protected by transport costs—at a price which is even slightly above the variable costs, the firm can increase its profit. It is conceivable that two such firms might try to invade each other's markets simultaneously. In fact, several firms might be invading each other's markets, selling at a price lower than they are charging in their own territories.

Note how this situation differs from the conditions under competition. Under competition no producer would consider selling below the going market price. It would be unnecessary to attempt it, since the entire output of the firm could be absorbed at whatever was the going market price. Under oligopoly, however, there is a choice. When firms produce a sizable part of total production, there is the opportunity for deciding to sell below the going market price. In time, therefore, the same type of instability we saw emerging from duopoly may arise where there are several producers of identical or similar products.

We can see why this is likely if we consider the role of modern technology in industrial development. Modern large-scale production methods, such as those used in steel, oil, aluminum, automobiles, glass, cement, and other industries, require large fixed investments in plant and equipment. Any firm that gets a running start on its competitors in the adoption of new large-scale methods has a price advantage because of rapidly decreasing fixed costs. It can systematically undersell smaller, less efficient establishments, winning away their purchasers. It may even acquire the smaller unit, once the latter is convinced that it can no longer survive.[4]

But what about the tendency toward equilibrium within the industry? Is there no limit to which this process can go before the diseconomies of bureaucracy and top-heavy supervision within the individual firm assert themselves? There may be, except for the injection of another contributing

---

[4] When this happens, it is usually reported in the financial pages as a *merger*.

307

influence—that of monopoly control itself. When increased efficiency through the use of large-scale production methods finally begins to level off, a further advantage from monopoly control asserts itself. Monopoly power is the power of control over large property holdings built up from profits plowed back into ever improving technological development. This can be viewed as an optimum-size firm which, feeding upon its power to command income, is continually expanding. National income instability—the ups and downs of the business cycle—contributes to this process, since weaker firms are more likely to be eliminated when large capital values are wiped out. Such a market will have arrived at what we have just described as oligopoly.

When firms of roughly the same size and bargaining power begin to undercut each other's prices, the result is price warfare. Here again, such "cutthroat" competition, if extended, will be recognized fairly soon as of little practical benefit to anyone but the purchasers. Unless there is hope of one firm winning a clear-cut victory, there will appear to be no point in continuing it. Even if a single powerful firm succeeded in outlasting the others, it probably would be a Pyrrhic victory, since government regulation would undoubtedly follow.

Thus industries characterized by oligopoly tend to gravitate toward a monopolistic price policy, accomplished ordinarily through some type of price leadership. Understandings need not be the result of formal agreement. Frequently they are not. They are the consequences of long experience, of trial and error, and burned fingers. A form of equilibrium is established, in which relatively stable income arrangements emerge. Large and small businesses through a variety of combinations and adjustments to one another find a *modus vivendi.*

In such situations it is not unusual for comparatively small firms to exist side by side with much larger, more powerful organizations, which might be capable of supplying the entire market. Considerable rivalry may be present, usually based upon practices other than lowering prices—personal favor, connections, and long-established business relations, which will persist as long as price differences are not involved.

It will be apparent that a model that could cover the wide variety of situations would become extremely complex. To treat them systematically would require many different sets of assumptions. The general relationship developed so far will be sufficient in succeeding chapters for the purpose of organizing descriptive and institutional data gathered from empirical studies of industries and firms. Meanwhile, we can bring this phase of our model of production for markets to a close with the analysis of variations based upon product differentiation.

Monopolistic Competition

In a general analysis of monopolistic competition we will find the short-hand of our cost and revenue curves to be useful. By now the derivation of these curves and their relations to one another should be sufficiently understood so that they can be presented as abstract forms without relating them specifically to the arithmetic behind them.

We can begin with the case of a monopolist whose control is based upon a newly patented product, or one based upon a secret process. Assuming that a price has been established which maximizes profit, the firm will have achieved an equilibrium position illustrated by Figure 30. At a price *OP,* an output *ON* will be produced. Total revenue will be represented by the rectangle *OPAN,* total costs by *OMCN.* The smaller rectangle *MPAC* represents the difference between the two, or monopoly profit.

If demand does not change the monopolist could continue to operate indefinitely at a profit. An increase in demand would enable the firm to expand output as well as profits. Suppose, however, a second firm enters the market with a product sufficiently different to avoid infringement of patent or trade-mark, but enough like the original to be an acceptable substitute for at least part of the market. At a slightly lower price such a competitor would attract potential purchasers from the original firm. To the latter this would appear as a decrease in demand. This situation is illustrated by the dashed *AR* and *MR* curves in Figure 30.

Now assume that the patent expires, or is broken, so that the possibility of restricting entry into the industry is removed. Since the industry has been showing substantial profits, new investment and new firms will be attracted.

How far will such a process go? It is unlikely to go so far that a purely competitive market results. What is more likely to happen is illustrated in Figure 31. Demand for the output of an individual firm may actually decrease to the extent that for at least some of the firms it falls below the average cost of production, resulting in short-run losses. The dashed *AR* and *MR* curves illustrate this situation.

Since losses cannot continue indefinitely, the least efficient firms (high-cost) may go out of business, convert to other production, or be merged with other firms, thereby improving the situation with respect to existing demand for the products of the remaining firms. Advertising and other sales efforts will be used frequently to increase demand for the whole industry. Equilibrium will be achieved when price in the industry is equal to the cost of production at the point where the *AR* curve intersects (is tangent to) the *AC* curve, as in Figure 32. Monopoly profit has disap-

Figure 30. Cost and Revenue Relationships
Under Monopolistic Competition

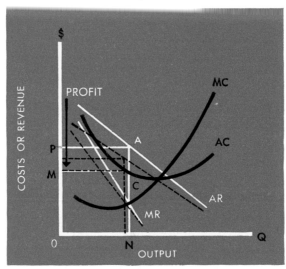

Figure 31. Cost and Revenue Relationships
in Overexpanded Industry

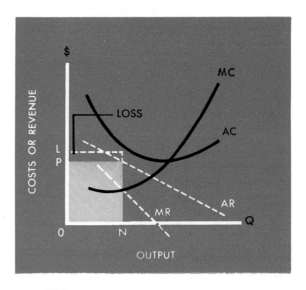

310

Figure 32. Long-Run Equilibrium Under
Monopolistic Competition

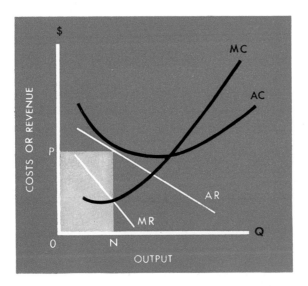

Figure 33. Effect of Advertising Costs on
Price Under Monopolistic Competition

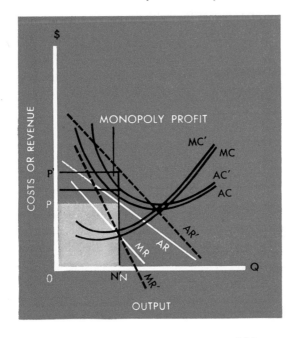

peared, but the existing firms will be covering average costs, including wages of management, interest on investment, and depreciation costs. This is an adjustment similar in many respects to equilibrium under pure competition. There is a difference, however. Because the demand for the output of the firm is less than perfectly elastic, it will intersect the average cost curve somewhere above its lowest point. The firm, accordingly, is not producing at its lowest cost. By producing more it could reduce its average costs.

Where a number of firms achieve equilibrium under conditions such as these, there will be unused capacity—factors of production (capital in particular) which, from the social point of view, are making no contribution to the real flow of income. While this may be less of a problem in a rich society than in a poor one, it requires notice. Under these conditions equilibrium is likely to be characterized by instability. In the absence of "understandings," such as price leadership or outright collusion, the individual firm stands to gain from price competition, provided immediate retaliation is unlikely. For by lowering its sales price and expanding sales the firm can reduce costs. A firm increases sales by attracting previously unsatisfied buyers as well as purchasers from other firms. Elasticity of demand for the output of a given firm is an important consideration. Where the number of firms is fairly small (oligopoly) this type of competition will be discouraged, for reasons already discussed.

Product differentiation, advertising, and aggressive salesmanship constitute the most widely used alternatives to price competition. For if by persuasive advertising techniques a firm is able to bind purchasers to it, the effect is a degree of monopoly. Demand becomes relatively inelastic, since convinced purchasers are not easily lured away even by price differences. Such advertising and sales methods frequently stress superior quality, greater prestige, or other features likely to contribute to satisfaction. The purpose is to establish the reputation of difference—difference which may be a quality of the actual product or a fiction created in the mind of the buyer.

Such selling costs are costs of production. Where they are effective they are recovered in increased revenue. Figure 33 is a graphic presentation of an effect of selling costs on price, output of the firm, and revenue. Average and marginal cost curves are raised; but so, too, are average and marginal revenue curves, with the likelihood that demand becomes more inelastic. Factors of production in the form of materials and human skills are required in increasing proportions to man the ranks in this battle of the advertisers.[5] Total real income may or may not be increased.

---

[5] Advertising will be treated more extensively in Part 4 under Consumption.

One further technique available to the firm under monopolistic competition in its pursuit of income is *price discrimination*. This is the practice of splitting a potential demand curve into segments, charging different prices to each segment of the curve. This will be illustrated by referring to an ordinary demand schedule.

A firm which charges a given price to all comers gives up that part of the demand curve which falls below the established price. At the same time buyers represented by the part of the demand curve which lies above the established price are able to acquire the good for less than they would be willing to pay. If a seller could charge every potential buyer exactly what he would be willing to pay in order to get it, profits would be greater. However, where the seller cannot know with precision the eagerness of a buyer, and where uniform treatment is the general rule of business, price discrimination must rest on other grounds than eagerness and ability to pay.[6] Consequently, producers of many branded products usually have several different grades of the same article. Where the firm has earned the reputation for a very high quality product, and is patronized by the "discriminating" trade, it will try to tap a lower segment of the demand curve with a lower priced product. In some cases the difference consists chiefly of an absence of the trade name. This amounts to setting up an additional demand curve. Profit maximization within these semiautonomous markets can then proceed, within limits, without shifts of purchases from "higher" to "lower" markets.

Monopoly on the Buying Side

We have considered instances in which the condition of a large number of buyers and sellers, necessary to the existence of pure competition, is lacking on the supply or selling side. When a small number of buyers face a large number of sellers, the effect on market price and income advantage is similar to that outlined above. The individual bidder becomes conscious of his influence in price determination. To distinguish between control over price by buyers, in contrast to producers or sellers, economists use the terms monopsony, duopsony, oligopsony, and monopsonistic competition.

Varying degrees of monopoly on the buying side are likely to be of small importance in consumption-goods markets. A watered-down version of the relationship is present in situations sometimes referred to as "buyers markets." Buying clubs and consumer co-operatives make use of the principle when they use mass purchasing power to influence prices.

---

[6] In certain professions fees frequently are assessed on the basis of an estimate of the client's ability to pay for the service.

However, the general principles of monopsonistic competition apply mostly in markets for factors of production. When a large firm is the principal user of a given factor of production (a specialized raw material, labor, machine tool, and so on), it can use its strategic position in the market to influence price. These principles are of importance, therefore, as they relate to distribution (which will be discussed in Part 4).

This completes our model of production for a market where the prices of the factors of production (costs) are given, and the prices of output are assumed to be determinable. In the following chapter this assumption is partially abandoned, and the consequences for production decisions are examined when prices are uncertain.

Discussion
Questions

1. The assumption of homogeneity of product is a heroic one, indeed. Nature is characterized by infinite variety. Moreover, men differ in their perceptions. Some see differences where none "really" exist. This propensity is grist for the mill of the advertiser and the monopolist. Comment.

2. Nearly everything has a substitute. However, these substitutes may be imperfect. Where substitutes are not perfect, and where the preferred good is controlled by a few, some degree of monopoly exists. Comment.

3. Good will is an enemy of competition. Comment.

4. Technological change is the enemy of monopoly. Show how this could be true in the case of a patented product.

5. If a powerful firm buys up patent rights on new inventions which might become substitutes for their own products, the effect will be to extend monopoly power. Comment.

CHAPTER 18

A More Inclusive Model of Production

IN THIS CHAPTER we will modify our model of production to take account of the experience of firms in situations which are not as clearly defined as the conditions posited in the preceding chapters. Many aspects of reality, of course, must still elude specific treatment because of the variety and complexity of economic behavior.

The first and most obvious limitation of the preceding analysis was the assumption that a firm's output consists of a single homogeneous product. Even with the most specialized firm in the business world this is rarely the case. The efficient use of raw materials and productive capacity will usually necessitate the development of by-products and secondary output. What might otherwise be waste material can often be turned to account in a separate market, emerging as an additional claim on income. Cotton seed, which once cluttered the grounds of ginning mills and had to be hauled away at extra cost, was subsequently developed as a source of oil, capable of carrying a part of the initial cost of the raw cotton. The protein solids or pulp of the seed were also converted into a meal, which found an outlet in still a third market as feed for livestock. Cotton linters, hulls, and a whole list of additional products eventually flowed from the single cotton boll.

Modern chemistry has multiplied examples of *joint supply,* by which is meant two or more distinct products which come from a common raw material. This has created new problems for the cost accountant in apportioning the cost of basic raw materials and plant overhead among products whose prices may vary quite independently, and sometimes in the opposite direction. It has also created a problem for the production engineer, since there are few cases where the proportion of the raw materials going to a single product is rigidly fixed. If the demand for one good increases, the production process may be geared to extract a larger proportion of that item from the raw materials. Moreover, an increasing demand for one of the joint products, with a resulting increase in price, will increase its capacity to bear more of the costs of production, both fixed and variable.

The different by-products may be sold at the plant (the point of separation) to other firms for which they constitute basic raw materials. Usually it has been found, however, that with relatively small increases in plant or equipment (fixed costs), the processing of by-products can be carried on parallel with the primary enterprise, adding to the revenue of the firm. When the output of the firm thus consists of multiple products, the usual practice is to attempt to maximize profit income for over-all production, allocating the fixed costs among those items best able to bear them. Alternatively, if the management thinks in terms of the income of the over-all business, it is not necessary to allocate all of the fixed costs among particular products. Certain fixed or overhead costs may be treated simply as necessary costs of doing business. Within the business, therefore, these are set aside to be paid out of total available revenues. When this is done, management can think in terms of the variable or working capital and the alternative uses for it. By comparing costs and expected revenues for a number of different alternative outputs, the management chooses those which promise the best returns and the greatest likelihood of paying all costs (including overhead). Those items that are dropped are visualized as opportunity costs for those that are retained. In other words, if in an oil refinery more gasoline is obtained from a given unit of crude, one cost of this gasoline is the revenue which might have been obtained from more fuel oil.

Dropping the assumption of a single homogeneous product for purposes of analysis complicates our model somewhat, but it requires no new concepts. We can illustrate with an example from agriculture. Mutton (or lamb) and wool are joint products of sheep. An increase in the price of wool, relative to mutton, will bring about shifts in production practices. It will result in greater care in the shearing and handling of wool, as well as in additional efforts and costs to see that as much wool as possible is taken from the sheep, that it is kept clean and dry (perhaps by means of better quality bags), and that it is properly warehoused. Technologically, it may result in a shift to a different variety of sheep, such as the Merino, which produces more wool but less valuable meat.

The test for the firm is the cost-price ratio. As long as the marginal revenue resulting from producing more wool exceeds the additional cost of producing it, profit-income can be increased by the shift in emphasis to the primary product, although it by no means implies abandoning the other product. A balance or equilibrium of different enterprises within the firm is achieved when the marginal cost of each product is equal to the marginal revenue attributable to it.

Indivisibilities

Another simplifying assumption was that of continuous variation or infinite divisibility. Some factors or resources occur in lumps or bunches. It is not possible to operate on a scale at which less than complete units are used. One man cannot operate a copper mine even at a low output level. A locomotive cannot be cut in two.[1] Indivisibility may be due not to physical characteristics alone, but to institutional rigidities as well. A farm of particular size may belong to an owner who is unwilling to rent less than the total acreage to an individual operator. A factory building, once constructed, may not be adaptable to partial use, or to uses other than that for which it was designed. In such cases the indivisibilities involve the owner in risks.

The development of modern financial institutions and legal property arrangements have helped to modify this problem somewhat, bringing greater flexibility into the use of such resources through sharing the ownership among a greater number of individuals or firms. A mining operation which would be beyond the capacity of a single owner can be undertaken by a corporation, under which the ownership is distributed widely through the sale of shares of stock (see discussion in Chapter 20).

Wherever inflexibility and indivisibilities exist, cost curves will not be smooth, as on the graphs used above, but will be jagged, and may show little change over a considerable range of output. In such cases there may be no neat coincidence or intersection of the various curves.

Expectations

Most production takes time. All adjustments in the supply and demand picture do not occur instantaneously. Our division of the production processes into the three time periods was a first approximation to the dynamics of change. These are useful analytically, but even they are simplifications of the production process which is the result of many interacting variables and differing rates of change. A motion picture of over-all production, viewed from the level of the firm, would be one in which there would be many lags and uneven processes of adjustment.

The real world is one of uncertainties and surprises. Plans do not

---

[1] Over a period of time, however, a changing technology may achieve greater divisibilities, without loss in production, as it has in the design of small tractors and motors.

317

work out and losses result (see pages 149–50). A firm plans its output on the basis of an anticipated price. When the product is ready the market may have changed. On the other hand, the surprise may be a pleasant one, in that high prices result in incomes larger than expected. If prices have been stable for some time, the producer may feel considerable confidence in adjusting his decisions to them. If present output is one that appears to maximize profit, it may remain constant. If prices are rising, either because of a shift in demand favorable to the particular good or because of a rise in the general level of prices, the producer may increase output on the basis of price expectations, particularly if costs do not change at the same rate. On the other hand, falling prices, which are expected to continue downward, will dictate caution.

In the first instance the entrepreneur's decisions to increase production may not affect the general level of national output, since increasing demand in one industry may be balanced by decreases in other industries. Where the instability is the result of changes in the general level of prices, so that all entrepreneurs' decisions are affected in the same way, the national product will be subject to fluctuations. An initial price rise, resulting from a factor outside production itself (such as an increase in spending), may stimulate entrepreneurs to undertake production expansion simultaneously, adding still further to rising prices and employment. This is an example of induced investment, discussed in Part 2. An initial fall in prices, affecting all entrepreneurs in much the same way, may start a wave of retrenchment in production. As this is taken into account in more and more production decisions, employment and resource use will fall, this time adding up to an over-all effect of declining national real income.

Taking account of such variations will require some modification of our precise supply and demand curves (Figure 34). Instead of the narrow lines with which we illustrate market price determination and output of the firm, we can show a band of possible prices and quantities. The heavy central core of this band represents the relationship between prices and quantities most probable in terms of present expectations. This line shades off into the less likely (but still possible) relationships. The market price, instead of one neat numerical statement, is likewise a band of possible prices. Where this band cuts the marginal cost curve of the firm, it gives a range of possible outputs, depending on which of the prices the entrepreneur believes to be most likely.

This improves the realism of our chart, but destroys the appearance of precision and the possibilities of exact prediction. It points up, however, why stability of the general price level is regarded as essential if the market

318

Figure 34. Price Relationships Under Conditions of Uncertainty

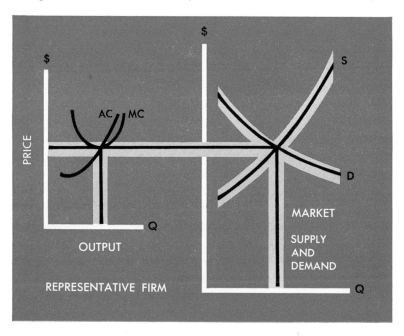

is to do its job of regulating production, and if consistent behavior by producers is to be realized.

Speculation

Speculation is a technique—developed in the everyday practice of the market place and incorporated into theory as well—which serves as a link between present and future prices. In some circumstances speculation reduces risks for producers by permitting them to *hedge*.

A speculator is an entrepreneur who is a professional risk taker. His job is to predict what prices are going to be in the future and back up his predictions with his own property. For the speculator to function there must be a market for goods in which he can buy and sell, not for immediate delivery but for delivery at some future date; hence the name *futures market*. The most familiar futures markets are those for commodities and securities, the Board of Trade, and the Stock Exchanges. There basic raw materials and property titles are traded. Wheat, to take an example, is quoted on the "board" for 6 to 8 months in advance. In April prices will be quoted for May, July, September, and December delivery. A contract to deliver a given quantity of wheat can be made in April, but the wheat need not be delivered until some future date, say December. Different

319

time periods are thereby linked together. The producer, who may be interested in the commodity at some date in the future, is given something of a preview of what his raw materials will cost him then and can adjust his production plans accordingly. He can also hedge.

Assume that a milling company has made a contract with a string of bakeries to furnish them with flour over a six-months' period.[2] On the basis of the current prices for wheat, the milling company quotes a price per barrel for flour that will take care of all costs of production. Ordinarily a milling establishment will not have facilities for storing enough wheat to fulfill such a series of contracts. If prices should increase, flour delivered at contract prices would result in losses. Of course, if the price should fall, thereby lowering variable costs, the firm would be able to make greater short-run profits. However, a producer, particularly in a competitive industry, may prefer not to take such risks. The firm's normal income comes from converting wheat into flour—the creation of form utility—not from price changes on inventories.

Hedging can protect income plans. To ensure that wheat purchased as it is needed to fill the flour contract will not cost more than prices used in determining the contract price for flour, the milling company can buy on the futures market an amount of wheat equal to its estimated requirement. Let us say that wheat for delivery now (April) is $1.75 per bushel, while the price being quoted for September delivery is $1.81.[3] The company's estimate of its requirements for September is 10,000 bushels. If between April and September the price of wheat should rise by 25 cents a bushel, this would mean that in fulfilling at least part of its contract the firm would be paying $2.06 per bushel. Such an increase could cancel any expected profit on the contract.

If the milling company buys a *futures contract* for the delivery of 10,000 bushels of wheat in September, the value of this contract will rise. When September arrives whatever is lost on the flour contract will be made up on the futures market. Should the price of wheat fall, the company will then lose on its futures purchase. However, it will then make up this loss by obtaining its wheat at a lower price and will make a larger profit on flour. Thus *hedging* eliminates the possibility of either gain or loss from price changes, and the producer's expected income is protected from this influence.

What is the role of the speculator in this process? Before the milling

---

[2] The bakery is interested in making such a contract because it will then be able to make more exact calculations for quoting bread prices.

[3] This spread between the two prices will be approximately equal to the cost of storing wheat for the period.

company could purchase a futures contract there had to be someone willing to sell. Such a person might be, and frequently is, a bona fide wheat producer or a dealer who has a contract with a producer. Ordinarily, however, there are other enterprisers operating in the market whose interest is purely speculative—buying and selling simply in an attempt to "outguess" the market. To back up their transactions they put up money (or securities), and in a sense "bet" that the market is going to go up or down.

In the language of the market place, those who sell with the expectation that prices will fall are called "bears"; those who buy in the belief that prices will rise are called "bulls." When the number of bulls and bears is about equally divided, the price is likely to be relatively stable. When the number is not equally divided, the price is likely to change in the direction of the predominant view.

When a free market is relatively stable, the speculator can contribute to short-run flexibility and long-run stability. A larger volume of trading makes the market more responsive to changes in the underlying determinants of supply and demand, and thereby promotes short-run adjustments in production. This prevents the changes from accumulating until the market has to absorb large adjustments all at once. Suppose that early in the growing season a large crop is in prospect. When the new crop is ready, the supply curve will shift to the right (increase). Unless there is a parallel increase in demand, lower prices are indicated. Lower prices will be necessary to encourage consumption, if the large crop is to be sold. Speculators, on the alert for possible profits and taking note of the crop reports, begin to sell wheat short. The futures market moves down. As the present moves into the past and the future becomes the present, much of the adjustment will have been made by harvest time. Since full knowledge and foresight is impossible, not all speculators will interpret the market information in the same way. It should not be inferred, however, that the bulls and the bears are separate groups. Unlike "producers," speculators move easily from one side of the market to the other.

Speculation may have a stabilizing effect when needed adjustments in price are small and associated with changes in the ordinary interaction between supply and demand. Where the general price level is rising or falling, however, the action of speculators may intensify the movement. A fall in effective aggregate demand, because of a decline in national income, may produce a wave of speculative selling which drives prices still lower. As falling prices begin to have their effect on the decisions of entrepreneurs, who reduce production to minimize losses, the general level of claims against income falls still further. During a period of rising prices speculative buying in important raw-materials and securities markets pushes prices much higher than is warranted by existing supply and demand conditions. It was this aspect of speculation that John Maynard Keynes presumably had in mind when he stated that:

Speculators may do no harm as bubbles on a steady stream of enterprise. But the position is serious when enterprise becomes the bubble on a whirlpool of speculation. When capital development of a country becomes the by-product of the activities of a casino, the job is likely to be ill-done.[4]

Insurance—the Sharing of Risks

Among the unforeseen events which may result in loss to the firm, and perhaps a reduction of its capacity or willingness to continue to produce, are fires, theft, accidents, storms, and so forth. When we assume full knowledge as a requirement for a competitive market, this would appear to do real damage to reality. Here again the growth of specialization and division of labor has provided a method for coping with uncertainties. There are firms that specialize in the bearing of risks for other firms (and individuals). The principle of risk sharing can be illustrated in the case of fire. Any enterprise is liable to suffer loss because of fire at any time. The loss can be greater than the net worth or total value of property owned by the firm, if there are debts. It would be extremely difficult for the enterprise to obtain credit and resume production. All firms must face the possibility of such a loss. The problem can be handled in each case by setting aside a reserve—so much each year to take care of this risk. On the other hand, if a large number of firms pool their risks and pay a small sum into a common fund, this can be used to cover losses when they occur. Such premiums become a fixed cost of doing business—a small but certain loss incurred every year in order to eliminate the possibilities of a much larger loss.

Insurance firms collect payments from large numbers of businesses and pay the losses of those that incur them. Where large numbers are involved, the element of speculation or uncertainty for the insuring enterprise is removed. When statistics of an area—city, state, or entire country —have been kept for an extended period on accidents, fires, theft, mortality rates, and so on, it is possible to construct an *expectancy table* based upon experience. Thus, while it is impossible to predict whether a fire will strike a particular building, it is quite possible to predict the number of fires that will occur in cities of a certain size during a year. The Na-

---

[4] Keynes, *General Theory*, p. 159.

tional Safety Council, for example, can predict with considerable accuracy the number that will be killed over a three-day week end. From such tables the insuring agencies estimate the losses likely to occur from various causes. Given this information, the cost of underwriting them can be determined.

Uncertainty

Some of the hazards of doing business, however, do not occur with any kind of regularity or pattern. Changes in buyers' tastes cannot be predicted, nor can specific technological changes which render equipment and techniques obsolete. Changes in the level of business activity itself, for the individual producer, cannot be predicted.

These represent uncertainties which all who engage in production have to bear. Workers run the risk of losing their jobs, their skills, their incomes, and in some trades their lives. Owners of property risk its loss, and with it their claims against income. Entrepreneurs risk failure—rejection by the market of their particular good or service. In an enterprise economy it has usually been the entrepreneur or the "undertaker" who has been singled out as the bearer of uncertainties. Profits (or the hope of profits), even if only for the short run, have been regarded as his reward and special claim against income. The burden of failure is loss of capital invested.

We will return in Part 4 to some of the problems posed here. There we will remove some of our other major assumptions, notably *given prices* for the factors of production. Now, however, we will fill in details of an institutional and historical character to supplement the more abstract relationships of the production process.

Discussion
Questions

1. What is your understanding of the term joint product? How does this complicate our model of productivity and efficiency?

2. A firm which uses large-scale machines in its production process has a cost advantage when it operates at or near physical capacity. A smaller firm, using a higher proportion of other factors, particularly labor, may have an advantage at smaller outputs. Explain, using the concepts of indivisibilities and fixed costs.

3. Uncertainty is the enemy of decision. When the future is uncertain, what criterion for action do people use?

4. In a large market with many buyers and sellers, most of whom are engaged in production, the speculator may serve a useful function. How can this assertion be related to hedging, discussed in this chapter?

5. Explain the function of experience tables in the field of insurance. How are they related to risk? Explain "statistical certainty."

CHAPTER 19

Economic Analysis and Economic Institutions

OUR PRESENTATION of the main features of production theory is now complete. Much of it is *received* doctrine, the logic and language developed by economists over the years to serve as a guide for inquiry into the processes of production. In this model a number of abstract relationships which influence production decisions have been highlighted. The main body of production theory is not something arrived at just from looking at things as "they are." It is rather an interpretation or meaning abstracted from the *first order facts* or observation of production activities.

We have abstracted from these facts to focus on general relationships and tendencies, neglecting all motivation except the goal of income maximization. We have also made the entrepreneur responsive to a single stimulus of "price" which he must use in the calculation of costs and profits. The solution of problems is a contingent solution, or the consequence of reasoning *as if* major assumptions were true. If any factor of production is limited (as usually is the case), the output of goods requiring its services will be maximized when it is employed in combination with more plentiful factors up to the point where its marginal product becomes zero. *If* an entrepreneur seeks to maximize profit, *then* he will expand output to the point where marginal costs equal marginal revenue, or as near to this point as possible, depending on the divisibility of factors. *If* the market is *purely* competitive, *then* the result will be a long-run normal price which equals the lowest average cost of production using an optimum combination of factors.

What this theoretical model provides, of course, is a framework for things that go together. Alone, theory is not enough. To extend our knowledge about income and production, it is necessary to maintain a continuing contact with "fact" at all different levels. From the production model we have concluded that certain variables—prices, production decisions, income goals—change together in related ways. These assumed relationships can be used as a basis for questions and predicted answers or forecasts.

These conclusions or predictions cannot be as precise as the theory makes them seem. But when these relationships are perceived in close conjunction with the carefully gathered and ordered observations relating to quantities, prices, effective demand, past sales volume, competing products, and other variables, they form a basis for judgments more reliable than mere guesses. Used this way the conclusions of the theoretical analyses become hypotheses to be tested in experience. Thus they are the starting point, not the end, in the task of accumulating systematized knowledge about the income processes.

The Role of Institutions

Even if the relationships derived from the production model were certain (in the long run and with other things remaining equal), the fact that they operate through human beings and human institutions would mean that they could rarely be observed in unadulterated form, just as the elements of nature rarely occur in a pure state.

Human institutions and social adaptations to environment are constantly changing. Balanced combinations are sometimes established which endure for a time, even while the conditions that produced them are modified. The *cultural lag*, as defined by the sociologist, can be viewed as a stabilizing as well as a retarding influence in society. It is only through discovering such constants and their rates of change that we can give operational content to the concepts of our model. While matter of the physical world varies according to central tendencies which appear as statistical constants—boiling points, atomic weights, speeds of light and sound—we have less evidence that human behavior does. The income flow that originates in economic institutions, and the relationships which cluster around it, also change.

Production decisions occur in an environment of social sequence and social distance as well as ordinary time and space. As observable "fact" they consist of millions of separate decisions and adaptations to one another by individuals and groups in a real world that includes them all. Each action has a history behind it of remembered experience, and each presumes an expectation of a future consequence. Through time they are fitted into arrangements of convenience. Thus Walton Hamilton:

> Men doomed to live together cannot carry on without some regard to the interests of each other. So arrangements gradually grow up

326

which curb the excesses of self-seeking; groove channels for individual effort; and subdue multiple activities into a trim pattern. In time agencies of control arise to impose something of a larger will upon members of society.[1]

These arrangements or patterns are not something known directly through the senses of the observer—the business executive or the economist. They are inferred from the broad uniformities that appear in accumulated observations. They are the central tendencies we get from statistical series, when large numbers of observations are brought together and summarized on the calculating machines, or in the more difficult to describe synthesis of intuitive understanding.

The firm of our model was treated as a homogeneous business institution. Within the firm the entrepreneur was a single individual, possessed of a knowledge of factor prices and the productivity of these factors, as well as of a reasonably clear perception of the market within which he operated. This situation, of course, is true only in the most abstract sense.

The business firms of our advanced industrial society differ in many ways. The most obvious difference, of course, is in the relative size. The popcorn stand on the corner and the American Telephone and Telegraph Company (the world's largest business institution measured by assets) are both operating firms. Both represent a centralized agency for making production decisions. Beyond this fact their differences far outnumber their similarities. By size is meant the aggregation of property claims, the power to command the factors of production, and thus ultimately to create output and command income claims. *Big business* and *small business* have become important distinctions in modern times, although the line between them is not always easy to draw. Volume of sales, value of assets owned, or number of workers employed are used as indices of size, but the dividing line between big and small is likely to be an arbitrary and shifting one.

Since the early nineteenth century the growth of large-scale enterprise has been associated with important changes in the institution of property itself. Foremost among these is the development of the corporation, which can only be comprehended against the background of a shifting legal and judicial process. This we will examine in the next chapter.

---

[1] Walton Hamilton, *The Pattern of Competition* (New York: Columbia University Press, 1940), p. 18.

The Impact of Technology on Production

Technology is not usually regarded as an institution. Dictionaries define it as "the science of the industrial arts." In "common sense" terminology it usually means machinery and tools and prescriptions for their use. The cumulative growth of machine technology has had such an impact upon society that it has revolutionized the relationship of men to one another. If we define *institutions* as the regularities or uniformities of those relationships, technology is certainly a continuing influence for upsetting and realigning them. Ours has been described as a *machine age*. Within this technical civilization the ordered patterns of individual and group adjustment have been subjected to an increasing tempo of change.

So far-reaching have been these changes that some "institutional" economists have given technology the status of an institution—a control which imposes "a larger will upon the members of society." A man with a plane or a hammer uses a tool of which he is master. The workman on the assembly line shapes his actions and bends his will to the requirements of the machine. In the words of Thorstein Veblen, "it compels the adaptation of the workman to his work, rather than the work to the workman."

Whether we give technology the separate status of an institution or whether we assign it a function in shaping human behavior, formerly performed by other institutions, we can nevertheless trace important changes in older institutions that have paralleled its growth. Not the least of its effects has been that on property, which, as we noted earlier, is a basis for control of factors of production and of claims against the flow of national income. The enterpriser who uses his own tools, and perhaps hires a few workers to produce goods or provide services for others, speaks with assurance and close adherence to fact when he refers to his business as "my property." He alludes to that which he is capable of defending by his person, if need be, and of instruments whose use touches the lives of only a very few people. When Henry Ford produced the first "horseless carriage" in his barn and spoke of "my property," the concrete object to which he referred was easy to comprehend, and was tied up with the interests of a half-dozen persons at most. Today the River Rouge plant, the direct descendant of that barn, signifies something else. It is scarcely private property at all. Henry Ford II cannot decide to close it down as his grandfather could close down his barn. He would involve in his decision the thousands of workmen employed there and a large number of other residents of the city of Detroit who depend on the Ford Company payroll for their income. The Ford Company no longer belongs to the Ford family in the sense it once did. It is a semipublic corporation.

There is another aspect of technological and industrial development which influences the productive activities of society as a whole. This comes to light when we contrast nations in different stages of development. The more backward a country is technologically, the larger will be the proportion of its people engaged in direct, simple production to satisfy basic needs, while the more technologically advanced a country is, the smaller will be the proportion so occupied.

Colin Clark, in his *Conditions of Economic Progress,* has suggested a system of classification and relationships to characterize the extent of technological development in a nation. He distinguishes three broad categories of production, which he calls simply *primary, secondary,* and *tertiary* production. Primary industries are those devoted to raw-materials production: agriculture, forestry, and fishing. Secondary industries include manufacturing, mining, and construction—the creation of *form utility* through processing raw materials and adapting them to their many different uses. Finally, the tertiary industries are those supplying services of various types: commerce, transport, and the professions.

As a society's technology develops, the requirements for human effort in the primary industries diminishes. Improvement in the agricultural arts releases an increasing proportion of people from mere subsistence occupations, making them available for employment in manufacturing and in the services.

Clark concluded from his study of the national-income statistics of forty countries that high real income is associated with a large proportion of the labor force employed in the tertiary industries. Low output, on the other hand, is associated with a high percentage of the working force in primary production. Where the former condition prevails, Clark asserts, the Malthusian hypothesis of population increasing at a faster rate than food supplies not only fails to be borne out but the reverse may even be true.

Specialization and division of labor, which accompany the growth of technology, change the groupings and the established relationships of persons. They create new bases of association for those doing new and different things. Broad new *classes* in the population have emerged, which show up in the vital statistics as "white-collar workers," business and professional groups, small and big businessmen, a new group of organized industrial workers (in contrast to craft or trade union workers), farm groups of various types, and many others. Based in large part upon associations which are related to the production process itself, these groups of individuals (created by industrial change) find expression in political alignments. As power groups they are of interest to the political scientist.

329

But as forces which affect the production process they cannot be ignored by the economist. They influence markets as well as the character and size of output. In terms of our theoretical model, such groupings show up in the mobility and divisibility of factors of production. In their various forms they can be compared to monopoly in their effect on markets and market price. We shall come back to this point later on.

One last feature of the impact of technology upon production should be noted, for later reference. This is related to the shift of the human factor away from primary production. The "back breaking" toil of wresting food and fibre from the land, and the process of transforming and adapting them are done more and more by the machine. This frees men for ministering to one another's "higher needs," the wants and desires further removed from basic physiological requirements. The production of these people, the creation of output and claims, is tied to a demand less stable than in a technologically backward society. The "higher needs" can be postponed in times of crisis. The fur coat, the trip to the mountains, the new car, even the new fall suit are goods that can be put off another year if need be. This characteristic of an industrial economy has already been discussed as an aspect of the social economy in Part 2. Here we view it as a factor affecting demand for the output of the firm and the industry.

Institutionalization and Professionalization of Management

The growth of mass markets and of large manufacturing and distribution establishments to supply them has induced changes not only in the size and complexity of physical plant and equipment. The entire process of management and control has also been revolutionized. Entrepreneurial decision has ceased to depend on the "genius" of the individual enterpriser, limited to a scope of operations completely understood and supervised by him. In his place is a composite function of direction, management, supervision, and execution of decision, representing a high-level division of labor in professional entrepreneurship. The affairs of giant enterprises like Du Pont, with a sales volume of nearly $2 billion and an output of hundreds of different commodities (most of them raw materials for other firms), are handled by executive and finance committees. The members of these committees are men of varied knowledge and experience—in sales, finance, public relations, commodity production, and ownership—who decide on major production plans by a majority vote, a procedure closely akin to the political process. Through the pooling of judgments, knowledge, and communicative skills, a consensus is obtained, which may be something quite different from the conviction of any individual member of the committees.

Where once the individual relied upon his own experience, organized and integrated into a system of "intuitive" judgment, plus whatever he was willing to accept by way of advice from others, modern management and entrepreneurship represents a synthesis of a much broader base in experience. It draws upon a wider area of social knowledge, which we can designate as *scientific management* or *managerial economics*. Thus management itself has been institutionalized in an elaborate set of principles, rules of thumb, and critical ratios. The purpose of these more elaborate techniques is, of course, similar to those of simpler societies and simpler situations, namely, to control the factors of production and to allocate them to the output of goods and services and the generation of income claims. This control is accomplished through the use, manipulation, and transfer of property claims.

In order to comprehend the internal functioning of its far-flung property holdings and production efforts, modern management has developed its own system of symbols and signs—the accounting procedures, the financial reports, and the sales and inventory reports.[2]

In practice, knowledge of unit costs and of prices of the factors of production is rarely so neatly given as we have assumed in the presentation of our model. These costs have to be discovered or estimated, frequently by methods that must be at best somewhat arbitrary. It is for this reason that businessmen are sometimes critical of theory, even to the point of denying that any such neat balancing of marginal costs and marginal revenues is possible or actually practiced. Some economists have replied to this criticism by pointing out that, whether the businessman recognizes it or not, the model represents (in its most general form) essentially what the businessman does (or ought to do) if he tries to maximize profits.

Does business management, in fact, view production decisions as the means to maximum profit? Confronted by such a question, it is likely that most businessmen would reply affirmatively. That is why they are in business. However, such a response is largely a reaction to language. As we shall discover in Part 4, the meaning of profit is rather ambiguous. Its most common usage is in connection with favorable income experiences of business. Business journals and the daily press invariably refer to high or increasing profits as symbolic of sound or improving "economic health." Businessmen themselves use profit as a criterion of business success or failure.

Further inquiry, however, may reveal that in day-to-day decisions

---

[2] We will examine some of the more common of these accounting and reporting techniques in the next two chapters.

immediate profit maximization is not a paramount influence. For example, as perceived by a management charged with safeguarding the fund of property values entrusted to it as well as with earning an income through its use, the amount of the immediate profit income will not be its only concern. In some circumstances, such as a period of falling prices, management is likely to be more concerned with a favorable ratio between liquid property holdings and other forms of assets, such as inventories. A business which fails to meet its debts (liabilities) may be totally immobilized by bankruptcy. Also a firm may be more concerned in the short run with holding its share of the market—thus ensuring larger profits in the longer period—than with maximizing profit or minimizing loss.

Today high profits for any given firm or industry often result in unfavorable reactions from other quarters. Larger earnings attract competitors, thereby spoiling the long-run expectations for earnings. They result in demands from the suppliers of factors of production, chiefly labor, for higher prices, which mean higher costs and smaller profits. Rates of return in excess of those of other firms in other industries also create an unfavorable "public" opinion, and bring demands that such business be regulated or taxed more heavily. Finally, there are indications that habit, customary procedures, and satisfaction with what is often called a "reasonable" profit, may play a larger role in business decisions than economists have believed.

We come again to the dual nature of much of economic doctrine: the distinction between economics as a social science and as a normative discipline. If production theory aims at predicting the behavior of those responsible for production decisions, any hypothesis about profit maximization needs to take into account any circumstances which modify behavior. On the other hand, if it is viewed as a normative discipline, the economist can say that *if* a firm seeks to maximize profits then it *ought* to produce to the point where marginal cost and marginal revenue are equal. Assuming this to be possible, the giver of such advice would still need to deal with the problem of how the entrepreneur *ought* to balance future profit expectations against more immediate realized income.

Recognizing certain weaknesses in overgeneralizing the so-called rationality of pure economic calculation, Von Neuman and Morgenstern have attempted to construct a mathematical model more suitable for describing economic behavior. They have used as their analogy the theory of games.[3] Their reasoning, simply stated, is as follows:

---

[3] John Von Neuman and Oscar Morgenstern, *Theory of Games and Economic Behavior* (Princeton: Princeton University Press, 1947).

An economic agent, such as an entrepreneur, operates in an environment in which he does not have, nor can he get, all the information he needs to decide a future course of action that would ensure him the largest possible profit. Like a chess or poker player, he is required by social and legal pressures to abide by certain rules of the game—rules observed also by his adversaries. He has certain information (such as the cards he holds), he can infer certain other information, and he knows the rules of the game; but other information he cannot know except as the game progresses, such as how his opponents or competitors will behave with respect to the information they have. Within these circumstances he can only proceed on the basis of assumptions, using the technique of strategy and bluff, modifying his own behavior as more information becomes available to him from the actions of his adversaries.

The producer operates in a market against competitors according to certain rules (laws) and customary procedures, aiming for the high stakes (maximum profits), while exercising the necessary precautions to protect himself against ruinous losses, withholding trump cards (liquid funds) for effective use if new information suggests better opportunities and pleasant surprises. In most strategic situations the existence of sizable reserves (property holdings) are an advantage. The large-scale enterprise in capable hands will experience in the long run the greater gains and the greater capacity to recoup losses and turn pleasant surprises to more favorable account.

Because of the relative newness of this approach, it is too early to assess the extent to which a hypothesis derived from such a model may prove fruitful for organizing observations regarding the behavior of producers and to what extent it will lead to a revision of the traditional model. We turn now to a more detailed examination of some of the institutional and accounting data relating to production.

Discussion
Questions

1. The modern entrepreneur differs in a number of important respects from his counterpart of a century ago. Can this be meaningfully discussed in terms of increased specialization and division of labor?

2. Make a list of inventions which have brought about great changes in our way of life.

3. Can you distinguish any important differences between the circumstances surrounding the release of atomic energy and those connected with the invention of the telephone, the electric light, and the wireless?

4. In what way can the introduction of a new technological process, or a new product, be related to the entrepreneurial function of uncertainty bearing?

5. Distinguish between a concept of short-run and long-run profit maximization. Are the factors generally taken into account likely to differ?

CHAPTER 20

Production Organization: Formal Aspects

In 1956 THE TOTAL NUMBER of firms in the United States was about 11 million. The Department of Commerce estimate of the number of separate business units was 4 million. This figure excludes enterprises devoted to agriculture, forestry, fishing, and the professional services. It also leaves out all individuals who were self-employed but who did not hire at least one other person. There are nearly 5 million farms. The rest of the total is made up of other business units, including self-employed professional people selling their services from "places of business" of their own. When these private firms are combined with the various government corporations and agencies which provide services, we get some measure of the separate production control units from which national product derives, and where claims against this product originate.

These firms are literally of many shapes and sizes, from the popcorn stand on the corner to such business empires as American Telephone and Telegraph Company and Standard Oil of New Jersey. Consider for a moment the case of a single industry such as agriculture. We may think of it as made up of individual farms that are much alike. However, the term refers to operations as diverse as mushroom production in an abandoned barn (if it returned a gross annual income of $250), the giant wheat farms in the West, and the King Ranch in Texas. Even the largest enterprise in agriculture, however, is small compared with such firms as General Motors or Du Pont.

As a next step in our inquiry, we will examine some of the differences among firms, according to legal classifications. The following classifications will be discussed: (1) the individual proprietorship, (2) the partnership, (3) the stock corporation, (4) the co-operative corporation, and (5) nonprofit organizations.

The Individual
Proprietorship

The simplest and numerically, the most important form of production organization in the economy of the United States is the individual proprietorship. It is also the oldest form of organization, in which many of today's largest corporations began their existence. As its name implies, it is a production unit built around the capacities and energies of a single person or family. Within limits the proprietorship is a one-man affair, in which responsibility, authority, and power of decision rests with the owner. The entrepreneurial function is exercised by him, although he may rely upon advice from others, and may enter into agreements by virtue of which he accepts limitations on his freedom of action. For example, to secure credit with which to carry out production plans, he can mortgage what he *owns,* thus sharing that ownership. He may convert an expected future income into cash in a similar way. Such encumbrances on the enterprise will involve a surrender of some freedom of action until the mortgage or note has been paid, although as long as interest payments are met and orderly reduction of the debt continues these restrictions are only potential.

The foundations on which such an enterprise can be built up are many and varied. An individual's skill or technical competence may constitute a starting point for business. If that is all he has, and if he can find someone willing to finance him, he can set up a shop or open an office, repay his creditors, and build up an equity or property holding out of earnings. Professional workers, mechanics, service workers, and others usually begin in this way. A small stake, an inheritance, a windfall, or accumulated savings often make it possible to start an enterprise on a modest scale. A reputation for hard work, thrift, and shrewd dealing may be the sole asset of the entrepreneur in a new undertaking.

This is the form of business organization we sometimes like to imagine as typical of the "American Way." As individuals, many of us have dreamed of the day when we might have a business of our own, one in which we would be boss, free to do as we pleased, and one in which we could be certain that whatever was produced, whatever claim against income was created, would be ours.

However, while the individual proprietorship is numerically the most important, its relative weight in terms of output and income is of declining significance except in a rather limited number of fields. It is predominant in agriculture, but as we have noted, agriculture has been declining in relative importance as far as value of goods and services

336

added to national product is concerned. The growing service industries make some use of the individual proprietorship, but even here the appearance of chain-services has become marked.

Exact information on the number of individual proprietorships is difficult to obtain, because it is the most fluid and mobile form of organization. In 1956 the Department of Commerce estimated the number of unincorporated enterprises at 10,700,000, but this included partnerships as well. The value of their claims against the national product was less than 25 per cent.

A number of factors have contributed to the decline of this form of production organization. Since it is the property (and usually the place of employment) of the individual owner, little distinction is made between his personal property or income and that of the business. To operate at all on a scale required by modern methods, using the most advanced technology, requires that virtually all that the owner possesses be made a basis for credit. Production risks involve virtually the whole net worth of the owner, his home, his car, his furniture, and sometimes his future income-earning capacity when a mortgage becomes (through court action) a *deficiency judgment*. Because the business of the individual proprietor is so much a personal thing, it must depend upon highly personalized lines of credit, which with the trend toward large investment institutions have become more difficult to obtain. The life of an individual is limited and uncertain. Creditors prefer to risk their loans on more enduring assets. Modern total war is particularly damaging to the small individual enterprise. Between 1941 and 1945 almost 1,200,000 businesses were discontinued, a large proportion of them small one-man affairs. There were about 1,400,000 new starts in the same period, but at the peak of war activities those businesses which were discontinued exceeded those which were started. After World War II new business starts rose rapidly, while failures and discontinuances increased from their 1945 low more slowly, partly because of the high-level income of the whole economy.

The special strength of the individual proprietorship is its adaptability and temporary nature. Perhaps for this reason it persists in large numbers, and adapts itself to the unique situations of local markets, to the particular talents of persons, and to the felt needs and necessities of the fringes of industrial society. But the force of technological development and change requires the main stream of production to flow through larger institutions, with a capacity to handle the intricacies of machine production based upon extensive capital and sources of credit, and also with a capacity to maintain costly research departments and sales forces.

337

The Partnership

A partnership, as a legal form of production organization, is a combination or a merging of the property and efforts of two or more individuals in a single enterprise. The substance of such an arrangement is the agreement which spells out how any income (or losses) will be shared. Here we see the emergence of the firm more clearly as a separate entity. It was, as far as can be determined, the earliest institutional arrangement which enabled individuals to pool their efforts for purposes of production. Partnership arrangements were common in ancient Rome, with the rights and responsibilities of the individual set forth in codes. Modern British and American law pertaining to partnerships derives from Roman law, modified by common-law practices, legislative enactments, and accumulated court decisions.

In both England and the United States efforts have been made from time to time to encourage the growth of partnerships, because of a belief that they perpetuate important features of an enterprise economy. *Limited partnerships* allow individuals to invest in such firms without involving themselves completely in their liabilities. Attempts in this country to secure the adoption in all states of a uniform partnership law have not been wholly successful, however.

Despite efforts in its behalf, the partnership has lost ground, comparatively speaking. There are in the United States approximately 200,-000 business firms that are partnerships. Partnerships are best adapted to the needs of the professions and agriculture, and are used by accounting firms, doctors, dentists, and other service occupations where specialists find it convenient to maintain a joint office. Brokerage houses (where individual responsibility is regarded as being in the public interest) are still most frequently either proprietorships or partnerships. In agriculture, where the individual proprietorship predominates, the partnership is a convenient device for transferring an enterprise from father to son (or son-in-law), while enabling both to share the income of the farm. Landlords also find it a convenient arrangement for sharing in the operation and income of a farm enterprise with a reliable tenant.

The partnership offers division of labor and specialization, while still preserving the initiative and flexibility of the individual proprietorship. A pooling of property and human skills, it allows the firm to benefit from greater management abilities than one man may command. This can improve the firm as a credit risk, even where the suppliers of capital do not actually associate themselves as silent partners.

Beyond a certain point partnership arrangements become unstable.

To secure enough capital to carry on mass production operations requires a group of participants much too large to function effectively. Because partners may be held liable for one another's debts, this form of organization can succeed only where personal confidence and mutual trust exist. This is usually possible only in relatively small groups. Even then many a partnership has foundered on petty jealousies and suspicion. A mutual dislike between partners' wives, not to mention too high a regard by one partner for the wife of another, may end the relationship and the continuity of the business. The death of one of the partners usually ends, or greatly alters, the firm, so that established business contacts are broken and the firm must be reorganized. Thus the continuity required in modern industrial growth is interrupted.

The Corporation

The corporation is an institution with a modern flavor. In its present form it represents a product of the advanced stages of technological and industrial evolution. As an idea its roots extend back into antiquity. It bears some resemblance to the chartered companies created by the English Crown to "further the trade and enhance the treasure of the realm" during the early periods of exploration and discovery. The charters granted to medieval cities and trading centers and to guilds and other organizations for the control of economic life were also early contributors to the technique of co-ordinating the activities of large numbers of individuals acting together toward a common goal.

After 1500, and particularly in the seventeenth and eighteenth centuries, the joint-stock company achieved widespread use as a device to raise money for financing expeditions to search for gold, to promote trade with natives, and to undertake ambitious colonization and land-development plans. Individuals were encouraged to participate in these ventures by buying shares of stock which gave them a claim against anticipated earnings. Following a number of spectacular failures which resulted in losses to stockholders, the most notable of which were the "Mississippi Bubble" in France and the "South Sea Bubble" in England,[1] the joint-stock companies fell into disfavor.

The English Bubble Act passed by Parliament in 1719 sought to

---

[1] Both of these ventures—the most famous of numerous schemes for development during the period—were called "bubbles" because of the tremendous inflation and profit expectations that accompanied their promotional periods and the suddenness of their collapse, bringing widespread deflation and losses.

limit the use of the joint-stock form to companies specifically chartered by the Crown.[2] Although the act remained on the statute books for more than a hundred years, it failed to accomplish what was intended. The new trading and industrial classes already had begun to challenge the authority of the monarchy (and the landed gentry which was its principal support) to grant monopoly trading rights to court favorites. Newly organized companies continued and gradually expanded their use of stock certificates to raise money to finance machinery and technical processes required for expanding production. The joint-stock company thus filled a breach that the partnership could not fill. Early in the nineteenth century legislation was passed to regulate and control what could not be prevented. Under the Act of 1825 and succeeding acts the joint-stock or limited-liability companies[3] were recognized as individual entities or legal persons, separate from their owners.

The history of the American corporation parallels that of its English counterpart, although legal definition has been complicated by the fact that the United States consists not of one government but of fifty so far as the regulation of production is concerned. The charters for corporations are issued almost exclusively by the separate states, with the exception of the nationally chartered banks. Initially, every corporation had to be created by a separate act of the legislature, but this practice gave way quite early, with New York leading the way in 1811, to the adoption of a general law under which any group of persons fulfilling specific requirements could be granted a charter and authorized to engage in production. Both federal and state laws have been modified, so that the legal status of a corporation as a "person" is now fairly complete.

What exactly is meant by the statement that a corporation is a legal person? It means that "before the law" all concerned will act as if the corporate firm were in fact a person. The corporation can hold property in its own name[4] and in its own right. This means that the agent for such an organization can transact business in its name in exactly the same way an individual person can. Debts may be contracted, property may be bought and sold, labor can be hired. Other individuals can sue it and be sued by it. Where liability for action rests with the corporation, the separate individuals who own the organization are relieved of respon-

[2] It is interesting to note that Adam Smith himself questioned the usefulness of joint-stock companies and predicted that they would never be very significant.

[3] British corporations usually affix "Ltd.," meaning limited liability, to the end of the firm's name, which is essentially the same as "Inc." (Incorporated) in the United States.

[4] Every corporation must have a name, and may have more than one, but no two corporations may have the same name.

sibility. In short, no person owning a part of the corporation, through the purchase of stock, stands to lose more than the amount he has invested.

Who owns a corporation? While one corporation may be owned by another corporation, somewhere along the line there is a *real* person or group of persons with the final claim against the property, the assets of the firm. What is perhaps more important, they have a claim against the income originating in its productive activities. Such ownership is only of that part of the property or income on which there is no prior claim. Debts owed by the corporation must be honored in full before the stockholders can be said to own anything. This point will be discussed more fully in the next chapter when we treat the purely financial aspects of control. Here our concern is with the control exercised by persons over the production decisions within the individual corporate firm.

Let us say that an individual decides to invest in a corporation. If he has converted part of his holdings into cash totaling $10,000, he can "reinvest" this in shares of stock in a given corporation. If the shares are selling for $100 each, he can obtain 100 shares. Now, assume there are 100,000 such shares. This particular stockholder has a $\frac{1}{1,000}$ ownership of the firm. This does not assure him any very direct voice in the management of his property. Even if he should regard management as unsatisfactory, he has little chance to express his opinion other than to sell his stock. The reason is, of course, that there are thousands of others like him holding stock, some of whom may have more "interest" in the business than he does. He can attend stockholders' meetings. He may be listened to politely and ignored in the voting.

The actual direction of the business under such circumstances, is only possible by delegation of authority. This is done in two steps: first, delegation by the stockholders to a board of directors; second, delegation by those directors to management (management can be drawn from members of the board; conversely, men hired for management jobs are frequently provided with stock and elevated to the board). All our lonely stockholder is entitled to do, by virtue of his stock ownership, is to cast his vote for a representative to the board of directors. Directors are elected by a "democratic" ballot, in which the voice of each stockholder is multiplied by the number of shares he has. If the board numbers twenty members, the twenty receiving the highest vote are elected. They are also likely to be individuals holding the largest number of shares—having voted for themselves in the election—except for some purely honorary members whose names and reputations lend prestige to company letterheads. The board elects a chairman, again on the basis of the number of shares they control (through ownership or proxy[5]), together with other officers. It appoints a manager, who may, but need not, be a member of the board. In production operations most boards determine broad policy, while the actual details of day-to-day decisions are left to management.

A board and management, once in control, are difficult to unseat. Without access to stockholders' lists (a means of obtaining proxies), and unfamiliar with the details of operation and with other inside information, minority members find it difficult to challenge those in power. Where the stock is widely held, the actual equity of the "majority" need not be large. As long as dividend payments remain satisfactory to stockholders, this is not usually regarded by them as a disadvantage. Most of them have neither talent nor taste for production decisions. Occasionally bad management may set off a revolt among stockholders and minority board members, with a consequent shift of control.

The increasing separation between ownership and management is a characteristic of corporate enterprise. Those who own no longer control the use of their property or the disposition of its earnings—at least in the case of the millions of small stockholders.

The Corporation and Economic Concentration

The corporation has undoubtedly contributed to the increasing size of the individual firm and at the same time to the declining number of firms comprising many major industries. This raises a question about the relationship between corporate property and monopoly.

In 1956 there were approximately 420,000 corporations in the United States. This was about 4 per cent of the total number of firms. However, slightly more than 55 per cent of the national income originated with these corporations. (Sole proprietorships and partnerships accounted for 25 per cent, government for 11.3 per cent, other private business for 5.4 per cent, and households for 3.3 per cent.) What is perhaps more significant is the proportion of this total which originated with a relatively small proportion of these corporations. The 500 largest corporations, a little more than one-tenth of one per cent of the total, employed nearly 9 million workers or close to 15 per cent of the total civilian labor force.

Firms with a long history, lines of communication, and reservoirs

---

[5] A proxy refers to one who exercises the voting right for a stockholder who cannot be present. By signing a proxy form, the stockholder transfers this right.

of good will in brand names and trade marks give continuity to contacts between sellers and buyers. Thus the modern giant business firm has in a sense become a "habit" in our national economy, an institutionalized system of relationships. The corporation as a property form serves as a device for the preservation and increase of wealth and income in an uncertain and changing world.[6]

In those industries adaptable to involved and costly technological processes the continuity of the corporate entity has been particularly useful for the merging of formerly independent firms. The decades on either side of the turn of the century were periods of giant mergers, when such organizations as U.S. Steel, Continental Can, and others combined existing firms. The decade following World War I was another period of mergers, and the process has continued to the present day.

A number of important industries now have no more than three or four firms accounting for their entire output. Aluminum ingots, until comparatively recently, were produced by a single firm.[7] Cigarettes, automobiles, steel, chemicals, tin cans, aircraft are among the products which have from 2 to 10 firms that account for a major share of the output. The advantage to the individual firm of a steady growth in size, with a corresponding reduction of rival companies, stems from two sources: (1) technological efficiency, and (2) monopoly power. Technological efficiency includes the higher productivity of large-scale operations, where assembly-line methods and large capital equipment are used. High fixed costs are spread over a large output. Today technology would also include the "know how" of scientific management, machine accounting, and rapid communication, which makes possible co-ordination and internal control. Monopoly power, once established, can often be maintained against newcomers through advertising, powerful sales campaigns, and established contacts.

Types of Combination

A combination or merger may take different forms. At the outset expansion often involves *horizontal combination,* combining under one management firms that formerly competed at the same stage of the roundabout production process. The merging of two or more separate automobile-manufacturing establishments, as in the case of General Motors, would be an example.

On the other hand, expansion can take place through *backward*

---

[6] The financial aspects of production organization are discussed in the next chapter.

[7] Since World War II, as a result of government policy in the disposition of publicly-constructed war plants, this number has been increased to three.

integration, or the action of a firm when it absorbs what had previously been an earlier stage in the production process. If a company begins operations by simply assembling parts of a product, it may subsequently absorb its principal suppliers. For example, an automobile manufacturer may purchase its carburetors, its ignition systems, its clutches, and other parts. If it eventually becomes the principal outlet for such firms, a merger becomes increasingly easy to accomplish. At various times the Ford Motor Company has acquired iron mines, rubber plantations, shipping lines, and other enterprises. The so-called captive mines of the large steel companies are coal-mining operations they own or control.

A third type of combination is usually called *forward integration,* a procedure in which the manufacturer or processor acquires (or sets up) wholesale and retail sales outlets for its output. The large oil companies, for example, own many of the service stations where their products are sold to motorists.

A given commodity may come under the control of a single firm at all stages of its production. To accomplish such complete "integration" requires very large funds of capital, and can only be done today through the devices of the corporation.

Industries vary in the extent to which the corporation has become the predominant form of organization. It has not been particularly adaptable to agriculture. Only about 7 per cent of farm output is produced by corporations. In contract construction the corporation accounts for about 36 per cent of the total output. On the other hand, 92 per cent of manufacturing, 96 per cent of mining, and 100 per cent of both electric power and telecommunications is carried on by corporations.

Closed and Government Corporations

The corporate form of organization is employed by firms that are essentially individual proprietorships. An individual owner desiring to use certain of the advantages of limited liability, may incorporate his business by selling a small amount of stock to two or more other persons. He thus retains control of his business but secures a separation between his business and personal property. Where the stock of a company is held by a small group, frequently the members of a family, it is known as a *closed corporation.*

Governmental or public agencies also find the corporate form of organization useful. The Federal government has made increasing use of the public corporation to achieve production objectives. The Reconstruction Finance Corporation, the Commodity Credit Corporation, and the Farm Credit Corporation are examples of agencies making use of publicly-subscribed capital funds to promote objectives closely related to production.

The Co-operative

Similar in many respects to the corporation is the co-operative, also a legal form of production organization with limited liability operating under a charter. But while it is similar in many respects, the co-operative is quite different in others. The greatest apparent difference is in the control of the affairs of the organization, and particularly in the division of claims against institutional income.

Where the corporation is controlled ultimately by the stockholders, in proportion to their ownership of common stock, the co-operative is controlled by its member-patrons (who may own one or more shares in the organization) on the basis of "one member, one vote."[8] Each member counts as much as every other member. In sharing the earnings (the excess of revenue over costs), members establish their claims on the basis of the amount of patronage they have given the firm, the amount of their sales to it or purchases from it.

Co-operatives may be classified into two broad types—*producer* and *consumer*. Producers' co-operatives are usually marketing and purchasing agents for their members. The producer member delivers his product to the co-operative, which usually makes an initial payment equal to the prevailing market price. The co-operative then markets the product, or it may process it further before disposing of it in a market. Theoretically, the good continues to be the property of the original owner as it passes through more advanced stages of production, acquiring added utility and value. Actually, of course, the output of any particular producer loses its identity, becoming part of the output of the co-operative firm. At the end of the accounting period the firm will have taken in certain revenues from the sale of members' produce. It will have incurred costs for handling and processing. If it has been efficient in its operation, it will have at the end of that period an amount of earnings usually called "savings." Claims against this fund are credited to the member patrons in proportion to the amount of their patronage.

If the enterprise is a consumers' co-operative or, in the case of some agricultural co-operatives, a purchasing association which buys equipment and materials used by the members, the firm sells to the member-patrons at prevailing prices. Again, if the co-operative is operated effi-

---

[8] Some co-operatives do have unequal control based upon proportionality of patronage.

ciently, it will have certain savings over and above its costs. Claims against these savings are remitted to the member-patrons in proportion to the dollar volume of their purchases.

Historically, the idea of the co-operative is a little more than one hundred years old. Credit for the explicit formulation of co-operative principles is usually assigned to a group of Rochdale (England) weavers, who in 1844 opened a small store. They decided to "pool" their limited funds and purchase their needs in larger volume. The members in effect turned over their money to the co-operative society, which was then commissioned to buy the things they wanted as cheaply as possible. Part of the savings were left with the organization to serve as working capital. The rules set up or evolved from experience by this association were seven: (1) one member, one vote; (2) a fixed return to investment capital; (3) no discrimination because of race, religion, or political beliefs; (4) purchase and sale at the going market price; (5) sharing of savings in proportion to purchases; (6) trading for cash only; and (7) member education in the principles of co-operation. From these small beginnings co-operative enterprise has grown to very large size, particularly in England and the Scandinavian countries. There both consumer and producer co-operatives are extensive. In the United States co-operative enterprise has been successful chiefly among farmers.

Co-operative enterprise is regarded by many of its members as a means for securing the efficiencies of large-scale production, while still retaining control of their products through more advanced stages of production. In parallel fashion large numbers of relatively small consumer purchasers can, by joining together, make contributions to a common capital fund, intercept goods more remote in the production processes, and achieve savings by doing their own processing. In this way money incomes earned in other pursuits may command a larger real income or purchasing power.

If markets were perfectly competitive, co-operatives could not expect to make large savings, since market price and average cost of production would be approximately equal. However, where monopoly exists the co-operative has been viewed as a means for injecting competition into the market, thereby increasing members' real income. The co-operative form of enterprise began as a protest against what was regarded as too much control over production by large property owners. The Rochdale weavers viewed their low incomes as a consequence of the sale of their labor in markets that were biased against them. They saw the returns to owners of capital as a consequence of their control of the economy. What they said in effect was, "We will improve our real income by using our com-

346

bined purchasing power to hire the services of capital as we are hired, at the lowest price."

Over the years, however, co-operatives have found that more is involved than just this. Only where co-operatives have been able to set up organizations that achieve greater efficiency through large-scale production have they succeeded in achieving their purpose. Where they have succeeded, for example, in Sweden, they become instruments for controlling monopoly.

Co-operatives as Institutionalized Controls

The tendency toward centralization of control through a separation of ownership and management was noted in the case of corporations. How about co-operatives? Where the co-operatives are most successful, and when they achieve a scale of operation that makes possible the fullest use of modern technology, the same tendency toward concentration can be noted. Co-operative societies with large memberships can only function effectively by delegating authority and responsibility to a board of directors and to a professional management. The individual member exercises control only through his vote for representatives on the board, which determines broad policies and selects the management. An indifferent membership may very well result in control by a small group which acquires power through default. There is one difference, however. The essential equality of individual members under the rule of one member, one vote provides a safeguard against concentration of power based upon property ownership. This is the basis for the claim of the co-operative philosophers that their organization is democratic and more equalitarian.

Could a large-scale co-operative organization achieve monopoly control? To answer this question a distinction must be made between producer and consumer co-operatives. Producer co-operatives, when they are organized around scarce factors of production, can be effective instruments for controlling the volume of output and for raising prices. An example frequently cited is that of lemon growers. Because of the limited area of land suitable for lemon production, the growers have been able to form an effective co-operative to process and market their output. Through this control of supply, the lemon producers over a time have been able to "regularize" marketings and practically double the price of lemons in relation to other citrus fruit. Thus, since producers' co-operatives are devices for increasing the income claims of a particular group of producers, they are no insurance against monopoly. Where the number of members is small, and control of scarce factors is complete, the effect is not essentially different from that of a corporation. In the case of consumer co-operatives, however, since everyone is a consumer, and since membership is open, the consequences of monopoly may be less pronounced on income distribution. Even if a monopoly were achieved, the broad base for distributing the savings from the enterprise would offset the concentration of income claims. We will devote further attention to consumer co-operatives in Part 5.

Although the co-operative is a relatively minor form of organization in the United States, it is not without significance. Agricultural co-operatives, which include both marketing and purchasing associations, numbered 10,125 in 1952. Total estimated membership was five and a half million, and they did a business in excess of $7 billion.

Other fields in which the co-operative form of organization has been used are credit, hospitals, housing, and numerous service activities. All told, in 1954 more people were members of co-operatives than owned common stock in corporations.

Nonprofit Organizations

Many activities, such as charity, the promotion of educational and cultural development, and the propagation of religious and ethical experience, have in our day acquired the dimensions of mass production effort. Command over factors of production and the creation of output and income link them unmistakably with the other production institutions contributing to the flow of goods and services. However, from a legal viewpoint, they are differentiated, and for taxation and other purposes receive separate treatment.

The nonprofit corporation has become an enterprise of ever growing importance, administering large funds, filling the needs of many, and giving employment to thousands. Great foundations set up by persons of affluence are dedicated to the advancement of research, peace, medicine, education, literature, and countless other objectives.

Discussion Questions

1. For income purposes, what is it that distinguishes an independent or separate firm?

2. In light of the discussion of this chapter, reread the sections in Chapter 3 on wealth, property, and capital. Relate this to the nature of property forms in the proprietorship, the partnership, and the corporation.

3. A share of common stock represents an abstract property form. Essentially, what property rights are involved?

4. What is the function of a board of directors in a corporation?

5. Who owns the capital of a government corporation?

CHAPTER 21

Production Organization: Financial Aspects

A SELF-SUFFICIENT household economy could measure the results of its production for the past year only by counting the additions to its herds, the containers of fruits and vegetables, the bushels of grain, the cards of wool, and the seed set aside for the next year's planting. The specialized, highly institutionalized production organizations of today consult their accounting records.

The language of the accountant is a convenient shorthand for describing the activities of a production organization during a specified period. We have already encountered the accountants' handiwork in the national-income accounts. Here we will see it within the framework of the separate firm.

We can gain insight into the function of a modern production organization and the sources of its basic information on costs, output, prices, and income by understanding the purely financial aspects of its ownership, sales, and control operations. Property is no longer a simple matter of possession and use. Except for personal or consumption goods, the things that are owned in most cases are the titles or claims, backed by a reciprocal obligation of someone else to turn over or deliver on those claims. Viewed by the person who holds title, these are *assets*. To the one against whom they are held, they are debts or *liabilities*. Both are but different sides of a personal relationship. Wealth consists to an increasing extent of what others owe you. Production is undertaken in large measure to get out of debt and to increase claims against others. We will be concerned in this chapter with two sets of accounting records kept by the firm: the financial balance sheet and the income (profit and loss) statement.

The Proprietorship

We begin with the simplest form of business organization, using a hypothetical case to show production history as reflected in comparative balance sheets and income statements. Assume that a truck driver has accumulated a modest fund out of earnings, or from an inheritance, which he decides to use as a basis for starting a business of his own. He organizes a bread delivery service for a bakery, in which his income will depend on his success in establishing a regular clientele among retail stores and restaurants. As capital equipment he requires a delivery truck, a few accounting records, and his own management skill and labor. Lacking the full amount needed to purchase the truck and maintain a cash reserve for working capital, he decides to obtain a loan from a bank, giving as security a mortgage on the truck. A balance sheet for the enterprise, just prior to obtaining the loan and purchase of the truck, would appear as follows:

Bill Jones, Bread Delivery Service

BALANCE SHEET
Dec. 31, 1955

Assets		Liabilities	
		None	
Cash Balance	$4,000	*Net Worth*	$4,000
Total Assets	$4,000	Liabilities & Net Worth	$4,000

On the day he begins operations, part of his cash will have been invested in a delivery truck. Half of the equity in the truck is held by the bank. His balance sheet will now appear as follows:

BALANCE SHEET
Jan. 1, 1956

Assets		*Liabilities*	
Cash Balance	$2,000	Notes Payable	$2,000
Truck	4,000	*Net Worth*	
		Assets—Liabilities	4,000
Total Assets	$6,000	Liabilities & Net Worth	$6,000

So far his business transactions consist of changing the form of his assets by converting cash into capital equipment. He now controls assets valued at $6,000 as he begins operations, although his net worth has not changed. By combining his labor and management abilities, it is his plan to (1) increase his income and (2) maintain the value of assets he controls.

351

On December 31, 1956, the balance sheet of the firm appears as follows:

BALANCE SHEET
Dec. 31, 1956

Assets		*Liabilities*	
Cash Balance	$1,000	Notes Payable	$1,000
Truck, less $800			
depreciation	3,200	*Net Worth*	
Accounts Receivable	1,400	Assets—Liabilities	4,600
Total Assets	$5,600	Liabilities & Net Worth	$5,600

As a result of one year's operations, we note by comparing the two balance sheets that a number of changes have taken place. The net worth of the business has increased by $600. As an entrepreneur Bill Jones has increased his property holdings by that amount. Among his assets are claims against others for $1,400. He has reduced his indebtedness by paying off one-half of what he owed to the bank on his truck. His equity in the truck is therefore increased, although the value of the truck has decreased by $800 (we have depreciated the value of the truck by 20 per cent, on the assumption that it will last five years).

The balance sheet tells nothing about the income of the firm, however. We do not know, for example, what Bill Jones as head of a household received from the business. The increase in net worth might have been accomplished by greatly restricted consumption. Earlier we defined income as the amount an individual or household can consume and still be as well off at the end as at the beginning of the period being considered. We will have to consult the income statement to find out.

Bill Jones, Bread Delivery Service
Operating Income Statement
Jan. 1—Dec. 31, 1956

Operating Revenue

Gross Receipts from Bread Sales	$15,000

Direct Variable Costs

Payments to Bakery for Bread	$8,000	
Truck expenses and gasoline	800	
		$8,800

Direct Fixed Costs

Depreciation on Truck	$800		
Interest on Note @ 5%	120		
		$920	9,720
		Net Income	$5,280

Imputed Costs

Interest on Investment ($4,000 @ 3%)	$120		
Salary	3,000		
	$3,120		3,120
		Profit Income	$2,160

From this income statement we can fill the gaps in our knowledge about the business. The delivery service paid its way to the extent of maintaining intact the $4,000 investment, adding $600 to it. Out of the net income the firm's indebtedness was reduced by $1,000 and the investment increased by $600. Subtracting this $1,600 from net income, we can infer that $3,680 was transferred to his personal or household account.

On the assumption that Bill Jones had previously earned $3,000 a year for his labor, and that the $4,000, if invested in government bonds at 3% interest, would have returned $120, we are able to determine further that the profit income which accrued to him was $2,160. However, this contains an element of management return also, since he has demonstrated an ability to manage an enterprise and to render a service for which others were willing to pay.

The records presented are limited, and intended only for illustration. The circumstances we have outlined are favorable ones. A series of such records continued over an extended period would undoubtedly show wide variation between good years and bad. Let us assume, however, that the enterprise is a successful one. Assets continue to increase; liabilities are reduced. In time, reserves are created out of income to replace capital equipment as it wears out and to take care of bad debts and other unforeseen contingencies. In addition, something new has been added. The net worth of the business is now something more than the investment from savings and accrued income. It is a going concern, returning an income from which the claims accrue to the capital value of the enterprise, to the managerial abilities of the proprietor, and to his actual labor.

Let us assume that the enterprise attains the status of debt-free ownership. With no expansion, the enterprise income provides a return on a fixed investment (with adequate depreciation reserves) and to labor and management, and a profit which presumably varies from year to year, but which maintains a fairly stable average. We can illustrate this with a hypothetical generalized balance sheet.

BALANCE SHEET

Assets		Liabilities	
Cash	$1,600	None	
Bonds (Sinking fund to replace truck)	3,200		
Truck ($4,000 less 80% depreciation)	800	*Net Worth*	
		Owner's Equity	$5,600
Total Assets	$5,600	Total	$5,600

What is the value of such an enterprise? What could the owner get for it if he were to sell it now to someone else? Or, conversely, what could someone else afford to pay for it? Needless to say, this is not an easy question to answer for so personal an enterprise as this one. First of all, we would have to assume that anyone taking over the delivery route could retain the *good will* built up by the entrepreneur. We would need some estimate of the relative return on his labor and his management skills. We could assume as a necessary cost of the enterprise a return on the stabilized investment of $5,600 at least as great as the going rate of interest. The problem of imputed labor costs (income) could be solved by choosing the next best income opportunity for the driver. If he could earn $4,000 as a driver for someone else, this would give us a figure of valuing labor costs and management ability in this field. If an audit of records showed that after allowing for all such fixed costs of operation (including continuous maintenance of reserves and insurance to offset depreciation and other foreseeable losses), plus all variable costs, an average profit income remained, this would be a starting point for answering our question.

Assume that the average *profit income* for a number of years had been $600. Our question now becomes, "How much could another entrepreneur afford to pay for such an enterprise?" We can answer this by asking how much money would have to be put to work at a *given* rate of interest to earn that much. The formula is:

$$\frac{P}{r_i} = C, \quad \text{or} \quad \frac{\$600}{.05} = \$12,000.$$

Another way to look at this value is from the point of view of the present owner. Assuming that he takes a job at $4,000, how much would he need to invest elsewhere, at the going rate of interest, to give him an income equivalent to what he is now receiving? The decision of both the owner and the prospective purchaser would finally have to rest upon expectations about the future prospects of the enterprise. If the owner has decided that he prefers greater security, and intends to invest in something more stable, he may be willing to accept less. If the purchaser believes that the profit figure is a maximum that can be expected, he would be unwilling to pay more.

We have illustrated here something of the problems of valuing an individual proprietorship, both from the standpoint of sale price and for purposes of borrowing against it. However, the materials presented illustrate the *method* of capitalizing profit income to arrive at a tentative value of a going concern. Essentially, the procedure is the inverse of that for determining compound interest. A compound interest table tells us the future value of a present sum of money which is increased by a certain percentage (its earning), say 5 per cent, each year. The interest for the following year is computed from the larger base, and is in turn added to it. Thus $1.00 compounded annually at 5 per cent will be worth $2.65 in twenty years.

Capitalization is a method for determining present value of future income, where the original investment is maintained intact. If profit income continues at its average rate, the value of assets will be maintained as part of costs, and in addition the $600 becomes a return on investment. Note now the changed financial structure of the enterprise. With a larger value of invested capital, profit income disappears and the income becomes wholly a return on invested capital. This is a capitalization of profits.[1]

Also illustrated are some of the complications involved in determining the income of the firm. If we define the latter as the amount that an owner can use for his own personal needs during the year and still be as well off at the end as at the beginning, we run into difficulties. A change in the interest rate will greatly change the net worth of the enterprise. A fall in rate, for example, would enable the proprietor to consume more than the net value added to goods or services produced in that year, and still be as well off at the end of the year (at the lower interest rate) as he was at the beginning (when the interest rate was higher). A fall in the price of services (or commodities), affecting profits, will likewise be reflected in the value of the enterprise as viewed by the entrepreneur.

---

[1] In Part 4, under Distribution, we will extend this process to other kinds of income. See also page 360 below.

The Corporation

In the financial structure of the corporation we can see most clearly the operation of the purely financial aspects of production control—what Veblen called "absentee ownership" and the "vested interests."[2] This is because the functions of labor, management, and property ownership, as they are joined in the production process, are more clearly defined. Management, as well as labor, is hired. Specialization is here carried to its greatest degree of refinement.

As was noted in the previous chapter, the modern corporation has made it possible, through limited liability and the issuing of stock shares, to bring together from many sources large amounts of money capital with which to finance the more costly technological production processes. Here we shall enlarge upon this statement to show how different methods of financing have made it possible to provide for varying degrees of financial participation. The principal instruments used by the corporation represent different techniques of financial control, as well as a means for graduating risks to suit the tastes of investors.

Common Stock. The simplest form of the corporation is that in which the *capital investment* is raised by issuing par-value common stock. We will take as our example a corporation financed by the sale of 10,000 shares of stock at $100 per share. This is how the projected balance sheet would look prior to production operations.

XYZ COMPANY, INC.

BALANCE SHEET — January 1, 1956

Assets		Liabilities	
Current Assets		Current Liabilities	None
Cash	$1,000,000	*Net Worth*	
Fixed Assets	None	Capital	
		10,000 shares of	
		common stock	$1,000,000
		Liabilities &	
Total Assets	$1,000,000	Net Worth	$1,000,000

[2] These may appear to be terms that are less than objective, due to the unfavorable connotation often associated with them in everyday speech. It certainly can be argued that Veblen himself meant them to be no more than descriptive terms. That is all they are intended to be here. An absentee owner is merely one whose claims against income arise not from direct participation but from some pre-existing property claim. Vested interest refers to a property right which is included in the bundle of rights upheld by existing institutions, and particularly by law.

On this balance sheet the capital stock represents a liability of the firm to the stockholders who own it. Now assume that the corporation acquires a plant, together with equipment required to begin operations. This change will be represented in the balance sheet as follows:

XYZ COMPANY, INC.
BALANCE SHEET — July 1, 1956

Assets			*Liabilities*	
Current Assets			Current Liabilities	None
Cash	$200,000		*Net Worth*	
Inventories	400,000		Capital	
Total		$600,000	10,000 shares of	
Fixed Assets			common stock	$1,000,000
Land	20,000			
Building	200,000			
Equipment	180,000			
Total		$400,000	Liabilities &	
Total Assets		$1,000,000	Net Worth	$1,000,000

This balance sheet is oversimplified. An instrument of such a type represents a still photograph of the business, as of a particular day. In getting organized, acquiring an inventory, and so forth, it is unlikely that there would be no outstanding current liabilities. However, our next balance sheet will show this added complexity. After six-months' operation the company's balance sheet might appear in the form shown on page 358. Note that a number of complicating entries now appear in the balance sheet indicating the results of production. Accounts receivable in the amount of $500,000 have appeared in the assets column. These are debts owed to the firm, representing the ordinary commercial delay or credits allowable in the regular course of business. On the liabilities side accounts payable are similar entries, except that they are debts of the firm. Under Paid-in Surplus and Dividends Payable is a total of $100,000. This represents earnings of the corporation for the six-months' period. Of this total, $20,000 has been set aside and declared as dividends, at the rate of $2 per share of common stock. The remaining $80,000 will remain in the business. By virtue of this accumulated surplus the value of the business as a going concern should now be $1,080,000. The value of the stock per share has presumably increased to $108. In lieu of the full $10 per share earnings made possible by the profits of the business for the six-months' period, the owners received a $2 dividend *plus* added value of stock shares.

357

XYZ COMPANY, INC.

BALANCE SHEET — December 31, 1956

Assets

Current Assets		
Cash Balance	$120,000	
Accounts Receivable	500,000	
Inventories	400,000	
Total Current		$1,020,000
Fixed Assets		
Land	$ 20,000	
Building		
($200,000 less depreciation)	194,000	
Equipment		
($180,000 less depreciation)	171,000	
Total Fixed		385,000
Total Assets		$1,405,000

Liabilities

Current Liabilities		
Accounts Payable	$ 85,000	
Notes Payable	100,000	
Total Current		$ 185,000
Long-Term Liabilities		
Bonds Payable		100,000
Net Worth		
Reserves		$ 20,000
Paid-in Surplus		80,000
Dividends Payable		20,000
Capital		
10,000 shares of common stock		1,000,000
Liabilities & Net Worth		$1,405,000

One other item in the liabilities column should be noted. Notes payable in the amount of $100,000 represent a use by the firm of commercial credit for short-term expenses. This will usually be *short-term credit* obtained from commercial banks so that wages and salaries and other regular monthly or weekly payments can be met independently of receipts that come in at irregular intervals. The firm's long-term expenses appear as Bonds Payable in the amount of $100,000.

For a more complete understanding of the changes in the balance sheet we will need to consult the income statement for the six-months' period.

XYZ COMPANY, INC.
INCOME STATEMENT
July 1 to December 31, 1956

Net Sales (Total Revenue)		$2,000,000
Total Costs		
Materials and services purchased from others	$1,300,000	
Wages and salaries, workers' benefits	500,000	
Depreciation	15,000	
Taxes, other than Federal Income & Social Security	25,000	
Federal Income Taxes	40,000	
Reserve for contingencies	20,000	
Total Costs		$1,900,000
Net Income for Period		$ 100,000

Two items are important to note in the balance sheet and the income statement because we will later refer to them in connection with internal financing. These are the depreciation reserves, a cost item, and the retained earnings or surplus.

Reserves for depreciation are funds made available out of gross income for reinvestment or replacement of worn-out or obsolete capital equipment. It has sometimes been the practice of corporations to invest these funds outside the business—in government bonds or other high-grade securities—so that they are available when needed for new equipment or for plant remodeling. However, another practice is to leave them in the business as working capital, where, particularly during prosperous times, their earnings will be greater.

The other internal source of funds for investment is the undistributed earnings or retained surplus. Decisions regarding net earnings to be paid out in dividends and the amount to be retained in the business are made by the board of directors. Occasionally surplus funds may be set aside during years of high income, to be paid out as dividends in years of low income.

Except for one bond issue, this corporation has relied on *equity capital*. In other words, land, buildings, machinery, and other assets are *owned* by the stockholders. As the net worth of the firm increases, through retained earnings, the value of the investor's equity increases. Because of a well established market for most corporate "securities," individual owners of these stocks can realize the full income by selling them on the stock exchange. In the corporation we have been considering, at the end of the six-months' period a total of $80,000 on $8 per share has been "plowed back" into the business. The value of these shares should presumably be $108. An owner of one of these shares might sell it on the market for that price. His income for the period, with the $2 dividend already received, would be $10, and his net worth of $100 would remain intact. However, if he were to sell his stock, more would be involved than the income for the period just past. This is stock in a going concern. If it appears that earnings will continue at this rate, there is future income to consider. At the rate of $10 for a six-months' period, the rate of earnings would be $20 per year. This amount capitalized at different rates of interest would be:

$$(1) \quad \frac{20}{.04} = \$500 \qquad\qquad (3) \quad \frac{20}{.08} = \$250$$

$$(2) \quad \frac{20}{.05} = \$400 \qquad\qquad (4) \quad \frac{20}{.10} = \$200$$

A rule of thumb, sometimes followed in the stock market for valuing securities, is to multiply the earnings by 10. Thus a corporation whose stock is traded freely, given a substantial earning per share, is likely to witness a gradual rise in the value of its stock. To prevent this from happening, to keep the value of its shares low, firms frequently issue stock dividends. This is called splitting the shares. In the spring of 1948, for example, when the value of its common stock had risen to $99 per share, Bethlehem Steel paid a stock dividend of two for one. Anyone owning a share of stock received two additional shares. The value of shares on the market dropped to $33.

During a period when a company's stock is rising trading may take place on the strength, not of actual earnings, but of the expected rise in value. The rise in value, of course, is not wholly independent of earnings. The prime mover, however, is the general price level. During speculative

360

"booms" in the stock market the prices of stocks have sometimes been "bid up" out of all relation to dividends or earnings. The stock market boom of 1929, for example, saw prices so far out of relation to earnings that some wit remarked that speculators were "discounting not only the future, but the hereafter as well."

During a rising stock market the holder of favored shares may be able to obtain what amounts to an income in the form of *capital gains.* This is a point to which we shall return in our discussion of distribution. Meanwhile, one other aspect of trading in equity capital is of interest. This is the technique of raising additional capital through the sale of no-par stock, a practice which has evolved from experience with stock prices in excess of par.

Assume that after a period of successful operation the above corporation desired to expand its operations by installing more efficient modern equipment. This would be an example of *autonomous investment* discussed in Part 2 (see page 162). One technique would be to offer additional shares (perhaps authorized in the corporation charter, but not issued) with no-par value, to be sold at existing market prices. If the record of the company were a successful one, and if the stock market were favorable, this might indeed be the easiest way to raise the capital. A larger amount of capital per voting share could be obtained than by issuing par-value stocks.

If for any reason the company desired to acquire additional capital without extending participation in company affairs, it could use other instruments. These instruments, while they are nonparticipating (carry no vote), may prove more attractive to investors than common stocks, because of their prior claims against income.

Preferred Stock. A corporation may issue stock which in some respects offers a status similar to that of the silent partner in a partnership. This is *preferred stock,* which pays a fixed return on a par value. For example, a $100 par value at 6 per cent would mean that such a share of stock would carry an assured annual income of $6. This assurance, of course, is contingent upon the income of the firm. However, preferred-stock dividends take precedence in their claims against income over common stock.

There are two principal types of preferred stock—cumulative and noncumulative. *Cumulative preferred stock* not only has a prior claim against income in any given year, but its claims, if not met, accumulate. This means that before common-stock holders can share in earnings all back dividends on the preferred stock must be paid up. *Noncumulative preferred stock,* of course, takes precedence only in any given year. Dividends passed need not be made up in the future. In case a certain number

361

of dividends are passed, owners of preferred stock are sometimes granted voting privileges.

Bonds. Bonds are hired money. They are agreements to pay, at specified rates, for the privilege of using someone else's liquid funds. Usually they include as part of the agreement a date when the money will be paid back, or the bonds redeemed. Like stock shares, the engraved paper evidence of company debt called bonds are usually *negotiable instruments,* meaning they are bought and sold in the securities markets.

From the standpoint of investors, bonds have the first claim against corporate revenues after the ordinary costs such as wages and salaries, raw materials, and so forth. Bonds may be backed by *liens* against specific equipment, which means that bondholders could foreclose and take over such equipment in case of default. These are called *machinery bonds.* Income bonds can lay claim only to the income of the company. In the event a company's income drops below what is required to meet the bondholders' claims against it, the latter may institute court action to take over the assets of the company. In such a case a bankruptcy court will appoint a receiver for such assets. The receiver will operate the company in the interests of the bondholders until their claims have been met. The assets will then be returned to the owners of the preferred and common stocks. Cases are on record, however, of bankrupt companies continuing to operate for many years under a receivership. In such cases equity capital has virtually disappeared.

From the point of view of the corporation, bonds have certain advantages as a means of raising operating capital. Bondholders have no voice in management, as long as their regular claims are met. On the income statement the interest payments on bonds appear as direct costs, and are therefore not regarded as corporate income, on which Federal income taxes must be paid. When earnings are high bondholders have no claim against profits. This enables the corporation to command greater quantities of the factors of production, and the profit income realized therefrom goes to management and the common-stock holders. If through bad management or falling prices, however, the income of the corporation declines, the financial structure of the company may become highly inflexible. Whereas equity capital or risk capital accepts fluctuating income, bondholders' payments are fixed and must be met.

During periods of high corporate earnings bonds become relatively unattractive to all investors except the most conservative, and a corporation may find it advantageous to raise its funds from risk capital. In times of unfavorable income outlook bonds become more desirable. Since 1929 bonds and borrowings from banks, plus internal financing, have increased relative to risk capital. High corporate income taxes are frequently credited with having brought about this shift, though there are reasons to doubt that this is the only influence.

Growth of
Financial Control

The wide variety of capital-raising techniques open to the modern corporation has sometimes lent itself to manipulation. One technique was the *trust,* which had rather widespread use in the last quarter of the nineteenth century. The formation of a trust was a simple adaptation of a very old legal device (which had long been used for other purposes) to get control over previously independent firms. The owners of a majority of the stock of operating companies turned over their securities to a board of "trustees." In exchange they received "trust certificates" entitling them to share, on a pro rata basis, in the combined profits of all operating companies. Thus the board of trustees came to control a group of operating firms in particular industries, with the result that they could be welded together into a closely integrated unit, or into what amounted to a single firm. This practice provoked public disapproval and resulted in the passage of the country's basic antimonopoly law. The Sherman Anti-Trust Act of 1890 declared such mergers illegal, if intended as devices to control supply and raise prices. After 1902 the trusteeship was no longer used in this way. It was replaced by the more effective methods of outright purchase of plant and equipment, or the use of the holding company. The latter is of particular interest because of its importance during the period between the end of World War I and the onset of the great depression in the 1930's.

The *holding company,* as its name suggests, is a corporation whose business it is to hold the securities of other companies. As an investment institution it can perform a service to investors by spreading their risks among a number of operating companies, so that they need not "put all of their eggs in one basket." Thus a corporation may be formed to raise capital from the public, that capital to be invested in the securities of firms engaged in direct production. Dividends paid on the stock of the operating companies become the source of income of the holding company (as holder of such securities), which income is distributed as earnings on the holding company's own stocks and bonds.

From a primarily investment institution, however, the holding company developed as a control device for welding separate companies into what amounted to a single firm. For a clearer understanding of this, we will need to reconsider how the control of factors of production is achieved within a given corporation. The corporation whose development we considered earlier began with a $1,000,000 paid-in capital, contributed by stockholders and represented by 10,000 shares of common stock. Now consider the change which would take place in the capital account of the balance sheet after a period of successful operation, with a substantial part of the earnings retained. Assume that the value of common stock has risen to $3 million. In the absence of additional issues of common-stock dividends, this would mean a value per share of $300. Total value of common stock in any event would be $3,000,000.

Such a company would be in an excellent position to raise additional capital by means of preferred stock and by bonds. For the purposes of our discussion we will take the case where the corporation has increased its net worth to $6,000,000, represented in the capital account as follows:

OPERATING COMPANY XYZ

Common Stock	$3,000,000
Preferred Stock	2,000,000
Bonds	1,000,000
Net Worth	$6,000,000

Since ownership of a majority of the voting stock in a corporation will give the owners control over the firm, anything in excess of $1,500,000 in common stock could control effectively the company's $6,000,000 net worth, and assets persumably in excess of that.

We will assume now that we have five operating companies with capital structures identical with that outlined above. Their total net worth would represent $30,000,000. This entire holding could be controlled by slightly more than $7,500,000 if properly invested in the common stock of the operating companies. Thus a holding company which acquired this stock would be in a position to integrate the policies of the five separate companies.

Now we will consider the formation of a holding company, organized to raise this amount of capital. Using the same methods of financing as the operating corporations, the promoters of the holding company can build up a capital account which appears about as follows:

HOLDING COMPANY A

Common Stock	$3,000,000
Preferred Stock	3,000,000
Bonds	1,500,000

364

Promoters of Holding Company A will be in a position to acquire a controlling interest in the common stock of the five operating companies. But note that control of the holding company rests with the majority interest of the common stockholders. In this case anything above $1,500,000 can exercise control over capital accounts totaling $30,000,000.

Promoters of a second holding company possessing a parallel capital structure can gain a controlling interest over Holding Company A. During the late 1920's this process of pyramiding control through successive holding companies resulted in the seat of final control over vast enterprises, particularly in the field of public utilities, as many as nine stages removed from the actual production organizations. Where the common stock of these corporations is widely distributed, effective control can be achieved with ownership of as little as three or four per cent. As a consequence of legislation passed in the 1930's, holding companies more than one stage removed from operations are now prohibited.

Discussion
Questions

1. What is meant by the expression "the value of a business as a going concern"?

2. Define or explain imputed cost. Why is it necessary to use such a concept? What difficulties does it involve?

3. When a company fails to make adequate provision for depreciation, what is happening to its investment? In a real or physical sense? In a money or property sense?

4. What determines the value of an asset? In the accounting sense? In an economic or income sense?

5. During a period of rapidly rising prices, what is likely to happen to depreciation reserves?

6. If a corporation retains part of its profit income, what, theoretically, should happen to the value of its common stock? To its preferred stock? To its ability to engage in debt financing?

Production

and Public Policy

MEASURED BY whatever criteria one might choose, the production economy of the United States is without peer anywhere in the world, its present performance unequaled before in all of history. In volume, in variety of goods, and in ratio of output to human effort the indicators continue to rise decade by decade.

Could it have done better? Has it produced the "right" things and in the "proper amounts"? Have we sacrificed quality for quantity? Is it true that we have "wasted" resources turning out things people don't really want, and then used additional factors of production in advertising (more than $10 billion in 1956) in order to make people want them?

When the voice of the critic is raised against things as they are, it is not because the United States compares unfavorably with any other nation in output per person. It is rather with some imagined state of affairs, some hypothetical criterion of efficiency or productivity, that comparisons must be made.

Once again we return to our three-way classification of policy prescriptions to inquire how they are translated into programs for action. The following chapter explains what these normative positions mean when they come to grips with the question of determining what to produce and how much.

CHAPTER 22

Who Should Make Production Decisions?

IN THE IDEAL MODEL of an enterprise economy the production decisions of millions of private individuals and organizations are co-ordinated and linked together in a communications system called the market. In the ideal model of a centralized economy production decisions are shaped to the design of some over-all plan set up in advance and co-ordinated through agencies of the state.

The Free Market

Where wants are often in conflict and subject to change, where new technology is constantly extending the horizon of possibilities, many argue that the market (which they regard as the best "allocator" of scarce factors) can function only for a system of private enterprise, of private ownership of the factors of production, and of private direction of the business firm in which the primary guide is the hope of profit income. Hence, their prescriptions for public policy in the field of production are likely to emphasize the importance of freeing the market from government influence. This viewpoint also rests on certain further judgments.

1. All governmental agencies are basically inefficient and bureaucratic in their allocation of resources. This is because the chief characteristics of the state are "enforcement and uniformity." The characteristics of society, on the other hand, under conditions of freedom, tend toward "voluntary co-operation and variety." To place the resources of a nation under the control of government must inevitably result in the creation of a monolithic administrative system of control, which must enforce a rigid compliance with planned production in order to prevent chaos. At the top some final authority or board must make the decisions on the use of the factors of production, including labor.

367

2. Once private property has ceased to exist among the factors of production, the very plan by which such an authority or agency could operate would become arbitrary, subject to the whim or caprice of the board or the dictator, for the following reason. Once private property has been abolished, there would no longer be a *market* for the various capital assets. Accordingly, there would be no process of social valuation, no price for the factors of production which could be entered in an accounting system to determine the cost of the goods produced. Even assuming that consumers had been provided with a money income (as payment for services performed or by means of some other form of social dividend), free consumer choice would not be effective, because the prices on things available for purchase would have been arbitrarily determined. Managers of public enterprises would have no way of deciding whether too many of the factors of production had been used for a particular good, say automobiles, and too few for what people would like to have, say television sets.

3. Over and above the previous objections to a government-planned economy, Friedrich Hayek has emphasized the progressive character inherent in a private enterprise, free-market economy. Where ownership of the factors of production is widely distributed, with each owner free to decide the use of his own property (according to which use will give him the largest income), each enterprise is potentially an experimenter, an innovator. This accounts in large part, he believes, for the tremendous progress that has been made in Western society during the last century.

By contrast, a centralized production administration could not possibly have in its possession information regarding all the infinite variety of resource characteristics and possibilities. It could not afford to experiment, operating as it must on the grand scale, where mistakes are costly if not catastrophic. The result would be an essentially static, unprogressive production organization, turning out goods of a highly standardized quality. Even if it should achieve a high level of output, this output would be attained at the expense of the variety which distinguishes a dynamic free society from a military state.

4. Finally, the "cost" of a merged political and economic system would be an increasingly arbitrary managerial state, in which all of the instruments of power would tend to gravitate to a self-perpetuating inner circle. Under these planners and administrators, who would be cautious and unprogressive lest costly errors upset the plan, mistakes would inevitably be made.

In a decentralized enterprise system the consequence of a failure of the individual enterprise is loss of income and perhaps bankruptcy. The penalties of bad judgment fall on a relatively small segment of society. But in a highly centralized collective economy this would not be the case. First of all, there would be no such "calling to account" of bad production judgment. There would be no reckoning of errors in this segment or that segment, since all would be concealed in the grand over-all plan. No bankruptcy, no receivership would be needed, since there would be no one to receive. Losses could be compounded, with only society to bear the consequences.

How about the people themselves? In a democratic, planned society would not such an accounting take place at the polls, where those who had demonstrated their lack of competence would be replaced by leaders with a program more in line with what the majority desired?

This might happen, say the critics of socialism. But the chances are against it. In the central authority of the planned society the distinctions between political and economic power disappear. There is one employer —the state. The dissatisfied worker could not quit his job because he could only be re-employed, if at all, in another branch of the giant firm-state. Against such an employer men would hesitate to speak out. More-over, such enterprises as the press, the radio, the publishing houses—all of which require access to the means of production—would also be in-cluded in the "plan." With these facilities at the disposal of the state, say the critics of planning, it is quite likely that any party in power would make every effort to keep itself in power. Moreover, as Professor Hayek has maintained, there would be a tendency for the "worst men to get to the top," since they would be the ones most willing to use all of these means to that end.

The picture which emerges from these projections of the most ardent advocates of private enterprise, when they describe the alternative to their "good society," is the slave state, "the road to serfdom." It is the *Nineteen Eighty-four* of George Orwell.

Theirs is perhaps the extreme position among those who would strengthen and extend the role of the market. Others who share their distrust of the state and of centralized direction or planning, do not minimize the difficulties involved in preserving the market in a complex industrial society characterized by giant corporations, whose property holdings represent an ever recurring problem of monopoly or private control. While Von Mises, reasoning from his model of the free economy, denies the possibility of monopoly control in the absence of government intervention, others like Corwin Edwards see developments in thought and action among producers themselves as threats to competition and its influence in maintaining a free market.

369

State Intervention to Keep the Market "Free"

Those who, like Henry Simons, propose a "positive program" for laissez faire see the dangers of state encroachment not so much in the degree of intervention as in what it does and what it fails to do. They recognize that a private enterprise not held in check by the forces of competition, may also be a threat to maximum performance.

In contrast to those whose position is described above, these advocates of the market economy would consider it of first importance for the state to *promote* an environment favorable to decentralized business decisions by maintaining stable money and credit systems. To this end they would approve interference with one part of the enterprise system to an extent greater than the United States has known, that is, with the commercial banks (see page 211). Aside from perhaps eliminating certain purely discriminatory taxes frustrating to enterprise and consumption alike, the other policy prescriptions of this school of thought would aim at the decentralization of "economic power," namely the elimination of monopoly advantage and control by such organizations as labor unions and trade associations. In those areas of production where competition has been shown to be impractical—the natural monopolies—they would accept public ownership on a local, state, or national basis.

The use of government as a means of enforcing competition is defended on the grounds that where monopoly exists it is more often than not the creature of government. Hence the strengthening of the market could be achieved as much by not doing some things now being done as in initiating actions to enforce competition. They would therefore recommend the following steps:

1. *Withdrawal of subsidies and protection from firms, and even whole industries, where the existing market price does not cover costs of production.* This stricture would apply principally to the tariff used by some industries to insulate themselves from foreign competition. However, it might be applied equally well to actions by local and state governments to make their areas especially attractive to particular industries by exempting them from taxation.

2. *Revision of patent laws to make the results of modern research more accessible to new firms.* Patents were originally issued to inventors, and were intended to stimulate new discoveries. Many advocates of reform question (a) whether a majority of inventions have been motivated only by the hope for monopoly, or (b) whether the inventors have been the principal beneficiaries of the law. Today the motivation is even less, since new discoveries are made in universities, government laboratories, and the research organizations of large corporations, where salaried tech-

370

nicians, drawing upon the reservoir of social knowledge, work in a co-operative setting.

3. *A general overhaul of legislation which legalizes collusion in re-sale-price maintenance and in various licensing practices.* State and Federal laws which parade under such euphemisms as "fair-trade laws" have become increasingly common. Often these are sponsored, in the first instance, by lobbyists of special-interest groups. While they are ostensibly for the purpose of protecting legitimate businesses from "unscrupulous" traders, who use price cutting in some lines as devices to attract the unwary consumer and "do him in" in others, such laws have in actual practice been used as forms of collusion between manufacturers and certain favored retailers. In the case of special licensing of privileged firms, particularly those producing foods, beverages, and even professional services, the initial intent was to uphold standards of sanitation, purity, and professional competence. As they have been administered, they have frequently become devices for keeping out new firms and for limiting output in order to maintain prices.

On the other hand, the prescriptions for positive action, which are inferences from the ideal model of an enterprise society, are perhaps even more far reaching in their implications than the preventive measures outlined above. They are also more controversial. This is because they involve the questioning of a number of assumptions which are rather widely accepted in business ideology, and the questioning of practices that are taken for granted.

Rights of the Corporation

That the corporate form of organization, through its limited-liability provision, has made it possible for modern industry to bring together the large aggregations of capital necessary to adapt production methods to modern technology is well accepted. Increasing the scale of operation has resulted in greater efficiency and made possible reduced prices. In this process, however, mere bigness has been glorified and oversold. Bigness does not ensure efficiency, particularly not mere size of the owning unit. Once a firm has expanded to the point where it is duplicating assembly lines and plants, there is at least a presumption that the advantages stem from monopoly rather than from efficiency. Accordingly, it is the contention of economists like G. J. Stigler that many of the industrial giants in our economy ought to be broken up. At least, Stigler maintains, the burden of proof to the contrary ought to be placed on the companies.

The rights to limited liability and other privileges of corporations are quite definitely special grants from government. They can, and ought

371

to be, withdrawn if the firm does not comply with orders to dispose of duplicating facilities and parallel processes. To do this it would simplify matters if there were a single incorporating agency. This *should* be an agency of the Federal government. Under present enforcement by the states, many companies have far transcended the provisions of their charters. Originally established to produce one commodity or a related group of commodities, they have expanded into other and far different fields. This has been accomplished by the organization of new, wholly-owned subsidiary corporations, capable of dominating entire markets. Such practices *should* be prohibited. Financial control through *interlocking directorates* (persons sitting on several boards of directors of presumably independent corporations) could and ought to be restricted, and the powers of the state invoked to prevent them.

Some would undertake these changes even at the expense of a small sacrifice of efficiency. The net gains from rooting out monopoly control—the systems of private collectivism—would be likely to outweigh such losses by creating a system of production organization more malleable, more responsive to the shifts in consumers' taste.

Centrally Planned Production

In contrast to the ideal model of a market-directed system of production, with its private ownership of the factors of production and decentralized decisions, is the centrally-directed or "planned" allocation of resources. The former relies on the pursuit of income by individuals (the motivation of economic advantage), disciplined and directed into socially useful channels by competition; the latter administers the means of production according to some co-operative plan which will allocate them directly to socially agreed-upon ends. Arguing that the vast majority of our wants are socially determined and must be co-operatively provided for, collectivists have always maintained that the maximum output of goods and services will be attained when a co-ordinated industrial system is designed to achieve that end (rather than leaving it to chance).

Like the plans or blueprints for a market economy, the models for a planned system of production are varied. Planners are not agreed among themselves. The Marxian communists, for example, believe that the forceful seizure of the factors of production and the establishment of a dictatorship is a necessary prelude to successful planning. Marxian socialists, confident that capitalism must inevitably break down because of its inner contradictions, organize and hold themselves ready to take over and set up a plan for orderly socialization when that day comes. The more moderate non-Marxian socialists, like those of the British Labour party, believe in the gradual nationalization of "basic" industries such as power, communications, minerals, etc. It may not be necessary or desirable ever to socialize or collectivize many types of production. Thus the moderates foresee a gradual growth of planning, working through the democratic processes, and the acquisition of the instruments of production now in private hands through purchase. Present owners would have continuing income claims from government bonds issued for the purchase of their properties.

How Would Production Decisions Be Made?

How would central authorities decide problems of allocation, lacking the clues provided by the "costs" of factors? Economists have outlined procedures by means of which a ministry of production in a socialist state might guide decisions on what kind and how much of goods and services to produce. One solution to the problem was outlined by the American classicist and defender of the enterprise economy, Fred M. Taylor. Other names associated with the economic theory of socialism are Enrico Barone and Oscar Lange.

How Costs Would be Determined Under Socialism

It will be recalled that the costs of the output of a private firm will be the prices of factors of production used to produce it. Since in a centrally-planned economy capital equipment and land would be publicly owned (and would not be bought and sold), there would be no prices for these factors, and no cost figures to be entered in the accounts of the public enterprise. Without such cost information, critics maintain, management of a socialized industry would lack important guides for pricing output and for the allocation of the factors of production.

This problem may be more apparent than real. The bookkeeping problem could be solved in a purely pragmatic manner. Any central management taking over a firm or group of firms would have at its disposal historical data which could be used in setting up the books of the industry. If the assets of the industry were acquired by purchase, these costs would be a matter of record in the government bonds issued to pay for them. If, on the other hand, the assets were simply seized, there would still be from the past history of the organization a set of valuations on the physical assets of the industry. These costs would be entered in the books, and together with the wages paid to labor would

373

be used for computing the costs of the output. This output would then be offered for sale to consumers at a price which would cover cost of production. All that would be required in addition would be income in the hands of consumers. These consumers, exercising their rights freely to use this income as they chose, would buy the goods offered on the market at the prices set by the *initial* cost of production. Now assume that on the basis of the initial price consumers decided that a particular commodity was too expensive relative to other commodities. The industry producing that commodity would find itself with rapidly accumulating stocks of unsold goods. If, on the other hand, the starting price were too low, consumers would desire to buy more than was available. Shortages would appear, and with the existing output the industry would not be able to satisfy the demand for its products. Suppose there were examples of both situations. If the inventories of shoes began to mount, while ships and sealing wax were in short supply, this would be a clue that too many shoes and too few ships and too little sealing wax were being produced. The solution, of course, would be to transfer factors of production away from the commodities which were being overproduced. As these adjustments are made throughout the industrial system, the allocation of the factors of production to the different things which people want will take place as management acts on these clues. The allocation of factors to the production of new capital equipment and the expansion of productive capacity could be geared to the indicators which show to what extent people prefer future real income over the present, as indicated by their savings.

In addition to the cost records which the managers of a planned economy would use in their accounting system, there would be records of past production and growth indicators suggesting what the output of important commodities ought to be. Allocation to important social services such as education, public health, parks, conservation, police protection, and defense would be made much as they are made now.

This is the *logic* of the socialist economic processes of production. Would it work in practice? Critics say that it would not. In such an economy plans would have meaning only if carried out, and where the requirements of the plan on where to work and what to do were different from the desires of the people, the final solution of this dilemma could only mean an arbitrary allocation of labor. On the other hand, the defenders of a planned economy maintain that free choice of occupation is less personalized and individualized than has been claimed. To attract people into less desirable areas, from the standpoint of hardship or uninteresting work, more attractive incomes would have to be assured.

374

This is a problem which cannot be answered by logic alone. Much would depend upon the conditions under which a planned economy were instituted and set in operation. Previously there was no basis in experience for judging what might happen if an industrial society decided to adopt a system of planned production. The "planned" society of Russia came into being only after war and revolution had nearly destroyed the meager industrial system that existed. In England the nationalization of certain industries also had a background of an economy badly out of joint, disorganized by a long drawn-out war and the loss of foreign investments. In Sweden, where war has been avoided, the circumstances are different, though the country is small and its population homogeneous. We can gain some insight by considering briefly how production decisions are made in these areas where approaches to a centrally-planned economy have been tried.

Production Decisions in the U.S.S.R.

We will neglect the political aspects of the Soviet system, concentrating on the more technical aspects of resource allocation, and noting only that the powers of decision rest with a small group in the Presidium which approves final plans as drafted by the state planning commission. This latter organization has at its disposal the statistical information on output and consumption for the over-all economy. The problem of resource allocation to conform with "free consumer choice" is not involved, though from time to time concessions may be required in this direction.

When the plants and other physical assets of existing firms were taken over by the Soviet government after the revolution, they were organized as industrial trusts. These trusts were management organizations to control a particular industry. A parallel state banking system was set up to provide credit for industries, enabling them to acquire additional factors as required. The labor supply has been administered through the controlled labor unions, and the plant managers negotiate with the union for their labor supply.

At the time of the revolution Russia was predominantly a nation of peasants and farmers. Expansion of the Soviet industrial system required the transfer of workers from the rural areas to the new and growing cities. Pressures have been used to secure this transfer, including the attraction of higher wages and special privileges in the purchase of scarce consumer goods, along with extensive "education" or propaganda campaigns.

Information on plant capacity and on factor needs is passed up from the lowest echelons or plants (of the steel trust, for example) and assem-

375

bled for top management of the national trust. Such information from all sectors is then passed on to the national planning board. The planning board has the records of past production. From this data it attempts to estimate the potential output in all areas for the coming period. Since during most of their successive five-year plans the Soviets have had need for expanded production in virtually all areas, the problem of shifting resources has been related to how rapidly heavy industries could be expanded. This expansion has been usually at the expense of the consumption-goods industries. This has been accomplished by raising the prices of these goods to discourage consumption. Prices have been used less as a measure of the relative scarcity of goods than as instruments for controlling the consumption.

Controversy has sometimes appeared in the Russian economic journals over just what ought to be a proper index for the allocation of capital. When it was discovered that certain managers were using "return on capital investments" as an indicator, these men were roundly criticized and accused of copying the practices of a "decadent capitalism."

To assume that all Soviet allocations are arbitrary, however, would be to underestimate the ability of her economic technicians and engineers. Although Soviet statistics available to the outside world are notably unreliable and confusing, there is some indication that the statistics they use in their own planning are more dependable. Through the manipulation of prices, income, highly differentiated wage scales, and so forth, there can be little doubt that many of the shifts have been accomplished with subtlety and finesse, so that Soviet citizens are given what appears to be choices regarding their own economic or income interests (this, of course, does not apply to the reportedly large group of "slave laborers," which has been an important factor in many capital improvements such as canals, river dredging, railroad construction, mining, and others). That the Soviet Union has made progress in its attempt to industrialize a backward agricultural economy is generally recognized. Industrial production has expanded to an estimated 40 to 50 per cent of that of the United States.

From all that can be learned about Soviet actions in the satellite countries, which were taken over during and after World War II, an important technique for the exploitation of such populations has been the creation of corporations in which Soviet trusts have acquired a majority control over industries. Soviet managers are assured the power to determine Russia's share of the industry's income and the allocation of the final product. Here too, the necessary workers are attracted by promises of special privileges, stores where scarce consumption goods may be pur-

376

chased at relatively favorable prices, and other special inducements. While these inducements usually turn out to be not as promised, there are also other means of discouraging workers from transferring to occupations regarded as less vital to the Soviet Union.

British Socialism

From 1945 to 1951 the British Labour party, with a small parliamentary majority, inaugurated their moderate socialist program aimed at the gradual nationalization of the production economy of Great Britain. Coal, transport, communications, civil aviation, steel, and the Bank of England were the more important basic industries to be socialized. In addition, an extensive social welfare program was initiated, but the treatment of this is more appropriate for later chapters when we discuss distribution and consumption.

With the return of the Conservative party to power in 1951, steel was denationalized, but the other industries were left under public administration. The Labour party, even in opposition, continues to be a significant political force in Britain and looks forward to the day when it will be returned to office. Meanwhile, however, members of that party are not in full accord on a future program. Except for a minority, British Labour has never advocated socialization of the entire production economy—at least not yet. Most would agree though that if the party were returned to power, further nationalization of "basic" industries would be undertaken.

Important opposition to parts of Labour's program for nationalization developed within its own ranks from the co-operative movement (this group has its own splinter party which operates within the Labour party under a working agreement). When proposals to nationalize insurance and certain distributive industries arose, the co-operatives objected. They contend that other forms of social ownership than nationalization can be effective and less open to rigid centralization. They point to their own extensive operations (some of which the Labour party would nationalize). They also regard municipal and regional ownership of some of the means of production as effective, less bureaucratic, and more responsible to democratic control. Some discerning socialists[1] in the party have called for and attempted a re-examination of first principles and a re-evaluation of nationalization as a means to greater productivity. In view of the Labour party's continuing influence, we shall ex-

---

[1] Cf. C. A. R. Crosland, *The Future of Socialism* (New York: The Macmillan Company, 1957).

amine briefly their methods and accomplishments during their tenure in office.

Acquisition

In line with the Labour party's policy of gradualism, nationalized industries were purchased at a "fair" valuation, and the owners paid with government bonds. Since most of the nationalized industries were large-scale and corporate in form, it was chiefly a matter of exchanging ownership certificates or common stock for government bonds. While the exchange of dividend-paying common stocks for government obligations paying a fixed and relatively low rate of interest undoubtedly represented something of an expropriation of property, this loss was less than it might seem, in view of the very high British income taxes.

Since nationalization was undertaken as part of a broader program of social welfare, and during a time of serious financial difficulties internationally, the management practices adopted possibly should be regarded as a rather special case, and not necessarily as an indication of what might have been done under other circumstances. Judgments regarding the success or failure of management in these industries are varied and conflicting. The program left the British economy still predominantly an enterprise society. It has been estimated that no more than twenty per cent of British industry was nationalized. It should be noted also that in the case of coal even the Conservative party favored such a solution to the problems facing that "sick" industry.

What criteria were used to decide which industries should be nationalized? Some claimed that only basic industries need be nationalized, but "basic" was not clearly defined. Others referred to an industry as "ripe" for nationalization, but this concept too is not easy to define. It was suggested that "ripeness" is related to the extent of monopoly or perhaps to the technological characteristics of the industry which makes consolidation desirable from an engineering point of view. If this criteria has meaning, it is that the productivity of an industry promises to be increased by large-scale investment, under conditions of decreasing costs, which could only be undertaken by a firm so large that it would involve some kind of monopoly.

Organization

What about the organization and management of the British nationalized industries? At the top, corresponding to the board of directors of a large corporation, is an industry board or policy-making agency as, for example, the Coal Board. Members are selected for background and experi-

378

ence in the industry, and include representatives of organized labor. The Board appoints the top management of the industry, delegating to that management the responsibility for operating facilities and executing policies. In some instances the managers chosen have been the same as those who worked for former owners. Their responsibilities and methods of operation have changed little, if any.

Bonds issued for the purchase of the industry's assets are fixed costs of the industry, together with new investments, and these costs must be met if deficits are to be avoided. Labor, raw materials, power, and other services are purchased in the market (sometimes from other national industries). Nationalized industries plan to cover costs and to show a net income no less than do private firms. Success of the management is judged by whether it can cover its costs and achieve the desired output at prices in line with previous experience and with other firms. If the industry does not cover its costs, including interest on the bonds, its deficit is made up by government. It remains to be seen whether such deficits in the long run will exceed the subsidies previously granted by government to some of the firms that have been nationalized.

Wages are determined by negotiation with the union. During the postwar period there were indications that negotiations between the management of nationalized industries and the union representatives were not all that had been hoped for by the union members. Where workers previously had felt free to strike against private owners, they were now subjected to greater social pressure not to use this traditional weapon of collective bargaining. They were told that such action would be embarrassing to the Labour government, which, they were reminded, was "their government." Thus, while the evidence is not conclusive, there is at least a presumption that when unions operate in nationalized or government-owned industries, they are likely to be subjected to a greater discipline than in privately-owned industries. There are, of course, other means of redress than the strike. There is always the appeal to public opinion, if the government itself is democratic and hence responsive to that opinion.

Prices and Price Policy

On the pricing policies of nationalized industries, as illustrated by the British experience, the evidence is inconclusive. Because the whole economy continued to operate after the end of the war under strict rationing and price controls, the industry boards had to make few decisions in this area. Prices were governed by the past. Relationships existing during some base period were maintained, with certain exceptions determined largely by expediency. With shortages existing in virtually all important areas, there was little opportunity for making difficult decisions in the use of factors of production between different sorts of goods, particularly those which are ordinarily classified as luxuries.

Great Britain is dependent upon foreign sources for raw materials. To obtain these it is necessary that she export finished goods. Because of the liquidation of overseas investments during two world wars, the British economy has been like a business operating on a shoestring. She must sell abroad in order to obtain the means for paying for her raw materials. To do this it has been necessary to meet foreign competition. As a result export prices have been characterized by differentiation, subsidy, and promotional techniques by means of which Britain has attempted to obtain foreign exchange, particularly dollars. In these circumstances it is understandable if the management and the industry boards of the nationalized industries had little opportunity to give serious consideration to their long-run price policies as part of the program of a planned or partially planned economy.

The Pragmatic Approach
to Production Policy

The idea of a mixed production economy is difficult to represent by means of a unified model. For those who prefer their "dream worlds" and their ideologies neat, internally consistent, and certain, the purely competitive ideal of production, on the one hand, or the planned allocation of the factors of production, on the other, is likely to be more satisfying emotionally as well as artistically.

Admittedly, the problem of evaluating policy prescriptions can be simplified if one asks, "Does this proposal, if accepted or imposed, expand the role of an *impersonal market* in factor allocation by increasing competition (minimizing the influence of individuals, groups, or government)? Alternatively, one can ask, "Does this action contribute to the achievement of production goals under the master plan?" Once the fact is recognized, however, that markets in the real world vary widely, and "imperfections" of the model are by no means minor exceptions in economic behavior, the single criterion of competition (or the promotion of competition) as a test for policy ceases to be convincing. When the only evidence we have of a centrally-planned economy indicates a disturbing disregard of human rights and preferences, the Utopian dream of the perfectly organized economy loses its power or argument as a directing principle.

The pragmatic approach to policy in the field of production is characterized by heterodoxy rather than unity or orthodoxy—either of the classical or the socialist tradition. Here, as elsewhere, economists interested in problems of public policy adopt a point of view that human behavior is much too complex, varied, and insufficiently understood to be contained by monistic principles of either the "right" or the "left." To the extent that they have an ideal model, it is that of the mixed economy. They recognize the role which government or collective action has played in economic growth. They can recommend actions by government to meet a specific problem, such as planned regional development or conservation, without feeling that an important value principle is being violated. They do so with the full knowledge that this will force adaptation and adjustment in the private sector, the full consequences of which cannot be predicted. They are likely to agree that where a relatively free market operates effectively cost and price indicators can be the least cumbersome and the most impartial guides to production decisions. Private and semiprivate firms following their own income pursuits (profits) can also contribute to the public welfare by assuring a flexible production economy responsive to consumers.

In general, prescriptions for an active role for government are likely to be at a minimum in the field of actual production. Many modern economists accept as a matter of policy government responsibility for high-level employment and stability of the general price level. If these objectives can be achieved, they believe, the resulting economic environment will be favorable to a predominantly private-enterprise system of production. Except for periods of war or national emergency, and except for public investments to provide essential services, the actual control of factors of production can be left to private owners or their agents. Government influence on production decisions can be indirect, and will be effected not through detailed plans for allocation, but through actions influencing income distribution. This aspect of government action will be treated more extensively in Part 4.

What of the influence of private monopoly on the production economy? Laissez faire advocates, we have noted, stress the importance of this problem as one of the few requiring government action. Collectivists, on the other hand, have tended to minimize the usefulness of policies aimed at reducing economic concentration, on the assumption that trusts and cartels (integrated industries) help to hasten the day when they will be "ripe" for nationalization.

While not unaware of the problems posed by increasing scales of operation and the growth of economic power, particularly the concentration of income, many modern economists no longer believe that atom-

381

ization of industries provides a solution that is either workable or desirable. It is unworkable chiefly because of the great complexity of modern property forms. It is undesirable because the size of many firms is geared to technology, including modern management techniques, and the evidence is not convincing that anything approaching the model of pure competition could be adopted without substantial losses in efficiency and total output. They are not opposed, however, to enforcement of antitrust laws, and a number of economists who tend to be pragmatic in outlook have advocated spelling out more carefully certain prescriptions as to what constitutes monopolistic practices.

Institutional economists, of whom J. M. Clark is one, have called on their colleagues to give attention to a model of "workable competition." Such a concept would need to take into account the complexity of the production and marketing structure and the rise of powerful merchandising firms, such as chain stores, mail-order houses, and the multiproduct firms with large amounts of free capital which enables them to move into product lines showing favorable profits. This amounts to calling for the development of new analytical tools as well as more realistic criteria than the traditional pure competition to serve as a measure of social contribution.

While giants in one industry may not be held in check by other firms producing the same commodities, other economic interest groups, such as retailers, labor groups, consumer organizations, and government, can offset the unfavorable income effect of monopoly. This is essentially the meaning of the concept of *countervailing power* elaborated by J. K. Galbraith in his *American Capitalism*.

Discussion
Questions

1. When the management of a private enterprise makes a wrong decision, the loss is borne by the owners of the enterprise. If the management of a nationalized industry were to make a mistake, everyone would be affected. Discuss.

2. Rigid adherence to plan is the enemy of change, and hence of progress. Discuss.

3. Giant modern production organizations must produce what people want or they will go bankrupt. However, large advertising expenditures are effective persuaders, paid for by the persuaded. Discuss.

4. The management of modern corporations are hired employees. It would not matter to them who owned the enterprise. Discuss.

5. Modern society is too complex for production decisions to be left to the chance co-ordination of individual plans, on the one hand, or to be forced into a mold of a single over-all plan, on the other. Discuss.

Selected References for Part 3

Boulding, Kenneth E. *Economic Analysis,* 3rd ed.; New York: Harper and Brothers, 1955.

Chamberlin, Edward. *The Theory of Monopolistic Competition.* Cambridge: Harvard University Press, 1938.

Conference on Price Research, *Cost Behavior and Price Policy.* New York: National Bureau of Economic Research, 1943.

Edwards, Corwin D. *Big Business and the Policy of Competition.* Cleveland: The Press of Western Reserve University, 1956.

Galbraith, J. K. *American Capitalism: The Concept of Countervailing Power.* Boston: Houghton Mifflin Co., 1952.

Hayek, Friedrich A. *The Road to Serfdom.* Chicago: The University of Chicago Press, 1944.

Henderson, H. D. *Supply and Demand.* New York: Harcourt, Brace & Co., 1922.

Lippincott, Benjamin E. (ed.). *On the Economic Theory of Socialism.* Minneapolis: University of Minnesota Press, 1938.

Stigler, George J. *Production and Distribution Theories.* New York: The Macmillan Co., 1941.

Whyte, William H., Jr. *The Organization Man.* New York: Simon & Schuster, Inc., 1956.

And very often the influence exerted on a person's character by the amount of his income is hardly less, if it is less, than that exerted by the way in which it is earned. It makes little difference to the fullness of life of a family whether its yearly income is £1,000 or £5,000; but it makes a very great difference whether the income is £30 or £150; for with £150 the family has, with £30 it has not, the material conditions of a complete life.

ALFRED MARSHALL

PART 4

DISTRIBUTION

Factor Allocation and

Income Shares

Introduction

WE COME NOW to what David Ricardo thought was the central problem of economic science. He believed that it was the economist's job to explain the laws or principles governing the distribution of income (wealth). While economists today are less confident of formulating their conclusions as *laws*, distribution remains an important area to be investigated by the empirically minded and an issue to be argued by supporters of opposing policies.

Claims against the national product originate in the production process. Part 4 is thus an extension of Part 3. For purposes of analysis it was assumed there that the prices of the factors were given—that they did not change for the period under consideration. We now drop that assumption. Figuratively speaking, the prices of factors of production are allowed to change while we are observing them. Since these factors are owned by the households, household income is some function of the prices of the factors of production.

A re-examination of the income-flow diagrams in Part 2 will help to make it clear that we are here concerned with the lower half of that circular flow, together with the incomes channeled through the government sector. We shall be concerned with income which accrues to labor services and property rights, together with income-transfer payments.

CHAPTER 23

Who Gets What and How?

In 1939 the Twentieth Century Fund published a book titled *Does Distribution Cost Too Much?* The authors of that study were concerned with something different than what we propose to treat here. They were asking, in effect, whether a particular group of enterprisers were getting more for their contributions to production than was justified. They referred to the firms which handle various commodities while they are in transit from the primary and secondary producers to the ultimate consumer. These would include transportation, warehousing, retailing, financing, selling, advertising, and other business activities which are part of production but whose contributions are largely of a service nature in the exchange process. This is a fairly common association of the term distribution. Automobile dealers are distributors for automobile manufacturers. A retail store in a particular town may be designated sole distributor of a certain branded product. The question that the authors of this book were seeking to answer was, "Do those who occupy the middle position in the production process get paid too much for the services rendered —the others too little?"

When the economic analyst talks about distribution he is concerned with how the claims of all who contribute to production (as well as those who do not) are finally established, and under what circumstances they might be different than they are. He is concerned with such questions as the following: How are the claims against a nation's output of goods and services finally determined for this individual or that, this group or that group, and what determines why the distribution of claims is as it is? When the national output (dividend) for any period is finally divided up, who gets what and how? What effect does this division have on persons and on the functioning of the economic system?

387

Functional and
Personal Distribution

It will be necessary to have the term distribution do double duty by meaning two slightly different things. We will accordingly differentiate two concepts which we shall call *functional distribution* and *personal distribution.*

Functional Distribution

Functional distribution refers to income claims established through the performance of specific functions in the production process. This meaning is related to the system of classification of the factors of production.

Beginning with the twofold division into services performed by people and those performed by physical objects or technical processes, we can examine in as much detail as we like the different sorts of services that may be interesting or important for our purposes. In the case of the human factor attention will be focused on the exercise of hand and brain which we call work or labor, and which is paid for in wages or salaries, fees, or simply by "payment for services rendered." The second type represents payments to persons for the use of property, such as land, buildings, machinery, patented processes, copyrighted printed materials, and so forth. These payments are called rents, royalties, and tolls. Finally, there are the "dynamic" income claims of interest and profit, whose link with the production process is more roundabout. To assist in conceptualizing these functions and their payments, we will again speak of markets, and treat such payments as prices which vary according to conditions that affect the demand for them and the influences which help to determine their supply.

These payments have already been encountered in the discussion of production. There they were treated as costs to the firm. To simplify the analysis there they were assumed to be given—that is, to be known and fixed. We will now inquire into the forces which operate to change the payments to the factors which are income to their owners and costs to the firm. In other words, we will be looking at markets for factors of production, where the prices they command in the market is the income claim per unit of the factor.

Economists find it useful to make a distinction between the demand for a factor of production and the demand for a consumer good. The demand for a consumer good arises because people want it for their own satisfaction and will pay for it. The demand for factors of production is a different sort of demand. It is a *derived demand.* Firms need the services of factors of production not because they satisfy personal needs, but

388

because they can be used to produce goods for which a demand exists. Hence the demand for factors of production can be said to derive from the demand for goods and services which these factors can assist in producing.

Just as particular consumer goods can be substitutes for each other, so too can factors of production be substitutes, within limits, for one another. A given output can be produced by different means. It can be turned out by hand, using only the most elementary tools. It can be produced with machinery, using proportionally less labor. If raw materials are cheap and labor relatively expensive, as at the cutting board of a dress manufacturer, for example, management may seek to get the maximum number of dresses from the scissors of the skilled tailor and disregard the material that is "wasted." Functional distribution, or the pricing of the factors of production, is important because it provides a guide for the allocation of the factors of production.

Personal Distribution

While a knowledge of functional distribution is helpful in understanding why the income payments to individuals (or households) vary, the picture of distribution in society has to be completed by bringing the various functional incomes together, tying them finally to persons. In our society households may get their income from a variety of functional sources. That is why modern economists, particularly those with an empirical bent, are concerned with personal distribution.

In the United States of the middle twentieth century there are no neat and rigid classes based upon income sources. The boundary lines between landowners, workers, and capitalists have become blurred. We will examine evidence that large income differences are closely correlated with property ownership. The largest personal incomes are derived from property. Property is very unequally distributed. This distribution is greatly influenced by our legal-institutional organization. However, individual income differences cannot be brought entirely within a model which assigns to property the causal role for inequality. The income of a Pat Boone or a Ted Williams will bear witness to this fact. Moreover, in these days of graduated income taxes personal incomes are modified through the agency of government and through the medium of economic change, which has done much to erase the importance of income differences by ending the most abject forms of poverty.

Difficulty in Determining Functional Distribution

Although it is possible to distinguish conceptually the contributions of the different factors which co-operate to create the national output or product, a precise determination of income distribution according to function is more difficult. This we can illustrate with an example from the breakdown of distributive shares which the Department of Commerce derives from national income statistics.

Table 18 shows this information for selected years, as aggregate shares and as percentages of total national income. The first category is reasonably unambiguous. Compensation of employees means payment for services rendered in the form of labor and mental effort, the wages and salaries received by workers and management executives.

The second category poses a problem. The income of unincorporated enterprises is the final claim of persons who operate their own businesses or render professional services. Most of these enterprises are small. Usually the owner works in the business himself, sometimes along with his employees, but often by himself or with members of his family. As owner he has capital invested and as entrepreneur he makes decisions and takes risks. Thus his income is a combination of functional returns. Similarly the income of farm proprietors is the return to the farm and in most cases to the farmer as the proprietor. Farm income is a composite of functional claims.

The fourth category is the return to owners of rental property. However, this income is not a pure rent. The owner of an apartment house may perform services such as the management and upkeep of the property. Hence his return includes a return on his own effort. Corporate profits are the net income of incorporated enterprises. Legally this income belongs to the owners of the business—the common-stock and sometimes the preferred-stock holders. It represents the returns on capital invested, together with profits. However, because a part of these profits, even a substantial part, may be retained in the business, they do not become income to the owners. Net interest is an income payment to enterprises that make a business of loaning funds.

Household Distribution

Personal distribution is household distribution of income. This unit, as has already been pointed out, is the basic consumption unit, and the one for which at least a hypothetical budget is kept. For the most part the household income is the tax base for the personal income tax, although persons who are members of a household—for example, husband and wife—are permitted to split the household income and file a joint tax return.

Although it is possible to define a household in an operational way as the income-receiving unit, the research worker who undertakes to as-

390

Table 18.   National Income by Distributive Shares in Selected Years

(amounts in billions of dollars)

	1929		1933		1939		1949		1956	
	Amount	%	Amount	%	Amount	%	Amount	%	Amount	%
Compensation of Employees	51.1	58.2	29.5	73.4	48.1	66.0	140.9	65.1	241.4	70.2
Business and Professional	8.8	10.0	3.2	8.0	7.3	10.0	21.4	9.9	28.0	8.1
Farm Proprietors	6.0	6.8	2.4	6.0	4.3	5.9	12.7	5.9	11.6	3.4
Rental Income of Persons	5.4	6.2	2.0	5.0	2.7	3.7	7.9	3.7	10.3	3.0
Corporate Profits	10.1	11.5	−2.0	−5.0	5.7	7.8	28.1	13.0	40.4	11.8
Net Interest	6.4	7.3	5.0	12.4	4.6	6.3	5.2	2.4	11.9	3.5
Total	87.8		40.2		72.8		216.2		343.6	

semble reliable figures on personal-income distribution is faced with many difficulties. For reasons mentioned above, income-reporting units are not quite synonymous with households. However, the Bureau of Internal Revenue, now that the personal income tax has become so inclusive, is able to supply considerable information. Using modern sampling techniques research organizations (both public and private) are able to collect the information which enables them to make estimates for the over-all economy. These are called "budget studies." Budget studies constitute the source of our knowledge about both income distribution and consumption.

Not all income is allocated for final disposition to the units of the private economy. An increasing portion has been taken by the various government units and is spent by them for goods and services, which we will call public consumption. These are the things for which we use our income as members of an organized society. Accordingly, we will examine in some detail the "government's share," the part of the national income reported in the public budgets.

The Importance of Distribution

On questions of practical policy, probably no aspect of the economic process receives more attention than the distribution of income. There are few attainments (in our culture at least) which so vitally affect the life of an individual and that of his family as the size and security of his income. This determines much of his freedom of action in so many spheres—where and how he will live, who will be his friends, how and where his children will be educated and thereby get their start in life. From the more material aspects of scales of living to the less concrete considerations such as status in the community, dependence on (and hence subservience to) others, the psychology of security and self-esteem, the differences in income distribution constitute a basis for perceived differences among people.

It is understandable, therefore, why concern over income inequality should loom large in the eyes of those who favor reform. Whether that reform takes the direction of leveling upward (through seeking to channel an ever increasing proportion of the gains from economic progress to those at the bottom of the income pyramid) or leveling down (through redistribution of the present income) the fact of inequality serves as a point of departure.

Those who oppose greater equality of income usually do so on the grounds that saving is an important source of investment funds. Saving, they maintain, is done by those with high incomes, who thereby perform an important function by promoting economic progress.

392

Discussion
Questions

1. When is a firm likely to decide to hire more workers? What is likely to be the effect if a number of firms decide to increase their working force of a particular skill simultaneously?

2. The rapid increase in population after 1939 has resulted in a steady rise in the demand for houses. How would you expect this to affect the demand for carpenters, bricklayers, and plumbers?

3. After World War II and the Korean war, veterans who returned to school received a monthly income from the Veterans Administration. Would you call this a functional income claim?

4. A family-owned and family-operated store provides a net income of $15,000. The husband and wife both work in the store. They own the building and fixtures. Their savings have provided the working capital. The venture is successful. What are the functional sources of income? How would this be reported by the Department of Commerce?

5. Why is it difficult to get reliable, inclusive information on personal income distribution?

Distribution

in Theory

and Experience

THIS SECTION contains the analysis of income distribution as it is usually presented in economic literature. For each of the functional shares, some of its theoretical history has been included. However, if analytical concepts are to be useful in providing an insight into the distributive processes, they need to be viewed in relation to the changing pattern of institutions and experience.

Whereas in earlier societies social conflicts and political action tended to revolve around the control of land and other "real" wealth, in modern industrial nations the focus is on income distribution. "Pressure groups" usually have an important income orientation. By influencing factor allocation they seek to control their own incomes.

The general relationships posited in the model—the opposing forces of supply and demand—are not rendered meaningless by monopoly influences in the factor market. Their consequences for factor prices, and hence for income, are the subject of our attention.

By acting through the agency of government to achieve their own income ends, pressure groups have been an important factor in the expansion of government's role in the economy. How government obtains its income is a significant influence on production decisions and hence on distribution.

CHAPTER 24

Simple Distribution and Allocation Theory

AN ANALYSIS of functional distribution can be approached by means of a simple analytical model. Like other such models used earlier, this one has been designed to illustrate concepts and relationships rather than to conform to familiar experience. It will include an assumed production function or set of productivity relationships that hold when factors of production are combined in different proportions to create an output. Real, rather than money, income relationships are emphasized.

Assumed Conditions

A single product (coconuts) is produced, making use of what amounts to five factors of production: labor of uniform skill (in other words, the individual laborers are perfect substitutes for one another), and four grades of land of differing productivity. We will neglect the product market (assuming a highly elastic demand), and we will eliminate the influence of money by assuming that the principal product is also the measure of value. Wages and rents are paid in units of the product.

The production arrangement is as follows: a South Pacific island is surrounded by a cluster of lesser islands which are the source of supply of the chief crop—coconuts. These coconuts are traded for manufactured goods with visiting ships. There are four classes of islands of varying productivity. In Class A there are 10 islands; in Class B there are 20; in Class C, 30; and in Class D, 40. The A islands are the most productive and the D islands are the least productive by virtue of being more remote.

These islands are owned by landlords, who received them by grant from the chieftain of the islands. Different combinations of workers are able to gather varying amounts of coconuts. This information, we will assume, has been learned in the trial and error of experience. The amounts which different combinations of workers can produce on each of the respective classes of islands is shown in Table 19.

Table 19.   Schedule of Productivities of Individual Islands with
Varying Amounts of Labor
(Production Function)

Number of Workers	A Island	B Island	C Island	D Island
1	100	90	80	70
2	185	165	145	125
3	245	215	185	155
4	265	225	190	160
5	275	230	190	160

Conditions are such that the workers cannot divide their time in any given day between the islands. In other words, a worker must work on one or another of the islands.

If the objective of this island economy is to maximize its collection of coconuts, which we will assume is the case, how will any given number of workers be allocated or distributed among the islands in order to achieve maximum output? If we can imagine new additions to the working force, we can then ask the question: Where will the additional workers be allocated? We will begin simply by stating a rule and then see if the rule holds up. The rule is this: *Assign the next additional worker to the island where his marginal productivity will be highest.*

If there were only one worker, there is no problem. He would be sent to an *A* island where he would be able to produce 100 coconuts. If there were 10 workers, each one could be assigned to an *A* island and the productivity of each worker would be 100 units. Suppose, however, that we have more than 10 workers to allocate. Where should they be placed? Two men working together on an *A* island would turn out 185 coconuts between them. Thus the second worker on an *A* island would add 85 units to total output. However, a single worker on a *B* island would produce 90 units. Hence a second worker on an *A* island would not be used until there was at least one worker on each of the *B* islands.

Now let us assume that a working force of 30 has been assigned and additional workers become available. Should they be sent to *C* islands, or should they be used as additional workers on the *A* and *B* islands? We come back to the *A* islands. Here the marginal productivity of labor or the productivity of an additional worker after the first is 85. This is more than an additional worker could produce on a *B* island, and more than the first worker could turn out on a *C* island.

This is how it would be done if the whole economy were under the direction of a single authority. But we have assumed that this is not the case. There is a group of landlords, each trying to maximize his own production and to hire the workers at wages that will give the largest rental income. If the working force were very small, it is warrantable to assume that competition among these landlords for the services of the workers would be active. On the other hand, if there were an abundance of workers, one could assume that the bargaining power would be in the hands of the landlords.

What would determine the upper and the lower limits of what the individual workers could demand, again assuming that each worker attempts to maximize his income; and what is the maximum the landlord could expect in the way of rent by virtue of his ownership of this material factor of production? We know that the total of all of the claims cannot be more than the total production. No economic system can distribute more real income than it produces. In a very rich economy, with a large accumulation of capital, it is possible to distribute and consume more goods and services during any period than are produced. But when this is done, of course, the economy is "living up" its capital. This does not apply to the present example because we have assumed that the only coconuts available are those which are being gathered currently. We can see what happens to the respective distribution claims when the total output varies. Since the total land area is fixed, we think in terms of an increasing supply of labor.

Table 20 is derived from Table 19 above. It gives the marginal productivity for each additional worker from one to five, on each of the classes of islands.

Table 20. Amount Added to Total Product by Additional Worker

Workers	A Island	B Island	C Island	D Island
1	100	90	80	70
2	85	75	65	55
3	60	50	40	30
4	20	10	5	5
5	10	5	0	0

Marginal productivity is computed by finding the difference between any given total and the previous total product as an additional worker is allocated to that particular island. By multiplying each marginal productivity by the number of units or islands, we can obtain the number of workers that can be accommodated at each value of the marginal productivity of labor.

Figure 35 shows this marginal productivity of labor for our small economy, with productivity measured on the Y axis and the number of workers on the X axis. Thus, if we read up from any given number of workers, we can read across from the curve to the productivity scale and see what the productivity is for that amount of labor. The shape of this curve gives us a clue to the productivity of labor as the amount of labor increases. If there is no change in the other factors of production—which, of course, by assumption in this case there is not—the trend of the curve is downward. This tells us that as the number of workers increases the marginal productivity tends to decline. We see illustrated here the influence of the "law of diminishing returns."

What will the landlords be willing to pay for additional labor? It will be apparent that additional workers can only be employed if they can be obtained at a lower wage rate. If the forces of competition are operating, this will mean that all workers will tend to get the same wage. Why does this follow? Let us take a very simple case, where the number of workers is five. This would be an extremely small labor supply. Total output will be maximized if these workers are allocated one to each of the A islands. Each worker would produce 100 coconuts and the total output

Figure 35. Marginal Productivity or
Demand Curve for Labor

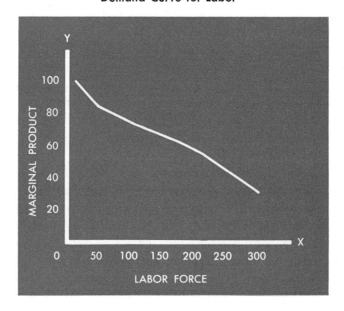

would be 500. There would still be five *A* islands without workers. In such a situation workers would be able to demand and get the entire product. Land would be so plentiful, relative to the labor supply, that there would be little point in owning the land. Any landowner who attempted to pay a smaller wage than 100 units would find his worker deserting him to go to one of the idle islands. This would be comparable to the situation which existed for a considerable period in the history of the United States, when a frontier of unused land provided an opportunity for men to leave land which belonged to someone else, or city employment if wages were too low, and seek a farm of their own.

Suppose, however, we start from a situation in which there are ten workers, one on each of the *A* islands. The *B* islands would be unused, and to use a term fairly familiar in everyday language they would be called *submarginal* land. Now let us say that the labor force is increased by one worker, making a total of 11. Where will the additional worker go? It is apparent that he will go to a *B* island where he can produce 90 units of coconuts. Now, however, a new situation exists. The workers on the *A* islands can no longer get 100 units in wages. The worker on a *B* island could always better himself by offering to work on an *A* island for, let us say, 99 or 98 units. This would be more than the 90 units he could produce on the *B* island. If we can imagine a process of bargaining taking place, a stable situation will be established only when all wages have fallen to the rate of 90. This means that the *A* islands will now have a surplus of coconuts after the wage has been paid to the worker. In other words, the island owner can now exact 10 units of coconuts for the use of his island, and this payment we call rent. There will be no rent on the *B* island since the total output will just equal the wage. The *B* island thus becomes the marginal or no-rent land. The *C* and *D* islands are still submarginal.

If we can now imagine that this process of growth in the labor force continues, and the new workers gravitate to the spot where their contribution to total production is greatest, the gradual reduction of wages will also continue. However, since total production will be increasing, and since the number of islands remains constant, this will result in a parallel rise in the amounts of rent that the landlords can command in the bargaining process. This is illustrated in Table 21, which shows allocation, rents, wages, and maximum total output. The process is carried through in successive steps until a total working force of 310 is reached.

This allocation would be described as the *optimum* for achieving maximum output. This is the allocation which a central production authority would make if it possessed the information we have assumed for this situation. It is also the allocation which presumably would be achieved through the bargaining process, if individuals in a pursuit of maximum

Table 21. Factor Allocation and Distributive Shares

Labor Force	Allocation of Workers				Rents				Wages Per Worker	Total Production
	A	B	C	D	A	B	C	D		
10	1	0	0	0	0	0	0	0	100	1,000
30	1	1	0	0	10	0	0	0	90	2,800
40	2	1	0	0	15	5	0	0	85	3,650
70	2	1	1	0	25	10	0	0	80	6,050
90	2	2	1	0	35	15	5	0	75	7,550
130	2	2	1	1	45	25	10	0	70	10,350
160	2	2	2	1	55	35	15	5	65	12,300
170	3	2	2	1	65	45	25	10	60	12,900
210	3	2	2	2	80	55	35	15	55	15,100
230	3	3	2	2	95	65	45	25	50	16,600
260	3	3	3	2	125	95	65	45	40	17,800
300	3	3	3	3	155	125	95	65	30	18,000
310	4	3	3	3	185	155	125	95	20	18,700

income were operating according to the rules of the game we have specified (private property in the physical factors and competition in the market), and if there were no upsetting influences, such as a change in technology or a change in demand.

As we move down the labor-force column and look across at what is happening to wages, we see that an increase in the supply of workers results in a decline in wages. At the same time rents on the four classes of land will rise. Less productive land is brought into production once the working force reaches a certain level. At the bottom even the poorest land is receiving a rent of 95 units, while wages have dropped to 20 units. In general, this has usually happened in heavily populated nations where technological or industrial progress has been retarded, as in China and India. Landowners are able to exact a very heavy toll in rents. Wages fall to a subsistence level.

There is another inference from Table 21 which it will be well to keep in mind. For each allocation of workers we have a total output figure. The total wage bill plus the total rent payments equal the total product.

There is another way of dividing the total. We can regard each factor combination as a firm. It represents a combination of land or capital and labor. If we compute the total output for each island of each class, and then multiply by the number of islands in each class, we should obtain a figure which is the same as that for total distribution. Thus, in the first instance, we were looking at "national income"; in the second, what we obtain is the national product. The two figures in this particular problem, given the static conditions assumed, are exactly equal.

Effect of Labor Organization

Let us assume that with a working force of 310 the workers decide to form a union to raise wages above the 20-unit price. Let us say they demand a wage of 50 units. If their organization is effective and no landowner can obtain the services of workers for less than that figure, what action can the landowners take? Since they want to continue to supply coconuts to the visiting ships, they will presumably meet the demands of the workers. Certainly they will still have larger rental incomes at this figure than they would if no coconuts were collected.

This wage is above the marginal productivity of labor when 310 workers are employed. If all 310 were to be used the total wage bill would be 15,500 units of coconuts. This would leave 3,200 units for rental payments. What would happen if the landowners decided to employ workers only up to the point where the marginal productivity of labor was 50— the wage demanded? If we look at the graph of marginal productivity above (Figure 35), it is apparent, on reading across from a marginal productivity of 50, that 230 workers could be employed at that figure. The same information is shown in Table 21. If 230 workers are employed, the total wage bill will be 11,500. However, total output will only be 16,600. Nevertheless, this will still leave the landlords better off, since it will mean a total product available for rental payments of 5,100 compared with 3,200. Under the rules of our economic system, 80 workers will be unemployed. The 230 workers will be receiving a total wage of 11,500, compared with 6,200 when all 310 were working for a wage of 20. In this situation then, if the union could collect from the employed workers and pay special benefits to those not employed, labor as a group could increase its share of the total national income.

What would happen if, in retaliation against the union, the landlords were to form a landlords' association and present a united front to the workers? The logic of our model cannot give us an answer to that question. The results would depend upon the relative bargaining power or perhaps staying power of the two groups. Whatever the outcome, there would presumably be some modification of the property system or the general basis for income claims. The workers, of course, might attempt a revolution in order to take over the land and to organize production under some arrangement of their own. This sometimes happens in backward agricultural areas when the majority of the population feel that rents are taking an "unfair" share of the joint production. Much would depend, of course, on the whole complex of institutions in any society where population pressure exists.

If we now complicate our economic system by assuming a monetary system, so that wages or rents or both may be paid in money, this underlying set of relationships has to be seen through the "veil of money." Whatever authority, centralized or private, makes the decisions on allocations and output, they will be made in terms of the unit of account. Productivity is measured not in physical units, but in value of marginal product, that is, the physical product multiplied by its price. The comparison will be between the money wage and the money value of marginal product. Under the conditions set forth above, wages under competition would tend to equal the *value of marginal product*. Under conditions of equilibrium the total value of money wages and money rents would exactly equal the value of total product. Thus the amount of money income equivalent to the total output would be distributed as functional shares.

Thus far we have developed the logic of productivity measurement for only one factor. In a more complex model the introduction of some additional factor, say some type of tool or machine, would have the effect of increasing output and raising the productivity of labor. This would appear as a change in the production function, or a change in the assumed values with which we started. What we have illustrated in the model is a change in the supply (relative scarcity or abundance) of factors of production when some factors are fixed and one varies. The same type of model can be generalized and used for the analysis of any factor of production. Such a model has been used extensively to show that if each factor of production is paid the value of its marginal product (marginal product in real terms), the total output will be exhausted.

Use of the Model

This logical model is a thinking tool. It does not have an analogy with reality except in the very special case where all of the assumptions could be verified in experience. One important conclusion of this theoretical model is likely to be true also of experience: no economy can distribute indefinitely more than it produces. If the owners of one type of productive services can control the supply of that service, they may gain at the expense of others. Such action may result in an actual reduction of total output. Whether it does or does not depends upon many other factors, particularly in a complex industrial economy.

402

Discussion
Questions

1. If the goal of a production economy is to maximize output, that goal can be achieved when the variable factor is allocated where its marginal productivity is highest. Could this variable be any of the factors of production?

2. In the production situation described in this chapter, assume that a new *A*-type island were acquired. What would be the effect on wages? On rents?

3. What would be the effect on the income of this economy if a foreign firm were to bring in processing equipment (capital) which converted the coconuts into oil and other products of higher value? In terms of value of total output? In terms of wages? In terms of rents?

4. If the foreign firm imported labor from the outside, what would happen to wages, if no further industry were established?

5. Assume now that, because of the higher income, other new industries are established to produce new types of goods for domestic consumption. What would be the effect, in terms of money incomes? In terms of real income?

CHAPTER 25

Wages

WHEN ECONOMISTS use the term *wages*, they refer to a functional income claim, which is at the same time a price for services performed by a person. This includes managerial effort such as supervision and decision making.

Approximately ninety-five per cent of all wages are paid in money.[1] The employer (the firm) is willing and able to make such a payment because the work performed has been incorporated (as a rule) into something of value which is the property of the employer. This work may have changed the form of a product, made it more valuable through a change of location in space or time, or merely assisted in the transfer of ownership incident to the many transactions involved in the flow of goods and services.

In the sale of labor, the employee sells something different from what the employer buys. The laborer gives his time, his energy, and his skills, while the employer receives a product modified through the application of energy. Thus when reformers and crusaders for social justice contend that labor is not a commodity,[2] their statement is perhaps an important half-truth, but no more. Demand for labor arises because a demand exists for the commodities it helps to create. To management, wages are a cost of production, which by law have a prior claim on the income of the firm. They are warranted from the point of view of management, if the resulting revenue is sufficient to pay them. Wages are linked as costs with commodities, and are meaningfully treated as a price. The laborer is not a commodity; but his service is.

---

[1] *Income in kind* is important chiefly in agriculture and the merchant marine, where board and lodging are provided by the employer. However, an increasing number of "fringe benefits" in industry may be most meaningfully placed in this category.

[2] The Clayton Anti-Trust Act, passed in 1914, specifically states that "labor is not a commodity."

Background of
the Wage Theory

Concern with wages as a distributive share of income and as a prime cost of the firm began with the establishment of a "wage system." This system is of comparatively recent origin. The master-slave arrangement which predominated in ancient times and continued into the nineteenth century (until 1863 in the United States) did not involve wage payments. The slave was the *property* of the master; he could be used in production or personal service, and what he produced was the property of the master. The only cost involved was his clothing and food allowance. Serfdom, which predominated in the Middle Ages and persisted (in Russia, for example) until after the middle of the nineteenth century, also had no system of wages. The serfs were tied to the land and were actually regarded as part of it, passing to the next owner with its sale or transfer. They had certain lands assigned to them from which to produce their own means of livelihood. In return for this privilege they cultivated the land or worked in the household of the landlord.

Artisans of the cities and towns worked with their own tools, organized themselves into guilds, and bartered the products of their labor. Their interest in what they produced, except for the apprentices, was proprietary. The wage system began with the factory system and the employment of free workers, many of whom had escaped from the land and were congregating in the cities once opportunities for such employment began. There is no precise beginning date for this shift, since it can be traced as an evolutionary process which varied from place to place.

In these early factories and shops the conditions of employment and manner of payment carried over many of the characteristics of the old *master-servant* relationship. Hours of work were from sunup to sundown, and rates of pay corresponded to the "just wage" determined by masters, whom Adam Smith saw "everywhere in collusion." As the Industrial Revolution gathered momentum, as markets grew and employment opportunities expanded, the question of wages began to occupy a prominent place in the thought of those seeking to understand the "nature of the economic process." While some of the theories purporting to explain how wages are determined now appear to resemble what the rising merchant and industrial groups thought they *ought* to be, the economists of that day believed that they had discovered the underlying forces which cause shifts and adjustments in wages. As a freer society evolved, and outlines of the new institutions became more distinct, these theories were modified or abandoned as they failed to coincide with experience.

405

Subsistence Theory of Wages

There was a deep-rooted belief among these early students of political economy that the wages of labor, while they might fluctuate with respect to time and place, tended to be equal to *subsistence*. Because of "natural scarcities," the amount of payment a worker could command (on the average) would tend to equal what was required to purchase the necessary food, clothing, and shelter to keep himself alive and able to work. A refinement of this theory was that subsistence must also include enough to provide for the rearing of the next generation of workers.

Malthus, in his theory of population, provided what was ostensibly a realistic base for the subsistence theory of wages. To increase wages above the level of subsistence, he believed, would merely call into operation the "natural law" of population growth—the tendency of a people to outrun its food supply. More babies of the working class would now be able to survive. More mouths would have to be fed. The increase would thus be whittled away until wages again were equal to subsistence. True, each new individual would bring with him two hands and only one mouth. But the law of diminishing returns decrees that, in the absence of technological progress, those two hands are less and less effective as the number of workers increases. Malthus, of course, did not foresee the tremendous technological development then in the offing. The subsistence theory of wages persisted in economic literature, and in policy arguments until cheaper food and a rising income level discredited it as a useful concept.

The Wage-Fund Doctrine

The wage-fund doctrine, most commonly associated with the name of John Stuart Mill, was a modified subsistence theory. It stated that wages, which are usually paid in advance of the sale of the product, must come from a fixed fund of working capital, accumulated from past savings. The average wage or price of labor was simply the total wage fund divided by the number of workers. Any attempt by one group of workers to organize for purposes of increasing their own wages could only result in lowering wages to other workers.

Although used vigorously for a time to deny the possibility of gains to labor through union organization, the wage-fund doctrine as a general theory for explaining variations in wages was eventually rejected by Mill and largely abandoned after 1850. Once a society develops a substantial stock of goods (capital) and a money and credit system, no individual employer with goods in process needs to depend on his own accumulated working capital for the payment of wages.

Exploitation Theory of Wages

The exploitation theory of wages is associated with the name of Karl Marx and his followers. At the hands of Marx it was used both as an explanation for wages and as an underpinning for his belief in the inevitable downfall of capitalism. Marx was convinced that the poverty he saw about him (and there was much of it during the nineteenth century, when population was increasing rapidly and the old agricultural society was disappearing) was due to the exploitive nature of the capitalist form of organization. Borrowing the labor theory of value from Smith and Ricardo, which stated that all value is created by labor, Marx then built on this foundation his theory of the exploitation of labor. If, the theory stated, all value is created by labor, then the full value of the product necessarily belongs to labor. The only claim of capital that is justifiable is an amount necessary to maintain that capital—in other words, the depreciation reserves. The existence of profits and interest demonstrates on the face of things that the capitalists expropriate from the workers that which is their own by virture of the workers having created it.

The rate of profit was a measure of exploitation. Marx believed that this exploitation would become more and more severe. As capital increased and became concentrated in ever fewer hands, the capitalist class (in order to maintain its expected profit) would force wages down even more, thereby intensifying the poverty and suffering of the working man. He believed this was inherent in the system of property known as private capitalism, and predicted that rising resentment among the workers would inevitably result in the overturn of capitalism, the socialization of the factors of production, and the appropriation of all income by the working class. This dogma is still given lip service by the communist followers of Marx.

The Marginal Productivity Theory

By now the marginal productivity theory of wages and wage determination should need little elaboration. It is the partial equilibrium analysis of supply and demand, generalized and applied to the factor market, in this case the market for labor.

In an enterprise economy the demand for labor derives from the demand for the products which labor produces. If the wage for a particular kind of labor is less than the value of the marginal product which it adds to the total, the firm can increase its profit income by employing more labor. If the value of the marginal product is less than the prevailing wage, then the firm can increase its profit or minimize its losses by hiring less labor. What is perhaps more significant, a high wage relative to the value of marginal product is likely to lead to a substitution of other factors for labor, particularly new capital equipment. Thus under conditions of equilibrium, and given time for adjustments (when competition is present), wages will equal the marginal productivity of labor.

Wage determination under conditions of monopolistic competition are more involved. If a firm or an industry possesses any considerable monopoly control in the product market, and if it acts to increase profits by restricting production, wages may equal the marginal productivity of labor, but under restricted conditions. Less labor is employed than would be the case if the industry were competitive. Laborers, unable to get jobs in the restricted industries, must seek employment in the more competitive industries. The effect there will be to drive wages down because of the increased supply of labor and the lowered marginal productivity.

When varying degrees of monopoly are set off against a large and powerful labor union (itself wielding a form of monopoly control over labor supply), the relationship is even more complex. If the industry is earning a monopoly profit, then the union may, by threatening to withhold the labor supply, share in that profit. Higher wages need not mean higher prices to consumers in this case, since if the firm or the industry is already charging a price which maximizes profit, it cannot improve its position by raising prices. This situation, of course, will vary, depending upon the level of employment and income. If the general level of income rises, then wage increases may be passed on in the form of higher prices. In this case union demands can be said to be contributing to inflation. During a period of falling employment and income the bargaining position of the union is likely to be weakened, although experience has shown that under these circumstances the union usually resists wage cuts. Some economists hold that this tends to increase unemployment.

The Bargaining Theory of Wages

There is no universal agreement among economists regarding the usefulness of the marginal productivity analysis as a technique for understanding how wages are determined in an industrial society such as that of the United States. One group of critics holds that the general approach is not easily adapted to empirical investigation. It might be useful if one were able to conduct an experiment in which all factors but one, notably labor, were constant. This, however, is not possible. Moreover, even through the use of modern statistical methods it is difficult to fit the data into the form of this logical model.

Because of the dynamic nature of the industrial process, which includes changes in the entry to and exit from the labor market, the influence of continuous technological improvement, and the rather large fluctuation in the relationship between wages and the productivity of labor itself, any attempt to order the statistics to determine the marginal productivity of labor is out of the question. Also, the fact that labor is by no means a homogeneous service—consisting as it does of literally hundreds of different skills and operations—makes the greatly simplified model of the preceding chapter too general for realistic application. Conclusions derived from it, if applied directly to policy, may be misleading.

Few would quarrel with the thesis that for any extended period of time labor as a whole (if that concept can be assigned any meaning) cannot obtain more income than the economy produces. Certainly, the workers in any firm or industry cannot claim the whole of income created without bankrupting the business.

While acknowledging that productivity sets the upper limit to wages, labor economists in particular, doubt that in a complex industrial society, with a large element of monopoly, labor is assured of getting that much. They recognize a zone of indeterminacy, the upper limit of which is set by the productivity of labor and the lower limit of which is determined by the relative strength of the parties at the bargaining table. They maintain that the degree of labor mobility assumed in the analytical model is neither possible nor desirable. Workers do not have full knowledge of all possibilities of higher wage rates or better job opportunities. Even if they did, it is not easy to shift from place to place according to the vagaries of the market. A majority of workers tend to settle in homes and prefer not to leave them except under special circumstances.

To this the marginal analyst will reply that the analysis does not require that all workers be in a state of perpetual motion. A large core of steady workers will, for the most part, stay put. It is the marginal worker, shifting about from one area to another and from one industry or firm to another, that brings about the equilibrating process.

The bargaining theory of wage determination probably derives from the experience of the increasing role of unions in the wage-determining process. American labor union tradition has always been predominantly one of business unionism (see page 478). In short, the union concept of its role in an enterprise economy is one of countervailing power. Management has superior bargaining power when it faces the individual worker. The union, representing workers as a group, seeks to offset this advantage. Depending on the strength of the two parties, a compromise is usually reached between maximum demands and minimum offers. Productivity can only be measured imperfectly, and bargaining power (at the present state of our knowledge of motivation psychology) scarcely at all. This is an important area for research, and much work needs to be done.

Wage Levels and
Wage Rates

The total wage and salary component of the national income, an aggregate figure, provides us with one type of information useful for analysis. As a percentage of the total national income, it tells us from year to year the relative share of the whole which has been assigned to the "human factor." This information is given for selected years in Table 18 above. While there is some variation from year to year, particularly during periods of high and low national-income levels, the percentage figure remains remarkably stable at around 65 per cent. During the depression when total national income was low, the share of wages and salaries rose to nearly 74 per cent, while profits declined. This was because wages have a prior legal claim against the revenues of the firm. It is undoubtedly true, also, that while many firms laid off large numbers of workers, as the demand for their output declined, many were kept on in anticipation of an eventual upturn, or for reasons other than purely economic.

Aggregate figures cannot tell us many of the things we want to know. For our examination of wages it is necessary to have greater detail. We could, for example, by dividing total wages and salaries by the number of gainfully employed workers, obtain an average wage. By comparing this average from one year to the next, we could learn whether payments for effort and skills were on the average increasing, decreasing, or remaining relatively constant. If the rate of increase or decrease were greater than that of the total national income, this would provide an indication of what was happening to the average real income of workers.

Grouping together all wages and salaries from the highest to the lowest, however, fails to give a picture of the wage structure in depth. For that reason the Bureau of Labor Statistics attempts to provide data on aggregates at a slightly lower level by gathering information for different industries and trades. By maintaining a record of the total labor force and the numbers of employed and unemployed, together with the number of wage and salary workers in different industries and rates of pay and weekly earnings, the statistical agencies provide the basic data for the study of wages and salaries and their variations. Table 22 is a compilation of information for selected years since 1929 (with certain gaps) on the number of wage and salary workers, the average weekly hours worked, the average

410

hourly earnings, and the average gross weekly earnings in selected industries. This is still not a picture of great detail, but it shows what has occurred from year to year with respect to shifting employment and wages. No single pattern emerges which would provide a clue to any very stable relationship between wages and the decisions of workers about where to work and for how long. This is not surprising. Vast and complex forces have played upon the economic life of the United States during this period. The general level of employment and income has varied widely, vast technological changes have occurred, new industries have arisen, while the requirements of war and defense have had prior claims on many workers and the things they produce.

The decade of the 1930's was a period of general "oversupply" of labor. The proportionate claim of workers, while relatively high in the aggregate, provided a rather low level of real income. This was because many were unemployed and were not making any contribution to production. Many could not buy new cars, as is shown by the low level of output of the automotive industries compared with 1929, which had been a peak year. Few bought houses, as evidenced by the large unemployment in the construction industry and the backlog of housing needs which began to show up during World War II and which became critical immediately afterwards.

On the other hand, the 1940's and the early 1950's were years of "short supply" in labor, except for a brief period in 1949, 1954, and again in 1958. Workers possessing critical skills continued to be employed at high wages, and even relatively unskilled workers kept their jobs.

Wages and Allocation

Relative wages provide clues for production planning. Cost reduction is a necessity if a firm is to improve its profit position. Wage reduction was once a means to that end. In the face of short labor supply and union opposition, wage and salary cuts are no longer widely used. Substituting machinery or improved organization as a means to greater efficiency is the more frequent road to lower costs. This requires that labor be treated not as a single factor of production, but as a composite of many different factors of production, some of which can be substituted for one another in the production process, and which may also be replaced within ever widening limits by the other factors of production, specifically by machines and technical processes.

When modern management discovers that a particular type of labor has a high price relative to its contribution to the production process, it will set its engineers or organization specialists to the task of finding some

411

Table 22.   Basic Data on Number of Workers, Average Work Week, Average Wage, and Average Weekly Earnings for Selected Years and Selected Industries

A. Average Number of Workers (thousands)

Year	Total Wage & Salary Workers	Manufacturing	Mining	Contract Construction	Transport & Public Utilities	Trade	Finance	Service	Government—Federal, State, & Local
1929	31,041	10,534	1,078	1,497	3,907	6,401	1,431	3,127	3,066
1933	23,466	7,258	735	809	2,659	4,999	1,225	2,614	3,167
1939	30,311	10,078	845	1,150	2,912	6,612	1,399	3,321	3,995
1949	43,315	14,178	918	2,165	3,949	9,513	1,765	4,972	5,856
1956	51,483	16,890	795	3,038	4,145	11,144	2,300	6,000	7,172

B. Average Weekly Hours of Work

Year	Manufacturing	Bituminous Coal Mining	Building Construction	Class I Railroads	Telephone	Wholesale Trade	Retail Trade	Laundries
1929	44.2	38.4	—	—	—	—	—	—
1933	38.1	29.5	—	—	—	—	—	—
1939	37.7	27.1	32.6	43.7	39.1	41.7	42.7	41.8
1949	39.2	32.6	36.7	43.7	38.5	40.7	40.4	41.5
1956	40.5	37.7	36.3	41.7	39.5	40.4	38.5	40.3

Table 22 (continued)

C. Average Gross Hourly Earnings

Year	Agriculture	Manufacturing	Bituminous Coal Mining	Building Construction	Class I Railroads	Telephone	Wholesale Trade	Retail Trade	Laundries
1929	$0.241	$0.566	$0.681	—	—	—	—	—	—
1933	.115	.443	.501	—	—	—	—	—	—
1939	.166	.633	.886	$0.932	$0.730	$0.822	$0.715	$0.542	$0.422
1949	.559	1.401	1.941	1.935	1.427	1.345	1.414	1.137	.843
1956	.725	1.98	2.79	2.79	2.11	1.86	2.01	1.57	1.05

D. Average Gross Weekly Earnings

Year	Manufacturing	Bituminous Coal Mining	Building Construction	Class I Railroads	Telephone	Wholesale Trade	Retail Trade	Laundries
1929	$25.03	$25.72	—	—	—	—	—	—
1933	16.73	14.47	—	—	—	$26.11	—	—
1939	26.86	23.88	$30.39	$31.90	$32.14	29.82	$23.14	$17.64
1949	54.92	63.28	70.95	62.36	51.78	57.55	45.93	34.98
1956	80.13	105.21	105.21	87.82	73.38	81.21	56.70	40.10

Source: Adapted from Economic Report of the President, 1957.

413

new combination which will result in greater efficiency. Time and motion studies, the identification of separate and distinct motor skills of workers, and the invention of machine processes to take over these skills when they can be reduced to their simple components are an important part of modern industrial management. In this area the contribution of the economists has been small. The knowledge and skills of the psychologist, the sociologist, and the engineer have been more to the point.

Since World War II "labor-market research" has received increasing emphasis. This research has sought to accumulate in greater detail than heretofore empirical knowledge about skills, wage rates associated with those skills, and other experience data which can be linked with what the economist has always called labor supply and demand. Such information is important in education and training, especially in courses intended to increase the productivity of workers, enabling them to move from a lower to a higher-paying skill.

There are two components which constitute labor as a factor of production—time and productivity. These are not easily distinguishable in experience, but in the hands of the analyst they are useful concepts for purposes of differentiation. Production is accomplished over a period of time. Output is a function of time and production—so many units per period of time. Wages also are usually specified on a time basis. Thus a worker may be paid according to some hourly, weekly, or even monthly rate. The choice of these time rates will ordinarily depend upon how effective the accounting system is in identifying a worker's time with a specific output. Central office workers and supervisory personnel cannot be assigned to any specific output, particularly in multiproduct firms. In the cost accounts of the firm their wages and salaries are treated as "overhead costs," the rates computed on a weekly or monthly basis being thus chiefly a function of time. Other workers who can be assigned to specific departments or specific operations are more often paid at an hourly rate.

Some wages are paid on a *piece-rate* basis. In other words, the worker is paid so much for each unit of a product he is able to turn out, and his total wages are a function of his productivity. Where it is possible to do so, management has usually preferred this method of payment, since it lends itself to control over costs. Labor unions, on the other hand, have sometimes opposed this method of computing wage rates. They believe that it lends itself to "exploitation" of the worker by pitting him against his fellows and through manipulation of the wage rate, extracting more work for less pay. They maintain that a worker's productivity and efficiency is related to the length of time he has been on the job. Thus they favor a

414

lower starting rate, on an hourly or weekly basis, adjusted upward over time as the worker develops greater proficiency in his work.

Patterns of Wage Differences

When we abandon the simplified assumption of labor as a homogeneous factor of production (which we make when we speak of labor in general), and relate wage differences to the differences in people as energy-releasing mechanisms, what do we find? A thought which may occur to anyone who reflects on the problem (partly because it is a belief of rather wide acceptance) is that wage differences are likely to be closely correlated with differences in *ability*. There is one difficulty with this answer. Ability is not a single-value concept, and is next to impossible to define in any operational sense of the word.

If one examines the records of workers at the lower end of the wage scale—those most frequently unemployed—composite "debility" would be apparent in a majority of cases. Many will be old, physically handicapped, emotionally unstable, or mentally deficient. Incapable of performing physical tasks requiring strength or endurance, incapable of working with others, or unable to perform any but the simplest types of labor under close supervision, these are human beings whose contributions to any productive effort will be small.

Beyond this tip of a wage and salary distribution curve, however, the relationship between wages and ability is more complex and more difficult to identify If we look at workers who do the same sort of job, the term ability may be easier to identify, and those who have more of it are likely with time to achieve the higher wages. If the job is one which demands physical strength and endurance, those possessing such characteristics in greatest measure will have the higher wage within that particular class of labor. In comparison with other classes of skills, however, this group is not likely to be found in the higher wage groups.

If, in addition to strength and endurance, one adds the variable of motor skill to the criterion of ability, the worker who makes a high score on a test designed to measure such skills is likely, with experience, to rise higher in the wage classification structure than those who make a lower score. Nor does our list of identifiable variables associated with ability end here. Intelligence, particularly the capacity to think abstractly, to see complex interrelationships, and to predict future consequences of present actions, is an important qualification of the human factor, especially in planning and supervising large-scale joint efforts. We move here into the wages of management, where some of the highest incomes are to be found. Here, too, will be found the complex abilities of those persons of great

415

technical achievement—such as successful surgeons, scientists, and engineers—where motor skills, capacity to think abstractly, and ability to coordinate these efforts are joined.

Today, as never before, human engineering and personnel management are receiving increased attention by those responsible for production decisions. Batteries of tests are used to identify these skills, to measure them, and finally to design techniques for teaching them. Enough has been accomplished to indicate that a knowledge of labor supply involves much more than counting the working population. The *Dictionary of Occupational Classification,* developed and widely used during World War II, lists more than 36,000 different occupations by title, with a brief description of what the worker does to accomplish his task.

Ability or competence alone does not determine the supply of a particular type of labor. Interest, drives, educational opportunities, background, and pure chance also enter into the picture. We know very little about why men work. Usually we assume that they work because they have to. We believe, as a first approximation, that they go to work where they expect to earn the largest income. We know from everyday experience that when shortages in a given occupation develop, and wages or salaries rise, workers, particularly those just starting out, move into that certain area. When Henry Ford announced his $5 a day wage rate in the Ford plant in 1916, he attracted workers from all over the country. The population of Detroit increased rapidly, and today it has a large reservoir of workmen with experience and skill adaptable to the automotive industries.

However, this easy first approximation does not give us all that we need to construct a model of the labor market in sufficient detail to make it useful as an instrument for prediction. There has been considerable discussion among economists about the shape of the labor supply curve. The simplest analytical model can be represented by the traditional upward-sloping supply curve. This assumes that the supply of any particular type of labor is a function of the price or wage rate. In other words, if the wage increases there will be an increase in the quantity of labor or labor time offered. This is illustrated in Figure 36. Of course, the rate at which the amount of labor offered increases (the elasticity of the labor supply) will depend upon such things as the skills required and the ease with which these skills can be learned, as well as the degree to which workers in other trades or industries can be substituted for the type of worker already in this particular labor market.

Many exceptions to this model have been noted. This is illustrated by the supply curve which turns back upon itself, as illustrated in Figure

37, a phenomenon obtained from a number of empirical studies. This curve tells us that as wages rise less labor will actually be offered than at a lower price. One explanation for this is that leisure is an important form of income. When wage rates are high enough to provide the worker with a specified income for a given expenditure of time, he may prefer more leisure to a higher money income.

Empirical evidence also indicates that the shape of the supply curve will vary considerably with the *level* of employment and income. At a rather low income level the supply curve is practically horizontal. In other words, as the number of job opportunities expands more labor will be offered even though there is no rise in wage rates. Also contributing to a relatively flat supply curve is the increasing influence of labor unions and the collective bargaining process. When a wage contract has been signed, new workers who come into the industry tend to be paid at the contract rate for their particular skill. A rise in wages usually occurs only when a new contract is negotiated. Thus labor supply can be depicted by a stair-step curve.

Wages and Technological Progress

Laboring people have long been fearful lest innovations in machinery rob them of their skill and of their jobs. Beginning with the English weavers who in the late eighteenth century banded together to smash the power-driven looms, there has almost always been concern over technological unemployment. Such concern is most pronounced during periods of de pression. Workers thrown out of jobs are very conscious of a machine which does the work that several workmen formerly did. When employment is high this concern diminishes.

Experience shows that, far from reducing wages (particularly real wages), technology has had the effect of increasing them. This can be stated most precisely in terms of our simple model developed in Chapter 27. An increase in capital can be perceived as a relative decrease in the supply of labor. In that illustrative problem, if at any given supply of workers the number of *A* islands could have been increased, productivity and wages would have risen.

Working with more and better tools, the productivity of labor in the United States has risen steadily. This is not to say that certain workers have not been adversely affected. When a machine takes over, skilled workers may not be able to find employment elsewhere at the same wage rate. For those no longer young the problem of readjustment may be a serious personal problem. Younger workers through re-education or training can "reconvert" without serious long-run loss of income.

417

Figure 36.   Supply Curve for Labor

Figure 37.   Backward-Sloping Supply Curve
for Labor

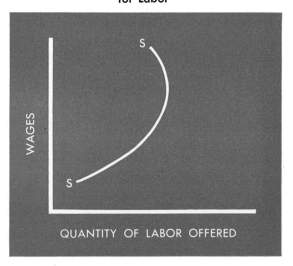

Changes induced by technological innovations are not accomplished without modification of institutional arrangements. For example, modern mass-production methods based upon the machine have greatly changed the structure and power relationships of the American trade-union movement. The modern *industrial union* has become increasingly characteristic of organized labor, which at one time was dominated by the *craft union,* This is discussed at greater length in Chapter 30.

Discussion
Questions

1. Why is labor not a homogeneous commodity?

2. What limitations on competition do you see resulting from the existence of noncompeting groups? Does this have any consequences for the marginal-productivity theory of wages?

3. Does the term wages carry a different common-sense association from salary? If so, what does the term wages of management connote?

4. What happens to the proportionate claim of labor on the national income during a depression? Why?

5. What does the term "up-grading" of labor suggest? When is it likely to occur?

CHAPTER 26

Rents

INCOME CLAIMS established through ownership of certain properties, most of which are associated with physical objects, are commonly called rent. Rent as an abstract concept used in economic analysis has a more specialized meaning which can be most easily explained in terms of its history.

This functional income claim was once thought to have unique characteristics because of the nature of land as a form of property. It is easy to think of land as material and very *real*. This association is evident in such terms as *real estate, realty,* and *real property,* usually contrasted with personal property and such intangibles as stocks and bonds. Land can be seen, measured, walked upon, and transmitted with seemingly little change from one generation to the next. Its ownership in a world of changing human relations gives a sense of security and stability to many.

Rent was undoubtedly the first stable form of property claim which gave a continuing income to its owner. In the ideology of medieval culture, rights of land ownership were believed to come from God and were closely linked to the divine right of kings.

Rents continued when land ownership was institutionalized in the legal structure of the emerging industrial society. However, when the interests of the landowners came into conflict with those of traders and industrialists, as they did in the struggle over the Corn Laws in England from 1815 on, landed property lost its claim for special treatment. Up to that time property in land had been closely linked with political power. Landed gentry dominated the legislative process by virtue of their control of the House of Lords, membership in which was reserved to them.

The Corn Laws consisted of a duty placed on wheat to discourage its importation. To a rising population, and particularly to the rapidly-growing working class in the new industries, this meant higher bread prices—an important item in the workers' scale of living. Rising wheat prices, on the other hand, meant an advantage to the landlords in rental income. Ricardo, who led the fight in the House of Commons against the Corn Laws, developed as an analytical tool and political weapon the concept of *economic rent*. His analysis was essentially as follows: The unique quality of rent as a distributive share of the national income derives from the characteristics of land as a factor of production. Defined as the "original and indestructible qualities of the soil," a free gift of nature (its quantity fixed for all time), land is the basic factor of production. As property, this factor of production entitles the owner to a share of the output to which it contributes. However, unlike the other factors of production, no matter how high the rents may go, this increase in the price of the services of land will not result in any increase in supply. The total land area of England cannot be increased. True, as wheat prices rise in response to the demand of an increasing population, the poorer land will be brought under cultivation. This only serves to enrich still further the owners of the better land.

Rents are determined at the margin of production. This idea was incorporated into the concept of *differential rent*. As the term suggests, this concept refers to the variation in rents due to differences in the grades of land. If we can return for a moment to Table 21 (page 400), the concept of differential rent can be concretized by means of an example. If we take the figures from the last line of this table, where 310 workers have been allocated to the different islands, we see that the islands labeled *A, B, C,* and *D*, respectively, command rents of 185, 155, 125, and 95. When these values are shown by means of a bar diagram, as in Figure 38, the concept of differential rent will be clear. The dotted line cuts across the entire chart at the exact level of the lowest rent. The parts of the diagram which lie above this line represent the differential rents on *A, B,* and *C* islands (land). *To what can these differences in rent be attributed? The answer is obvious. Differential rent measures the differences in productivity of these lands, as determined by their original fertility, or location.*

When the fight against the Corn Laws had been won, and the British market opened to the wheat of the Western Hemisphere, the supply of land was increased. The levy of the landlords against the British economy was ended.

It should be apparent that the situation with which Ricardo was concerned was based upon a particular set of circumstances which paralleled the built-in assumptions of our model of simple distribution theory in Chapter 24. The limited lands of the British Isles, as long as the landlords were in a position to impose their own interests on the economy, could not be expanded as rapidly as the demand for the wheat they produced.

Figure 38. Differential Rent

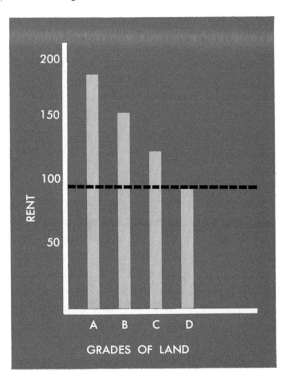

Although the circumstances disappeared, the analysis remained, and an older generation of economists devoted much space in economic literature to the controversy over whether rent was *really* a cost of production. Was the price of wheat high because rents were high, or were rents high because the price of wheat was high, and could landlords charge what the traffic would bear because of the limited supply of land? The problem is, in fact, a semantic one. The answer depends upon whether the frame of reference within which the problem is viewed is an aggregative one or that of an individual firm. It is true that, viewed in terms of the total land area of a country or of the world, the available land supply is pretty well fixed. However, if the point of view is that of the individual firm, or even a whole industry, the land supply is not fixed. Land is used to produce more than just wheat. It is used for pasture, for the production of corn, barley, rye, oats, and other crops. If the demand for wheat increases relative to these other products, then the owners of land can demand a higher rental income and the firm can afford to pay the higher rent, but the price mechanism will result in a greater allocation of land to wheat. To the firm the amount paid for the land is a cost and represents a cost of production. Even the differential rent is related to cost, since it represents a higher productivity, which translated into costs will mean greater efficiency.

Our discussion of rent might end here were it not for the fact that a phenomenon very similar to that observed by Ricardo can be distinguished in other circumstances. In the United States during the latter part of the nineteenth century Henry George created something of a stir with his impassioned book titled *Progress and Poverty*. In this book he inveighed against the so-called unearned increment, and his proposal for a tax policy to expropriate what he regarded as a vicious thing received widespread attention.

Henry George grew up in San Francisco during a period of its most rapid expansion. As in the case of all boom towns, the value of real estate rose together with its rental charges. Early arrivals on the scene, who had acquired lands of little or no value, found themselves possessed of great wealth when the population expanded and demand for land increased. Many had made no improvements whatever on the land to increase its physical productivity. Viewing the poverty which existed alongside riches, Henry George felt that there must be some connection between the two. Property holders who had contributed little or nothing to society had gained at the expense of others who wanted and would put to productive use the land in question. George maintained that society, not the landowners, had created this value and ought to appropriate it for society's use. From these beginnings there eventually evolved his scheme for a single tax, which would take from landowners the full value of the *unearned increment*. According to his calculations, such a tax could provide sufficient revenue to pay all of the costs of government, thereby returning to the "public" that which really belonged to it in any event.

Here again there are analogous conditions to those observed by Ricardo. A factor of production, limited in its supply, which becomes increasingly scarce relative to the other factors which are used in production, is able to exact an increasing income claim. It did not matter that California was a very large state with vast unused lands, since those lands most in demand were the ones located favorably with respect to the growing cities and their bustling trade. Not just land area, or even the fertility of the soil, is involved in this problem, but the factor of location as well. Distance constrains the economic activities of men, and those locations most favorably situated gain most.

Recognition of this fact of experience has been incorporated into the analysis of modern urban land values. This is implied in the term *situs*, which means literally situation or location with respect to "economic activity." In the modern large city land values and rentals are highest in the crowded center of the city. Businessmen who operate the shops on Fifth Avenue must pay very high rentals. Prices in these shops are high. If asked about the problem, the businessman would probably say that he has to charge high prices in order to pay his rental charges or to earn a return on the capital he has invested in the expensive land. Merchants in adjacent areas sometimes advertise their goods by urging customers to save money by trading outside the high-rent district—"walk upstairs and save a dollar," or "a few blocks from Main Street but miles from Main Street prices." Here again the inference is that rent as a cost is the cause of high prices. Economists have usually pointed out that it works the other way round. The reason a merchant on Fifth Avenue can afford to pay the rent he does is because of the large crowds that pass his store each day, who see his merchandise, and who come there to shop when in search of goods. Thus the capital and rental values of the purely situs aspect of land are traceable to space limitations, to property rights in favorable locations which cannot be duplicated.

Quasi Rent

Economists (and others) long regarded *physical capital* as a factor of production distinct from the "gifts of nature." This factor is capable of being expanded, hence an increase in its price will (sooner or later) result in an increase in its supply. When a particular form of capital goods brings to its owner a favorable return, because the demand for its services is great, the owner of that capital good cannot retain any permanent claim against a higher income, because similar facilities will be produced and competition will drive down any purely rental income.

However, it was recognized that under certain conditions returns on a capital good do have rent-like characteristics. Buildings and many kinds of machines require time to be produced. Free or money capital must be accumulated and invested in such assets. During this time period existing equipment may experience increasing demand for its services and income claims greater than anticipated at the time the original investment was made. This has been called *quasi rent.*

During periods of rising income and rising prices—in short, during inflation—most capital assets or physical factors of production acquire an increasing claim against income and will rise in value. This is known as a *capital gain.* Those properties in an unusually favored position with respect to the market show the greatest gains. Thus, while there may be a general rise in the level of property values, some physical assets gain more than others.

424

These capital and income gains have frequently been the object of special treatment by the taxing authorities, on the grounds that such income claims bear no relation to production in any real sense. In other words, here is a distributive share of income not paralleled by an output of goods and services. Following World War I, when most European countries went through a severe inflationary period, a capital levy against property holdings was widely advocated and put into operation in a number of countries. It was argued that by this means great inequities in the distribution of property claims were corrected. Landowners and others were forced to sell part of their holdings to pay this tax.

There is, of course, another side to this picture. During periods of deflation the situation is reversed. Rental payments for physical assets tend to fall and with them the value of the assets. This has always been a stumbling block to Henry George's proposal for a single tax, which presumably would work in only one direction. It leaves unanswered what should be done with capital *decrements,* and what the effect would be on government revenues during falling prices, if revenues and spending were based only on a single tax.

A More General Theory of Rent

We have examined some specific cases in which the phenomenon of a rising functional income claim not associated with a parallel increase in productivity has been linked first to land and then to other forms of physical capital. The theoretical models of those who attempted to analyze what they experienced or saw were of necessity abstractions from reality. What at first appeared to be peculiar to land was later recognized as a characteristic of physical factors generally. In our time the same can be said for even the less material embodiments of property. Patented processes, a favored name, and many other forms of more abstract capital may be the basis for rent-like incomes.

Nor does the process end there. When war breaks out, when a whole population goes through a process of changing its mind on what it wants, on what it values, there occurs a rearrangement of social valuation. At the outbreak of World War II welders were in great demand. Additional welders could not be trained overnight. Consequently, until more welders were trained, and until wage and price controls were imposed, persons with such skills experienced rapid relative increases in the incomes they could command.

How does this differ from the phenomena we have been discussing? The answer is, it doesn't. The forces associated with such income gains are the same as those for the real assets described above. In each case an inelastic supply of the factor in question resulted in an increase in its relative claim on income. Often such gains are temporary. Given enough time for adjustments to take place, there will occur a shift in the factors of production, so that similar or substitute factors become part of a new supply. Where there is no possibility of increasing the supply, because of an extremely limited resource or skill, the property owner may continue to realize large gains. These too, however, pass away. Property owners do not live forever. A new owner who acquires the asset pays the new higher price, and the return on his investment approaches something like the "normal" or the going rate. True, there are families who for generations have held title to the choice locations of lower Manhattan island. These families have continued to live off rentals that are high when computed on a per-acre or even per-square-foot basis. Meanwhile the rest of society has adapted itself to the new situation. Buildings have been pushed ever higher in order to use more intensively the ground space or situs.

It will be apparent that we are approaching a phenomenon similar to that which we called monopoly in another context. This monopoly is a more or less rigid property form. The institution of property, adapted to a particular set of social and economic relations during a given time, tends to persist even though times and circumstances change. If, in the eyes of the public, gains to individuals attributable to the lag in institutions are "unjust," property forms themselves may be changed through the agency of government. We saw in Part 2 how this happened with gold. Property rights are maintained by organized society and usually will be upheld only if they are regarded as "just," measured by some criterion of social justice shared by at least a majority of members of society.

Rent control after World War II is a case in point. Although price controls, which had been in operation for a large number of commodities and services during the war, were rather suddenly removed in 1946, rent control continued. Although viewed as unjust by some, a majority regarded the removal of rent controls as contributing to still greater injustice. At the war's end there were tremendous shortages in housing. Experts estimated that it would probably require ten years for new construction to catch up with the demand. The supply of house room was highly inelastic. To have removed rent control, many believe, would have resulted in a rapid rise in rents. This rise would not have resulted in anything like a parallel increase in housing. Landlords would have been enriched, but the unsatisfied demand of tenants would have remained. To encourage the construction of new housing, controls were taken off new houses. That the gains or losses which resulted from rent control

426

were unequally distributed among tenants and landlords is probably true. Many tenants of old houses continued to pay low rentals, even as their own incomes rose during the period of prosperity which followed the war. Builders of new houses were able to secure substantial benefits. It is at least arguable that removal of rent controls and the siphoning off of large gains in the form of income taxes might have distributed them more equitably.

The Capitalization of Rents

We have referred from time to time to the parallel rise in the value of a physical asset and the rental income it commands. The two are actually different sides of the same coin. The value of an asset is based upon its rental or income-earning capacity. The process is similar to that involved in valuing a business enterprise. Ownership of a productive factor entitles one to a rental income. Let is say that a piece of property returns a net rent of $1,000 per year. If we capitalize this figure at a given rate of interest by dividing it by the interest rate, say 5 per cent, we arrive at the figure $20,000. In other words, a prospective owner who desired an income of $1,000 per year would be justified in paying $20,000 for this piece of property, since that is precisely what he would earn on that amount of money loaned out at that rate of interest.

Rent on property is often a compound functional income claim. Thus the owner of an apartment house collects rent from the tenants. Part of this represents payment for his time and effort in managing the property. Part pays for depreciation and real estate taxes. The remainder can be treated as return on investment. If this return, because of favorable location, is higher than a normal return, the difference is called *economic rent*.

Discussion
Questions

1. What does the phrase "original and indestructible powers of the soil" mean to you?

2. What were the three fairly distinct classes of society, at the time of Adam Smith, whose incomes were based upon wages, rents, and profits?

3. In the eyes of Henry George, who created the "unearned increment" he proposed to tax away?

4. In a university town, rates on hotel rooms frequently are higher on football week ends. This can be explained by increased demand. What is the explanation from the supply side?

5. Businesses sometimes advertise that because they have moved from the high-rent district their prices are lower? Can you think of certain other costs of doing business which might offset higher rental costs?

CHAPTER 27

Interest and Profits

In this chapter our concern will be with the twin claims to income—interest and profits—which rest upon a base somewhat less "real," much less directly linked to the observable actions and materials associated with production. It has become a convention to describe these claims as dynamic. This is another way of saying that their connection with the production process is ambiguous, not easily represented by a system of relationships that can be fitted into a logical model, measured precisely or predicted with confidence. Both are aspects of the purely money-income flow described in Part 2, although they must be finally linked to the real-income process.

Interest

Interest, as usually understood, is the price we pay when we hire, rent, or borrow money. Since it seems a little awkward to speak of the price of money, tradition dictates that we speak of a *rate of interest,* and that rate is usually some fraction of the unit of money which is borrowed. A five per cent interest rate means that for the use of one dollar (100 cents) for a year we will pay five cents. Literally, the lender is entitled to his dollar back at the end of a year and an interest or share (to the extent of five cents) in whatever else the borrower owns. For the lender this interest is income.

While this simple description will suffice to define the paying and receiving of interest as such, economists try to go behind the immediately perceived events to understand the relationship between the income claim and the function to which it can be assigned. They have sought to explain (1) why people are willing to pay interest, and (2) why they have to pay it.

Semantic Background

Few words have a more complex pattern of meanings or "double in brass" more often than the term *interest*. The dictionary distinguishes many different meanings. All suggest involvement of one sort or another, from the "interest of one person in another," to the "vested interests" which Veblen used when he referred to absentee owners in the modern "pecuniary economy."

In order that we may understand the particular meaning of interest as we use it here, a brief review of its history will be helpful. This history begins with the earliest approaches to money. Aristotle is credited with the observation that "money is barren." Other forms of property or wealth were viewed as either capable of self-reproduction or useful in the production process. Money in itself, however, contributed nothing to an increase in useful things. This doctrine was taken over by the Church in the Middle Ages and provided the basis for the so-called stricture against usury. *Usury* was any payment for the use of money. Since money had been declared barren, to charge for its use was regarded as wrong. The lender was entitled to no claim against the borrower, no interest in the borrower's property, beyond the face value of the loan. The term usury as used by the Church philosophers meant essentially what we understand by interest today.

Some have speculated about what it was in those times which led people to this attitude toward payment for the use of money. One hypothesis is that most loans, which were undoubtedly made during that period, were consumption loans; and there was no obvious link between the possession of money and the ability it gave to acquire factors of production. With the rise of commerce and trade and with the beginnings of manufacturing, men became aware of opportunities to increase their incomes through the use of money in hiring labor and purchasing raw materials and goods for further exchange. Consequently, they were willing to promise an "interest" in these earnings, if someone with cash loaned it to them.

Strictures against usury continued after the use of liquid funds as an aid to production became more general. However, men began to reason as follows. If a man had money in his possession, he could use it in production to increase his own income. If he were to loan the money to someone else, he would thereby give up such an opportunity. Thus to claim an "interest" in the income earned by the borrower was a way to compensate him for what he gave up when he loaned the money. Because of the official Church attitude against usury, merchants of the late Middle Ages frequently resorted to borrowing from Jewish moneylenders, who were not bound by such strictures on the taking of interest, and thus rather neatly got around the problem—a subterfuge dramatized in Shakespeare's *Merchant of Venice.* As this practice spread, the attitude of the Church gradually changed, and requiring "interest" became established procedure.[1]

We now have a tentative answer to the two questions posed earlier. Men are willing to pay interest because the money which they borrow enables them to employ other factors, to increase production, and thereby increase their incomes. They have to pay interest because the owner of money could otherwise do the same thing for himself. These answers, however, require further development. How does the borrower decide when it will be to his advantage to seek a loan and to pay for its use? What are the conditions under which the holder of money will surrender it to another in return for a given interest payment?

Interest and Capital

The amount of interest a borrower (usually an entrepreneur representing a firm) can pay will depend upon the plans for using the money. It is true that "idle" money does not multiply in the sense of creating additional income claims. But used to purchase factors of production for the creation of an output of goods and services, it may create additional income claims. This is why we refer to "money capital." How much the borrower can earn by acting in this manner will depend upon the productivity of real capital (in terms of our model the marginal productivity of capital). Translated into strictly economic terminology the criterion would be the *marginal efficiency of capital.* Suppose that the management of a corporation estimates that by purchasing a new machine of modern design it can earn on such an investment (after all additional costs such as depreciation have been paid) a return of seven per cent. If it can borrow money with which to purchase this machine for anything less than seven per cent, then it will be able to increase its profit income. Thus the ratio between the expected return (seven per cent) and the interest rate becomes a measure of the marginal efficiency of capital. The expected returns from the use of capital for investment is therefore related directly to the *demand* for capital.

Such an analysis led earlier economists to classify interest as the *functional return* on capital. Although interest is paid directly for the use

---

[1] The term usury is still used, although its meaning has changed. Today it refers to the charging of interest, but specifically to the charge which is excessive. Most states have laws which specify that moneylenders, particularly those who lend to low-income groups, shall not charge a rate higher than a certain percentage of the value of the loan.

431

of money (or liquid capital), the ability to pay this interest stems ultimately from the use of these funds in production. Even where the money
was used to hire additional workers or to acquire raw materials, but not
to purchase machines, it was classified as *working capital,* a liquid asset
which makes possible the creation of form, place, time, and ownership
utility, and thereby establishes a claim to income.

In the allocation of the factors of production the interest claim
serves as a cue to be acted on by the entrepreneur in deciding between
production for present demand and investment in capital goods which
will result in the expansion of consumer goods and services for future
use. When the marginal efficiency of capital is greater than the prevailing interest rate, it will pay (be profitable) to invest. When the interest
rate is above the marginal efficiency of capital, investments will not be
expected to pay off. Thus the conditions for an equilibrium will be present when the two rates—the marginal productivity of capital and the
interest rate—are equal, or when their ratio is equal to one.

The classical economists illustrated this relationship by means of the
ordinary supply and demand curve. Behind the demand curve for money
capital, and thus determining its shape, would be the estimates of various
firms and industries of their opportunities for making profitable investments. At a very high rate of interest, these would be few. At a very low
rate of interest, there would presumably be many more. Thus the curve
would have a downward slope typical of any other demand curve.

What about the supply curve? The supply of investable funds would
be constituted by the savings of income receivers. Such a supply would
come into existence as a consequence of income being received but not
spent on consumption.

What determines the size of these savings? Economists tried to answer this question in terms of observations or assumptions about human
behavior. They reasoned that people save (abstain from spending on consumption) from present income in order to be able to consume more
later on. However, present consumption is always more attractive than
future consumption. We live in an uncertain world, in which human
life is finite and plans for future consumption may never be realized. On
a *time-preference scale* the present is weighted more heavily than the
future. For this reason the same amount of money available for future
consumption would appear smaller in time perspective than the same
amount spent on present consumption. In balancing a future income with
the present income for consumption purposes, the sum of money for future
spending must be larger than the present sum in order for the two to be
equivalent. Therefore, people save for future consumption purposes when

432

they can anticipate the growth of the saving through the addition each year of a certain increment, which is the interest rate; and the higher that rate, or the larger the expected future income, the greater will be the savings and the supply of capital. Thus the supply of savings or of funds to be invested will be positively related to the interest rate and can be represented by an ordinary supply curve. The market rate of interest under these conditions will tend to equate the marginal efficiency of capital (demand) with the time-preference schedule of households at some point. A rise in the interest rate will encourage saving and discourage investment, while a fall in the interest rate will have the opposite effect. In this way the interest rate brings about a balance between consumption and investment, or the allocation of factors of production between production for present use and production for future use.

Saving represents a postponement of consumption and an anticipation of future income. Accumulated money or generalized property claims against the economy (society) can be made available for lending or investing in future income claims—an "interest" in future production for the saver, and a means to facilitate expanded production by the borrower, who uses it to obtain factor services. In view of the time preference of individuals or households, only the promise of interest will offer a positive inducement to save.

Because different types of enterprise have different prospects for success, or must undertake varying degrees of risk in an uncertain world, lenders will ordinarily expect a higher rate of interest if they loan to an enterprise where there is more risk involved. This accounts for the fact that at any given time there will be a *range of actual interest rates* rather than one interest rate. The differences will be related to the degrees of risk. Ordinarily, the chance for unfavorable surprises to occur will be greater the longer the period of time involved. Thus the long-term interest rate will be higher than the short-term rate.

Pure interest can be conceptualized as the return on a loan if there were no risk. In terms of the preceding analysis, it is the payment for waiting or abstaining from consumption, pure and simple. In experience, the form of investment most free of risk is the obligation of a strong government. That is why interest on government bonds is used as a rough approximation to the pure interest rate. Other interest rates are largely determined from this base.

Interest and Liquidity Preference

Where earlier economists assigned interest (as a functional income claim) finally to capital, and explained it as a necessary claim against production on the grounds that it was a reward for waiting, Keynes used as his starting point a more immediately perceived fact of experience. Interest, he maintained, was a payment for the use of money, the most liquid form of asset or property. It is adequate for an understanding of economic behavior to recognize that it is necessary to pay people interest to persuade them to give up liquid assets. Otherwise, they will prefer to hold cash and avoid risk. Under certain conditions, people prefer to hold cash or near cash. That is why they save. This behavior and its motivation Keynes called liquidity preference. People may be induced to give up their liquid position if they can expect an expanded future income from interest. Saving is not entirely a rational or a calculating form of behavior. People save from habit. This is particularly true in a rich economy such as in the United States, where high income renders saving easy, and those who receive very large incomes would be hard pressed to spend the entire amount even if they tried.

In Part 2, where we discussed the propensity to save, we examined the evidence that as income rises the proportion saved increases. If this is true, then saving depends much more on the level of income than on the interest rate. In other words, the rate of interest is a less important inducement to save than the earlier economists believed.

The desire to hold cash is related to what people ordinarily do with cash. Reasons for holding liquid assets have already been discussed. They were classified as the transactions motive, the contingencies motive, and the speculative motive. During periods of rising income and prices the need to hold cash on two of these accounts will ordinarily increase. With higher prices more pocket money is needed to make ordinary purchases. Unforeseen events, such as sickness and accidents, will also cost more. However, when prices are rising there is no particular advantage in holding cash for speculative purposes. It is more "profitable" to get such funds into real property. Money will be loaned even at a lower rate of interest.

These are the more important influences on the supply side of the liquid funds market. What about the demand side? Here again modern economic analysis gives much less of a role to the interest rate as a factor in production and investment decisions. This is evident during the upswing of the business cycle. Under such conditions business profits are likely to be increasing more rapidly than the prices of the factors of production. Influenced by these profits, entrepreneurs are encouraged to make new investments on which they can ordinarily expect higher returns. In other words, the marginal efficiency of capital will be high. Such investments are the induced investments described earlier. Since the interest payments for the use of borrowed funds are small, relative to the other costs of

434

production, it appears unlikely that the rate of interest can act as any very great deterrent to investment. During the downswing of the business cycle, on the other hand, two of the reasons for holding cash on the part of households and firms will decrease, while the speculative motive will increase. When prices are falling the incentive to have ready cash in order to take advantage of special advantages will be greater. During such periods business firms are likely to be motivated to make an autonomous type of investment, or one which promises to be cost reducing in its effect rather than revenue increasing. However, when business expectations are pessimistic the firm may be willing to undertake investments only if the interest rate is particularly favorable. On the other hand, those with funds to invest may be highly skeptical of business risks and hence unwilling to take less than a given rate of interest, which may be higher than the marginal efficiency of capital. Thus once again the interest rate is given less of a role in bringing about adjustments in the economy, and particularly adjustments between present consumption and investment which looks to future consumption. The over-all impact of this analysis is to reduce the importance of the interest rate as an influence on investment.

Interest and Commercial Banking

Since interest is a payment for the use of liquid claims, no discussion of this distributive share of income would be complete without relating it to the banking and credit institutions. Savings banks, investment banks, insurance companies, and other financial institutions perform the function of bringing savers and investors together. By collecting interest from those who borrow and by paying something less than this amount to the lenders, these institutions earn an income and facilitate the earning of income by the savers. They contribute to production by making it possible for the firm to invest in the capacity to produce.

However, it is the commercial banks with their capacity for "creating" loanable funds that are likely to have the greatest influence on the interest rate (other than that of government), and which are likely to be most responsive to the interest rate when the market is relatively free. These banks receive cash from households and firms which becomes, with the paid-in capital, their reserves. In exchange they create demand deposits. They also create demand deposits by making loans at interest. Operating under a system of fractional reserves (described in detail in Part 2), these banks earn an income by making loans to various types of borrowers, particularly on commercial paper which represents the financing of current production. These deposits are the banks' liabilities. By keeping a close balance between current assets and current liabilities, so that as obligations to the

435

bank are paid off new loans are made, the bank is able to maximize its income. For reasons of safety the bank will ordinarily have in its portfolio assets of a highly liquid character, such as government bonds and high-grade industrial bonds. Interest earned on these investments comes very near to a pure rate of interest, since the purpose of this part of the portfolio is to avoid risk or unnecessary delay in converting the assets into cash if necessary in order to meet the demands made against the bank by its depositors. By raising or lowering the rate of interest, now done largely through the Federal Reserve System, and by encouraging or discouraging borrowing, the banking system has an influence on the volume of production.

The Interest Rate and the Value of Government Bonds

We learned above that interest on government bonds approximates interest in its pure form. During a downswing of business activity, when prices are falling and the risks of engaging in production are great (and liquidity preference is high), savers prefer government bonds paying a low, fixed rate of interest, but providing an income that is secure. If the demand for government bonds is increasing, this will result in a rise in the price of such bonds and a consequent fall in the interest rate. In other words, if a government bond having a par value of $100 pays an interest income of $3.50, any rise in the price of that bond would result in a fall in the *effective rate* of interest, since the higher purchase price of existing bonds would still command only a $3.50 interest income. Conversely, during a business boom, when profits are high and investors are eager to borrow money to invest in production, the demand for government bonds, with their comparatively low return, will decrease and only the most conservative investors will prefer government bonds. Now, however, a fall in the price of a government bond paying a fixed rate of interest will be equivalent to a rise in the interest rate. Let us say that the price of a government bond, maturing in ten years with a par value of $100 and paying $3.50 a year interest, falls to $96.50 in the market. This would mean an effective rise in the interest rate.

Compound Interest

A phenomenon which has long fascinated many as an aspect of the modern pecuniary economy is that of *compound interest*. The way in which it operates can be defined essentially as follows: If a given sum of money is loaned out at interest, and if the interest is allowed to accumulate (being added to the principal sum at certain intervals, so that it too begins to earn an interest), at some specified date in the future the original sum will have

436

expanded by a predictable amount. Tables have been constructed which tell us how much one dollar invested now will be worth at some future date, say ten years, if the interest is compounded annually or semiannually.

There is an almost magical quality to the picture. As would be expected, the growth curve of such a value rises at an increasing rate. In other words, the original sum grows at an increasing rate as the time during which interest accumulates increases. As an interesting game, mathematicians have sometimes calculated what one cent placed on compound interest at the beginning of the Christian era would be worth today, if it had been allowed to accumulate. The sum is astronomical.

The educational or advertising programs of banks stress to the saver the magic of letting money work for him. Superficially, at least, it would almost appear that the observations of Aristotle and the scholastic philosophers who maintained that money was barren are contradicted by experience. Lest one be fooled by appearances, however, it is necessary to know just what is implied by these figures. Before this money claim can behave in the fashion described, it would have to be used continuously to facilitate production and the generation of real income. It is the cumulative growth of the capacity of an economy to produce which makes possible the creation of these cumulative claims. The flaw in the example of one cent being invested at the beginning of the Christian era is that there has never been such a long-run, uninterrupted growth in the capacity of society to produce to that extent. In this time span production plans have often been interrupted by wars, revolutions, the complete overturn of many property institutions, and the passing of many generations of peoples, whose interests in income could not possibly extend much beyond a normal lifetime.

Profits

Profit theory is the least satisfactory of all the theories of functional distribution, and is perhaps the area with least agreement. The classical economists, reasoning from their model of perfect competition, concluded that in the long run, under conditions of general equilibrium, profit in the *pure sense* would not exist. While they believed that the hope of profit was essential to get goods produced, such hope in their ideal world of an enterprise economy was doomed to continuous frustration. Under conditions of monopoly, profit can and does exist, although completely "undeserved" as far as a functional claim to income goes.

Professor F. H. Knight, in one of the more exhaustive analyses of the phenomenon, concluded that profits rest upon the function of "uncertainty bearing." In a world where the future cannot be exactly predicted, to act requires that we act blindly or on the basis of incomplete and imperfect information. Those who undertake the production of goods in anticipation of sales (the entrepreneurs), risking their property on the outcome of a venture, are the ones who earn and get the profits on the successful ventures. Some of these situations can be identified.

Profits Defined

In assigning income claims to specific functions, it is necessary that both the share and the function be identified as precisely as possible. We will note at the outset the ambiguity of the term profit in everyday speech.

Profit is often used as if it were synonymous with *net* business income. This is the accountant's definition, and it designates what remains of gross income after all expenses or costs owed outside the firm have been met. It does not ordinarily allow imputed costs.[2] If a building is owned debt-free by the firm, no rental charge is subtracted from net income. If the firm's cash, rather than funds borrowed from a bank, was used as working capital, no interest is charged.

Here we have an anomaly. Two firms with identical outputs and identical efficiency would show different profits, if one firm owned its own building and used its own cash, while the other firm rented the building and borrowed its working capital. This is not to say that the accountant is in error for doing what he does. His job is to determine the net income of the *business*. Whether it be assigned finally to capital, to management, or to pure profit does not interest the accountant. His designation of net income as profit is only misleading when used for functional analysis.

By profit the economist understands the net income of a firm or an owner after all costs including imputed costs have been deducted. This is pure profit. Thus defined, on what can such an income be said to rest? Suppose a firm has been producing an output which has a stable demand, earning an income which just covers all costs of doing business. Capital is earning the "going rate," management receives a salary equal to anything it might earn elsewhere, and the liquid funds used for working capital earn an interest return equal to the going rate. All other costs have been met. The net income is zero. Now suppose the management of the business decides to start production of a totally untried product. Production costs are incurred, an investment in advertising is made, and the firm embarks on a campaign to get customers for the new product. If the product goes

---

[2] An imputed cost is a cost to the firm which is not associated with an outside transaction. It is arrived at through an imaginary transaction between the firm and the owner.

438

well and there is no other competition in the field, the price obtained is such as to bring in earnings much greater than had previously been experienced. By deducting all costs, including imputed costs, there is now a profit residue. Can this be linked to any specified product or service? As a consequence of the action taken, consumers are now supplied with a product which they did not previously have. From their action in buying we can infer an increase in or the experience of a new satisfaction.

This is what economists mean by an *innovation,* and the returns called profits can be linked to this type of activity. Ordinarily, such gains from an innovation will not be of long duration. Unless there exists some kind of monopoly control to prevent others from entering the field, sooner or later imitators seeking the same type of return will offer competition either through a duplicate item or a close substitute, which will over the longer period reduce earnings. An innovation in the form of some cost-reducing invention gives the innovator an advantage in the market for a short period. If the advantage of a particular firm originates from a patented process or from the ownership of a resource of superior productivity, this advantage may continue for a longer period. In such cases the profit income of the firm resembles the rents discussed in the last chapter. In other words, such advantages are related to what we may call the dynamics of a changing world, in which special advantages, not entirely possible to predict, redound to the advantage of a few. They may be buttressed and protected by an institutional or property arrangement established prior to the new development. This is what is suggested by the expression, frequently used in economics, that "profits are dynamic in their origin and institutional in their appropriation."

Even such profits are unlikely to persist indefinitely. Particularly is this true today, when the existence of strong labor unions makes it likely that demands will be made for an increasing share in this profit income. Public opinion, in the face of what is regarded as exorbitant profit, is likely through the agency of government to sanction regulation which reduces such profit. If this does not occur, even the fear that it might occur tends to exert a leavening effect on the fullest exploitation of profit advantage.

Corporate Profits

Today the largest aggregation of profit is in net corporate income. The 200 largest corporate organizations conduct a major part of that research which is the most important source of innovation. Financed on a long-run basis, these laboratories are able to turn out a succession of innovations which tend to secure to the firm a continuing profit. Part of this is now siphoned off by heavy corporate income taxes. Of that which remains,

439

part is paid over to the owners of the corporations, and part is used to finance the internal expansion of the firm.

To whom do these profits belong under existing institutional arrangements? Legally, they are the property of those who own the common stock. An examination of the record of dividend payments will show, however, that less than half of these profits are returned to these legal owners. Of the remainder, some are used rather frequently to pay bonuses to those who exercise the executive and management function. Most of it, however, is retained in the business, either to provide reserves against less prosperous times or to finance the development of increased production.

When it is thus invested, this fund is returned to the income flow in the form of wages, salaries, and payment for other materials. In periods of high-level employment and income, at least, a substantial part of corporate profits do not represent a final income assignment, but re-enter the income stream, where they contribute to other income claims which may be finally assigned.

Discussion
Questions

1. Explain the difference between time preference and liquidity preference as the hypothetical basis of interest. Why is it necessary to pay interest? Why are people willing to pay interest?

2. What is the present-day connotation of the term usury?

3. Why do people save? (Turn to pages 146–47 in Part 2 and review the discussion there.)

4. What do you understand by the term marginal productivity of capital? How would you relate this concept to the marginal efficiency of investment?

5. Profit has sometimes been defined as a payment for risk bearing. Can you distinguish between risk and uncertainty bearing? See pages 319 to 323 for discussion of risk. Is there a relation between innovations and uncertainty bearing?

6. Long-run profits, not associated with innovations, are similar to economic rent. Discuss.

CHAPTER 28

Personal or Household Income Distribution

PERSONAL OR HOUSEHOLD income distribution is simpler to define in an operational sense than is functional distribution. It is the amount of money or the value of new claims which "comes in" during a given period to an individual or to the household which that individual heads. Where more than one member of the family earns such an income, it is the sum of all such claims made available to the household during the income period.

The simplest concept of personal income distribution can be obtained by dividing aggregate national income by the total population or by the number of spending units in the nation. These are figures we often see quoted as *per capita income* or average family income. In 1956 these were $1,935 and $5,600 in current prices respectively, before taxes. All these figures tell us is how much individuals or households would have received if the national income had been distributed equally. However, since this is a hypothetical case, these concepts are limited in their use. To get the information needed for present purposes is more difficult, and the results not so neat. We must, in fact, begin our inquiry from the other end. This means the collection of information from the basic units, assembling and arranging it so that the resulting statistics preserve more of the details of the actual distribution.

Budget Studies as Sources of Information

Facts on household income distribution are not easy to obtain. People are often reluctant to give information on their personal incomes. Investigators in other areas of the social sciences have been able to collect data on the most intimate details of individual behavior, but ask a man how much money he made last year and his response is likely to vary from evasion to outright refusal to answer. When the Bureau of the Census, in preparation for the 1950 decennial census, announced that figures on income would be requested from every tenth household contacted, there was a storm of protest. Important as this information may be for many purposes, both public and private, it is still regarded as an invasion of an individual's private life to try to find out about it. Such reactions are not easy to explain. They are no doubt culturally determined, reflecting a long history of resistance to attempts by tax collectors (often representing an arbitrary and not very sympathetic government) to discover new sources of wealth against which to levy tribute. Moreover, in a society such as ours, where status, security, and self-evaluation are closely associated with income, responses to questions about the size or amounts of earnings are very often psychologically determined. Information obtained will contain deviations from fact that range from outright lies to lack of knowledge due to inadequate records and short memories. Respondents may fear that their friends, their wives, or the government may discover their earnings, and for one reason or another they may not want the facts known.

Skilled interviewers, using questionnaires that are carefully designed and adroitly administered, do obtain information that is both reliable and usable. To gather information in this way, however, is costly, and accounts for the fact that all-inclusive studies of income distribution have seldom been made. Using modern sampling techniques, carefully designed so that errors will be distributed at random (and hence tend to cancel each other out), estimates can be made which have a reliability that is at least better than conjecture. These are supplemented by information of various types from indirect sources such as consumer purchases, savings, and income tax returns. Because so many now pay income taxes, whereas formerly only a few had that privilege, the Bureau of Internal Revenue has become an increasingly rich source of knowledge about personal incomes. Because of exemptions, loopholes written into the law, and the possibilities of evasion, the raw data of income tax returns cannot be taken at face value, however. They are important supplementary sources for our knowledge about the incomes of households.

Before discussing the more important studies of household income distribution, we will examine some of the difficulties involved in framing a concept of personal income. It can be defined as the claims against goods and services which become available to a household during a given period, usually a year. In our society this ordinarily means a money claim. We will ignore for the time being attempts to convert these money claims into real income, since that will be our problem in Part 5. Here our purpose is to derive a money value which represents the final claim of the household from all sources.

If a family received its entire income in the form of wages and sal-

442

aries paid weekly or monthly, it could, by simply adding up its pay slips, arrive at a definite figure. The same would be true of dividends, rents, pensions, cash gifts, government benefits, and gains from any increase in the price of assets carried over from a previous period, but sold during the year. In the case of assets whose value has increased, there is a problem in assigning the income to a particular year, since this gain has taken place over several income periods. To assign it all to the year in which the gain is finally realized by being converted into cash will overstate income for that year. The researcher who is investigating income distribution must make allowances for this.

Another problem arises in connection with income in kind. This is a form of income in addition to the goods and services which members of a household provide for each other, and which, as was indicated in Part 2, are largely ignored for income purposes. The term used to designate this is *household production,* and it is neglected chiefly because it does not pass through a market and cannot be valued for that reason. *Income in kind* is something different. It occurs chiefly in agriculture, where products which might have been sold are used for home consumption. This poses a practical problem of determining a money value for such goods. Should the products consumed at home be valued at a price the family would have received had the items been sold? Or should the price be what the farm family would have paid had it purchased the goods from the market, paying the markup which urban consumers would have paid for the same items. The decision must be an arbitrary one, and the practice usually followed is to value these goods at market price to the farmer. Thus, in estimating the income of the household, the value of goods produced and consumed at home is added to whatever is received in cash. Farm households therefore have an advantage not apparent on the face of most income estimates, and this fact needs to be taken into account when the generally lower income level of farmers is considered.

Budget Studies

Estimates of the income of particular groups in a society, as well as of a representative sample of households for an entire nation, are usually referred to as *budget studies,* or as income and expenditure studies. These studies have usually had other objectives than the knowledge of income distribution. They are used for determining the weights to be used in price indices, and for determining comparative levels of living. As a result, they are more representative of lower- and middle-income groups than of the higher-income groups.

There are on record a few studies of income distribution, particularly

443

among the lower-income groups, which date from the early years of the Industrial Revolution. Gregory King, a Mercantilist, made some studies in Europe during the latter half of the seventeenth century, and the Reverend David Davies made studies of the very poor in different parishes in England. It was the work of Frederick Le Play (1806–1882) in France and his student and follower Ernst Engel (1821–1896) in Prussia, both empiricists and engineers, that provided the inspiration for later budget studies. Carroll D. Wright, a statistician who headed the Massachusetts Bureau of Labor Statistics from 1873 to 1885, and then became U.S. Commissioner of Labor, was inspired by the work of these two Europeans and others to undertake the earliest budget studies in the United States. Between 1888 and the outbreak of World War I a spate of income and expenditure studies were made in various cities and industries to determine, among other things, the earnings of workers. Parallel studies were made in Europe for the purpose of comparing incomes of American workers with those of European workers (this was inspired, in part, by the desires of manufacturers who were concerned with competition from foreign goods). During World War I, induced largely by the rise in prices and cost of living, income and expenditure studies were undertaken in response to the demands of organized labor for higher wages. They argued that higher incomes were needed to maintain the efficiency of workers in war industries.

As statistical and interviewing techniques improved in this century, an increasing number of special studies (carried on by both private and public agencies) were able to provide greater detail in our knowledge of income distribution. However, it was in 1935–36 that the most ambitious study ever undertaken in the United States was made. This was a survey of the distribution of income and expenditures which sampled all income groups in the country. A co-operative project among the Bureau of Labor Statistics, the Bureau of Home Economics, the National Resources Committee, and the Central Statistical Board, the sample included some 300,-000 families from different income groups, occupations, and areas. Estimates based on these data were eventually made for 29.4 million families and about 10 million single persons living alone or as lodgers. This represented about 91 per cent of the households of the country at that time. Since then sample surveys by various government agencies have provided a basis for revising the findings of the 1935–36 study.

Immediately following World War II the Federal Reserve System sponsored a continuing study of household incomes together with other aspects of consumer finances. Using the most up-to-date sampling methods and interviewing techniques, this research program has provided us with one of the most useful continuing estimates of household-income distribution on a year-to-year basis. With information from various other sources, which include the greatly expanded research programs of government agencies, universities, and private organizations, we now have more reliable statistics on income distribution than previously. Many gaps still exist between our knowledge of aggregate functional income estimates and household income, but that gap appears to be narrowing.

What the Studies Show

The 1935–36 income-expenditure study was conducted at a time when the effects of the great depression were still widespread. It showed considerable concentration of income distribution. When all households together were considered, more than two-thirds received in that year less than $1,500. City incomes ranged somewhat higher, and in New York about two-thirds of the consumer units had incomes below $2,000. The highest 5 per cent of the households for the whole United States received 27 per cent of the aggregate income. This was nearly as much as was available to the lowest 60 per cent of consumer units. This also was a time when the total national income was $56.8 billion, and unemployment was nearly 11 million. With nearly 20 per cent of the labor force unemployed, and with a farm income of less than $5 billion, these figures on income claims probably should not have occasioned the surprise they did.

As an aid in representing the facts of household income distribution, economists make use of the Lorenz curve (Figure 39). The percentage of income received is measured along the vertical axis. The percentage of households receiving a given percentage of income is measured along the horizontal axis. If income were equally distributed, the resulting curve would be the straight line shown on the diagram, rising at a forty-five-degree angle from the point of origin. On this curve 10 per cent of the households would reveive 10 per cent of the income, 20 per cent would receive 20 per cent of the income, and so forth. Actual distribution of income among households would be shown on a curve concave upward. The greater the dip of this curve toward the right-hand corner, the more unequal would be the income distribution. Estimated income distribution for three selected years is given on the chart.

On the basis of the best evidence we have, during the years since 1935–36 we have had not only a rapid increase in the size of the national income, but also a greater equalization in its distribution among households. A study by Simon Kuznets for the National Bureau of Economic Research points up the magnitude of some of these changes. Studies of the 1929 income distribution indicated that the highest 5 per cent of the

445

Figure 39. Distribution of Income in the United States
Measured by Lorenz Curve, 1935-36, 1948, and 1955

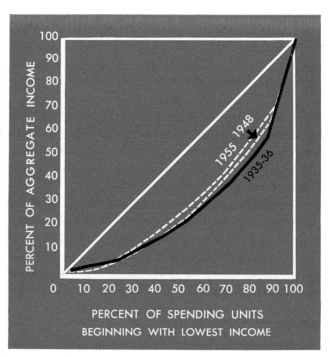

Source: Data from National Resources Committee, *Consumer Incomes in the United States*, Washington, 1938, p. 96; *Federal Reserve Bulletin*, Jan., 1950, p. 23; and *Statistical Abstract of the United States, 1957*, p. 309.

income recipients received 34 per cent of the total disposable income of individuals or households. This was after the deduction of Federal income tax payments. Ten years later the share of this group had dropped to 27 per cent of total income. In 1946 the proportionate share was 18 per cent. Comparing 1929 and 1946, the share going to the top 5-per cent group declined 16 points.

By reducing income inequality for the top 5 per cent by a total of 16 points out of a possible 29 points, the income concentration at the upper level has been reduced by a little more than half. When the top 1 per cent instead of the top 5 per cent is considered, the reduction has been even more pronounced. This group in 1929 received 19.1 per cent of the total national income, in 1946 only 7.7 per cent. Thus at the very top the reduction in the concentration of income distribution is about two-thirds. Of course, these two classes represent only two points of a Lorenz curve of

446

income distribution in the United States, and the estimates cannot be treated as absolutes; nevertheless, they do indicate an important change in household claims against income in the United States. As Arthur F. Burns has pointed out, in the annual report of the National Bureau of Economic Research where these findings are reported, this amounts to something of a social revolution and perhaps one of the great shifts in social relationships of history.

While substantial inequalities still exist, if the full range of income distribution is considered, there can be no mistaking the fact that in recent years the growth of the total level of national income has been associated with a trend toward less inequality. There is evidence, too, that the changes in distribution have occurred chiefly near the middle of a Lorenz curve, which means that the middle-income groups have gained in relation to both ends of the distribution array.

What has brought about this significant shift in the income claims of households? To ask this question is to inquire into the nature of other changes in the economic or income relations in our society which are associated with such a change. To answer it we will do well to consider some of the factors which have always been identified with the existence of the unequal distribution of income among households.

Inequality in Household Distribution

In our analysis of functional distribution we have already examined the relationship between productivity and the price, or functional income claim, of the factors of production. Productivity in the human factor, it was pointed out, can be loosely identified with ability or skills, provided these terms can be defined to relate to the contributions to production. Fertility of land, favorable location, effectiveness of machine and plant design, relative scarcity of resources, and exclusiveness of property rights were identified as influences affecting relative productivity and the functional income claim of the other factors.

Household income, which may be derived from a combination of different types of functional claims, can be expected to vary according to the quality and quantity of the factors it owns or controls. Since nearly 80 per cent of all income claims can be traced to human skills, circumstances which affect those skills can be regarded as important in determining household income. If the earning members of the household are very young or very old, their capacity to contribute to production will be less than that of the heads of households who are in the middle years of their productive life. Those with no schooling receive less income than those possessing a technical education. Those who from choice, lack of oppor-

447

tunity, or lack of learning capacity have failed to develop their skills will ordinarily be found in the lower-income class, and their households the recipients of smaller claims against the rest of the economy.

In an industrial society such as ours, with its advanced technological development and the concentration of the industries in urban centers, the statistics on income show higher incomes in cities than in rural areas. This can perhaps be described as a kind of social dividend which accrues to people who share in the benefits of co-operative economic effort, characterized by a high degree of specialization, division of labor, and possibilities for more efficient production. Prices and costs of living are higher in the cities too, a factor tending to reduce real-income differences. This in turn may be again offset by greater public contributions to the household. Cities, in general, provide better schools, sanitation and health facilities, clinics, public parks, art galleries, recreation, and other facilities, which are similar to income in kind and reduce the household requirements for money income.

Households headed by women will ordinarily have lower earnings than those headed by men. This is because of two influences. In the first place, most women do not seek or receive training to equip them for the higher-paying professional and management positions. Because a large majority of women usually become housewives, parents do not feel justified in making any investment in this sort of training. For the same reason professional schools and professional associations discourage the use of limited facilities for training persons who may not use the training once they have it. Secondly, there is evidence to support the claims of women that in our culture they are discriminated against. Traditionally, woman's place has been in the home, and even though in the long run an increasing number of women have sought employment, the existence of this tradition helps to explain why women workers receive lower pay for the same jobs than men. Many women go into primary and secondary school teaching, a profession which has long had a relatively low valuation in our society.

Household incomes also differ with location. In other words, when we arrange the information we have on personal-income distribution, it falls into different patterns according to geographic location. Plotted on a map of the United States, shaded to bring out state and regional income distribution, a pattern emerges (Figure 40). While we are not justified in saying that geography causes income differences, the arrangement we see is useful if we can link these patterns to other influences already discussed. Areas with large urban concentrations will show up high on the scale of average-household or per capita income distribution.

448

The industrial northeast, most industrialized states of the east central area, such as Ohio, Michigan, and Illinois, together with the west coast area, will be relatively high on such a scale. Middlewestern and south central states occupy a middle position, while the lowest income area will be found in the south and southeastern part of the country. Nevada, a state of sparse population and rich mineral resources, occupies a high place on the income distribution scale. In 1929 such a map would have shown almost the entire southeastern section as a great white expanse, indicating a very low level of income. Since that time shifts have taken place, and the vast blank space is now mottled with some evidence of an increase in income distributed to that area. In the predominantly agricultural areas those with the most fertile land, the richest mineral deposits, and the relatively low concentration of population will show up highest on our income-measuring rod.

Another set of statistics on income distribution in the United States can be used to highlight an important aspect of social relations in our very complex society. This is in the field of race relations. The best evidence we have shows a rather wide income variation closely associated with racial groups, particularly the Negro and Spanish-American. While there are exceptions, and in recent years the differences have been reduced, household income among these minority groups is to be found rather consistently in the lower brackets. This is in part related to productivity. A high proportion of the Negro population in the United States is concentrated in the deep south, an area which is itself characterized by low incomes. If the Negro households are arrayed and related to the geographic areas where they live, the lowest income concentrations will be found in southern rural communities where more than 50 per cent of the Negro households (in the budget studies of 1935–36) received annual incomes of less than $500. Cities in the same area show the Negro families there to have slightly higher income claims and the north central cities provided an average household income of $1,000 or more for nearly 50 per cent of such families. These families are concentrated in areas where school facilities and other opportunities for training are poorest. A long history of segregation in the schools has relegated the minority groups to the poorest schools even in that underprivileged area. Thus, while it can be said that the productivity of these groups largely determines their income, such an analysis does not go very deeply into some important problems which are reflected in unequal income distribution.

The Influence of Property

When household-income distribution data are arranged on a scale corre-

Figure 40. Per Capita Income Payments by States, 1955

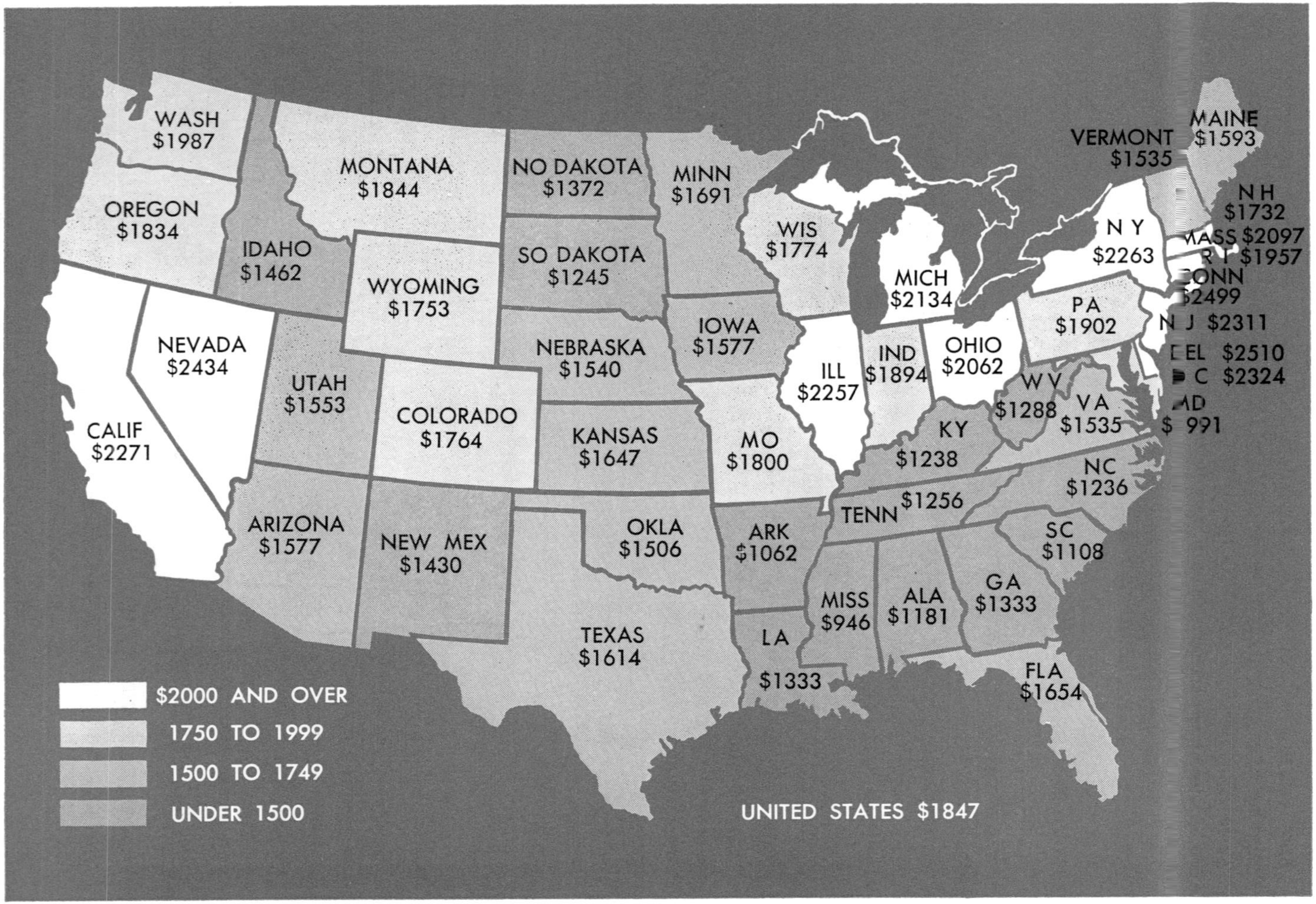

WASH $1987
OREGON $1834
CALIF $2271
NEVADA $2434
IDAHO $1462
UTAH $1553
ARIZONA $1577
MONTANA $1844
WYOMING $1753
COLORADO $1764
NEW MEX $1430
NO DAKOTA $1372
SO DAKOTA $1245
NEBRASKA $1540
KANSAS $1647
OKLA $1506
TEXAS $1614
MINN $1691
IOWA $1577
MO $1800
ARK $1062
LA $1333
WIS $1774
ILL $2257
IND $1894
MICH $2134
OHIO $2062
KY $1238
TENN $1256
MISS $946
ALA $1181
GA $1333
SC $1108
NC $1236
FLA $1654
VERMONT $1535
N Y $2263
PA $1902
W VA $1288
VA $1535
MAINE $1593
N H $1732
MASS $2097
R I $1957
CONN $2499
N J $2311
DEL $2510
MD $ 991
C $2324

UNITED STATES $1847

$2000 AND OVER
1750 TO 1999
1500 TO 1749
UNDER 1500

sponding to each of the variables described above, certain relationships appear to hold, although in most cases our knowledge is far from complete and difficult to generalize. There is one factor, however, which does appear to be more positively associated with differences in income than any other single variable. That is property ownership. Income and property, of course, are not independent of each other. In a relatively free society, where the chance operations of the market are not interfered with, there is a tendency for the effects of property holdings to become cumulative. We often hear it said that "it takes money to make money." While the implication of this statement is broader than money as such, property holdings which are the basis of credit give great freedom of action in earning an income. Studies of great family fortunes show that substantial property holdings passed on from generation to generation are important in keeping members of those families high on the distribution scale.

There is another common expression which says that "from shirt sleeves to shirt sleeves requires about three generations." Many examples can be cited to support the conclusion that the children and grandchildren of those who, through good fortune, thrift, hard work, good management, and high-income motivation, have amassed a fortune often possess fewer of these qualities than their forebears. When they come into possession of a substantial property, therefore, they rather quickly dissipate it. However, trusteeships, professional investment services, hired management, and other institutionalizations of estates have offset this tendency. The history of many of the great family fortunes will back up this observation.

Studies of the graduates of universities and colleges show a notable tendency for the "products" of the "Ivy League" schools to outdistance the other institutions. Many of these graduates, and sons and daughters of graduates, come from families of substantial means, and not the least of the advantages of the old school tie are the contacts and connections which are useful in later life, as far as income advantages are concerned.

Let us examine some of the evidence of the influence of property. Statistics from the U.S. Treasury Department show that in 1930, 98 per cent of incomes greater than $1 million had their origin in property claims, while only 2 per cent came from personal service. For incomes between $25,000 and $50,000, 70 per cent came from property and 30 per cent from personal service. In the $5,000 to $10,000 group, 38 per cent of the income was traceable to property, while 62 per cent was from personal service; and in the $1,000 to $2,000 class, only 18 per cent came from property and 82 per cent from personal service. Below $1,000, however, the trend shown in the above figures is reversed. Property again becomes of increasing importance. This is because many of those receiving relatively low annual incomes are old people, retired and living on the small savings they have built up over a lifetime in insurance policies or holdings of other types of property. They are also the widows and orphans of modest inheritance.

W. I. King, reporting in 1927 on the distribution of wealth, estimated concentrations of wealth or property claims as follows: the wealthiest 2 per cent owned 40 per cent of property; the middle 33 per cent owned 45 per cent of property; and the poorest 65 per cent owned 15 per cent of property. In that year property concentration corresponded fairly closely to the range of income variation.

We have already noted some important modifications in income distribution. Can we find to what extent shifts in distribution are related to modifications in the institutions of property? Since property in any society is secured for its owners through the laws and institutions of government, it is to government and changes in public policy that we will look for hypotheses concerning these shifts. There is some evidence that they can be traced to (1) the increasing role of government itself in the taxing and spending of income; (2) the greater reliance of government on the income tax, which has more and more been graduated to tax away a higher proportion of large income; (3) the use of inheritance and gift taxes, which reduce the size of property concentrations passed on from generation to generation; (4) the growth of Social Security and other measures, which have compelled large groups of income receivers to accumulate claims in various retirement funds; and (5) the fortuitous circumstances such as war and government defense spending which have resulted in the longest sustained period of high-level employment in our history. Other measures, such as control of the interest rates, taxes on "excess profits," and rent control, have had the effect of retarding increases in income based largely upon property holdings. We will examine each of these in turn.

The Increasing Role of Government

By the increasing role of government we mean an expansion of the public economy, so that a larger proportion of income flows through the public sector and is allocated by agencies of the state. Taxes reduce the disposable income of those from whom it is collected. Spending by government generates income for households and firms, and these may be different groups from those who benefit from an undisturbed private spending.

452

An expanding public economy results in an increasing allocation of resources to the production of goods and services comprising the government part of the national product. Real income and levels of living may change as a result of this expansion, depending upon what groups actually use public properties and services. A shift of shore line from private to public beaches, for example, will increase the real levels of income for lower-income groups and reduce those of the higher.

The spending and distribution of money income in the private economy may also be changed. There has long been a certain stability of income derived from government sources. Authorized spending by government agencies frequently precedes the raising of revenue, and much of it is assured from year to year. Government employment has been generally recognized as providing a secure, if not always generous, income. But because of its stability, public employees over a lifetime frequently experience a greater total income, and business in areas with a large number of public employees often shows great stability.

Government, particularly the Federal government, has ready access to credit, and when it is used the effect is to stimulate investment. When used in a compensatory manner to maintain employment and income, the effect is to increase the long-run income of those at the lowest level by preventing the erosion of income, and perhaps more important the wiping out of small savings, through unemployment.

Income Taxes

Since 1914 the Federal income tax has become a principal means for raising revenue. From its inception a certain minimum income has always been exempted from the tax. Above that minimum the tax rate rises progressively, so that those receiving higher incomes pay a larger percentage in taxes. This tax, then, becomes an instrument for reducing the inequality of disposable income. Over the years the progressiveness has been increased, particularly during and after World War II.

A number of states and some cities use the income tax, although many of these are much less progressive, and some are actually regressive—a point which will be developed in the next chapter.

In terms of a total tax structure, progressive or graduated taxes must be set off against taxes that fall most heavily on incomes at the lowest level, together with income transfers to the higher-income groups— interest on the public debt, for example. There is no universal agreement among experts concerning the net effect of taxation on personal income distribution, although considerable evidence exists to indicate greater equalization.

453

Inheritance and Gift Taxes

Taxes on estates, inheritances, and gifts have long been used in Western industrial countries to influence income distribution by reducing concentration of property ownership. Originally little more than the cost of a seal with which to validate the documents to permit property transfers at the time of death, these taxes have tended to become more progressive. They are effective in that they reduce the concentration of property income which we have already noted as a significant influence on the concentration of personal-income distribution.

Social Security Measures

The term *social security* refers to action by some agency of the state to set up or accumulate funds over a period of time for particular individuals or groups. This can be regarded as an automatic or involuntary form of saving out of income. These funds become property or income transfers from certain individuals to others, or for the same individual from present income to income in some future period.

For example, Workmen's Compensation is based on an accumulation of funds (through a special tax) from industry to be used in providing an income to those incapacitated in industrial accidents. Unemployment Insurance operates on funds accumulated primarily from employers (while the worker is employed), to be paid out when the employee is laid off. Old Age and Survivors Insurance operates on funds collected by government to provide for a continued income for retired workers or for surviving members of a family in case of death of the income earner.

High-Level Employment

It is at least arguable that an important factor in bringing about a greater income equality in the United States since World War II has been the particular combination of circumstances resulting in stable, high-level employment. By whatever means that employment has been maintained without serious setback, it has meant sustained use of most of the factors of production, with a resulting output of goods and services of all kinds much greater than for any comparable period in the past.

Unemployment contributes heavily to inequality of income distribution. The first to lose their jobs are usually the relatively unskilled, those already in the low-income brackets. Other workers with modest savings (property holdings) are forced to liquidate these during unemployment. This has kept them from realizing even modest property incomes.

High-level industrial income has meant a sustained demand for food and fibre, the output of agriculture. This, coupled with certain

454

government supports and subsidies to agriculture, has meant some gain for farmers, who are in another low-income group.

At times in these postwar years government has acted to control the rise in such functional income returns as rents, interest, and the profits of incorporated businesses. It has transferred income to veterans, many of whom would fall in the lower-income groups. These are mostly the negative influences on income concentration. On the positive side we could list the upward mobility of workers, from lower-paying to higher-paying skills, during periods of relative labor scarcity. Veterans who took advantage of the educational opportunities offered under the G.I. Bill thereby increased their productivity and ultimately their incomes.

Discussion
Questions

1. Why is reliable information about household or personal income distribution more difficult to obtain than data on wages, interest, rents, or profits?

2. J. K. Galbraith, in his *The Affluent Society,* argues that the problem of poverty, of unequal income distribution, is of much less concern than it was a half-century ago. Why might this be true?

3. Personal income depends not only upon personal ability, but also upon the ability of your ancestors, on where you were born, and upon race and sex. Discuss.

4. Both the high- and the low-income groups depend rather heavily on property income. Discuss.

5. From Figure 40, find the per capita income of the District of Columbia. Compare with other areas. Would you expect this income to be more or less stable than that for other areas? Explain.

CHAPTER 29

Government Income

THROUGH THE INSTRUMENT of taxes, local, state, and national governments appropriate for their use money claims owned by individuals, or by firms in which the ultimate ownership rests with individuals. These taxes are usually paid annually, although payments may be made in installments. When these claims are spent they become income to persons in the present or in the immediate future. Sometimes they are balanced by return transfers to the same people at some future date.

The factors of production which are allocated through the public economy by the use of taxes (and government credit or borrowing), create the services we receive from government agencies. What these services are and how taxes are spent will be discussed in Part 5.

Special Characteristics of Government Income

There is a difference between our purchase of government services and the things we buy in the private economy. This difference centers on the act of choice. In the case of most government services we are not permitted to weigh the pros and cons of spending our money for them rather than for something else. There is no balancing of· the merits of paying or not paying taxes; either we pay them, or our property is confiscated, or we go to jail. (We have already noted that in estimating the national product, since there is no market for such services, the value of government production is entered in the aggregate accounts at actual cost— whatever has been necessary in taxes and borrowing to pay for them.)

The methods of raising and spending tax funds are such that a direct comparison between the services received and the amount paid by the individual is difficult to make. Decisions to spend are made by the elected representatives of the particular government or taxing unit, usually on the basis of what is judged necessary or desirable by the body politic. At

456

the local and state levels, tax levies may be voted upon directly, as when residents of a school district vote on a special bond issue to build a new building or to provide playground facilities. Residents of a city may vote on the desirability of improvements, such as parks or boulevards, and the citizens of an entire state may be asked to vote upon a measure which proposes a tax increase for welfare purposes or other services. Otherwise, citizens participate in these decisions through their votes for candidates, or through influencing their elected representatives. To the individual, therefore, the actual decisions to spend are remote and indirect. Decisions to spend are usually made in advance of tax collections, so that direct comparisons between services and costs are difficult.

The Long-Run Growth of Government Expenditures

Newspapers unfriendly to the political party in power and associations of large taxpayers are among those who sometimes call attention to the contrast between the present government budget and that in George Washington's time. Needless to say, the amount of money which passes through the hands of government agencies has expanded greatly. It is doubtful, however, that such a comparison serves any very useful purpose, since so much in our national life has changed, that any contrast between periods so widely separated is almost meaningless.

Other less dramatic comparisons tell a similar story, although the relationships are easier to conceptualize. Since the turn of the century the proportion (as well as the total amount) of government income has increased. In 1909 expenditures by all government bodies were equivalent to roughly 7 per cent of gross national product. Compared with earlier periods (although our data are not nearly so reliable), this seemed like gross extravagance to some. However, the proportion in 1925 was 11 per cent and by 1956 was 19 per cent. In 1952 the figure was slightly more than 22 per cent, but by 1956 was back to 19.4 per cent.

The rate of increase has not been constant. The curve representing public expenditures is characterized by a number of sharp peaks, each representing one of the major wars in which this country has been involved. Following each of these periods, the curve drops again, but has never returned to the level of the prewar period.

The fact of increased government expenditure and of increased tax collections need not be labored. They are part of the experience of all of us. More people have demanded of government that it do more things,

457

and when it does, workers, raw materials, finished goods, machines, and public buildings are required. Even with no increase in services, the role of government would necessarily have expanded as population grew. But with growth has come urbanization—millions of people crowded together in relatively small areas—and merely keeping order, safeguarding health, and protecting persons and property require proportionally greater effort and expenditures. These things, however, do not explain all of the cumulative expansion we have had. The jars and tensions of a complex society go far to explain the increase. Wars and the threat of wars have been dominant factors. The obligations to veterans, the debts to those who contributed their labor and property in wartime represent the claims of many against the nation as a whole, which only the agency of government can discharge. A slowly rising price level has had a significant impact on the actual size of government expenditure, as it has on all values.

Finally, experience indicates that tasks which cannot be done by individuals and small groups can be accomplished by all working together. This is likely to be the procedure in the democratic countries when there are wide differences in wealth and income. There is a story told of Lloyd George, Liberal Prime Minister of Great Britain, which illustrates the point. George had presented to Parliament a bill calling for increased expenditures for social welfare purposes. Asked from the floor, "Where will you get the money?" he swung around and pointed to the right side of the chamber where the Tories, representatives for the most part of the well-to-do, were seated, and replied, "We will get it there, where the money is."

Organized pressure groups working through their representatives in government have discovered the means to achieve their ends through collective action. Their representatives in turn have responded by applying taxes "where the money is." This has meant a search for an expanding tax base, to which a tax rate can be applied with the expectation of raising more revenue.

Tax Bases and Rates

Literally, the *tax base* is the thing taxed. Ultimately, of course, taxes are paid by persons, and the money which is paid as taxes comes out of someone's income. The amount of tax is determined by multiplying the base by some *rate*. Table 23 tells the story of government revenues given as totals for selected years. Methods of raising these funds have varied, but the collections, like government expenditures, have risen steadily through the years.

Table 23. Total Tax Revenue for Selected Years
(millions of dollars)

Fiscal Years*	Total	Federal	State	Local
1902	1,386	526	156	794
1913	2,272	663	301	1,308
1922	7,586	3,570	947	3,069
1927	9,562	3,475	1,608	4,479
1932	7,971	1,807	1,890	4,274
1934	8,815	2,903	1,979	3,933
1936	10,554	3,853	2,618	4,083
1938	13,012	5,407	3,132	4,473
1940	12,712	4,902	3,313	4,497
1942	20,797	12,270	3,903	4,625
1946	46,128	36,037	4,937	5,157
1950	50,967	35,053	7,930	7,984
1952	79,066	59,744	9,857	9,466
1954	84,476	62,409	11,089	10,978
1956	91,593	65,226	13,375	12,992

* Data prior to 1946 not strictly comparable with later years.

Source: The Conference Board, The Economic Almanac, 1958, p. 428.

It has long been a moot question out of whose income a given tax comes. In the dynamics of the income process a tax may be passed along from one individual or group of individuals to another. This process is known as *shifting*. For example, indirect business taxes or sales taxes may be paid over to the tax-collecting agency by a business firm. The firm may add an amount equal to the tax to the price of the good or service. In this case, the tax is *shifted* to the purchaser. However, if the price of the good is already one which is calculated to maximize the profit income of the firm, due consideration having been given to the price elasticity of demand, a smaller number of units will be sold as a result of adding the tax, thus reducing profits and passing at least a part of the tax back to the business firm and finally to its owners. The point at which the burden of the tax finally falls is known as the *incidence* of the tax.

Shifting and Incidence

Economists who were specialists in public finance once thought and wrote a great deal about shifting and incidence. It was considered desirable to use a tax which could not be shifted, or which could be shifted only with great difficulty. Tax specialists believed that the consequences of such a tax could be most easily predicted in terms of its effect on free consumer choice and the incentives of producers. A tax that is shifted to consumers by being added to the price of the good or service would theoretically result in a smaller amount being taken than before the tax, either because it would now be too expensive for those purchasers just able to afford it before, or because other substitute goods would be relatively more attractive. In either event, the unsold goods and the change in expectations of business firms would be likely to result in an alteration of production plans, the withdrawal of factors of production from the areas taxed, and the further upsetting of other adjustments in the use of resources. Should the tax result in altering the output of a given product, not only would this lead to changing the patterns of production, but would be self-defeating as far as the tax itself was concerned. Depending, of course, on the elasticity of demand for the good, the revenues from such a tax would be unpredictable.

In the search for a tax base least likely to change the pattern of resource use, thereby affecting the exercise of free consumer choice, some economists recommended taxing the so-called surplus in the distributive shares. Thus it was maintained that a tax on economic rent, if it could be levied, would not result in significant changes in resource allocation, since no contribution to production corresponds to this particular functional return. The tax on differential rents, for example, would not cause the owner of the particular resource to withdraw it from production, providing he was already using it in such a way as to maximize income. A tax on quasi-rents would not be likely to result in withdrawing the physical capital from production. As John Maynard Keynes has pointed out, however, this would not necessarily hold if there were involved important "user costs." By this he meant a factor which may be depreciated or depleted more rapidly through use than if it were held in idleness. A tonnage tax on minerals extracted from the earth, or upon timber cut from forest land, might well result in these resources remaining unused, at least until more favorable demand conditions arose. Economic surpluses would also include, of course, monopoly profits which arise from a restriction of production rather than production expansion.

The interest in shifting and incidence can be linked with the search for some kind of *tax justice*. While the classical economists believed that competition tended to regulate the prices of other goods and services in order to keep them in line with something like a "just" or "reasonable" price in a market economy, no such force appeared to operate on the costs of government.

Criteria of Tax Justice

Two criteria of tax justice have been advanced. The first is called the benefit principle. According to this criterion, people ought to pay taxes in accordance with the benefits they receive. While this principle appears on the face of it to be a reasonable one, it is by no means easy to apply. Do all citizens, for example, benefit equally from the protection of the law or from the security provided by the Army and Navy, regardless of their station in life or how well they have fared under existing laws and institutions? Do not the rich and well-placed, with large property holdings, receive a greater benefit from such protection in view of the fact that it helps to secure them in the "enjoyment" of their property? At least some students of government will answer affirmatively. Here, however, emphasis shifts to the second of our criteria—ability to pay. Those having the greater wealth, the larger income, possess the ability to pay taxes. Taxes levied there can be collected, because that is "where the money is." It can be argued, moreover, that possession of such ability implies an obligation, since a large part of government expenditure is devoted to maintaining security and order, thereby safeguarding such persons in the use of their property and income. Even if we accept the principle of ability to pay, however, the problem does not end there. For how are differences in ability to be measured?

Taxing authorities, while not unaware of the problems of tax justice, have not often been bound by it. Principle has usually been tempered by expediency, and taxes have been raised where they could be raised. Some wag has described this as the principle of "getting the most feathers with the least squawking." As a result, most countries have inherited from the past a hodgepodge of things taxed and of rates which apply to them. When these are classified and arranged in some kind of order, the result is usually referred to as the *tax structure*.

Few people like to pay taxes if they can avoid them. Most taxpayers have a criterion of their own which they apply whenever called upon to pay taxes: whatever tax is paid is too much. The inverse of this criterion would be: others pay too little. As a consequence, there has never been a time when there has not been active some association of taxpayers seeking reform of the tax structure.

Classification of Taxes

A tax classification useful for comparison and evaluation is a four-way division based on the relation between the thing taxed, that is, the tax base, and the tax rate. These are:

1. *Equal.* An equal, or equivalent, tax is one which treats all taxpayers exactly alike. The old poll tax or capitation tax is an example. All male citizens between the ages of 21 and 45 were required to pay annually a specified sum or its equivalent. Used principally by local or township governments, proceeds usually went for the upkeep of roads. The poll tax as a means of raising revenue has all but disappeared in the United States, although it still persists in some areas as a means of controlling the exercise of the voting franchise. Certain licenses and fees which are entirely uniform could also be placed in this classification.

2. *Proportional.* A proportional tax is one for which the tax rate remains constant while the base varies. Thus the total amount of the tax will vary in proportion to the size of the base.

3. *Progressive.* A progressive tax is one for which the tax rate varies directly with the size of the base. In other words, as the base increases, so does the rate. Such a tax may be mildly progressive, in which case the rate increases just slightly faster than the base, or steeply progressive, in which case the rate rises much more rapidly than the base.

4. *Regressive.* A regressive tax is one for which the tax rate varies inversely with the size of the base. In other words, a small base will be taxed relatively more heavily than a large base.

Principal Forms
of Taxation

Over the years legislators and other tax authorities can scarcely be criticized for lack of imagination. Few points along the income flow have escaped their notice. A complete inventory of tax bases and rates would require a volume much larger than this book. By simplification, and by treating them in broad categories, however, we can examine the more important forms of taxation.

General Property Tax

Historically, the *general property tax* is the oldest form of taxation. When property was made up chiefly of land, crops, livestock, and the tools for cultivation, a man's holdings constituted very tangible evidence of things to be taxed and of ability to pay taxes. The early tax collectors roamed the countryside appropriating for the use of the sovereign, often on a commission basis, some part of men's worldly goods. When a money and credit system developed, providing a means for valuing tangible possessions, it became more convenient to levy against property some specified percentage of its value. An early distinction was made between *real property,* usually land and buildings, and *personal property,* which could be moved about and associated with the person of the owner.

Division of labor in the tax-collecting business came about when officials experienced in the valuation of property took over their task as *assessors,* while others determined the rates and levied the taxes. As the economic or income process became more complex, property claims more abstract and easily transferable, a new form of property described as *intangibles* came into being. These are property claims not easily discovered by the eyes of the assessor or the tax collector—forms of wealth that can be secreted in strong boxes and vaults, like stocks and bonds or cash. Tax authorities had to rely more and more upon the honesty of the taxpayer to declare such property forms at the time tax assessments were made. When such a trust proved to be too great a strain upon the veracity of many citizens, the taxation of intangibles at anything more than a nominal rate was largely abandoned.

The property tax as a base for determining government income is still widely used in the United States, although it has now become the preserve chiefly of local government. Townships, counties, school districts, and municipalities derive a major portion of their revenues from the property tax. The tax rate, usually called the *millage rate,* is determined by dividing the amount of revenue desired by the total assessed valuation of property in the district. Thus, if a school district had determined that $1,000,000 was required to operate the schools for a year, and if the total assessed value of property in the district were $200,000,-000, the mill levy for schools would be .005. A property owner with a $10,000 house would thus be liable for a tax of $50. Another property holder with a $20,000 house would have to pay $100. Thus the property tax can be classified generally as a proportional tax. Differential treatment for different types of property is usually achieved by establishing an assessed valuation different from "actual" valuation. Thus the assessed valuation of a home may be fifty per cent of its sales value, while an industrial property which returns an income may be valued at seventy per cent of its "actual" value.

Uniform valuation, particularly where assessors are not well trained or where they are elected by the property holders whose property they value, poses a continuing problem for those governmental units using the property tax. The problem is particularly pronounced at the state level, because different tax districts may attempt to avoid their proportionate share of the state tax by undervaluing their property.

Because of the great diversity and complexity of modern property forms, the general property tax has become an increasingly erratic measure of ability to pay. We have already noted that it is now applied chiefly to tangible property. A piece of tangible business property, which during full employment and high level business returns a substantial income to its owner, may return little or nothing during a slump. A house built during prosperity may have to be sold for taxes during depression.

Excise Taxes

An *excise* is a levy which has as its base some good or service which is widely traded. During World War II a variety of "luxury items" were taxed as a means of raising additional revenue. Such items as cosmetics, leather goods, long-distance telephone calls, and theater and sports admissions were taxed at varying rates levied against their sales prices. Since the war rates on some items have been reduced, some have been abolished, but others remain. Most indirect business taxes are a form of excise tax.

Two items of consumption in particular have been extensively taxed at virtually all levels of government. These are tobacco and alcoholic beverages. Such taxes are justified on the grounds that these items are habit-forming, their consumption socially undesirable, and hence to be discouraged. Legislative bodies have usually regarded them as useful tax bases for exactly the opposite reason. Taxing them does not discourage their consumption, because the demand tends to be inelastic, and the tax yield therefore stable and predictable.

An excise tax which has become increasingly important is the Federal and state gasoline tax. Revenues derived from this source are used chiefly for highway construction, and it is one tax which might be characterized as conforming to the benefit principle, since it is paid by those who use the highways.

Another form of excise tax, long popular with national governments, is the tariff. This is a tax levied on *goods of foreign origin*. As a tax it is easy to administer, since all goods coming into the country must enter through some port where they can be counted, valued, and the tax levied. The rate may be either *ad valorem* or *specific,* the first a percentage of the value of the item, the second a set rate or tax per unit. During the early history of the United States the tariff or import duty constituted the most important source of Federal revenue. The individual states are proscribed from levying import duties under the Constitution. Following the Civil War the tariff became increasingly a device for restricting imports or, in other words, a *protective tariff*. A protective tariff, if it were successful in its objective, would return little or no revenue.

464

Excise taxes are rather difficult to classify with respect to the relation between their bases and their rates. They are probably proportional, since the amount of tax paid depends upon the size of the purchase. To the extent that they are levied against commodities (so-called luxuries), purchased by wealthy persons, the effect may be progressive, but this interpretation involves a subtle shifting of the tax base in the middle of the analysis.

General Sales Tax

The *general sales tax* is very old. As commerce and trade developed, it is understandable that governments did not overlook the opportunity for levying a tax on transactions or sales at the point where they were made. Thus a sales tax is literally the application of a tax rate to the value of a sale, collected from one or the other of the parties to the exchange. The most common form in general use is the retail sales tax collected from the purchaser at the time of sale. Another form is the gross sales or income tax levied against firms, which is simply the application of a tax rate against the total volume of revenue collected, no allowance being made for costs.

In the United States the general sales tax is used principally by the states. West Virginia, which instituted such a tax in 1921, was the first to adopt it as a means of increasing state income. During the 1930's, when government income from other sources (particularly the property tax) fell off, and when demands for relief and other types of social welfare measures were increasing, thirty-one different states imposed a general sales tax. Twenty-six have retained it. In addition, the sales tax is used by about two hundred municipalities. A Federal sales tax was proposed during the depression—in 1931—but was defeated. Following the outbreak of the Korean war in 1950, some proposed a Federal sales tax as an anti-inflation device, but it was never seriously considered.

The most common rate for the sales tax is 2 per cent, although in some states it is higher. Provisions vary among the different states, some of them applying to the sale of all commodities and services not covered by excise taxes, others exempting "necessities," such as food purchased at the grocery store. In most cases the tax is shifted to the purchaser or consumer, and this is usually the intent of the law. While this tax might appear to be proportional, the amount collected varying directly with the amount of the purchase, it is usually classified as regressive. This is because the effect is evaluated with respect to income. Low-income households spend most of their income on items that are taxed. High-income households, which spend much more on rents, personal services,

465

and investment or savings, can avoid the sales tax for a substantial part of their income.

Since states are prohibited from collecting sales taxes on purchases made in other states, many have adopted the subterfuge of a "use tax." Theoretically a tax on the use of a commodity purchased outside the state, it is in fact a sales tax on such a purchase. A difficult tax to collect, it is effective principally on automobiles, which require registration if they are to be used in the state. Mail-order houses and other merchants selling across state lines frequently collect and remit these taxes under a "gentlemen's agreement."

Income Tax

An *income tax* is a levy against a household or firm, having as its base the income received or realized during a specified period. The sum taxed is not necessarily the same as the "actual" income of the receiver, since income for tax purposes is defined by legislatures, administrators, and the courts and may be different from the economic or accounting definition. This is why firms in particular often keep more than one set of books on their income accounts—one for tax purposes, and one or more for other purposes.

Within the family of taxes (the tax structure) used by governments to raise revenues, the income tax is a comparative newcomer in the United States. Its development parallels the increasing complexity and interdependence of the economic system which has resulted from changes in the nature of property. It is in part a recognition of money income as the ultimate measure both of ability to pay taxes and of benefits received, since it is a standard of what the household or the firm is getting from the society of which it is a part.

Wisconsin inaugurated the first income tax in 1911, and it has been in continuous use by the Federal government since 1913. The idea of such a tax is, of course, much older. As an emergency measure, and an unpopular one, it was used to raise revenue during and following the Civil War (1861–72). The Federal government passed an income tax law in 1894, but this very mild proposal was declared unconstitutional by the U.S. Supreme Court. In 1909 a proposed amendment to the Federal Constitution, authorizing the central government to tax the income of persons, was submitted to the states, and its ratification paved the way for the first such tax on a permanent basis four years later. At the present time twenty-nine states, in addition to the Federal government, use the income tax.

466

Income for Tax Purposes

Taxable income and actual income differ in the first instance by the amount of personal exemptions. This is an amount (now $600) which a household can receive for each of its members before liability for payment of the Federal income tax begins.[1] Personal exemptions are the same for all households regardless of the size of income, and constitute an acknowledgment by tax bodies that some minimum requirement for family living needs to be recognized before liability begins. In addition to personal exemptions, allowances can be claimed for contributions to religious and charitable organizations. After such deductions have been made from actual income, the remainder becomes taxable income, to which varying rates are then applied. From the beginning the income tax has been progressive. This progressiveness is achieved by applying a graduated tax rate or surtax to different levels of income. At the outset the United States Federal income tax was only mildly progressive. However, the increasing size of government expenditures has made the rate more steeply graduated, and for incomes of more than $50,000 a major portion is now taken for income taxes. State income taxes generally have more liberal exemptions and lower rates, and are less steeply graduated. More recently a number of cities in states which do not make use of the income tax have adopted their own municipal income tax. These taxes carry low rates, and tend to be less progressive than state and Federal income taxes.

Since 1909 the Federal government has levied an income tax on corporations. Initially it was called an excise tax on the business of corporations, largely to avoid the issue of constitutionality raised when the personal income tax was declared unconstitutional in 1895. However, the *corporate income tax* has continued, and now amounts to 52 per cent of net income. Whether or not a corporation has an income, in the sense that an individual or household has an income, is a much debated question. However, the fact that the corporation has been declared a legal person, with rights of limited liability, has tended to make it easier for legislators to justify such a tax. If, however, one maintains that the income of the corporation belongs to its owners, and if this income is taxed twice—once as corporate income, and again when it is paid out in the form of dividends to the stockholders—this raises the issue of *double taxation*.

Until World War II taxpayers were liable for their income taxes on

---

[1] Also deductible from the gross income receipts are all expenditures of the household (or firm) which have been allowed as direct costs of earning the income.

467

March 15th following the year in which the income was earned. During the war the practice of collecting income taxes at the source, on all wages and salaries, was instituted. Employers deducted from the weekly or monthly pay check of their employees an amount equal to the proportionate tax liability for that amount of income. This had long been advocated by many students of taxation on the grounds that it avoided the difficulty arising when the income receiver has spent his entire income and finds it difficult to meet his tax payment during the year following its actual receipt. Now, on April 15 of the year following, the taxpayer submits a tax return which states the amount of his taxable income and the amount that has already been paid. If the tax paid is in excess of the liability, he submits a claim for a refund; if the amount paid is less than the liability, he remits the remainder.

All of the difficulties encountered in measuring or estimating income precisely show up in taxable income as well. Even after a long series of court decisions which have attempted to define taxable income equitably, some inequities or differences of treatment still exist. The difficulty involved in estimating a precise value for income in kind has been mentioned. Another notable inconsistency is when a household which owns its own house is compared with one which rents. If a household has invested in a house, and lives in this house, then presumably it is realizing a return on the invested capital. Implicit rent would therefore be added to other income. In practice this is not done. On the other hand, a household which pays rent for its home is not authorized to deduct this amount from its income. Thus home owners and those who rent are treated differently.

Other differences in treatment occur in deducting costs of earning an income. Farmers who transport their produce to market in the family car are allowed to deduct these costs from their income. Workers, however, cannot deduct cost of transportation to and from work each day.

Death Taxes

When a person dies, the residual property claims he owned pass to someone else. In one sense the receipt of such an inheritance is similar to income. On the other hand, it is linked by long tradition to the institution of the family and to the transfer from one generation to the next of accumulated family property. Advocates of equal opportunity for the members of each new generation have long favored taxing such inheritances. Legislators, while sometimes accepting the argument that death taxes protect equal opportunity, have also been guided by expediency, since estates are well adapted to the levying of a tax. The services of the

468

courts are required in the settlement, and valuation is necessary for this purpose.

Death taxes are of two types. *Estate taxes* are levied against the residual value of the property of the deceased. *Inheritance taxes* are levied against the separate shares of the heirs who receive bequests. The Federal government has collected an estate and gift tax since 1926 (*gift taxes* were imposed to prevent the giving away of an estate in anticipation of death to avoid the estate tax). While state and local death taxes vary among the states, the inheritance tax is the most common form. Because death taxes have long been regarded as the province of the state, the Federal government allows 80 per cent of its estate and gift taxes to be forgiven, if the states collect an inheritance or estate tax. One reason for the adoption of a Federal tax was to discourage some states from offering themselves as havens for wealthy retired citizens, hoping thereby to attract large concentrations of property.

Payroll Tax

Another tax which has income as its base is the *payroll tax*. Proceeds from this tax are used to establish a claim to income at some future time or under specified conditions. Examples are the old-age and survivors' insurance, the unemployment insurance, and certain other retirement plans. Under these arrangements a percentage of the earnings of a worker is withheld from his pay, matched by a tax on the employer and by government contributions. These funds are paid to a government agency, in return for which the government obligates itself to pay an income to the earner under the conditions set forth in the law. Thus the old-age and survivors' insurance provides that when the income earner reaches the age of 65, he or she is entitled to retire and to receive a specified income. Under the Unemployment Compensation Act the worker is entitled to an unemployment benefit payment from the state for a specified length of time, which varies somewhat from state to state both with respect to amount and length of time.

A New Outlook on Taxes

There has been a shift in emphasis in recent years with respect to taxes. As was pointed out in Part 2, the government budget has two sides to it. While it may be useful for some purposes to study the proportion of income going to government for further disposition, it is equally important to inquire into the effects of that disposition. Income distribution is not a static thing but an ongoing process, the results of which are likely to be reflected in changes in total income available for distribution to the income-receiving units. For this reason much less emphasis is put on shifting and incidence than formerly. This does not mean that any idea of tax justice is a dead letter. It is simply a recognition that income distribution cannot be evaluated by a static model. Taxes today are more likely to be appraised for their effect on income flows, on total household spending, on saving, on investment, and on liquidity preference, which are likely to change as the general levels of prices and employment change. That taxes should be evaluated only by their contribution to inflation or deflation is the extreme view. We will return to this problem in the next section, where we consider alternative judgments on how income ought to be distributed and what ought to be the role of government in this distribution.

Discussion
Questions

1. As the nation and its economy have grown, government revenues have expanded not only proportionally but also relatively to the national income. Can you account for this increase?

2. Do you think that the income tax fits the ordinary concept of tax justice?

3. All taxes are paid, ultimately, from income. Discuss this proposition.

4. How would the effects of a general sales tax differ from those of an income tax, in prosperity and depression? In terms of government revenues, and in terms of spending in the private economy?

5. Differentiate between a progressive tax and a progressive tax structure.

CHAPTER 30

The Role of Interest Groups in Distribution

THE TERM *pressure group* is usually applied to organized political effort. In modern society there is a proliferation of groups and organizations of like-minded persons joined together to influence government policy and to work toward common objectives. Many such groups have a predominantly economic or income orientation. The common bond is usually a conflict of interest (real or imagined) with other groups. Among their objectives are: (1) a shift in income distribution favorable to the members, to their commodity, or to their industry; (2) an agreement on standards to be adopted by members of the group and imposed upon others; (3) the sharing of knowledge gained from individual experience, as in professional associations, and (4) the counteracting of similar activities by others. These actions have a direct bearing on resource use, and thus on size and composition of output, and ultimately on distribution itself.

Our purpose is not to evaluate such groups. They are to be noted as "facts" of economic life which have a bearing on income. We note only that their role has been a matter of concern to many. Fainsod and Gordon, two students of the American scene, have stated this as follows:

> Many have expressed concern lest the tendency of organized groups to put primary emphasis on their own economic interest lead to a dispersive type of group utilitarianism, which completely loses sight of the general welfare and transforms the political arena into a "battle royal of interests."[1]

Lest we get the impression, that these associations have become a prob-

---

[1] Merle Fainsod and Lincoln Gordon, *Government and the American Economy* (New York: W. W. Norton & Co., 1941), p. 45.

471

lem only in our day, however, the following classic passage from Adam Smith may be worthy of note:

> People of the same trade seldom meet together, even for merriment and diversion, but the conversation ends in a conspiracy against the public, or in some contrivance to raise prices.

While recognizing that actions of such groups may be to the disadvantage of others, Smith believed that it would be difficult to prevent them by law, save at the expense of freedom. He relied on individual self-interest to mitigate such influences. There is less faith today, perhaps, in the corrective powers of competition and individual action than in Smith's day. Modern institutional economists look to the neutralizing effect of opposing and competing *groups* to safeguard the general interest. In historical perspective, it is arguable that the formation of one organization which seeks to influence income claims in its own favor sooner or later finds its objectives offset by an opposing force in some competing group.[2]

Owners of commercial and industrial establishments, the employers of labor and the principal producers, because of their smaller numbers and greater geographic concentration, were the first to organize around their common interests—especially their relations with labor and their interest in the tariff. Again we can find pertinent comment on this point in Adam Smith:

> Masters are always and everywhere in a sort of tacit, but uniform, combination, not to raise the wages above their actual rate.

Today, unlike the period in which he wrote, such combinations are set off against combinations of the workers themselves. Even farmers, as transportation and communications have reduced their geographic isolation, have formed associations of regional and national scope. They too meet together for purposes other than merriment or discussions of the weather and crop conditions.

Each of these groups tends to see the general welfare in terms of its own well-being. To the extent that they neutralize one another, their influence on distribution may be minimized. A net result of their activities has been to increase the role of government as a regulator of production as well as other aspects of economic life. We shall now consider some of these groups and their influence on output and income shares.

---

[2] Compare J. K. Galbraith, *American Capitalism.*

Organized Business and
Professional Groups

In the theoretical model developed earlier for the analysis of production decisions, the concept of an industry was derived by a simple additive process—the combining of separate firms having in common the production of similar goods. This concept was expanded in later chapters to show how the institutionalization of financial control has brought an increasing number of these firms together, in some cases into industry-wide organizations.

Here we will be concerned with influences less direct, less a part of formal production organization, but which nevertheless play a role in management decisions and in factor use and payment. The usual form of such organizations is the association, and the one with which we are most familiar is the *trade association*. Its counterpart for the service industries is the *professional association*. What are these associations? What are their principal functions?

The Bureau of Foreign and Domestic Commerce of the U.S. Department of Commerce has published numerous studies of this type of association. It has estimated that there are approximately 3,000 national and interstate trade associations, grouped according to industries, such as food, textiles, machinery, distribution, transportation, foreign trade, and others. Through surveys ranging over a number of years, information has been collected on nearly 11,000 organizations, of which 8,000 are trade associations. This number includes state and local groups. There are, for example, some 3,000 chambers of commerce, mostly on a local level, and these are loosely associated in a national federation.

Mutual Interests

An important function performed by these organizations is the purely social one of bringing together individuals with similar interests. However, a more frequent motivating influence in their formation is the opportunity afforded for discussing matters of mutual economic concern. These discussions include topics which in some countries would be trade secrets. Experience has shown that in a nation such as the United States, with its high level of education and the general application of scientific knowledge to industry, trade secrets are difficult to keep. Moreover, in the give and take of free discussion, about as much is gained by the individual firm or establishment as must be surrendered. Nor is this kind of sharing, comparing of notes, and mutual assistance necessarily detrimental to the

473

public interest. In the words of a Department of Commerce analyst, "When wisely guided by their boards, committees and staffs, so that general public welfare is kept first in mind, trade associations can more effectively undertake the handling of many types of business problems than can the average individual proprietor."

Standardization and quality control are examples of two kinds of problems which can be so handled. The application of science to the production processes has multiplied the materials and designs useful in the production of goods. It has also increased the possibility for disguising inferior substance, so that it cannot be detected immediately by the untrained observer. Because of cost advantage, such goods are sometimes sold to the unwary buyer at what appears to be a favorable price. Producers of superior quality goods regard this as "unfair competition," detrimental to them and to consumers, and have pressed for adoption of minimum standards. In the professional associations, actions along similar lines have led to the framing of *codes* of ethical practice.

Enterprises with inadequate knowledge of modern accounting and control practices, and because of failure to estimate their costs accurately, may subject an industry to periods of price instability and loss of income, resulting in business failures and irregular supply. Another function of some trade associations has been to develop uniform accounting methods and cost procedures.

Co-ordination

New products, little known to consumers, can quite often benefit from industry-wide advertising—co-operative projects financed by firms otherwise in competition with one another. The trade association can co-ordinate such industry-wide efforts. Finally, when the problems of standardization and definition of accepted practice cannot be met by common agreement, the trade association provides an effective instrument through which to work for legislation at the state and national level to impose such uniformities on the industry.

So far we have considered the socially favorable features of trade associations as their activities affect the production and distribution processes. There is, however, another side. The association may serve established members in a manner that discourages the entry of new firms into the industry. This restricts competition and diverts factors of production to other uses less preferred by the public. The development of uniform accounting procedures for cost determination has been at times a means for promoting monopolistic practices. Price leadership, without actual collusion, has been fostered by aggressive secretaries of trade associations, working as agents of the dominant firms in communicating price policies. Where successful, this has meant an income advantage for those concerned. In some instances these secretaries have also become highly paid lobbyists for the industry, promoting legislation and public policy, as well as promoting the income interests of their particular products.

The technique of income transfer with the longest history is that of the protective tariff. This subject will be treated in Part 6.

Professional associations, no less than trade associations, have important consequences for income distribution. By setting up standards of required competence and ethical practice, they have rendered a public service in safeguarding people against quackery and malpractice. Their professional journals provide first-rate communication media. On the other hand, they have appeared at times to be interested chiefly in restricting entry into the profession in order to preserve an already favorable income advantage. This effectiveness shows up in the income statistics. Physicians and dentists, for example, whose average incomes are among the highest of any group, have extremely active and vocal organizations.

Organized
Labor

During the last quarter-century organized labor has become a force to be reckoned with in production decisions and distribution. Sumner H. Slichter of Harvard University has characterized our system of production control as "laboristic," in contrast to the "capitalistic" production of a generation ago. However, this phrase needs elaboration.

We usually think of organized labor in association with distribution rather than as a direct participant in production decisions. We noted in our discussion of organization controls of the business firm that policies aimed at maximizing profit income and the stability of asset values determine production decisions, particularly where monopoly control is important. Organized labor, which seeks to influence wages (the size of labor claims against the revenues of the enterprise), has gained a type of control in the factor market which may approach monopoly.

Raising the price of labor, unless productivity also increases, will result in higher variable costs and a higher average cost per unit. With a given demand for the product, this will mean either a decreased output or a smaller profit, if the firm exercises any degree of monopoly control. There is, of course, what may seem to be a way out. If the general level of prices is rising, with a resulting upward trend of national income, the appearance

475

of rising wages can be achieved even as real wages remain constant or even decline.

The immediate goal of organized labor is to increase the functional claims of its members by raising the price of labor as a factor service. Its influence on production decisions, the allocation of all factors, is indirect, but it is there. In addition to the actual wage or labor income, unions also influence the hours and conditions of work in a manner reflected in the costs of firms.

Development of Organized Labor

The growth of labor union strength and effectiveness parallels that of the large-scale, corporate firm and the business and trade associations of producers. Although the idea of collective action has its roots in the past, the story of organized labor's real growth in the United States is largely of this century, and almost of the past twenty years.

In 1897 there were in this country less than a half-million organized workers. Of this number roughly two-thirds were in the American Federation of Labor, the principal organization of national and international unions. The rest were in so-called independent unions. Among these the Railway Brotherhoods were the strongest and had the longest tradition, chiefly because railways were the first truly national industries. By 1930 slightly more than 3.5 million workers were in unions, this total representing a decline from the peak of 5 million attained in 1920. The total labor force in 1930 was nearly 30 million. Union membership had increased to 9 million by 1940, and in 1956 it was approximately 18 million in a civilian labor force of 67 million.

Something of the changing pattern of production can be traced in the evolution of labor organization. The first to attempt an association of working men were the skilled artisans or craftsmen. As early as 1794 cartwrights, printers, hod carriers, carpenters, and other skilled tradesmen were making crude attempts to form local organizations. Their principal concern was the control of apprenticeships, the sharing of sickness and accident expenses, and occasional resistance to the introduction of "labor saving" machinery. By 1827 efforts to organize city-wide councils had begun.

In 1834 the early efforts at organization coalesced in a National Trades Union, an association which was instrumental in securing a ten-hour day for workers in government service. From then on, until the last quarter of the nineteenth century, many efforts were made to form workingmen's associations on a larger scale, but one after another they were frustrated by depression or diverted to various reform programs.

476

Union leaders again and again used their associations to further Utopian objectives—co-operation, free silver, socialism, and so on. Not infrequently the movement, and particularly its treasury, was diverted to the personal benefit of the leadership.

However, these early struggles did exert some influence. Aside from purely economic considerations, they contributed to social and political reforms which broadened the base of suffrage, regulated the use of prison labor in production, modified laws relating to debt, promoted land reforms which enabled workers to escape the cities to new lands during periods of depression and unemployment and supported free public education. With the rise of modern technology and large-scale production methods, they served to call attention to the possibility of shorter work days—a movement repeatedly resisted by employers.

The inception of a primarily "economic" unionism, with a distinct income orientation, began after the Civil War. Following a long period of conflict, of fruitless opposition to labor-saving machinery, and numerous ventures into politics, the American Federation of Labor was founded in 1886, under the leadership of Adolph Strasser and Samuel Gompers. This association dominated organized labor in the United States (and Canada) from the time of its founding until the middle of the 1930's. The Railway Brotherhoods paralleled the AF of L, on an independent basis, in outlook and method.

Union Structure

Students of organized labor usually classify trade unions according to *structure* and *function*. Structurally, both of these dominant organizations were built around the crafts or skills of their members, organized in local labor markets and linked only by a relatively loose confederation. Their leaders emphasized the control of the labor supply in each of the separate trades, as differentiated and separate factors of production. The more highly developed the skill, the more likely it was to be limited by human capacity and the easier to control.

The organization structure adopted by the American Federation of Labor has become characteristic of the labor movement in the United States. Local associations (locals) are joined together in the national (or international, if the union has locals outside the United States) association. Examples of national organizations are the United Automobile Workers, the United Steelworkers, the Brotherhood of Teamsters, and the United Mine Workers. The nationals issue charters to local organizations, and come to their assistance during strikes and membership drives. Liaison is maintained through field representatives and organizers working

477

out of district officers. The national officials arrange for the national conventions, where elected delegates elect (or re-elect) officials and enact the "laws" which govern the affairs of the union.

In addition to the principal line organizations, unions function through city, district, and state councils, which comprise an important network of interim communication systems and administrative machinery. Direct member contact with the union occurs chiefly at the local level.

Functionally (as well as structurally), the AF of L appears to have established the pattern of unionism in the United States. Often characterized as "business unionism" or "bread-and-butter unionism," organized labor in this country has traditionally rejected long-run political and social reform (other than as it affects the jobs of workers) for a larger slice of the "national pie" now. Initially, the objective was to be accomplished by controlling the acquisition and use of the human skills or crafts involved in the particular job at hand. However, one after another the skills on which their organizations were based fell victims to advancing technology. The greater precision and standardization of the machine process made more and more crafts obsolete, and reduced workmen to machine tenders, replaceable with a bare minimum of training. Workmen no longer owned their tools. They owned no particular skill. Their control over the production processes receded.

A new group of labor leaders emerged, stressing the organization of a single large union which would encompass the workers of an entire industry. Soon after the turn of the century the revolutionary Industrial Workers of the World began extensive organizing and propaganda activities for "one big union" which would encompass all workers. While this organization registered some successes, it was never accepted by the bulk of American workers, and during World War I it ran afoul of the government and was specifically rejected by the general public and workers alike. The idea of industrial unionism, however, continued to gather supporters, and during the 1930's leaders in twelve unions in the AF of L were appointed to a committee—the Committee for Industrial Organization—which undertook to investigate the feasibility of forming industrial unions in the mass-production industries, such as steel and automobiles. The United Mine Workers, already organized on an industrial basis, was an important moving force and contributor to the effort. When division occurred in the ranks of the AF of L, some of the older unions, together with those newly organized by representatives of the Committee, split from the parent group and later formed the Congress of Industrial Organizations (CIO). The effect of this was widespread. In addition to

478

setting up a separate organization composed entirely of industry-wide units, the CIO further modified the basic philosophy of the AF of L, weakening the control of crafts over labor organization. Early in 1955, under a younger leadership, the two organizations reached an agreement for a new merger of the two groups into the AFL-CIO.

The coming of industrial unionism has strengthened the effectiveness of organized labor. Not the least of this strength is related to the fact that mass membership has encouraged wider participation by labor in politics, working through government to achieve income objectives.

Operating Methods

From the earliest times the exercise of economic power by organized labor has centered in the *strike*. While in form the strike consists of withholding a major factor of production, in substance it represents a capacity to deny income to the firm. Without labor, or a significant part of it, few plants can operate. Idle plants create no output, no income. With fixed costs and other commitments to meet, a recalcitrant management can be persuaded to negotiate an issue in dispute as the least costly course of action. Such an exercise of power, of course, is not all to the advantage of the union. For while business is denied income, the strikers themselves must also forego income. Relative bargaining power between the contending forces is measured chiefly by the ability to withstand such denial of income. An individual worker, threatening to withdraw his services and the increment of profit income it would represent, has very little power. A firm's entire working force has much.

When labor unions were young and weak their power was small. Management could even turn the tables and execute a kind of strike in reverse—the *lockout*. Recalcitrant workers kept long enough from their jobs would return hungry and contrite. This device is much less used than formerly, partly because to close down a modern plant is a costly affair. Moreover, a much stronger labor organization with substantial strike funds can keep its members out for longer periods. What is perhaps more significant to the labor unions of our time is the favorable climate of public opinion within which they operate. During much of the nineteenth century, when laissez faire was the dominant ideology, labor unions were faced not only by hostile employers but also by an unfriendly state. Time and again intervention by the police, the militia, and even Federal troops —ostensibly to preserve order—proved effective in ending a strike to the employer's advantage. Subdued workmen, returning to the job, often found themselves locked out. In seeking other employment they were con-

479

fronted with a *blacklist,* circulated among employers as a means of barring active unionists from jobs anywhere.

After 1890 the Sherman Anti-Trust law became an important strike-breaking device. On a charge of conspiring to raise prices, courts would issue an injunction against unions on strike, holding its officials in con tempt if the strike persisted. When the Clayton Act of 1914 specifically exempted labor unions from provisions of the antitrust laws (by denying that labor is a commodity), strike breaking by injunction persisted under the *yellow-dog contract.* An employer could require workers to sign a contract not to join a union during the period of their employment. Then, if a union succeeded in organizing a plant, management could seek a court injunction against the members on the grounds of contract violation.

Public Opinion

In the 1920's public opinion appears to have shifted to a more sympathetic understanding of union activities. Following the failure of the great steel strike of 1919, labor unions adopted a generally nonmilitant policy. Dominated by the American Federation of Labor, led by Samuel Gompers until his death in 1924, organized labor attained a certain respectability. During the industrial prosperity of the 1920's, while jobs were easy to get, labor did little more than attempt to hold the members it had, and it did not succeed even in this.

In 1932 a new era of public policy began. The Norris-LaGuardia Act passed that year outlawed the yellow-dog contract. When Franklin D. Roosevelt became President in 1933 the shift in policy was accelerated. Section 7a of the National Industrial Recovery Act of 1933 (legislation intended to aid business) provided that all firms taking advantage of this act must agree to bargain collectively with the representatives of organized labor. When it was declared unconstitutional by the Supreme Court in 1935, new legislation in the form of the Wagner National Labor Relations Act was passed. Referred to in union circles as labor's "Magna Charta," the Wagner Act reinstated collective bargaining and created machinery in the National Labor Relations Board to enforce the law. This law remained in effect essentially as drafted until the passage of the National Labor-Management Relations Act (Taft-Hartley) of 1948 instituted provisions somewhat less favorable to unions.

The economic influence of labor unions is a fact of our time. Public sanction of collective bargaining, while not universal, is at least given verbal expression. Union leaders continue their search for effective exercise of power to justify themselves to their members. In contract negotiations they press for the *union shop*,[3] an arrangement wherein the union acts as the exclusive bargaining agent for members, and to retain a job the worker must remain in good standing in the union. Failing this, they insist on a *maintenance of membership* clause in contracts, whereby dues of members are collected by management and paid over to the union treasury during the life of any contract; here, too, a member must remain in good standing. In addition to *wage-rate* increases, fringe benefits, such as paid vacations, company retirement funds, and health and accident insurance, have become bargaining items.

Unions now exercise controls in the production process through collective bargaining that once were regarded as the prerogative of management. These include the setting of standards of performance, conditions of work, seniority or precedence in hiring, and wage differentials for overtime. Even the replacement of men by machines is regulated within limits. Reorganization of the production processes around labor-saving machines may be resisted until assurances are obtained that no more than a minimum of workers will be replaced. When this practice is extended indefinitely, so that surplus labor (which renders no service) is kept on the payroll, it is known as "featherbedding."

Nearly 80 per cent of the labor force now works for wages or salaries. If agriculture (where the individual proprietor predominates) be excepted, the percentage is even higher.

The actual results of organized labor's activities have not always been as intended. Actions to raise wages have undoubtedly hastened the adoption of labor-saving machinery to replace the high-cost services of man. This has worked to the disadvantage of individual workers whose skills are involved, but it can also be argued that it has on the whole improved labor's lot, since improved technology has meant greater productivity and higher real wages.

More recently, organized labor has received considerable adverse publicity as a result of Senate investigating committee findings. The exercise of power by some union officials has been criticized not only from the standpoint of the public interest, but also from that of the union members themselves. The accumulated reserves from membership dues of the largest unions, built up during years of prosperity and comparative industrial peace, confer great economic power on those who control them. Union welfare funds are also large reservoirs of accumulated capital requiring

---

[3] The *union shop* differs from the *closed shop* in the degree of union control. A closed shop arrangement requires workers to join the union before being hired. In a union shop they may be hired first and join afterward.

capable management if they are to contribute to economic growth and development.

Organized
Agriculture

Throughout much of American history farmers have lacked the cohesion of the dominant business and industrial groups. Since the time of the Civil War, in contrast to labor, they have become increasingly a minority group. Since 1910 the number of persons engaged in agriculture has declined both relatively and absolutely (see page 231).

As long as farmers were a majority, they were unable to achieve unity of action with respect to production and income problems. While the Western lands were in the public domain and remained to be settled and captured from the wilderness, and while immigration provided new additions to the farming population, the restless westward movement across the frontier created a climate of opinion in which the most common single element appears to have been the continuing desire for new lands. In the pursuit of this shared objective, the immigrants acted as individuals or family units—a factor to which the historian Frederick Jackson Turner gave great weight as a force in our national character. Because they were widely scattered over great distances, farmers were more often divided over sectional interests than they were united on anything approaching a common interest.

There were times, however, particularly during the forty years following the Civil War, when it appeared that a union of farmers might be achieved. During periods of low prices in the 1870's and again in the 1880's, first the Grangers and later the Populists appeared on the verge of seizing political power in order to impose their "rules of the game" on the rest of the economy.

As was true of the labor unions, these early efforts of the farmers failed because of being tied to short-lived political issues, such as paper money, free silver, and other schemes designed to remedy the seeming lack of purchasing power, as well as because of overambitious cooperative ventures. When prices improved, enthusiasm for these movements subsided, and farmers reverted to the pursuit of their individual income interests.

Partly as a consequence of these movements, however, regulation of the railroads and of farm commodity markets were among the several types of government intervention which took place. Public sponsorship of research in improved agricultural technology was another consequence. The establishment of the land-grant colleges, the agricultural experiment

482

stations, and finally, in 1914, the Agricultural Extension Service, contributed to the increasing productivity of agriculture, which in turn contributed to the recurring problem of surplus farm commodities, low prices, and depressed income for the producers of food and fibre.

Since 1920 farmers have learned to work through the offices of government to achieve what they could not achieve on their own. The farm bloc in Congress, which cuts across party lines on issues involving agriculture, emerged during the decade following World War I. Repeated efforts were made to achieve a political solution for what was called the "farm problem." After 1933 a series of government farm programs of far-reaching nature undertook to regulate the use of agricultural resources in the interest of achieving higher farm prices and incomes. Production control, crop storage, price supports, government purchase, financing of soil-conservation programs, and more recently the soil bank program have been adopted to control surpluses which depressed prices and farm incomes.

The principal farm organizations have been influential in the framing of these programs. The largest of these farm groups is the American Farm Bureau Federation. A significant fact in terms of institutional development is that this organization is an outgrowth of a government-sponsored association created to co-operate with the county agricultural agents provided for under the Smith-Lever Act of 1914. From these beginnings the Farm Bureau has developed into a powerful organization in its own right, consisting of forty-five state federations and claiming a membership of more than one million farm families and three million farm people. The greatest concentration is in the Middle West and the South. As an organization the Farm Bureau represents the income interest of the larger commercial farm producers, the corn-hog farmers of the Middle West and the cotton growers in the South. In recent years this organization has exercised the greatest influence on the various "parity" programs of price support and production planning sponsored by the U.S. Department of Agriculture. Since 1950 the leadership of the Farm Bureau has favored liberalizing the more rigid features of price and production control.

The second largest general farm organization is the National Grange, lineal descendant of the Granger movement of the last century. The local granges, which form its base, are concentrated in the northeastern part of the country and in the Pacific Northwest. The National Grange claims a membership of approximately 900,000.[4] A high proportion of Grange members are dairy farmers, poultry and vegetable producers, small gen-

---

[4] Grange membership is conferred upon all members of the farm family, in contrast to the Farm Bureau which is based upon a family membership.

eral farmers, and in the Pacific Northwest, wheat growers. As a consequence, the Grange is more concerned in its organizational activities and its policy prescriptions with the protection of these markets from outside competition or imports, and with assuring the greatest freedom for the individual farmer to work out his production problems, as he sees them, within the family farm. The Grange has usually been critical of government production-control programs, but has consistently argued that farmers ought to be assured "cost of production."

The third general farm organization, in terms of size and influence, is the Farmers Union. Its membership of 145,000 farm families is concentrated chiefly in the west central states and the South. Hence it represents, for the most part, the farmers of the Great Plains states, an area of high risk and limited possibilities for diversification in the use of resources. In its public statements the Farmers Union usually stresses the importance of the family-size farm as a protector of basic American values. It advocates liberal government credit for agriculture, and during the depressed period of the 1930's was most active in promoting the activities of the Farm Security Administration. Of all the farm groups it has been most vocal in urging the co-operation of organized labor and organized agriculture.

The general farm organizations, as such, do not engage directly in business enterprise. They do sponsor co-operatives, but these are separately incorporated organizations. As purely membership organizations, all three devote most of their attention to pressure group activity to promote public policies which they believe will further the income and social interests of their members.

The Commodity Associations

Apart from the general farm organizations, other farm groups have emerged to promote the interests of the producers of particular commodities. They are parallel organizations to the trade associations in business, industry, and the professions. Among the larger and more active of these groups are the National Livestock Association, the National Wool Growers Association, the California Fruit Growers, and the National Cooperative Milk Producers Association. The work of these associations is usually carried on by a secretary, and includes activities of a promotional and public-relations nature. Most of these secretaries work for public legislation favorable to the income interests of their members.

Distribution and the Farm Problem

Despite the efforts of farm groups and despite a variety of government

484

programs over nearly thirty years, the income position of large groups of farmers remains unsatisfactory to them and a concern to elected public officials. Year after year large numbers leave agriculture for jobs in industry, but rising production on the one hand and a relatively higher birth rate among farm people on the other prevents the kind of adjustment which would raise the marginal productivity of the human factor. Agricultural economists speak of "underemployment" in agriculture. This is not the same as unemployment in industry. There is no lack of work to do on a farm. Many farm families work hard for long hours. But it is work that results in low-income returns because it is not productive.

Not all farmers have low incomes, however. Of the 4.9 million farms, perhaps 2 per cent provide very high incomes. These are the large commercial farm enterprises which account for roughly one-fourth of farm output. At the other end of the scale slightly more than 40 per cent of the farms produce less than 10 per cent of the output. Their incomes are correspondingly small. The rest of the farmers, somewhat more than half, comprise the broad middle of the family-size farms and earn an average annual income of about $4,000. Even at the lower end of this group there are many with incomes well below the modal income of the whole country.

Moreover, not only are farm incomes relatively low, but they are also quite unstable, depending on weather, pests, disease, and other natural factors. A large crop and an increase in supply (under relatively free market conditions) will result in falling prices. Demand for food and other raw materials tends to be inelastic with respect to price. Falling prices do not perform their function of moving the greater supply into consumption. Surpluses pile up to exert a still greater pressure on prices, with resulting adverse income effects. Nor do rising incomes in the rest of the economy help very much. For some commodities consumption is actually less at higher levels of income—commodities such as wheat, potatoes, beans, dried fruits, rice, and other "inferior goods."[5] Technically, the income elasticity of demand is less than 1. Even when total expenditures for food and fibre increase, as income increases, the additional expenditures, are for more refined commodities, that is, products that contain a higher proportion of secondary and tertiary production. The modern housewife who buys a prepared cake-mix contributes a smaller proportion of her food dollar to the wheat, poultry, and dairy farmers than her grandmother did.

Prosperity for the great majority of farmers has occurred mostly

---

[5] This concept will be developed in Part 5.

485

during wartime, when total demand increases rapidly. American agriculture has risen to the occasion twice in a single generation to expand its production to meet such an urgent need. Each time when the war ended, however, the existing excess capacity has kept farm income from increasing as rapidly (on a par with) as other segments of the production economy. This experience helps to explain why farmers are price conscious, and why most of the farm programs have included price supports aimed at achieving some type of *parity*. Such prices encourage greater production, however, and require parallel output restrictions. Income depends upon both price and quantity. Even though a small crop may be worth more than a large one (inelastic demand), the farmer who is already farming a small acreage receives little benefit from government restrictions.

As we have noted previously, farmers have been caught in a long-run downward trend—the declining need for people in primary production. Those who have been able to expand the size of their operations—larger landholdings worked with tractors and other capital equipment—have been able to increase their productivity and hence their incomes. The average size of farms has risen from 138 acres in 1910 to 242 acres in 1955. This figure, again, is an average. Many still continue to apply family labor in a combination of factors, which only results in inefficient production.

The movement out of agriculture, although steady, is relatively slow, and in the face of technological advances has not been fast enough. When employment in industry and the services is available, it is the young who leave the farm. Some have expressed the hope that the increasing rate of population growth characteristic of the last two decades may help to solve America's perennial farm problem by creating a demand related to more mouths rather than higher income. Whether or not it will, only time can tell, for this will depend also upon the continuing rate of technological progress.

Discussion
Questions

1. From the reports of Congressional hearings, find examples of pressure-group testimony which seeks to influence public policy in a manner favorable to the income interests of members of the group.

2. The argument is sometimes advanced that what is good for business is good for the country. When might this be true? When might it not be true?

3. Labor leaders frequently argue that wage increases are always good because higher labor income will mean increased demand for goods and services. What are the merits and shortcomings of this assumption?

4. "When the farmer is prosperous, everyone is prosperous." Evaluate this slogan.

5. Distinguish between a general farm organization and a commodity organization. Between a craft union and an industrial union. Reform and business unionism.

Distribution

and Public Policy

FEW WILL QUARREL with the opinion that the final claims against what society has to offer ought to be tied somehow to productivity, since the sum of all distributive shares or claims "logically" cannot be greater than total output. Linking productivity and distributive "justice" also serves a useful function to the extent that it stimulates effort. If men believe that they get what they produce and "deserve," they may be motivated to work harder and create more. There is a limit, however. The cruel fact of the real world is that at any given time, and in any institutional setting, all cannot be rich and equal. Where does inequality cease to serve a useful function in reducing the economic problem of scarcity? At what point do purely "economic" values begin to conflict with other value systems? These questions come into focus in the problems associated with distribution. There is no very neat answer, and that is why men differ in their opinions and in their proposed solutions.

CHAPTER 31

How Should Income be Distributed?

In this chapter we shall inquire into proposed policies derived from conflicting ideologies, which attempt to answer the question of how income ought to be distributed.

Market Determination of
Distributive Shares

Adam Smith and many who followed him had implicit confidence in the essential "justice" of some natural system of distribution, which would be realized if only men were given a maximum freedom to follow their interests as they saw them. Later refinements of classical and neoclassical economic doctrine attempted to demonstrate that if each factor of production receives its marginal product, the total output will be distributed, and the distributive shares will be a true measure of the contribution to production.

Alfred Marshall was quite aware that such a system of distributive justice meant an unequal distribution of household income, because property is unequally held. The return on capital, even assuming it is assigned no more than its marginal productivity, would cause incomes to be unequal. As long as property holdings did not become monopolies (and Marshall believed monopoly was of minor importance), this was not regarded as undesirable.

Large incomes were regarded as an important source of savings, and it was taken for granted that savings would be invested in capital expansion, resulting in a long-run increase in productive capacity. Only through increased productivity could there be any improvement in the lot of man or any solution to the basic economic problem of scarcity. If incomes were equally distributed, Marshall believed, the share of each would be small and the wealth of nations quickly dissipated in immediate consumption. In 1920 John Maynard Keynes, who then regarded himself as a representative of the classical tradition, described the psychology and the accomplishment of the society in which this faith was dominant.

> While there was some continuous improvement in the daily conditions of life of the mass of the population, Society was so framed as to throw a great part of the increased income into the control of the class least likely to consume it. The new rich of the 19th Century were not brought up to large expenditures, and preferred the power which investment gave them to the pleasures of immediate consumption. In fact, it was precisely the *inequality* of the distribution of wealth which made possible those vast accumulations of wealth and of capital improvements which distinguished that age from the others. . . . The immense accumulations of fixed capital which, to the brief benefit of mankind, were built up during the half-century before the war, could never have come about in a society where wealth was divided equitably. The railways of the world, which that age built as a monument to posterity, were, not less than the Pyramids of Egypt, the work of labor which was not free to consume in immediate enjoyment the full equivalent of its efforts. Thus, this remarkable system depended for its growth on the double bluff or deception. On the one hand, the laboring classes accepted from ignorance or powerlessness, or were compelled, persuaded, or cajoled by custom, convention, authority, and the well-established order of society into accepting a situation in which they could call their own very little of the cake that they and nature and the capitalists were co-operating to produce. And on the other hand, the capitalist classes were allowed to call the best part of the cake theirs and were theoretically free to consume it, on the tacit underlying condition that they consumed very little of it in practice. The duty of "saving" became nine-tenths of virtue and the growth of the cake the object of true religion.[1]

If we read today the writings of many of the economists of this earlier period, and their defense of the free market, they may seem to be calloused men. They opposed all attempts by government to regulate the hours and

---

[1] John Maynard Keynes, *The Economic Consequences of the Peace* (New York: Harcourt, Brace & Co., Inc., 1920), pp. 18–20.

conditions of work, even for women and children forced into the mines and factories to supplement their meager household incomes. Nassau Senior, for example, argued that it would be doing neither them nor society any favor to attempt to improve the lot of workers, since such action would dull initiative and shrink production. Only greater efforts, only more production, could finally remove the blight of poverty and the spectre of hunger.

Yet, despite the seeming callousness of these men and their times, there was a distinguishable overtone of humanitarianism and equalitarianism in their perceived goals. Especially was this true of John Stuart Mill and Alfred Marshall. Present consumption, it was believed (and to a considerable extent this belief was confirmed), was in effect being exchanged for a larger future income—one in which all would have a share.

Return to Laissez Faire

Those who argue for the return to or an enlargement and strengthening of the "free market" stress the fact that income inequality is an important inducement to initiative and sustained effort. The drive to "get ahead" by those who are behind is thereby harnessed to the social need. "The hope of the carrot (income) rather than the fear of the stick (compulsion) becomes the driving force of ever expanding production." In the normative system of laissez faire the hope of profit income, the expectation of a constantly expanding claim against the rest of society, is the motivating force which induces those with imagination and insight to invest in the new and to risk their accumulated property claims in more efficient methods. The force of competition, in the long run, will ensure that profit income will not be large.

Philosophers of the free market like Von Mises would argue that the mere absence (or the holding in check) of government interference would be a sufficient public policy. Even the spectre of monopoly, stressed by others, does not concern him, since where monopoly exists it is *by definition* the creature of government. To preserve order, to protect persons and property, to safeguard national security, and to enforce contracts (freely and openly arrived at) would require only the minimum in government financing. The raising of the necessary funds to carry out these functions ought to be accomplished with as little administrative cost as possible. A small number of direct taxes would suffice, and these *ought* to be paid at the time and place most convenient to the taxpayer; and above all such taxes *should* leave unchanged the relative distribution of income and wealth. Because the personal income tax cannot ordinarily be shifted, this is the tax base most likely to be accepted by those of this persuasion in the modern world. However, in keeping with their principles of tax justice, they insist that the tax rate *should* be strictly proportional. Whatever the amount finally deemed necessary, they would presumably be strongly in favor of a continuously balanced government budget, with a neutral effect on the private sector. This is admittedly an extreme position. As the ideal model of those who would make of economic freedom an all-embracing value, however, it can serve as the basis from which criticism and argument begins.

No realistic value system could require that the income claim of every *individual* be tied exclusively to individual productivity. This would exclude infants, the very old, and the incapacitated from any income. Societies are known in which nonproductive persons other than children are allowed to starve. But these are the most backward in economic and cultural development. In the comparatively rich industrial civilization of the West responsibility for the dependent has been carried forward from the past in the sanctity of family and kinship ties. Most students of social organization believe that this responsibility was extended beyond family and kinship group as political and economic life developed around expanding social and political units. Feeling for the general welfare and individual responsibility toward the larger group was an acquired or learned response to a social environment. It has been incorporated into most ethical systems, although its applicability to the *in* group or the *out* group varies widely. In the Judaeo-Christian ethic, and in the legal-political-ethical system of democracy, it has perhaps achieved its widest application, idealized and symbolized in the concept of "the brotherhood of man." In the evolution of the state, it has been slowly recognized that this agency possesses useful techniques for providing on a collective basis at least a minimum income for the less fortunate members of society. The almshouse and the workhouse in England were public institutions for dealing with poverty. In the United States the county home and the poorhouse were organized almost as early as schools and churches. Many "relief" organizations, set up for the purposes of income transfer, have operated outside the structure of the state, though usually dependent upon it for legal status and such privileges as tax exemption. It is these private, spontaneous organizations the laissez faire exponents would encourage.

Those who hold a less extreme position, but nevertheless fear the inherent evil of big government, believe that the ultimate determination of income distribution ought to be left *primarily* to the free play of the market and individual decisions. While acknowledging that such an arrangement will result in inequalities in distribution, they believe this is not wholly undesirable. If government acts to preserve and strengthen competition, such inequalities will correspond to contributions to production. If monopoly is prevented, such inequalities need not be large. By keeping the way open for all to invest and to exercise their ingenuity and ambition, savings from the larger incomes will be largely channeled back into the national-income stream, raising the level of income by creating new opportunities and new jobs. At the same time those who do not place a high value on money income (preferring rather the pursuit of leisure or other goals), can be free to follow their preferences.

Relief and social welfare work ought to be a local and state responsibility, with the Federal government providing supplementary aid only in hardship cases. This is perceived as the way to preserve local autonomy and responsibility, and to keep the control and administration of such measures in the hands of people close to the recognized needs, and where the bonds of organization are strongest.

If, through the "proper" administration of its monetary and credit system, the Federal government were to ensure a stable price level, the need for income transfers would be less acute. Alternating periods of inflation and deflation, which favor some unduly and penalize others harshly, would be minimized. Then if loss of income were made clearly identifiable with improper allocation and misuse of resources, the argument for special treatment would lose its force.

Even the less extreme proponents of the free market would favor a balanced budget, if not on an annual basis then over a somewhat longer period. They would allow borrowing for durable improvements, the returns from which would be forthcoming over longer periods of time. But such investments would be restricted to fields where government effectiveness could be demonstrated. Their preference for the personal income tax as the principal source of government revenue is based on the belief that it is least likely to have "uneconomic" effects on the over-all economy. Most of them would favor estate and death taxes, since these are levied at a time when a general rearrangement of property claims occur in any event. Because of the apparent connection between property income and concentration, they would accept progressive tax rates on estates, in the interest of preserving equality of opportunity. Mostly they oppose the corporate income tax on the grounds of double taxation and because the evidence is not at all convincing that corporate income taxes cannot be shifted.

The defenders of a predominantly private enterprise society, who base their argument on a belief in individual liberty (either of the extreme or the modified view), place "economic freedom" high on their value scale, if not in fact at the top.

493

Distribution
Under Planning

The defenders of a centrally-controlled or planned economy bring up their heaviest artillery when they deal with distribution. In their discussions of distributive justice the term *economic democracy* appears frequently. While the meaning of this term is not always clear, there is an implied parallel with political democracy which stresses the principle of equality as a criterion of distributive justice.

The stated goals of collectivist economists range from complete income equality to perhaps a little more equality than exists at the present day. Karl Marx developed no explicit principles for determining distribution in the socialist Utopia he envisioned. He did suggest that in the future socialist society income would be distributed according to the principle, "From each according to his ability, to each according to his need." While ability might be understood to mean productivity, the concept of need is less easily defined.

If one characterizes laissez faire in its extreme form as a value system based upon maximum responsibility of the individual for his own income, collectivism can be described in its extreme form as a value system in which the general welfare is central. The individual is advised that his own income aspirations rest finally with the planned development of society or the state. The psychological roots of the socialist Utopias are fairly clear. The mutual aid and security of the primary group is generalized to include the larger social environment of the nation or beyond. In nineteenth-century socialist thought the thread of internationalism was strong. Those who were known as Christian socialists identified themselves with all humanity, and spoke of the co-operative commonwealth of man. The so-called scientific socialists identified themselves with the "working class," which they extended to include the "workers of the world."

The history of the United States during the nineteenth century contains examples of numerous experiments in community effort and income sharing. Many of these communities were inspired by religious beliefs, although some, such as Brook Farm and New Harmony, were founded on idealistic principles regarded as the "essence of rationalism." Some relied upon the judgment of the elders, the church fathers, or the leader in the distribution of rewards and punishments, both economic and other. Some tried elaborate plans for sharing work and product, with clearly defined classifications of payment for different kinds of jobs. These worldwide "experiments" were small islands of socialism or communism in a sea of expanding private enterprise. Not until the twentieth century were

494

political parties with a socialist orientation to achieve power as national governments. When they did, the gap between socialism as "dream" and socialism as "reality" was often wide indeed.

While the goal of socialist planning has sometimes been absolute equality in the distribution of income, this has not often been attempted in practice. When it has been the effort has usually failed. Possible exceptions would be those situations of extreme scarcity, when only enough food or water exists for bare survival. Then the members of a closely-knit group may share alike the misery and poverty. Even within the primary social unit, the family, equality is usually not desired or practiced.

Soviet Russia, immediately following the revolution (during the period now described as "war communism), tried a policy of equal distribution of whatever that war-torn land had to offer. But this soon gave way to Lenin's "new economic policy" (NEP), which made the ultimate income claims contingent upon contributions to production.

Socialization of Property Income

Models of collectivist states are usually predicated on an abolition of most property income, if not at once, then as a long-run objective. Socialization or nationalization of the means of production, of land and capital, has usually been assumed to be the necessary prelude to ending the "exploitation of man by man."

What, then, would be the source of the income claims of individuals and households? The answer usually given is that it would be based upon human effort alone, except where society itself makes provisions for those unable to work, or those not yet old enough to work. This would mean the elimination of a *rentier* class. All who were able would be expected to make some kind of personal contribution to production. This, it was long presumed, would result in substantial increases in output and would mark an important milestone on the road to plenty, where more of both leisure and income would be available to all.

Decisions to save and invest would be in the hands of the state and the duly-elected representatives of the people, where the regime was one of democratic socialism, while they would be in the hands of the planning agency or the dictator (leader) in an authoritarian system. Having decided on what proportion of output to allocate to consumption goods, and how much to allocate to new capital construction, the amount of money income distributed would be just sufficient to take available goods and services off the market. Control of aggregate money income presumably would be the function of a central banking system, closely coordinated with the central planning organization.

495

Distribution in Soviet Russia

We now shift our attention from dreams of the ideal to experience. What can we say (on the basis of limited sources of information) about distribution in Soviet Russia? How is income shared? How are claims established? How much of it becomes household income, and what part of it is available for final disposition by agencies of the state?

All capital equipment, the land, the mines, the factories, communications and transportation, are property of the state, its subdivisions, or their agents. New construction and maintenance, and therefore investment, is a function of state agencies. Investment plans are co-ordinated through the State Planning Commission; final approval is by the Presidium or central authority.

The principal saving is what might be called "forced saving." Prices are devices for limiting the consumption of goods and services so that factors of production (including labor) can be allocated to capital formation. Since 1929, when the first of the Five-Year Plans was initiated, rapid industrialization of the country has been a primary objective. Since the Russians have been unwilling to accept foreign investments for the expansion of industries and development of resources, "forced draft" capital accumulation has been accomplished through increasing production and the limiting of consumption. Indirect taxes, which are added to the price of consumer goods produced by the various *trusts,* make it difficult to draw a line between the part of price based upon costs (as they are recorded in the accounting systems of firms) and the taxes collected by government. All profits from industry, which can be defined as the difference between accounting costs and revenues, are channeled back to government.

In agriculture the government has several sources of revenue. On the state farms where workers are paid a wage the entire output becomes the property of a government agency, which in turn sells it to the processing trusts or the export trusts, also government agencies. All income above the cost of operating the state farm becomes government income.

A major part of the farm land is nominally the property of *collectives.* In lieu of taxes the collective pays over to the government a specified percentage of its production in kind. This is disposed of by government agencies in the same way as the output from state farms. Government tractor stations supply machine services to the collective farms, and for this service the government collects an additional payment in kind. The rest of the collectives' output (not required for use on the farm) is purchased at a fixed price by government agencies, or may be sold on the so-called free market. Raw materials thus collected become the food sup-

496

plies of the working population of the cities. Since these goods are processed in state-owned factories and distributed in state-owned stores, the profit at each stage in production becomes revenue to the government. When factories or collective farms make new investments, credit is supplied by the central bank (Gosbank).

What about household income? This can come from wages and salaries, or from the funds set aside for pensions, bonuses, or other special purposes.[2] Distribution through bonus and subsidy is a means for rewarding workers and attracting them to industries scheduled for expansion. Many factories operate their own stores, where employees are entitled to buy goods which are not otherwise available or which are sold here at favorable prices. These goods are usually rationed. Additional quantities may be purchased on the "free market," where prices are higher and the government's profit income proportionately larger.

Within a particular industry wage rates are based upon an elaborate system of job classification, which in turn is related to types of skills and the training required. Skills and training are linked with productivity. To stimulate effort, piece rates are widely employed, with rates set sufficiently low to insure maximum effort. Bonuses are offered, both in industry and agriculture, for outstanding production records; and liberal use is made of medals and decorations, which give status to those whose "contributions to the state" are outstanding. Prior to World War II the term Stakhanovite (derived from Stakhanov, an unusually productive coal miner of the Donets Basin) became a title of distinction conferred upon those of outstanding production achievement.

Although most saving is by government, households can save and participate in investment through the purchase of government bonds. Since the purchase of such bonds reduces income available for consumer goods, such saving is encouraged.

While exact information on the range of income differences is not available for the Soviet Union, most experts on the Soviet economy believe that it is considerably greater than that of most Western nations. A clue to distribution policy shows up in the revision of Marx's famous stricture which is now the slogan, "From each according to his ability, to each according to his productivity." In view of the fact that the Soviet Union is still a relatively backward country industrially and a substantial part of investment goes into the military establishment, it can be presumed that productivity is low compared with the United States.

---

[2] At one time households could "invest" in government bonds and thus "earn" an interest income. More recently such interest payments have been deferred.

Also, the preceding discussion leaves out of account the untold numbers of prison laborers whose only income claim is the meager subsistence they receive.

Distribution Policies of the British Labour Party

A more equitable distribution of income has long been central to the socialist program of the British Labour party. While security and dignity for those who work (and the use of political power for these ends) are its stated objectives, a larger share in the national income is the means to these ends.

Party leaders maintain, of course, that their plans for the "rationalization" of industries will mean more production and better products. The hope of sharing in such increased productivity, it is maintained, will be the factor most likely to induce a greater effort by workers.

When it came to power in 1945 the Labour party inherited from the preceding coalition government an intricate system of price controls, steeply graduated income taxes, and rationing. These had been adopted during the war on the grounds that when the national security was in danger, and when so much of the country's productive capacity had to be allocated to war production, the remaining limited output *ought* to be shared as equally as possible, so that none should bear a disproportionate burden of the sacrifices. Distribution was based on a rough approximation of need, so that children and the sick received proportionally more protective foods. Those doing heavy manual labor were given a larger ration of energy-producing foods.

Because of the precarious financial position of Great Britain at the end of the war, with her foreign investments dissipated and twelve billion dollars owed to India and other Commonwealth nations, controls and wartime taxes were retained to limit consumption and make a greater amount of the national output available for export. Exports were required to procure raw materials which Great Britain could not produce at home. The Labour government retained these controls, since it intended to effect a more equitable sharing of whatever productivity could be attained during and after conversion to peacetime production. Nationalization was to be a safeguard against any return to the unequal distribution which had prevailed before the war.

Rationing continued for a longer time in England than in most other countries; longer even than in the Soviet Union. Even though incomes rose, price control, rationing, and food subsidies prevented an increase of prices (which would have reduced the real income of the workers). The rationing system continued to make special provisions based upon

498

need, and it was a claim of the Labour party that milk consumption by children was greater, on the average, than at any previous time.

Simultaneously, the Labour government embarked upon an extensive social-welfare program, which provided without direct costs services which previously had been purchased on an individual basis. These included medical and dental care, drugs, artificial limbs, and other items for the handicapped. Income previously allocated for such items by low-income households was now available for other uses. Taxes remained high and steeply graduated. The effect was a further equalization of incomes. Municipalities and other government agencies undertook the reconstruction of houses destroyed or damaged during the war, and rents on existing houses were controlled. However, much of Labour's program did not originate with the socialists. Public construction of houses had been instituted after World War I under a Conservative government. The leading exponent of the health program was Sir William Beveridge, a member of the Liberal party and long an advocate of the use of government fiscal policy to stabilize and maintain high-level employment.

Within the Labour party there is a wide range of opinion. This was true while the party was in power and has become more marked since it has been out of power. The Cooperative party, which accepts the discipline of the Labour party whip, has become increasingly critical of nationalization, particularly in industries which have a substantial cooperative sector. In his *Future of Socialism*, C. A. R. Crosland acknowledges the fact that the modern "mixed economy" has gone far toward achieving distributive goals formerly espoused by British socialism.

The Scandinavian countries have had Social Democratic or Socialist governments for extended periods. New Zealand and Australia also have had Labour governments, dedicated to increasing the income of the lower-income groups. In all of these countries socialist governments have functioned in a democratic political environment with strong opposition parties, so that progress toward the objectives of their ideal models has necessarily been gradual, with credit for "social advances" sometimes going to their adversaries.

The Pragmatic Approach
to Distribution

How is distribution treated in the thinking and policy prescriptions of the pragmatic approach? Dedicated neither to the dogma of a free market nor to comprehensive economic or income planning, the pragmatists' criteria of distributive justice are not so neatly logical and consistent as

the others. Principle is tempered by expediency (which implies a compromise of many principles) and a recognition that in a world of relative,
and sometimes conflicting, values distributive justice, like other forms of
justice is subject to change in the face of shifts in public opinion and
political action.

There is explicit recognition of the fact that people have never accepted completely the decisions of an unregulated market to decide "their
fair share," and have acted as individuals and groups to influence it.
Where conditions in the "real world" have approximated the postulates of
the competitive model, income has been determined with a minimum of
social tension. But there is also the recognition that over a period of time
these conditions have become increasingly difficult to maintain. Changing
technology and the drift away from personal ownership and identification
with real property have resulted in concentrating the control of capital
and the powers of decision in fewer and fewer hands, so that the link
between contributions to production and income claims is less clear-cut.

In a political democracy the central belief in equalitarianism and the
freedom to associate for the purpose of correcting economic injustices
(real or fancied) have resulted in an increasing role for pressure groups.
Working through government to influence markets by restricting competition and free entry, and by seeking income transfers through subsidies
and government matching of "security funds," these groups have used
political action to promote their income interests.

When those dedicated to a policy of laissez faire profess to see in
present trends a definite drift to socialism and loss of freedom, the pragmatic or modern liberal points to the gains of freedom in other areas—
freedom from want and freedom from job insecurity, both of which have
been achieved through positive government action in maintaining income
flows and employment. When the advocates of planning profess to see
in the increasing size (and reduction in numbers) of firms the threat of
private monopoly control of economic life, the pragmatic liberals call
attention to the increasing real flow of new mass-produced goods, developed through research and made available at declining relative prices
(in the long run) by "big business."

Modern economists have found justification for a more equalitarian
distribution in aggregate income analysis. As we learned in Part 2, lower-
income groups spend a higher proportion of their incomes. Households
with high incomes save a larger proportion. The more unequal the income
distribution, the greater must be investment to offset savings and maintain
the level of income and employment. However, since investments are
made by individuals and groups in their capacity as entrepreneurs or

managers of corporations, they are sensitive to aggregate demand or total spending on consumption. A disproportionate number of low-income families will mean an aggregate demand insufficient to clear the market, especially in the short run. Policies which result in increasing the incomes of those with a high propensity to consume can stimulate demand, helping to maintain output and employment. Most modern economists would hold that a government fiscal policy which prevents the national income from falling is of first-order importance. By keeping people employed the most damaging causes of unequal income distribution can be prevented. Just as the trend toward more equal income distribution of the last decade can be attributed, in no small measure, to full employment, so also can the unequal distribution of a period of low economic activity such as the middle 1930's be attributed to the fact that many people did not have jobs.

While the argument for more equitable income distribution on the grounds of "economic need" in maintaining purchasing power is a meaningful one, and one seemingly devoid of the sentimentality of the so-called "do-gooders," it is not the only one advanced for pragmatic reasons. Helping the lowest income groups to secure a larger share in economic progress can be justified for social reasons as well.

Few would argue for absolute income equality, although economists like A. P. Lerner have presented the case for this as a long-run goal. Democratic political organization lends itself to equalization of income. This was anticipated by the more conservative members of the Constitutional Convention, when they argued for property qualification as a basis for the franchise. However, equalization of income is now accepted as a fact of experience by defenders of the mixed economy, who approve the use of public policy to hasten improvement in the lot of the least privileged members of society. Even the late Senator Robert A. Taft, never one for hasty modification of existing institutions of the enterprise system, favored Federal subsidy for housing and education as a means of improving the real-income position of the lowest twenty-five per cent of the population, thereby strengthening the "social fabric." The progressive income tax is defended as a practical expedient of gradual social reform. Graduated tax rates, coupled with liberal family exemptions, have the effect of leaving low-income families with a larger disposable income.

Intervention in the distribution process through income transfers is regarded as more practical than attempts to rearrange basic property holdings, either by breaking up giant firms on the one hand, or by socializing them on the other. This, of course, does not necessarily imply a total neglect of antimonopoly policy. The pragmatic liberals regard the increasing role of government as an adaptation which our society has made to science and technology. Technological change has upset old institutional and property relationships. As groups have learned from experience that, by acting through government, their own income interests can be served, such actions have spread by precept and example. There are dangers, of course, in too great acceptance of things as they are, even for practical reasons. The "money illusion" is very strong, and the pursuit of an ever increasing money income, a larger relative claim against the pie of real income, may come to naught, if each group succeeds in getting a larger and larger slice of a pie that fails to increase or actually gets smaller.

The strength of the belief of those who favor the ideal model of the free market is that when it works it does the best job of keeping the money-income and real-income flows in balance, while preserving the illusion of impartiality. The logic of the controlled or planned economy rests on the assumption that the distributive shares can be determined in advance, so that they must equal the value of available consumption goods and services. The experimental model of the mixed economy is not so neat in its logic. Its adjustment must depend finally upon compromise, experiment, and the solution of specific problems as they arise.

Modern social science provides some evidence that we can rely, in part at least, on old habits and old ways of thinking to preserve a central core of stability in our society. As long as the income distribution of the recent past does not change drastically, particularly in an unfavorable direction, perceived income needs and the income received are not likely to be far apart. Economists and other social scientists, as scientists, can continue to make their greatest contribution to distributive justice by their research into patterns of human behavior, including economic behavior. There is still much we do not know about the relation between income needs and the psychological needs of people, and what this implies for human motivation.

Discussion
Questions

1. The free market is an impartial dispenser of distributive justice. When it does its job well, there is no one to thank for one's good fortune, no one to blame for misfortune. Discuss.

2. While productivity may be difficult to measure, the criterion of need as a basis for income distribution is vague and difficult to apply. Discuss.

3. J. K. Galbraith argues that as industrial societies become more affluent

the incentives for production, particularly in the private economy, become weakened, because people are further removed from any pressing sense of need. He therefore argues for an expanded public economy, especially for investment in people through education. What is your opinion?

4. More has been achieved in alleviating poverty in the United States by increased production than by reform programs aimed at redistributing income. However, this progress has not been achieved by unrestrained private enterprise either. Discuss.

5. Income is easier to redistribute than property. Discuss.

Selected References for Part 4

Allen, Frederick L. *The Big Change*. New York: Harper and Brothers, 1952.

Blough, Roy. *The Federal Taxing Process*. New York: Prentice-Hall, Inc., 1952.

Chamberlin, Edward H. *The Economic Analysis of Labor Union Power*. Washington: American Enterprise Association, Inc., 1958.

Daugherty, Carroll R., and Parrish, John B. *The Labor Problems of American Society*. Boston: Houghton Mifflin Co., 1952.

Department of Commerce. *Income Distribution in the United States by Size, 1944–1950*. Washington: U. S. Government Printing Office, 1953.

Drucker, Peter F. *America's Next Twenty Years*. New York: Harper and Brothers, 1957.

Groves, Harold A. *Financing Government*. New York: Henry Holt & Co., 1954.

Heilbroner, Robert L. *The Quest for Wealth: A Study of Acquisitive Man*. New York: Simon & Schuster, Inc., 1956.

Lerner, Max. *America as a Civilization*. New York: Simon & Schuster, Inc., 1957. Chapters V, pp. 265–353, and VII, pp. 465–541.

Schickele, Rainer. *Agricultural Policy: Farm Programs and National Welfare*. New York: McGraw-Hill Book Co., 1954.

Simons, Henry C. *Personal Income Taxation*. Chicago: The University of Chicago Press, 1938.

Wootton, Barbara. *The Social Foundations of Wage Policy*. New York: W. W. Norton & Co., 1955.

Annual income twenty pounds, annual expenditure nineteen, nineteen six, result happiness. Annual income twenty pounds, annual expenditure twenty pounds ought and six, result misery.

CHARLES DICKENS
Micawber,
in *David Copperfield*

PART 5

CONSUMPTION

The Final Use of Income

Introduction

OUR INQUIRY into the transactions and relationships which underlie the national-income figures, first presented in Part 2, has taken us through the complexities of production decisions and distribution. We turn now to the problems and choices which face the ultimate consumer in the use of income.

As economic agents, that group of persons loosely described as "the consumer" is the most inclusive we can imagine since in a very real sense it includes us all. Defined in this way, the term has meaning for some purposes. However, it has been overworked. Rarely does a special-interest group plead its case in the press or before a Congressional committee without claiming that its proposals are in the consumers' interest, or at least not contrary to it. Because the concept is used in popular discussion to include everybody, and everything anyone does, it includes nobody in any very precise sense. A systematic study of consumption can begin with the behavior of household units in the use or spending of income.

As we learned in our analysis of the national-income accounts, spending or saving by consumers constitutes the largest feedback into the income system. At the same time it is meaningful to regard consumer expenditures as dependent upon income. By investigating the response of consumer behavior to changes in income (both in the short run and the long run), economists seek to discover relationships and patterns useful for understanding and predicting economic events.

Other factors than size of income are also significant. Standards of living are useful dimensions for comparing and contrasting cultural characteristics of national and regional groups. Attitudes about the use of income reflect other value commitments of individuals and groups. These are some of the data and ideas treated in Part 5.

CHAPTER 32

Consumption in an Industrial Society

REDUCED TO ITS SIMPLEST (and therefore most general) form, our inquiry into the economics of consumption will be concerned with how people use the resources of their environment to satisfy their needs. Like all simple statements, this one requires development; and like other aspects of our subject, this development involves us almost at once in language, with concepts which are meaningful for the purposes at hand, and with data to serve as evidence in the search for knowledge about the subject.

We begin by asking what is the meaning of the verb *to consume*. In ordinary usage, it serves in many different contexts. "Fire Consumes Dwelling" screams a newspaper headline. Livestock being fattened as part of the production process consume vast quantities of grain and supplements. The coke *consumption* of a blast furnace in extracting a ton of pig iron may serve as an index of its efficiency. When used to refer to many aspects of the "real world" of human affairs, the ultimate consumption process usually means "destruction in use" of scarce goods. But what does it mean to destroy a good by consuming it? Certainly it does not mean the destruction of matter, which we know is indestructible.

The act of consuming has usually been defined in economic literature as the destruction of utility. If production is defined as the creation of utility, then we can say that consumption is the act of undoing what has been done in the production process.

For the individual household, the goal or end to be served by consumption can be described as the use of available means to achieve immediate or long-run satisfaction. In our society this process *begins* with the use of money (income). Accordingly, we can ask of the basic data on consumer behavior, "How do households, individually and in the aggregate, actually use (spend) this scarce means?"

In a frame of reference tied to the income process the concept of

507

consumption will be different from that of the home economist, although the two can be linked in what we shall call the technology of consumption. It will be recalled that in Part 2 consumption was defined, for purposes of aggregate analysis, as the spending of income, and was distinguished only from saving. Here, as inquiry brings us nearer to the problems of the micro or household level, the definition will be consistent with that used earlier, but it will be deepened and enriched with other experience data. By the ultimate consumer we mean those economic agents (as individuals or representatives of households) who, in planning the disposition of income, exchange liquid assets or property forms in their control for goods and services better suited to the satisfaction of perceived needs. As part of the income process subsequent acts of consuming or using up these goods and services result in reducing household net worth, which can only be renewed through further access to income.

Consumer Behavior

Consumer behavior is an important source of knowledge about the economic process—one that has been neglected by economists, except for a nod of approval and acknowledgment that it is important. Adam Smith thought that the interest of the consumer was central to the whole economic problem, and he believed that the benefit of the producer should be attended only insofar as it contributed to the interest of the consumer. Having made this acknowledgment, however, he gave most of his attention to production and government, on the grounds that what he had said about consumption was so self-evident that it required no further exploration. What he and others assumed was that consumer tastes and income are *given,* that consumers know what they want and act rationally to satisfy their wants. For purposes of analysis it will sometimes be useful to make this assumption as a starting point. To understand the role of the consumer in the economic process, however, it will usually be necessary to abandon such an assumption once we take our hypotheses back to experience for testing.

Modern psychologists recognize that consumer behavior (which is part of general behavior) is not a completely consistent and rational phenomenon. This is not to say that there are no determinants of behavior, that such behavior cannot be predicted or understood. What is implied is that in an environment which is subject to change, where new experience and new knowledge make consumption as much of an adventure as a plan, consumer behavior will display a wide range of variation correlated with other factors.

To the management of producer organizations, forecasting consumer

508

behavior is a necessary function. While demand creation through advertising and salesmanship has always been part of the merchant's tools, the solid core of production plans is based upon knowledge gained from experience of what steady customers will buy. With the mass markets of today, demand analysis and market forecasts based upon past records and trends in buyer preference have become staff functions in most large firms. Advertising media, such as daily newspapers and national magazines, perform a continuing service for their customers by conducting attitude surveys and consumer-preference studies. Research organizations, like the Survey Research Center at the University of Michigan, use their nationwide sampling organization to assemble regular information on houshold plans (which is later checked against performance) in order to build a more reliable basis for statistical prediction of consumer behavior.

Maximum Satisfaction

It may be helpful, as Kenneth Boulding has suggested, to think of the household as a miniature firm whose objective is the maximization of total satisfaction from available means. These *means,* which have been called the factors of consumption by Elizabeth Hoyt, are the *income,* the *time,* the *energy,* and the *management ability* of the purchasing agent of the household. Of these, income is likely to be of overwhelming importance, although within limits the other factors mentioned may be substituted for it. It is an important fact of everyday life that some families are able to "do more" with a given income than others because of the abilities, the energies, and the knowledge of the principal agent.

The technology of consumption will consist then of the way income is used. Efficiency and productivity of the household is measured by whether or not the given income is spent in such a way that later experience does not lead to regrets. Because it is easy to spend money and difficult to earn it, Wesley C. Mitchell, in an essay which has now become a classic, addressed himself to the "backward art of spending money." In that essay he pointed out the more important problems and the obstacles which stand between the housewife and effective use of income. Lack of knowledge, lack of clear conceptualization of her role, and the complexity of her task are the most important.

Economists have developed an abstract model which classifies the important variables and significant relationships. In the next chapter this will be presented as the simple theory of consumption. This theory will then be applied to the problems of the individual household budget.

Decisions are made in a social environment characterized by the variations of income and by technological change which is constantly providing means for satisfying new needs, or is providing new goods to satisfy old needs. This environment, as consumers perceive it, has become increasingly complex. It is not merely a passive surrounding from which to select, but an active force affecting and being affected by people. The consumer is both end and means.

The question of consumer direction of the economy depends in part on the point at which inquiry begins. If, somewhere in the repetitive and roundabout cycle of production, we had focused attention on a particular good or service, following it through all the stages that have been described up to now, the time and place at which we might arrive (and perhaps take our leave, unable to bear the sight of our economic good being destroyed in the final act of consumption) would be where ownership passes to some consumer. One could say that this was how it was *intended* from the beginning, and the process is now complete.

The Act of Choice

We shall dramatize the act of choice for purposes of concreteness. We have all watched a child standing in front of a candy case, a coin clutched tightly in her hand, eyeing the display, some part of which can be hers with the simple act of surrendering the coin. Arranged before her in some pattern of color and design to attract attention are many different sorts and sizes of things, intended to satisfy the inner craving we have called a want. We see her, the ultimate consumer, making up her mind. The possibilities are many, each separate unit having its special shade of want-satisfying capacity. Some, though larger than the others, may lack the quality or intensity of sweetness or lasting chewiness which is a special delight. But what they lack in quality they make up in size, and while the range of possible satisfaction is immense, the means to that satisfaction is limited, concentrated for the moment in the single coin in the hand. Sooner or later the decision will be reached. Perhaps *only* after a number of inquiries have produced the information that this or that item costs more than a nickel, is the coin surrendered and possession exercised over the desired item.

The possibilities in this little drama of the ultimate consumer have by no means been exhausted. We could go on to speculate on why the particular item was chosen. For some purposes this too would be included in a definition of consumption, along with the process of eating and enjoying the good. Our frame of reference, however, is more limited. Our interest in the transaction tapers off at a point where the money changes hands and shifts to the events that follow as a result of the choice. The psychologists, the physiologists, and the sociologists, take over to explore in more detail the forces behind the choice, the sense of security and satisfaction which

510

attend the consuming of the item. Our attention moves to the empty space which once contained the bar of candy, and to the fact that it must now be replaced. We are led back again into the series of events with which our discussion of production began. For when enough of these ultimate consumers have exercised this choice, the one who sold the candy will be forced to replenish his own stock from the wholesaler and the wholesaler from the manufacturer.

The little consumer in our economic drama was purposely given a high degree of freedom of choice. No dominating mother was there to influence her. Sometimes, and particularly with children, this would be an unrealistic portrayal; for children often are not granted that special capacity of knowing what they want (in particular what is good for them), and hence the ability to exercise freedom of choice. This capacity is usually reserved for adults.

We could extend the dramatization to a broader field. It can be observed or inferred from the behavior of the housewife at the food market, dress department, at the auto show, or in the real estate office. Conceptually, we can extend it to all decisions by the consumer where limited resources are involved, to the weighing of this advantage against that, and to the final act of decision when the owner of liquid claims makes a choice among different goods or services and the money changes ownership.

The consumer has been purposely cast in a feminine role. Estimates vary, but for some of the more important consumption items as much as 80 or 90 per cent of the income passes through the hands of women. In a majority of households it is the task of the housewife to determine how the income for food, clothing, house furnishings, and a large part of the recreation expenditures and medical care will be spent.

The size of the family income plus the extent of the household credit determine the claims which can be exercised against the market. The judgment of the housewife will determine the allocation of income among several broad categories of the budget. The exercise of choice is thus bounded on the one side by the prices and qualities of goods available, and on the other by the amount of income, tastes, and perceived needs. At any given time complete freedom to dispose of a given income is usually limited by previous commitments and plans.

Consumer Sovereignty

If the production organization of a nation is so administered that decisions to produce are regulated by consumer choice, *consumer sovereignty* is said to prevail. It is analogous to the concept of sovereignty used in political science, where the referent is power. There we ask the question: "Who

511

decides ultimately how the coercive authority of the state shall be used?" If control over its use is widely distributed among individuals or groups, the situation is described as *popular sovereignty*—the power distribution associated with democracy. Thus the concepts of consumer sovereignty and democracy share a common core of meaning. The casting of "dollar votes" in the market place has been compared to the casting of ballots at the polls. Households vote for the continued production of goods and services by purchasing them. They vote for larger production by increasing their purchases. They vote for smaller production by decreasing their purchases.

This is a useful analogy, but it can be carried too far. Complete freedom rarely exists in either area. If consumers are free to spend their money for goods and services others have already decided to produce, this is not what most economists have in mind when they refer to consumer sovereignty. Choice cannot be exercised when an authoritarian government decides what *ought* to be produced, and then by propaganda convinces the population that this is what it needs and *ought* to buy (particularly if the output of consumer goods is so small that having any item is better than doing without). Neither does it exist when private producers decide what their output shall be, and spend millions of dollars on manipulative advertising to convince consumers that this is what they *really* want by appealing to emotions, prejudice, insecurity, and wishful thinking. Free consumer choice is an ideal, a goal that a society may try to attain. Practically, it can be imagined as a situation in which people are able to choose from a variety of goods and services they know from past experience, and in which new products can get a chance to compete for consumer approval.

Consumer choice cannot be divorced from distribution. When votes are by dollars, influence in the market will be in rough proportion to the number of dollar votes cast, and the market will be biased in favor of high-income groups. This is a problem to which we shall return later. However, mere income differences do not provide a unique criterion of consumer freedom, since tastes also are likely to be related to income, which means that consumer satisfaction or utility will be judged by different *standards*.

If a concept of consumer sovereignty is to be useful for analysis, its function will be to raise questions for further inquiry. To what extent do consumers actually determine factor allocation? Given the behavior pattern of people as consumers, is the ideal of consumer sovereignty an attainable goal in a complex industrial society?

A part of the problem which attends any discussion of consumer sov-

512

ereignty is semantic. That our use of language permits us to refer to *the* consumer clouds the fact that *the* consumer does not exist. Wide differences of interest among people as consumers is merely a special case of the "economic problem" which originates in the rivalry for the limited resources to be shared. In the striving for income, groups emerge in which members share a common interest. The pressure groups discussed in Part 4 are examples. There are no such clear-cut examples among consumers, except insofar as standards are characteristic of such occupational or class groups. Individuals act in many different roles. Their achievements as producers are likely to "pay off" more handsomely in terms of status, security, and general emotional satisfaction than the most efficient use of income. It is perhaps for this reason that consumer consciousness as a socio-economic force is largely ineffective.

Of the things people consume—the goods and services they use to satisfy their needs—not all are obtained by spending private income. As the free gifts of nature (which once could be freely appropriated) have diminished, an increasing volume of services used by everyone has been provided by the public economy. The private automobile, as well as the public carrier, travels over roads supported by taxes. Water supply, electric power, parks, scenic areas, postal service, education, and many other important items of consumption that contribute to "scales" or "levels" of living, and which in their immediate "enjoyment" appear to be free, are paid for by all of us acting together (although not at equal rates). No inquiry into consumption can neglect this fact, particularly if we are concerned with changes in consumption over a period of time. As part of our inquiry into the final use of income, therefore, we will learn how the different agencies of government spend their income, that is, on the goods and services they provide for households and individuals. Finally, we shall close the examination of this aspect of the economic process with a discussion of important policy questions and ideal criteria as they affect the use of income by people.

Discussion
Questions

1. A household with $3,000 in savings decides to buy a new car for that amount. Show what entries would be made in an imaginary balance sheet for this household, and in the balance sheet of the dealer, upon the completion of the transaction.

2. Would the purchase of a car by a household be regarded as an invest-

ment or a consumption expenditure? How would the Department of Commerce treat it? Suppose the $3,000 had been used as a down-payment on a house. Would it be treated differently from the car in national-income accounting?

3. A considerable amount of food purchased by American households actually goes into the garbage pail. Would this, ordinarily, be something an economist would study? A home economist?

4. How would you define an "unwise" consumer expenditure?

5. Make a list of factors which you regard as important in determining consumer tastes. What part does habit play in taste? Emulation?

Consumption

in Theory

and Experience

IN THIS SECTION we will develop more systematically the concepts and relationships introduced in the preceding chapter. The formal representation
of the logic of choice, as it usually appears in economic analysis, is introduced first. We then link this purely formal solution to the operation
called budgeting. In succeeding chapters, a concept of taste is given empirical content by referring it to what large groups of households actually
buy (as revealed in budget studies), and to how these purchases vary with
time and circumstances. Such information leads meaningfully into a consideration of levels and standards of living. At each stage, criteria for
measuring change and variation are discussed in some detail.

CHAPTER 33

A Simple Theory of Consumption

FROM THE POINT OF VIEW of the individual consumer or household agent, the problem of *effective* income use is essentially one of allocating income (the principal factor of consumption) among alternative or competing goods and services. The starting point for decision is the felt need or (what is perhaps more accurate) the structure of wants and activities which are perceived as requiring satisfaction. This structure can be described as an ordering or ranking which at the moment of decision at least rates some things as more important than others. The judgment on which this ordering is based we have called taste. This includes wants which derive from biological need as well as those induced by social obligation and custom.

We can assume that for any act of decision these will be given (or known), even if seldom explicitly formulated. If income and tastes are given, then we can formulate a *general* solution for the problem of income allocation.

Income is the scarce means at the disposal of the household. Price tags, the symbols of the money which must be surrendered in order to effect a change of ownership of desired goods, are in this instance the constraints to attainment of satisfaction. Prices of the various goods and services differ. These prices, as we learned in Part 3, are related to the costs of producing them, and to the type of market in which they are offered for sale. Decisions to buy can be treated as a problem of allocating limited income (over a time) among alternative goods and services, each having different degrees of importance or utility and different prices. To choose more of one good ordinarily involves giving up money which might be spent on something else. Given a knowledge of wants and prices, how can disposable income be allocated among the different goods to achieve the greatest (maximum) satisfaction or utility?

516

Diminishing Marginal Utility

Before proceeding with the solution of this problem it will be necessary to consider another variable which will have a bearing on it. Any given need or want which motivates a drive to achieve its satisfaction is not unlimited. It can be reduced or satiated by obtaining different amounts of the means of satisfaction. For any time period the drive intensity can be reduced and an equilibrium re-established in the organism. Credit for first noting this characteristic of human wants is usually given to H. H. Gossen (1810–1859), a German pioneer in mathematical economics, although he was accorded little recognition during his lifetime. He developed the concept of marginal utility, and his solution to the problem is essentially the one we will now present.

The willingness to surrender a given money claim in order to obtain a particular good will diminish as each additional unit of that good is acquired, and the intensity of the drive to acquire more is reduced through being satisfied by actual consumption or by having the means in one's possession. We can use an analogy with the simple theory of production and the law of diminishing returns as it was discussed in Part 3 (see page 247). Allocation of income to a particular commodity is similar to the input of a variable factor. The output is the *desired satisfaction* of a want. If the need is intense, the first units of the good acquired will result in a substantial increase in satisfaction. But as the desire is satisfied, additional units contribute progressively less and are perceived as less important. Thus diminishing marginal utility or satisfaction is a parallel concept to diminishing marginal returns. Total utility from a particular good rises to a maximum and then declines. More units of the same thing become less and less important, until at the point of maximum total satisfaction marginal utility becomes zero, and then negative. This is what is known as Gossen's "first law."[1]

If we combine this relationship with those already noted, we shall be in a position to arrive at a logical solution to the problem of choice. Let us look first at the relationship between expected satisfaction (utility) and price. If in the structure of tastes a particular good or service ranks high, it will have a prior claim against income. If its price per unit is high (or if the number of units required is large), then the total claim against available income will be large. However, it will not be infinitely large. Sooner or later diminishing marginal utility will result in the weakening of the claim of any particular good against income, and the impor-

---

[1] This was treated in a preliminary way in our discussion of demand in Part 3 (see page 265) as a partial explanation of the downward-sloping curve.

tance of some other want will assert itself. The process of balancing satisfactions against one another, and against available income, will continue until one cannot (by allocating more income to one good and taking away from others) achieve a greater total satisfaction. This equilibrium will be achieved when the last small unit of income or money allocated to each particular good or service results in equivalent satisfaction. This is called the balancing of utilities at the margin. This is Gossen's second law of consumption.

We can illustrate this principle by means of a series of ratios between the price or cost of an additional unit of each particular good and its assumed "marginal utility." We will use a simple example of three goods (a, b, and c), whose combined purchase will exhaust a given income (or fraction of that income):

$$\frac{MU_a}{P_a} = \frac{MU_b}{P_b} = \frac{MU_c}{P_c}.$$

Assume that the values for these particular ratios are as follows:

$$MU_a = 10 \qquad P_a = 5$$
$$MU_b = 2 \qquad P_b = 1$$
$$MU_c = 12 \qquad P_c = 3$$

Our series of ratios now becomes:

$$\frac{10}{5} = \frac{3}{1} = \frac{12}{3}.$$

The conditions for equilibrium have not been met, because the ratios are unequal. For each additional unit of expenditure (say one dollar) on good a, two units of satisfaction or utility are obtained; for each unit of expenditure on b, three units of satisfaction are obtained; for each unit of expenditure on c, four units of satisfaction are obtained. Clearly, income transferred from a and b to c would result in greater total satisfaction, because the marginal utility of a and b would rise and c would decline. If transfers were accomplished until the ratio in each case were the same, then no further improvement could be realized as long as income or tastes did not change.

We can call the above conditions necessary for the maximizing of satisfaction. Are they also sufficient conditions? Clearly, they could only be met if we knew or could measure the utility of all possible goods. They would also require full knowledge of prices and of present and expected income.

The Concept of Substitution

Modern economists have tended to place less stress on the concept of utility, except as a term of convenience. When, for purposes of illustration, we give it some numerical value we suggest that it is capable of measurement.

Whether it can be or not is debatable. An individual, it is true, can say, "This is more useful to me than that." But can he also say with assurance, "This is twice or three times as useful as that?" If he can use some exact criterion of usefulness, as when he evaluates two classes of the same commodity for some specific purpose, then a measure of utility exists. An example would be the relative lives of synthetic and natural rubber tires when subjected to the same treatment in a testing laboratory. However, most consumer goods are judged by multiple criteria; and therefore to impute to persons the capacity to conceptualize utility precisely in the allocation of their income is unwarranted. Nor is it needed. We can start from a simple observation that people do choose, and that there does appear to be some kind of order in these choices. Their market behavior in the spending of income is a fact of experience.

We have noted previously that in making choices (where means are scarce and ends are many) the economic agent can be visualized as acting to rearrange his property claims in a manner to improve his preference position. In production this consisted of the use of liquid claims to acquire the service of factors to be transformed into an output which would increase the likelihood of a profit income. In distribution this took the form of giving up property claims or labor services to that agent which promised the greatest income claim. It will be useful to think in a similar way about the household.

At any given time the household will have some combination of assets or goods in various forms, including real assets and others of varying degrees of liquidity. Ordinarily, the household will have an inflow of claims or money. Agents of that household will also have time and energy to devote to shopping—the act of transforming assets into a different form to satisfy perceived needs. Income, or expected income, initiates the process. Cash assets are less desirable than real goods and services capable of satisfying various needs.

Substitution in Real Terms

To illustrate the process of transformation we can begin with an example in which we use concrete physical goods. Assume that a household has come into possession of 100 oranges. With this abundance of oranges, compared to immediate need, each individual orange will appear relatively insignificant. If the opportunity were presented to exchange oranges for grapefruit, the household might be willing to give up 10 oranges for 2 grapefruit, depending on their preference for the two fruits. The oranges will then have been reduced in number, while the initial taste for grapefruit has been satisfied. If the exchange were continued from there, the

519

willingness to exchange oranges for grapefruit would perhaps be at a ratio of 9 for 2. Now the number of oranges is reduced to 81, the grapefruit increased to 4. As this transformation continues, the importance of each orange will tend to rise, the importance of having another grapefruit will fall. Thus oranges will be exchanged for grapefruit only if more units of grapefruit are offered per unit of oranges. Conceivably, if the terms of exchange were favorable enough, all oranges would be exchanged for grapefruit.

If we construct a curve to describe such a transformation, using the Y axis to measure the number of oranges and the X axis to measure grapefruit, we can plot a sequence of points showing combinations of oranges and grapefruit that would be equally attractive or equally acceptable. This curve is called an *indifference curve,* since the various combinations are all equally acceptable. If the logic followed above holds, then this curve will be concave to the point of origin of the axes. This is because of the diminishing marginal rate of substitution (oranges for grapefruit as we move upward to the left, grapefruit for oranges as we move downward to the right). It is apparent that this relationship is similar to that of diminishing marginal utility, but here we do not need to assign cardinal utility to the good in question.

For each point on such a curve, there would be a position to the right which would be superior, since it would represent a combination of both grapefruit and oranges larger than that represented by the original curve. To the left (in the direction of zero on both co-ordinates) would be an inferior position since it would represent less of both. Thus we can imagine an entire family or map of such indifference curves, ranging from lower to higher levels of satisfaction (Figure 41).[2]

Substitution with Price as a Variable

We can now introduce the variable of price. Assume that we are given the indifference map for oranges and grapefruit outlined above. At existing prices, with a specified sum of money, the entire amount might be spent on (converted into) oranges. The number that could be purchased is indicated by point L on the Y axis. If the money were converted into grapefruit, the total amount that could be purchased can be indicated by K on the X axis. The ratio of lengths of these two lines O-L and O-K is the same as the ratio of the relative prices, since price times quantity (if the units are equivalent) gives total value.

---

[2] Since indifference curves connect points of equal satisfaction, we can compare them to contour lines on a map. Indifference curves are contours on the mountains of satisfaction.

If we now connect these two points, the straight line will touch (be tangent to) an indifference curve. This will tell us how much of each will be purchased at existing prices to maximize satisfaction, given the preferences of the particular household. A change in the price of either of the two goods will result in changing this line, as shown by line *A* in Figure 42. What can we infer from the change that results? With a reduction in price (of either good), the price line will touch a higher indifference curve. Thus the decrease in price has made it possible for the household to improve its consumption position by increasing its claim over the total quantity of real income. This is because of two effects of the price change. First of all, if exactly the same quantity is purchased as before total expenditure will be less. This amounts to an increase of income for the household, and is known as the *income effect*, a money income concept. Secondly, the cheaper good may be substituted for the other, since more of it can be obtained for satisfying wants. This is known as the *substitution effect*. Whether more of one good will be purchased than the other will depend upon the income or the substitution effect.

A presentation on a two-dimension graph does not permit us to deal with more than two commodities at a time. However, if we can imagine a situation in which one particular asset can be compared with all others, we can generalize our model of the psychological process whereby the consumer can arrive at an equilibrium position. Money is such an asset. If we designate the *Y* axis as the measure of our most general asset or property form and compare it with each of the other commodities (thereby establishing its importance in terms of tastes or needs), then we can approximate in our theoretical model the process of equating the preference for the various items in a household budget until the disposable income has been transformed into other assets. When the available liquid assets have been allocated, and when there is no further point in converting other assets into cash so they can in turn be reconverted into more useful goods or services, we have made the best bargain with necessity that we can make.

A More Complex Model

So far we have considered each good or service as a separate and completely independent entity. We know from experience that this is not realistic. Some things go together in pairs or in complexes. The purchase of a car, for instance, necessitates the purchase of other things. Before committing income or other assets to the purchase of an automobile it is necessary to take into account the gasoline, the oil, the tires, and the repair bills required to keep it running. Automobile, gasoline, and tires

Figure 41. Indifference Map for
Oranges and Grapefruit

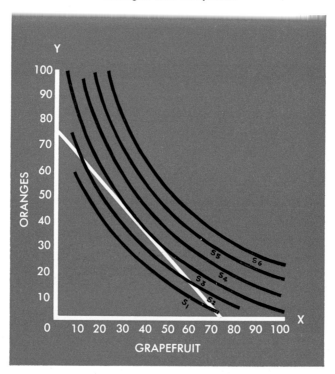

complement each other, and in economic analysis are called *complementary goods.* Thus the purchase of a car will cause the buyer to commit more from prospective income or accumulated savings than the purchase price in any planned expenditure of income.

On the other hand, some goods will be regarded as alternative or *competing goods.* This is the same as saying that one is a substitute for the other. For example, a vacation may compete with a new car, the down payment on a house, or any one of other large expenditures. The final decision, the perceived need in such cases, will not be an entirely rational matter, as we shall learn in a succeeding chapter on standards of living.

What is the significance and what is the use of the abstract model just presented? It represents a set of relationships which appear to correspond in certain respects with the market behavior of people when they plan the use of income. It has been derived from observation and hypotheses by economists, as an aid for the ordering of observations and

Figure 42. Effect of Change in the Price of Grapefruit

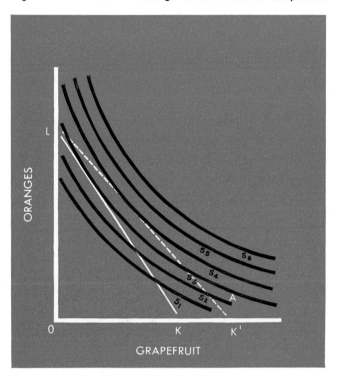

for thinking about a planning budget. We will now make these concepts more concrete by relating them to budgeting as it is practiced by many households, and as it is recommended by specialists in household or personal finance.

Planned Use of Household Income

Budgeting means the planned use of household income. A budget can be conceptualized as a system of controls which assist the household in achieving consumption goals.[3] A sequence of annual budgets can serve as a record of past experience against which to evaluate future expenditures.

---

[3] The meaning is analogous to that used in the business firm, except that there it is used as a means for achieving such goals as maximum profit income, protection of net worth, etc.

Want Classification

The starting point in any household budget is some system of classification
of needs or wants, which experience has demonstrated to be of a sufficiently repetitive nature to be anticipated or predicted in advance, so that
their claims on income can be included in planned expenditure.

Most households find it useful to make a distinction among their
wants on the basis of time. Within limits, this ordering of time can be
related to the market periods discussed in Part 3 (see page 281). The
period of market supply would correspond to those purchases the household needs immediately, or which they purchase on a daily, weekly, or
monthly basis. The short-run demand period would comprise the needs
likely to be encountered during the next year, while the long-run demand
period would in all likelihood include the objectives to be realized over
a decade or even over a lifetime. Many items ordinarily included in this
latter period are of a durable nature, such as a car, a home, education
for children, insurance, savings for old age and other situations of dependency. A lifetime budget would anticipate the filling in of valleys
and the leveling off of peaks, representing the expected gaps between
expenditures and income which occur as part of the experience of any
household.

The founding of a new household will usually involve an excess of
expenditures over income, since this, on the average, is the period of relatively low earning power and property accumulation. With experience,
income can be expected to rise to a peak, varying with occupation and
capacity, while as children grow up and start homes of their own, the
required outlays will ordinarily diminish. In our wealthy industrial
society credit has become an important means for balancing income and
outgo, with a normal expectation of income transfers between periods.
Thus savings can be viewed as the inverse of going into debt in anticipation of future income claims.

Against this general pattern of expectations, the typical household
lays its plans, makes commitments, forms its habits in the use of income,
and adjusts its behavior as experience verifies or invalidates its expectations. Successful prediction tends to reinforce habitual choices as they
contribute to household satisfactions, while failure tends to modify these
choices.

The Limits of Planned Expenditure

Within this broad system of want classification, which necessarily includes
many commitments of a fixed or contract nature, the household sets up
its more detailed budget for allocating income to the specific goods and

services within each category, where the range of choice is more flexible. These will ordinarily include expenditures on food, clothing, household operation, amusement and recreation, medical and dental care, and items of personal expenditure for individual members of the household.

Budgets tend to fall into a fixed pattern as experience accumulates and the allocation of available or expected income assumes a habitual pattern. Experience, however, is subject to variation because of changes within the household and in the social environment around it. The process of growth and aging results in a changed perception of needs and wants. New knowledge of relative price changes, the appearance of new goods, imitative behavior to conform with shifts in style or fashion, as well as fluctuations in employment and income, all have their impact on wants. Habitual patterns of expenditure are subject to review in the light of new information, and it is in this context that the problem of balancing the budget, or of transforming assets and reallocating income, occurs.

For a given act of budget analysis, our model of the marginal rate of substitution or the balancing of marginal utilities and costs is suggestive. Given the relative importance of the different broad items within a budget, together with previous fixed commitments such as rental contracts, payment schedules for durables, tax obligations, and insurance payments, the household will have made the best possible bargain with necessity when, through reflection and the trial juggling of figures, it is no longer possible to achieve a more favorable use of its assets by transferring income from one item to another.

The greatest freedom of action and choice during the short periods is likely to occur within budget items. It is there that most important substitutions are possible. While expenditures on food may represent a relatively constant proportion of the total budget for a given income, the individual commodities for which income is spent will vary with what the market has to offer in favorable prices, variety, and the capacity to command the attention of the household agent. To a lesser extent this flexibility is also present in the clothing budget, and the recreation and amusement budget. Purchases of durables, which occur less frequently during a lifetime, offer fewer opportunities for such weighing of judgments.

Within limits, the time and energy of the principal household agent can be regarded as substitutes for income in the consumption budget. Knowledge of the market, of the variations in quality of similar goods and services, of price differentials among competing firms, and of the preferences of household members constitute the technology of consumption and basis for maximizing satisfaction from any given income. Such skills are admittedly unequally distributed and, as Mitchell noted in his

525

classic essay,[4] are difficult to acquire by the housewife whose job is more diverse than that of a purchasing agent for a firm (and who is rarely selected on the basis of these particular abilities). Partly as a consequence of the increasing complexity of modern production methods (and the possibilities for transforming materials through the application of science), the task of the consumer has become even more difficult. Evaluating the qualities of new synthetic fibres, in relation to the standard wool, cotton, linen, and silk fabrics, is difficult for anyone without knowledge of results gathered in the testing laboratory. Reprocessed wool and other fibres can be treated, so that when they are new, inferior qualities can be detected only by the expert.

With this complexity and the concurrent possibilities for disguising inferior quality have come new sources of information and protection, however. The Federal government, through the Bureau of Standards and the investigators of the Federal Trade Commission and other public agencies, has undertaken to safeguard the health of consumers and to check the dissemination of false or misleading advertising. Local governments also maintain inspection services. Private testing agencies, such as Consumers' Research and Consumers' Union, have found an increasing demand for their services, particularly since World War II,[5] in providing objective criteria for the rating of a wide variety of goods and services offered by different firms. Departments of home economics in colleges and universities, numerous testing bureaus of magazines, the Bureau of Home Economics in the Department of Agriculture, and organizations of housewives carry on a continuing program of research devoted to giving operational meaning to the phrase "your money's worth."

Business firms that once operated according to the principle "let the buyer beware" today find it to their advantage to discover through research, and manipulate through advertising, the preferences of those for whom their output is intended. To the modern marketing specialist, knowledge of the market is not something that is given, packaged, and ready made. Techniques for sampling and analyzing consumer preferences for anticipating wants in advance have become important tools for the research worker. Information gathered in this way is a major influence on production plans of retail and manufacturing establishments. Although advertising and selling skills have been aptly described as *demand creation,* the work of the researcher can be characterized as *demand discovery.* Similarly, our knowledge of how households use their income, and of

[4] *The Backward Art of Spending Money.*
[5] See E. R. Beem, "Consumer-Financed Testing and Rating Agencies," *The Journal of Marketing,* January, 1952, pp. 273–85.

how the allocation of income varies with time and changes in its level and distribution, comes from the research of economists and other social scientists.

Discussion
Questions

1. Maximum satisfaction for a consumer consists of the best compromise between what is most desirable and the limitations placed upon him (or her) by such environmental constraints as income, credit, time, and custom. Explain.

2. While it is difficult to state precisely the maximum amount of any particular good or service it would be desirable to have, most people have a fairly well defined notion of their minimum requirements. Discuss.

3. A concept of utility is a linguistic convenience, and we probably couldn't get along without it. However, it is not a single-value term, and accordingly it is very difficult to assign a precise value to it. Discuss.

4. What are the similarities and differences between the concept of diminishing marginal utility and the concept of the diminishing marginal rate of substitution?

5. Explain in your own words the income effect and the substitution effect of a price decline for an important item in the consumer budget.

Consumer Budgets and Consumer Spending

BUDGET STUDIES, which were discussed in Part 4 as a source of information about income distribution, are also a source of information on income spending. Economic historians, searching for and classifying evidence from the past, have sometimes found the account books of systematic householders useful evidence of how people lived, as revealed in the goods and services they purchased to satisfy their needs and reward their efforts.

Such bits of information, when fitted into data accumulated from other sources, such as diaries, books, and newspaper articles written at the time, give an impression of what life was like in a given period (its material aspects at least). Thus E. W. Martin, an economic historian, was able to recapture in *The Standard of Living in 1860* a feeling of the "content" of life in that predominantly agricultural society. The high proportion of income spent for food and other staples indicates how much effort must have been devoted simply to providing enough to eat and wear. Martin's descriptions and broad perspective, and his familiarity with many recorded impressions over a broad time span, also give us a sense of the gradual shift from concern over "enough to eat" to other consumption experiences in a society of increasing real-income capacity.

Economists and other social scientists have undertaken more systematic inquiries into family or household spending to give detail to an understanding of consumption. Modern sampling techniques and methods of observation have improved the data and given us measures for describing levels or scales of living.

Early Attempts to Study Consumption

The pioneers in the investigation of household income and its use were sometimes motivated by concern for family "welfare." Gregory King, while not quite in this company, conducted studies in Europe during the latter half of the seventeenth century as part of an attempt to understand the effect of consumption and war expenditures on national income. Like other of his Mercantilist contemporaries, who spoke for the group of traders enjoying special privileges from the Crown, his concern was with strengthening the state rather than understanding the conditions likely to promote widespread consumption by all classes of the population. The Reverend David Davies, during approximately the same period, investigated consumption of the very poor in different parishes in England. Many of these households were victims of the early Industrial Revolution, which was bursting through the seams of the comparatively stable feudal society, and had cast many families adrift to suffer privation before they could be absorbed into the new industrial order.

The problem of poverty and its attendant consequences of disease, unrest, and revolution led Ernst Engel to investigate the income and expenditures of European peasant families early in the nineteenth century. His studies established a pattern which was widely copied and expanded. Engel was a statistician, trained in the methods of that emerging discipline. From his systematic and detailed observations he derived the set of relationships which has since been associated with his name, and which has sometimes been dignified by being called the "law of consumption."

The households which Engel studied had incomes ranging from a rough equivalent of $300 to $1,000 a year in 1857. He wanted to discover any tendencies in the spending of given incomes that might lead to generalizations about the relative welfare of the spender. He assumed that family living could be measured and understood by the quantities of different types of items consumed. He believed that the percentage of family expenditures used to obtain nourishment were an "accurate and truthful measure of the material well-being of a people." After compiling and summarizing data gathered from many family budgets, made possible by his attachment to the German statistical office, Engel stated his generalization as follows:

> The poorer the individual, a family, or a people, the greater must be the percentage of the income necessary for the maintenance of physical sustenance, and again of this a greater proportion must be allowed for food.

Other relationships, which seemed to emerge from the statistics, and which were the basis of certain of the conclusions drawn, can be stated briefly as follows:

1. As family income increases, the amount spent on food increases, but at a lower rate than the increase in income.

2. The amount spent on clothing expands at approximately the same rate as income.

3. Expenditures on rent, fuels, and light increase at about the same rate as income.

4. The amount spent for education, health, recreation, amusement, etc., increases at a rate greater than that of income expansion.

Engel concluded, therefore, that the most useful single index of family welfare is the proportion of income spent on food.

The importance of Engel's study today lies less on the basis of his conclusions, which he regarded (rather rashly) as a kind of natural law which would hold at all places and for all time, than in the stimulus it has provided to other investigators. Many early American studies were influenced by his work. In search of a universal key to welfare, he selected as his single criterion a "material" translation of household income. If, in his premature enthusiasm, he believed he had found it, it can perhaps be pointed out that he, like others of his time, had not yet become aware of the much greater complexity of the "real world."

Somewhat in contrast to Engel's method and conclusions was the work of Frederic Le Play, a French mining engineer and sociologist, whose studies of family life were carried out during approximately the same period. While his studies were less extensive than those of Engel, Le Play paid greater attention to the total family situation—to the social, economic, and religious environments as factors affecting consumption and over-all well-being. He too generalized from his studies far more than would seem warranted today, using his conclusions to justify a rather thoroughly conservative attitude toward social policy. Le Play's work also influenced subsequent studies in the United States and Europe, and traces of his point of view, though not necessarily his conclusions, linger in some concepts of the standard of living which will be treated in the next chapter. In sociology he is acknowledged as a founder of the *situationist* school of thought, which holds that individuals and groups need to be viewed in a setting of total environment. To the extent that the income levels of households are associated with important environmental differences, the approaches of Engel and Le Play can perhaps be linked together. Both pioneered in the field of social and economic observation at a time when the impact of modern technology and industrial organization was just beginning to produce the vast changes which have at last made possible

530

the consumption of goods and services, actual and potential, that we know today.

However, even if one assumes that their generalizations were realistic for the society of their day (and thus could be used as a basis for predicting the behavior of the household as its income changes), would these same relationships hold in different economic and cultural settings? Within limits, it can be demonstrated from later studies that some of the tendencies Engel noted do persist, particularly at the lower-income levels. At a very low level, an increased income is likely to result in an immediate increase of food purchases. Beyond some point the quantity of food does not increase, but purchases are shifted to higher quality foods involving a larger proportion of services. This may mean a greater than proportional increase of expenditure on the "food budget." However, as the size of the total assets or wealth held by a family rises, the relation between consumption and income may shift, since consumption can be divorced from current income through the use of credit and other means. Before considering some of these other relationships we will examine some of the studies undertaken in the United States, beginning in the latter half of the nineteenth century.

Budget Studies in
the United States

Interest in that aspect of human satisfaction which can be comprehended through the goods and services a household is able to command developed in the United States partly in response to Engel's studies. Since the period following the Civil War also witnessed the growth of the labor movement and an increasing consciousness of labor problems, it seems warranted to assume that the concern with the *real* content of living reflected important changes in "economic life" as well. Immigrants and native-born were crowding into the cities to man the expanding industries. Their concern with wages, now the principal or only source of income claims, was basically a concern with what those wages would buy.

A Bureau of Labor was created in 1884 in the Department of the Interior, which up to then had been concerned chiefly with lands of the public domain and Indian affairs. Subsequently transferred to the Department of Commerce, Labor emerged as a full-fledged executive department in 1913.

During this period, and later, an apparent contrast between the promise of American production and the actual levels of living of various groups in the nation (especially workers' groups) stimulated economists

531

and others to investigate the important "facts of life" through budget studies both in the United States and abroad. The demands of manufacturers seeking tariff protection for their goods, on the grounds that high wages made their costs greater than those of their foreign competitors, provided added incentives for *comparative* budget studies. Much of the early work was done by the departments of labor in the more industrialized states, but some of it was undertaken by private welfare agencies concerned with problems of poverty and relief. With the establishment of a Bureau of Labor, and ultimately a Department of Labor, budget studies on a continuing basis were set up, and today they comprise the source of much of our data on household expenditures, particularly among urban workers. Since 1922 the Bureau of Home Economics in the Department of Agriculture has performed a similar function for farm households.

Early Efforts

Between 1870 and 1900 more than 100 studies of family living were made in various communities in the United States, according to an estimate by Dorothy Brady, a contemporary authority on empirical investigations of consumer behavior. Many of these early studies were conducted on a simple "income-versus-outgo basis."

The criterion usually adopted for a "good" budget was the ability to save a part of the income. Some followed Engel's technique in an effort to establish a norm for proportional expenditures as a measure of well-being. Others, particularly those undertaken by social welfare agencies and reformers, were inspired by a desire to focus attention on the conditions of the "underprivileged." Although the years between the 1870's and World War I saw a rapid growth of production, living conditions for many (for immigrant workers particularly) were low. The "full dinner pail" became a successful political slogan during the middle of this era, and Father J. A. Ryan, a liberal Catholic economist, published his book on *A Living Wage*. The name of Carrol D. Wright, a statistician, stands out as the organizer and sponsor of such inquiries. Wright was chief of the Massachusetts Bureau of Statistics of Labor from 1873 to 1885, when he was appointed U.S. Commissioner of the newly created Bureau of Labor.

During his stewardship of the Massachusetts bureau Wright collected data on the expenditures of 397 wage-earning families in his state. When broken down into comparative expenditures on different budget items, American households were found, according to these relatively gross measures, to spend more on food than their European counterparts of similar income. Two studies were undertaken between 1888 and 1890, the first of 2,490 wage-earning families in North America (770 in Europe), and the second of 5,284 (of which 965 were in Europe). These were concerned chiefly with money receipts and expenditures, analyzed on the basis of "normal families." Between 1899 and 1902 (mostly in 1901), under Wright's direction, a large-scale survey covered 25,400 working-men's families, including 124,108 persons in 33 states located in the principal industrial centers. None of those included earned more than $1,200 per year. In average figures, the expenditure pattern per household for urban workers in the United States (averaging 4.88 persons), with total annual income of $749.50, was as follows:

Food	$312.92
Rent	118.40
Fuel	31.06
Light, etc.	7.53
Clothing	94.99
Miscellaneous	145.37

Slightly more than half (12,816) had savings averaging $120.84, while nearly one-sixth had debts averaging $65.85. This study probably represented the expenditure pattern of skilled and semiskilled workers (lower middle class) rather than the unskilled and lowest income classes. While the principal concern in this study (published in 1903) was with income, expenditures, and prices, the Labor Commissioner supplemented it in the following year with information on working hours for a wide range of industries.

Norms of a "Living Wage"

As a part of a drive for minimum wages and the regulation of working conditions, particularly for women, numerous other studies were carried out, in which actual expenditures were compared with a norm which represented an attempt to give content to the concept of a "living wage." One of the best known among these studies was one made with the support of the Russell Sage Foundation and directed by R. C. Chapin, chairman of a special committee for the New York State Conference of Charities and Correction. The income range of the 391 families included in this survey was from $500 to $1,000. An analysis of expenditures from 224 families earning an income of between $600 and $900 showed the following divisions:

	$600–699 Av. Income $650	$700–799 Av. Income $748	$800–899 Av. Income $846
Rent	$154	$161	$168
Carfare	11	10	16
Fuel and light	38	37	41
Furniture	6	8	7
Insurance	13	18	18
Food	279	314	341
Meals out	11	22	18
Clothing	83	99	114
Health	14	14	22
Taxes, dues	8	9	11
Recreation and amusement	3	6	7
Education	5	5	7
Miscellaneous	25	32	41
	$650	$735	$811

Quantitative data on real income gathered at the same time served to emphasize a number of important "facts" about the content of living for the period. By nutritional standards current at the time, 70 per cent of families getting less than $600 and one-third of those getting up to $800 were "underfed." Rents, due to rapid population increase and rather severe crowding, claimed nearly one-fourth of incomes of $600. Since some kind of shelter was required, funds for rent came out of the food budget—a deviation from Engel's findings. Chapin estimated that 75 per cent of those getting less than $600 were "underclothed" by any "reasonable" standard, and 40 per cent of all families could be classified in the same way. Health expenditures showed such a wide range of variation that any average would have had little or no significance. However, nearly 40 per cent received free medical assistance. The over-all conclusion of the study was that a large number of these people lived near the border line of dependency, so that illness, accident, or other unforeseen contingencies usually necessitated public or private assistance.

The first decade after the turn of the century was one of rising prices, and budget studies based upon purely monetary expenditures tended to obscure the "real" facts of consumption. This situation was intensified by the outbreak of war in Europe in 1914 and the subsequent entry of the United States in 1917. As prices rose, workers demanded higher wages in order to maintain levels of living, arguing that efficiency in war production required at least some minimum level of consumption.

534

In 1918–19 the Bureau of Labor Statistics conducted a large-scale survey in which it sought an over-all view of the expenditures of working families, together with information on prices, in order to determine what these expenditures would buy. Interviewers contacted in their homes nearly 13,000 families in all sections of the country. Households were chosen on the basis of (more or less) uniform size, consisting of a husband and wife and at least one dependent child. Dependent families were excluded, as were certain other households regarded as not "typically American." In comparison with the results of the 1901 study, when the average expenditure on food of an almost equal number of families was 43.13 per cent of total income, the average expenditure in 1918–19 was 38.2 per cent. Average total expenditure had risen from $617.80 to $1,434.36. On the basis of Engel's thesis, these figures appeared to indicate an improvement in the levels of consumption. However, the results were not conclusive, and an analysis of some of the food schedules indicated that, judged by the nutritional standards of the time, many families were living on a rather low level.

Figure 43. Percentage of Income Spent on Different Budget Items
by American Families at Different Income Levels, 1935-36

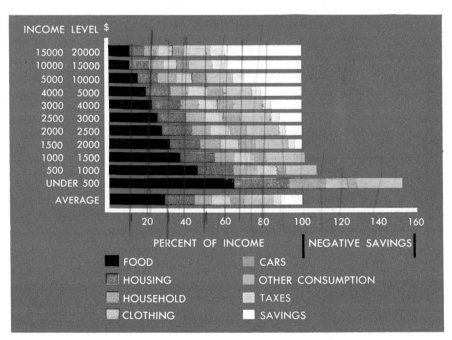

Source: National Resources Committee, *Consumer Expenditures in the United States*, Washington, 1939.

535

This survey became the basis for the "cost of living" or consumers' price index which has since been maintained, with periodic revisions, by the Bureau of Labor Statistics, and which is treated more fully in an appendix to this chapter. Studies of farm living conditions were instituted by the Bureau of Home Economics in 1922–24 in co-operation with colleges and universities. These results were published as a survey of the consuming habits of 2,886 white farm families in areas selected to represent "average conditions."

In 1934 the Brookings Institution brought together from various sources data on *America's Capacity to Consume*. This was a companion volume to *America's Capacity to Produce*, and its objective was to measure the utilization of existing production. Using combined data from the Bureau of Labor Statistics, the Heller Committee for Research in the Social Sciences of the University of California, and various other agencies, this study tried to determine how income was, on the average, utilized at each income level. In general, the tone of the study was pessimistic, in that it suggested the improbability of attaining a "liberal" diet and "reasonable" standard of living for each and every person of the United States in the near future.

In the extensive income-expenditure survey of 1935–36 much was learned about the budget items on which households at different income levels spent their income, and the proportion of total expenditure devoted to each of the different budget items. This information is graphically presented in Figure 43. It will be apparent that for this set of observations the tendency noted by Engel for expenditures to change as the location of the household on an income scale shifts, is borne out. The percentage spent on food declines slowly at the lower level until an income of approximately $1,200 is reached, after which it declines steadily as income rises. Clothing expenditures increase moderately, as do housing and household expenditures. These represent the hard core of the living requirements of any household, and help to explain the essential stability of consumption expenditures noted in the discussion of the propensity to consume in Part 2. Among the remainder of the budget items many appear which were unknown in the nineteenth century. These are the new consumption goods which advancing technology and the accumulated wealth of an industrial society have made available. At the lower end of the income scale, where a high proportion of income goes for food, there is evidence to support a belief in the essential stability of a sizable part of consumption expenditures and a relatively high marginal propensity to consume.

Further insight into the household use of income can be gained by examining what happens to different budget items, in the aggregate,

536

when incomes change. This time the comparison is between the years 1940 and 1954. Disposable income in 1940 was $76.1 billion. In 1954 it was $254.5 billion, an increase of approximately 234 per cent. The figures in Table 24 show the relevant changes in aggregate expenditures for each of the major budget items.

Table 24. Personal Consumption Expenditures by Budget Item, 1940 & 1954

	Expenditure (billions of dollars)		Percentage of Yearly Total		Percentage Increase in Total Expenditure
	1940	1954	1940	1954	from 1940 to 1954
1 Food & related products	22.2	78.6	30.9	33.2	254.0
2 Clothing, accessories, and jewelry	8.9	24.5	12.3	10.4	175.2
3 Personal care	1.0	2.8	1.4	1.2	180.0
4 Housing (rents)	9.3	29.8	13.0	12.6	220.4
5 Household operation	10.5	30.8	14.6	13.0	193.3
6 Medical & death expenses	3.5	11.8	4.9	5.0	237.1
7 Personal business	3.6	11.4	5.1	4.8	216.6
8 Transportation	7.1	26.9	9.9	11.4	278.8
9 Recreation	3.8	12.2	5.2	5.2	221.0
10 Private education & research	.6	2.6	.6	1.1	333.3
11 Religious & welfare activities	1.0	3.2	1.4	1.4	220.0
12 Foreign travel & remittance	.2	2.0	.3	.9	900.0
Total Consumption Expenditures	71.9	236.5			228.9
Durables	7.8	29.3	10.8	12.4	275.6
Nondurables	37.2	120.9	51.8	51.1	225.0
Services	26.9	86.4	37.4	36.4	222.0

Source: U.S. Department of Commerce.

Thus far our examination of the available materials on income and expenditure can be viewed as serving two purposes. First of all, it provides us with empirical data (admittedly lacking in preciseness), which throw light on how American households in fact meet the problem of allocating available income to the goods and services our economy can provide. Secondly, it tells us something of how this allocation changes when disposable income, the most important determinant of consumption, changes. This information is important insofar as it provides insight into consumer behavior and how the household performs its role in the income process.

The data provide little information about savings. In fact, it is very difficult to secure reliable information on this important budget item. What, for example, is meant by household savings from income? If savings could be regarded simply as the accumulation of liquid assets, such as cash or near cash (savings accounts, government bonds, and other equity and debt ownership easily converted to cash), the problem of the researcher would not be so difficult. However, for some purposes any increase in the net worth of the household—such as life insurance policies, a reduction in mortgages on the house, or the purchase of durable equipment, the service of which is to be rendered over a considerable span of time—also represents an accumulation from income claims. These can be translated into spendable funds by using them as a basis for credit or by selling them to others possessing liquid funds.

Recent Budget Studies

Since 1945 the Survey Research Center at the University of Michigan has conducted a continuing study of consumer finances, an important part of which has been devoted to household spending and saving. These observations regarding saving have been more systematic than earlier studies. Although the number of households included is smaller than in earlier investigations, the sampling techniques are designed to provide a more representative picture.

In defining savings, this study has adopted a compromise solution for the problem mentioned above. Important purchases of durable consumer goods are regarded as consumption expenditures. However, the purchase of houses or improvements on the house are treated as savings. Other forms of savings or additions to net worth include increases in holdings of government bonds and various kinds of bank deposits, purchases of securities and real estate, repayment of debts, payment of life insurance premiums and contributions to retirement funds, amounts lent, new investment in family owned business, profits left in the business, and the purchase price of farm machinery. Withdrawals in each of these categories represent dissaving. Net difference between the two tells whether the household saved or dissaved during the period.

Practical difficulties arise in finally isolating actions that result in savings, however. Insurance payments contribute to savings, but they also buy protection. In proprietorships business savings left in the business are different from household savings, although they may be difficult to sepa-

538

rate. In all cases decisions on how to treat separate items must be made somewhat arbitrarily, although insight and judgment can provide important clues. For purposes of measuring change, these judgments do not constitute imponderable shortcomings, provided the decisions once made are consistently applied.

The results vary widely, as is true of almost any empirical findings in the social sciences. In his interpretation of the results, Professor George Katona, program director of the Survey Research Center, has gone into considerable detail to distinguish between the many social and psychological variables associated with savings. However, since our concern here is with the relation between income levels and savings, we will confine our attention to his remarks on that subject. Katona sums up what his observers have found:

> What is the relation of saving and dissaving to the level of income? . . . the proportion of savers increases with income . . . the "zero" savers . . . are most frequent among low income people. With respect to negative savers . . . they are equally frequent at most income levels. . . . The top income receivers saved a substantial proportion of the aggregate[1] savings. . . . The top income group . . . those 10% of the spending units who had the largest incomes were responsible for most of the net saving of the economy.[2]

Thus the evidence collected from a sample of household spending units in our most recent continuing budget studies does not warrant our rejecting those hypotheses concerning the propensity to save in an industrial society which were presented in Part 2.

Variations in Consumer Behavior

While position on the income-distribution scale and changes in the level of national income are important variables associated with differences in consumer expenditures, they are by no means the only ones. That is why the modern social scientist is extremely cautious in his use of such terms as the law of consumption. Enough evidence exists to conclude that the manner in which individual households rank the various budget items according to their importance varies widely, and is related to other variables of a highly personal nature and to factors in the economic and social environments. We know that geographic differences, for example, are

---

[1] Positive.

[2] George Katona, *Psychological Analysis of Economic Behavior* (New York: McGraw-Hill, 1951), p. 153.

significant. Expenditures on food, housing, and clothing will differ between northern and southern regions. Patterns of expenditures will differ with occupations, even when the size of income is equivalent. The jobs people hold, the groups and associates they regard as important for the success of their own income pursuits, create different forms or standards by which they guide their expenditures (we will return to this point in the next chapter in our discussion of normative standards). The type of community is also an important influence on expenditure patterns. As a rule, rural people, with equivalent incomes, will spend less and save more than those living in urban communities.

Long-run social and political trends, as well as economic or income trends, tend to accumulate and exert a subtle influence on people by changing attitudes toward consumption. Our own forebears, living in a relatively undeveloped environment, had an attitude toward spending on consumption goods quite different from our own. Then, in anticipation of a more abundant future for themselves or their children, saving and accumulation was itself an important virtue. Changes in production and in the composition and size of real income have changed perceptions of need. Because human beings have been able to manipulate and shape the physical environment, they have, in a sense, changed themselves, consciously at times, but more frequently in an unconscious manner.

Discussion
Questions

1. Why, in your opinion, was concern with poverty a stimulus to early budget studies? Do you think this same emphasis is warranted today?

2. To what extent is it possible to make a general statement about welfare, based upon a single consumption index? Is such an index a useful first approximation?

3. As a household rises on the income scale, what are the principal changes that take place in the way in which it uses its income?

4. Why is our present consumer price index a more reliable index of economic well-being, when combined with household income, than it would have been (had it existed) in 1860?

5. What would be the limitations of a single "cost-of-living index" which included the purchases of all households, from the lowest income classes to the highest?

540

Appendix to Chapter 34

A Note on the
Consumer Price Index

BECAUSE OF ITS EXTENSIVE USE in scientific studies (as well as the constant reference made to it by press and radio), the consumer price index merits a more extended treatment. Like all indices, it has its limitations. For translating household income into "real" terms, this instrument serves a useful purpose. However, we must recognize that it is subject to error and must be used with caution, if we are to avoid unwarranted conclusions.

The present index, published by the Bureau of Labor Statistics, had its origin in the budget studies made in 1918–19. During World War I the wholesale price index was the only available index for use in adjusting workmen's wages. A recognition of its limitations was the inducement for developing a "cost-of-living index." A survey of expenditures was a necessary preliminary to the construction of a usable index, since only the proportion of income spent on the different budget items could provide the relative weights for the individual prices.

This survey collected information on spending and prices for six major budget components: food, clothing, housing, house furnishings, fuel and light, and miscellaneous. On the basis of these findings, an index was constructed going back to 1914. It has been maintained continuously to date (Figure 44). A major revision of the index (and a change in its base) was undertaken following the income-expenditure studies of 1934–35. This revision was first published in 1937. Initially issued four times yearly on the basis of quarterly surveys, the index has been published on a monthly basis since World War II. The title of the index was changed from "cost of living" to "consumer price" index in 1945.[1] The most recent revision of the index, aimed at taking account of new expenditure patterns, was completed in 1952 and publication started in January,

---

[1] The full title of the present index is "Index of Change in Price of Goods and Services Purchased by City Wage-Earners and Clerical Worker Families to Maintain Their Level of Living."

Figure 44.   Consumer Price Index, Annually, 1914-1957

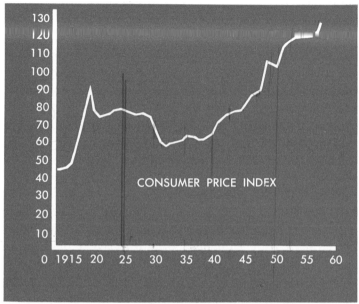

Source: U. S. Bureau of Labor Statistics.

1953. Since previous years have now been recomputed, using the base adopted in 1953, we shall describe the index as it is now derived and computed.

The principal concern of this index (as described by the Bureau of Labor Statistics) is with the retail prices of "food, clothing, house furnishings, fuel and other goods; the fees paid to doctors and dentists; prices in barber shops and other service establishments; rents; rates charged for transportation, electricity, gas, and other utilities; and sales and excise taxes."

In popular presentations the weightings or composition of goods or services priced for the index are represented as a "market basket" which contains the regular purchases of urban wage earners and clerical-worker households. It is the content of the basket that is determined by the budget surveys. Between revisions, the assumption is made that the contents of the basket do not change. Thus the index measures only the changes in the purchasing power of the consumers' dollar income attributable to changes in prices.

Such a market basket could not possibly include all of the thousands of different items actually purchased, particularly all of the different grades of each item. For example, some households may buy center cuts of pork chops, others may buy end cuts. These are of different quality, and the prices differ accordingly. In the price surveys, investigators collect price data only on one cut, and always the same cut. The same principle holds for other items where different qualities exist. The assumption is made that prices of the different qualities remain relatively stable, and that if the price on the reported grade changes, the other prices change in the same direction and by the same proportion. Thus this index would not register the consequences for the real income of families attributable to substitution, if the prices of some qualities or grades change relative to others. Nor does the market basket take into account new products which come on the market between revisions.

Constructing the Index "Market Basket"

In 1950 the Bureau of Labor Statistics conducted a new survey to find out what wage earners and clerical-worker families were buying. As an indication of the number of such households involved, it is estimated that more than 18 million such households in 3,000 cities and towns in 1950 made up the urban consumers. To collect detailed information on all purchases of these households would be a stupendous undertaking. Instead, a carefully designed sample was collected from a relatively small number of households. First, a representative sample of cities and towns was chosen, which included all of the twelve largest urban areas with populations of more than a million and representatives of large, medium-sized, and small cities. The effort was made here to include different kinds of cities based upon the following characteristics which affect the spending of household incomes: (1) size, (2) climate, (3) density of population, and (4) level of income in the community. In all, 97 cities were surveyed. In each city the Bureau investigators chose a representative group of families, and an interviewer obtained a record of kinds, qualities, and amounts of goods purchased during 1950.[2] Heads of these families included craftsmen, factory workers, laborers, clerks, and sales and service workers. The average size of the households (families) included in the survey was estimated to be about 3.3 persons, and their average income was $4,160 after taxes (households with more than $10,000 after taxes were excluded). This sample was regarded as representative of about 64 per cent of all people.

On the basis of these findings, the following are the weights given

---

[2] Since 1952 was to be used as the basic index market basket, the averages were later adjusted for changes between 1950 and 1952.

to prices in the broad budget categories, and the number of items included in each:

All Items	Importance (100) Relative	Number of Items Priced (298)
Food	*30.1*	*87*
Cereals & Baking Products	3.1	9
Meats, Poultry, Fish	8.0	16
Dairy Products	4.2	6
Fruits and Vegetables	4.5	32
Other Foods	5.7	18
Food Away From Home	4.6	6
Housing	*32.0*	*72*
Rent	5.3	1
Other Shelter	11.9	14
Gas & Electric	1.0	3
Solid Fuels & Fuel Oil	2.2	7
House Furnishings	6.6	35
Household Operation	5.0	12
Apparel	9.7	78
Transportation	11.0	18
Medical Care	4.7	18
Personal Care	2.1	13
Reading & Recreation	5.4	8
Other Goods & Services	5.0	4

Within these broader categories, the subclasses of items are also determined and their relative weights assigned. Full detail is not necessary here, since the information provided should make clear the principle involved.

How Price Data Are Gathered

After selecting the "standard" for each of the 298 separate items (the standard being carefully identified and described), these are priced at regular intervals and price changes noted. Collections are made in 46 of the 97 cities covered in the expenditures survey, including the 12 largest, 9 other large cities, 9 medium-sized cities, and 16 small cities. Prices are reported by representative stores and all other types of establishments where the households of wage and salary workers do the bulk of their buying, including chain stores, independent stores, and department and specialty stores. Prices reported by the different types of stores are weighted according to their relative importance as shopping places for the relevant households, and all prices are averaged together to obtain the index for each city. Collections are made in each city at intervals which range from once each month to once every four months. For the more important items, and those subject to frequent change such as food, prices are secured every month. In the five largest cities most items are reported monthly. Orderly procedures are followed, such as training agents and spot checking information sources reporting by mail, to insure the greatest possible accuracy.

How the Index is Computed and Reported

Price changes, as measured by the consumer price index, are expressed in percentages of some past period. The index itself is a composite or weighted average of the price changes of all items included. In the present index the past period which forms the base is the average for the years 1947–49. When, in May, 1958, the index stood at 123.6 (base 1947–49 = 100), this meant that prices were 23.6 per cent higher, on the average, than during that base period.

Changes in the index are published each month, and prices at each date are compared to the base period. Thus, if the index were to rise from 110 to 112 from one month to the next, the price rise for that period can be computed as follows:

$$\frac{112 - 110}{110} = \frac{2}{110} = 0.018, \text{ or approximately } 1.8\%.$$

The general index, as it is published, represents price changes for all urban places. In addition, the Bureau of Labor Statistics publishes an index for each of the twenty largest cities.

The actual calculation of the index is accomplished by means of a standard statistical formula. A constant weight of the relevant items is multiplied by the prices, and the value of the market basket for the two dates compared. For example, if the basket contains 20 pounds of pork chops, and these are priced at 75¢ per pound at one time and 80¢ at the next, the value would be $15 and $16 respectively. The percentage change would be computed as follows:

$$\frac{16 - 15}{15} = 6.6\%.$$

All other items, calculated in the same way, would be added together and divided by the number of items. This would give the percentage change in the total cost of the basket attributable to price changes.

A measure of the change in the purchasing power of the household dollar is obtained from the reciprocal of the consumer price index. For example, if between the present month and the base period the index had increased by 20 per cent, the value of the consumer dollar would be $\frac{100}{120}$ or 83.3 cents, compared with the base period. However, this information alone would not tell us whether the household were realizing a smaller real income than before. If money income had remained constant, real income would be smaller. If it had risen by 20 per cent during the same period, and if changes in prices on all items had been the same, real income could be unchanged. It can be assumed that this would be an unlikely case. If the price index is applied to the incomes of those very low on the scale, or those very high, conclusions about changes in real income may be spurious, since it is intended principally to apply to the urban workers whose preferences have determined the weighting of the items included.

CHAPTER 35

Scales and Standards of Living

IN THE PRECEDING CHAPTER we were concerned with the development of budget studies as sources of information about consumer expenditures. The primary emphasis was on money-income flows, the transformation of assets in the income process when members of households seek finally to use their claims for satisfying wants. In this chapter we shall examine a number of concepts and operations used by economists and other social scientists to translate money symbols into their real-income meaning, and finally into norms. This will involve us in the associations of a group of terms already familiar.

Scales (or levels) and standards of living are terms used in everyday affairs more or less interchangeably. Specialists in the field of consumption economics have attempted to reach an agreement on a more precise meaning for them, although not always with success. The meaning usually attached to *scale* and *level* of living comes very close to what is implied when we use the term "real." *Standard* is used to designate what we usually associate with "norm" or "ideal," as a criterion or as an expected or desired goal. Again, however, there are shades of difference which range from an ideal which can be operationally defined (for example, in terms of nutritional requirements for bodily maintenance) to the purely emotional associations of the "Walter Mitty world" of each of us. While the term standard can apply to what the clinical psychologist or the psychiatrist might discover from our answers when we are asked, "What would you do with a million dollars?" it is more usefully conceived as what a household, a cultural group, or an entire nation has come to expect or hope for on the basis of past experience.

People whose command over goods has been increasing (as in the United States it has) are likely to entertain a "reasonable" expectation that this will continue. On the other hand, those whose lot has been hard (as for so much of the world's population it has always been) learn to adapt to an environment where hopes cannot rise very high.

When we hear it said that the people of the United States have the highest standard of living in the world, two associations may be implied. It can mean that in terms of empirical or real content people here have more things, more of their physiological and social needs satisfied than elsewhere. It can also mean that we have learned to expect more, that our consumption goals are higher and that we can reasonably expect that these goals will be realized. There is a large body of evidence to demonstrate that both meanings are true. However, this does not mean (though it is sometimes interpreted in this way) that Americans are happier or better adjusted, or even that they achieve greater satisfaction. The adjustment to real life situations, the physical and emotional balance which psychiatrists and physicians attribute to a satisfied and healthy person, consists of some kind of balanced equilibrium in which available means for the satisfaction of perceived needs are present or attainable in sufficient quantities to prevent continued frustrations.

Interpersonal and intercultural comparisons of standards are difficult, since those who have much (but expect more) may be less well-adjusted or happy than those who have less in the way of real income but whose expectations are lower. Here our speculation enters the realm of *psychic income*, where the training of most economists does not make them competent to speak. The aid of the psychologist is required, or perhaps the literary artist.

The Link Between Scales and Standards

Nevertheless, there are practical considerations which impinge upon the field studied by the economist. For example, when the Ford Motor Company established a branch plant in Berlin during the 1920's to produce cars for the German market, Henry Ford is reported to have issued instructions that wage rates (in reichsmarks) were to be made the equivalent of the dollar wages of his Detroit workers. Domestic entrepreneurs and German officials, when informed of the policy, were greatly concerned. Such a pay scale would have been much higher than those prevailing in Germany. This, it was argued, could only lead to social dislocation and a disturbance of orderly economic life. To resolve the conflict, the Ford Company employed a group of social scientists to study wage structures in both Detroit and Berlin. The company's Berlin workers were then given an income status "with respect to those of other firms in the community" comparable to that of its Detroit workers.

An analogous situation, although perhaps not strictly comparable (be-

548

cause of the underdeveloped nature of the economy), was reported by Elizabeth Hoyt[1] following a visit to Guatemala shortly after World War II. She stated that she had at last observed a situation in which the scale of living for a substantial number of households was raised above prevailing standards. A nationalist government, elected on a platform proposing that "foreign corporations" be made to "pay," imposed an arbitrary wage scale on nondomestic companies (principally fruit growers) greatly in excess of those prevailing in domestic trades. This sudden rise of income had the immediate consequence not of stimulating desires for more comfortable homes, more nutritious foods, better dress, education for children, medical and dental care, and so forth, as might have been expected, but rather of excesses of drunkenness and idleness which disrupted family life, heightened social conflicts, and generally disturbed institutional arrangements.

Such an adaptation, of course, is one that has long been recognized and associated in literature and the drama with the *nouveaux riches*. This is not to suggest that adaptation to such changes in the economic environment will not be made eventually. New standards emerge as the consumption potential of a higher income level is realized—higher, not in any mystical sense, but in varieties of experience and in possibilities for exercising a wider range of choice.

How then do standards of living originate? How are they assimilated by people so that they eventually come to be accepted as "normal"? From what we can infer from changes in scales or levels of living, it appears that something of a pattern may exist. The *real* content of living will ordinarily consist of the goods and services which a production economy can make available (given the quality and quantity of the factors of production, the institutional characteristics of the society, and trade relations with the "outside"). The consumption habits of a population are established through historical experience or the awareness of what seems reasonable to expect. If the production economy is progressive, if science and technology operate to increase the real income level, then those who gain access to this expanding output develop expectations of rising levels and standards.

This hypothetical relationship between scales and standards of living, while admittedly crude and lacking in verifiable stability (at least on the basis of present knowledge), can be linked meaningfully with our earlier discussion of the propensity to consume. The assumption of the classical economists that consumer wants are capable of indefinite expansion may be valid as a basis for understanding and predicting long-run consumer

---

[1] In conversation with the author.

behavior (which, of course, was their assumption). Certainly, the capacity of consumers in the United States for finding a place in their plans for the great variety of new things made available by science and technology appears to have been demonstrated.

Whenever the income process has generated a sustained level of income flows, making it possible for households to acquire such goods, items viewed as luxuries in one period have become social "necessities" in the next. Automobiles, at the turn of the century, were regarded as playthings of the well-to-do. Today they are a necessity for many workers as a means of getting to their jobs.

Consumer Expectations

However, if income experience of the recent past (and the expectations based upon it) are the clues acted upon in consumption plans, there is reason to believe that expenditures will tend to lag behind income changes. Economists differ in their interpretations of the aspect of income experience most closely related to *expectations*. Some believe that the amount or actual level of income is the item most heavily weighted in determining how consumers will act to maintain that standard. Others believe that it is the rate of change which is perceived as important. Thus a rate of change in income (or prices) for any period in the past, if it persists, may be projected into the future, exercising the most important effect on decisions to spend. An increase in income may not result in an immediate expansion of expenditure, in which case the tendency will be to save a higher percentage of the additional income, and the marginal propensity to save will be high. If the income continues to rise, or becomes stable at a higher level, then the propensity to consume may rise, and the household will move to a higher level of living. An opposite pattern of behavior would be associated with an income decline. The most likely immediate short-run reaction would be to attempt to maintain the previous level of living, the accepted standard, if necessary by decreasing savings. After a lag, however, expectations of a further decline would command attention, with a rising liquidity preference and a rise in the propensity to save. This is the point at which the impact on the production economy, in the form of a decline in effective demand, begins to assert itself, contributing to a cumulative downward spiral of deflation.

Some economists, in an initial burst of enthusiasm over the working tools provided by aggregate analysis, concluded that a policy which resulted in increasing the income of low-income groups, through income transfer, would have an immediate impact on effective demand because of the high marginal propensity to consume in those households. Further reflection and investigations, however, have tended to emphasize the importance of taking into account other factors, namely, the importance of social or cultural considerations. Individual households do not exist in isolation. They are members of groups with similar backgrounds and similar tastes. "Keeping up with the Joneses" is an important influence in consumer expenditures, but each social group has a different Jones. In other words, the *standard* is generated through interaction within that group. Each occupational group, geographic region, and income class tends to develop a level and a standard with which it lives.[2]

These factors, as well as size, age, and sex composition, and health and training, all influence household standards. Some can be regarded as randomly distributed, and hence likely to cancel one another out in aggregate behavior. On the other hand, among broad groups the reaction of consumers to national income change, where standards are shared, tends to be cumulative. Until we know these standards in greater detail, predicting changes in the marginal propensity to consume is likely to be hazardous. This may be why, in part at least, the leverage effect on national income is relatively unstable (see page 168).

Members of low-income groups, conforming to group norms, would be likely to respond to a sudden increase in income according to habits of long standing. This could mean that their marginal propensity to consume might not be any higher than that of higher-income groups. Since the lack of saving among low-income households results more from a lack of ability than desire, there is at least a reason for doubting any very great difference in the desire to spend in the short run. If this is in fact the case, then it will provide a reason for doubting the effectiveness of a policy which seeks to promote greater income equality as a means of raising the average propensity to consume in the short run.

Normative Standards

We have described how levels or scales of living tend to become subjective standards. We can now look at the concept of a standard of living in a slightly different way. Normative budgets have already been mentioned. The efficiency budget used during World War I was an example. When average material requirements for food, clothing, house room, medical care, and so forth, calculated to maintain the worker's energy and

---

[2] In a series of articles in Fortune Magazine, W. H. Whyte has made some penetrating and amusing observations on the consumption standards of corporation executives. He points out the importance to the rising young executive of knowing when to move from the Buick class to the Cadillac, or when to graduate his wife from Persian lamb to mink.

morale, had been agreed upon and translated by means of prices into a money income, such a budget became a normative standard. It could then be used for purposes of comparison with existing incomes, and treated as a goal to be achieved through wage increases. A subsistence standard adopted during the 1930's, as a criterion of wage payments on the WPA and other relief projects, was another such norm. Other normative standards, described variously as "minimum health and decency," "liberal," or "comfortable," have been suggested from time to time by different agencies. Except perhaps those for nutritional requirements for food and certain objective measurements for house room, few of these norms are capable of precise statement. Even calorie and vitamin requirements can be met by a small range of monotonous food items, as was illustrated by George J. Stigler when he undertook to show that an annual food budget of as little as $40 in 1939 and $60 in 1944 could provide the nutritional requirements recommended by the National Research Council for a moderately active man. In a series of investigations among various occupational and professional groups, the Heller Committee of the University of California has attempted to derive *normative standards* comprising the average requirements of these groups. In other words, a normative standard which includes the "social" requirements for the household of a practicing physician, a lawyer, a college professor, and others is outlined, and a money statement of that standard derived. Thus, in the tradition of Le Play, a norm is created which takes into account the total situation in which the household lives and moves.

Norms or Standards and Consumption Research

Specialists in consumption economics have devoted increasing attention to the construction of normative standards as criteria of consumer welfare, and as aids to the ordering of empirical data. Where in the past investigators proposed to let the "facts" speak for themselves, the tendency more recently has been to rely upon the judgment of experts from the outside to provide norms. In the older studies the desirable standard was perceived as that level of living which individuals and groups, on the average, had attained or found necessary for their sense of satisfaction, when they compared their lot with others about them. As a norm, this average or typical level could serve both as goal and a measure of failure or achievement for the household (or for the economy). Those whose level was below the standard had some measure of the "theoretically attainable," and for them it served as a goal or spur to action. Those whose attainments exceeded the average were provided a base against which to evaluate their achievement or good fortune.

552

Although distilled from the raw data of experience, any such standard will be somewhat arbitrary in a changing world, particularly when one translates money income into real terms or vice versa. Thus, when a committee of consumption specialists is asked to decide on a "reasonable" standard of living for a workingman's family, how is it to determine whether the husband should have a new suit once in two years or once every year? Should the budget provide for tobacco and, if so, should it include cigarettes for the wife as well as for the husband? Need such a standard include an electric washer, or ought a household in this social group aspire to such heights? Time and again experts have disagreed among themselves, each tending to impose his own feelings of what is correct for the particular group, especially if it is a low-income group.

For some items specialists in other fields may offer usable suggestions. Nutritional requirements, based upon physiological needs, will sometimes determine limits for estimating what a budget should contain by way of calories and vitamins. Housing specialists, architects, psychologists, and others can provide meaningful criteria for space and privacy which will allow for satisfactory adjustment of the individual. Modern architecture (an adaptation of design to function and materials) has been viewed as a trend toward adaptation to the "needs" of people who live in a predominantly urban culture. Clothing experts, who adopt a functional approach to the problem of attire, make meaningful suggestions for comfort, appearance, and durability in materials and styling.

We are left with the fact of social experience, however, that the many variables which determine the attitudes of individuals and groups toward what they would like to have and can reasonably expect, as reflected in the use of income, cannot be reduced to any neat, logical statement. It is particularly evident that the knowledge which the economist has and the tools which he has developed are not sufficient for the task of completely comprehending consumer behavior. The attitudes and tastes of an individual are an expression of needs which have their roots in biological or physiological requirements. These needs, developed and conditioned as they are in a social setting, take on a specific form generally approved by these groups, and take into account the role of the individual with respect to other members.

Finally, the broader cultural setting of the larger society, the nation, or even the family of nations, when contacts are maintained across boundaries, affect the limits which help determine the possible and the desirable. In our own industrial civilization, with its great emphasis on the scientific and the technological, the facts of novelty and change need to be taken into account.

553

Thus beyond a certain point the economist once again finds it useful to link his inquiry to the studies of consistencies and trends discovered by the other sciences.

The Market Basket as a Norm

As the refinement and general use of the consumer price index has progressed, it has been adopted more and more as the basis for a standard or norm aimed at maintaining levels of living attained during some base period. Labor unions use it at the bargaining table to argue for wage increases. An increasing number of contracts contain provisions for an automatic adjustment in wage rates when the index changes, particularly in an upward direction. Where such contracts also contain provisions for merit increases to take account of greater productivity, security and progress are both primary considerations.

Whether written into contracts or not, the general opinion appears to presume that levels of living, once attained, ought not to recede. This has been especially evident since the close of the depression decade of the 1930's. Even where a full understanding of index numbers (their exact meaning and limitations) is lacking, the practice of thinking loosely in terms of these numbers has spread. A decline in the purchasing power of the dollar is emphasized in popular discussions during periods of inflation. The cost of the market basket is played up. During a period of deflation, however, decreased income, rather than the increase in the value of the dollar, is likely to be stressed.

Fostered by an awareness of rising prices, such as have prevailed since World War II, increasing numbers of individuals and groups have watched with mounting interest the announced changes in the "cost of living," using this index as a kind of mental bench mark for judging their own economic welfare. In such circumstances the well-being of the "consumer" acquires some meaning in terms of the everyday experience of people, rather than as a purely abstract idea or a self-evident proposition requiring no further examination.

Discussion
Questions

1. Describe or define your present scale of living. Then describe the level which you hope to attain ten years after leaving college. What was your standard for giving content to your expectations?

2. How would you describe the "American Standard of Living"?

3. Now describe in real terms what you would call a minimum standard below which you would not want to fall. What money income, at present prices, would you have to earn to support this standard?

4. During the inflation which has characterized the U.S. economy since World War II, which groups have experienced the greatest reductions in their levels of living?

5. What basic assumption lies behind escalator clauses in labor contracts, and the lobbying of civil servants for cost of living increases?

CHAPTER 36

Consumption and the Public Economy

NEARLY ONE-FIFTH (19.3 per cent) of the gross national product was accounted for by government purchases in 1956. As a consequence of this spending, goods were produced and ultimately used by people in a manner determined by government through its legislative bodies and administrative agencies. The public services we use every day are often taken for granted, and we rarely think about them except when we pay taxes or if we try to imagine their sudden withdrawal. Only occasionally are such consumption items associated with immediately perceived personal needs.

Government employees and service personnel work in buildings and sometimes live in homes that are owned by public agencies. A few buy in commissaries operated by these same government bodies. Workers in government buildings eat in cafeterias operated by nonprofit organizations created by the government or by private contractors under a leasing agreement. National parks are maintained and kept open at nominal admission charges, so that scenic spots of the country may be visited and admired by people on vacation. National and state forests are managed by civil servants to ensure reserves of lumber and to protect watersheds and provide space for recreation. Government corporations, like the TVA, provide services ranging from flood control to power for whole regions. A public school system provides primary and secondary education, and publicly supported universities provide higher education at less than costs. State and county hospitals are maintained for the use of the indigent aged and infirm. A public postal system dispatches communications of various types throughout the country and the world, while postal savings offer a type of banking service. Some idea of the number of separate units of government at different levels can be gained from Table 25.

Each of the units has a source of income, either from taxation, sale of services, or by assignment from other governmental units. Each has a

Table 25.   Units of Government in the
United States, 1957

Federal	1
States	48
Counties	3,047
Municipalities	17,167
Towns and Townships	17,214
School Districts	50,453
Special Districts*	14,423
Total	102,353

* Totals change from year to year because of the disappearance of
old units and the creation of new ones. For example, the number
of states, constant for nearly a half-century, was increased to 49
in 1958. Special districts include irrigation districts, housing authorities, soil conservation districts, etc.

Source: The Conference Board, The Economic Almanac, 1958, p.
429.

budget and spends its income. In the more efficient agencies budget procedures are well organized, and allocation is made according to some
ranking of public needs.

The determination of such "needs" is not an easy matter, however.
Alternative uses for limited government income are many. These alternatives often appear as the "special interests" of different and sometimes
rival groups, while to those groups themselves they appear as the "essence"
of general welfare. Because a clear-cut concept of the general welfare is
usually lacking, it is difficult to determine when or if the maximum attainment of goals has been achieved. Indeed, general welfare goals seem
always to be in the process of being discovered, as rival claimants and competing needs seek public support. They are finally determined, however,
through political means (including compromise and political expediency),
and once they are they become part of the broader income process.

Systematic budgeting, for governments as well as for households, is
a means for establishing controls and for linking expenditures more directly
with intended goals. Specialists in public administration contend that the
development of more orderly procedures has become a requirement for
modern big government. We shall now examine the background of budgetary procedures for the public economy, beginning with that of the Federal
government, since it is the largest.

The Federal Budget

The Constitution of the United States made no provision for the planning of income receipts and expenditures. Full powers for raising and allocating revenues were placed in the hands of the lower house of Congress. Responsibility for carrying out the intent of Congress on fiscal matters rested with the President as head of the executive branch.

The Secretary of the Treasury was among the first cabinet positions to be established under President Washington. The first two secretaries of the Treasury, Alexander Hamilton and Albert Gallatin, were strong men, and it was evidently their intention to make of this office an effective finance ministry. Later actions by Congress frustrated these plans, and the Secretary of the Treasury only assumed powers equivalent to those of the other heads of departments in the President's cabinet.

Before the Civil War the Federal budget was actually made up by the Committee on Ways and Means in the House of Representatives. In its deliberations this committee considered bills providing for both the raising and spending of government income. In 1865 the power of this committee over financial affairs was split up and distributed between two other committees—Appropriations, and Banking and Currency. Further diffusion of control over the Federal budget continued, and after 1885 there was little legislation in support of orderly budgeting until 1935.

Presidential Budget Making

About 1909 a movement was started by the executive department and Congressional leaders to increase the responsibility of the executive branch for assembling and presenting to Congress information and recommendations on the revenues and expenditures of the Federal government. This culminated in the Budget and Accounting Act of 1921, which placed the responsibility for controlling and planning expenditures with the chief executive. A central budget organization, the Bureau of the Budget, was set up in the Treasury Department, making the President more or less the business manager of the executive branch of government. The Bureau itself occupied a position analogous to that of the comptrollership in a large business organization. At the outset, however, the Bureau was limited in what it could do, for its own budget was limited. In 1935 this limitation was removed, and the Bureau was allowed to assemble a staff adequate for its assigned task. In 1939 it was removed from the Treasury Department and located in the executive office of the President. From a budget of $354,710 in 1939, allocations to the Bureau increased, until in 1956 they amounted to $4,400,000.

Estimates of "need" for all branches of the Federal government are compiled by the Bureau of the Budget for use by the President in submitting his budget message to Congress. Like the ordinary household budget, or that of a business firm, the budget which the President recommends to Congress is not a completely new and different instrument each year. It has links with the past and purportedly attempts to estimate the future. Moreover, the recommendations of the President do not become the budget of the Federal government until they have been discussed and amended by Congress and finally passed as a number of appropriation bills. The combined appropriation bills of Congress are a statement of what the Federal expenditures are intended to be during the next fiscal year. Some of these are more or less permanent appropriations representing long-term commitments, such as special funds set up for particular purposes, which have their own sources of revenue. Also included are supplemental and deficiency appropriations, which correct the failure of the previous budget to estimate total expenditures correctly.

Under the original act creating the Bureau of the Budget, the President was supposed to estimate the tax and other receipts and to propose new revenue legislation so that receipts and expenditures might be expected to balance. However, the Treasury Department still retains the major responsibility for the revenue portion, assisted more recently by the President's Council of Economic Advisers. Thus the President's budget is chiefly an estimate of expenditures.

In many respects Congress and the executive branch still view the raising of revenue and the spending of income as two separate operations, although much less so than formerly. Most specialists in public finance and administration generally believe that a more careful planning of the two sides of the budget in closer relationship to each other would make possible a more orderly system of choice making and a link between expenditures and goals.

Another proposal made with increasing frequency is for a separation between the government's so-called capital budget and its current or year-to-year budget. At present the public is aware only of a lump-sum figure which represents what the government is to spend or commit during the year. A substantial part of expenditures, however, are of a long-run nature, returns from which will be realized in the form of various services over a much longer time span. From the standpoint of consumption or use, to separate the two would represent a meaningful distinction.

Real Income from Public Spending

In terms of real content, what does the nation get for these expenditures? A detailed breakdown of all the things for which the Federal government spends money is obviously impossible, and would not serve our present needs. In 1956 the Federal budget was an imposing decument of 1,164 pages, plus an appendix. However, something of an overview can be had by referring to the broad classifications used for arranging items in the budget. Table 26 and Figure 45 tell us in a general way what it is that citizens of the United States get for that part of the national income which passes through the agencies of the Federal government. The government's

Table 26. Major Categories in U.S. Federal Budget for 1956
(in millions of dollars)

Items	Amount	Per Cent of Total
National Security	$ 40,641	61.1
Interest	6,846	10.3
Veterans' Services and Benefits	4,756	7.1
Natural Resources	1,104	1.7
Social Security, Welfare, Health, and Education	2,301	3.5
International Affairs and Finance	1,846	2.8
Agriculture and Agricultural Resources	4,913	7.4
Finance, Commerce and Industry, Transportation, Communications, and Manpower	2,503	3.7
General Government	1,629	2.4
Total	$ 66,540	100.0

Source: Bureau of the Budget, Department of the Treasury, as reported in The Economic Almanac, 1958, p. 433. Individual items do not add to total due to rounding.

fiscal year ends on June 30. If we examine the figures in each of the broad categories, we can get a general idea of what it is that all of us together are buying with our public-consumption budget.

National Security

By far the largest item in recent annual budgets has been that for the maintenance of a military establishment, including assistance to foreign governments to support military organizations which presumably supplement our own. In the present state of international relations, it appears that the major part of our public expenditures are likely to continue to be for national defense. As an item of consumption, this is perhaps the most difficult of all to measure, to concretize in any very specific sense. Its real content, of course, consists of the guns, naval vessels, the aircraft, guided missiles, military vehicles, the bases and military posts in this country and other parts of the world, together with the services of the members of our armed forces who are devoting their time and energy to the defense of the country. The satisfaction, insofar as it can be comprehended at all, is

560

presumably the psychological sense of security and confidence which permits a people to go about its ordinary affairs of producing and consuming the other things which satisfy their needs.

Interest

The second largest item in the Federal budget is interest on the public debt. This is an income transfer payment. To those who receive it, it represents income. To all of us who help in one way or another to pay it, this item represents a necessary payment to the government, in return for its not exercising its full authority to tax, and thereby avoiding whatever rearrangement in property ownership and control would be necessary if the balanced Federal budget were to be maintained at all times.

Veterans' Benefits

Expenditures which appear under this heading represent the costs of maintaining a Veterans' Administration and the services which the nation provides for those who have served in the defense of the country. These include the costs of maintaining hospitals, veterans' allowances for education and re-training, payment for disabilities suffered while in the service of the country, and, in general, payment for the kinds of risks undertaken individually and collectively by those who have served in defense capacities.

Natural Resources

In the early days of this country's history, following the establishment of sovereignty over successive broad tracts of territory, the ownership of natural resources was vested in the Federal government, or the public economy. As farm lands were settled and claims were staked out to forest and mining lands, ownership passed into private hands with rights guaranteed and protected by the state. Some of these resources remained in government hands, since no private individual wanted or could be permitted to own them. Important rivers and lakes could not be owned by private persons, and their control could not reside in the states because of conflicting interests. Substantial areas such as the national parks, the forest reserves, and sites for public structures were eventually reserved. From time to time these have been expanded as the Federal government has purchased additional lands from private owners.

The administration of these vast holdings requires personnel and equipment. Some income from these resources flows back into the national treasury. For example, the Forest Service, which manages the national forests, sells logging rights to private companies. Ranchers are authorized,

Figure 45. What Federal Expenditures Bought in 1956-57

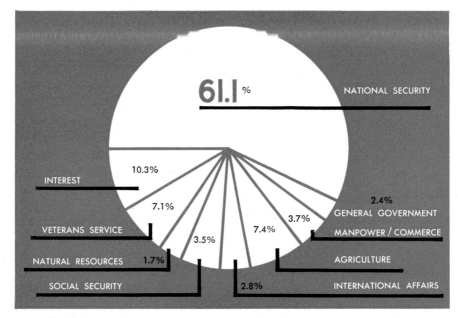

Source: The Conference Board, *The Economic Almanac, 1958,* p. 433.

for a fee, to graze livestock on these lands. A small admission charge is made at most national parks and monuments; and concessions for providing food and lodging, gasoline, and other services are leased to private persons. In the aggregate, however, most of these public properties do not pay the full cost of their maintenance and are supported from tax funds.

Welfare, Health, and Education

Public expenditures for "welfare" and "social security" have become increasingly important, particularly since the 1930's, when large-scale unemployment and the disappearance of accumulated savings caused suffering and widespread anxiety. Both terms have been so widely used, their associated meanings so distended, that unless fairly carefully defined, they can be made to cover almost anything government agencies do.

In its narrowest sense the term welfare expenditure was long associated with the poor relief administered by local governments and the care of county charges and the infirm aged. More recently, with the growing participation of the Federal government in economic life, the term has come to mean those government expenditures intended to maintain and

562

improve the levels of living of individuals and households, usually through income transfer. A new Department of Health, Education, and Welfare, headed by its own cabinet secretary, has become the official agency for co-ordinating and planning the expenditure of such funds. Three broad categories of such expenditures can be distinguished: (1) funds to provide for education and health, which can be regarded as an investment in people, in the development of their minds and bodies; (2) old-age pensions and other income transfers to dependent individuals, aimed at preventing suffering and deprivation due to lack of income, of which the Old Age and Survivors Benefits has its own source of revenue from the payroll taxes and contributions of workers and employers; and (3) unemployment insurance, aimed at providing income to workers when they lose their jobs, as well as a means of underpinning effective demand. Unemployment insurance is principally a state function but certain payments are made to the Federal government. These are remitted to the states to cover administrative costs or held as a fund for loans to the states.

International Affairs and Finance

In the present condition of world affairs, expenditures for items listed in this category overlap and supplement those in the national security category. Defense and international relations have become practically inseparable. At all times, in a world characterized by separate national states, a long tradition of diplomacy requires that each nation devote certain economic resources to promoting favorable relations with other states. When nations are not at war with one another, each maintains in the capital and principal cities of the other an embassy, consulate, mission, or legation, charged with looking after the affairs of its nationals, promoting trade and the exchange of information and ideas, as well as attempting to determine attitudes and intentions in a world where conflicts of interest may lead to hostilities. In the most favorable circumstances money spent on international activities may be interpreted as good neighborliness, or a recognition that shared interests and responsibilities redound to the benefit of all. Then these expenditures can be regarded as furthering understanding and mutual aid. In the least favorable circumstances they are the price paid for being informed about events which may have adverse consequences.

Since World War II the United States, as the world's most advanced industrial nation, has made substantial contributions to the reconstruction of war-torn countries and to technical assistance for underdeveloped areas. This type of aid has developed partly as an instrument of policy in the diplomacy of the Cold War.

Agriculture

Although there is considerable overlap between the expenditures for this category in the Federal budget and those which come under natural resources, historical precedent and convenience dictated the creation of a separate department to administer affairs concerned with the people and the business organizations which cultivate the soil and produce the food and fibre, the raw materials, on which our industrial society depends. The Department of Agriculture was created initially to promote the efficient use of the nation's landed resources and minister to the needs of the people who tilled them. This responsibility has become increasingly complex, and now includes the administration of a large system of credit agencies for farmers, the promotion of soil conservation, the maintenance of farm income, and in general the promotion of the welfare of farm people.

Commerce and Manpower

The development of a national transportation and communication network can be regarded as part of the responsibility of the Federal government, as provided under the Constitution for the regulation of commerce and trade among the several states. This includes the handling of problems associated with a national highway system, the co-ordination and regulation of railroads, the promotion of civil aviation, a system of navigation aids, and the assignment and regulation of the airways for radio and television. While a large amount of these expenditures are for regulatory activities (the determining and setting up of the rules of the game where conflicting interests are involved), these expenditures are also of a promotional nature amounting to subsidies for the development of services to industry, commerce, and the consumer.

With increasing urbanization, shifts in population, the increasing size and complexity of business and financial institutions, and the growing importance of labor-management relations, a whole new class of public services has developed. Aid to housing and urban development, to business and industry (particularly those connected with war production), has taken on an importance (as measured by expenditures) approximately equal to that of natural resource development.

General Government

In the category of general government we find provision for those services which once constituted virtually the whole of the public economy. The salaries of public officials in the legislative, judicial, and executive branches of government and the civil service, together with materials and supplies, are of relatively minor importance in the total picture, although the aggregate expenditure is substantial. The cost of administering territories and possessions, together with the District of Columbia, also come under this budget heading.

Budgets of
the States

Only six of the forty-eight states have a provision in their constitutions for the operation of a basic budgetary system. All states, however, have provided for a budget by statute where it is not required in their constitution. Between World War I and the early 1930's those states which had not already done so developed some standard form of budgetary procedure.

Considerable variation exists among the states with regard to budgetary procedure. Most common is the executive type of budget, under which the governor, or a board appointed by him, is responsible for preparing a budget. In some states a combined legislative-executive budget is prepared, and one state has a legislative budget. The wide variation in practice makes a summary of state receipts and expenditures difficult and generalization almost impossible. Special funds, such as highway funds, which have their own continuing sources of revenue, are often omitted. Almost the only uniformities that exist are those which have been imposed through provisions for grants-in-aid by the Federal government, such as, for example, tax collections for unemployment compensation. A number of states show in their budget statements as little as one-half or less of existing revenues and expenditures.

Specialists in public finance have frequently noted that state governments are most often remiss in systematic procedure for estimating revenues and planning expenditures according to any criterion of need or orderly development in any over-all sense. Moreover, state practice has often run counter to fiscal policies of the Federal government. During periods of high-level employment and income, state legislatures increase their expenditures, frequently by borrowing. Then at the first sign of recession in the private economy, they cut expenditures and reduce employment.

Although there is a lack of uniformity in budget reporting, accounting methods, auditing procedures, and aggregate amounts spent on different kinds of services for their population, there is a certain uniformity in what the states use their income to provide. The Bureau of the Census of the Department of Commerce compiles an annual report of state government finances. These reports show in some detail the amounts of revenue, their sources, expenditures for various purposes, debt, and cash and security holdings. Also included is a brief summary of total state expenditures and a breakdown under broad classifications of the use of income.

In fiscal 1956 general state expenditure for all purposes amounted to more than $21 billion. On a percentage basis, the state tax dollar was allocated among the following functions:

Education	30.1%
Highways	28.4
Public Welfare	14.2
Health and Hospitals	8.5
Miscellaneous	8.3
Natural Resources	3.6
Public Safety	2.8
General Control	2.6
Employment Security Administration	1.1
Non-highway Transportation	0.3
Housing and Community Redevelopment	0.1

Allocations to education comprise the largest expenditure of the states (see also Figure 46). Although primary and secondary education are the responsibility of local communities and school districts, all states make grants-in-aid to local school boards, chiefly because of the superior capacity to the state to raise taxes. Per capita expenditures on grants-in-aid ranged from $2.97 in New Hampshire to $54.24 in New Mexico. In addition, all states have universities and other institutions (schools for the blind, the deaf, and the incorrigible), and it is the combined support of all these institutions that amounts to approximately $35 per capita.

The second largest category is for highways, and in all states a gasoline tax is used principally, although not exclusively, for the building and maintenance of roads. Other welfare expenditures, the third largest category, go for the support of the poor, the indigent, the physically and mentally incapacitated, and for the criminal and penal institutions. Expenditures on public health and hospitals (also representing chiefly grants-in-aid to the local governments), plus inspection services, make up the fourth largest expenditure. Most states maintain a department of conservation for natural resources, fish and game, state parks, and forests.

The remainder of the regular expenditures cover the costs of the rest of the services performed by the states, including the various regulatory functions, the salaries of state officials and payments to the state legislators

Figure 46. How the States Spent Their Incomes in 1956

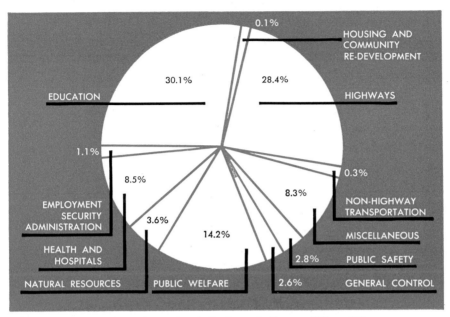

Source: Adapted from The Conference Board, *The Economic Almanac, 1958*, p. 447.

and the state courts. Three categories of expenditure are of a special kind. The unemployment compensation expenditures are financed with funds collected specifically for that purpose under a co-operative arrangement with the Federal government, which makes grants-in-aid to the states for purposes of administration. Most states now maintain a system of retirement funds and pensions for state employees and teachers in the school systems to provide retirement income. A number of states have their own systems of liquor stores, and the management of these institutions requires expenditures, although the stores themselves provide revenue sources.

Local Government Expenditures

New York City collects and spends annually a larger income than any other government unit except the Federal government. The demands and needs of approximately eight million residents (as well as the large transit population which works there, transacts business, and comes for amusement) require vast resources and the services of many workers. Despite revenues which exceeded $2.7 billion in 1956, the bonded indebtedness of New York was more than $5 billion, indicating the problem it faces in meeting its obligations from available revenues. While the dilemma of

567

New York is the most spectacular, it is not substantially different from that of scores of other cities. Modern urban centers in the United States, where a majority of the population live, find it increasingly difficult to preserve order, maintain sanitary living conditions, supply pure drinking water, support schools and recreation facilities, cope with traffic, light streets, heat buildings, and provide communications facilities. Although they represent the unit of government closest to and touching most intimately the lives of individual citizens, the city and other local governments are not independent agencies. The city is a creature of the state, and in many cases must depend on revenue sources not already pre-empted by the state. At the same time demands made upon them increase in an almost geometric ratio to the increase in population. Cities have spread out to engulf the functions of the earlier local governments—the county, the township, and the school district—although vestiges of these agencies still remain.

The combined expenditures of all local governments in 1956 amounted to slightly more than $24 billion.[1] The following breakdown tells how it was spent:

Education	45.4%
Highways	10.6
Public Welfare	6.3
Health and Hospitals	5.3
Police and Fire	7.8
Housing and Community Development	5.4
General Control	1.7
Interest on Debt	2.8

Long dependent upon the property tax, local governments have had to be supported by "kickbacks" and grants-in-aid from states and the Federal government. State aid to schools is now practically universal, and some specialists believe that eventually Federal support for schools will be necessary if equal opportunity is to be assured for all children.

Discussion
Questions

1. It is very arguable that, in terms of a modern standard of living, we get more for our tax dollar than for any other dollar we spend. Discuss.

---

[1] Adapted from The Conference Board, *The Economic Almanac, 1958*, p. 453.

2. In your opinion, what would be the impact on the whole economy if government suddenly ceased to be as good a customer as it has become?

3. What factors make budget planning more difficult in the public than in the private economy?

4. How would a capital budget for the public economy be of assistance in the evaluation of public expenditures?

5. Not all public expenditures derive from taxes. What are some examples, at the three levels of government, of income which does not come from taxes?

Consumption

and Public Policy

IN THIS FINAL SECTION of our concern with consumers we shall examine the normative prescriptions which vie with one another for the beliefs and feelings of men in the market place of ideas. As in other aspects of the income process, men differ in their interpretation of economic experience and in the goals to which they give first importance.

What kind of economic environment and what broad policies are likely to contribute most to the satisfaction of peoples' wants and needs? In one sense, this question has been in the background of much of our preceding discussion. In the following chapter attention is brought to bear directly on this issue.

CHAPTER 37

Attending the Interest of the Consumer

How CAN THE INTEREST of the consumer best be attended? Adam Smith suggested one answer; Robert Owen proposed another. In fact, almost every economist has had an opinion on this matter. It is easier to describe the broad value positions from which policy prescriptions derive than to catalogue the exponents whose ideas have furnished the justification and argument. Normative assumptions regarding the "consumer interest" are discussed under the three classifications used previously: (1) laissez faire, (2) central planning, and (3) the pragmatic or mixed economy.

The Free Market
and The Consumer

Consumer advantage has always been high among the *stated* ideals or values of those who have argued for a free market. Whether the position be that of complete laissez faire or the positive program which would have government intervene to "free" the market, the objective has been to create an economic environment in which the expressed preferences of people as consumers can guide factor allocation. With any given distribution of income, the decisions of consumers to spend can be counted on to remove currently produced goods and services from the market in a manner described in preceding chapters. Business firms, responding to these purchases, will continue their output of particular goods and services, expanding when demand increases, contracting when tastes change. A free market is a prerequisite to the fullest exercise of consumer choice.

To the critics of the market economy (who stress the inequality of income as an important constraint upon the range of free choice, particularly among the lower-income groups), the laissez faire idealists refer back to their policy prescriptions for production and distribution. If a competitive market is maintained, permitting free entry of new firms into any industry with greater than "normal" profit, income concentration can be held to a minimum—the minimum required for new capital formation and economic growth. Rising levels of living are provided with a solid underpinning of production expansion, made possible by the voluntary saving which holds consumption in check. The hope of greater consumption provides the stimulus for effort. As economic progress continues, the rising level of output "trickles down" to the lower levels and their range of choice is enlarged. Thus do levels and standards of living rise. At the same time the individual consumer, afforded the widest latitude for the exercise of free choice, acquires his taste from an expanding range of experience.

To the more extreme representatives of this position, the greatest threat to such free consumer choice, and thus to consumer sovereignty, is the encroachment of public (government) control over resource allocation. The part of household income diverted to the public economy reduces the proportion of national product subject to continuing approval in the market by consumers. As public expenditures fall into a fixed pattern, the possibilities for reconsideration become increasingly remote. Moreover, government intervention in the economy has the effect of strengthening and increasing the area of monopoly control. Politicians are responsive to the lobbying activities of pressure groups. Interference in the market in behalf of organized pressure groups favor some goods or services over others. Since no parallel influence by consumers has ever been particularly effective, government intervention restricts consumer choice by distorting prices, bringing into play the adverse income effects which force many households to substitute the less preferable for the more preferable goods.

Support for the interest of the consumer is admittedly indirect. The particular value attended to is that of maximum freedom—flexibility in the production economy which makes it capable of responding to a consumption economy in a continuous state of changing its mind. All that is required is that the consumer "know" his mind, as well as his market. Time and again *sumptuary legislation* has been opposed on the grounds that if consumers are to fulfill the responsibilities of freedom, they must be prepared to take its consequences. Only thus can the individual learn from his experience. "Let the buyer beware" was once a slogan deriving from this normative position in its crudest form.

On this point, critics of the market as a guardian of "consumer welfare" have made their strongest stand. Market ideology, they maintain, rests upon an assumption of a rational behavior which does not exist. The presumption of perfect knowledge, both of wants and the market, adopted initially for analytical convenience, is imputed to the individual consumer in the real world of experience. When these assumptions are withdrawn, the policy prescriptions based upon a purely logical system of thought which has *reified* freedom cannot be defended.

Some economists have denied the validity of such criticism. Defense of laissez faire and the free market does not necessarily presume that people know what they want or even what is good for them. All that is needed, is the presumption that the individual or household agent knows these needs or wants better than any government agency.

David McCord Wright, a normative economist, goes further in his defense of a primarily market-directed economy than some. The exercise of free choice is posited as a value in itself. The assumption of private responsibility in making choices, spending income, and accepting the consequences constitutes an integral part of the development of a society of free men. Freedom, Wright believes, is indivisible, and freedom to own, to work, and to consume are the foundations upon which responsible people must stand.

Thus, although consumer sovereignty and free consumer choice are placed at the top of the hierarchy of values of the free-market ideology, the route is indirect. Public policy prescriptions aimed at benefiting the consumer *should* be limited to such things as improving and enforcing standards, facilitating the flow of information, and otherwise abstaining from acts which interfere with the satisfaction of given wants, which are the voluntary transactions and associations of free people.

Central Planning for Consumer Satisfaction

The idea of planned direction of production aimed at the satisfaction of human needs has been, with some exceptions, most attractive to those at the bottom of the income pyramid. In our time the appeals of communism have found willing ears in the "have-not" nations and among the poorer groups in the more developed nations.

The claim of socialism's critics that it is a doctrine proposing to "divide up the wealth," while greatly oversimplified, contains an important half-truth. While the naive socialist idealist may believe that simple redistribution of existing wealth (or income) would be sufficient to the task of ending poverty in the world, the more sophisticated socialist economist would argue the case on the grounds of planning a more effective, co-operative effort in meeting the problem of scarcity. Socialists will usually acknowledge a preference for more equitable distribution of income, so that the factors of production, directed by consumer choice as expressed in purchases, can take account of the wants of a wider representation of people.

In the nineteenth century collectivists emphasized the importance of producing fewer yachts, luxurious mansions, and extravagant consumption goods (when they were not promising these things for everyone), so that vastly greater numbers might have comfort, fuller lives, and less back-breaking toil. In the face of what appeared to be the gloomy predictions of political economists like Malthus and Ricardo, Carlyle's characterization of economics as the "dismal science" struck a responsive chord. At that time the great insecurity and low level of living for many (which attended the early development of industrialism) was revolting to sensitive minds, and the Utopias they designed as alternatives ranged from a return to the pastoral society of the romanticists to the model industrial communities of Robert Owen. In all such designs of a "good life" for all, the starting point for argument was the disparity in levels and standards of living between the few and the many.

Frederick Le Play rejected a material test of living standards, emphasizing rather the concepts of total family living, including the security of religious identification and the "satisfaction of sacrifice in the name of country." It was on this basis that he rationalized the necessity for authoritarian government.

Karl Marx, who claimed for his system the authority of science, was contemptuous of those he labeled "Utopian." He claimed to have discovered the laws of the "natural" evolution of society, according to which the institutional arrangements of capitalism were to be replaced by one calculated to universalize the "good life" for all. The abolition of economic (income) classes he regarded as the necessary (and inevitable) prelude to the consumption economy, in which the individual would contribute what he could and would be entitled to consume "according to his need."

Time and the transformations of science and technology have rendered obsolete most of the value symbols of nineteenth-century socialist thinkers.[1] In industrial nations, at least, where the harnessing of inanimate energies to do man's work has greatly expanded output and raised the

---

[1] For a recent discussion of this point, see C. A. R. Crosland, *The Future of Socialism* (New York: The Macmillan Co., 1957).

574

general level of life, the contrast between the wealth of the few and the poverty of the many no longer stirs the imagination of sensitive people as it did once. On this point, as J. K. Galbraith has said, "In the United States, in recent times, for most people the biological minimums of foods, clothing, and even shelter, have been covered as a matter of course." As a consequence, to address prescriptions for a "better world in birth" to the "prisoners of starvation" is to expect but scant genuine response from feelings based on experience in a majority of people in the industrial nations.

The appeal is rather to the possibility of eliminating a characteristic insecurity of our time. During the great depression, when mass unemployment was eroding traditional levels of living and "poverty in the midst of plenty" took on a very real meaning for many, the underconsumption theory of capitalist business cycles was listened to with renewed interest. Marx's thesis of "increasing misery" for the masses had a period of renewal in communist organizations, while various other movements based upon a wide range of nostrums—from the Townsend pension plans to Technocracy—presented programs for consumer's Utopias.

Concern with private monopoly, by no means limited to the advocates of central planning, is the basis for their prediction of the inevitable breakdown of an enterprise society. Even those who reject the class-struggle theory of Marx see the evolution of monopoly as a force which will sooner or later prevent the production economy from delivering as much as it could. Joseph Schumpeter, himself no admirer of the idea of central planning, believed that capitalism was doomed, not because it delivered little, but because it promised so much.

No longer able to maintain the thesis of increasing misery of the masses in the face of so obvious an improvement in levels of living, the extreme left has focused on what they call "capitalist imperialism" as the factor which will finally deny people, as consumers, the full benefit of modern industrial production. Because the working population of any nation is unable, finally, to buy back what it is able to produce, markets have to be found abroad in the underdeveloped parts of the world. This drive for outlets for the "excess" production leads inevitably to clashes among nations and the dissipation of output in wars and preparation for wars. Thus the "war economy" which brings into being full employment and high-level output, and rising income and consumption, appears as a boon to consumers, but it can never be more than temporary.

Consumption in the Soviet Union

As long as the referent of collectivist discussion could be some faraway "dream world" of the future, there was little to restrain the imagination. Freedom from want, freedom from toil, freedom from disease, as well as security to consume and enjoy, needed no bounds. Under central planning in our time, however, the dream of "plenty" remains a promise of the future. Under a succession of five-year plans, no population has been asked to accept greater present sacrifice than that of Soviet Russia. To free factors of production for use in an ambitious industrialization program, and to maintain a large military establishment, consumer goods of the most basic kind have been rigidly restricted. This has been accomplished, in part, by means of administered prices intended to keep goods and services not absolutely essential beyond the reach of the great bulk of households. Perhaps as a means of avoiding any reasonably approximate measure of levels of living, the Soviet Union has never published a reliable index of consumer prices. Such measures as the outside world has been able to obtain show a level of living far below other industrial nations. Hours of work required for the purchase of such basic goods as shoes, clothing, meat, and shelter seem far out of line with Western experience.

Shortly after the death of Stalin in 1953 the new Premier, Malenkov, announced a policy of increased consumer-goods production. Pressure was exerted to raise farm output to provide food for a growing population. Less than two years later, however, a new regime was calling once again for sacrifices of current consumption. Present satisfaction gave way once more to the hope of abundance in the remote future.

British Socialism and the Consumer

During the British Labour party's term in office after World War II public policy was designed to provide security for consumers at a relatively low level. A war rationing system designed to ensure equal access to limited consumer goods was retained, modified only by certain other criteria of "need" based upon nutritional and health standards. Freedom of choice was allowed to operate within limits by a point system in rationing coupons, which permitted alternative purchases within broad classes of the budget. Foods might be substituted for one another. Different articles of clothing could be purchased with the same coupons.

Labour party spokesmen maintain that the austerity program served as a means for rebuilding Britain's international economy, while at the same time providing for equal sharing of sacrifice. As rationing was lifted, strict exchange control was used to regulate the composition of imports on which the British consumption economy is highly dependent. At the same time, meager though the level of living had to be, security in the basic necessities for the masses of the population was maintained, and the nutrition of children was improved over what it had been in the period between the two world wars.

The other accomplishment for "consumers" of the Labour government was the assumption of the cost of medical care by the public economy. In the national health insurance program participation was made compulsory, so that medical and dental care from the cradle to the grave was "assured" for all on a more equal basis.

Consumer Control Through Co-operation

While the "philosophers" of the co-operative movement would undoubtedly maintain that their design for control of the income process in the interest of consumers is a far cry from the centralized planning of socialism or communism, there are a number of very practical reasons for including this ideology among the designs for central planning.

First of all, from the beginning the advocates of consumer co-operation have argued that its tenets for control of the factors of production are basically different from those of capitalism or an enterprise economy controlled by the owners of private property in production goods. The Rochdale Pioneers, who set up their buying club in England in 1844, announced to the world their intention of hiring the services of capital on the same basis that they sold their labor services—for the lowest price obtainable. Equity capital was to be subscribed in small amounts by the many. Control was to be exercised, not on the basis of property ownership, but on the basis of one vote per member. Earnings of the firm, including all returns to capital above the necessary minimum, were to accrue to the patrons on the basis of their use of the co-operative's services.

Secondly, in those nations where the co-operative movement has had its greatest success—in Great Britain and the Scandinavian countries—association with the labor and Social Democratic parties is close. While the consumer groups have usually acted to safeguard their own autonomy, a large common denominator of membership with the working classes has contributed to the similarity of social goals. While the co-operative organization has insisted on its right to separate existence outside the direct control of the state, in nearly all cases special legislation defining its legal status has been required. With the rise of the corporate income tax, this has involved exempting co-operative "savings," when paid out as patronage dividends, from this assessment.

The conventions of the co-operative societies (in the Scandinavian countries, particularly) receive as much attention as those of the political parties. In fact, the latter often make up factions in the co-operative congresses, and electioneering for delegates is vigorously carried on.

Aside from contributions to real income claimed for consumer co-operatives, through the distribution of patronage dividends, consumer sovereignty can be made effective in three ways. Household agents, who are at the same time members, make their wants known directly through their purchases. Moreover, as owners of the firm, they can communicate directly with management whenever they feel that their needs are not being met. Finally, as voting members with equal voice, they influence decisions on investment, expansion, and research.

From modest beginnings the consumer co-operatives of England and Scandinavia have broadened their operations to include not only the maintenance of retail outlets, but also the manufacturing and production of raw materials. Sidney and Beatrice Webb, historians of the British co-operative movement, were responsible for introducing to the language the term co-operative commonwealth. The vision they presented was of a society completely organized around the ideal of consumption. Only in such an organization, they believed, would the real emphasis on consumption in the economic process be given perspective.

Despite the signal success of consumer co-operatives in a number of countries, they have never had other than limited, and usually purely local, influence in the United States. Under the aegis of government, rural users of electricity have organized to provide this increasingly important service for themselves. Farm producers co-operatives have been quite successful in marketing commodities and in purchasing materials and equipment used in production. Some of these have expanded into the field of durable consumer goods for the farm home. Credit unions and mutual insurance companies have achieved considerable success in the financial field. In general, however, the organization of people in the United States around their interests as consumers for the planning and control of production has created only a minor ripple in the economy. A tradition of individualism, the diversity and mobility of social classes, and the high productivity of private enterprise have usually been cited by economists as the factors responsible for this lack of success.

The Pragmatic Approach
to Consumer Sovereignty

Is the conflict of freedom and security a real problem, or is it merely apparent in the language with which economists have traditionally described the world of consumer experience? In order to understand the growth and development of our own mixed economy and its performance in behalf of consumers, the pragmatist does not find it useful to frame inquiry and argument in terms of the opposing ideologies of freedom and planning. Freedom and security, far from being the mutually exclusive values they seem to be when argued from extremist positions, are both terms which refer in experience to what are apparently rather universal psychological needs. They suggest two "opposite conditions of man," which are at the same time antidotes for each other, but they are meaningfully experienced in varying combinations.

In real life situations people appear to differ in their needs for independence or security. At the extremes we find individuals who identify themselves strongly with one goal or the other. The beachcomber, the hobo, and (as a group) the gypsies seem most satisfied with a minimum of social ties and community control. At the other extreme are those whose dependency and need for security are so great that they accept the sinecure of family or public subsidy, conforming to the behavior standards which are imposed. Between these extremes the great body of mankind appears to waver between the satisfactions derived from a sense of independence on the one hand, and the security of belonging and group identification on the other.

We do not know the best combination of the uncertain and the secure to provide the most satisfactory human adjustment. In economic literature competition, rivalry, uncertainty, and fear of want have usually been glorified as conducive to initiative and effort in the individual. Psychologists and anthropologists are not in full agreement on this question, although the weight of modern opinion inclines toward security.

While this contradiction is a phenomenon with which most of the social sciences (not to mention the humanities, philosophy, and religion) have dealt, it is nowhere more recurrent than in the area of our present concern—consumer satisfaction as a general principle. As we have noted, money income can be perceived as a claim against the rest of society. Access to a major part of what we consume is obtained by surrendering these claims—by spending money. When expectations are for a fairly definite future income (and when the amount provided for in the institutional setting is substantial), the attitude is likely to be one of independence and freedom. A wide range of choice becomes possible and is desired. On the other hand, if the income experience has been variable, if there have been periods of deprivation caused by a "lack of money," individuals are likely to be less concerned with the range of choice, more

579

concerned with ways and means of securing a standard of living that is at least as high as the best they have had.

Changing Pattern of Security

Modern property forms, the abstract evidence of equity and debt, make up a complex structure of claims against the national product which can give both the appearance and substance of security. Public and semi-public organizations have emerged to administer funds, the purpose of which is to provide an "insured" level of living for an expanding number of the population. In a monetary economy these reserves take the place of storage bins and larders which earlier were maintained by the self-sufficient household. Access, however, is more roundabout and indirect.

The activities of pressure groups, which were discussed earlier as an aspect of distribution, take on additional meaning in connection with consumption, if they are viewed as organized efforts to secure some level of living. Through the use of political power, they work through the agency of the state, which ultimately determines what is and is not property.

Philosophers and proponents of the mixed economy, in contrast to the advocates of the free market, are inclined to minimize the threat of welfare programs (and other such funding of income claims) to consumer sovereignty or free consumer choice. Nor do they view them, as do the advocates of centralization, as "logical" stepping stones to the complete socialization of income. One reason why the increasing "prior commitment" of income is not viewed as a threat to consumer choice-making is that much of our present standard of living transcends any conventional concept of "need." Food, clothing, and shelter in abundance are forthcoming almost as a matter of course to a large part of the population, as long as the flow of household income is maintained. During periods of high-level employment, the diversion of income to such security funds as unemployment insurance and old-age retirement, and funds for dependent children, the aged, and victims of industrial accidents, represents small sacrifices of current levels of living.

One of the more comprehensive arguments for the pragmatic welfare position is that of William H. Beveridge, whose *Report on Social Insurance and Allied Services* has become something of a classic. Beveridge, himself a long-time liberal economist, says of this report, formally presented in 1942, that it ". . . takes freedom from Want as its aim and sets out a plan of Social Security to achieve this aim. Want is defined as lack of income to obtain the means of healthy subsistence—adequate food, shelter, clothing, and fuel. The Plan for social security is designed to secure, by a comprehensive scheme for social insurance, that every individual, on condition of working while he can and contributing from his earnings, shall have an income to keep him against want when for any reason he cannot work and earn. In addition to subsistence income during interruption of earnings, the Report proposes children's allowances to insure that, however large the family, no child need ever be in want, and medical treatment of all kinds for all persons. . . ."

Laissez faire critics of this position, as would be expected, object to it on the grounds that the income commitments involved in welfare programs constitute a limitation on free consumer choice, particularly with respect to time preference. If individuals prefer present consumption (as sometimes they do), increasing deductions for welfare funds will mean that the household is denied the right to choose alternatives, to change its decisions. The impounding of income will influence the allocation of the factors of production in such a way that they are not subject to the continuing test of consumer preference. Over a time this can result in a diversion of factor allocation from what consumers would really prefer.

Pragmatic economists like Barbara Wootton[2] have replied essentially as follows:

1. Even with a comparatively free (competitive) market, there is no objective means for determining whether the allocation of factors of production is optimum from the point of view of consumers. If we could assume that market prices were equal to the necessary minimum cost of production (which we cannot do if monopoly profits or economic rent exist), the influence of unequal distribution would still be present. With more equal distribution, or even with a distribution different from that which exists, what would happen to consumer preference? There can be little doubt that it would be different. Thus we are left with little basis for preferring one allocation over another, in any objective sense, ruling out, of course, ridiculous extremes which we can imagine but which have little reference to existing conditions or to the habits of people.

2. The idea of consumer sovereignty has been overgeneralized and overplayed. In our highly complex society the individual is seldom conscious of any control over the use of factors of production far removed from the point at which purchases are made. Consumer sovereignty, in this sense, is highly abstract and largely incomprehensible to anyone other than trained economists. It does not play an important role in consumer behavior. In a rich industrial society, aside from periods of war mobiliza-

---

[2] Specifically in her *Freedom Under Planning* (Chapel Hill: The University of North Carolina Press, 1945), pp. 41–69.

tion or crisis, the volume and variety of goods and services available offer a wide range of alternatives. Consumer preferences are not fixed and unalterable, the possibilities of substitution are very great, as the volume of resources devoted to advertising will make abundantly clear.

In contrast to the laissez faire critics, the more extreme advocates of central planning criticize the pragmatic position on consumption as piece-meal and half-hearted. While they admit that each expansion in social welfare provisions can be viewed as progress in the direction of an inevitable socialization of property income and planned allocation of the factors of production in the interest of people as consumers, they regard these partial concessions as only delaying actions.

This argument, too, is rejected by most proponents of the pragmatic or mixed economy. Consumer experience in the Soviet Union has heightened skepticism regarding rigid central planning for household "need." Granting even that the Soviet Union has an industrially underdeveloped economy, that cultural and political factors have determined events there, and that a wealthy industrial society might do considerably better by consumers, the ideology of rigid central planning is still heavily discounted. Planning, in the public economy, is accepted as both necessary and desirable, but a substantial area for private and semiprivate enterprise, operating through reasonably free markets for the co-ordination of production, is retained as effective and hence desirable.

Approach to Consumer Satisfaction

We can now summarize the principal elements which shape policy prescriptions as they affect consumers in the pragmatic frame of reference. Flexibility is the prime consideration, not rigid dedication to any single value or ideology, even the ideal of consumer freedom. People and institutions, not wants or the monolithic plan, are taken as given—the starting point for projection and control. The pragmatists' "realistic" model of the consumption economy, admittedly varied and lacking in logical neatness, is built upon the most dependable empirical knowledge available from the history and the most recent trends in consumer behavior. The development of attitudes, habits, and institutions in the mixed economy is treated as something of a "pragmatic" adaptation to the problem of "economizing," the continuing compromise between the realities of changing experience and the more desirable economic world of imagination.

The esssential instability of household income, discussed in Part 2, is given first attention by modern economists concerned with levels and standards of living. If the over-all economy cannot be stabilized, then planned spending and saving by individual households is doomed to re-

582

peated failures. Such frustrations are likely to be most destructive of "rational" or systematic budgeting, and thus of consumer satisfaction. Reasonable adaptation by the household to its economic and social environment cannot be accomplished if that environment is too unstable. This problem can be dealt with only at the higher level of group action, which means, increasingly, the agency of the state. To this end, therefore, fiscal policy receives primary emphasis as a means for giving stability and predictability to the budget plans of households. Household agents are counseled to support, in their roles as citizens, government taxation and spending practices which offset the destabilizing effect of savings, of the short-run rise in liquidity preference, and of the correlated variations in the investment plans of business firms. With the "economics of control" this form of governmental budget planning is a necessary, if not sufficient, prerequisite of the maintenance of household income.

Unemployment compensation, retirement income, and other transfer payments serve to sustain aggregate demand, employment, and income, as well as levels of living. In contrast to the laissez faire advocates, who would make the provision for such contingencies the responsibility of the individual household, the pragmatist believes that experience has demonstrated this to be ineffective. He therefore accepts aggregate provisions which assure at least "minimum freedom from want." In addition to securing some such level of living (which in a progressive economy will also have a tendency to rise), the effect will be to sustain production.

Minimum Standards

By stabilizing income flows sufficiently to sustain the minimum requirements for food, clothing, shelter, and medical care, the pragmatist (in contrast to the central planners) seeks to preserve for the private sector of the economy the more dynamic types of want-satisfying goods and services. This part of the modern standard of living is something quite new. The privilege of leisure-time activities, of indulging the satisfaction of conspicuous consumption in the new and untried, of spending without always counting pennies, was once the prerogative of the aristocracy and the well-to-do. In the "unseemly economics" of a rich economy it comes within the reach of more and more people. Such, in substance, is the judgment of economists like J. K. Galbraith, who insist that an understanding of this fact is basic to understanding much of modern "capitalism." By leaving this area to the market, there remains a wide scope for the enterpriser and the innovator. In the allocation of factors, the "market" simply does the job with less bother than other means. While some attention should be given to keeping such markets open and reasonably free, a form of "workable competition" is accepted as about the best that can be achieved. If a nation is productive enough, that is all that is needed.

There are other implications which derive from this view of the consumption economy. Advertising, frequently treated in an earlier frame of reference as a form of "waste" as far as consumers are concerned, is accorded a more productive role, although less perhaps than the advertising fraternity claims. Where information (always acknowledged as a proper function of advertising) is not sufficient to the task of demand creation, manipulation for purposes of generating new wants can be defended on the grounds that it helps to maintain production, to keep income flows from declining. In our society this is important.

Galbraith points out that this use of the factors of production in a "poor" society would be destructive of general welfare, because it would deprive people of goods more urgently needed to sustain life and comfort. It would not be countenanced in such an environment because it would be superfluous. Hungry people need not be advised of the advantages of eating rice or wearing clothing. In an affluent society, even though consumers must bear the cost of such advertising, they are too rich to care very much. This does not suggest the elimination of all restraints on the advertising copy writer. The pragmatist, unlike the free-enterprise idealist, does not propose to abandon information sources to the undisciplined imagination of the ad writer, leaving it to the individual consumer to "beware." But his concept of consumer protection would not differ substantially from the spirit of existing legislation and the activities of the Federal Trade Commission, which restrains the production of goods which are physically harmful or socially repugnant and attempts to control (not always with success) advertising claims that are factually untrue.

Consumer Credit

An earlier generation of economists was inclined to view with much alarm the rise in the use of consumer credit. In our economy of high consumption potential it has come to be accepted as an important device for sustaining aggregate demand in the short run. American households in 1957 were "in debt" to the extent of some $42 billion. This was exclusive of mortgage indebtedness on homes.

There are two factors in particular which have contributed to the expanding use of credit: (1) the increasing proportion of consumer expenditures on durable items, and (2) the relatively unequal distribution of income, which makes it necessary for large numbers of households to share their equity in durable items with other property owners. If income and employment are maintained at a high level, there can be little doubt

584

that the use of credit by many households makes possible satisfactions derived from such goods far in advance of the time it would take to accumulate the full purchase price. Such purchases, moreover, serve to sustain and regularize aggregate demand, thereby maintaining income and employment. The existence of such receivables is viewed by many students of the economy as one more incentive for following co-ordinated monetary and fiscal policies to insure against their being defaulted.

An increasing number of modern pragmatic economists, influenced in part by the analytical concepts and policy prescriptions of Keynes (but also by the growth of the "socialized nature" of modern consumption), predict and accept the necessity for an expansion of publicly-owned and financed services. At present a disproportionately large percentage of that consumption is comprised of items calculated to provide security in a troubled world. In the event that world tensions are reduced in the next few years, many students of the economy believe that it may be necessary to provide for a still larger volume of public services domestically. Modern roads, urban renewal, schools, hospitals, public parks, fish and game propagation, waste disposal, and the prevention of air pollution are the most likely areas for development. These all require capital investments linked with budget items showing the greatest growth during the postwar years of high-level employment. Given the continued expansion of scientific knowledge and its application to technology, the possibilities for a standard of living which includes still further comforts and conveniences for all seem likely, and the release from still more of the constraints of scarcity, in the narrower sense, appears to be indicated.

How this added real income will be used, or how it ought to be used, is an open question. How much of it should be allocated collectively to the common use of all, how much secured for the exclusive use of "covered" households, and how much left "free" for venture consumption are questions which the pragmatist does not attempt to answer. They will not be decided, in any event, by economists. However, the economists, as well as other social scientists, may influence the decisions which people make, to the extent that they are able to advance knowledge and understanding of the income process.

Discussion Questions

1. Few attempts to organize people around their interests as consumers have been successful, particularly in the United States. Why do you think this has been the case?

2. The greatest limitation on free consumer choice is limitation of income. Discuss.

3. Excise taxes restrict free consumer choice more than income taxes. Discuss

4. Is modern advertising destructive of free consumer choice?

5. How does monopoly restrict consumer sovereignty?

6. Would you favor the creation of a cabinet post dedicated to the advancement of the interest of people as consumers? Why?

Selected References for Part 5

Cochrane, Willard W., and Bell, Carolyn Shaw. *The Economics of Consumption*. New York: McGraw-Hill Book Co., 1956.

The Consumer Price Index: A Layman's Guide. U.S. Department of Labor. Bulletin 1140. 1953.

Davis, J. S. "Standards and Content of Living." *American Economic Review*, XXXV (March, 1945).

Duesenberry, James S. *Income, Saving and the Theory of Consumer Behavior*. Cambridge: Harvard University Press, 1949.

Katona, George. *Psychological Analysis of Economic Behavior*. New York: McGraw-Hill Book Co., 1951.

Norris, Ruby Turner. *The Theory of Consumer Demand*. New Haven: Yale University Press, 1941.

Smithies, Arthur. *The Budgetary Process in the United States*. New York: McGraw-Hill Book Co., 1955.

Stigler, George J. "The Early History of Empirical Studies of Consumer Behavior." *Journal of Political Economy*, LXVII (April, 1954).

Williamson, Harold F. *The Growth of the American Economy*. New York: McGraw-Hill Book Co., 1955.

The benefit of commerce does not consist, as it was once thought to do, in the commodities sold; but since the commodities sold are the means of obtaining those which are bought, a nation would be cut off from the real advantage of commerce, if it could not induce other nations to take any of its commodities in exchange; and in proportion as the competition of other countries compels it to offer its commodities on cheaper terms, on pain of not selling them at all, the imports which it obtains by its foreign trade are procured at greater cost.

JOHN STUART MILL

PART 6

INTERNATIONAL TRADE AND INCOME

Introduction

IN THE PRECEDING CHAPTERS of this book we have structured our analysis, examined data, and explored value positions in the frame of reference of a closed economic system—the nation. We now propose to broaden the scope of our inquiry to develop an *open system,* which will enable us to take account of income originating in trade with the outside.

Foreign trade, like domestic trade, makes it possible for people to obtain, indirectly through exchange, things they either could not produce directly or which they could only produce at a greater sacrifice of other goods and services. International trade, therefore, contributes to a reduction of the scarcity problem, and in that sense is simply an extension of the various processes and relationships we have already discussed. Production for foreign markets likewise generates a flow of property claims or income.

International income flows (real and money) deserve separate attention chiefly because they are *perceived* as being different. In a world marked off by boundary lines defining national states, goods and services (and people) which cross these lines are counted, incorporated into official statistics, taxed, and regulated. The basis for separate treatment is thus largely political. Economists have sometimes made a considerable point of the conflict between economic and political forces in international trade. Some have implied that the forces leading to trade are "natural" and therefore "good," while the political forces are arbitrary and artificial. These and other positions will be discussed in more detail when we consider commercial policy. Before we can treat such questions meaningfully, however, it will be necessary to develop basic analytical concepts and to examine the data.

CHAPTER 38

The Trade of Nations

TEXTS ON introductory economics usually begin their treatment of foreign trade with the question, "Why does international trade take place?" Adam Smith, one of the first to argue against discriminatory treatment of foreign goods (with certain exceptions), answered this question in terms of the logic of his analysis of specialization and division of labor, predicating all trade on a "natural propensity" of man to truck, barter, and exchange one thing for another. J. B. Condliffe, a contemporary specialist in the field of international economic relations, dissents somewhat from this view. On the basis of research by modern anthropologists and historians, Condliffe concludes that "the verdict is that the propensity to trade is not an original principle of human nature, but a painfully acquired accomplishment."[1] Evidence from the practices of primitive peoples suggests that early trade grew out of gift exchanges intended to buy good will, and gradually evolved as part of the process of cooperation and social organization. With the progress of communication and transportation the trade area expanded, constantly pushing across borders of the organized tribes and clans. With the establishment of settled national boundary lines, trade crossing these lines became "foreign trade."

However trade began, and devious though its acceptance and growth may have been, there is no need now to speculate on why such trade takes place. It exists as an important fact of our everyday experience. Our purpose here is rather to answer the question "How?", to describe the conditions associated with its ebb and flow in the changing climate of international relations, and to assess the consequences for national income of its growth or restriction.

---

[1] J. B. Condliffe, *The Commerce of Nations* (New York: W. W. Norton & Co., 1950), p. 11.

591

For many important items the significance of foreign trade is clear. Goods and services we use every day simply would not be available to us unless they were imported. Coffee is an example. As a nation we grow no coffee. We might be able, at very high cost, to create a man-made environment in which coffee would grow, or with modern chemistry produce a synthetic substitute. Whether it would taste the same or have the same qualities we now prefer is doubtful. Certainly, the American public, which has become one of the world's greatest aggregations of coffee drinkers, could not indulge this taste to the extent that it now does without giving up other things. In time, people might acquire a taste for substitutes, or learn to do without coffee at all (as some individuals do now), but presumably they would not do so from choice. There is no compelling reason to do so, and therefore coffee is one of our largest imports, permitted to enter the country without restrictions or duty.

Coffee is one item in a long list of goods which would not be available to us without foreign trade. It happens to be an important raw material and consumption good. Other consumer-goods items add variety and satisfaction to our life. Nonconsumer-goods that are imported because they do not occur or are not produced in the United States include a number of basic minerals and energy sources vital to an industrial economy. All of these are items which would be classified as those in the production of which other nations have an *absolute* advantage (see also page 253).

Additional items traded by a nation include those which are produced domestically, but for which the demand exceeds the supply. These, too, are consistently imported year after year, varying with the level of income and employment. There are also still other goods and services, which can be produced at home, but which are imported in varying quantities because it "pays" to import them. A combination of factors gives the foreign producer a *comparative advantage,* sometimes temporary, which shows up in the price at which these goods can be imported and sold.

Factors Affecting Trade

The volume and kinds of goods traded by a given country will be related to a number of factors. The most obvious, of course, are: stage of industrial development, size and quality of population, extent and variety of known natural resources, and location. Industrially advanced nations with large production economies require substantial raw materials, and in turn usually find markets for part of their output in foreign nations. If the area of the country is large, the population highly urbanized, and resources plentiful, the major markets will be at home. This is the situation in the United States. If a country's area is small, its resources limited or highly specialized, and the population density high, the major markets will very likely be abroad. Table 27 shows a measure of the trade with the "outside" for a selected list of nations, derived by expressing imports and exports in percentages of gross national product.

Table 27. Imports and Exports as Percentages of Gross National Product for Selected Countries, 1955

Country	Imports %	Exports %
Netherlands	42	35
Japan	36	30
Belgium-Luxembourg	33	32
Norway	32	19
Denmark	28	26
New Zealand	28	26
Austria	26	18
United Kingdom*	22	17
Australia	18	16
Greece	18	8
Canada	18	16
Brazil*	10	8
United States	3	4

* 1954.

Source: Computed from International Monetary Fund and United Nations data.

These figures tell us something of the importance of trade for the individual countries. They do not show the importance of a country's trade in the total movement of goods and services among the community of nations, nor do they show the full consequences of trade for the individual country. Compared with the others, the 3 and 4 per cent of national income derived from imports and exports in the United States appears insignificant. Because of the size of the American economy, however, this small percentage figure represents an important part of total world trade. In 1956 the total value of exports from all leading countries of the world was nearly $92 billion. United States exports were nearly $19 billion, or a little more than 20 per cent of the total. If this same movement of goods be viewed as imports, the share of the United States becomes slightly more than 14 per cent. The value of exports from the United States was more than twice that of the United Kingdom, the second largest exporter. The imports it received from the "outside" were valued at 1.2 times that of the United Kingdom, also the second largest importer, and a nation highly dependent, because of limited natural re-sources, upon other areas.

To examine the particular factors influencing the pattern of trade for each of these countries would make this book too long. We shall therefore limit ourselves to the experience of the United States, using it as an example to illustrate the variables mentioned above.

Characteristics of United States Imports

The value of commodity imports into the United States, as we have just noted, amounts to roughly 3 per cent of the national product.[2] Aggregate value of these imports in 1956 was $12.5 billion. Compared to a gross national product of $435 billion, this seems small indeed. The comparison, however, is misleading. In many instances the real content of these imports is vital to the actual output of the much larger volume of goods and services which constitute the national product.

The United States production economy turns out approximately 40 per cent of the new products (income) of the world. We hear repeatedly that in a world of self-sufficient nations, the United States would stand the best chance of attaining this "ideal." But even in the United States self-sufficiency would be attained at the cost of substantial reduction of output.

The following are some of the vital minerals, with the percentage of new supply imported in 1955:

Industrial Diamonds	100%
Tin	100
Chrome Ore	99
Nickel	97
Cobalt	95
Manganese Ore	83
Asbestos	94
Tungsten	57
Bauxite	76

Foodstuffs for which we depend exclusively or very largely on foreign sources are:

---

[2] This percentage varies from year to year, of course, and since 1929 has been as high as 4.2 and as low as 2.5.

594

Bananas	100%
Cocoa	100
Coffee	100
Crude Chicle	100
Tea	100
Sugar	48

Other selected products in the same category include:

Copra	100%
Jute Fibre and Burlap	100
Manila Fibre	100
Natural Rubber	100
Raw Silk	100
Newsprint	78
Wool	56

These imports represent only a small part of the total product of the United States. They were selected because of their importance to the much larger output of goods and services into which they are incorporated, or because they represent items of consumption characteristic of a high level of living. For example, of the minerals listed, tin, chrome, nickel, and manganese are essential for the production of many types of high-grade steel. Precision tools and modern high-speed machinery, now turned out in great quantities, would be limited or could not be made at all without them. Tungsten is necessary for many kinds of electrical equipment. Asbestos makes it possible to safeguard men and equipment from the tremendous heat generated in many manufacturing processes. Bauxite, the basic raw material of aluminum, has become increasingly important. Finally, industrial diamonds are essential for many rapid cutting operations and for the mass production of machine tools.

Additions to the variety and attractiveness of our diet are apparent in the foodstuffs imported, while the fibre and the natural rubber serve many purposes not fulfilled, or not fulfilled as well, by American-produced materials. Imported newsprint is essential to feed the presses of our newspapers and magazines.

A longer list of imports would include items for which we are less dependent but which nevertheless are important supplements to our own output. Raw materials like Turkish tobacco and Egyptian cotton, consumption goods such as fine wines and hand-made linens, fabricated goods like cameras, watches, and surgical instruments, all are imported to supplement home-produced goods. Ships of foreign registry help to carry goods and passengers to and from our shores, with the risks involved in their movement borne by foreign as well as domestic insurance companies.

Structure of Imports

It is helpful to regard any country's imports as the composite of goods and services which have been found through experience to supplement and complement its own national product in ways that increase its usefulness and value. At any given time the *structure* of imports will reflect the countless decisions of firms searching by trial and error for new and improved sources of supply, for strategic factors of production; of households (with tastes acquired in other places and other times) seeking satisfaction for their wants; and of governments striving to promote or impede the movements of such goods. Among the industrial nations of the world, which possess a high degree of growth and change and of rapid transportation and communications, a historical record of what has been imported (and exported) tells part of the story of their industrial growth and development.

The following percentage figures for United States merchandise imports (in broad categories) averaged for two ten-year periods tell the story of our industrial progress.

	Per Cent 1851–60	Per Cent 1941–50
Crude Material	9	31
Crude Foodstuffs	12	18
Manufactured Foodstuffs	15	11
Semimanufactures	13	22
Finished Manufactures	51	18

During the ten years from 1851 to 1860 finished manufactures made up more than half of the slightly more than $250 million of purchases from abroad. Consumption goods and machinery were the principal items. Only 21 per cent of imports were crude materials to be incorporated into finished goods by domestic industry. The United States was then a predominantly raw-materials producing area just entering the period of rapid industrial development. By 1941–50 the United States, transformed by technology and more heavily populated, was itself a substantial part of the "workshop of the world." Finished manufactures had decreased to 18 per cent of imports, though with an average volume of more than $5 billion this still represented a large aggregate. The importation of raw materials (including crude foodstuffs) had practically replaced finished manufactures in relative importance compared with the earlier period.

In 1850, 71 per cent of United States imports came from Europe (Great Britain, particularly), since the nations of that continent then contained the major industrial plants of the world. The other nations of North America contributed 12 per cent and South America 9 per cent. Asia, then the center of spice and silk production, contributed 7 per cent, while less than 1 per cent came from Africa. By 1950 our neighbors on the North American continent accounted for 35 per cent of our imports—reflecting a heavy dependence on Canada, particularly, for lumber, pulpwood, and minerals. Europe's share had fallen to 16 per cent, while the South American countries, reflecting the large imports of coffee, petroleum, and other crude materials, supply 22 per cent of the total. Asia was the source for 19 per cent, while Africa contributed 6 per cent and 2 per cent came from Australia (see Figure 47).

Characteristics of United States Exports

Imports are a means of supplementing that which our own production economy provides. Exports are the supplements to other national economies, and ultimately are the means by which we obtain imports. While this relationship between exports and imports is highly complex and often obscured, it needs to be kept in mind when we think about international economic relations. Accordingly, when we are examining the record of exports of a country like the United States, it is to be expected that changes in the pattern will show parallel but opposite tendencies to those of its imports.

For example, the following percentage distribution of exports gives us companion information to that presented above for the same periods.

	Per Cent 1851–60	Per Cent 1941–50
Crude Materials	62	10
Crude Foodstuffs	2	5
Manufactured Foodstuffs	16	11
Semimanufactures	4	10
Finished Manufactures	12	64

The relative positions of geographic areas taking our exports have likewise shifted (Figure 48). In 1850 Europe was the recipient of 75 per cent of our predominantly raw-materials exports. Other countries of North America took 17 per cent, the nations of South America 5 per cent. Asia

Figure 47. Source of United States Imports, by Continent, in 1850 and 1950

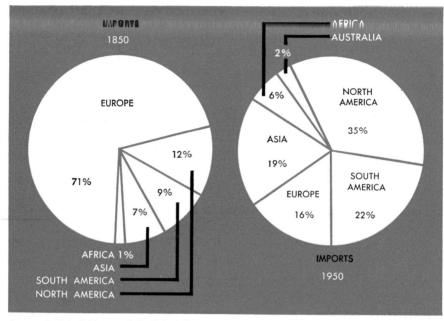

Source: *Statistical Abstract of the United States.*

and Africa received almost negligible amounts. In 1950 the other North American countries, of which Canada was by far the most important, took 35 per cent of our exports (predominantly finished goods), while European nations were customers for 30 per cent, Asia 16 per cent, South America 14 per cent, Africa 4 per cent, and Australia more than one per cent.

If we now combine, in an overview, this two-sided transaction of the United States with the outside world (and if we imagine similar relations among the other nations of the world), we begin to perceive the total system of multilateral trading, by means of which goods and services, many of them peculiar to certain nations and regions, are exchanged. Figure 49 is a graphic portrayal of this web of relationships.

When we view these exchanges in "real terms," the exchange of American automobiles and typewriters for Brazilian coffee, or Malayan rubber, and more particularly when we observe changes in the *rate* at which they are traded—*x* number of tons of coffee for a Ford in one period compared with .9*x* in another—we have the referent for a concept frequently employed in trade circles. This is the *terms of trade*. Viewed in the

598

Figure 48.   Purchases from the United States, by Continent, in 1850 and 1950

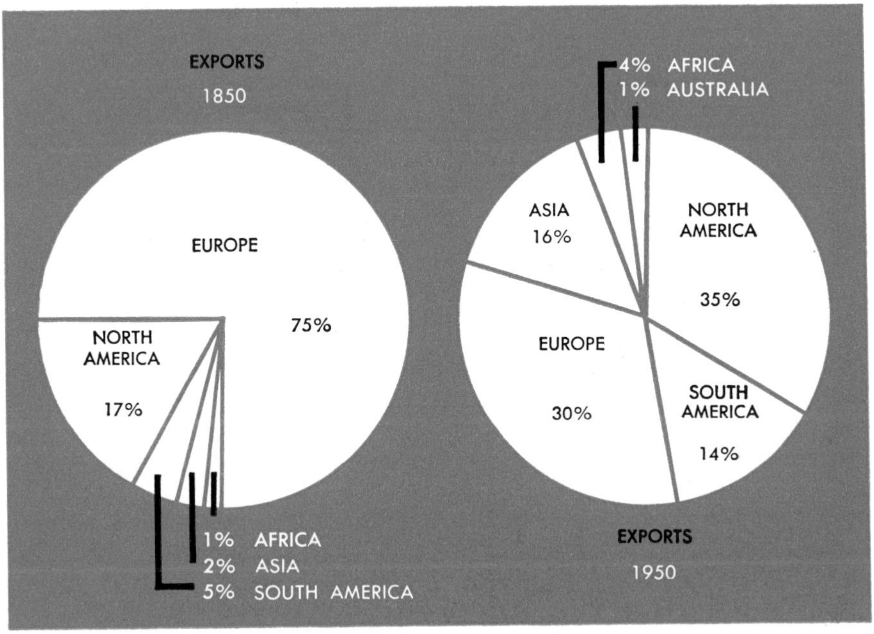

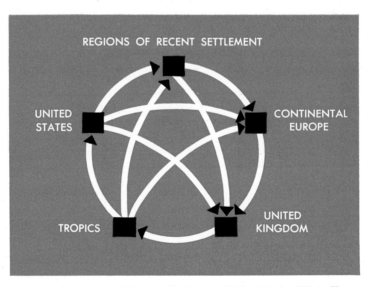

EXPORTS
1850

EUROPE
75%

NORTH
AMERICA
17%

1%   AFRICA
2%   ASIA
5%   SOUTH AMERICA

4%   AFRICA
1%   AUSTRALIA

ASIA
16%

NORTH
AMERICA
35%

EUROPE
30%

SOUTH
AMERICA
14%

EXPORTS
1950

Source: *Statistical Abstract of the United States.*

Figure 49.   Circular World Trading System,
as It Operated Between the Two World Wars

REGIONS OF RECENT SETTLEMENT

UNITED
STATES

CONTINENTAL
EUROPE

TROPICS

UNITED
KINGDOM

Source: Based on League of Nations, *The Network of World Trade,* 1942, p. 78.

599

frame of reference of a given country, it means the amount of exports required to balance a *given* quantity of imports.

In barter transactions this relationship is easily perceived between any two commodities or services. For combinations of exports and imports, the "real" relationship cannot be comprehended directly; hence we are once more faced with the problem of measurement which was discussed in Part 2. Here, however, the problem is even more complicated, because the monetary measures of value differ among countries, and often the problem of translating one into the other is confusing. We shall postpone our discussion of this problem until the next chapter.

Balance of Trade and Balance of Payments

So far in our discussion of imports and exports we have emphasized merchandise, raw materials, and to a certain extent such services as shipping and insurance. This is the concrete, more or less identifiable part of cross-boundary trade. When we treat exports as the means of paying for imports, an exchange in which the transaction is fully completed (with the cross transfer of ownership of the properties involved) is called a balanced exchange—hence the term *balance of trade*. As the term is used conventionally, it refers to the relationship between the value of imports and exports, exclusive of gold which has long been, and still is, a balancing item. During the period of mercantilist dominance in economic thought, when an excess of exports over imports resulted in an inflow of gold to the exporting country, the phrase *favorable balance of trade* was used. The very concept suggested the desirability of exporting more than was imported—a belief that Adam Smith attacked as unsound. Subscribing as they did to a labor theory of value, Adam Smith and the classical school he founded believed that goods were exchanged according to the ratio of their labor content, and that by specialization and division of labor a given nation could increase its *real income* (wealth) by exchanging what it could produce with the least labor cost with other countries, which would also be doing the same thing (see page 630). In the long run the labor involved in transactions would be in balance, but all parties gained, in terms of goods, because exchange enabled them to obtain their real goods where they were produced most efficiently.

Modern economists can no longer organize their thinking around so simple a model. With the complex property forms that have evolved, the highly developed technological processes used in production, and the intricate money and credit structures which play an active part in determining relative prices, the exchange process cannot be so neatly described or explained. The total value of goods exported by any nation need not *balance* its imports even for a long-run period. The United States has been sending abroad a greater aggregate than it has imported since 1873. Great Britain has imported more than she has exported for about the same length of time. The means by which this is accomplished is to be found in the parallel but opposite flow of abstract property claims, including gold.

A balance sheet of the flow of claims, called the *balance of payments,* shows the total of all transactions which create or extinguish claims between one nation and the rest of the world during a period of time (year). Like all balance sheets this one has equivalent debits and credits. The goods and services section (balance of trade) is seldom in balance for any given year, frequently not for decades. The other sections record the the capital transactions by means of which the two sides are brought into balance.

Table 28, which is a simplified balance-of-payments statement, shows the consequences of foreign trade operations of the United States for 1956. During that year business firms, households, and government exported goods and services valued at $3.7 billion more than the value of imports. In other words, on the basis of current transactions the United States had an *active balance* of this amount. Foreign nations failed to balance their imports from the United States with an equivalent value of goods and services. In addition to an excess of goods and services, foreigners acquired long-term investments in the United States in the amount of $542 million, and they (together with international institutions) acquired liquid dollar holdings of $1,302 million (combined in the table with errors and omissions of $692 million). Thus the total deficit or excess of exports amounted to $5,938 billion. How was this offset? The answer is to be found in Item II—unilateral transfers; Item III—U.S. capital outflows; and Item IV—gold purchases.

Unilateral transfers are gifts (income transfers) made by private persons and by government under military and foreign aid programs. These amounted to $2,332 billion. Capital outflow represents property claims acquired abroad—stocks and bonds, bank deposits, and plants constructed by American firms.

These balancing items show us why a nation's trade in goods and services need not balance. They also show the nature of payments balances, because what figuratively moves back and forth across boundaries is residual property rights—properties which are themselves expected, under stable conditions, to earn future money incomes. When American citizens "invest" in foreign enterprises, the United States expenditures are transformed into "real" capital improvements abroad and provide money income to the foreign residents who participate in the construction.

601

Table 28.   Balance of Payments of the United States, 1956
(millions of dollars)

	Exports (credits)	Imports (debits)	Excess of Exports	Excess of Imports
I. Goods and Services				
1 Merchandise	$17,321	$12,791		
2 Transportation	1,619	1,432		
3 Travel	705	1,275		
4 Miscellaneous Services Excluding Military	1,059	784		
5 Military Expenditures	156	2,910		
6 Income on Investments:				
a. Private	2,464	464		
b. Government	194	154		
Total	$23,518	$19,810	$3,708	
II. Unilateral Transfers				
1 Private (net)		$ 637		
2 Government (net)		1,695		
Total		$ 2,332		$2,332
III. Capital Movements				
1 Private (net)		$ 2,980		
2 Government (net)		626		
3 Foreign Long-Term Investments in U.S.	$ 542			
Total	$ 542	$ 3,606	$ 542	$3,606
IV. U.S. Gold Sales (purchases —)	$ —306		$ —306	
V. Transfer of Funds between countries, and errors and omissions	$ 1,994		$1,994	
Total U.S. Payments	$25,748	$25,748	$5,938	$5,938

Source: *Economic Report of the President, 1958,* p. 194.

As the expanded facilities come into production, new income (money and real) beomes available. Part of that income (in the form of interest or dividends) can then be used to pay the claims of the investors.

Long-Run Tendencies of Trade

Trade routes, the networks of transportation and communication, which today tie together the remote areas of the globe, have developed through an evolutionary process. The Phoenicians were among the first "traders," in the sense of an orderly process of commercial intercourse and not simply the sporadic contact of plunder and booty. The Greek and Roman civilizations carried on commercial relations with many widely separated areas, and even during the Dark Ages some movement of goods and services took place.

Trade in the modern sense, however, dates from the beginning of the Industrial Revolution and the steady improvement in productivity which it has made possible. Industrially developed areas, as their need for raw materials and markets expanded, made contact with less developed areas and eventually established a pattern of trade with them. Through diffusion and integration these areas too have come under the influence of science and technology, gradually adapting to their own production practices the processes of the machine. Progress has been uneven and sometimes interrupted because of other influences (usually political, but sometimes geographical and cultural), so that there remain today areas

Figure 50. United States Exports and Imports of Merchandise, with Trade Balance, Annually, 1916-1956

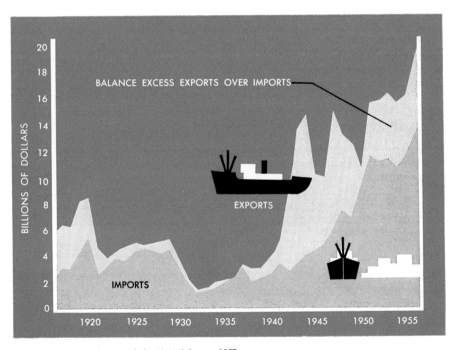

Source: *Statistical Abstract of the United States, 1957.*

described as *underdeveloped*. The economic development of these areas usually begins with the application of technology to agriculture, mining, and forestry, and the building of roads and other forms of transportation and communication. This is how the export of capital from the more advanced areas begins. It continues in the development of light and then heavy industries, where resources and the labor supply warrant it.

With the development and economic progress of the more "backward" areas, patterns of trade undergo changes, such as we have already noted in the case of the United States. Thus the amounts and composition of imports and exports are characterized by a continuous adaptation, as if approaching some stable balance or equilibrium based upon productivity and efficiency.

Levels of Income and Trade

In Part 2 when we discussed the growth and levels of national income, we noted that its history was one of long-run expansion and short-run setbacks. As one might expect, this pattern is repeated in the statistics of international trade. Figure 50 is a graph of United States exports and imports from 1916 to 1956. The same peaks and valleys which characterize domestic indices are characteristic of this one.

For the long-run trend and the shorter-run variation in merchandise imports and exports, the changes in the rate of growth from decade to decade (in current dollars) are revealing. The following figures show the percentage changes of United States imports and exports in ten-year averages from 1861 to 1950.

Decade	Percentage Change Imports	Percentage Change Exports
1861–1870	+ 16.9	+ 3.3
1871–1880	+ 58.1	+139.7
1881–1890	+ 29.3	+ 30.4
1891–1900	+ 10.2	+ 47.46
1901–1910	+ 51.7	+ 57.95
1911–1920	+118.9	+175.26
1921–1930	+ 47.6	+ 1.71
1931–1940	− 44.6	− 42.05
1941–1950	+142.7	+318.81

For the entire period, only during the decade of the 1930's did the dollar volume of exports and imports show an actual decline. The early years of this decade saw the rapid decline of income and employment in all industrial nations with a predominantly enterprise form of economic organization. We have already examined the experience of the United States for this period (see page 132). Figure 51 is a very revealing graphic representation of what happened month by month to the volume of international trade.

In economic literature, generally, the interpretation of these data has a frustrating "hen and egg" quality. Those with a high international trade orientation emphasize the magic quality of foreign markets for restoring and expanding the level of economic activity. There can be no doubt than an expansion of sales abroad can have a salutary effect on producer decisions at a time when aggregate domestic demand is declining and surpluses are accumulating. This is particularly true when such sales are made on short-term credit, so that they are not balanced by imports.

If a country has been exporting at a rather high level and the foreign demand decreases, the effect is similar to a decline in domestic demand. This is how business recessions are, in fact, transmitted from one country to another, and why, as Figure 51 illustrates, the cumulative downturn in any industrial nation eventually is transmitted through international trade to other nations.

Do such depressions originate in the foreign trade field? Arguments can be made on both sides. The advocates of protection for domestic industry have always been quick to point out the national advantages of restricting imports to provide an incentive to domestic producers. In practice few nations have ever resisted the temptation to interfere with trade—either by promoting exports or restricting imports—to further the interest of domestic industry. The statistics tell us that national income and the volume of trade move together and in the same direction, though not necessarily in perfect timing. There is no agreement on what the connection is between the two, in a causal sense. On policy questions, particularly, the modern view inclines toward emphasizing domestic levels of income as of first importance. A further discussion of this point, however, will have to wait on our more systematic inquiry into international trade in theory and experience.

Discussion Questions

1. Countries depending chiefly on agriculture, particularly at a rather low level of self-sufficiency, were once described as backward. More recently they have been described as underdeveloped. What are the implications of this latter term? Underdeveloped in what sense?

Figure 51. Month by Month Contraction of International Trade During the Great Depression, 1929-1933

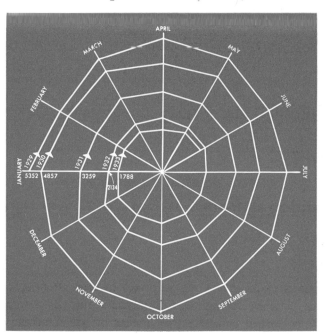

Source: League of Nations, *World Economic Survey, 1932-1933* (Geneva, 1933).

2. The United States has often been described as the largest free-trade area in the world. Do you think this fact has any relation to the levels of output and income attained? What does it suggest with respect to size of markets, specialization, and division of labor?

3. In 1850, 75 per cent of U.S. exports were to western Europe. By 1950 exports to that area comprised only 30 per cent. Does this mean that our trade with Europe was smaller in 1950 than in 1850?

4. Distinguish between balance of trade and balance of payments. Which, in the short run at least, need not be in balance?

5. What is a unilateral transfer? In the early twentieth century unilateral transfers from the private economy abroad were quite large. Can you think of an explanation? With what have unilateral transfers been associated in recent years?

606

SECTION TWO

International Trade

in Theory

and Experience

In the preceding section we purposely focused attention on the broad similarities between foreign and domestic trade. By treating trade in general as a learned procedure, by means of which people and nations acquire wants for goods and services that do not occur in the immediate environment, developing and extending lines of communication and exchange by producing for organized markets, we minimized certain problems and attitudes of mind connected with the movement of goods and services across national boundaries.

At the same time we cannot completely ignore the fact that these problems exist and have given rise to an extensive literature and some highly complex and elegant theories. In the tradition of British classical economics, particularly, the theory of international trade was singled out for special attention. The fact that Great Britain depended on trade and opened up many of the important trade routes undoubtedly accounts in large measure for this interest. For about a hundred years England was *the* center of a world trading network. Beginning as a source of supply for many of the world's consumption and capital goods, she subsequently emerged as world banker and source of capital. Lombard Street in London became the nerve center of world financial operations, and decisions made there affected production decisions in every part of the world. The theory of international trade carried authority by virtue of the success of the British experience.

Now the situation is different. Lombard Street has given way to Wall Street, and Downing Street in London to the less easily described centers of power in Washington, D.C. Moreover, the unity of philosophy and action that once prevailed in England does not exist in the United States. While trading widely, and in substantial volume, the United States has never "collectively" made up its mind with respect to foreign trade. Part of the discussion of this ambivalent attitude will be reserved for Section Three.

Meanwhile, however, the shift of emphasis in economic science has also changed the frame of reference of international trade theory. Where once the *terms of trade,* the international equivalence of relative prices, occupied the center of attention in trade theory, the *balance of payments,* or level of international income flows, is now stressed. In the analysis of international income flows, levels of national income and employment are the starting point. Comparative costs and the terms of trade have now been replaced in importance by the acceleration effect of changes in world demand and the multiplier effect of investment. This does not mean that comparative advantages in production are not important; but for prediction and control they are of secondary importance.

CHAPTER 39

Balance of Payments, Foreign Investment,

and Levels of Income

INTERNATIONAL TRADE, like domestic trade, begins with a transaction— the sale of a good or service by an economic agent for a firm or a government to a buyer abroad. The reciprocal of this transaction is a purchase. Ownership or possession of the good passes to the purchaser (frequently through one or more intermediaries), while title to some abstract property claim flows in the opposite direction.

A transaction between two economic agents who are residents of the same country can usually be treated as a relatively independent event involving only the parties to it, particularly if the exchange medium is money. A transaction across national boundaries involves others from the beginning. Intermediaries in foreign trade are banks and brokerage firms dealing in foreign exchange. Through their offices the transfer of financial claims or credits are made.

An import will bring into being a supply of domestic "money" earmarked for foreign exchange (e.g., dollar exchange), since it usually becomes a deposit owned by a foreigner. Simultaneously, a demand will be created in the exporting nation for the counterpart in foreign "money" (e.g., pound exchange). The purely financial aspects of such a transaction were discussed earlier when we discussed the nature and functions of money (see pages 204–07). It will be useful to repeat part of this example here. For the time being we will take as given an exchange rate between the two national currencies, since without it an importer could not determine the costs or relative value of the goods. Later we will examine the process by means of which this rate is established.

Assume that an American importer in New York arranges to purchase sweaters from a London firm. Payment for these sweaters will be made to a bank or broker, probably after they have been delivered. The bank arranges with its correspondent bank (or branch) in London to pay the English exporter the equivalent amount in pounds,[1] and credits the dollars it has received from the importer to the account of the English bank. Stated in terms of the two economies, the United States has acquired ownership and possession of a consignment of goods, while England has established a claim in the form of a bank deposit.

The willingness of the English bank to accept such a claim rests upon an expectation that sooner or later it can be used in some countertransaction. In the usual course of international trade this occurs when an English importer purchases goods or services in the United States. We can now assume, for purposes of simplicity, that an English textile firm purchases a shipment of cotton of equivalent value to the sweaters, and pays over to the London bank an amount in pounds equivalent to its New York dollar deposit. The bank orders the New York bank to pay that amount to the New Orleans cotton merchant. The cotton passes to the possession and ownership of the English firm. The prior claim of the British economy is extinguished.

When the flow of exports and imports between two nations is in balance—when the value of imports is balanced by an equal value of exports—the accounts of the two countries will be in automatic balance. Money payments originating from imports will be used to clear money claims created by exports, that is, the money withdrawals and the money payments to the national income flow will result in a balanced trade account for the foreign sector.

If we can now imagine a model of international income flows analogous to the circular flows presented in Part 2 for the national economy, it may help to conceptualize this exchange process. Across the top the twin lines or pathways moving in opposite directions can represent exports. The outer line, whose direction is from the exporting nation to the importing nation, will represent a flow of goods or services. The opposite line represents a *credit flow* (which could be perceived as a potential money flow if an international currency existed). Connecting the bases of our national economy models would be another pair of lines also moving in opposite directions. The outer line, with a reverse direction to the outer line at the top, will represent imports. The inner line indicates the *debit flow* or the opposite money flow to the one above. If the value of the real flows is equivalent, the money flows figuratively disappear, and the export-import process becomes simply a matter of *clearing*.

---

[1] Such credit arrangements are usually made in advance of the transaction.

610

This simplified analogy of the flow of goods and services and the flow of liquid claims can serve a useful purpose as a starting point for analysis, but no more than that. For, as we noted in the previous chapter, a balance or equilibrium of trade is a rare exception. (Sometimes *bilateral* trade agreements result in a situation approaching this. The transactions between these nations are then closely akin to *barter*.)

Development of Financial Institutions

In the evolution of trade relations among nations, market and financial institutions have been organized to reduce the need for immediate, direct balancing of real transactions by substituting credit arrangements. This enables an importer, for example, to act without reference to specific exports, since if he desires to purchase foreign exchange drawn upon a particular nation (say Canada) he will usually find the exchange market ready to supply it at a price quoted in his own money. That price is the *rate of exchange*. For example, in 1957 the average price of Canadian dollars (in U.S. dollars) was $1.048+, the British pound was $2.796+, the Australian pound $2.223, the New Zealand pound $2.762, the German mark $.237, and the French franc $.0028.

The organized financial systems of all trading nations (those possessing at least a degree of sovereignty) are linked together in a communications system which we can call the foreign exchange market. Just as in a national banking and credit system, connections are maintained through interbank deposits and the maintenance of correspondent relationships. The largest institutions dealing in foreign exchange have their branch offices in different countries.

Each nation's *payments* can be perceived as a type of running account kept in double entry by the banking institutions. Merchandise exports and imports are the easiest to follow. An American importer who buys woolens in England buys a pound draft from a New York bank which he pays for with dollars. The dollars are credited to the account of the bank's correspondent (or branch) bank in London and the draft is forwarded to that bank, which will then pay out the specified number of pounds to the woolen merchant and debit the New York bank's account. The transaction is listed as a debit to the balance of payments of the United States, because either some previously acquired claim has been exercised over real goods or payment is made through a short-term credit arrangement to be paid back subsequently. Perhaps at about the same time a London textile firm will be purchasing a dollar draft on the British bank to pay a New Orleans broker for an equivalent value in cotton. The bank will accept his pounds, to be added to the account of the New York bank, ordering payment from its dollar account in New York to the cotton broker. This transaction is listed as a credit to the United States balance of payments, because dollars that formerly belonged to a British firm have passed to the ownership of an American firm.

In addition to the merchandise transactions there are payments for such services as transportation (e.g., American goods moved in foreign vessels), insurance for goods in transit, the expenditures by tourists in foreign countries, the servicing of debts, and so forth. The financial operations which parallel the opposite flows of real transactions thus consist of building up and drawing down reservoirs of liquid claims in two national currencies available for foreign trade.

As in the case of aggregate national-income flows, our conception of international trade relations is facilitated if we generalize the process, combining millions of individual transactions into classes, and simply pay attention to the aggregates. Each of the individual transactions will affect the balance of payments in a given direction, by increasing a nation's claims against or obligations to the outside. Current transactions—mostly involving the movement of goods and services in the production and consumption processes—offset one another through a process of "clearings." If trade were always in balance, this would always be true.

Trade in a
Relatively Stable World

The flows of trade in opposite directions seldom balance. Creditors have to be found to hold some form of debt. The debtor may borrow, which means either that someone is induced to save (abstain from exercising claims over real assets in goods or in gold) or that credit is expanded by bank action. During the ascendancy of Great Britain in international trade, London was able to balance its payments rather handily by raising or lowering the interest rate. An excess of imports would mean that, on balance, more was owed to the outside than was due. Since an attractive interest (income) was offered for leaving these funds in London, they would be "invested" there on a short-term basis until British claims could again rise and provide the means for payment.

Britain's long-term claims were balanced through the operation of a long-term investment program which began with Britain's early emergence as an industrial nation. Early surpluses, along with an aggressive navy and a succession of military victories, enabled the British to establish substantial property claims abroad. A series of long-term loans established others. In the nineteenth century, when England had emerged as a leading manufacturer and trader and then as the leading banker, the returns on overseas investments provided a ready supply of "foreign exchange" with which to purchase the raw materials which fed her industries and to import, year after year, more than she exported. Out of an expanding income and employment at home the British people were able to realize a steadily rising level of living. Their claims against the outside, together with a national gold reserve, made the British pound sterling the symbol of financial stability and confidence. England had become a *mature creditor nation,* a status she was able to maintain until 1939. The balance of payments of such an economy showed a consistent debit balance (excess of payments over receipts) on goods and services but a large credit balance (excess of receipts over payments) on income from investments.

Trade and Growth

During the period when England was achieving world leardership in international trade and finance the United States was progressing through a series of stages with respect to the outside, which now places her in a position closely approximating that which England once had. In the early years of its development the United States was a rather heavy borrower, from England especially. This fact showed up in the balance of payments in the form of a heavy debit on current accounts and a heavy credit (receipts) on long-term capital accounts. This is the mark of an *immature debtor* with a high potential for economic (income) growth.

Between 1873 and World War I a shift occurred in the balance of payments of the United States, occasioned largely by the rapid industrial growth during and immediately following the Civil War. A large excess of merchandise exports over imports showed a large credit balance, while the long-term accounts showed a large debit balance for interest and dividends. These are the signs of a *mature debtor,* one that has ceased to be a net borrower, and which is meeting its interest and dividend obligations.

World War I forced Great Britain to liquidate many of its overseas holdings in the United States in order to purchase war materials. With greatly increased production, the United States literally produced itself out of debt, acquiring domestic ownership over properties which were formerly owned by foreigners. In addition, substantial intergovernmental loans were made by this country, and during the 1920's large overseas investments were made by American nationals. However, the excess of commodity exports over imports continued, so that the United States was literally lending foreigners the money with which to buy her products. This position with respect to the outside is that of an *immature creditor.*

These four methods of classifying balance of payments have been treated rather extensively because of their relation to world economic trade and development. Economists once assumed that the four stages of development were "natural stages," through which all nations were destined to pass in the steady progress of the world economy. Like the old theory of the "agricultural ladder," by means of which a farmer graduated by stages from hired hand to tenant to mortgaged owner to full owner of his farm, progress through these stages was to be the reward for a nation that followed the rules of industry and thrift and a "wise" economic policy. During much of the period from about the 1870's to World War I, when the British navy maintained a reasonably peaceful world order and British merchant ships circled the globe with their cargoes, this did indeed appear to be the prospect. If colonial areas at times complained of "imperialism and exploitation" because of unequal bargaining power, this was dismissed as undue impatience for income benefits before they had demonstrated their productivity and efficiency.

Economic policy consisted chiefly of maintaining a stable rate of exchange through adherence to the gold standard, the development of a sound money and banking structure, and abstinence from the overuse of credit for consumption, either at home or abroad. A stable rate of exchange was regarded as essential to orderly trade relations, just as a stable domestic price level was thought to be most conducive to a progressive national economy.

Trade in a
Disorganized World

It is at least arguable that World War I marks a turning point in economic experience, particularly in international affairs.[2] For a time after the war ended an effort was made to return to practices followed before 1914. The gold standard—or an approximation of it—was reinstated. Great Britain announced a program for conversion of her exchange at the rate of £1 = $4.84. Such action was regarded by the government as essential if the confidence of other nations in sterling was to be restored. But many of Britain's overseas investments were gone, she (along with France) had borrowed heavily from the United States, with the expectations of paying these loans from German reparations, and her general price level was high.

---

[2] Some qualification of this statement is necessary. The world has had many periods of disorganization and change. The change in 1914 was a departure from a way of belief that had lasted about 100 years.

The United States, while ostensibly adhering to the gold standard, violated one of its fundamental rules by restricting imports through successive tariff increases. At the same time, in a mature industrial nation with a large accumulation of capital, American citizens and investment institutions embarked upon an ambitious program of overseas lending. Loans to Germany, particularly, enabled her to make reparations payments (after two successive downward adjustments) to the Allies (except the United States, which demanded no reparations), and they in turn maintained the form of paying their war debts to the United States.

Structural Changes

Great Britain, in particular, experienced considerable difficulty throughout the 1920's. Since the rate of exchange had been re-established at the pre-war level, foreign buyers, in order to purchase goods and services, had to pay a relatively high price for pound exchange. For them to have found British goods attractive, prices there would have had to be relatively low. They were not. An attempt to lower domestic prices, particularly wages, through a deflationary policy led to a general strike in 1926 and an abandonment of the effort. In consequence, Great Britain was saddled with an employment problem throughout the 1920's, particularly in the shipping industry. Accordingly, income failed to expand as rapidly as it did, say in the United States. Lacking many raw materials, particularly agricultural raw materials, Britain was forced to continue a heavy import program. Since she no longer had the returns on foreign investments she once had this meant a continuing threat of a passive balance of trade. In order to meet her short-term obligations Britain was required to increase her short-term borrowing, export gold, or devalue the pound. The threat of devaluation made it difficult to borrow on short terms, since investors feared getting caught with a falling exchange rate which would make it difficult for them to recover the full value of their funds, measured in other currencies.

The expansion of the American economy, coupled with its overseas investments (the two, we now believe, were not unrelated), seems to have provided sufficient underpinning to world trade and world production to give the appearances of full recovery from the disorganization of war. There were problem areas—agriculture in the United States was one— but these were regarded as laggard islands that sooner or later would catch up. Political strife and disorganization continued for a time, but appeared to subside as "recovery" progressed.

Of interest now is the American effort in the early 1920's to solve the "farm problem" and bring agriculture under the canopy of industrial

615

prosperity. To the advocates of the tariff (the so-called American way)[3] the high level of prosperity prevailing during that decade was directly traceable to protection from "outside" competition. Their prescription for agriculture, accordingly, was an effective tariff. This, however, posed a problem, because the United States exported rather than imported substantial quantities of the principal farm crops. One proposed solution was *export debenture*. What this plan provided, essentially, was the reservation of the American market for that part of domestic production which could be sold at an agreed upon price, calculated to maximize farm income. The rest of the output was to be "dumped" on the world market for what it would bring. A tariff could then be levied to prevent the reimportation of these exports, and prices received by farmers would be "equalized" between the two markets. Provisions such as these were actually incorporated in the McNary-Haugen Bill, twice passed by Congress and twice vetoed by President Calvin Coolidge. Such unilateral action, to be taken in almost complete disregard of its effect upon the rest of the world, is perhaps a minor incident in history, but it was some indication of things to come.

Depression

The great depression, world-wide in scope, exploded suddenly and with unprecedented severity in the 1930's. The stock market crash in the United States in late 1929 and the bank panic which began in Vienna in May 1931, spread to Germany in June, and by September had forced England off the gold standard, wrought havoc with the credit structure of most important industrial nations. Foreign lending by the United States, which had begun drying up even before the stock market crash, virtually ceased.

In this chaos of liquidation and falling prices, production, and income, nations acted unilaterally to protect their remaining gold reserves, and used various devices to limit imports and expand exports. The consequences for foreign trade we have already noted in the preceding chapter. Speculators, those traders in foreign exchange, spot and futures (see page 319), who during periods of relative stability operated in all of the markets of the world, and whose actions in anticipating changes in exchange rates could be stabilizing, now were contributors to panic. If one currency were falling relative to another because of a minor disequilibrium in debit and credit operations originating in trade, selling short in the falling market and long in the rising market could speed the adjustment

---

[3] This will be discussed more fully in Section Three.

and restore stability. But when all currencies were unstable, because of the general contraction, attempts to anticipate a decline frequently brought such a decline about. While the gold standard was retained, those with actual claims would attempt to convert them into gold, then transfer this gold to a nation whose balance of payments exhibited greater stability. When this action was coupled with short selling by speculators, the exchange rate, far from being stabilized, was further upset.

After the worst panic of world-wide deflation had passed the more important trading nations began to take action to stabilize their domestic economies and their exchange rates. The United States, England, and France created *exchange stabilization funds* to maintain stable exchange rates for the dollar, the pound, and the franc. These funds were used to buy or sell foreign exchange for the particular nation involved. For example, if in the short run the supply of dollar exchange originating from an active balance of payments exceeded the demand, putting pressure on the rate of exchange, the treasury could buy up the surplus and thereby relieve the pressure. Government became the willing creditor.

At the same time, other actions were instituted to reconstruct world trade, raising it from the low level to which it had fallen. Some of these were purely "nationalistic" in their conception. The United States government, for example, appropriated capital funds for the Export-Import Bank,[4] an institution designed to promote the export of American goods by extending credit to purchasers.

Following the devaluation of the dollar in 1934 (the increase of the price of gold from $20.67 an ounce to $35.00 an ounce) the United States became the principal market for gold reserves and new production. The figures in Table 29 on the value of United States monetary gold stocks tell part of the story of American trade during the years following 1933. American exports rose, balanced to a considerable extent by gold imports. The later years, of course, show the effect of the approach of World War II, the purchase of war material by the Allies, and the widespread transfer of credits because of the greater security of the United States.

In 1934, under the leadership of Secretary of State Cordell Hull, the United States embarked upon its program of Reciprocal Trade Agreements, aimed at reciprocal reduction of tariffs and trade restrictions on specific traded items. These agreements, which are still in effect, were designed to create an international environment more favorable to the foreign trader.

---

[4] This bank was set up initially to help finance trade with the Soviet Union soon after recognition in 1934. It was later permitted to expand its operations.

617

Table 29. U.S. Monetary Gold Stocks, 1933–1942

End of Year	Value of Gold Stock (millions of dollars)
1933	$ 4,038
1934	8,238
1935	10,125
1936	11,258
1937	12,700
1938	14,512
1939	17,644
1940	21,995
1941	22,737
1942	22,726

Source: U.S. Bureau of the Census, *Historical Statistics of the United States, 1789–1945*, p. 276.

World War II

Before any of the numerous endeavors to restore orderly economic relations among nations could be effective, however, the world was caught in the grip of approaching war. Emergent nationalism, nurtured by anxieties and old resentments, and reinforced by the recent trauma of economic breakdown, could not be contained. Once the drift to war had been recognized as more or less inevitable, the general economic climate changed markedly. Governments, fortified with vast purchasing power based upon their ability to borrow and tax, became a dominant force in virtually all markets. Surpluses, which throughout the 1930's had continued to "drug" the markets, disappeared into the ownership of government agencies responsible for preparing for and prosecuting the war. The unemployed (nearly 9 million in the United States in 1939) were put back to work, and rapidly turned their newly acquired purchasing power into effective demand. Output rose, and for the first time in decades people were made aware of the full potential of modern industry. Producers, long jealous of their vested interests in domestic markets, accepted foreign-produced raw materials and semifabricated goods as they found difficulty in keeping their supply lines filled.

Two world wars and a great depression, followed by an uneasy peace (all in one generation), proved to be powerful forces for changing practices and beliefs of nations and peoples. The techniques of central banking, in addition to the weight of the fiscal operations of government, have altered the environment in which trade takes place. In earlier chapters

618

we discussed the consequences of these events for economic inquiry and analysis at the national level. How have the concepts and relationships discussed there been translated into thinking tools in the field of international trade?

Trade Theory from 1814 to the Great Depression

For nearly one hundred years preceding World War I, but particularly during the second half of the period, the world was a fairly orderly place. Population increased rapidly, and the volume of trade rose apace, with London as its financial and trading center. The theory, by means of which economists and others sought to understand the order of events, was likewise neat and orderly. Political economy tended to de-emphasize the gloomier predictions of its founders, Malthus and Ricardo, as the necessities and comforts of life actually became more plentiful. Social Darwinism, the belief in progress, gradually moved into a central position. Such progress was acknowledged to be slow and long-run in nature.

Basic to the theory which emerged was the concept of *comparative advantage,* which rested upon the physical facts of unequal distribution of the factors of production and the restrictions on mobility, particularly of labor, between nations as compared to intranational movement. This was an inducement to specialization and hence to trade, with each nation that was party to an exchange gaining more in real terms than they could realize from self-sufficiency.

At the center of this theoretical system, then, was relative or comparative cost (however measured), and ultimately the terms of trade which measured the possible gains from trade in real terms. With specialization, both parties to trade could gain more goods and services by exchanging what they produced best for what they could not produce as well. How this gain was divided depended upon the relative bargaining power, the elasticities of the two demands, and the stages of industrial development of the countries involved. Entrepreneurs or the business firms in search of profit income would search for those transactions that were advantageous. In this way goods and services would be moved about until supply and demand in all trading countries could be brought into a stable relationship. This did not mean that prices would be everywhere the same, since there would be "real" cost differences based upon transportation, indivisibilities, and other dynamic factors, such as changing technology and changing standards of living. But within these limitations the tendency was for trade to "redistribute" goods and services in such a way as to reduce the so-called economic or scarcity problem. This was the meaning, in real terms, of the belief that international trade was in the general interest—general interest being understood here as world welfare. Further refinements of this theory, and the meaning of *terms of trade*, will be developed in the next chapter.

Monetary Aspects of Stable Trade

Prior to 1914 monetary theory was tailored to fit the comparatively stable political and economic situation. As long as a belief in long-run progress and stability persisted, a premium was placed on monetary and banking practice regarded as "neutral." In the field of international exchange this meant a stable exchange rate. The gold standard provided a technique which appeared well suited to this end.

The greatest contrast during much of the nineteenth century was between the underdeveloped areas of the world and the industrialized economies of western Europe, particularly England. Living in a comparatively wealthy industrial country, with steadily rising income, British nationals, through their banking agents, had wide ranges of choice on where to invest their savings. Underdeveloped countries with substantial resource potential were likely areas for investment. In technical terms, the marginal efficiency of capital was high in underdeveloped areas. Imports were paid for in part by raw materials and semimanufactures. With an excess of imports, the foreign exchange of the debtor would build up in foreign accounts. But if foreign nationals were using this exchange to purchase equities in the developing industries, these funds became available to hire labor and purchase materials for new industrial equipment. Out of the eventual flow of new production came new income for servicing and repaying the debts, plus a rising level of living for the younger nation.

According to the prevailing theory, liquid funds, the reserves represented by gold, would gradually be shifted about among the trading nations in a proportion representing the relative level of production or economic activity. As this relationship changed, because of growth in the newer areas, passive trade balances would result in further shift. Investors, recognizing more profitable opportunities elsewhere, could decide to hold their property in gold (liquid form) temporarily, until its transfer could be effected, at which time they would again convert it into other equities.

The stable exchange rate, accordingly, was the symbol of security, convertibility, transferability, and economic development, in directions indicated by improving terms of trade and comparative advantage. Although alternating periods of prosperity and depression tended to upset long-run trends for short periods, adherence to the rules of the gold

620

standard was regarded as essential if credit were to be forthcoming when it was needed and deserved. Students of political and economic affairs were to argue later that the essential stability of this period, and the "reasonableness" of the theory, stemmed not so much from the fact that the gold standard was the stabilizing influence but that it rested upon the "Pax Britannica" of British diplomacy and force. Perhaps another factor should be added—the comparative liberality of British commercial policy.

Breakdown of Traditional Trade Theory

With the wholesale abandonment of the gold standard after 1930, and the attendant breakdown of trade, economists and others attempted to construct a theory more in line with the practices of the times. The question was asked, "What determines the *rate of exchange* between two currencies having no common denominator in a gold standard?" Or, alternatively, "When rates of exchange are determined solely by supply and demand for foreign exchange, what is to prevent the short-run rate from fluctuating between zero and infinity?" A hypothesis advanced in the nineteenth century by the Swedish economist Gustav Cassel and others was revived and widely discussed. This was the *purchasing power parity* theory of exchange. It posited that two national currencies will exchange with each other according to a ratio of their relative purchasing powers under equilibrium conditions. According to this hypothesis, if the pound and the dollar exchanged at the rate of £1 = $4, then the bundle of goods and services the pound could command in England would be equivalent to that commanded by four dollars in the United States. A £1,000 income in England would represent a real income equivalent to a $4,000 income in the United States.

Any departure from this rate would, under free trade, set in operation forces to restore it. Assume, for example, that price levels in the two countries remained stable, but that the exchange rate were set at £1 = $3.50. Then $3.50, exchanged for a pound, would purchase the equivalent of $4.00 in England. Imports from that country would rise, the supply of dollar exchange would increase, and the value of the dollar in foreign trade would fall until the equilibrium rate had been re-established.

On the other hand, suppose that because of inflation in the United States the price level rose ten per cent. The $4.00 which one could exchange for a pound would now buy only the equivalent of $3.60 compared with the base period (equilibrium). Again it would be advantageous to purchase goods in England. But now the mounting surplus of dollar exchange would force the value of that currency down in international trade. What would be the new equilibrium rate?

Assuming that United States prices had risen by ten per cent, it would now require $4.40 to buy what $4.00 had purchased in the base period. Thus, if there had been no price change in England the new equilibrium exchange rate would be £1 = $4.40.

How reliable is this hypothesis for explaining exchange rates between currencies that are not backed by gold? On a common-sense basis, the hypothesis would appear to have considerable validity under relatively free trade conditions. As an instrument for precise prediction, however, it has serious limitations. First of all, the selection of a base period with stable domestic prices and an equilibrium exchange rate would be extremely difficult. Moreover, even if a usable base from which to measure change were agreed upon, it would be equally difficult to decide what prices to include in the price index. Should it include only such items as move in international trade, or should it include all items traded in the two economies? We have already learned that when inflation (or deflation) occurs, not all prices move up or down together. Much would depend on what prices were included. Also, any interference with trade, such as tariffs, quotas, and exchange control, tends to influence price relations between economies, and thus complicates any analysis which attempts to work its way through the maze of interactions using price as a variable. Following the development of aggregate analysis, a new approach to international economic relations involving income and employment appeared to offer more promise.

Aggregate Analysis
and Trade Theory

Near the close of World War II, when asked what the United States should do to help foster foreign trade and world recovery, Keynes is reported to have answered, "Maintain full employment." Behind those words, from the man who had so greatly influenced world economic thought between the wars, was as a whole shift of emphasis. The implications of that shift for the approach to national-income analysis and policy have been covered. We now propose to examine some of the concepts and relationships as they apply to international trade.

When the nations of the world were abandoning the gold standard in the early 1930's, each one adopting more or less unilateral measures for moving its mounting surpluses abroad (while seeking to limit imports), traditional analysis and policy prescriptions still had official status and nominal approval. Conference after conference among the representatives of trading nations ended with an official pronouncement in praise of balanced budgets, stable exchange rates, and international co-operation.

622

These were usually followed by further exchange devaluation, unbalanced budgets, and other attempts to cope with unemployment and falling income.

Income Flows in Foreign Trade

The analysis which emerged from the impact of Keynes's *General Theory* was admittedly *national* in its orientation. In substance, what it assumed was that in a world of sovereign nations with a substantial amount of private enterprise in economic affairs international trade can take place on a relatively stable basis only when it can be integrated with consistent *national* goals.

If most nations can be expected to act in their own self-interest (as they see it) to protect the level of income and employment, then it will be useful to perceive international trade in terms of the concepts and relationships used to interpret the national economic phenomena. For the national economy this involves consideration of a fourth budget, the international account.

An active balance of trade, an excess of exports over imports, means an injection of income claims into the national-income flows not balanced by a parallel flow of real income, since the goods and services produced pass to the control of the "outside." The effect is analogous to an increase in aggregate demand, bringing into operation the income leverages. A passive balance of trade has the opposite effect. Real-income flows—the supply of goods and services—expand, while the expansion of money-income flows occurs outside. These two situations can be comprehended with the concept of a deficit and a surplus budget for the foreign sector. The effect of the first on prices is inflationary, which means higher income expectations, especially for the profit income of firms. The effect of the second, of course, is the opposite.

If an economy is operating at less than full employment, the inflationary effect of an export surplus will be "damped" by expanding production. An economy operating at or near full employment will experience a damping of inflationary pressures from imports. But a national economy with less than full employment will experience further deflation from an excess of imports. A balanced budget for the foreign sector presumably will be neutral.

These effects were always apparent to men of practical affairs in business and government. This is suggested by the persistence of the designation of an active balance of trade as a "favorable" balance, even though economists insisted that such a state of affairs is a long-run impossibility. But men live and act in the short run. A theory which professes to be reasonably *realistic* needs to take this fact into account.

623

Saving and Investing Through International Trade

A nation with an active balance of trade with the outside will be accumulating foreign accounts abroad. The domestic effect of this surplus in the foreign sector is an expansion of incomes, since claims are generated in the production of exports. From our analysis in Part 2 of the propensity to consume, we will assume that part of this increase will be spent on consumption, and part saved. If some of the increased demand is for imports, then in part, at least, supply has created its own demand. To the extent that the increased savings result in a willingness to lend abroad and to create conditions which lead to investments there, an expansion of the output potential of the creditor nation results. Such "export" of capital is most likely to be feasible for a relatively high-income, advanced industrial economy.

The relationship between income flows and foreign investment is essentially the same as that between income flows and domestic investment. A deficit budget in the business or government sector brings the multiplier into operation, increasing income and employment by more than that involved in the initial expenditures. As income rises, the increased aggregate demand will be primarily for domestically produced goods, although (depending on the income elasticity of demand for imports) part of it will be fed back into effective demand for foreign produced goods. In this way the general expansion within a nation is transmitted through trade channels to other trading countries. Expansion in employment and income may continue until something like full employment is reached. To the extent that further expansion beyond this level is stimulated by credit expansion, by deficit financing in any of the four income sectors, the consequence will be price inflation. To the extent that net surplus budgets result in contraction in the income flows, with resulting deflation, this too will be passed on through trade channels, depending on the size of the economy where it originates and the relative importance of its trading operations.

In foreign operations, as in domestic ones, what passes for saving (once contraction begins) is a rise in preference for liquid assets or gold. A nation, caught in such circumstances with a negative trade balance, with mounting surpluses of its own foreign exchange compared with demand for it, is faced by unwilling creditors.

Experience Since World War II

Events since the close of World War II have tended to support Keynes's thesis. Except for three minor recessions, in 1949, 1954, and 1957–58, the United States has experienced a more or less steady rise in employment and income. For many sectors of the American economy, the export markets provided that important margin of demand which kept industries producing and made room in the labor force for the net addition of new hands each year. At the same time imports also rose. A prosperous America was a good customer, although on balance a substantial part of her exports had to be financed by loans, gifts, and direct investments. To an extent hitherto unknown, a national government made direct grants and loans to other nations. In one sense, these can be viewed as investments by the whole American economy in the reconstruction and development of other economies. Between the end of World War II and June 30, 1956, these grants and credits amounted to more than $56 billion. Nor was this the whole story. By the end of 1955, direct investments by American firms and individual investors were valued at a little more than $19 billion. A substantial part of this was in petroleum, manufacturing, and mining, and more than two-thirds of it was invested in Canada and South America, areas of substantial undeveloped resources which are only now gathering momentum in their industrialization programs.

It is probable that when Keynes stressed the importance of maintaining full employment in the American economy he had rather serious doubts that it would be able to do so. He, along with others, had no evidence on which to base a belief that the United States, once the Axis was defeated, would behave as it has. That it did is perhaps attributable largely to the politics of the Cold War, rather than to design. But in the circumstances created by the rival nationalisms of two superpowers some evidence has been forthcoming which has a bearing on our ability to describe at least some necessary conditions for sustaining and expanding the levels of international income.

If the most advanced industrial nations, because they are generating sufficient income to permit substantial saving, extend credit to encourage investment in less industrial areas, the leverage effects of such investments will maintain an environment favorable to rising levels of trade. Such trade will, in turn, help to sustain the levels of employment, income, and output in the advanced industrial country. It is doubtful, given the almost instinctive reactions of people who are citizens of national states, that the process would ever occur in the reverse order, through the increase of imports at less than high-level employment. A sovereign state can pass on the benefits of its own rising income level. It will not act to alleviate the effects of its falling income on others, and if we are to judge from the experience of the 1930's, the result will be quite the opposite. "Beggar my neighbor" policies and the export of unemployment through various techniques to increase exports and restrict imports are more likely to become the rule once depressions get under way.

Organizing for Trade

Near the end of World War II (1944) a group of the world's leading economists and statesmen, hoping to build on insights gained from the changed frame of reference of economic thought, as well as from the experience of the war, met at Bretton Woods in New Hampshire to discuss the reconstruction of orderly trade relations in the postwar world. A belief many of them shared was that trade could not be left to chance, or to the discretion of the United States which had emerged as the economically and politically dominant nation. Many foresaw a return to conditions similar to those that had existed in 1939, and they believed that this would result in a revival of economic nationalism, which had been shown to be destructive of the international economy. They hoped that out of the political co-operation imposed by the necessities of war a small transfer of economic sovereignty could mitigate the need for unilateral action.

The International Monetary Fund

From the Bretton Woods conference and subsequent meetings there emerged the design for two monetary and credit institutions to serve two kinds of credit needs. The first, the International Monetary Fund, was conceived as a kind of international commercial bank which could supply short-term credit when it was not otherwise available. This institution, it was hoped, would step in to provide foreign exchange to any country whose balance of trade had remained negative long enough to create anxieties among creditors. By borrowing on short-term accounts, that nation would not then need to resort to exchange control, exchange devaluation, or other forms of import restrictions. The Fund began with $8.8 billion of capital subscribed by the leading trading nations on a pro rata basis determined by gold reserves and relative volumes of trade. One-fourth of the capital was to be subscribed in gold, the rest in the country's own currency, and this capital would be the basis for international short-term loans. Keynes, who was an early contributor to the thought behind the plan, had favored a clearing union rather than a fund. Under such a plan member nations would have paid into the clearing union only when imbalances developed. Each nation's commitment would have been indeterminate. The American plan, which was adopted, provided for the creation of the capital fund as it exists.

Borrowing from the fund was not to be painless, in a financial sense. In other words, there was no intention to encourage reckless use of credit. When a nation borrowed the foreign exchange of another, it was required to deposit with its own central bank an equivalent amount in its own currency, earmarked for the fund. Moreover, interest on loans was to increase progressively with time, so that extended borrowing would become very costly.

One of the requirements for membership in the fund was an agreement by the member nation that it would not devalue its own currency more than ten per cent without consulting the other members. This was to guard against the competitive devaluation characteristic of the 1930's.

The International Bank

The other institution to be set up was the International Bank for Reconstruction and Development. In contrast to the Fund, this was to be an *investment bank,* its function that of providing long-term loans for investment in new capital construction.

The Bank was launched with a capital fund of $9.2 billion, again subscribed by the member nations, and again 25 per cent in gold. The value of its subscribed capital was to set the limit of the Bank's lending operations. Loans for projects judged "sound" could come into being in one of three ways: (1) the Bank could loan its own paid-in capital funds; (2) it could raise funds through the sale of its own bonds; or (3) it could commit funds without actually lending them by underwriting or "insuring" the loans of financial institutions in the capital-surplus nations which were unwilling to assume the full risk of such loans otherwise. In any event, the total of such loans, by whatever means accomplished, could not exceed the capital and surplus of the Bank.

Both the Fund and the Bank were located in the United States, since it was recognized that this country would be the principal source of capital. As the largest subscriber of funds to both institutions, the United States was able to exercise considerable control over their affairs.

To date the Fund and the Bank have not exercised the influence over international trade that was predicted at the outset. The East-West political division has stood in the way of universal membership. The organization for political stability has taken much longer than had been thought, and important as economic stability is, it cannot be achieved in an environment of political uncertainty. However, both institutions are in being, their operations have been moderately successful in a "financial" way, and they give some promise of becoming useful devices for international co-operation for trade and development purposes, if and when the nations of the world achieve a reasonably stable (predictable) relationship with one another.

627

Discussion
Questions

1. A foreign investment is essentially a claim against the future income of the country in which it is made. Explain.

2. During the 1930's many United States investments in Latin American countries were for purposes of constructing luxurious government buildings and presidential palaces. Would you regard these as sound investments? Why?

3. How does a country export its unemployment when it devalues its currency?

4. What financial or property relationships enabled the United States to have a "favorable" balance of trade year after year following 1873?

5. What characteristic difference would you expect to find between the balance of payments of a mature debtor nation and a mature creditor nation?

6. Over the long run a country must import as much as it exports. In what respect is this statement true?

CHAPTER 40

Patterns of World Production and

the Terms of Trade

IN THE PRECEDING CHAPTER we examined the thesis, and the evidence from experience on which it rests, that a sustained level of income flows, however attained, is a *sine qua non* of any substantial volume of international trade. In the pecuniary culture of the modern world, in which people have learned to respond to the almost universal symbol of money, there can be no retreat to the real world of just things without doing serious damage to expectations of one another's economic behavior.[1]

At the same time our model of the monetary economy, the flow of income claims, cannot be taken too literally. Behind these flows, and linked with them, are the real flows of each of the millions of transactions and the final acts of use or consumption into which they are translated. Goods do get traded for goods, and from time to time out of the highly complex process comes the awareness of what was received in return for what was given up. The money income of the household is translated into scales of living. The foreign exchange generated by the export of automobiles and typewriters and tobacco and wheat is translated into Brazilian coffee, Venezuelan oil and iron ore, Canadian lumber and wood pulp, and Malayan crude rubber, which in due course find their way into those scales of living.

We are involved once again in a dual system of logic, a macromodel for the analysis of aggregates, and another model for the analysis of microphenomena. Decisions to import or to export are made at the level of the

---

[1] This does happen on occasion when the financial system of a nation breaks down completely, as in a runaway inflation. Then people fall back on barter arrangements, in which goods are exchanged directly for goods.

individual firm, and are based upon calculations using comparative prices, motivated by the desire for profit income.

These decisions are influenced by a general economic environment of income flows and price levels. Rising incomes, rising prices, and an accelerated rate of transforming assets in production and exchange influence the expectations of the producers. Rising incomes are a clue to *increased transactions and rising volume of trade*. They do *not* enable us to predict what will be traded or where the expansion will take place. This was a problem of primary concern to an earlier generation of economists. Comparative advantage, the heart of their theoretical model for explaining *why* trade takes place, was essentially a concept of productivity, of factor combination, and of the relationship between input and output. Specialization, a key concept in international production (as it was in domestic production), was a means of still further increasing productivity. The concept of comparative advantage in foreign trade, however, needs to be translated into another relationship—*opportunity cost,* or the quantity of a particular good that has to be sacrificed if a given combination of factors is to be used to produce something else. We will illustrate with a very simple example, using a single factor—labor—and two goods, either of which could be produced in two countries.

	Output		
	Wheat (bu.)		Corn (bu.)
Country *X*, productivity per man-day of labor is	20	or	40
Country *Y*, productivity per man-day of labor is	10	or	15

In Country *X* labor is clearly more productive in the output of both wheat and corn than in Country *Y*. Its greatest advantage is in corn. To produce additional wheat by shifting labor from corn to wheat, Country *X* will have to give up 2 bushels of corn to get 1 bushel of wheat. In Country *Y*, to produce an additional bushel of wheat will involve giving up only 1.5 bushels of corn.

If these two countries were to specialize in one crop and obtain the other by trade, it would clearly be to *X*'s advantage to concentrate on corn and for *Y* to specialize in wheat. If by exchange *X* could get 1 bushel of wheat for anything less than 2 bushels of corn, it would be to its advantage to do so. On the other hand, if *Y* could get anything more than 1.5 bushels of corn for 1 bushel of wheat, it could have more of both crops than by trying to produce both. Let us say that the rate of exchange between the two commodities is 1.75 bushels of corn for 1 bushel of wheat. Clearly, both countries would gain. This is the meaning of the terms of trade for the two countries. X would exchange 1.75 bushels of corn for 1 bushel of wheat; Y would be getting 1.75 bushels of corn for 1 bushel of wheat. From time to time the terms of trade might shift nearer to one or the other of the two limits, depending on the relative supplies and the elasticities of demand in the two countries.

This type of illustration had its origin in the labor theory of value. As we have framed the problem, the relative labor content is the criterion by means of which the two goods are valued in terms of each other. Actually, of course, the *costs* of output will be all of the factors that went into their production. Here, the analysis presented in Part 3 will again have relevance. With specialization, other input-output relationships come into effect. Economies of scale, the efficiencies of large-scale production, will operate as the market abroad expands. Still lower costs will heighten comparative advantage. If costs continue to decrease, specialization may be complete. Otherwise, two or more nations may share in the production of a commodity. The type of market, whether competitive or monopolistic, will also be a factor influencing the extent of gains from trade. These considerations complicate the analysis, and make it more difficult to predict precisely what goods will be traded. In practice, of course, transactions are made on the basis of comparative prices (costs to the importer). If the firm (or a nation) can buy more of the foreign commodity than it could have obtained by spending the same amount on domestic factors to get it produced, then it is assumed that there is a "real" gain. When a situation arises that forces up the price of the foreign commodity, relative to the price received for the domestic good, the terms of trade become less attractive, and foreign trade has become less "productive."

There are a number of hidden assumptions in this analysis. One is that the market mechanism has done its job so well that when we make the transition from productivity to cost and to price we do not lose any of the so-called real relationships. Another is that all factors are fully employed, so that to get more of one commodity at home we must necessarily give up something of another. Finally, this type of analysis neglects such influences as technological change and the fact, as Professor John Williams of Harvard University once expressed it, that the terms of trade may be improving for both parties in the sense that the gains are not alone from trade but from the mutual influence of science and technology.

Of course, economic analysts who were interested in the logic of "pure" relationships did not necessarily assume that the events of the

631

real world were so neat. They intended only that their analogy should give some insight into the process, some meaningful explanation for the existence of trade. The relationships or principles they derived were described as *long-run.* By this they meant that where the differences in productivity were real, that is, based upon underlying physical, techno logical, or human capacities, these would be detected over a period of time and would show up in what men do and where specialized production takes place. For the most part, of course, they were thinking within the frame of reference of *economic* advantage alone. Their outlook was influenced by the assumed conditions of laissez faire, and their objective was to show the benefits of specialization, irrespective of national ambitions, different cultural value systems, and the other biases of human behavior generally.

In those instances of significant *absolute advantage,* events in experience appeared to confirm the reasonableness of the analysts' beliefs. Coffee production in Brazil, rubber in Malaya, tea in Ceylon, corn in the black earth regions of the world (particularly in the United States), copra in the tropics represent the clear cases of advantages in productivity. Even in these instances, however, variations exist, and other areas with "poorer" factor characteristics dabble in the production of these items. Coal and ore deposits of lesser concentration get into production during brief periods, and under temporary conditions that show up in price differences.

For the kinds of production activity less clearly attached to specific locations and to specific skills, where potentialities are diffuse and widely distributed, the problem of acquiring a knowledge of the "advantages" is infinitely more complex and ambiguous. Furthermore, where even these are but vaguely perceived through the intervening variable of a price system (with ambiguities of its own), reliable information for the use of production planning is even more difficult to obtain.

Yet much is known, individually and collectively, by those in the workaday world, in the laboratories, in government statistics bureaus, and in financial and investment circles. Consistencies which show up in production patterns and trends give us a knowledge of what has been happening, and at least a rough approximation of what to expect. Lines of communication and trade, once established, have survival value and do not change abruptly. Thus, for a time at least, those with the knowledge and experience know where to find the most likely price advantages.

Historical Patterns of Trade Movements

We have referred from time to time to a traditional pattern of exchange between the industrially more developed and less developed regions. Since the first application of machine processes to production, industrial areas have evolved as centers of population concentration. These centers require a tremendous flow of food, fibre, and other raw materials, which modern transportation has made available. A traditional pattern of trade, accordingly, has been that of raw and semiprocessed materials moving in one direction and a flow of finished goods in the other.

With time, however, this flow has usually been subject to change. Technology has moved out from the industrial centers nearer to the sources of supply. In part, this has been induced by purely technical considerations. From a cost standpoint it is more efficient to transport goods that have undergone partial processing to remove extraneous weight and waste materials. In part, it has been due to politico-economic considerations. Wherever trade of this kind took place between semi-independent nations, the terms of trade seemed always to favor the more wealthy industrial economies over the "hewers of wood and drawers of water." It should perhaps be noted that this situation existed even when the regions were part of the same national economy. For many years the agricultural south of the United States has believed, with considerable feeling and some justification, that the terms of trade between it and the industrial north have been unduly biased in favor of the latter.

Primary production, as we have already learned (see page 329), has traditionally had a lower income status than secondary and tertiary production. Within the nation this has been a factor in the population shift from country to city. Between nations it has been a stimulus for industrialization in the overpopulated, underdeveloped areas. The process is observable in the historical development of the United States. It provided the early argument for tariff protection of the "infant industries." Alexander Hamilton, in his *Report on Manufactures* in 1791, urged the rapid industrialization of the new country, so that not only would manufactured items be available near at hand, but markets for the then predominantly agricultural output would also be close by. Today this is being repeated in Canada, South America, and many of the former colonial or semicolonial countries. India is perhaps the best example. And in a different political setting the communist-dominated nations are industrializing under forced draft.

This entire process has been intensified by the fact that modern warfare is mechanized, and only as industrial nations can they hope to maintain the minimum show of power necessary for the exercise of sovereignty. War has become an overburdening fact of the real world, its requirements a force in shaping economic need and the terms of trade as well, since it changes the relative importance of many products.

633

Trade Among Industrial Nations

Because of the early predominance of trade between more developed and less developed areas, some students of economic processes have raised doubts about the future of trade. If the long-run practice of industrial nations is to export their technology and to contribute, through investment, to the industrialization of the less developed nations, will not this practice in time reduce existing differences and hence the advantages or need for trade? Men of practical affairs in business and government, acting on doubts generated by similar expectations, have repeatedly tried to prevent the export of ideas and capital equipment, lest developing industry abroad reduce the need for trade by changing the terms on which it takes place.

Industrial history is filled with incidents of the subterfuge necessary to get machines, designs, and even ideas out of a country. Some of the early machines constructed in the United States came from plans memorized by departing English emigrants and reconstituted on their arrival here. Brazil tried desperately to prevent seeds and cuttings of the rubber plant from being taken out of the country. But the present dominance of Malaya and Indonesia in natural rubber, while Brazil specializes in coffee, attests to its failure to do so.

Experience, so far, at least, appears to demonstrate that such fears of the future of international trade are largely unfounded. In the almost infinite variety which characterizes the real world, and the process of change induced by accumulating knowledge (science), new possibilities for the application of human effort emerge constantly. When production shifts from one location to another, it rarely leaves a void where there is any degree of human ingenuity and flexibility.

After World War I the United States became the world's leading industrial nation, more productive and financially more powerful than any other. Great Britain, which had once occupied this position itself, continued to be an important trading and financial center. Despite the fact that these two nations were rivals in a number of markets, trade between the two, and American trade with western Europe, continued to be substantial. Great Britain's balance of trade with the United States was passive—her imports exceeding exports. On the other hand, British trade with southeast Asia was active, while that of the United States was passive. By means of a *triangular clearing*, Britain accepted payment from southeast Asia in dollar exchange, which she then used to balance her payments to the United States. Similar clearing arrangements with other regions provided for the *multilateral trading system*, giving flexibility and freedom to seek out goods and services where prices were most favorable.

The breakdown of this system, coupled with the increasing drive for self-sufficiency attending depression and impending war in the 1930's, served to focus attention on the advantages to be gained from seeking out and developing sources of supply near at hand. Even Keynes, writing in the early 1930's, in a mood of frustration with the growing complexities of the international economy, argued (albeit mildly and tentatively) the case for *autarky* and the possible gains from such a course. "Ideas, knowledge, hospitality, travel—these are the things which should of their nature be international. But . . . and above all let finance be primarily national."[2] His later efforts at organizing institutions to build world trade, however, indicate that he at least continued to hope for the widest possible movement of people and goods for the mutual aid and sharing of all mankind.

The benefits from mutual aid and exchange were rediscovered during World War II, as the need for materials and supplies from abroad to realize "full production" became apparent. This had a modifying effect upon attitudes and practices so prominent during the 1930's. As shortages appeared, and labor for many tasks became difficult to obtain, there was less emphasis on keeping men employed at less "productive" tasks. Moreover, the drains on raw materials in industrial nations pointed up the fact of unequal distribution over the earth's surface of many important substances and energies on which a mechanized world depends. When men could find jobs where they were more productive, the "waste" of setting them to work at any job at all was obvious.

However, there were other tendencies here as well. Spurred on by acute shortages, research workers were set to tasks which brought into existence an entirely new flood of products and substitutes. Synthetic compounds turned out by modern chemistry proved not only to be adequate substitutes for old products, but even to be superior. Synthetic rubber, internal combustion fuels, quinine, and fibres and food sources were developed to replace old products that had previously been specialties of particular areas (e.g., quinine in Formosa, rubber in Malaya).

Finally, the unleashing of the energies locked in the inner structure of the atom opened up entirely new areas for possible uses in material transformation, power, and destruction. What this development portends for the future cannot be clearly anticipated. Atomic energy may reduce the dependence of one region on another. Thus far, however, it has increased the movement of people and goods. As men push into hitherto unexplored areas in search of uranium, and to mine and process it when it

---

[2] John Maynard Keynes, "National Self Sufficiency," *Yale Review*, XXII (June, 1933), 758.

is found, the effect has been increased trade and income. If the time should come when, through the use of tremendous energy concentrated in small volume, men succeed in transforming the physical environment—thereby creating greater uniformity over the earth's surface—the movement of persons and materials for income reasons might be reduced from what it is now. However, in the light of all that experience has to teach us of infinite variety and change, it appears unlikely that differences in cost ratios would disappear even then. In any event, that time has not yet come, so that for the foreseeable future the advantages from trade among regions and nations seem likely to persist.

Much effort is needed to bring a large part of the world's population up to levels of living even approaching the requirements for "health and decency." Such a goal is not only a possibility, but an imperative. Large areas of the world, where former subject peoples were once reasonably content with low and static standards of life, are undergoing change. The levels of aspiration are rising, and one phase of reconstructing a reasonably stable world order involves holding out a greater prospect for improvement to these people.

New Role of the United States in World Development

Since the end of World War II the United States, as the world's largest industrial nation and its most formidable military power, has been thrust into a position of leadership and responsibility which was not sought and not particularly desired. A significant body of opinion exists which is openly opposed to involvement in world politics and even more critical of the economic obligations involved.

This is not the first time that a nation on the threshold of great economic influence and power in world affairs has found itself divided over the wisdom of continuing such a course. In England in the second half of the nineteenth century, when a new burst of expansion was manifest (after 1870), a group described as the Little Englanders argued against further expansion of the British empire on economic and moral grounds. They lost the struggle, and British capital and trade followed the flag around the globe. British imperialism became a term of opprobrium, as one after another of her colonies and subject peoples awakened to national aspirations, and as other industrial nations sought military glory and markets. Students of history are not agreed on the net effect of British policy during her period of world hegemony. There can be little doubt that in terms of productivity, and of the transformation of agricultural and industrial methods, her influence was on the side of increased wealth and income.

636

The United States, accordingly, gravitates to the position of leadership at a time when this position is more complicated and difficult than at any previous time. In the struggle for the hearts and minds of men, the promise of a greater sharing in the potential flow of "man's worldly goods" has emerged as a persuasive argument, though admittedly not the only one. On this score the United States has much to offer. During the current period of disorganization and uncertain loyalties following World War II the United States has donated much from her large and varied output. But in the long-run organization for doing the world's work and sharing the product, free gifts from the United States can scarcely be a permanent arrangement.

Important characteristics of the American political and economic system present added difficulties. Not the least of these is the balanced character of the production economy. In addition to the great mass-production industries, the United States has a large and efficient agricultural system. With the exceptions noted in Chapter 38, there are hardly any commodities of which the United States is the world's largest consumer that she is not also the largest producer. For many items the present rates of production outdistance the effective demand of the domestic markets. Some of these—for example, cotton and wool—are at the same time being hard pressed by the new industrial fibres. The domestic policies aimed at supporting the income of producers, particularly in agriculture, are the sources of conflicts between international goals and domestic objectives.

The existing Cold War has not made the task of the United States easier. Defense requirements are offered on every hand as arguments for producing one item after another at home, lest the outbreak of war find the country dependent upon supply lines that cannot be defended. On the other hand, trade itself has become an instrument of strategy for strengthening countries outside the areas of communist control and influence.

Discussion Questions

1. The period of the most rapid expansion of world trade and production was also a period of the greatest political stability. What does this suggest to you?

2. If a country wishes to gain the greatest advantage from free trade, it will ordinarily have to have considerable flexibility in its production planning. Why?

637

3. Although most nations believe that to be prosperous they must develop large-scale industry, Denmark has achieved one of the highest levels of living in the world, based largely on agricultural production. How has this been accomplished?

4. Distinguish between absolute and comparative advantage in production. Except at the extremes, why is absolute advantage difficult to measure in practice?

5. Chile once had an absolute advantage in the production of nitrates. Why does she no longer have it?

6. Outside of certain agricultural products, where does the United States have its greatest comparative advantage?

International Relations

and Commercial Policy

FOREIGN RELATIONS, in a world of separate sovereign states, are the prerogative of central governments. While foreign trade, in the West at least, has been regarded as having something of a separate existence of its own, it has rarely had the same treatment as domestic trade. Foreign relations and trade relations intermingle in the area usually referred to as *commercial policy.*

Commercial policy can be defined or perceived as those consistencies which characterize a nation's treatment of its trade with the "outside." Whether such policies are the result of conscious design or simply the consequence of opportunistic adaptations to situations which cannot be fully controlled, and in which principles and compromise intermingle, is a debatable question. Sir Henry Maine once observed that "substantive law emerges from the interstices of procedure." By analogy, one might say that commercial policy is to be discovered in patterns that emerge as we study the day-to-day and year-to-year actions of governments as they pursue their over-all income objective through procedures that take other sovereign powers into account.

Trade routes, lines of communication, and points of contact among nations and cultures intermingle. Advocates of international trade have long emphasized the role of commercial contact in cultural diffusion and the growth of understanding and friendship, since such trade serves mutual economic needs. Economic determinism—the hypothesis that the manner in which people gain access to income (i.e., to goods and services) is the most important influence shaping all other values—is an idea that per-

639

sists. Most dogmatically stated in the Marxian ideology, it runs as an important thread through other systems of belief as well.

Thus one can maintain that commercial policy reflects the "economic interest" of a nation. We would have to add, however, that economic interest is an ambiguous term. Economic goals, in ordinary experience, are not neatly separable from other objectives. This is true for both individuals and groups up to and including nation-states. For the nation as a whole, however, the intermingling is infinitely more complex, and ostensive policy reflects the attitudes and influences of subcultures and pressure groups comprising the national culture.

Among economists the principal criterion by which commercial policy is evaluated derives from its effect on the income process. Foreign trade has been promoted because of the belief that, for the long run at least, world real income will be larger and the participants will share in the economic consequences. However, economists too must eventually take other values into account when prescribing in the realm of policy, and as a consequence they sometimes differ among themselves. Whether international trade can be promoted best indirectly or by design is an issue on which not all economists agree. To what extent should government influence either the level or terms of trade? This and similar questions are the subject matter of the following chapter.

CHAPTER 41

Alternative Routes to Optimum Trade

IN THE PREFACE to the second edition of his *Conditions of Economic Progress*,[1] Colin Clark offers the following judgment:

> . . . the situation may perhaps be summarized by saying that, while there is a good deal to be said for nationalism so long as it remains associated with competitive enterprise, and a good deal to be said for socialism so long as it remains internationalist in outlook, the alliance of Nationalism and Socialism produces a monster which threatens to devour the world, and Nazism is not the only form which it has taken or may take.

In this restatement of a very old dilemma, Clark in a sense gives a nod in the direction of the free-trade, laissez faire position, only to counter it with an equivalent recognition of the centrally-planned economy. Both, however, are circumscribed by conditions. These conditions serve to call attention to the chinks in the armor of each, which their respective adversaries have always used against them. To the laissez faire capitalist, who has pictured his dream world of a perfectly competitive order, the socialist has always countered by calling attention to the "ugly" fact of monopoly, of international combines, and of the inordinate influences on national governments of such powerful economic groups. To the socialist, whose perfectly planned society, in which workers of the world have united to usher in the brotherhood of man, and in which the distinction between economics and politics has largely disappeared, the advocate of minimum government points with horror to the single monolithic power and the all-embracing state. He is also quick to point out that the clash between two

---

[1] New York: St Martin's Press, 1957 (3rd. ed.).

socialist states is not likely to be milder than it has been between national states of more limited authority in economic affairs.

The dilemma of the normative economist is increased by the fact that the whole world today stands in the shadow of potential conflict between two superpowers. One, the United States, has an ideological commitment to limited government in the area of economic affairs. At the same time big government even here is an inescapable fact. Moreover, in the area usually described as the "free world," big business, big labor, and organized agriculture have made it necessary to re-examine the substance of competition as a regulator of economic affairs. In the other superpower, the Soviet Union, the ideological commitment is to communism or central planning. Such trade as exists with the outside is handled by a giant *state trading corporation*. Its bargaining power is supported by the financial weight of the monolithic state.

In the rivalry which takes place in the market place of ideas, where normative choice must be the best compromise between the desirable and the possible, the problem of evaluating claims and counterclaims is not easy. Old loyalties never die. They just appear in new symbolic garb. Accordingly, it will be useful to review the value assumptions behind the *ideal types* that have become familiar in the course of our inquiry, as they apply to the field of international economic relations.

Free Trade
or Laissez Faire

In its simplest meaning, the concept of *free trade* refers to a commercial policy which makes no distinctions between foreign-produced goods and domestically-produced goods in the national markets. If a tax or regulation is levied against a domestic good, usually for revenue purposes, the same tax will apply to its foreign equivalent; but no special tax for imports is sanctioned. *Protection* has always meant special treatment for a particular good. The tariff, once the most common type of protection, is a tax levied against the product of an outside producer (but not on the domestic counterpart) which is intended to increase its price to the domestic user. In this way the domestic producer is "protected" from outside competition. The foreigner may absorb the tariff into his cost structure, in which case it becomes less profitable to export. If the tariff is high enough, of course, access to the domestic market can be prevented entirely.

Historically, the consistent advocate of laissez faire or a minimum of government has maintained that foreign trade *ought* to be free, just as domestic trade ought to be regulated by competition in the market place. This position was first enunciated by the Physiocrats in France, and was later stated in its classic form by Adam Smith in *The Wealth of Nations*. Even Smith, however, had some reservations, in that he approved the British Navigation Acts which favored domestic shipping.

On what set of facts and what value assumptions did this position rest? Did it favor one class, the rising industrial and commercial groups, as some have charged? Did it neglect an important human loyalty—that of patriotism? Modern industrial society emerged from the gradual breakdown of a largely local feudal society. Getting rid of local tolls and restrictions on commerce and trade resulted in gradually expanding markets, an increasing flow of goods and services, and rising levels of living. As the number of purely local authorities capable of taxing the movement of trade diminished, incentives for specialized production emerged, rigid prices maintained by the guilds were undermined, and the wealth, or property holdings, particularly of the merchants and traders, increased.

Although the Physiocrats were the first to advocate a laissez faire policy for domestic affairs, Adam Smith carried the argument further and elaborated it for foreign commerce as well. His general argument, of course, rested upon specialization, division of labor, and exchange. Advantage in production sets the limits within which the terms of trade are determined, and the exchange which follows results in a general increase in real income, which is shared according to other factors in the supply and demand situation, such as bargaining power, elasticities of supply and demand, and temporary variations related to changes in technology, large and small crops, and so forth. In the long run, however, the process of competition was necessary to diffuse the general gain from trade. The temporary advantage of those who took the initiative in promoting trade, and in producing for the expanding markets, was acknowledged. To society, however, this was a cost of getting the job done—a temporary cost outweighed by the long-run increase in wealth and real income, as goods were transported from locations of relative surplus to places where they were scarce and high-priced.

As to the charge of a lack of patriotism, a lack of concern over the primacy of the "national interest," there is some evidence that David Hume (Smith's friend and teacher), Smith himself, John Stuart Mill, Alfred Marshall, and others who contributed to the laissez faire argument were rather more cosmopolitan than some of their detractors. There is nothing to indicate that they were anything but loyal Englishmen. Their stand was taken on other grounds. Free trade and equal treatment for foreign traders, they believed, could be defended purely on the grounds of

643

enlightened self interest, and the long-run increase in wealth for all nations.

An extreme form of this argument was contained in the doctrines of the Manchester school. This group, at the outset, centered around the Manchester Chamber of Commerce, which spoke for the manufacturing interests of that city, particularly the textile industries. Two of its leading figures were Richard Cobden and John Bright. Cobden, a textile manufacturer and Member of Parliament, was active in the repeal of the corn laws and influential in the complete abolition of British tariffs. An ardent champion of laissez faire, he also dealt with the special economic factors related to war, colonial policy, and factory legislation.[2]

The members of this school were perhaps the extreme believers in the efficacy of commercial contracts and trade as contributors to peace and international understanding. Their influence, particularly on British commercial policy, was tremendous. Through organization and "public education," their program was advanced over several generations until at last in 1869 Britain in effect removed the last of her preferences for domestic production and cast her lot with free international trade. This final step was taken with the full intention of showing the way, by precept and example, to free-trade relations. Even prior to this step, Great Britain had followed the practice of incorporating in her trade treaties an unconditional *most-favored-nation clause*. This clause provided that whenever a tariff concession was made to any country, it would be generalized to apply to all other nations. No nation would then fare worse in the British market than the most favored nation. This gradualism was finally abandoned, and England took the lead in the free international trade movement. This policy persisted, sometimes in the face of considerable domestic opposition, until it fell a victim of the great depression. Great Britain provides the single significant example of complete laissez faire, or nonintervention by government, in international trade relations. It is this experience that is weighted most heavily in the thinking of economists who emphasize the desirability of free trade.

In the United States, academic economists, influenced as they were by the British tradition, usually took an antiprotectionist position. They were usually in conflict, however, with a substantial body of public opinion and the practice of the Federal government. It has been said of F. W. Taussig, professor of economics at Harvard University, that he taught free trade to more students, and turned out more practicing protectionists than any other teacher in America. The anomalies of United States trade policy, however, are worthy of separate treatment.

---

[2] Cobden's speeches abounded in the use of the word freedom. One of his detractors has suggested that, if wherever freedom appears the term cotton were inserted, his speeches would make more sense.

Laissez Faire and the "American System"

A minimum of interference by government in economic affairs was not something that was achieved in the United States after a long struggle. When independence from an outside authority had been attained through revolution, the citizens and the more influential leaders were in essential agreement on founding a national government of strictly limited powers. Thomas Jefferson (whose influence as revolutionary leader, ambassador of the young republic, and President was substantial) emphasized repeatedly that the "least government was the best government." The frontier peoples, at the outset, resented even the comparatively light taxes imposed by the Federal government on certain commodities—a resentment which found at least one overt expression in the Whiskey Rebellion.

In its search for revenue sources, the Federal government singled out foreign imports as an easy and obvious base for raising revenues. The separate states, however, were proscribed from levying taxes specifically against goods of foreign origin or from discriminating against the products of other states. But while the laissez faire tradition was very strong with respect to domestic affairs, opinions on foreign trade were divided, and as time passed became even more so. Hamilton, in his *Report on Manufactures,* strongly recommended a program of rapid industrial development, fostered and supported by the Federal government.

The War of 1812 and the close of the Napoleonic wars in Europe in 1816 mark something of a turning point in United States commercial policy. During the embargo, just prior to the conflict with Britain, a considerable number of American firms sprang up in the New England and Middle Atlantic states for the production of manufactured goods. With the cessation of hostilities in Europe, manufacturers in England were poised for expansion into the American markets. Fearing this competition, the so-called infant industries demanded and eventually received tariff protection. The tariff act of 1816 was the first to include a distinct protective feature. From that time forward the argument for protecting domestic industry built up gradually until it reached a crescendo in the decades following the Civil War. The infant-industry argument was simple and logical. Small firms in their formative stages, with limited capital and experience, could not hope to meet the competition of the established foreign firms. An implication usually present in the protectionist argument was that once the industry of a young nation had achieved maturity it would be able to compete on an equal footing with those of the more mature trading nations.

Three names stand out as contributors to the rationale for protection in the United States. Mathew and Henry C. Carey were a father-son combination, whose publishing house and personal tracts and speeches were influential in promoting tariff legislation and government sponsorship of internal improvements. Friedrich List was a naturalized American, whose advocacy of protection and national development had influence both in his native Germany and his adopted country. His books were published in the United States under the Carey imprint. Corresponding to the Cobden-Bright political advocacy of free trade were the careers of Daniel Webster and Henry Clay, spokesmen of the manufacturing interests of the North and East.

Protectionism as a political credo was successful in the United States, and after the Civil War it remained almost unchallenged as a prescription for economic progress, as well as an explanation for industrial expansion. Farmers, particularly the producers of important export crops, were never entirely convinced of the benefits of the tariff (the cotton South was certain that the opposite was true), and as giant combines and trusts began to appear in the protected industries their doubts increased. Their situation was somewhat ameliorated by the fact that as a debtor nation the United States could continue an active trade balance, exporting year after year more than was imported, with the knowledge that the growing wealth and property of the American economy was "paying" itself out of debt to the outside.

For the success of the "American System" the free traders have this explanation. Despite the fact that in many cases the United States acted unilaterally, and in a manner which in other circumstances would have invited retaliation, its immunity rested upon the size and diversity of its own territory. Opportunity for growth and expansion, an ever recurring need for new investments, was ready-made at the frontier. When the empty spaces had been occupied, a vast expanse of local markets were at hand, with no bothersome boundary lines and no separate systems of currency to complicate the income flows. The United States had emerged as the largest free-trade area in the world.

This has not precluded the rise of regional inequities and of roadblocks to the uniform movement of goods and services and the realization of equal benefits, however. For a long time the South experienced many disadvantages and failed to keep pace with other regions. Freight differentials, social and cultural differences, and political discrimination combined to make the South, in the words of President Franklin D. Roosevelt, "the nation's number one problem area." This is a partial answer to the free-trade enthusiast, who believes that the elimination of international trade restrictions is the solution to the world's ills.

To the firm believer in laissez faire, the future of world trade lies in the return of export-import decisions, and ultimately decisions to invest,

646

to the control of private enterprise and the semiprivate investment institutions that channel savings into capital construction and new developments. For the most part, laissez faire economists were at first critical of the new international institutions, such as the International Monetary Fund and the International Bank, on the grounds that these organizations are controlled by governments and are for this reason likely to be more responsive to political considerations than to sound economic considerations. By "sound" is usually meant productivity and profitability as judged by the criteria of conventional business practice.

To be successful, private enterprise must be able to operate in a monetary environment of stable exchange rates, maintained by a gold standard or some workable equivalent. Tariff reduction and the removal of quotas and government rationing of foreign exchange (with full convertibility) are viewed as essential for a return to stable world trade, and the fullest realization of comparative advantage and specialization in world production.

International Trade and Central Planning

While the socialist dream of a better world is framed in the symbols of the international brotherhood of workingmen, this is admittedly an ultimate achievement, not something to be attained at once. The language suggests that most socialists see the process of transformation as beginning with the individual state. *Nationalization* is a term used most frequently to refer to the technique for achieving social ownership of the factors of production.

The objective of social ownership of the factors of production in the domestic economy is a more equitable distribution of income, based upon contribution and need (see page 495). Saving and investment decisions become functions performed by the planning authority. Decisions to produce and decisions to import would be made on a similar basis.

What criteria would such an authority use in deciding whether to import or to depend on domestic production? In the literature of central planning the answer to this question is not clear-cut. There is, of course, a presumption that the differences in productivity which lie behind comparative advantage would be as relevant to production decisions under planning as under a private-enterprise economy. Some goods and services would be secured at a lower opportunity cost if imported from abroad than if produced at home. With favorable terms of trade, levels of real income could be increased through exchange.

An office of foreign trade, with export and import branches, would co-ordinate (through the central planning authority) an invoice of needs for foreign goods and cultivate the most likely outlets for domestic production. Such an arrangement, the central planner would argue, should make immediately clear the relationship between exports and imports. The "illusion" of a favorable balance of trade would not exist, since for an integrated economy it would be apparent that here was something sent abroad for which nothing was received in return. A program of foreign investment to insure future supplies of goods and credit would not be ruled out, of course.

Moreover, a planned economy, with a state monopoly in foreign trade, would have certain advantages when it operated in foreign markets, where other traders were firms from free-enterprise economies. The bargaining power of such a monopoly would be great, and for goods with several possible sources of supply this power could be used to secure favorable prices, that is, favorable terms of exchange.

What of trade relations between two centrally-planned economies? Would there be an objective basis for determining rates of exchange and the terms of trade between two such economies, comparable to that provided by market prices in a relatively free world market? In Part 3 we examined the proposed solution to relative pricing and the allocation of factors in domestic production under planning (see page 373). This involved a set of "bookkeeping" costs, a process for adjusting the allocation of factors to provide something akin to an equilibrium price. If two centrally-planned economies were following similar cost and allocation procedures, then presumably the international comparison of prices might be possible. If the number of such economies were to increase, and relations among them were friendly, then presumably a system of multilateral trading could evolve a similar structure of relative prices for use in trade decisions. This was the implication of Colin Clark's judgment that there is "a good deal to be said for socialism so long as it remains international in outlook."

Again, it should perhaps be repeated that planning and socialist theorists are not entirely clear on the details of how such an international system should work. The basis for their proposals must be partially inferred from their criticisms of the enterprise system, the "evils" of which their ideal system is supposed to correct. The weakness of the free-trade argument, they have always insisted, stems from the fact that conditions assumed for its success do not exist. Trade does not take place between firms of equal bargaining power under competition. Trade is between the "capitalist giants," backed up by their governments, on the one hand, and the small, less organized producers of the underdeveloped nations, whose governments cannot give them the same support, on the other. (This, incidentally, was the argument also of the principal spokesmen for the American system. The Careys and List maintained that the free-trade arguments of England were calculated to serve her interests at a time when she had a virtual monopoly of many industrial goods.)

This was essentially the implication of the term "imperialism" as it was used by the communists and by certain of the latter-day liberals, to condemn the commercial policies of major industrial nations. Lenin and Rosa Luxemburg defined *imperialism* as the last stage of capitalism—the beginning of a drive to extend authority over colonial areas in order to expand markets, secure raw materials, and generally to establish property rights over resources. Following the analysis of Marx, the communists maintained that this was the inevitable evolvement of the "capitalist" process, and the cause of war when rival imperialisms came into conflict.

With less dogmatism in their arguments, perhaps, non-Marxians like J. A. Hobson and H. E. Barnes also stressed the use of national policy in the promotion of the economic interests of the richer, more powerful nations in the underdeveloped areas. The implications of much that they wrote was that American, British, German, French, and other "capitalists" used the backing of government to secure and defend investments. The favorable terms of trade there benefited the creditor nations disproportionately.

Soviet Nationalism and the New Imperialism

Two developments of recent times have served to weaken traditional collectivist arguments and the assumptions on which they were based. First, the status of the colonial powers has been greatly altered. The imperial powers of the last century, England, Germany, France, Japan, and Italy, have now "known better times." The national ambitions of the former colonial peoples have erupted in a way to make old relationships untenable. Moreover, the United States, the dominant industrial nation of the West, has disavowed any interest in becoming a colonial power, and has acted to terminate such quasi-colonial relationships as existed, as, for example, with the Philippines. The second development is that of the neo-imperialism of the Soviet Union.

Like the frustrated plans of the Nazis for world domination, the Soviet techniques for subjugation of the satellite areas include, in addition to the naked power of the Red armies, the subtle manipulation of property forms for the diversion of income to the Soviet economy. New corporations or trusts have been set up with the majority of capital stock in Russian hands. According to the rules of the game, control over production and pricing

649

thus rests with the dominant power, and integration with the central plan is assured. Terms of trade favorable to the Soviet Union permit the appropriation of a large share of the satellite output, and gives them in return a smaller real income in Russian-produced goods. By maintaining a rising level of prices in the occupied areas, even when income adjustments are made to provide incentives, the administered price system performs its function of limiting consumption. Substantively, then, we see being repeated under communism the "economic imperialism" which was the basis of collectivist criticism of pre-World War II industrial capitalism.

The Pragmatic Approach to World Trade

If we attempt to organize our beliefs about commercial policy in terms of the arguments of laissez faire or central planning, we end in an impasse. The assumptions on which both views rest appear to diverge so sharply from events and relationships of the real world that the dilemma posed by Clark appears to be one from which there is no escape. Neither approach appears to offer any assurance of harnessing nationalism to international organization and the growth of the *international economy*.

Recognition of mutual advantage and the growth of interdependence through specialization and trade, once the strongest argument of classical economists and the Manchester school, seems not to have survived World War I. The most devout free trader finds it difficult to argue the case with conviction (in other than a very abstract sense) that all that is required, even for as strong a nation and as wealthy an economy as the United States, is the removal of all trade barriers to usher in world prosperity and security. There appears to be no reason to hope that any sovereign government will surrender control over its own affairs to the extent of allowing its exchange rate to fluctuate until an equilibrium is established in international income flows, particularly when this may mean even comparatively brief periods of unemployment and falling income. Powerful economic groups cannot be resisted, when it appears obvious that foreign goods and the flight of short-term capital are intensifying the forces of deflation.

On the other hand, all the experience we have to go on indicates that centrally-planned economies show little tendency to be less nationalistic than predominantly private-enterprise economies. In fact, the monolithic state is especially well adapted to the use of total power in a more effective imperialism than that which excited socialists and liberals during and after World War I.

650

The principal efforts of internationalists since World War I have been directed toward the creation of some type of world political authority capable of curbing the most destructive features of nationalism. The League of Nations and now the United Nations have been the main organizations for this purpose to date. An important hypothesis behind such efforts is that if war as an instrument of national policy is to be controlled, the world must organize to that end. The goal is to learn to deal effectively —through discussion and agreement on mutual interests—with the conditions that create tensions and lead to the state of mind that makes war appear to be a necessary action.

The student of economic processes understands these conditions to be "the economic causes of war." To the economic determinist, of course, the causes of war are viewed as *entirely* economic. To the modern social scientist, however, aware of the great complexity of human motivation and behavior, single causes are likely to provide a shaky foundation for understanding, explanation, prediction, and control. That irritations, aggressions, and insecurities arising out of income and trade relations contribute to the tensions that produce war is acknowledged by most historians, political scientists, and psychologists. Policies designed to reduce such tensions can contribute to, if not assure, greater stability in international affairs.

The problem of the normative economist, accordingly, is to use the most reliable knowledge of the economic process at his disposal in shaping economic policies and goals, and in our present area of concern in influencing commercial policy. To the pragmatist in economic affairs, the counterpart of organization for international political relations is organization for international trade, such organization to be undertaken in the light of the best available knowledge and judgment on income flows, patterns of production, and levels of economic development. For economic science the goal is to predict the most likely response (given the present politico-economic structure) to different courses of action.

The economic and social organizations attached to the United Nations have been set up in accordance with such a philosophy. The fact that each sovereign nation is likely to insist upon responsibility for and control over its own economic development and trade relations is a starting point for the design of international institutions. In the belief that rising levels of trade and international investment are consistent with national economic (income) objectives, an attempt has been made to remove the blocks to these flows. The International Monetary Fund (see page 626) attempts to remove pressures for unilateral action in exchange devaluation by making short-term credit available. Similarly, in the field of investment and economic development, the International Bank seeks to regularize the flow of investment funds into projects that contribute to increased productivity and rising levels of income. These organizations do not replace existing private sources of short-run and long-run capital, but are intended to offset rigidities and such monopoly powers as exist. Also, they work through national governments so that consistency with national objectives can be maintained.

The importance of high-level employment and income—an emphasis that has stemmed from modern aggregate income analysis—is now generally acknowledged. In the absence of general agreement on effective monetary and fiscal policies for achieving this goal, the stress is on continuing research and consultation.

Other nations watch with interest, and with some concern, the actions of the United States as the dominant economic force in the world. Following World War II much of the rest of the world was not convinced that the United States had committed itself fully to this goal. Not the least of these, apparently, was the Soviet Union, whose doubts stemmed not so much from a belief that the United States lacked the resolve to maintain full employment, as from the conviction that the collapse of a capitalist economy was inevitable after a great war. By her actions the Soviet Union has done much to contribute to sustained high production in this country. She has also stimulated American assistance, through the Marshall Plan and other foreign aid programs, in the reconstruction and development of nations outside the Russian-controlled areas.

With high-level income and employment, the solution of other upsetting problems of trade are made easier. However, in the event of widespread depression, transmitted throughout the world through trade channels, it is unlikely that a return to unilateral and discriminatory actions could be prevented.

Recent Developments in U.S. Trade Policy

Meanwhile, developments in American policy since World War II, not entirely predictable from past actions, have tended to allay some of the skepticism in the "free world" and perhaps created doubts in communist circles. The Reciprocal Trade Agreement program, a mainstay of American trade policy in the 1930's, has been continued and extended. The General Agreement on Tariffs and Trade (GATT), which was proposed by the United States, formulated in preliminary form at Geneva in 1947, and ratified by fifty-four signatory nations at Havana in 1948, represents an attempt to generalize the process of negotiating trade agreements. This is to be accomplished by simultaneous negotiation among all signatory powers for the reduction of trade barriers.

A proposal of the United States State Department for the formation of an International Trade Organization (ITO) was also presented at the Havana Conference, after having been widely discussed in earlier conferences. The purpose of this organization was to create a formal structure for developing a generally acceptable code of behavior in matters pertaining to international trade. The proposal outlined four major areas within which such codes were to be prepared for mutual agreement.

1. *Policies for achieving and maintaining full employment.* It is proposed to set up machinery to provide for continuing consultation among members on their experiences in the attainment of full employment, in the belief that simultaneous action on all fronts in the event of a downturn in economic activity can make full employment easier to achieve for any single nation. Because of the observed historical tendency of such weaknesses to spread through the channels of trade, action to check a recession at its source seems worthy of trial.

2. *Policies for dealing with private monopoly and cartels.* One of the difficulties of laissez faire as a policy has been its inability to cope with increasing areas of concentrated economic power. Through the ITO, it is hoped that (again by consultation and joint action) cartel arrangements can be restrained. Cartel agreements have always been extralegal in the United States. In many countries, however, they have been able to exist with state sanction, their provisions enforceable by law.

3. *Policies for dealing with government monopoly.* Many governments maintain a monopoly of the trade in certain commodities. Centrally-planned economies have a monopoly of all trade. Through consultation and agreement, it is proposed to draft codes of fair conduct by government trading corporations. Under these codes would be agreements against "dumping"—sale at prices below some reasonable cost of production—and arbitrary restrictions by government to raise prices, such as the Brazil coffee valorization.[3]

4. *Policies for the regulation of commodity agreements.* Following the general breakdown of world trade in the 1930's the principal producing nations of a number of raw materials negotiated mutual agreements for production quotas and the sharing of markets. Like the valorization schemes, these agreements became devices for raising prices to consumer nations.

A justification for commodity agreements has been the extreme instability of raw-materials prices (for example, wheat, rubber, and cotton),

---

[3] A plan whereby coffee was purchased by the Brazilian government and actually destroyed in order to maintain prices. The same type of program has been used by the U.S. Department of Agriculture.

653

with resulting instability of income to producers. The prices of most industrial goods are already administered under various degrees of private monopoly. Only through government action can equivalent stability of raw materials be achieved.

Proposed agreements in this area under the ITO would provide representation for important consuming nations, so that their interests would be taken into account. The argument that primary production has unique characteristics is accepted. The supply of these basic commodities tends to be inelastic. The transfer of factors out of production is extremely difficult, either of natural resources or human factors. Primary producers are less mobile, and it is usually only the younger generations who shift to the higher-income secondary and tertiary industries. Again through consultation and co-ordination, it is hoped that reductions in production will be achieved through subsidizing the transfer of factors to other products when continuing oversupplies depress markets for extended periods.

Although proposed by the United States State Department, the ITO agreement was never ratified by Congress. Consequently, the process of generalizing reciprocity for the reduction of trade restrictions has been hampered. However, in 1955 representatives of most of the major trading countries outside the Soviet bloc (including the United States) drafted an agreement for the establishment of an Organization for Trade Cooperation (OTC). Less ambitious perhaps than ITO, this organization proposes to formalize and make permanent the machinery for supplementing GATT, originally intended to be only an interim measure.

An alternative proposal for dealing with surpluses of raw materials, particularly of food, was that of Sir Boyd Orr, first director of the Food and Agriculture Organization, who advocated the creation of world-wide buffer stocks to be used for famine relief and alleviation of undernourishment wherever it occurred. An international "ever-normal" granary would be set up to buy stocks of materials during periods and in areas of glut, which would be released in times of shortages and in famine areas. This proposal was rejected, largely at the insistence of the United States, on the grounds that it was impractical and would interfere with the regular channels of trade.

Partly as a consequence of the mounting tensions between East and West, the United States has embarked upon a number of international assistance programs on a unilateral basis. The Export-Import Bank has expanded its operations, facilitating the access of foreign nations to American-produced goods through more liberal credit. A technical assistance program, fortuitously labeled Point Four by virtue of its position in President Truman's Inaugural Address in 1949, contributes to the economic progress of underdeveloped areas. As part of the strategy of the

654

Cold War, the Foreign Operations Administration rendered a form of assistance, largely military, which eased the burden of rearmament in friendly nations, stimulated investment, and contributed indirectly to economic development.[4]

Other Regional Developments

As a means of modifying the impact of extreme nationalism on international relations at a lower level, other regional economic arrangements have evolved to supplement the work of the United Nations organizations, or to cope with problems which cannot be handled by the larger organization because of the present world division.

    1. The Economic Commission for Europe was organized as a research and co-ordinating agency to further trade and the extension of markets in a purely pragmatic manner.

    2. For the rationalization of the western European iron and steel industry the Schuman Plan has created machinery to plan investments and allocate the output of mines and factories. A commission representing management, labor, and the countries involved has begun the process of developing economic criteria for improving efficiency, expanding markets, and generally raising the productive level of the region. The six nations most directly involved in the iron and steel community—Belgium, France, West Germany, Italy, Luxembourg, and the Netherlands—have also inaugurated a program for setting up a common market looking toward eventual free trade among themselves.

    3. In south and southeast Asia the Colombo Plan, organized within the British Commonwealth of Nations and placed in operation on July 1, 1951, seeks to further economic development of the area through joint action. The initial members included Ceylon, Malaya, India, British Borneo, Pakistan, and Singapore in south and southeast Asia, and the United Kingdom, Canada, Australia, and New Zealand outside the area. Cambodia, South Vietnam, Laos, Nepal, Burma, Japan, Philippines, Thailand, and the United States have since joined.

    Two goals are specified under the plan: (*a*) to increase goods production sufficiently to keep up with population growth, and prevent further decline in levels of living; and (*b*) to lay the groundwork for industrial and agricultural development, with a view to raising living standards.

    Again, the hope is that by means of this plan the transformation of a basically agricultural area into a more balanced industrial economy can be hastened, beginning with the application of modern technology to

---

[4] The FOA was abolished by executive order, effective June 30, 1955, but its functions were continued by the Department of State and the Department of Defense.

agriculture. An investment of more than $5 billion for the first six years' operation is the goal. Funds for technical assistance were pledged by the United Kingdom, Australia, Canada, and New Zealand. About two-thirds of the investment funds are scheduled to come from internal resources of the countries themselves, the remainder to come from public borrowing from foreign investors, and from government investments by other Commonwealth dominions.

Numerous other proposals for regional economic development have been made, to be supported by government and private investments, with the objective of stimulating the general level of economic activity to full effective employment. In the underdeveloped areas, in contrast to the rich industrial nations, problems of co-ordinated development are likely to be of first importance. Whereas the older industrial nations have evolved gradually over the last century and a half, the present underdeveloped nations are attempting to catch up under forced draft. However, with heavy emphasis on industrial expansion and outside sources of capital, there is a danger that the production of some items may expand more rapidly than their markets. The income generated in their production could become effective demand for an output that not only is not expanding but may actually be contracting due to shifts in factors. To provide a safeguard against such a distortion of the economic structure and too great a departure from productivity-based absolute and comparative advantage, the pragmatist would support the retention of a flexible price system and a market to provide clues for factor allocation.

Some Unsettled Issues in U.S. Foreign Trade Policy

There are indications that an impressive weight of business and public opinion in the United States is shifting in favor of more liberal treatment for foreign-produced goods. The high income levels since the end of World War II have made possible a volume of travel abroad never before equaled. This, coupled with the number of service personnel who spent time overseas during the war, has served to create a demand for foreign goods. Domestic shortages after the war also permitted substitutes from abroad to gain entry. Some of our largest mass-production industries look to overseas markets for partial outlets for the volume they can produce. With the level of efficiency prevailing in many of these companies, the infant-industry argument is no longer convincing, and the industries themselves no longer feel impelled to make it. Industrial leaders like Henry Ford II and Paul Hoffman are on record in favor of more liberal import policies. Economic experience in a mature industrial, creditor nation (with fewer resources in relation to production) has forced a recognition of the dependence on foreign resources. In addition, the political climate created by two opposing superpowers has also served to foster an awareness of other types of dependency.

This shift of opinion, while significant, is by no means universal. Influential persons and groups still maintain old beliefs and habits. This has had the effect of creating the impression to the outside world of an international trade policy shot through with contradictions. Despite official pronouncements outlining the need for "good economic neighbors," arbitrary and unilateral actions to the contrary occur. Some of these are based upon a "reasonable" desire of a nation to exercise control over economic changes, and the corresponding rate of adjustment. In many cases, however, they have all of the appearances of unwarranted discrimination, rooted in old habits and procedures. A significant segment of Congressional opinion still holds to the older traditions, while officials in such administrative agencies as the Tariff Commission and Customs at times impose restrictions more stringent than a majority of Congress intended. These areas of dualism and policy conflict can be classified under the following headings: (1) peril points and escape clauses; (2) principal supplier technique; (3) tariff classification; and (4) "Buy American" legislation.

1. *Peril Points and Escape Clauses.* Treaties negotiated under the Reciprocal Trade Agreements program have been subject to the restraints of peril points (since 1951) and escape clauses (sine 1943).

A *peril point* is the minimum level to which a tariff on a commodity can be reduced without putting domestic producers "in peril." Such points are determined by the Tariff Commission, in advance of treaty negotiations, for all commodities to be included. While the President may authorize a reduction below this level, he must justify it to Congress.

Escape clauses are linked with the peril-point concept, but refer to a different and broader field of action. Incorporated in all Reciprocal Trade Agreements (since the Mexican Treaty of 1943), these clauses provide an "out" for the United States. Such clauses state that:

> No reduction in any rate of duty . . . shall be permitted to continue in effect when that product . . . is . . . being imported into the United States in such increased quantities, either actual or relative, as to cause or threaten serious injury to the domestic industry producing like or directly competitive products.[5]

The language of the law is so broad that it lends itself to rather loose interpretations of what constitutes injury or "peril." Suppose that the demand

---

[5] From Public Law 50, 82nd Congress, 1st Session, June 16, 1951.

for a particular commodity is increasing. If in such circumstances the proportion of domestic demand supplied by imports tends to rise, is the industry (which is also experiencing increasing sales) placed in peril? Is not the interest of consumers and exporters to be considered?

It is true that the United States has taken advantage of these clauses in relatively few cases. They have been used especially in the case of certain agricultural commodities, where higher American prices might encourage imports which would imperil the domestic support programs. However, the continued insistence on escape clauses in all treaties does provide some basis for skepticism among other nations regarding our stated intentions to foster freer trade. This skepticism is not allayed by the vigorous activities of many high-tariff pressure groups.

2. *Principal Supplier Technique.* For many years, in its commercial treaties, the United States operated under a *conditional most-favored-nation clause.* This clause provided that when tariff concessions were made to a particular nation, they would be extended to others only if they met the same *conditions* as the treaty nation. In this way American concessions were limited in their generality, particularly when protection-minded officials were the sole judges of another country's fulfillment of those conditions.

Under the Reciprocal Trade Program the principal of unconditional most-favored-nation treatment has applied. However, the spirit, if not the language, of the earlier provision has been preserved through the technique of negotiating only with a *principal supplier.* By negotiating only on items thus limited as to source, the liberalizing of restrictions, even for more favorable treatment for American goods, can be minimized.

3. *Tariff Classification.* Tariff classification is an official listing of commodities for purposes of assigning import duties. This may seem like a simple problem, but its very complexity becomes the basis for effective trade restrictions. Because of the bases for levying the tariff—*ad valorem* or *specific*—and because of the difference in rates applied (including a free list), the decision on how to classify a given commodity becomes very important. Ambiguity exists because most goods are not simple things, but rather combinations of materials and efforts. They are also designed or suited for particular purposes. They can be described (and classified) according to their principal component (e.g., wood), according to their stage of manufacture (e.g., wood pulp), or according to the use to which they are to be put (e.g., newsprint). It is not always easy to determine the principal component, if there are several; the stage of manufacture may vary according to intended use; and the final use may be defined as potential use, rather than intended use (a customs official, for example,

has defined ping-pong balls as ammunition, because they could be used in toy air guns). In cases of doubt authorities have been inclined to assign goods to the class carrying the higher rate.

This is a complex problem, and a simple, logical system of classification is difficult to apply, particularly when the purpose of the tariff is ambiguous. Tariff rates themselves are pretty much of a hodgepodge, that have been built up over the years to satisfy powerful interest groups, and later modified by treaty and legislation. For the pragmatically minded, tariff classification is a challenging area for effort.

4. *"Buy American."* Restrictive trade legislation carried forward from the depression years still remains part of United States law. Called the "Buy American" Act, this legislation gives preference to domestic firms in the bidding for major equipment purchased by government. Foreign firms, in order to have an equal chance of receiving a contract for large capital items, such as electrical generators, turbines, and other equipment, *must* bid at least 15 per cent below the lowest domestic bidder. With the large volume of purchases now made by the Federal government, foreign nations could increase their dollar earnings in an area already characterized by administered prices, without significantly affecting levels of employment, if this restriction were eliminated.

Pragmatism and the Mixed Economy

In the preceding discussion it has undoubtedly appeared that the term pragmatism has been used as a justification for a multiple criterion, compounded of opportunism, compromise, expediency, and avoidance of firm principle. In a sense it is. That is the nature of a *mixed economy.* Acceptance of pragmatism as an approach to the "real world" is an acknowledgment that there are no absolutes to guide us in a complex and troubled world. The insights into the economic processes provided by the assumptions of laissez faire economists and those in favor of central planning can be suggestive of long-run goals for which to strive. But progress toward these goals, given a maze of other goals and interests, cannot be along a straight line.

Discussion
Questions

1. Why is a consistent commercial policy difficult to maintain in the face of national rivalries?

2. What is the infant-industry argument for tariff protection? Could new industries be assisted by other means?

3. Rank the techniques for controlling international trade in the order of their restrictive impact.

4. Why is it difficult to get trade restrictions modified through Congressional action?

5. Why is unemployment likely to be more destructive of international trade than the tariff?

6. The United States has become a leading advocate of freer trade. Are her actions and her stated policies always in accord?

Selected References for Part 6

Condliffe, J. B. *The Commerce of Nations.* New York: W. W. Norton & Co., 1950.

Ellsworth, P. T. *The International Economy.* Rev. ed.; New York: The Macmillan Co., 1958.

Myrdal, Gunnar. *An International Economy.* New York: Harper and Brothers, 1956.

Snider, Delbert A. *Introduction to International Economics.* Rev. ed.; Homewood, Ill.: Richard D. Irwin, Inc., 1958.

Towle, Lawrence W. *International Trade and Commercial Policy.* 2d. ed.; New York: Harper and Brothers, 1956.

Epilogue: A Simple Restatement

A truism now widely believed is that science is more genuinely understood by one who is familiar with its historical background and, conversely, that history which fails to include an account of scientific development is but half the story—and perhaps not the better half.

CARL R. BOYER[1]

WE HAVE NOW COMPLETED our introduction to economics as a field of inquiry—a body of fact and information, a historical survey of the development of doctrine, and the characteristic patterns of normative judgments. If many unanswered questions and unsettled issues remain, then this book has served the purpose for which it was intended. The problems which have been discussed here have troubled the minds of men as far back as we can discover. At times answers that were at best tentative have been treated as final, only to be found wanting in the ever changing pattern of man's experience. Yet it is from that changing experience and its interpretation that we can gain insight and understanding to help us in our own world view and adjustments.

Economic literature is concerned with the study of human experience, abstracted and organized around the problem of scarcity. It is the language, the records of observations, and the interpretations which men have given over time to man's adjustment to that fact of the "real world." Economizing behavior, by general consensus, has come to mean those adjustments men make to the fact of relative scarcity, as it is mirrored in the acts of choice.

Scarcity is a broad term, and applies to many different circumstances. The world in which we live has "too little" of many things. Judged by

---

[1] *Science,* 15 April 1955.

the dream world of most of us, there is not enough kindness, not enough love, not enough tolerance, not enough happiness, and not enough time. In the broadest sense, all behavior can be viewed as economizing behavior—making do with what we have or can obtain. But, quite obviously, this is not what is meant by the subject matter of economics as a discipline. Its association, over time, is with a narrower slice of experience. The behavior covered by economics is principally that which establishes *claims* against the scarce materials and services required for the satisfaction of man's perceived needs. These claims have usually been comprehended by some concept of *property*. In the modern world property forms have become exceedingly complex, and are tied together in our thinking largely by means of a concept of *income*.

In this book we have made income our central focus of attention, and everything else which economists are concerned with has been linked to it. The scarcity problem in a monetary economy is in fact perceived principally as a scarcity of money income, relative to what we want to do with it.

How does a household, a firm, a government, a nation get its income? How is it shared and how is it spent? What are the factors that have determined its size in the past, and what is the most likely estimate of its future trend? To answer these questions takes us back over the ground we have covered, and that by now should be acquired knowledge.

What can be done to increase the size of income? How ought it to be shared? How should it be used? These are knottier questions to handle. However they are answered, some will be certain to disagree. In a sense, therefore, each must arrive at his own answer. But that answer will be better or worse, as the best evidence of the *possible* is used to give substance and realism to the *desirable*.

Index

Ability to pay—criterion of tax justice, 461

Abstraction, defined, 3

Acceleration principle, 163–5

Accounting
earliest treatise on, 21n.
for the firm, 350ff.
national-income, 111ff.

Advantages in production
absolute, 241, 592
comparative, 253, 593, 619

Advertising costs, in monopolistic competition, 311

Aggregate demand
concern of Keynes, 38
and trade theory, 622

Agriculture, organized, 482

Allen, F. L., 229n., 504

Allocation of factors, 395
and distributive shares, 400
effect of unions on, 401
optimum allocation, 399

American Farm Bureau Federation, 483

American Federation of Labor, 477

Anarchism, extreme laissez faire position, 65

Anti-trust laws, 293, 363, 480

Aquinas, Thomas, 22

Aristotle, on property, 51

Autarky, Keynes's defense of, 635

Autonomous investment, 162

Average costs, 252, 279

Average product, 248–9

Balance of payments
defined, 600
of U.S. in 1956, 602

Balance of trade
active, 601
favorable, 600

Balance sheet
corporate, 357–9
individual proprietorship, 351–4

Banking
development of, 183
function defined, 141

Bank notes, state, 190

Banks
central, 184n., 186
commercial, 186
investment, 184
organization of, 186–8
"wildcat," 191

Barger, Harold, 231n.

Barker, Ernest, 69

Barnes, H. E., 649

Beliefs, contrasted with feelings, 8

Bell, Carolyn Shaw, 587

Benefit—criterion of tax justice, 461

Bentham, Jeremy, 24

Beveridge, Sir William, 499, 580

Blacklist, 480

Bohm-Bawerk, Eugen, 257

Bonds, industrial, 362

Boulding, Kenneth, 88, 509

Boyer, C. R., 662

Brady, Robert A., 238n.

Bright, John, 644

Brook Farm, 494

Brookings Institution, 536
Bryan, William Jennings, 168
Budget studies
  and income distribution, 443
  comparative, 532
  in U.S., 531
Burns, Arthur F., 171
Business sector, 111
Business unionism, 409

Capital
  defined by Smith, 23
  dimensions as concept, 52
  dynamic factor of Classicists, 29
  equipment, 85
  equity, 560
  investment, 152
  result of waiting, 54
  working, 432
Capitalization
  of profits, 255
Carey, Mathew and Henry C., 645
Carlyle, Thomas, 48, 242, 574
Cartels, proposals to control, 653
Chamberlin, Edward H., 33, 504
Chapin, R. C., 533
Check, defined, 183
Choice—aspect of economic problem, 14
Civilian labor force, 86
Clark, Colin, 329
  on socialism and free enterprise, 641
Clark, J. B., 257n.
Clark, John M., 74n., 167, 225, 328
Classical economic thought, 22
Clearings
  international, 205, 634
  principle of, 197-9
Closed shop, 481n.
Cobden, Richard, 644
Cochrane, Willard W., 587
Commercial policy, 369
Commodity agreements, control of, 653
Commons, John R., 32, 74n.
Communism, derivation of term, 71
Competing goods, 522
Competition, monopolistic, 309
Competitive market, 274
Complementary goods, 522

Concepts—extension of symbols, 10
  in ordinary language, 8
  scientific, 9
Condliffe, J. B., 591, 661
Congress of Industrial Organizations (C.I.O.), 470
Conservative, ambiguity of term, 64
Consumer behavior, 508
Consumer credit, 584
Consumer expectations, 550
Consumer price index, description, 541-6
Consumer sovereignty, 511
Consumers Research, 526
Consumers Union, 526
Consumption
  by budget items, 537
  expenditures, 151
  function, 155
  unit, 100
  variety of meanings, 507
Consumption indifference curves, 520
Co-operatives
  consumer, 577
  form of organization, 345-9
Corporation
  balance sheet, 357
  closed, 344
  development of, 339
  form of organization, 339
  income statement, 359
  relation to economic concentration, 342
Costs
  determination under socialism, 313
  long-run, 290
  short-run, 277-80
Countervailing power, 382
Cournot, Antoine, 33n., 297n.
Credit, consumer, 584
Creditor nation
  immature, 613
  mature, 613
Crosland, C.A.R., 377n., 499
Cultural lag, 326
Currency act of 1873, 173

Daugherty, C. R., 504
Davies, Rev. David, 444
Davis, J. S., 587

Debt
  negative property, 56
  use as money, 138
Debtor nation
  immature, 613
  mature, 613
Deduction and induction, 11
Deficit budget, defined, 138
Demand
  creation, 526
  curve, 261
  elasticity, 267
  perceived by individual firm, 275
  schedule, 266
Depreciation, defined, 117
Depression, 35
Dewey, John
  on pragmatism, 73
  on symbols and signs, 4
Dialectical materialism, 72
Dillard, Dudley, 225
Diminishing returns, physical law of, 247
Distribution, 387
  and allocation theory, 395
  and farm problem, 484
  functional, 388
  national income by distributive shares, 391
  personal or household, 390, 441
Distributive justice
  and economic democracy, 194
  in Judaeo-Christian ethic, 492
  in Marxian system, 494
Draft, 183
Drucker, Peter F., 504
Duesenberry, James S., 587
Duopoly, 305

Economic Commission for Europe, 655
Economic history, 43
Economic holism, 74
Economic man, 25
Economic problem, 20
Economic progress, 43, 243
Economics
  as a discipline, 5
  as a social science, 14
  as a symbol, 4
  Historical school of, 32
  what economists do, 4
Economic system, 21
  as model, 8
Economic theory, 44

Economic thought, tentative nature of, 6
Economies, 291–2
Economize, different verbal forms, 19
Economy
  private, 104
  public, 105
Edwards, Corwin, 369
Efficiency
  budget, 551
  economic, 241–3
Einstein, Albert
  on scientific concepts, 7
Elasticity
  price, 268–9
  related to monopoly, 296
Ellsworth, P. T., 661
Empirical tradition, 9
Employment Act, 223
Energy sources, 235
Engels, Friedrich, 31
Engle, Ernst, 529
Engle's Law, 529–30
Enterpreneur, in classical thought, 26
Error, defined, 11
  related to feelings, 12
Escape clauses, in trade treaties, 657
Establishment, 57
European Common Market, 655
Exchange rate, 205
Exchange stabilization funds, 617
Expectations, 317
Expenditures, family, 533
Exports
  characteristics of U.S., 597
  percentage of GNP, 593
  structure of, 596
Ex post identity, 152

Facts, defined, 6
Fairs, 56
Farmers' National Grange, 483
Farmers' Union, 484
Federal budget, 557
  major categories, 560
Federal Deposit Insurance Corporation, 203
Federal Reserve System
  founding of, 195
  map of districts, 194
  ownership of Reserve banks, 196
  relative size of Reserve banks, 197

Firm, 57
Ford, Henry
    and private property, 328
    on comparative living standard, 548
Foreign exchange, 204
Foreign exchange market, 611
Foreign relations, 369
Foreign trade and income, 623
Frank, Philipp, 76
Free market and the consumer, 571
Futures market, 319–20

Galbraith, J. K., 329
    on countervailing power, 382
    on standards of living, 583
Gallatin, Albert 558
General Agreement on Tariffs and Trade
    (GATT), 652
George, Henry, 423
Gold standard
    clause in contracts, 181
    defined, 177
    nominal, 182
    role in foreign exchange, 619–21
Gold stocks, U.S., 618
Goods, concept of, 58
Gossen, H. H., laws of consumption, 517
Government
    growth of spending, 457
    income, 456
    sector of income accounts, 111
Government expenditures
    federal, 560
    local, 567
    state, 565
Gresham's Law, 143n.
Gross national product, 113
Groves, Harold A., 504
Gruchy, Alan, 74

Hamilton, Alexander
    on economic development, 633
    on monetary standards, 176
    Secretary of Treasury, 558
Hamilton, Walton, 326
Hansen, Alvin H., stagnation thesis, 218,
    225
Harrod, Roy M., 167
Hart, A. G., 225
Hayek, Friedrich
    on private enterprise, 209, 368
    on socialism, 70

Hazlitt, Henry, 209
Hedging, 319
Hegel, F. W., influence on Marx, 32
Heilbroner, Robert L., 504
Hildebrand, Bruno, 32
Hobson, J. A., 649
Holding company, 363–5
Household sector, 111
Hoyt, Elizabeth, 509, 549
Hull, Cordell, 617
Hume, David, 23

Imperialism, 649
Income
    as object of inquiry, 40
    as social benefit, 18
    disposable, 116
    in kind, 404n.
    per capita, 441, by states, 450
    period, 150
    source in international trade, 130
    statement, 359
Income distribution
    in Soviet Russia, 496
    under British Labour, 498
Income effect of price change, 521
Index numbers
    simple, 95
    weighted, 127–8
Indivisibilities, 317
Industrial corporations, twenty largest
    in U.S., 237
Inequality
    in distribution, 489
    of household income, 447
Innovation, relation to profit, 439
Innovators, 173
Institutionalist, 32
Institutions, 328
Insurance, relation to risk, 322
Integration, forward and backward, 344
Interest
    and marginal efficiency of capital, 431
    as factor payment, 429
    compound, 436
    effective rate of, 436
    pure, 433
International Bank, 627
International Monetary Fund, 626
International trade
    contraction in depression, 606
    relation to political stability, 612

International Trade Organization, 653
Investment
    autonomous, 76
    defined, 159–62
    foreign, 609
    induced, 162

Jackson, Andrew, 191
James, William, 73
Jevons, W. S., 35, 171, 257n.
Joint supply, 315
Juglar, Clement, 35

Katoma, George, 539, 587
Keynes, J. M., 33, 216, 225, 257, 322,
    434, 460, 490, 625
King, Gregory, and expenditure, 528
    studies on. distribution, 444,
King, W. I., 452
Knies, Karl, 32
Knight, F. H., 437
Kondratiev, N. D., 135
Kuznets, Simon, 133, 445

Labor, defined by Smith, 23
Labor force, 86
Labor organization
    AFL-CIO, 479
    development, 476
    structure, 477
Laissez faire
    and employment policy, 209
    as ideal model, 16
    as normative system, 65
    favored by Smith, 24
    relation to competition, 292
Land, defined by Smith, 23
Lange, Oscar, 373
Language
    as sign, 4
    different uses of, 12
Lasswell, Harold, 18
Legal tender, 179
Le Play, Frederick, 444
    on consumer behavior, 530
Lerner, A. P., 74, 501
Lerner, Max, 504
Leverage effect, 167
Liberal
    ambiguity of term, 64
    tradition, 27

Liquidity preference, 433
Lockout, 479
Logico-empiricism, 10
Lombard Street, 608
Lorenz curve, 445

Maine, Sir Henry, 369
Maisel, S. J., 225
Malthus, T. R., 24, 218
Management, professionalization of, 330
Manchester school, 644
Marginal cost, 286
Marginal firm, 289
Marginal land, 399
Marginal product, 247
Marginal propensity to consume, 154–5
Marginal revenue, 283
Marginal utility, 517
Market
    concept of, 56
    periods, 281–5
    role of, 241
Market-basket norm, 554
Marshall, Alfred, 25, 33n., 37, 58, 81,
    225, 257, 489
Martin, E. W., 528
Marx, Karl, 30, 31, 54, 81, 256, 574
Mathematics, as language, 4
Means, Gardiner C., 74n.
Menger, Carl, 257
Mercantilist writers, 22
Microanalysis, 228
Mill, John Stuart, 25, 406
Minimum budgets, 552
Misplaced concreteness, 13
Mitchell, Wesley C., 39, 52, 74, 82, 133,
    509
Monetary policy, instrument of Federal
    Reserve System, 200–3
Money
    as measure of output, 97
    as property, 55
    derivation of term, 54
    fiat, 179
    lawful, 179
    motives for holding, 146–7
    representative, 179
    token, 179
Money and banking function, 140
Money flow, 92

Money illusion, 41
Monopoly
  basis of, 303
  market characteristics of, 294
  social consequences of, 300
Monopsony, 313
Montagu, Ashley, 20n.
Morgenstern, Oscar, 332
Most favored nation, 644
Multiplier, 166–7
Myrdal, Gunnar, 76, 661

National Banking Act, 192–4
National Bureau of Economic Research, 135
National income
  defined, 115
  development of concept, 80–3
  industrial origin of, 233
  table of accounts, 120
National inventory, 84
Natural resources, 85
Net national product, 115
Neuman, John von, 332n.
Nonproductive occupations, 49
Normative systems, 16
Norris, Ruby Turner, 587
Norris-LaGuardia Act, 480

Objectivity, in economics, 7
Observation, in scientific method, 9
Occupational groups, 232
Oikonomia, 22
Oligopoly, 306
Operational definition, 10
Opportunity costs in international trade, 630
Optimum firm, 288
Organization for Trade
  Cooperation (OTC), 654
Orr, Sir Boyd, 654
Orwell, George, 369

Pareto, Vilfredo, 82
Parrish, John B., 504
Partnership, 338–9
Pecunia, 54
Peril points, in reciprocal trade, 657
Personal income, defined, 115

Physiocrats, 51
Pigou, A. C., 37, 62, 76
Plato, on property, 51
Pocioli, Luca, 21n.
Point Four program, 655
Polanyi, Karl, 76
Political economy, 22
Population changes, U.S., 230
Pragmatic approach to policy, 72–5
Pressure groups, effect on distribution, 471
Price
  central concern in economics, 26
  competitive, as just price, 27
  discrimination, 313
Pricing under socialism, 379
Primary industries, 49, 329
Principal supplier, 658
Product differentiation, 304
Production
  advantages in, 253
  as part of income process, 88
  decisions in U.S.S.R., 375
  distinctive features in U.S., 236
  household, 443
  roundabout, 240
  simple theory of, 245
Professional associations, 473
Profit, 258–9
Profits, 437
  corporate, 439
  defined, 438
  distributive share of income, 241, 437
  pure, 437
  relation to uncertainty, 437
Propensity to consume, 152
Propensity to save, 152
Property
  characterized by Proudhon, 49
  defined, 49
  influence on income distribution, 449
  rights, contrasted with human, 51
Proprietorship, 336
Prosperity, 35
Psychic income, 46
Purchasing power parity, theory of exchange, 621
Pure theory, abstract symbols of a discipline, 16

Quesnay, François, 81

Racial groups and income distribution, 449

Rapoport, Anatol, 76

Real income, 40

Realized savings, 150

Real world, 9

Redistribution of income, influences on, 453–5

Reichenbach, Hans, 76

Rent
  as cost of production, 422
  capitalization of, 427
  differential, 421
  general theory of, 425
  payment to land, 420
  quasi, 424
  Ricardo on, 421

Rentier, elimination under socialism, 495

Ricardo, David, 24, 256, 386, 421, 423

Robertson, D. H., 146, 225

Robinson, Joan, 33, 76

Robinson Crusoe, economic man, 26

Rochdale principles, 76

Roscher, Wilhelm, 32

Ruskin, John, 48

Russell, Bertrand, 73, 76

Ryan, Father J. A., 532

Savings and investment
  equivalence, 123
  international aspects, 624

Say, Jean Baptiste, 26

Scales of living, 547

Schickele, Rainer, 504

Schmoller, Gustav, 32

Schumpeter, Joseph, 39n., 71, 133, 172, 575

Scientific knowledge, 8

Seasonal variations, 134

Senior, Nassau, 491

Sherman Anti-Trust Act, 293, 363, 480

Simons, Henry C., 70, 504

Situs, as basis for economic rent, 423

Slichter, Sumner, 223

Smith, Adam
  consumer interest, 571
  evaluated by Toynbee, 28
  founder of discipline, 22
  interest in long run, 37
  on division of labor, 227, 242
  on joint-stock companies, 340n.

Smith, Adam (Cont.)
  on labor theory of value, 256
  on trade balance, 600
  perception of aggregate, 37
  reservations on free trade, 643

Smithies, Arthur, 587

Smith-Lever Act, 483

Snider, D. A., 661

Social accounting, 91

Socialism, derivation of term, 71

Social ownership, 71

Social policy, 13

Speculation
  defined, 319
  Keynes on, 322

Standard of living, 347

State banks, development of, 190

State budgets, 565

Stigler, G. J., 587
  on competition, 371
  on subsistence budgets, 552

Stock; *see* Capital

Strike, 479

Substitution effect, of price change, 521

Supply, of particular good, 269

Supply curve for labor, 418

Surplus budget, defined, 138

Systems analysis, 228

Tableau Economique, 81

Tariff classification, and trade policy, 658

Tastes, 264

Taussig, F. W., 645

Tawney, R. H., 28n.

Tax
  base, 458
  incidence, 459
  rate, 458
  shifting, 459
  structure, 461

Taxation, double, 467

Taxes, 462–9
  death, 468
  excise, 464
  general sales, 465
  income, 466
  payroll, 469
  property, 462

Tax justice, criteria, 461

Taylor, Fred M., 373

Technocrats, 96
Technology, 15
Terms of trade, defined, 598
Tertiary industry, 232
Testing, in scientific method, 8
Theory, as model, 10
Thorpe, W. L., 133
Thunen, J. H. von, 261
Time preference, theory of interest rate, 432
Towle, L. W., 661
Toynbee, Arnold, 28
Trade associations, 473
Transfers, income, 100
Trend, secular, 135
Trusts, 363
Tugwell, R. G., 74n.
Turgot, A. R. J., 249
Turner, F. J., 231
Turnover, 108

Uncertainty, 323
Underdeveloped areas, defined, 604
Union shop, 481
U.S. trade balance, 1916–56, 603
Usury; *see* Interest
Utility
  form, 240
  place and time, 241, 265

Value added, 98
Value judgments, 13
Veblen, Thorstein, 32, 74n., 328, 356n.
Von Mises, Ludwig, 209, 491

Wages
  bargaining, 408
  exploitation, 407
  iron law, 406
  marginal productivity, 407
  piece rate, 414
  rates and levels, 410
  relation to ability, 415
  subsistence, 406
  table of rates, 412–3
  and technological progress, 417
  theory of, 404
Walras, Leon, 82
Wants, defined, 58
Wealth
  as national inventory, 87
  concept of, 48–9
  Smith's concept of, 23
Webb, Sidney and Beatrice, 578
Weber, Max, 28n.
Whitehead, A. N., on political economy, 30
Whyte, W. H., 551n.
Wicksell, Knut, 34n.
Williams, John, 631
Williamson, H. F., 587
Wooton, Barbara, 504
  on consumer interest, 581
Wright, Carroll D., 444
  empirical consumption studies, 532
Wright, David McCord, 573

"Yellow Dog" contract, 480

Zweig, Ferdinand, 76

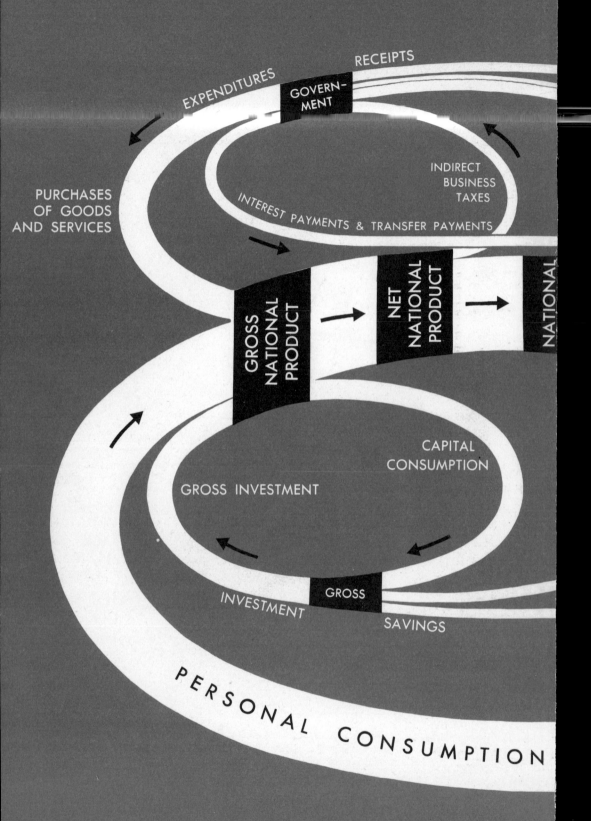

Based on J. F. Dewhurst and Associates, *America's Needs and Resources: A New Survey* (New York: The Twentieth Century Fund, 19...